Samuel Sharpe

The History of the Hebrew Nation and Its Literature

With an Appendix on the Hebrew Chronology. Fifth Edition

Samuel Sharpe

The History of the Hebrew Nation and Its Literature
With an Appendix on the Hebrew Chronology. Fifth Edition

ISBN/EAN: 9783337205836

Printed in Europe, USA, Canada, Australia, Japan

Cover: Foto ©Thomas Meinert / pixelio.de

More available books at **www.hansebooks.com**

THE HISTORY

OF

THE HEBREW NATION

AND

ITS LITERATURE;

WITH AN APPENDIX ON THE HEBREW CHRONOLOGY.

BY

SAMUEL SHARPE,

AUTHOR OF THE "HISTORY OF EGYPT."

FIFTH EDITION.

WILLIAMS AND NORGATE,

14, HENRIETTA STREET, COVENT GARDEN, LONDON:

AND 20, SOUTH FREDERICK STREET, EDINBURGH.

—

1890.

LONDON:

G. NORMAN AND SON, PRINTERS, HART STREET,

COVENT GARDEN.

PREFACE.

THE Hebrew nation had a history of about twelve hundred years, from the time of the Judges to the destruction of Jerusalem by the Romans. The earlier traditions about the Patriarchs and even the residence in Egypt, we can hardly include under the name of history. We first find the nation divided into several little tribes of herdsmen, some dwelling among the conquered natives on the east of the Jordan, and some struggling against the unfriendly Canaanites on the west of that river. The river did not make any marked division among the Hebrew tribes. The strong division was between the northern and the southern tribes. When the needs of war led them to choose a king, they chose Saul of the tribe of Benjamin, a middle tribe whose feelings were with the north. On his overthrow by the Philistines, David of the southern tribe of Judah made himself king. His warlike skill subdued most of the Canaanites, and thus he united all the Hebrew tribes and the subject races into one monarchy. He made Jerusalem his capital.

His son Solomon was a man of peace; and during his reign the country was prosperous. He built the Temple of Jerusalem for the worship of Jehovah, established the Levites to conduct the worship there, and surrounded his throne with magnificence. But his heavy taxes raised discontent among his subjects; and upon his death the northern tribes revolted from his son Rehoboam. Henceforth the nation was divided into two kingdoms; and our history is very much limited to that of Judah.

These two little kingdoms were unfortunately often at war with one another. Judah was usually the stronger, and it increased in wealth until the reign of Ahaz, who unwisely paid the neighbouring Assyrians to help him in his wars;

and from that time Judah continued tributary to that overwhelming power. In the next reign, that of Hezekiah, the Assyrians wholly conquered the northern Israelites, and carried them into captivity. They also crushed Judah to the ground, killed off a large part of the population, and were only checked in their course by troubles at home, probably a rising of the Babylonians. This saved Judea for a time but left it a tributary country.

During the first three hundred years of the monarchy, the priests in Jerusalem had steadily risen in power with the wealth of the people. They had been able to dethrone kings, they had made the whole nation tributary to the Temple of Jerusalem, and had burdened consciences with a strict ceremonial law. Towards the close of this period the prophets arose; and their bold speech may have been some little check to the priests' power; but a still greater check was the poverty of the people caused by the Assyrian invasion.

For a hundred years more the Jewish monarchy lasted, but usually paying tribute to Assyria, until Assyria was overthrown by Babylon. Then the Jews found that they had fallen into equally cruel hands; and they were soon conquered and carried off as captives by the Babylonians, as the northern Israelites had been before carried off by the Assyrians.

The Captivity of the heads of the nation in Babylon lasted nearly seventy years; while the poor of the nation were left behind to till the soil for the conquerors.

In B.C. 538 the Medes and Persians conquered Babylon and all its provinces; and then Cyrus allowed the Israelites and Jews to return home, and to raise up their fallen country as one of the provinces of the great Persian monarchy. For two hundred years they lived quietly under the mild despotism of the Persians.

When the Persians were overthrown by Alexander the Great troublous times again began, because the rival Greek kings of Syria and Egypt each claimed Palestine as a province. The cruelty of the Greco-Syrians led to a revolt under the Maccabee family; and for one hundred years Judea was governed by the Maccabees, first as high-priests and then as kings, until the last of that family was deposed by the Romans, who put the government of Judea into the hands of an Aristocracy.

It was during these last one thousand years that the

Hebrew Scriptures were written; and as **the aim** of the present writer is to compare the literature **with the** doings of the nation, and thus to judge when and why **each** Book was written, here **our** History will end. We do **not** enter upon the century and a half **of** Roman sway over **Judea**, which ended with **the** final dispersion of the Jews, and their ceasing to be **a** nation. That portion of history **may** be left **to a** writer on the Christian Scriptures, **as the** former **portion is needed** by **the student** of the **Hebrew** Scriptures.

The History of **the** Hebrew **nation must** be carefully studied **if** we would understand **the Bible.** The Hebrew writings **are** the **well-**spring of our religious thoughts; they furnish the key **to the** Christian Scriptures, and they **are** the Ark which during **so many** centuries **has** held safe from **the** attacks of Paganism that great religious truth that the Almighty Creator of the world is One, simple and undivided. But these writings have come down **to** our time in a very confused condition; that part of **the** Bible called the Old Testament contains writings, some **of** which must be dated in every one of the eleven centuries before the Christian Era. Not only are they put together with very little regard to date, but the writers in **many** cases did not scruple to weave their new matter into **the** old fabric. Writings which have been handed down **in** manuscript, at **the** mercy of every scribe who made **a new** copy, were naturally altered from time to time, both **by** receiving additions, and by suffering curtailment, and again **by** having **two** pieces joined into one, **or** one piece cut into two. It **is** easy to **show cases** of all **the** alterations. Thus the Pentateuch, of **which the** earliest part may have belonged to David's or **Solomon's** reign, received additions long after the fall of the **monarchy.** The Books of Ezra and Nehemiah **seem** both **to have been** curtailed of matter that they once **contained.** **The** Prophecies of Isaiah cannot have been the work of **fewer** than six authors living at as many different times; **nor** can the short Book of Zechariah be otherwise than **made** up of writings belonging to three **different** centuries. Prophecies written after the events have **been** added to the writings of Jeremiah and others; they **are** blots which it is the critic's business to remove **by** pointing out. The Psalms belong to every century from David's reign to that of Antiochus Epiphanes. Such being the confused state in which the Hebrew Scriptures have reached us, no commentary

on them can be so valuable as the attempt to determine the
date of each part. In this way the contradictions in the
Laws may be explained by showing that they were written
in different ages.

These writings, though religious, are most of them also
political, and they speak of the events of the day as if well
known to the reader, and without adding such explanation
as is now needed. Hence often arises an obscurity which
can only be removed by our inquiring into the history of
the times. Moreover, they are often purposely obscure;
because a writer, living under the tyranny of the Assyrian,
or Babylonian, or Greco-Syrian conqueror of his country,
wrote always guardedly, and indeed often enigmatically, as
when Joel and Amos speak of the Assyrian army under the
name of destroying Locusts, and as when Jeremiah gives
the name of Sheshak to Babylon, and as when the Book of
Ezekiel denounces Antiochus Epiphanes under the name of
the barbarian Gog of the land of Magog.

When these writings are set in due order, according to
the time when each was written, they present us with a
history of the Hebrew religion. It began with narrow
priestly ceremonialism, which was fostered under the
monarchy by wealth and prosperity, until checked by the
Assyrian conquest and the captivity in Babylon. After the
return from captivity, moderate prosperity, under the mild
rule of the Persians, allowed ceremonies again to gain a
feeble footing in the second Temple, and in some measure to
undo the work of the prophets who had written during the
nation's sufferings. At a later time, Greek philosophy and
scepticism came forward to play their part in moulding the
Jewish mind; and then Jerusalem was left in the hopeless
struggle between Pharisaic bigotry and Sadducean doubts.
Such was the preparation for the Light which afterwards
burst from Nazareth in Galilee.

In determining the age of a Book, the style alone must
not be relied upon, because in passing from copier to copier
the old form of words may easily have been made more
modern. Indeed, it is only on the supposition that such
liberty has been very much used by the copier, that we can
understand how there is so little difference in the language
between the oldest and the latest books. It is by the help
of the numerous copies, and of the numerous printed copies
in particular, that modern languages are kept from changing
more than they do; but the change in the English language

during the four hundred years that printing has been in use is greater than that which now appears between the language of the oldest of the Hebrew Books and that of the newest. Their age therefore must be determined by their contents compared with the History. For this reason, the Author has woven his description of the Books into a slight history of the Nation; and in the history he has dwelt chiefly on those facts which throw light on the Literature. He has rarely enlarged on the motives and characters of the kings; he has rather tried to show the motives of the writers, and thereby to determine the age of their writings. There are some of the Books so wholly free from any mention of events, that it would be rash to try to fix their date within two or three centuries; such are the Book of Jonah, many of the Psalms, and parts of the Pentateuch. But for the larger number of the Books the attempt to say when they were written is by no means hopeless; and the Author has here done his best to give to each its place in history. In doing this he may often have been mistaken; and if he has written with an appearance of too great positiveness, it has only been to spare the reader from the ever-needed words of "perhaps" and "it is probable."

We have now no Hebrew manuscript of the Bible older than A.D. 900. About that time a revision of the text was made, and it was so generally accepted as to cause the older copies to be destroyed for the sake of the parchment on which they were written; as the accepted revision of the Greek Bible in the fifth century was the cause of our losing the older Greek copies.

It is in the Pentateuch that we meet with the greatest difficulty in giving a date to each part, because it has been woven into one continued narrative, and has been put before us as if wholly written before the Israelites entered the land of Canaan. But, as the Levitical Law was unknown to Saul, David, and Solomon, we look to the events of the following reigns for the occasions which may have caused each part to be written; and there are certain deep lines drawn across the history of the nation which may be traced in these Books, and which enable us to say of many parts, with some certainty, to what period they belong. Such are the deposition of queen Athaliah by the high priest, the Assyrian invasion, the Captivity in Babylon, and Return from Captivity, and the rebuilding of the Temple. Moreover, it may be safely granted that among the Israelites, as

in every other nation, laws were not written until the
occasion for them had arisen. When the king's preparations
for the Passover were not finished in time for the fourteenth
day of the first month, then, and not before, was the Mosaic
law made that, under such circumstances, the feast might
be celebrated in the second month. When the priest was
authorized by the·king to sit as judge, and declare the
Judgments of Jehovah, then were those Judgments written
into the Law, in continuation of the Ten Commandments.
When it **was** found that the free-will heave offering did not
bring in money enough for the support of the Temple and
priests in Jerusalem, and that it was necessary to levy a
poll-tax, for that express purpose, a law was naturally made
to authorize its collection. These laws, indeed, are all said
to have been delivered by Jehovah to the Israelites on their
march out of Egypt; but this was only the priestly manner
of saying that these laws were agreeable to the will of God.

Many of the narratives also seem to have been written for
a controversial purpose. Thus, when the northern king set
up two golden calves for his people to worship, his conduct
is blamed by means of the story of·Aaron's golden calf. So
when the southern king set up a copper serpent within the
Temple-yard of Jerusalem his conduct is justified by the
story of Moses's copper serpent.

Relying upon these and other historic landmarks, the
Author has endeavoured to put many of the principal
portions of the Pentateuch into chronological order, and has
mentioned each portion at the time when it seems to have
been written. It is this part of his book for which he must
claim most indulgence, as it by no means can be supported
with the same certainty as the dates given to the other
Books of the Bible. There are two classes of critics who
differ from the Author as to the motives for which the
Ceremonial Laws were written, and therefore as to their age.
They both adopt so much of the old opinion as to think that
they were written for future use rather than to meet the
present needs. Some critics think that they were written
in the time of Samuel, with a view to create a priesthood;
and some, on the Return from Captivity, with a view to
revive the prosperity of the priesthood after its overthrow.
Both these opinions the Author rejects, and thinks that the
laws were written when the priesthood was most flourishing,
as the need for them arose.

The larger part of the Books were, no doubt, written in

Jerusalem; but not all of them. We shall see reasons, in the course of our History, for thinking that the account of the Garden of Eden in Genesis ii. 4—iv. may have been written in Hebron; the Book of Judges in the land of Ephraim; some of the Psalms in Babylon, where also the Books of Kings may have been put together; Esther and Daniel i. in Persia; Jeremiah xlv.—xlix., by Baruch, in Egypt; Ezekiel xxvi.—xxvii. and xxix.—xxxii. in Tyre, or one of its dependencies; Ecclesiastes in Antioch, on the Orontes; and the Book of Job by one who had lived in the desert of Uz, but had returned to Judea after a journey to Egypt and Nubia.

A critical examination **of the earlier of the Hebrew** writings shows us how very much the writers allowed their imagination to help them in their attempts to reduce tradition into the form of history. When they would speak of the origin of a tribe, they created for it a founder or forefather; and to him they gave the name of the tribe or nation, and joined him, as well as they could, to the tradition which had come down to them. Thus, for every one of the twelve tribes of Israelites, or, with the Levites, of the thirteen tribes, they created a father or patriarch. These are said to be the sons of Israel, as the father of the collected nation must be named Israel. In order to join this on to the tradition. Jacob is declared to be Israel; and as tradition has given him a celebrated son named Joseph, eleven of these patriarchs are called Joseph's brothers, and two of them Joseph's sons. So, as the Edomites are closely **related to** the Israelites, Edom, their imaginary father, is **said** to be the same person as Esau, Jacob's brother. The names of Jacob, Esau, and Joseph had come down to them by tradition, more or less trustworthy; but the names of Israel, Edom, Ephraim, Judah, and the rest, are the names of tribes, not of single men. So, from the word Rechab, *a chariot*, the Arabs who drove the chariots were called sons of Rechab, and Rechab became the name of their forefather; **and** the word Aron, *an ark*, seems to have given to the priests who carried the Ark the name of the sons of Aaron. Many names in the early genealogies seem to have been formed in this way.

The great value of the Hebrew books arises first, from the writers' firm belief in one God as the creator and governor of the world, and from the readiness with which they acknowledge His will **as** the cause of everything that befalls the nation; and, secondly, from their belief that the voice of conscience was the voice of God, speaking from within, and hence their strong hatred, according to such knowledge as they possessed, of all that they thought evil. Their misfortunes are treated as God's punishment for their sins; and they should be accepted in humility, for "Whom Jehovah loveth he correcteth." (Prov. iii. 12.) Their blessings are his rewards for obedience to his will, and hence the prayer, "Teach me **to** do thy will, for thou art my God." (Ps. cxliii. 10.) The nation's hopeful trust **in** God appears, with few exceptions, in every Book of the Bible. When **ruin** came upon **their** country, the Jews never faltered in their trust that they should be taken care of, and that the monarchy would be restored. When on the Return from Captivity they met with very little of the expected outward prosperity, their hopes and wishes were turned towards a time when peace and righteousness should reign upon earth. When they were disappointed also in this, they turned their thoughts to a future life of happiness after death. They always looked forward. Devout hope and humble trust in God never failed them. So strong was their trust in God's guidance that they thought that not only conscience but reason also spoke his direct commands. The prophet whose zeal in the cause of justice and religion raised him to become a teacher of his countrymen, claimed to have a message from Jehovah; and the priest who gave answers **to** the questions that were brought before him, whether **of** moral duty or of civil justice, spoke in the name **of** Jehovah. When Jeremiah thinks it well to purchase a field, **he** says that he does it by command of Jehovah. It is this strong religious feeling which gives to the Hebrew books their value. But as nothing human is free from faults, so even the Bible must be read with judgment and discrimination.

The distinction is not always clearly made between the eternal Moral Law which is commanded by God, and the Civil Law which is commanded by the magistrate. Even **the** voice of blind passion and of violent selfishness is often mistaken for the voice of conscience; and in these cases also the Hebrews thought, and their writers sometimes tell us, that they spoke the command of God. Thus, when they spoiled the Egyptians, seized upon the lands of the Amorites and Canaanites, and slaughtered the Amalekites, they said that they were obeying the will of Jehovah. But whether they were acting right or wrong, their writings everywhere remind us that we are living under an all-powerful governor, whose will ought to be the sole guide to our conduct. In the earlier writings He is for the most part a God to be feared, and in some a God of the Hebrew nation only; but with the improved views of religion which were gradually opening upon the nation, He becomes, before the fall of the monarchy, a God also to be loved, and a God of all the nations of the world. Hence these writings, not only those of them that are devotional, but those also that are historical and political, have had a most remarkable influence upon the world for good; and have by no means lost their value since the rise of Christianity. Indeed, the New Testament cannot be properly understood without the previous study of the Hebrew Scriptures.

"Whoever shall understand this had better keep silence." Such are the words of Aben Ezra in his commentary on the Pentateuch, when coming on one of those passages which, if properly explained, would prove the Book to be more modern than had been usually thought. Such also has been the rule usually followed by commentators, whether Jewish or Christian, who are bound to some standard of orthodoxy. Hence the reader need not be surprised at meeting with much that may be new to him in the following pages. He, however, who would understand the Bible properly, and form a sound opinion about the age of the books, must either go to the original Hebrew or use some translation more correct than the English Authorized Version. King James's translators were thinking of theology, not of antiquarian peculiarities; and they wished to make their work readable by the many, rather than instructive to the historic inquirer. Their translation thus conceals from us many interesting particulars, such as that Deuteronomy (i. 1) uses the language of Jerusalem, and says that Moab was "beyond" the Jordan; that the Book of Kings (I. iv. 24) uses the language of Babylon, and says that Solomon's dominions were "beyond" the river Euphrates; that David's sons were "priests" (2 Sam. viii. 18); that the heave offering, which was a free-will offering in Exodus xxv. 2, became at a later time, in xxx. 13-15, the fixed tax of half a shekel; and that the Court of the Priests (2 Chron. iv. 9) was a terrace, or raised platform. These instances are enough to show the necessity for a more exact translation of the Bible for those who would understand its contents critically; and if in some few cases the Authorized

Version in the passages referred to in this History seems not wholly to support the statements advanced, these instances of false renderings will plead a possible excuse. The Author usually quotes from his own translation.

The Author first published his opinion of **the** age of the several parts of the Bible in his " Historic Notes," 1854. In that work he described the books nearly in the order in which they stand in the Bible. But further study has led him to believe that the grounds upon which he forms his opinions can be best shown to the reader by describing the Writings together with the events of history in the order of time, as he has done in this volume.

32, Highbury Place, N.

TABLE OF CONTENTS.

c

THE HISTORY

OF THE

HEBREW NATION AND ITS LITERATURE.

THE history of **most** countries begins with an account **of** the arrival of a **tribe** or number of families from **a distance**, and of its settlement peaceably or forcibly **among the** weaker or less civilized inhabitants of whose yet **earlier** settlement no tradition remains. The Books placed **at** the beginning of the Bible contain three early traditions of the arrival of the Israelites in the land of Canaan.

One tradition, contained in the **Life** of Abraham, **relates** that a family, or tribe, from Chaldea, at the sources **of the** river Euphrates, moved first southward **into** Syria **of the** Rivers, the plains where the several streams unite **to form** that great river; **and** then again **moved** into **Southern** Canaan, and settled near Hebron, **as servants rather than** as masters of the Hittites, who were there already.

A second tradition tells us of a migration of Israelites **from** Syria, who, on reaching the **east** bank **of the** Jordan, divided into two parties, one of **which,** under Jacob, settled in Northern Canaan, near to Shechem, and **the** other, under his brother Esau, went further southward, beyond Hebron, and settled at Seir, in Edom.

A third tradition tells us that a **body of** Israelites, **a** part of those who settled in the north, **went** yet further southward into Lower Egypt, and settled **on** the east bank of the Nile. There they found **a** people stronger **and** more civilized than themselves; and hence had no choice but to remain as servants. But what they lost in freedom they gained in knowledge; and after a time **their** descendants escaped from Egypt, conquered the Amorites on the east bank of the Jordan, and then crossed that river into Northern Canaan, and helped their countrymen, who had before settled there, **to** become masters of the Canaanites, **rather than servants, as** perhaps they had hitherto been.

1

These three traditions relating to **the two** tribes **of** Southern and Northern Israelites, the later writers united into one continued narrative, giving the greater importance to the last, as being the one which relates **how** the wandering herdsmen became a settled independent **nation.**

We **have no** knowledge of when the Israelites first **committed to** writing this tradition that the forefathers, or rather the founders of their nation, had at one time been in bondage in Lower Egypt. But the belief was so firmly held by them, that there can be no reason to doubt it, although the histories which record it were written long after the events. The Israelites from Egypt may have left that country some time between 1600 and 1300 years before the Christian Era. Both from the tradition that we shall repeatedly meet with, and from what we learn from the name of the nation, we see that they at first settled on the eastern side of the Jordan; and hence, as the language and its expressions come to us from Judea, we find them called the *Beyond-men,* or the Hebrews.* Moreover, on that bank of the river was a village, or rather a district, called Ije-Abarim, or the *Mounds of the Hebrews,*† and the mountains in the neighbourhood were called the Mountains of the Hebrews.‡ Hence we can understand that, when, at a later time, the descendants of the Egyptian bondsmen crossed the Jordan, and conquered the country between that river and the Mediterranean Sea, they carried with **them** into Canaan this name of Hebrews, which may then **be** understood to mean *those who have crossed over.* This name, however, by no means displaced the more fixed name of Israelites. But the name of Israel, though it was never given up, yet after a time, in part received a new meaning. Having once meant the whole of the nation, it was used, after the division of the kingdom, by the northern tribes only; while the southern kingdom, consisting of Judah, Simeon, and part of Benjamin, was called the kingdom of Judah. And thus, throughout the whole of the Historic Books after the death of Solomon, and throughout the whole of the Prophets, the reader of the Bible is left in doubt whether the name of Israel includes both kingdoms, or only the northern kingdom. In the same way, the name of Jew has had two meanings; at first it belonged to the tribe of Judah only, but now is used by every one who

* Jerem. xxii. 20.   † Numb. xxi. 11, and xxxiii. 44.
‡ Numb. xxxiii. 47.

claims descent from Jacob. For this reason, it is more convenient to call our history that of the Hebrew nation, which includes all Israelites and Jews, whatever meaning may be given to those words.

The history of their flight out of Egypt under Moses, and of their conquest of Canaan under the generalship of Joshua, is related in the Pentateuch and the Book of Joshua. But those books are so far modern, that we find it difficult to determine what portion of historic truth they contain. The name of Moses, their leader, must, in Isaiah lxiii. 11, be translated the *Raiser-up*, as if so named because he raised up the nation; and the unhistoric character of the narrative of the march out of Egypt is further shown by the speeches on the occasion, which contain the whole body of the Jewish ecclesiastical law, with much civil law. These laws belong not to one age; but they were the growth of the centuries during which the nation lived under its monarchs; and the priestly legislators from time to time put them into the form of commands from God to Moses in order to gain for them a religious sanctity. The laws that were added, after the fall of the monarchy, are mostly of a moral character.

We naturally try to link the traditional history of the Israelites' flight out of Egypt with the better known history of that more civilized country, and thus to gain a knowledge of when it took place. But the hints in the Book of Exodus are too slight and too uncertain to be of much use. Possibly Thothmosis III, as he was the first Theban king who ruled over the Lower country, may have been "the king who knew not Joseph," who had not heard of his services, and who thus began to ill-treat the Israelites. He reformed the Egyptian calendar in the year B.C. 1322. His successor, Amunothph II, may thus have been the Pharaoh from whom the Israelites escaped.

According to the Book of Judges, which seems to be the oldest book in the Bible, the Israelites, on arriving on the east bank of the Jordan, having been refused a passage through the lands of the Edomites and Moabites, defeated Sihon, king of the Amorites, who dwelt between the rivers Arnon and Jabbok, and then seized his country, and Heshbon his capital city, and dwelt there for three hundred years, before crossing the Jordan.* This would place the flight out of Egypt about B.C. 1600. The Book of Numbers

---

* Judges xi. 15-27.

1 *

also mentions the Israelites seizing Heshbon and the land of the Amorites; but it differs from the Book of Judges in supposing that, without more delay than was necessary, they at once crossed the Jordan into Canaan. This would place the flight out of Egypt about B.C. 1300. If the Israelites who had escaped from Egypt crossed the Jordan at once, there may have been others who had dwelt between the Arnon and the Jabbok ever since they first went down into Egypt; for the nation could hardly have gained the name of Hebrews, or the *Beyond-People*, unless they had dwelt for two or three generations beyond, or on the east of the Jordan.

The Book of Numbers also tells us something of the history of the people who lived on the east of the Jordan before the Israelites arrived there; namely, that Sihon, king of the Amorites, had gained his country from the Moabites; and as an Arab in the present day will quote a national ballad to support his narrative if its truth is questioned by his hearers; so for its authority the Book of Numbers quotes the following very ancient piece of historic poetry:

> Come unto Heshbon, let it be built,
> And let the city of Sihon be prepared;
> For a fire is gone out of Heshbon,
> And a flame out of the city of Sihon;
> It hath consumed Ar of Moab,
> And the lords of Bamoth on the Arnon.
>   Alas for thee, O Moab!
> Thou art undone, O people of [the god] Chemosh!
>   He hath given his sons into flight,
>   And his daughters into captivity,
>   Unto Sihon, king of the Amorites.
> And their sown fields hath Heshbon destroyed unto Dibon,
> And their waste fields unto Nophah, which is by Medeba.[*]

Perhaps this may claim to be the earliest remaining piece of Hebrew ballad poetry. It is quoted a second time in Jeremiah xlviii.

The Book of Joshua, which described the crossing over the Jordan, and the defeat of the native inhabitants by the Israelites or Hebrews, is of about the same age as the Book of Deuteronomy, and was written or compiled by some unknown author, during the last few years of the Monarchy. It is the most misleading book in the Bible. It takes no notice of the two earlier settlements of the Israelites in Canaan, one of which is hinted at in the Life of Abraham,

---

[*] **Numb. xxi.** 21-30.

and the other in the Life of Jacob. It describes those who
had fled from Egypt as at once crossing the Jordan and
conquering the land to which they were strangers, and in
which they had no friends to receive them. It is true that
when we overlook this book, we have only a very meagre
account in the Book of Judges of the Eastern Israelites
crossing the Jordan to free their brethren from the yoke
of the Canaanites; and we have to wait until the reign of
Saul before we hear of any attempt on the part of the men
of Judah to become free. But if we rely upon that slender
narrative only, we shall go less astray than if we attend to
the Book of Joshua. As a history, it is of no authority;
but as a work on the geography of Palestine, it is of great
value; since, when it describes the division of the land
among the twelve tribes, it gives us a faithful picture of the
country at the time when the survey was made. The name
of the Israelite leader, Jehoshua or Joshua, may be translated
Jehovah saves; Oshea, as it was first written, is simply the
Saviour, or *Conqueror*.

Thus, passing by for the present the Pentateuch and the
Book of Joshua, we keep to the Book of Judges; and from
this we gain the earliest authentic glimpses of the Israelites
in the land of Canaan. This is in the thirteenth century
before the Christian Era. They were at that time broken
into a number of scattered tribes or families. These several
tribes were formed of a population far more numerous than
the small body of men who could have been living in the
land of Goshen in Lower Egypt, or even than that larger
body which afterwards crossed the Jordan to attempt to
gain land in Canaan. Those who entered the country with
arms in their hands were no doubt welcomed by others
whose families had never been in Egypt. It would seem as
if some parts of Canaan had been for a long time previous
quietly inhabited by men of the Hebrew race who "had not
known any of the wars of Canaan," which we now read of
in the Book of Joshua. "They dwelt among the Canaanites,
the Hittites, the Amorites, the Perizzites, the Hivites, and
the Jebusites; and they took their daughters to be their
wives, and gave their daughters to their sons; and served
their gods."*

Our earliest knowledge of the country is limited to the
middle and northern parts. Here the Israelites were in
continual warfare with the native inhabitants, among whom

* Judges iii. 1-6.

they had settled, and whom they were striving to dispossess
from their lands and houses. These were known under
various names, some of which merely describe their habits,
or manner of life. Such were the Hivites and Avites or
villagers, the Perizzites or *country people*, the Amorites or
mountaineers, and the Anakites or *giants*. The better
marked tribes on the west of the Jordan were the Canaanites
in **the** middle of the land, the Jebusites of Jerusalem, **the**
Sidonians near Mount Lebanon, and the Hittites in the
south, and Philistines of the south-west country. On the
east of the Jordan the enemies of Israel were the Midianites,
the Ammonites, and the Moabites. Of these tribes **the**
Moabites were the most quiet, and the Philistines the most
warlike and troublesome. The neighbours with whom they
had frequent wars, but whose more barren territory they
did not attempt to gain, were the Edomites on the south,
and the Amalekites on the south-west. But the name of
Edomite, like that of Israelite, has two meanings. It sometimes means the less civilized people of the desert, called
also Kenites; and sometimes a more civilized people touching
on the Calebites of the Negib, or south country of Judah.
These latter Edomites, like the tribe of Judah, worshipped
God under the name of Jehovah.* The others were more
wandering and more allied to the Amalekites. But though
we place the seat of the Midianites in the eastern desert,
and that of the Amalekites in the desert between Egypt and
the Philistines, yet we sometimes meet with Midianites **in**
the south, and Amalekites in the east; as these Arab tribes,
like the Ishmaelites, were very little fixed to one spot. To
the north of the land of Canaan dwelt the Syrians, who were
divided into three or four tribes, and who were too strong
to be conquered by the Israelites.

The first war mentioned in the days of the Judges is with
the Syrians, at a time when **the** Israelites, or a northern
portion of them, were held in servitude for eight years by a
king whose name, Cushan-rishathaim, which may be translated the *Most Wicked Negress*, seems to place him in the
region of imaginary tradition rather than of history. He
was defeated by a body of Calebites from Southern Judah,
who may very possibly have been driven to migrate northwards **by** the heavy hand of the Philistines, which pressed
upon them in their own country.† In the north these Calebites may have formed the tribes of Issachar and Zebulun,

---

* Amos ix. 12.   † Judges iii. 9, 10.

as those tribes were connected with Judah; and when the
later historian reduced the tribes into one family, those two
were said to be sons of the same mother with Judah. Moreover there was a small territory on the Syrian frontier to
which they may have given a name; it was called Hamath
of Judah.* This servitude under the Syrians, like the other
misfortunes in the time of the Judges, the historian, or
rather the later editor of the book, devoutly says, befell
them because they had done evil in the sight of Jehovah.

There was, about the same time, another migration of
Calebites northward from Hebron, to the City of Jearim
and to Beth-lehem. This we learn from the genealogies in
1 Chron. ii.; and it explains much that we shall soon meet
with, as to the agreement between those three towns in
religion and political feeling, when we find the Ark of
Jehovah in the City of Jearim.

The next war mentioned was an invasion by the Moabites,
who, being joined with a body of Ammonites and Amalekites, harassed the Israelites of the neighbourhood of Gilgal
and Jericho. This tribe of Israelites were named Jaminites,
or Ben-jaminites, a name which may be connected with that
of their enemies, the Children of Ammon, or Beni-ammon,
who seem to have had a settlement in that spot. After a
servitude of eighteen years under the Moabites, Ehud, a
Benjamite, found an opportunity of stabbing Eglon, the
king of Moab; and shortly afterwards the Benjamites were
relieved by a body of their neighbours from the hill country
of Ephraim. The Israelites then defeated the Moabites, and
seized the fords of the Jordan to stop their retreat, and slew
them all to a man.†

While this war was going on, on one side of the land,
the Philistines from the south were harassing those of the
Israelites who were nearest to their country. From this
trouble the Israelites were for a time released by Shamgar.‡
From the after mention of Shamgar, it seems probable that
he dwelt in the land of Ephraim, and that the Philistines
were invading some part of that country, not that Shamgar
was attempting to free any part of Judah from their iron
rule.

The history then carries us back to the northern Israelites,
and we hear of their struggle with the Canaanites of that
part of the country which was afterwards called Galilee.
These Canaanites were under a king named Jabin, who had

* 2 Kings xiv. 28.   † Judges iii. 13-30.   ‡ Judges iii. 31.

nine hundred chariots of iron; and they cruelly oppressed the men of Naphtali and Zebulun, who were among the most northerly of the Israelites. After a suffering of twenty years, the two tribes of Zebulun and Naphtali, under the leadership of Barak, rallied against their oppressors, and called to their help their stronger neighbours, the men of Ephraim. The tribe of Ephraim was the most settled portion of the Israelites, and they had adopted some form of government, while the other tribes were stragglers scattered over the land, every man doing what was right in his own eyes. The Ephraimites were at that time governed, or, in their own language, judged, by a brave woman of the name of Deborah, who rose to that post by the wants of society at the time. Laws there were none; but a member of a tribe who had the courage and the honesty to give a fair opinion on right and wrong, when a difficulty arose, and whose good sense so far gained the approval of the others that they were willing to act upon it, became Judge of the tribe. Evil-doers were then punished by their neighbours according to the award of the judge.

Deborah, after quieting her own tribe as a judge, was also called to act as a general; and she led her followers, together with some of the Benjamites, to the assistance of Barak, the leader of Zebulun and Naphtali; and, at the foot of Mount Tabor, near the brook Kishon, their united forces defeated Sisera, the general of the Canaanites. Sisera fled, and was murdered by Jael, a woman in whose tent he had sought for refuge.

On the occasion of this victory over the Canaanites, we have a very remarkable poem attributed to Deborah, the leader and judge of the Ephraimites, who was a prophetess or poet. It is a spirited triumphal shout of an early date, but its enumeration of the tribes shows that in its present form it belongs to a time after David had surveyed and divided the land. In particular the three lines which mention Zebulun a second time, with Asher and Naphtali, may have been added after David's division of the country into its well-known twelve districts. It was natural that a popular song should receive changes as time goes on. If it had not been altered it perhaps would not have been saved; for a nation's ballads get forgotten when historians begin to write.

It gives glory to Jehovah for the nation's success :—

For the leaders undertaking to lead in Israel,
For the self-devotion of the people, bless ye Jehovah.

We have some thoughts relating to the march out of
Egypt, which we do not find in our books of Exodus and
Numbers, as when the writer says,

> O Jehovah, when thou wentest out from Seir,
> When thou marchedst out of the field of Edom,
> The earth trembled.

The poem describes the **desolate** and disturbed state of
the country previous **to Deborah's** rule, and the sad want of
weapons among her brave troops :—

> In the days of Shamgar the son of Anath,
> In the days of Jael, the highways were unoccupied,
> And the travellers on foot journeyed through by-paths.
> Rulers of villages had ceased **in** Israel, they had ceased,
> Until I Deborah **arose, I** arose a mother in Israel,
> They had chosen **new gods;**
> Then there was **a war at the** city gates.
> Was there **a shield seen, or** a spear,
> Among forty **thousand in** Israel?
> My heart is toward the lawgivers of Israel,
> That devoted themselves for the people :
> Bless ye Jehovah.

In the same noble strain it relates that the men of
Ephraim, Benjamin, Machir or Manasseh, Zebulun, Issachar,
and Naphtali united their forces against the common enemy;
but that the men of Reuben and those of Gilead or Gad, on
the east of the Jordan, and the men of Dan and of Asher on
the coast of the Mediterranean, did not join their brethren
in the struggle. They were too far **removed** from the
danger. Thus ten of the tribes are mentioned by name.
The eleventh and twelfth, the men **of Judah,** and Simeon,
may be those called Jehovah's people, of whom only a small
number came with the others ;

> Then came down a remnant of the mighty ones,
> Jehovah's people came down for me against the warriors.

Perhaps at this time the hand of the Philistines **was** too
heavy upon them for a larger body to be able **to** help their
northern brethren;* or perhaps they had **few** feelings in
common with them ; as we see that the eastern tribes also
did not cross the Jordan to make common **cause** against the
Canaanites.

The next war that we are told of **is an** invasion by the
Midianites and Amalekites and Children of the East. The
last-named people were probably the Ammonites or Children

* **Judges iv. ; v.**

of Ammon. These three tribes crossed the Jordan to attack
the men of Manasseh, who were at the same time struggling
with the Amorites, the natives who dwelt amongst them.
Gideon, the leader of Manasseh, called together the fighting
men of his own tribe, together with those of Asher, Zebulun,
and **Naphtali.** The men of Gilead, who had come over to
help him, seem to have deserted him. Gideon, however,
routed his enemies, and then he summoned the Ephraimites
to guard the fords of the Jordan, and to cut off the fugitives.
This they did, and they gained an amount of booty that
reconciled them to the affront of not having been summoned
sooner. The release from the invasion by the Midianites
was long remembered with feelings of thankfulness pro-
portioned to the danger felt. Five centuries later the prophet
Isaiah compared Judah's escape from the joint invasion by
Israel and Syria, to the "day of Midian."

This victory of Gideon, or Jerubbaal, as he was also
named, marked him out as a man fit to be the ruler of
Israel, and to save them from the troubles that arose from
the want of a single head to lead them against the enemies
that surrounded them and dwelt among them. Accordingly,
he obtained the rank of chief of all the northern Israelites.*
His name, Jerubbaal, tells us that he worshipped God under
the name of Baal, although the later editor of the book of
Judges has added a story, with a wish to give to Gideon's
second name the opposite meaning.

Gideon had dwelt at Ophrah in the land of Manasseh, on
the east side of the Jordan; but his son Abimelech, who
succeeded him in his high post, was born in Shechem, in the
land of Ephraim, and had thus gained the friendship of some
of that tribe. Abimelech put to death all but one of his
brethren, the other sons of Gideon, and got himself made
king at Shechem; and he was the first who bore that title
among the Israelites. Shechem, his capital, was a place of
some religious importance. It stood at the foot of two hills,
upon one of which the son of Jerubbaal, who worshipped
God under the name of Baal, or *Lord*, may have had an
altar; as the hill at a later time bore the name of Ebal, or
the ruins of Baal. The other hill was called Gerizim. Near
the town was a sacred grove, or oak, called the Oak of the
Cloud-observers, or soothsayers, and also the Oak of Moreh,
or *teaching*, because the will of God was there taught by the
priests.† Shechem was for a long time the capital of the

* **Judges vi.; vii.; viii.**   † Gen. xii. 6.

northern tribes. The men of Shechem used also in worship
the name of Baal-berith, *Lord of the Covenant*, and El-berith,
God of the Covenant. This shows that, before the present
Levitical law was published, they believed that they were
living under a divine covenant, that as long as they were
obedient to God, they would receive in return his guardian
care.*

Abimelech's thus violently seizing upon the power was
the cause of a civil war between Ephraim and Manasseh,
which ended in the death of the usurper Abimelech, and the
transfer for the time of the chieftainship to another tribe.†
Tola, a man of Issachar, was then made Judge, or ruler of
the northern tribes. He fixed his residence, not within the
limits of his own less important people, but at the town of
Shamir, afterwards called Samaria, in the land of Manasseh,
though at that time said to be in the land of Ephraim.‡
The commonly received division of the land was probably
not made until David's reign.

After Tola, says the historian, Jair of Gilead judged Israel,
as if the seat of government had been removed from one
part of the country to the other. But we may more reasonably suppose that it is the narrative only that changes to the
east of the Jordan, shortly to return again to the successors
of Tola. Jair and his successors may have ruled in the east
at the same time that Deborah and Gideon and their successors were ruling or struggling against their oppressors in
the west.§

Jephthah of Gilead is the next great captain mentioned.
He is called the son of Gilead, after the Hebrew peculiar
use of the word Son, and according to the not unusual
custom with the Hebrew writers of creating a father for any
man or class of men, out of a descriptive adjective. He was
called to his post by the necessity felt among the people of
finding a leader who could unite their scattered forces
against the enemy. The Ammonites, who dwelt in the more
desert country to the east of Gilead, had made a serious
incursion on the Israelites on both sides of the Jordan; and
the men of Gilead, in their distress, sent for Jephthah, who
was then living at Tob, in Syria, whither he had fled from
a quarrel with his brethren. When he arrived they made
him their captain at Mizpeh, in the land which is sometimes

* Judges viii. 33 ix. 46.   † Judges ix.   ‡ Judges x. 1.
§ Judges x. 3.

described as that of the eastern half-tribe of Manasseh, but which then may have been part of Gilead.

It seems that the Ammonites invaded Gilead on the plea that they had possessed that land before the Israelites arrived there. To this plea Jephthah answered that the Israelites had dispossessed the Amorites under Sihon, king of Heshbon, and that the Ammonites had not dwelt in that part of the country; and he gives the history, which we have already quoted, of the Israelites' arrival on the banks of the Jordan. On coming out of Lower Egypt, they crossed the desert to the Red Sea, and then came to Kadesh. From thence they asked leave of the Edomites and Moabites to pass through their territory; but, being refused, they went round Moab till they came to the northern bank of the river Arnon, an eastern tributary of the Jordan. There they were attacked by Sihon king of the Amorites; and on defeating him they seized his territory, which lay between the Arnon and Jabbok. There the Israelites had dwelt quietly for three hundred years, without fighting against either the Moabites or the Ammonites; they were not strong enough to attack them. This is a most interesting narrative, both for what it tells and for what it omits, as compared with the longer narrative in the Pentateuch. It tells us that the Israelites had asked, and been refused a passage by the Moabites, and that they had dwelt for three hundred years between the Arnon and the Jabbok, before crossing the Jordan; and it explains how the Amorites, whom we find on the west of the Jordan, had been driven there when dispossessed of their own land. It omits all mention of the delivery of the Law, and of the Ark, and of any supernatural events as having happened on the march, and of the fighting with Og, king of Bashan, of whom we shall read in the Book of Numbers.

To return to our history. Jephthah defeated the Ammonites, but before the battle he made a vow to Jehovah that he would offer up as a burnt-offering whatever first met him from out of the doors of his house. On his return home his daughter, his only child, came out with music to greet him after his victory. And he accordingly performed his so-called religious vow, after allowing her two months to wander on the mountains and bewail her fate in dying unmarried. The writer, as if to prove the truth of the story, adds that the young unmarried women of Israel celebrated a lament for Jephthah's daughter for four days every year. But this goes rather to disprove the tradition, as it tells us that the writer lived long after the event; and it makes it probable that the sad story was invented to give a reason for the yearly custom. The story, however, tells us that the custom of human sacrifices was not wholly unknown.

After Jephthah's **victory over** the Ammonites, **a** body **of** the Ephraimites **crossed over the Jordan** to help him, **or** rather to claim a **share of the booty** for which they had **not** fought; and he then had to fight against his allies. But he defeated them, and slew a large **number of** them on their retreat homewards at the fords of the Jordan. The Ephraimites, when they wished to cross the **river**, were known by their pronunciation. **The two tribes** gave a different sound to the letter S; **the men of Gilead** called **upon** the fugitives to say the **word** Shibboleth, **and when they said** Sibboleth they **slew them.***

The **narrative now returns to the western tribes;** and we **are told of Ibzan** in Bethlehem of Zebulun, who judged **Israel** for seven years; then of Ajalon, a second Zebulunite, **who** judged for ten years; and then of Abdon, an Ephraimite, who judged for eight years.† We shall often, **in** later times, have to note a want of union among the northern tribes of Israel, and shall **see** that Issachar and Zebulun yielded the leadership of the north very unwillingly to their greater neighbours, Ephraim **and** Manasseh. This **may** perhaps explain why, in these early **days, the** judgeship **of** northern Israel **was** shifted about from **Zebulun** to Ephraim.

Hitherto we **have** hardly met with **the name of** the **great** tribe of Judah, **which** afterwards **plays so forward a part in** our history. But **we** now learn **that** part **or all of Judah** was held in quiet servitude **by the** Philistines; **and this,** indeed, we only **learn,** as if **by** accident, in **the history of** Samson of the tribe **of** Dan. So complete **was the** servitude at least of some parts of Judah, **and** so little hope had they then of freedom, that they were alarmed **at** Samson's rashness in attacking **the** Philistines, which **they feared** might increase the severity of the bondage **under which** they were suffering.‡ The rout of a small body **of** Philistines by Shamgar, as before mentioned, seems **not to** have been followed by any attempt of the tribe of Judah to shake **off** the bondage of those powerful and warlike neighbours. This **continued** superiority of the Philistines over **the**

* Judges x. 6—xii. 7.　　　† Judges xii. 8-15.
‡ Judges xv. 11.

Israelites is easily explained by their possession of iron for
weapons of war, an advantage which the Israelites were
without.* The Philistines probably received their iron
from the island of Cyprus by means of the Phenician traders.
But over how large a part of Judah the Philistine power
reached, cannot be determined, because we have no history
of that important tribe at this time.

The tribe of Judah is almost unknown to us before the
time of David. But, though not yet independent, its later
history leads us to think that it was not less advanced in
civilization than the northern Israelites. Its chief city,
Hebron, was the seat of the Levites,† and, no doubt, of
Levitical learning. Near it was the sacred grove of Mamre,
and an altar to Jehovah, said to have been built by Abraham.‡ This was the chief spot for the worship of Jehovah
before the Ark was moved to the City of Jearim, and before
Jerusalem robbed both those towns of that honour.§ Near,
also, to Hebron, was a town called Debir, *the Oracle*, a name
afterwards given to the Holy of Holies in Solomon's temple,
when the voice of Jehovah was thought to be heard there.
This town of Debir was also called the city of Sepher, or
Writing,‖ from which we judge that learning was there
cultivated; and perhaps we shall not be wrong in giving to
it the credit of those Jehovistic writings which were written
before Jerusalem became the capital. The lost Book of the
Wars, quoted in Numbers xxi., was a Jehovistic poem, and
it may have come from the City of Sepher. The Ten Commandments, in Exodus xx., which are Jehovistic, and have
been grafted on to the Elohistic narrative; and the
Jehovistic history of the creation in Genesis ii. 4—iv.,
which we shall speak of presently as older than the narrative
into which it is inserted,—both of these may have come
from the City of Sepher. These early hints explain the
high rank which the tribe of Judah took among the other
tribes, as soon as it became independent of the Philistines
and Hittites.

The difference in religion was probably very slight, between the northern tribes who worshipped God under the
name of El, and its plural, Elohim, and Baal, *Lord ;* and the
southern tribes, who used the name of Jehovah, a word
which perhaps meant *He that is.* They both employed the
sacrifice of animals as a mode of worship, and had High

* 1 Sam. xiii. 19.   † **Josh. xxi. 13.**   ‡ Gen. xiii. 18.
          § 2 Sam. xv. 7.   ‖ Judges i. 11.

Places where the sacrifices were performed, and where the will of God was to be enquired for; but the southern tribe had a sacred Ark, or box, containing the Tables of the Law, a moveable oracle, as Jehovah was thought to be always present with it. The northern tribes usually had a house, or temple, near the altar of sacrifice; while the Ark of the southern tribes had always lived under a tent until the reign of Solomon.* The northern people had no regular body of priests; among them any man might be appointed to the priesthood, as in the case of Samuel; and a man might act as his own priest in the house near the altar.† They claimed to be a holy nation, a kingdom of priests.‡ But the southern people had the Levites as a class of priests; and their ceremonies were, at a later time, embodied in the Levitical law, while the clanship of these priests gave a steadiness to society, which was much needed in the north. The rite of circumcision belonged at first to the northern people, they may have brought it out of Egypt; § but the observance of the seventh day, and the distinction between clean and unclean animals, belonged more particularly to the south. As the national feasts were regulated by the harvest and the crops, the northern people kept their chief feast a month later than it was kept in the south.‖ These outward differences between the north and south continued until the fall of the two monarchies.

The story of Samson is too fabulous, and perhaps too modern, to throw much light upon these early times. He was an Israelite of the tribe of Dan, living among the Philistines, from whom his countrymen had not been able to wrest the possession of the soil. His mother brought him up as a Nazarite, or *one set apart* unto God, who was neither to drink wine nor ever have his hair cut. As long as he conformed to this rule, he possessed a strength more than human; and, among other heroic deeds, he routed the Philistines at a hill called Lehi, *a cheek*, so called, perhaps, from its form; from which name seems to have arisen the story that Samson's weapon was the cheek-bone of an ass. After a time, Samson disclosed to his wife the secret of his strength, and she cut his hair off in his sleep, and then the Philistines took him prisoner, put out his eyes, and carried him to Gaza. There, as his hair grew, he recovered his strength,

---

* 2 Sam. vii. 6.   † 2 Kings xvii. 32.   ‡ Exod. xix. 6.
§ Exod. iv. 25; Josh. v. 5; Herodotus ii. 104.   ‖ 1 Kings xii. 32.

and he pulled down upon the heads of the assembled Philistines the temple of their fish-god Dagon.*

At this time, while the Israelites were living in huts or tents, without a settled form of government, Egypt was the greatest kingdom in the world. It had lately been united under one sceptre. Thebes, its capital, enriched by the Nubian gold-mines, had been ornamented with massive temples, covered with sculpture, and surrounded by colossal statues. Its kings could keep large armies in their pay : and they enjoyed the power of invading even distant countries. It was about the year B.C. 1200, that Rameses II, one of the greatest of the Egyptian kings, on marching through Palestine, carved his boastful monument on the face of the rock at Beyrout, on the coast of the Mediterranean Sea, a few miles to the north of Sidon. He had travelled more than a thousand miles from his capital; he had brought his army through the desert and Palestine, more than five hundred miles from his frontier city, overthrowing every resistance that he met with on his route. The Philistines, through whose country he crossed, must have been great sufferers; and very possibly the Israelities may have felt a relief by the check given to their enemies' power. How much farther northward the Egyptians marched and conquered, we are not told. Nor are we told that the Phenicians carried supplies for them in their ships; but the Egyptian trade was too profitable to the cities of Tyre and Sidon to allow us for a moment to suppose that they were otherwise than friendly to Rameses II.

We have no means of learning very exactly when the wars which we have been reading of within the land of Canaan took place; but the reign of Rameses II in Egypt must, at any rate, fall within the time when the Israelites were ruled by their Judges. It is important to notice in our history that this great invasion of the land of Canaan is not mentioned by the Hebrew writers. This circumstance, however, is explained by remarking how small a portion of the country the Israelites had yet occupied. They had not advanced to the west of the hill country; even two or three centuries later the strong cities of Gath and Gezer were both held by their enemies; and between these cities and the Mediterranean Sea there was ample width of country for the Egyptians to march and pillage the weaker inhabitants without their inroad gaining the notice of the Hebrew

* Judges xiii.—xvi.

writers. The sculpture left by Rameses on the rock at
Beyrout, does much to disprove the history in the Book of
Joshua as to the early occupation of all Canaan by the
Israelites.

In those days, before there was a king in Israel, and when
every man did what was right in his own eyes, some of the
Danites, who had not succeeded in winning an inheritance
for themselves from their strong neighbours the Philistines,
among whom, or near whom, they had settled, determined
to look for it elsewhere, where the owners of the soil might
be weaker and not so well armed. They had learned, by
means of spies, that there was at Laish, near the sources of
the Jordan, on the eastern slope of Anti-libanus, or Hermon,
a small tribe, perhaps Canaanites, or perhaps Syrians, allies
or subjects of **Sidon, who were** weak and unprepared for
defence, and **too far** from their friends the Sidonians to receive
immediate help from them. Accordingly, the Danites set
off, six hundred in number, and well armed, to see if land
could not be seized more easily there than in **the** south. In
order to gain a religious sanctity for their violent undertaking, they began by robbing an Ephraimite named Micah,
near whose house they passed, of his **wooden** Teraphs, **or**
household idols, of his silver images, and of his Ephod, **or**
priestly garment, and they carried them off together with
their owner's priest, a young Levite, of the family of Judah,
who was willing to be the priest of a tribe rather than of
one man. They then marched northward, they put the
unoffending men of Laish to the sword, and built there their
new town of Dan, which in more modern times has been
known by the names of Paneas and Cæsarea Philippi.
Micah's graven image remained an object of worship in Dan
as long as the House of God was in Shiloh ; that is, **until**
all sacrifices out of Jerusalem were forbidden, by **the**
authority of **the Sons** of Aaron, in that city. The descendants of Micah's Levite remained priests there **until** the
northern tribes **were** carried away captive in **the** year B.C.
722.* This migration of the Danites is the **third** migration
from south to north, all caused as we may suppose by a
wish to escape the Philistine oppression, and on learning
the success of the northern Israelites in gaining their
independence.

Here, for the first time, we have met with the Levites,
who seem to have been a humble, wandering class of men,

* Judges xvii. ; xviii.

like the Preaching Friars among the Catholics, whose poverty
may have added to their character for holiness. They were
not yet classed into a tribe apart from the tribe of Judah.
At least, this Levite was of the family of Judah. Micah,
the Ephraimite above spoken of, had made for himself, out
of eleven hundred pieces of silver, a molten image, and a
graven image. In addition to these, he had some Teraphs,
perhaps wooden household gods, and an Ephod, perhaps a
priestly dress, which gave a religious character to the wearer.
He had, moreover, appointed one of his sons to be his family
priest, and placed in his hands the offerings which were to
be burnt before these images. This "filling a man's hands"
with the offerings was at all times, among the Israelites, the
act of consecration to the priesthood. With these arrangements, Micah's religious establishment seemed complete;
but when the young Levite passed by, Micah thought that
he should do still better if he could gain his services; and
upon the promise of his victuals and a suit of clothes and
ten pieces of silver by the year as his wages, the Levite
agreed to remain with him as his priest. This he did
till, as we have seen, he deserted him for what seemed a
better lot.

The last narrative in the Book of Judges is of a very
modern character. Upon the occasion of a gross and wicked
outrage committed by the inhabitants of Gibeah in Benjamin,
the whole of Israel, from Dan to Beersheba, were summoned
together to revenge it. They met before the altar of
Jehovah at Mizpeh, in Benjamin, in number 400,000 armed
men. They then went to ask counsel of God at Beth-el,
where, at that time, was the Ark of the Covenant, under
the charge of Phinehas, the grandson of Aaron. There they
were told that Judah was to begin the battle. After a first
and a second repulse, they slew of Benjamin 25,000, leaving
only 600 out of the tribe alive. They burnt their cities,
and, as it would seem, slew all the women and children.
But, after a time, the conquerors repented of their severity,
and more particularly of a vow that they had made that no
one should ever give a daughter to a Benjamite to wife, a
vow which points to an early belief that the tribe of Benjamin were part of the children of Ammon, and had been
rather unwillingly admitted into the family of Israel. This
vow, if acted upon, would destroy one of the tribes of Israel,
as all the women of that tribe had been slain. But they had
also made a second vow, that whoever came not up in

obedience to the summons to the great meeting at Mizpeh, should be put to death. As they learned that the men of Jabesh in Gilead had not come up to Mizpeh, they put them and their families to the sword, saving only four hundred young women, whom they gave to the Benjamites. But, as these were not enough, they gave them leave to go to Shiloh, and to seize upon such young women as were yet wanted from among those who came out of the city to dance at the yearly religious feast there celebrated to Jehovah.*

In this improbable story there are a number of circumstances not belonging to this early age, such as the common action of all the Israelites dwelling between Dan and Beersheba; there being at Shiloh a yearly religious festival to Jehovah, rather than to Elohim the northern name for God; the answer of Jehovah instead of Elohim at Beth-el, *the House of Elohim*; and the Ark of God being at Beth-el under the charge of Aaron's grandson, and Judah being the leader in the war. These are all circumstances inconsistent with what we have been reading about. The story may have been founded on wars between the Israelites and the children of Ammon, who had once held the land of Benjamin. But, with the exception of the history of Samson, and of this story in the last three chapters of the Book of Judges, and with the exception also of the Introduction, chap. i.-iii., 6, which is a continuation of the Book of Joshua, this book must be considered of a very early date.

At this time, called the time of the Judges, we have the picture of a people living in a very rude state, many of them without laws and without magistrates. Their wars were begun for the sake of plunder, and carried on with such unrelenting cruelty, that the women and children suffered equally with the fighting men. None were spared but such as were willing to live under tribute, and cultivate the soil for their Israelite masters. No doubt the larger number of the conquered did submit. In that case the Israelites and the Canaanites lived quietly together; and notwithstanding what we read in the Levitical Law about not joining in marriage with the Canaanites, we shall meet with proof that the two races were very much moulded into one. During this time, the scattered families were gradually arranging themselves into towns and states, guided, no doubt, by the ties of blood; and the necessity of putting themselves under the command of a captain when going out

* Judges xix.; **xx.**

2 *

to battle may have quickened the growth of regular government and taught them obedience to law. But that no part
of the ceremonial law was yet written, is probable from our
as yet finding no mention of it, and in particular no mention
of an established order of priests.

The land was as yet by no means all brought into cultivation; nor had it in every **part** an owner, other **than** the
tribe that claimed sway over **it.** The inhabitants of the few
walled towns, owned the pasture lands around; but the
larger part of the **people** lived in **huts,** or tents made of
skins, grouped together into an encampment, perhaps
surrounded with stakes. Such had been the thicket-camps
and hill-top camps of the Canaanites; and such were the
early dwellings of the Israelites. Within the tribe every
man might feed his flock or herd wherever he could find
herbage; and he was allowed to claim as his own such portion of the open field as he **could** till; for **it** was common to
the whole tribe before **he had dug** a well and given a value
to the soil by his labour.

The tribes which the Israelites **dispossessed of** their lands,
as also those neighbours against **whom they** occasionally
fought, were mostly of the same race as themselves, speaking dialects of the Hebrew, Syriac, and Arabic languages;
yet, in the history of the descent of the several nations
of the earth, in Genesis x., the writer has made a wide
separation between them and the Israelites.

The Edomites,[*] the Ammonites, the Moabites,[†] **the
Syrians,[‡]** the Amalekites,[§] and the Midianites,[||] who all
lived on their borders, they acknowledged as of their own
family, and they classed them with themselves as Children
of **Shem; but** the others, amongst whom they settled, and
with **whom they very** much intermarried, notwithstanding
the laws against it, **and** whom they, sooner or later, conquered, and whose lands at last they succeeded in gaining,
they classed with **the** Egyptians, their former masters, as
children of Ham.[¶] These were the Canaanites, the Amorites, the Jebusites, **the** Philistines, **and** others whom we
shall afterwards **meet with,** whose exact geographical place
in Palestine it would not **be** easy to fix. As **we** never read
of interpreters being needed by the Hebrews in their intercourse with these tribes, whether the neighbours around or
those **in the** midst of them whom they conquered, we must

---

[*] Gen. xxxvi. 1.   [†] Gen. xix. 37, 38.   [‡] Gen. x. 22.
[§] Gen. xxxvi. 12   [||] Gen. xxv. 2.   [¶] Gen. x. 14, 19.

suppose that they all spoke nearly the same language. In Isaiah xix. 18, Hebrew is called the language of Canaan.

We may stop to remark that all the little tribes here spoken of, whether friends or enemies, together with the Israelites themselves, are, in the Hebrew books, often called the Peoples, as distinguished from the Nations; this latter word is more particularly given to the more powerful Egyptians, Assyrians, and Babylonians.

The last-mentioned of the peoples, the Philistines, were the latest to be conquered; they did not submit till all Israel was united into one strong monarchy. Their origin and history are obscure and tantalizing from their importance and uncertainty. They were also called Caphtorites,* and were said to have been new settlers in the land, to have come there from the island of Caphtor, and to have violently dispossessed the Avites of Gaza and that neighbourhood, where they established themselves in several strong cities, occupying the territory which the Jewish geographer in the Book of Joshua assigns to the tribes of Simeon and Dan, and to part of that of Judah. The island Caphtor has been thought by some to be Crete; but it was more probably one of the marshy islands in the Egyptian Delta, near to Pelusium. There these warlike people, without a distinctive name, seem to have settled as new comers some time before the Israelites arrived in Lower Egypt. They lived under kings of their own, who are called by Manetho, in his "History of Egypt," the Hyksos or Shepherd-kings. They ravaged the neighbouring territory, and put much of Lower Egypt under tribute, till they were driven out shortly before the Israelites settled in the same country. In the History of Joseph, we learn that the name of a Shepherd was hateful to the Egyptians,† which may perhaps have been caused by the injuries which the Egyptians had received from the Hyksos. The word Philistines means simply the Foreigners, and it is translated in the Septuagint. The name of their city in Egypt, Pelusium, seems to be derived from it. In the Egyptian language, a foreigner is called Shemmo. In Egypt both the hated Shepherds and the Israelites would be included under the same name; and both carried it away with them on leaving Lower Egypt. Thus it seems doubtful how far the Philistines were of the same race as the Israelites. Like the Edomites they did not practise circumcision. The Hebrew historians speak of their whole race as Sons of

* Deut. ii. 23.   † Gen. xlvi. 34.

Shem,* or Shemites, and again they give to those families
who settled among the Philistines the name of Simeonites,
which is simply the diminutive form of Shemites. The
reason for the Philistines having been thought by some
critics to have been Cretans, is because, in later days, they
were called Cherethites.† But they had this name more
probably because these skilled warriors were chosen by
David and his successors as their body-guard or axe-bearers;‡
and it may be derived from the word Chereth, *to cut.*

With regard to the religion of these tribes, they were
most of them idolators, each worshipping its own god or
gods, except the Edomites, the Midianites, and the Amalekites.   For these three tribes we hear of no worship of
strange gods; and these tribes were classed with the
Israelites, among the children of Abraham.   Of the Edomites we are particularly told that they were worshippers of
Jehovah, like the neighbouring tribe of Judah.§   Indeed,
the Edomites seem to have been almost as closely related to
Judah, as Judah was to the northern Israelites; and before
the end of our history **we** shall **find the** southern half
of Judah united to Edom.   The Amalekites, with the
Ismaelites,‖ including the Arabs, practised circumcision like
the Hebrews and Egyptians.   The Philistines worshipped a
Fish-god, named Dagon;¶ **and** were reproached as being
uncircumcised.   Some of the Canaanites seem to have
worshipped the sun, as we meet with several towns named
Beth-shemesh, and one named Ir-shemesh, *the city of the
sun.***

ELI, JUDGE AT SHILOH IN EPHRAIM.

We have already been told that there was at Shiloh, in
the land of Ephraim, about **ten** miles to the south of
Shechem, a house of Elohim, **or** God, of more than local
importance;†† and then, rather in contradiction to that statement, that there was a yearly religious festival to Jehovah
in that city, to which the neighbouring tribes resorted.‡‡
We are now again told of a temple to Jehovah in that city,
containing the sacred ark, and of a priest of Jehovah in
that temple, named Eli, whose priesthood and judgeship
would have been hereditary in his family if it had not been

---

* Gen. x. 22.   † Ezek. xxv. 16.   ‡ 2 Sam. xv. 18.
§ Amos ix. 12.   ‖ Gen. xvii. 23.   ¶ 1 Sam. v. 4.
** Josh. xix. 22, **38**   xxi. 16; xix. **41**.   †† Judges xviii. 31.
                ‡‡ Judges **xxi. 19.**

forfeited by the wickedness of his sons. To his care, in order to be educated as a priest, the young Samuel was intrusted by a pious mother from the land of Benjamin. Eli's judgeship may have begun about the year B.C. 1100. It lasted forty years, but to whom he succeeded of the Judges hitherto mentioned we do not know.

While Eli was yet judge, but quite an old man, the Philistines had met the Israelites in battle at Aphek, near the south-western corner of the land of Benjamin, and had defeated them. In their alarm, the Israelites sent to Shiloh to fetch from thence the " Ark of the Covenant of Jehovah, who dwelleth between the cherubs," which they hoped, as a sacred talisman, would ensure to them victory by its very presence in the army. But they were again defeated; the two sons of Eli were slain, and the Ark of God, or of Jehovah, for it has both names, was taken by the Philistines. Eli the Priest, when he heard of the disaster, fell down dead, after having judged Israel for forty years.*

Eli is said to have been warned by Jehovah that his family should be put aside from the priesthood in favour of a faithful priest, who should have a sure house and should walk before God's anointed, or the king, for ever. This points not to Samuel, but to Zadok, in whose favour Eli's descendant, Abiathar, was put aside in the beginning of Solomon's reign. It also helps us to the date of the Jehovistic colouring to the Life of Eli.

SAMUEL, JUDGE IN BENJAMIN.

On the death of Eli and his sons, Samuel, who had been brought up under his care at Shiloh, and had already made himself known to all Israel as a prophet, succeeded to the judgeship, not by election, nor by any appointment to the office; but his wisdom made him to be accepted as such by his countrymen. Samuel dwelt at Ramah, in the land of Benjamin; and here our history changes to a more southern part of the country. Hitherto the great tribes of Ephraim and Manasseh have been those chiefly spoken of; but now the wisdom and good qualities of one man raised the little tribe of Benjamin to the first rank. Samuel's judgeship was the time of a great improvement in the nation. The even administration of justice, bringing with it security to life and property, had tamed the wildness of the people, and

* 1 Sam. i.—iv.

allowed society to improve. The other tribes could not help following the example of Benjamin.

It would seem that as yet when in our history God has been called by the name of "Jehovah, who dwelleth between the cherubs," it has been by a mistake of the writer. But now the tribe of Benjamin, with the adjoining parts of Judah, become the chief actors on the scene : and the name of Jehovah is more often used for the Almighty. Now begins the history of a series of wars against the Philistines, in which the little tribe of Benjamin always stands in the front of the battle, and which ends, as great military struggles often do, in making an important change in the political government.

Seven months after the Ark had been seized by the Philistines, they sent it back of their own free will to the Israelites. It was said to have brought trouble in a wonderful manner upon every city into which it was carried. When brought back it was left, not in Shiloh, from whence it was fetched, but in the City of Jearim, a little town in the woods, and it was placed on the neighbouring hill of Gibeah. There it remained twenty years. The City of Jearim and the hill of Gibeah are in Judah.*

This story of the Ark, and all that relates to it before we find it at the City of Jearim, we may safely reject as untrustworthy, not only as to the wonders that it wrought among the Philistines, but, what is very important to our history, we must reject the statement that it had ever been at Shiloh. The religious customs of the northern and southern tribes were not the same ; the Ark belonged to the southern tribes. No temple for it had yet been built. Nathan in the next century assured David that it had never rested otherwise than in a tent, since it came out of Egypt.† The story of the Ark being carried about in the land of the Philistines may represent its removal from Hebron, from which place it may have been brought by the Calebites who came from Hebron to the City of Jearim ; ‡ as we must suppose that Hebron, the early seat of Levitical worship, was the original place of the Ark. But all that we can trust to in the early history of the Ark is summed up in two lines of Psalm cxxxii. :—

" Lo, we heard of it at Ephratah (or Bethlehem),
     We found it in the fields of the Forest (or Jearim).

* 1 Sam. v.—vii. 6.   † 2 Sam. vii. 6.   ‡ 1 Chron. ii. 45 and 50.

The placing it first at Shiloh, and then removing it into
the land of Judah, seems a narrative written with a purpose,
and intended to link together the religious feelings of both
people. The writer wished to show that the sovereign rule
among the Israelites had, in the north, **been sanctioned** by
the presence of Jehovah, and had removed from Shiloh
further southward.   In the same improbable way, Samuel
is said to have made his sons Judges in Beersheba, at **the**
very southern boundary of the land **of Judah.*** That
Samuel's authority should have reached so far, **we** cannot
easily believe. For, though we are told that **all** Israel, from
Dan to Beersheba, knew Samuel as **a prophet to** whom the
word of Jehovah had come in Shiloh,† **yet we** find him living
entirely within the land of Benjamin, and judging **his** people
only **by moving** about **in a** yearly **circuit to** the four neighbouring **towns of** Mizpeh, Ramah, Beth-el, and Gilgal. No
towns **within the** tribe of Judah are mentioned as being
visited by him.‡   Samuel's altar at Ramah, near to his own
house, was probably dedicated to Elohim, or God, rather
than to Jehovah; as we shall be told again and again **in the**
later part of our history that the name of Jehovah was not
in general use so far to the north as the towns in which
Samuel acted as judge. **Samuel does not appear to have**
been a Levite, though he was **afterwards claimed for that**
tribe by the writer of the Book **of Chronicles,§** who at the
same time rejected all knowledge **of Eli, and all connection**
with the town of Shiloh.

In order to **understand the history of the Ark, it is** necessary to say something of the town **in which we for the first**
time hear of **it in a** trustworthy manner. The **City of**
Jearim, literally **the** *City in the Woods*, was the most
northerly town of **the tribe of Judah.** It had been peopled
by Calebites from Hebron,‖ who may have brought **with**
them their Levitical **customs. It** was near the **western**
border of Benjamin. It stood at the foot of a hill **on** which
the people worshipped and sacrificed to Jehovah ; **and** when
the hill was embraced within walls, it was called **the** City of
Gibeah, *the hill.*¶ **It** was also called **Nob,** *the hill.* Here
the priests of Jehovah in charge of the **Ark** dwelt.** The
hill was also called, from its sacred use, **the** Hill of God,
Gibeah of God.††   It afterwards **became** an important

---

* 1 Sam. viii. 2.   † 1 Sam. iii. 20.   ‡ 1 Sam. vii. 15-17.
§ 1 Chron. vi. 28 and **33.**   ‖ 1 Chron. ii. 42 and 50.
¶ 1 Sam. vii. 1.   ** **1 Sam** xxi. **1.**   †† 1 Sam. **x. 5.**

stronghold, and was also called Gibeon.* It was within the
land of Judah, and must be distinguished from Saul's city,
Gibeah of Benjamin, which was also called Gibeon. We do
not hear that Hebron, which had its own altar to Jehovah,
had also its own ark. But very possibly when the Calebites
of Hebron migrated to the City of Jearim, they may have
carried the Ark with them. This would account for the
story of its wandering through the land of the Philistines.
However, the ark at Gibeah of Judah is the only ark that
we hear of. In later days, when the priests of Jerusalem
reproached all sacrifices except those at their Altar as Baal-
worship and idolatrous, they nicknamed the City of Jearim as
Baalah and the City of Baal.† A rival place of worship was
called idolatrous, as among Christians it is often called
heretical.

Now, for the first time, we are able to mention in our
history the Two Tables of the Law in Exodus xx. 1-17,
containing the Ten Commandments. They are brought to
our notice by the ark which contained them being mentioned for the first time in a trustworthy manner. The
earlier mention of the ark, in the case of Eli at Shiloh, seems
of doubtful authority, and may be by a later writer. That
these Tables belonged to the tribe of Judah, not to the
northern tribes, is probable, because the name of Jehovah,
therein used for God, and the ark that held these Tables,
and the Levites who had the care of the ark, seem all to
belong to Judah. Our knowledge of Hebrew civilization had,
before David's reign, been limited to the northern tribes ;
but in his reign the two ancient streams unite in one. The
northern tribes bring to the common stock the history of
the Judges and of Saul's reign ; but the tribe of Judah
brings a far higher proof of its being a people more
civilized than the nations around, it brings the Ten
Commandments, words which were reverenced for their
antiquity as well as for their religious worth. In the narrative
of the march out of Egypt, as we now have it, these remarkable words are said to have been written by the finger of
God on two Tables of Stone. In this way, the Levites
marked their reverence for this early code, which deserves,
and has received from Christians, a respect little short of
the words of Jesus Christ. It is stamped with the chief
feature in the nation's character, the opinion that morality
finds its best support in religion. It sets forth the heads of

* 2 Sam. ii. 12.   † Josh. xv. 9 and 60.

the eternal Moral Law of right and wrong, in six short laws, which it places last. At the beginning it places the great Theological Truth that there is one only God, the maker of those laws; and this is followed by three Religious Laws which arise out of it; namely, that He, and He alone, is to be worshipped; that no image, or likeness, of anything in heaven above, or in the earth beneath, is to be bowed down to; and that His name is not to be taken in vain, to give sanction to a falsehood. These are followed by one Civil Statute, namely, that one day in seven should be set apart for **rest,** a rule wise for ourselves, and humane towards our servants and cattle. We must suppose that this custom of resting from work upon four days in every month **had** been established for a very long time, before it was thus classed among the great moral laws. Here we have the fountain head from which first the Jewish religion, and afterwards the Christian religion, must trace its birth; a clearly pronounced morality accompanied by a belief in one God, the only safe foundation upon which the welfare of mankind can rest. As the early narrative of the march is Elohistic, and this is a Jehovistic writing, however much earlier it was written, it **must be** classed as an after addition to the narrative, **inserted in the time of** David, **or soon after, and as the** first **of** the series of laws which **were added from time to time** during the next five hundred years.

The early Judges **in** this history, **not** even excluding the prophetess Deborah, were all soldiers. Eli, who followed, was a priest; **but** his two sons were **at** the same time Judges, priests, and soldiers. Samuel **was** not a soldier; he was simply a priest acting as Judge, and therefore little fitted to be chieftain of **his** tribe in times of danger from invasion. Though he **was** respected by his countrymen for the justice of his rule,* **and** reverenced as a prophet and priest, yet the continual **wars with** the Philistines, and the defeats arising **from** bad generalship, had taught the Israelites the need for a more active **ruler.** They saw the advantage that their enemies gained from being governed by a soldier; and therefore, without throwing off Samuel's authority, the heads of the people came up to him in a body at Ramah, and called upon him to appoint a king, who should govern them as the nations with whom they were surrounded were governed. Samuel consented very unwillingly. **He** warned them of the **tyranny** that they might hereafter **look** for. But the **imme-**

* 1 Sam. xii. 1-5.

diate danger, both from the Philistines and from the Ammonites, was far more pressing, and they would have a king.*
Accordingly, he assembled the heads of the tribes at Mizpeh
in Benjamin, and there fixed upon Saul, a warrior of more
than usual height and approved valour, and we may suppose
of approved wisdom. Saul was of the tribe of Benjamin, and
dwelt **at** Gibeah of Benjamin, and his authority rested for
the **most** part on the warriors of his own tribe; for **a very**
natural jealousy made many of **the others** unwilling to obey
him; and they would contribute nothing to the expenses of
the government and of the war.†   Taxes of all kinds were, at
this time, evidently unknown. The priest was supported by
gifts; the soldier by his own means and by plunder; and
now the king also, on his appointment, expected gifts for his
support. That tithes had not yet been enacted, we learn from
the writer making Samuel warn the people that hereafter they
will have to bear that burden as the price of royalty.‡

According to another, but more **modern** and less trustworthy account, given side by side with **the former,** Saul had
been fixed upon by Samuel, and privately **anointed** by him
as king by the command of Jehovah, before the **tribes** met at
Mizpeh to choose a ruler.§

SAUL, KING OF ISRAEL, B.C. 1026—1017?

When Saul was chosen king he was not young. His son
Jonathan was already of an age to lead the troops. His
reign was short; and as at his death the son who succeeded
him was forty years old, Saul may already have been fifty
years old. He **is one** of the very few kings who have risen
from a private **station to** that high rank without being guilty
of either fraud **or violence.** As Judges had been before made
because the irregular **lawlessness** of a tribe led them to wish
for a ruler, and led them **to give to** that ruler power to say
who should be **punished; so** danger from foreign enemies
now led them to wish **that the** ruler should be a soldier. Saul
was chosen because he **was the** soldier best fitted for the post,
at a moment when it was **a** post of difficulty. He was made
king, with power to call the people **to** arms, because the danger
was pressing; and he immediately took the field against the
Ammonites, **who,** from their table-land on the east of Gilead,

* 1 Sam. viii.   † 1 Sam. x. 17-27.
‡ 1 Sam. viii. **15.**   § 1 Sam. ix.—x. 16.

had overrun that country, and were besieging the City of
Jabesh. Saul sent messengers through the whole of the
tribes of Israel, and thus gathered to his standard at Bezek,
in the land of Issachar, a larger army than had yet obeyed
any Israelite leader. Marching from thence he thoroughly
routed the Ammonites; and on his return southward, after
his victory, on crossing into the land of Canaan by the southern
ford, he again received the homage of the people as their
king, in a more formal manner, at Gilgal.* The ceremony
was accompanied by a sacrifice on the altar, as the historian
of Samuel's life says, to Jehovah. But this is in part contradicted by what we are afterwards told, that Saul's first altar
to Jehovah was built at a later time.

In this muster of the Israelites under Saul, one-tenth part
of his army were men of Judah. Thus, at present, the tribe
of Judah takes no great part with the northern tribes in their
struggles against the inhabitants of the land; but, henceforth,
we shall find it rising year by year in importance, till at length
the whole chain of history runs along the kings of Judah. In
the meantime, we shall often be puzzled by the writers' use
of the word Israel; as they sometimes leave us in doubt,
when they speak of the Israelites, whether they mean the
whole of the tribes, or only the northern tribes, to the exclusion of Judah.

Gilgal, where Saul was this second time declared to be
king, was a fortified camp, on the low ground called the
Circle of the Jordan, between the hills and the river, not far
from the most southerly ford. It was in a barren district,
very unsuitable for a city; but it was important as a military
post as long as it was necessary to guard the passage of the
Jordan. It was probably the first spot in the land of Canaan
in which the Israelites had entrenched themselves when they
came over to attempt the conquest of the land. This may
have given to it a religious rank in the mind of the nation
beyond what its size deserved, and this may have made Saul
wish to receive his appointment as king there.

The next year Saul was sorely pressed by the Philistines,
who had occupied, first Gibeah of Judah, and then Michmash,
a little to the north of Jerusalem. They are said to have had
an army of thirty thousand chariots, six thousand horsemen,
and foot-soldiers as the sand of the sea; while Saul had on
his side only three thousand men. But these figures only
prove the historian's little regard to exactness. Saul himself

* 1 Sam. xi.

had to retreat to Gilgal, near the Jordan, thereby gaining the
power of crossing the river if he should be further pressed by
the enemy.   From Gilgal, those Israelites who had joined him
from the land of Gad and Gilead deserted him, and returned
to their homes.*

Other battles followed in the same neighbourhood, but
they are not told with the clearness that would enable us to
understand the narrative satisfactorily.   The Israelites were
badly armed; they did not possess that knowledge of working
in iron that the Philistines had.†   Saul and his son Jonathan
alone in the army had weapons of metal.   While the Philistines were at Michmash, Saul kept himself at the very extrem-
ity of the land of Gibeah, at Migron, which was, probably,
like Gilgal, near to one of the fords, by which he had the
power of retreating across the river.   But the young Jonathan,
the hero of the army, leaving his father there, went forward
and defeated the Philistines.   Though fighting under great
disadvantages, the Israelites now began to be successful.
Many of the tribe of Judah who had hitherto served the
Philistines, and very probably had been fighting on their side,
now deserted from their masters, and joined Saul and Jonathan.   These men from Gibeah of Judah brought with them
the Ark of God into Saul's army; and Jehovah saved Israel
that day.   Those also who, in their alarm, had fled to the
hill country of Ephraim, now returned to Saul's camp.‡   The
Philistines were again defeated, and were driven from Michmash to Ajalon, beyond the limits of the land of Benjamin.
Then Saul built his first altar to Jehovah.§   This would
seem to have been done in gratitude to the men of Judah.
To adopt the religious customs of a friendly power was a
mode of showing gratitude which we shall often have occasion to mention.   Saul had driven back his enemies on every
side, defeating, or keeping at a distance, the Syrians of Zobah
in the north, the Moabites and Ammonites in the east,
and the Edomites and Philistines and Amalekites in the
south.||

Saul is now the acknowledged king of all the land of
Canaan, except those territories which the geographer has
allotted to Simeon and Dan in the south; these were still
held by the Philistines; and excepting a few strong cities
on the hills, such as Jerusalem and Gezer.   Throughout the
rest of the country the natives submitted quietly to the

* 1 Sam. xiii. 1-7.   † 1 Sam. xiii. 8-23.   ‡ 1 Sam. xiv. 1-22.
§ 1 Sam. xiv. 35. || 1 Sam. xiv. 47, 48.

Israelites. The larger part of Judah was now free from the heavy yoke of their warlike neighbours, the Philistines; but how much of that country had been held in bondage, or by what struggles they got free, or how far they owed their freedom to Saul, does not appear. It is in Saul's reign, however, that the great tribe of Judah first rises to any importance. On that tribe coming under his rule, he built, as we have been told, his first altar to Jehovah. This important remark of the historian further confirms our opinion, before advanced, that the name of Jehovah was that **given to** the Almighty by the tribe of Judah, while the **name of** Elohim, or *God*, and sometimes Baal, or *Lord*, was used **among** the northern tribes. The tribe of Benjamin may have **used** either name, according as it was connected politically with the north **or the** south. It **is true**, indeed, that in the Book of Judges, which contains history exclusively northern, the writer often describes the northern people as worshipping Jehovah. But in books that have come down to us through the hands of countless copyists, it is not safe to insist upon a word. A copyist may, perhaps, either in carelessness or devoutness, have changed the name of Elohim into Jehovah. And it is clear that the First Book of Samuel, which also insists on the worship of Jehovah, has certainly been freely altered, having had its original political **narrative mixed up** with modern portions of a priestly bias. In support **of the** above opinion, it may be further remarked that the worship of Jehovah was peculiar to the Levites, and that they belonged to Judah; and, again, that the older parts of the Pentateuch, which were written before the rise of Judah, speak only of the worship of Elohim, whilst most of those parts that speak of Jehovah seem modern additions. When, in Deborah's song, the other ten tribes are all mentioned by name, the mighty ones, who are called Jehovah's people, can only be the men of Judah, including Simeon. In the history of the monarchy, when a northern king asks for help from a king of Judah, he is often said to turn to Jehovah; and, after the captivity in Babylon, when the northern tribes are invited to a union with the south, they are asked to return to Jehovah.

It seems probable that it was in the time of Samuel that a large part of the Book of Judges was written, giving us the history of the early struggles of the northern Israelites. It seems to be the oldest book in the Bible, beginning at chapter iii. 7 to xii., and continued at xvii., xviii.; and its narrative

shows that neither the Book of Joshua, nor any part of the
Ceremonial Law in the Pentateuch, had been then written.
Had the Book of Judges been written later, when the southern
portion of the country became more settled and more important, the early wars and difficulties of the tribe of Judah
would not have been wholly overlooked, nor would so low a
rank have been given to the Levites. The writer, by his
knowledge of places, leads us to suppose that he lived in the
land of Ephraim. It was re-written, or put together in its
present form, at a much later time, when the first two
chapters and the last three may have been added, and elsewhere modern words and thoughts, in particular the use of
the name of Jehovah for God, may have crept in, either
by the carelessness of a scribe, or by the design of an
editor.

Now that King Saul was governing the tribes, Samuel was
relieved from many of the duties which before fell upon him.
He continued, however, the respected priest, and as such he
acted as judge in civil cases. Moreover, he was a prophet,
which means a ready speaker, and he was also a writer, either
by his own hand or by that of a scribe. Hence it would
seem not unreasonable to suppose him the author of parts of
the Book of Judges, and some of the earliest parts of the
Pentateuch.

No mention is made in the Bible of the art of writing being
new to the people ; and hence we may suppose that they had
possessed it when living in Lower Egypt, where it had been
already practised for many centuries. The Israelites had,
however, improved upon the Egyptians by having only one
character for each sound. But the art at this time can have
been understood by very few. It was by no means required
by a priest, to enable him to perform his duties, which were
chiefly those of sacrificing and burning incense. It was rather
more needed by the general of an army, who had to keep a
list of his soldiers. The military Scribe is often mentioned in
Jewish history ; the earliest, perhaps, are the captains spoken
of in Deborah's song, who led the men of Zebulun to battle.
But if writing was equally necessary to the general and the
priest, it was among the priests only that there could be found
men and opportunities for teaching it, and learning it, and
thus for handing down and improving the art from generation
to generation.

To the time of Samuel, however, we may assign the earlier
and simpler portions of Exodus and Numbers. Modern

criticism has shown that the Pentateuch is a book of very various ages, and that some parts belong to an early time, though others bear the marks of the reigns of the later monarchs, and others seem to have been written after the fall of the monarchy. The days of Samuel seem to be the earliest in which quiet was so far established that we can suppose any literary work to have been produced. But as soon as the historians had made a record of the wars and other doings of the people in their own days and of those within the memory of the old men around them, their next step would naturally be to inquire for such traditions as may have been handed down of the early fortunes of their nation; and first in importance among such scattered recollections would be the flight of their forefathers out of Lower Egypt, their forcible settlement in the land of the Amorites, and their then crossing over the Jordan to attempt the conquest of the land of Canaan. It is the fate of history to be written backwards. The writers first record what is more certainly known, as belonging almost to their own time, and then inquire for the traditions of the past. Among these, the history of the Exodus would be more particularly valued and remembered, because it was by the help of the civilized arts, then brought out of Lower Egypt, that they had been thus far successful in gaining so much good territory from the less civilized owners.

These early notices of the past we must search for in the Books of Exodus and Numbers. They may in part be distinguished by the use of the word Elohim for God, but they are interwoven with more modern additions, and they seem to have been very much disarranged. We may put them into better order by the help of the map, and of Numb. xxxiii., in which some later writer has given us a list of the several stations at which the Israelites rested on their march. We may suppose these older passages to be the mention of their ill-treatment by their task-masters, with the birth of Moses and his marriage with Reuel's daughter (Exodus i. 8—ii.; v. 6-14); their setting out from Rameses or Heliopolis with unleavened dough because they had not time to prepare proper food for their journey : their removal to Succoth, the Scenæ of the Roman Itinerary (xii. 37-39); their going by the way of Sinai to avoid the land of the Philistines (xiii. 17-20); their journeyings through the desert of Shur and the desert of Sin (xv. 22—xvi. 1); their battle with Amalek, near Rephidim (xvii. 8); their encamping in

3

the desert of Sinai (xix. 1); then at the Burial Place of
Taavah (Numb. xi. 34); then at the village of Paran (Numb.
xi. 35); their removal to the foot of Mount Serbal, the
Mount of God, where Moses delivered to them the Law
(Exod. xix. 2-8); their asking Reuel's son to accompany
them as a guide (Numb. x. 29-32); their journey to the desert
of Paran (Numb. xii. 16); their spying out the land near
Hebron (Numb. xiii. 21-24); their moving to Kadesh in
the desert of Zin (Numb. xx. 1); their asking leave of the
Edomites to pass through their country (Numb. xx. 14-21);
and on being refused, their journeying round Edom (Numb.
xxi. 4, and 10-20); their forcibly dispossessing the Amorites,
and then settling on the east bank of the Jordan between
the Arnon and the Jabbok; and, lastly, their after excursions
northward as far as the hills of Bashan, where they defeated
King Og, and added that fertile pasture land to what they
had gained from the Amorites (Numb. xxi. 21—xxii. 1).

Og, perhaps the same as Gog of more modern writers, was
the name of the monarch whose imaginary castles, seen upon
the mountains in the distance, the traveller thought it not
wise to approach. They were at the limits of all geographical
knowledge. At this early time this fabulous king held
Mount Bashan; in the time of the Greek geographers he
had retreated to the shores of the Caspian Sea; and some
centuries later the Arabic travellers were stopped by him at
the foot of the Altai Mountains in Central Asia. His with-
drawing before the advance of geographical explorers proves
his unreal character. He is not mentioned in the Book of
Judges, in the earlier account of the Israelites settling in
the land of the Amorites; it is only in the Book of Numbers
that he is attacked and defeated in battle, and only in the
more modern Book of Deuteronomy that we learn about his
iron bedstead of nine cubits of length.

The Ten Commandments, or some similar commandments,
would seem to have stood originally, not where we now read
them, but immediately after Exodus xix. 6. The careful
reader of the Bible will observe that, in Exodus xix. 2-8,
which seems to contain the original narrative, Moses goes
up the Mount of God, and receives certain commands
which he delivers to the people, and these commands the
people promise to obey. These commands, as we shall see
hereafter, were put aside by the later writer to make way
for the more important words which are to follow. In xix.
20, Jehovah calls up Moses a second time, and soon after-

wards delivers to him in spoken, not written words, the Ten Commandments, which afterwards, in xxiv. 12, and xxxi. 18, he delivers to him written on the Tables of **Stone**. From all this, it appears that the present Ten Commandments **are** in addition to the original narrative and not part of that **which** we have thought belonged to the time of Samuel. **This** conjecture is strengthened by remarking that the one **writer** uses the word God, and the other the word Jehovah. In what we suppose the original narrative, by an Elohistic writer, there was probably no priesthood, no tabernacle, no ark, no Aaron, no breaking of the Two Tables and delivery of a second pair.

This history of **the march out of** Egypt, written three **or** four hundred years **after the** events happened, and handed down, as we must suppose, by memory, cannot be relied upon for the small particulars. But the unvarying belief of the Israelites establishes the great fact of their leaders once having been bond-servants in Lower Egypt; while the geography of the march is confirmed by our modern travellers over the same route. The spots may some of them be recognized by the description, and some by the translations of the names in the Roman Itinerary. Thus Rameses is Heliopolis, both named from the sun. Succoth, *the tents*, is Scenæ. Etham is Thoum. Hiroth is Heroopolis, and Pi-hahiroth, the Bay of Hiroth, is the Bay of Heroopolis, which then reached to the northern end of the Bitter Lake, Dophkah, the *Crushing* place, Alush, the *Pounding* place, and Rephidim, the *Spreading* place, all point to the copper-mines of the Egyptians. The Burial place of Taavah, or the Tih range, is yet marked by the Egyptian tombstones. Mount Shephar (or Sephar, *writing*) is known to be Serbal, by the inscriptions on the rocks.

The particulars of the last narrative, namely the conquest of the Amorites, were handed down in a poetical form in a writing entitled The Book of the Wars, of which about eight lines now remain to us. Thus :—

> Jehovah showed himself at the **Red Sea**;
> And at the brooks of the Arnon;
> And at the source of the brooks that turn to Shebeth-Ar,
> And lean upon the boundary of Moab.

As this is a Jehovistic poem, it was probably afterwards added from sources not in the possession of the Elohistic **writer**, who probably belonged to the **tribe** of Ephraim. The

3 *

other four lines, which were perhaps part of the same poem,
are—

> Spring up, O Well (Sing ye unto it);
> O Well, which the princes digged,
> The nobles of the people hollowed out,
> With the staff of power, with their staves.*

These few lines are valuable as telling us that the early
history of the Hebrew nation, as of many other nations,
was at first handed down in ballads, which have been long
lost. By the help of such the history of the march out of
Egypt may have been written.

To this simple narrative of the march out of Egypt, which
may well have been committed to writing in the time of
Samuel as an introduction to the history of the Judges,
later writers added, as a new introduction, a narrative of
earlier times, the supposed account of their first settlement
in Egypt, and then one of yet earlier times, with the origin
of their family in Syria among the sources of the Euphrates,
and then a conjectural account of the supposed origin of the
human race and of the creation of the world. In every
case, the history of the earlier times was written last. And
during the years that these portions of the Pentateuch were
being added at the beginning, other large portions were being
mingled in with the narrative of the march, and being added
at the end. The additions contain the whole remaining
portion of the Jewish law, partly ecclesiastical and partly
civil, which is given to us in the form of commands spoken
either by God to Moses, their great leader on the march, or
by Moses himself to the assembled people. Of these, the
earliest laws were the Ten Commandments, written on Two
Tables of stone, which were no doubt part of the contents
of the sacred Ark which we lately heard of in the City of
Jearim, and which we shall hear more of in the coming
history. The later laws were added from time to time during
the next five hundred years, as they were called for by the
growth of cities, the more settled ownership of the soil, the
changes in the temple-service, and by the rise, and then the
decline, of the priestly power. Some of these later laws
will be hereafter mentioned in what we venture to think
their proper places in the history.

Before the end of Saul's reign, says the historian, it

* Numb. xxi. 14-18.

repented Jehovah that he had made Saul king. Saul had
not been so severe upon the neighbouring idolaters as the
priests, or rather the priestly historian, thought he ought to
have been. When he led his troops against the Amalekites
of the south, he was ordered by Samuel to put to death
every living creature in their country, not only men, women,
and children, but even the cattle. But in these religious
wars, the soldier was not quite so cruel as the priest. Saul
thought he had obeyed the command when he had slain
every soul that he met with, except Agag, the king, whom
he brought as a prisoner to Gilgal, with a few of the best of
the cattle. But Samuel was displeased at this tenderness for
the conquered king, and at this greediness for spoil, though
Saul said that the cattle were meant as a sacrifice; and the
prophet told Saul that God would punish him by taking
away the kingdom from him. Samuel then had Agag brought
to him, and with his own hand he hewed the prisoner in
pieces before Jehovah. The friendship between Samuel and
Saul was at an end.* So Samuel remained at Ramah, and
came no more to see Saul at Gibeah.† The marked difference
in character between the warlike, perhaps the irreligious Saul,
and the pious priest and prophet Samuel, gave rise to a
Hebrew proverbial question, meant to express surprise at
something improbable, " What ! is Saul among the prophets ? "
And out of the proverb may have grown up the doubtful
story, that in a mad fit he went to Ramah, and, stripping his
clothes off, prophesied naked before Samuel.

Saul was now evidently losing favour with the people,
whose eyes were turned to a young warrior in his army of
the name of David, a native of Beth-lehem in Judah. We
have two stories of David's first introduction to Saul, and of
their whole intercourse, as we had two stories of Samuel's
making Saul king. In one, the priestly narrative, written
in Solomon's reign after the publication of a collection of
Psalms had given to David the character of a musician, he
is brought to King Saul to play before him on the harp, and
amuse him in times of illness when an evil spirit troubled
him.‡ In the other, the earlier narrative, he is first known
to the king on his stepping forward as the champion of the
army, and slaying, with his shepherd's sling and a pebble,
Goliath, a well-armed giant, the champion of the Philistines.§
At first he was a great favourite with Saul, and Saul's son,

---

* 1 Sam. xv. 1-33.　　　　† 1 Sam. xv. 34, 35.
‡ 1 Sam. xvi. 14-23.　　　　§ 1 Sam. xvii. 1—xviii. 5.

Jonathan; and Saul promised to give him his eldest daughter in marriage. But after a time Saul became distrustful of his young captain. David's popularity with the people had alarmed Saul for the safety of his throne; and his jealousy was naturally roused when the women, **who** came out to meet the army on its return from one of David's victories over the Philistines, sang in answers as they played on their harps, "Saul hath slain his thousands, and David **his** tens of thousands." In one of his moments of fretful passion, he even hurled his spear at him, and tried to kill him; and he gave his daughter to another. But Saul's son, the young Jonathan, whose goodness of heart was equal to his bravery in war, was warmly attached to David, and befriended him from his father's madness, while Saul's younger daughter, Michal, fell in love with him, and married him, and helped him to escape.*

David fled first westward to Nob, in the land of Judah, where he was among friends. Nob, *the hill*, was probably another name for Gibeah **of** Judah, **where we** before met with the Ark of Jehovah, when it had **been** brought to the City of Jearim; and at Nob the priests **dwelt.** There they not only possessed an ark, but had at least so much of the Levitical worship as to have an Ephod, and a Presence Table, on which the holy bread was set out in the presence of Jehovah. From Nob, David fled to Gath, in the land of Dan, a district where the Israelites lived among the Philistines, for there the Israelites, had not yet been able to dispossess the owners of the soil. In Gath he offered his services to the Philistine king Achish; but he was distrusted and not received.†

Upon this, David withdrew to the cave of Adullam, a few miles to the south of Bethlehem in Judah, his native place. There he **was** joined by his brothers, or rather by his nephews, and by a body of discontented adventurers; and he soon found himself the captain of four hundred men. These were not enough at once to raise the standard of rebellion against Saul, but they were able to earn their livelihood as freebooters, whether they should think fit to attack the Benjamites or the Philistines.‡ And here, it may be said, begins the history of Judah, which henceforth runs side by side with the history of the northern Israelites,

---

* 1 **Sam.** xviii. xix. xx.   † 1 Sam. xxi.
‡ 1 Sam. xxii. **1, 2.**

to which we have been hitherto confined. It begins with the war between Saul of Benjamin and David of Judah. David had been Saul's captain, but was now in arms against him. The small number of four hundred men, here given to David, makes us remark on the greater trustworthiness in regard to numbers, in some writers than in others; for Saul was before said to have been attacked by the Philistines with 30,000 chariots and 6000 horsemen, beside the **foot**-soldiers.

In preparation for war against the Benjamites, David placed his father and mother in safety with the king of Moab, a tribe friendly to Judah, for he was so far in rebellion that Saul had put to death eighty-five priests of Jehovah at Nob, as friends to David, because one of them had helped David in his flight. As before remarked, the worship of Jehovah belonged to the tribe of Judah, not to the northern tribes under Saul. One only of that body of priests escaped to David with the linen Ephod, the mark of his office. He was thus able to give to David's wars the apparent sanction of Jehovah; and he lived to receive from David, as his reward, the office of high priest to the altar of Jehovah in Jerusalem, when David became king of the whole of the twelve tribes. But David's first battle was against the Philistines, who were plundering the men of Judah at Keilah, on the border between the two nations. He defeated the Philistines, and saved the men of Keilah; but still he would not trust himself to remain with them. Saul was marching against him; and he feared that the men of Keilah would deliver him up to the king. So he left that city with **his** troop, which had now increased to about six hundred men.*

He then retreated to the desert of Ziph, to the south of Hebron, where he dwelt in what we may call a thicket-camp, probably a village of huts, intrenched with shrubs and ditches, such as those in which the helpless country-people were glad to seek for safety. But David, on finding that the men of Ziph would willingly give him up to Saul, retired still farther south, into the desert of Maon, and then sought safety among the Edomites, between whom and the people of southern Judea there was very little distinction of race, and no attempt to draw a boundary line. There he took refuge in the city of Sela, *the Rock*, better known by its Greek name, Petra. It seems also to have borne the name Mibzar, *the fortress*. This **is a** remarkable fastness entered

* 1 Sam. xxii. 3—xxiii. 13.

through a narrow cleft in the rock, and it is valuable for its
spring of water, while the country round is a desert. But
even there Saul would have followed, had he not been called
back by the news that the Philistines were making an inroad
upon his territory at home.* On Saul's retreating, David
came northward as far as Ain-gedi, near the southern end of
the Dead Sea. There Saul again came down upon him; and
the historian has two interesting but improbable stories of
David having an opportunity of killing him in an unguarded
moment, but refusing to do hurt to the "anointed of Jehovah."† As he afterwards put to death seven of Saul's
unoffending sons and grandsons, he is not likely to have so
spared his enemy, Saul himself, if he had at any time fallen
into his hands. While living in the southern desert, David
married a third wife, namely Abigail of Carmel in Maon.
He had before married Ahinoam of Jezreel, a village near
to Maon. But Michal, Saul's daughter, who had been given
to him as a wife, had since been taken away from him and
been given to another man.‡

David, however, did not feel himself safe in any part of
the land of Israel while Saul was thus pursuing him; so he
again turned to the Philistines; and his former friend Achish,
king of Gath, gave him the city of Ziklag for a residence,
where he settled with his two wives and his six hundred
men. The difference between the men of Judah and the
Philistines was not then so wide as it became after Judah
had joined northern Israel to make one kingdom. Ziklag
was in the South Country, and it might with equal reason
be called either a city of the Philistines, or of the Edomites,
or of Judah. From thence David could conveniently make
excursions for booty. His first attack was upon the Amalekites and their neighbours in the south-west, where he destroyed everything that he met with. But, in order to gain the
confidence of his Philistine friend, Achish, and to prove the
earnestness of his enmity to his own people the Israelites, he
told him that his attack had been upon the southern parts of
Judea.§ At this time stealing was thought wrong, coveting
and attempting to grasp a neighbour's possessions was thought
wrong; but open robbery with violence against a stranger
was an honourable employment, blamed by nobody. He
wished to be employed by Achish against Saul; and Achish
was willing to trust him. But the other Philistines thought

---

* 1 Sam. xxiii.   † 1 Sam. xxiv. xxvi.
‡ 1 Sam. xxv. 43, 44.   § 1 Sam. xxvii.

it dangerous to employ him; and when the Philistines marched against Saul, David had to be left behind.*

Of the several battles which the brave Saul may have fought, on his retreat before the advancing army of the Philistines, we are not told. We last heard of him in Southern Judah, and we next hear of him preparing for what was to be his fatal overthrow in the very northern **end** of his kingdom.

Saul, on hearing **of the** approach **of the** Philistines, and feeling his own **weakness,** would **have** been glad of the advice and religious support of Samuel. But Samuel **was** now dead; and Saul inquired of Jehovah, by the prophets, and by dreams, and also by Urim, which may have meant by casting lots **in** the presence of the priest. He could, however, get **no** satisfactory answer. But his superstition increased with **his** fears and as the danger became more pressing. When he **was** in prosperity, he had forbidden his **su**bjects to consult wizards, but now he hoped to obtain some comfort from them himself. So he went for the advice of a wise woman, who professed to be able to call up the dead and question them. She was probably something of **a** ventriloquist; she had a large jar or bottle, out of which the voice of the person raised from the dead seemed to **come.** She lived at Endor, or Ain-dor, near Mount Gilboa, where Saul had retreated with his army, and was expecting the attack of the Philistines. When Saul came **to** her, she asked whom he would wish to have brought up. He answered, "Samuel;" and presently **a** voice **out of** the bottle asked why **he** had disturbed him. Saul **saw** nobody, but trusted to the woman's description of the prophet. Saul said that he was in fear of the Philistines, and could learn nothing about his future fate, either by dreams or from the prophets. The voice then told him that Jehovah would shortly take the kingdom from him and **give it** to David, and would deli**ver the** Israelites into the hand of the Philistines. Such **was** the method by which **the** fortune-tellers, both **among** the Israelites and among **the** Egyptians, professed, **by means** of their speaking-bottles, **to** receive from the dead answers to their questions; and there is nothing improbable in the story of Saul, in his distress, having consulted **such a** woman.†

Whether the voice from the speaking-bottle really gave such an answer to Saul may be doubted; the answer was probably gathered from the event that followed. The Philis-

---

* 1 Sam. xxix.   † 1 Sam. xxviii.

tines attacked the Israelites near Mount Gilboa, and routed
them thoroughly. Saul and Jonathan, and two other sons,
who were with him in the battle, were all slain. The
Israelites in the valley of Ajalon forsook their cities, and
fled, leaving it to the Philistines to take possession of them.
So thorough was the defeat that the Philistines even crossed
the Jordan, and laid waste the lands on the east of the river,
though they did not think **it worth** while **to** make a settlement
there.*

This thorough defeat of the northern Israelites by the
Philistines brought no increase to the Philistine power, **but**
rather the reverse; it transferred the sceptre from Saul to
David, from Israel to Judah. So slight was the separation
between the Philistines and the tribe of Judah that the
Philistine victory was Judah's gain. The ranks in the
Philistine army may have been filled with men of Judah,
men whom the Hebrew writers propose to call the Tribe of
Simeon.

Saul, as we learned from the name of the son who succeeded
him, was a worshipper of the Almighty under the name of
Baal, *lord* or *master;* but we have no reason to think that
he was an idolater. His son's name was Ishbaal, *the man of
Baal,* which the southern writers, in their horror of the word
Baal, altered reproachfully into Ishbosheth, *the man of Shame,*
the name by which he is best known. Saul had also a
grandson, known by the two names of Mephibosheth, *the
utterance of Shame,* and Meribbaal, *the Rebellion of Baal.*
Both of these seem to be only reproachful nicknames. The
real name may have been Mephi-baal, *the utterance of Baal.*
Gideon also, the early hero of the tribe of Ephraim, had
borne the name of Jerubbaal, and had been called by a
southern writer Jerub-bosheth.† Hence we may reasonably
suppose that the worship, by the Israelites, of God, by the
name of Baal was by no means always idolatrous. But,
as the name of Baal was at the same time given by the
surrounding nations to one of their numerous gods, the use
of it was dangerous, and was strongly objected to by the
Levites, and by the tribe of Judah, who insisted upon the
use of the word Jehovah, their distinctive name for God.
Three centuries later, we find the prophet Hosea describing
Jehovah as ordering the Israelites not to address him as
Baali, *my master.* Thus we see that, though the name was
objectionable, the use of it did not prove idolatry; and when

* **1 Sam. xxxi.**   † 2 Sam. xi. 21.

the southern writers reproach the northern tribes with the worship of Baal, **it** does not of itself prove that they had deserted the worship of the One God. It proves, however, that the name for God was not the same in the north as in Judea; and it goes far to confirm our former conjecture, that the early writings by authors who belonged to Ephraim and Benjamin did not use the holy name of Jehovah, and that it has, in some places, crept into these writings by the carelessness of the later scribes who belonged to Judah.

DAVID, KING OF JUDAH. ISHBAAL, OR ISHBOSHETH, KING OF ISRAEL. B.C. 1016.

Upon this rout of the Israelites at Gilboa in the north, there remained at the moment no body of troops strong enough to hold together and to secure for Saul's surviving son the kingdom of his father. David, with his six hundred followers at Ziklag in the south, was for the moment without a rival. He accordingly marched to Hebron, the chief city of Judah. There he was among friends. The men of Hebron were akin to the men of Beth-lehem, David's native place; and in Hebron his countrymen anointed him king. This may have been about B.C. 1016. The tribe of Judah, however, alone obeyed him.*

David then sent messengers **into** Gilead to invite the obedience of the eastern tribes, well knowing that he had less favour to expect from the northern tribes. But, in the meantime, Abner, the captain of Saul's army, had hastened across **the** Jordan with Saul's only remaining son Ishbosheth, and brought him to Mahanaim, a fortified camp, at that time the military capital of the country on the east of the Jordan. There he was well received, and was proclaimed king over Gilead; and the whole of the northern tribes, including Benjamin in the middle, followed the example. Thus the country, which under Saul had been united into one kingdom, though by very slight bonds, was now broken into two. David was king of Judah, and Ishbosheth was king of Israel, while Simeon and the southern land of Dan were held by the Philistines. This name Israel is, however, used very inexactly, sometimes meaning the twelve tribes, and sometimes the northern and eastern, as separate from Judah. And **henceforth, when we meet with** it, we are often left in doubt

* 2 Sam. ii. 1-4.

whether the writer means by it the whole of the tribes, or
only a part of them.*

This division of the tribes into two kingdoms was followed
by a civil war, in which David's best warriors were Joab,
Abishai, and Asahel, the sons of his sister Zeruiah; while
Saul's son, Ishbosheth, relied chiefly on the support and
zeal of Abner, a member of his family. Their battles were
fought with only a small number of men in each army. The
first battle was at Gibeon or Gibeah, of Judah, which, **as**
being **the** most northerly post of the men of Judah, it **was**
of importance for Ishbosheth's party to gain. There at first
twelve men on each side met and slew one another, **as**
champions for the rest. After this beginning, the army **of**
Israel was routed by that of Judah, and fled across the
Jordan to Mahanaim; but Abner, Ishbosheth's captain,
killed David's nephew, Asahel, who had pursued him too
rashly in his flight. In this, perhaps the greatest of their
battles, David's little army lost twenty men, while those
slain on Ishbosheth's side were three hundred and sixty.†

Now that David was king of Judah, and at war with
Israel, he proposed to strengthen himself by an alliance with
one of the Syrian kings. The Geshurites were a small tribe
of Syrians dwelling between Bashan and Damascus;‡ and
David obtained from Talmai, king of Geshur, his daughter
Maachah in marriage. It does not however, appear that he
gained any support in his war from this alliance. Maachah
became the mother of David's favourite son Absalom. But
this marriage did not hinder David from taking three other
wives while he lived at Hebron.§

So slight was the tie of blood between the southern and
the northern tribes of Israel, and so slight also the separation
between either of these tribes and the tribes around, that
David, when attacked by Saul, had not hesitated to ask help
from the Philistines on the west; and had placed his father
and mother for safety with the king of Moab, as with friends
in the east. So now, in his war with Saul's son, he made a
similar friendly alliance with Nahash, king of the Ammonites,
on the east.‖ Ishbosheth's difficulties could not but be
increased by some of his troops being needed to oppose the
inroads of the Ammonites.

After the war had continued for some time with not a

---

* **2 Sam. ii. 5-11.**   † 2 Sam. ii. **12-32.**   ‡ Josh. xii. 5; **xiii. 13.**
    § **2 Sam. iii. 1-5.**   ‖ 2 Sam. x. 2.

little suffering to both nations, David gained a great accession of strength in the treachery of Abner, who had received an affront from Ishbosheth, and who may have seen that he was on the losing side. Abner sent to David to propose to make a private agreement with him, and to bring over all Israel to his rule. David was willing to treat with him, but first required him to send to him his former wife, Saul's daughter Michal, who had been taken away from him and given to another man, and who could now be of great service to him as uniting him to Saul's family. Moreover, if she were sent, it would be a proof that Abner had both the will and the power to help him in his ambitious aims. Ishbosheth must have been a very weak man, entirely governed by Abner, for he allowed him to send Michal to David, who, by recovering her, might again be called Saul's son-in-law, and thus gain a title to the throne second only to that of Ishbosheth, whom he was trying to overthrow. Abner then, pursuing his treacherous design, addressed himself to the Israelites, and to the Benjamites in particular, urging them to take David as their king. He then came himself to Hebron, and trusted himself in the power of David, against whom he had lately been fighting. David received him favourably, and sent him back to continue his endeavours to bring over the northern tribes. During this interview between David and Abner, David's nephew Joab had been absent on a plundering expedition ; and on his return with his booty, he reproached his uncle for having allowed Abner to go back alive. He had not forgotten that his brother had been killed by Abner, and he also thought that Abner intended to deceive David, not to betray Ishbosheth. He accordingly sent some messengers after Abner, who brought him back to Hebron ; and Joab there slew him, stabbing him under the fifth rib. Against this act of Joab, David thought it necessary to protest publicly, and he washed his hands of the treachery by complaining of his nephew's disobedience. But his lament over Abner amounted to little more than blame for his folly in allowing himself to be slain by treachery.*

The death of Abner was immediately followed by the ruin of Ishbosheth, and he was soon assassinated by two of his own captains. He had reigned two years.† But his death did not immediately make David king of the whole country.

---

* 2 Sam. iii. † 2 Sam. ii. 10.

The northern tribes would seem to have remained five years
longer in a state of confusion without a leader, for no one
seems to have proposed to make Ishbosheth's lame nephew,
Mephibosheth, king. But at the end of that time the heads
of the northern tribes came to David at Hebron, and promised obedience to him; and they made him king over all
Israel as well as over Judah. This was B.C. 1008. He had
already reigned seven years and six months in Hebron over
Judah alone, and was now thirty-eight years of age.[*]

DAVID KING OF BOTH ISRAEL AND JUDAH. B.C. 1008-976.

David's rebellion against Saul may have been forced upon
him by Saul's conduct. His being made king in Hebron
over the tribe of Judah may have been by the willing choice
of his countrymen. But his seizing upon northern Israel
was an act of lawless violence; and a throne gained by the
sword, and held by the right of conquest, must be supported
by the sword.

No sooner was David king of both halves **of** the country,
than he felt the want of a capital for his kingdom. His
own city, Hebron, was too far southward, and to live there
would be to turn his back upon the larger half of his
subjects. Saul's city, Gibeah of Benjamin, was little better
than an open village, or as its name tells us, a hill-top.
Gibeon, the fortress, held by his own friends the men of
Judah, may have been too small. To fix upon a city in
Ephraim or Manasseh would have been to place himself in
the middle of his less trusted subjects, and at a distance
from Judah, to whom he looked for his chief support. The
strong city of the Jebusites, since known as Jerusalem,
built on Mount Zion, a rock at the boundary between
Benjamin and Judah, which was still in the hands of the
native inhabitants, was in every way suited to his purpose.
Its strength had gained it the name of Salem, *peace, safety,*
and hence Iru-salem, *the City of Safety.* He had only to
seize upon it as he had done in other cases; and if it were
stronger than any he had before taken, so also was his
army. The Jebusites boasted that even the blind and the
lame would be able to defend its walls against an enemy.
But Jerusalem is wholly without wells, and dependent on
the neighbouring pools for its water, which was brought in
by an open trough or aqueduct, from the high ground near

[*] 2 Sam. v. 1-5.

the north-west corner of the city. By this water-course David's soldiers stormed the place, and they thus gained for him the possession of this city, now so celebrated. He at once strengthened the walls, and in particular built a strong tower or castle, called Millo and Beth-millo, to keep the conquered inhabitants in obedience. It probably stood on the high ground at the north-east corner of the city, where the Castle of Antonia stood in more modern days.* Jerusalem was henceforth the chief city of the Israelites. But the Jebusites were still allowed to dwell there, if not in Zion, the city proper, at least in the northern suburb, under the threatening walls of Millo.† We may suppose, from the situation of their city, that they were a part of the tribe of the Children of Ammon, who once held that land. We shall hereafter see that David lived on friendly terms with Araunah, the king of the Jebusites.‡

Now that David was king of a larger country than before, he showed his increased importance in that truly eastern style of adding to the number of his wives and concubines. At Ziklag he had two wives; when king of Hebron he had six wives and as many sons; and in Jerusalem, with his larger number of wives, eleven more sons were born to him.§ This debasing practice of having numerous wives was followed by all David's successors, and by many of their nobles, and must be counted as one of the most certain causes of the nation's ruin. And we remark, in passing, that one of David's youngest children had the double name of El-iada, *God knoweth*,‖ and Baal-iada, *the Lord knoweth*,¶ showing that the name of Baal was at this time by no means set aside as idolatrous.

In order to terrify his enemies, and mark his future conduct, David had seven of Saul's sons and grandsons impaled or crucified in Saul's own city Gibeah, sparing, however, the lame Mephibosheth, whose weakness rendered him powerless as a rival. This act of cruelty was said to be done to satisfy the Gibeonites, a remnant of the native race who were living in the land of Benjamin. But we may rather suppose that the Gibeonites, whose death was to be avenged, were the priests of Jehovah, whom Saul slew at Nod, which was another name for Gibeon, or Gibeah of Judah. And again we may be sure that as Saul's family

* 2 Sam. v. 5-10. † Jos. xv. 63.
‡ 2 Sam. xxiv. § 2 Sam. iii. 1-5; v. 13-16.
‖ 2 Sam. v. 16. ¶ 1 Chron. xiv. 7.

were "impaled on the hill before Jehovah," it was at Gibeah
of Judah, where the altar to Jehovah stood, not at Gibeah
of Saul, that seven victims of a selfish policy were made a
sacrifice to Jehovah.* This took place in the first month
of the year, at the beginning of the barley harvest, which
was of course the time of the Passover-feast. It was no
doubt from religious reasons that public executions were
appointed to take place at that solemn time. In the same
way the Egyptians put their criminals to death as a sacrifice
to their god Osiris. When this was done in either country
to give a religious solemnity to a dreadful act of justice, to
show that life was destroyed, not in haste or anger, but
after delay with due thought, we need not class it with
the human sacrifices of savages; but here in the case of
David's slaughter of Saul's grandsons, the making use of
the name of Jehovah seems to add to the wickedness of the
deed.

David's being made king of all Israel did not intimidate
the Philistines or check their eagerness for spoil; and their
troops spread over the land, and even into the Valley of
Giants on the north-west of Jerusalem. But there he twice
defeated them, and drove them back from Gibeah to the
strong hill fortress of Gezer in the land of Ephraim.†

David as soon as he was at leisure proposed to give a
religious sanction to his new capital, and for this purpose he
removed the Ark of God, "whose name is Jehovah," from
Gibeah. This was done with much ceremony, but in a
manner wholly unlike that afterwards ordered in Numbers
iv. After allowing it to rest for three months outside the
city, he went forth and joined the procession of dancers and
musicians; and being himself clothed with a priestly linen
robe, the Ephod, and dancing with the rest, he brought it
into Jerusalem, and lodged it under a tent there pitched for
it. Then, on an altar placed in front of it, he offered burnt-
offerings and peace-offerings to Jehovah; and with the latter
he feasted the assembled people.‡ The Ark and the Ten
Commandments written on the Two Tables within it, belonged to that part of the Israelites who worshipped God
under the name of Jehovah, and it can now claim a more
important place in history. It can have had no cover of
solid gold, like that of Exodus xxxvii., nor did David, when
he brought it up to Jerusalem, bring with it the Tent under

* 2 Sam. xxi, 1-14.   † 2 Sam. v. 17-25.
‡ 2 Sam. vi.

which it stood; he **left** that behind at Gibeah.* Zadok and
Abiathar the Levites were in authority in Jerusalem when
the Ark was brought into that city by David; and with
them began the ceremonial worship of Jehovah there, which
was continued by their successors with such costly rites and
sacrifices. Whether the prophet Samuel called upon the
name of Jehovah, as stated in his life, or upon Elohim, God,
seems doubtful.

These peaceable doings, however, did not long detain David
from his wars. He again defeated the Philistines, and then
took the City of Gath their chief city in his neighbourhood,
and that which gave a great strength to their marauding
inroads. This capture of Gath the Hebrew historian calls
snatching the bridle on his chief city out of the hands of
its enemies.† The Philistines seem to have carried on
the war for plunder, and against them David fought in
self-defence.

On the other side of his country, David was stronger than
his neighbours, and there in his turn he looked for plunder.
He invaded the land of Moab, and cruelly slaughtered two-
thirds of those that he took captive. He laid them on the
ground and measured them with a line, slaying two measures
of men, and leaving one measure alive. The country of
Moab then remained tributary to David. During this and
the following reign, the few Jews who dwelt there, called
the tribe of Reuben, may have been masters of the land to
the north of the river Arnon. That half of Moab which lies
to the south of the Arnon, and is less fertile than the
northern half, they left to the Moabites, an unsettled race
of herdsmen, whose strength lay in the poverty of their
country. The deep chasm through which the Arnon flows
was a good **natural** boundary between them and the
Reubenites.

Modern and more civilized ages justly criticize the cruelty
with which these wars were carried on. The policy has been
nearly the same in all times. Might was thought to give
right. A king's aim was to widen his dominions and to
gain more tributary subjects. If a neighbouring state
consented to pay a tribute, the conqueror was satisfied. A
time perhaps soon came when it could venture to withhold
the tribute. Then followed more cruel wars, and probably
a second conquest.

After the conquest of northern Moab, David marched

* 2 Chron. i. 3.   † 1 Chron. xviii. 1.; compare 2 Sam. viii. 1.

against the Syrians, who were at that time quarrelling among themselves. The Syrians, like the Israelites, were divided into several tribes, or little states. These were the Syrians of Zobah, the Syrians of Hamah, the Syrians of Damascus, and the Syrians beyond the river Euphrates. This confederacy of little states, the Hebrew writers sometimes term an assembly of bulls with their **calves.***
Hadadezer, king of Zobah, had gone towards the Euphrates to recover his boundary, which used to be at that river; and David defeated his troops while he was at a distance, and brought away horses for one hundred chariots. The Syrians of Damascus then hastened to succour the king of Zobah; but David defeated them also with great slaughter, and placed garrisons in Damascus and the neighbouring towns, and for a time made that little state pay a tribute to him. His treaty with the king of Damascus may be the original of that between Laban and Jacob, in Genesis xxxi., when Bashan was allowed to belong to the Syrian, and Gilead **to** Israel. Mizpeh, *the* watch-tower, **was** Israel's frontier post.

Toi, king of Hamath, with whom Hadadezer had been at war, sent a willing tribute to David, and became his servant, as the other Syrians were forced to do unwillingly. On the south David was equally successful; he conquered the Philistines, the Amalekites and the Edomites, put garrisons in their cities, and made them also tributaries.† The wish for plunder, which was at times the king's chief source of revenue, rather than passion or quarrels, seems to have been the cause of most of these early wars. As little or nothing was spent on the military preparations, a successful war was always a source of profit.

Perhaps the conquest of Edom should be placed rather later in **David's** reign, because a child named Hadad, one of the family **of** the kings of Edom, who escaped from the slaughter brought upon the Edomites by Joab, David's captain, and was carried off into Egypt as a place of safety, lived to trouble the Israelites, and to gain the throne of his forefathers, towards the end of Solomon's reign.‡

David was now safely seated on his throne, and at leisure to attend to his civil affairs. His chief officers were his nephew Joab, who was his captain, a recorder, a scribe, a captain **of** his body guard of axe-bearers and runners, and

* Isaiah xxxiv. 7.   Psalm lxviii. 30.
† 2 Sam. viii.   ‡ 1 Kings xi. 14.

two chief priests. These two priests, Zadok and Abiathar, were Levites; but the priesthood was not limited to the Levites, as David's sons were also priests, though probably only the eldest son of each wife, and David must have claimed the same rank for himself when he wore an Ephod. David then remembered the kindness that he had formerly received from Saul's son Jonathan; and in order to make him some return he fetched Jonathan's son Mephibosheth, whose lameness made him no object of political jealousy, and allowed him to live near to him at Jerusalem, and gave him a maintenance from the royal table.*

We may here place two of David's acts which the historian mentions late in his reign, but which seem to belong to the earliest time after he was safe upon his throne; namely, his numbering the people, and his raising an altar to Jehovah on the hill on the east side of the capital. The latter act, in particular, was not likely to be delayed long after his priests had been established in the city. David's proposal to have a careful numbering made of the people of his kingdom, was made probably with the view to a regular collection of taxes for the support of his government. Though regular taxation existed in Egypt, it was unknown among the Israelites. Joab and the other captains earnestly endeavoured to dissuade him from this unpopular act; but David was firm to his purpose, and he committed the task to the captains of his army. It probably could not have been performed without some little display of force. These officers passed through the whole land from north to south, and on both sides of the Jordan; they made some kind of rough survey of the land; and at the end of nine months they brought back word to the king that he had in Judah five hundred thousand men of the military age, and in Israel eight hundred thousand. This act of making a register of the population would seem to have been with a view to a levy of soldiers, or of labourers, or perhaps to the introduction of a land tax, that known by the name of the tithe. In Egypt, when the Israelites were there, the king claimed one-fifth part of the produce of the land for the support of his government and army.† But that would have pressed too heavily upon the poorer land of Canaan. We have lately read of the prophet Samuel warning the Israelites that, if they appointed a king to rule over them, he would claim a tenth of the produce of their land for the support of

* 2 Sam. viii.; ix. † Genesis xli. 34.

4 *

his numerous servants.* And this is what David probably aimed at. At what **time** the Levites received or claimed the tithes for themselves we shall find a difficulty in fixing, in consequence of the difficulty of determining when the several laws relating to the tithes were added to the Pentateuch. The Levites were, in the first **instance,** maintained by the heave offerings and freewill offerings of the faithful, and by a share of their peace offerings, and they seem never to have claimed the tithe while the king **was** able **to** collect **it.** If this numbering of the people was for the purpose **of** collecting a tax we can well understand why it was so unpopular. A pestilence, which soon afterwards came upon the land, was thought to have been sent by Jehovah as a punishment for this act.†

When David thus surveyed the country and numbered the people, he probably divided his kingdom into its well-known twelve tribes, as set forth shortly after this time in the history of Jacob's family. Zebulun had hitherto claimed to reach to the furthest north, even to the Sidonians;‡ and not till David had driven out the Syrians, was that great district lessened, by making Napthali and Asher into two new tribes. In the south, his conquests **were not** so complete, nor the tribes so real. The Simeonites did not so far overcome the Philistines as to gain the lands assigned to them; nor did the Reubenites wholly gain that portion of Moab which they claimed as their own. The Levites were, about the same time, declared to be a thirteenth tribe, though no lands were given to them. They lived upon the offerings of the worshippers.

It is not impossible that we may have some of the results of David's survey in the Book of Joshua, as we know of no time after Solomon's death when the boundaries of all the tribes were likely to have been surveyed and described. **This** early information may easily have found a place in the newer book.

The author of the Books of Chronicles, writing five hundred years later, describes among the several sources of the king's income, the large crown lands, and gives the names of the overseers who had charge of the tillage. But this information relates to some of his successors, perhaps to Uzziah, who gave much attention to husbandry. No such lands are mentioned by the Book of Kings, even in Solomon's **more** quiet reign. It was for want of such

* 1 Sam. viii. 15.   † 2 Sam. xxiv. 1-17.   ‡ Gen. xlix. 13.

sources of income that most of the nation's wars were undertaken. With our modern system of **warfare, war has** become
very expensive; but it was not so when life was less valued,
and therefore the means of defending and of killing were
less carefully studied and prepared. In those less civilized
times, the booty seized from the enemies that resisted
invasion, and the tribute wrung from those that quietly
submitted, **were** looked to as the chief sources of a monarch's
income.

The **next act** in David's reign, **one** which gains great
importance from the after history of the nation, was his
raising an altar to Jehovah on Mount Moriah, a hill **on the**
east side of Jerusalem. The bare rock on the top **of the hill**
had **been used** as a threshing-floor, according to the custom
of the **people,** who brought their corn from the country
around to be threshed on such **a** spot, because there the
wind would blow away the chaff. It was the threshing-floor
of Araunah, king of the Jebusites.* It was usual with the
Israelites, both of the north and the south, to place their
altars of sacrifice on such hills. Such a hill was called
Bahmah, *a high place*, and hence, perhaps, the Greek word
Bomos, *an altar*. Samuel had sacrificed on such a High
Place at Ramah.† There was also a great High Place at
Gibeon, or Gibeah, of Judah, of more than usual holiness.‡
Probably every part of the land had its **own** High Place,
where the people of the neighbourhood sacrificed to Heaven
in their own fashion. Hence it was very natural for David,
now that he had established **his** seat of government in
Jerusalem, a foreign city, where the God of his fathers had
not hitherto **been** worshipped, to look out for a suitable hill
for a High Place or altar. When it had been chosen,
he bought **it of** Araunah, and there offered up his burnt-
offerings of **oxen to** Jehovah on behalf of himself and of the
nation.

The hill on which David sacrificed received the name of
Mount Moriah, **or** *that sheweth*, because the **will of** Jehovah
was there declared by the priests. Other holy spots had
gained a name for the same reason, such as the Oak of
Moreh, near Shechem.§ The rock on which the altar stood,
the threshing-floor of Araunah, is **now** inclosed under the
dome of the Mosque of Omar.

The next war which engaged David's attention was against

* 2 Sam. xxiv. **18-25.** † 1 Sam. ix. 12.
‡ 1 Kings iii. **4.** § Genesis xii. 6.

the Ammonites. This people had been David's friends
while both were at war with Saul's son, Ishbosheth; but as
soon as David was the acknowledged king of Eastern Israel,
the friendship cooled and then quarrels between them arose.
The Ammonites had put an affront on some of David's
servants, who had been sent to them with a friendly message.
In preparation for David's attack, the Ammonites now hired
a large body of Syrians from Rehob, Zobah, Tob, and
Maacah. They formed their camp in front of the city of
Medeba, near Heshbon on the table-land of Moab. But
their joint forces were defeated by the Israelites under
David's two nephews, Joab and Abishai. The Syrians then
made the war their own; and Hadadezer, king of Zobah,
sent for a larger body of men from his countrymen beyond
the Euphrates. Upon this, David marched out in person;
he crossed the Jordan, and defeated the allied Syrians,
who thereupon made peace with him and returned home,
leaving the Ammonites to suffer the consequences of David's
anger.*

It may have been at this time that the two little Syrian
tribes of Geshurites and Maachalhites sunk into the kingdom
of Israel.†

David's difficulties in the east were increased by the cold-
ness of his eastern subjects, who had opposed him as long as
any one of Saul's family claimed the throne. The eastern
tribes were only kept in obedience by his placing among
them, at Jazer in Gilead, a body of his most faithful troops
from Hebron, in number two thousand seven hundred. These
men were the lords over the Reubenites, the Gadites, and
the half-tribe of Manasseh.‡

In the following year, "at the time when kings go forth
to battle," a mode of dating which explains the frequency
of these marauding inroads, David sent Joab with troops
against the Ammonites, and they laid siege to Rabbah, the
chief city in that country.§ Joab was so far successful that
he took an important suburb, called the City on the Waters;
so called, probably, from the tanks or pools, which gathered
in a supply of water for the city, and made it weaker on
that side. On this Joab checked his troops, and like a true
friend to David, he sent to invite him to come and complete
the conquest in person, and thus receive the honours of the
victory. David did so; he took the city, placed the crown

---

* 2 Sam. x.; 1 Chron. xix.   † Josh. xiii. 13.
‡ 1 Chron. xxvi. 32.   § 2 Sam. xi. 1.

of the Ammonite king on his own head, put the inhabitants to death by the cruellest means, such as saws and harrows of iron, and returned to Jerusalem with a great spoil, after treating the neighbouring cities with equal cruelty.* Humanity had as yet placed no limit to the rights of the strong over the weak.

It was while the army was engaged on this siege of Rabbah, before Joab's success, that David took to himself Bathsheba, the wife of Uriah. To get rid of the husband, he sent him to join the army, with the cold-blooded instructions written to Joab that he should place him in the front of the battle, and then withdraw the soldiers from him, so that he could not fail of being slain. Joab showed no hesitation in joining in this murderous plot; Uriah soon met with the death which David had planned for him, and Bathsheba was then openly acknowledged by David as one of his wives. The crime, however, was strongly rebuked by the prophet Nathan, in a parable which is like an oasis in the desert of violence and wickedness which these early histories disclose. But, when we thus moralize about the crimes which we meet with among the Israelites, let us consider that these were probably far less wicked and less common than those which were committed among the idolatrous nations around.†

Another crime of this time was the outrage of David's eldest son Amnon against his half-sister Tamar. This led to Absalom, another of David's sons, killing Amnon, in revenge for the injury done to his sister. Such doings were only a part of the evils which arose from the king's having so many wives. The natural relationship of families was thereby very much destroyed.

Absalom, to avoid his father's just wrath, then fled to Geshur in Syria, of which place his mother was a native; and there he dwelt for three years among his mother's friends.‡

But Absalom was David's favourite son, and David, after a time, began to pine at his absence. David's nephew, Joab, who in all his difficulties had been his best friend, saw what was wanted, but did not himself venture to ask for Absalom's pardon. He therefore employed a wise woman, one who had gained some kind of sacred character, to obtain it from David. This she did by means of a parable which she related to him. So Joab was allowed to go to Geshur and

* 2 Sam. xii. 26-31.　　† 2 Sam. xi. 2—xii. 23.　　‡ 2 Sam. xiii.

to fetch Absalom to Jerusalem, where he had leave to dwell
in his own house; but it was two years more before he was
received into his father's presence.*

Absalom had been a spoilt child, and he was not content
to live in Jerusalem out of favour. His personal beauty
may have **helped** his high rank to make him popular with
those that he came near; and he now took all possible means
to gain that favour with the people which he had lost with
the king **his** father. He moved about in state in his chariot,
with fifty runners to go before him; but he, at the same
time, showed himself eager to redress the wrongs of any who
had been injured, and when any man offered to do him reverence, he took him by the hand familiarly and kissed him.
In this way he stole the hearts of all men.

Absalom's aim after popularity was so far successful that
he began to think that the throne itself was within his reach.
His ambition cannot have escaped the notice of David.
David, it would seem, had not been able to keep the friendship of both halves of his kingdom. He was always surrounded by a body of six hundred foreign mercenaries, men
of Gath. Though living in Jerusalem on purpose to be near
the northern tribes, he had never been able fully to gain
their good will. The friends of Saul were numerous in
Jerusalem, and still more numerous among the northern
Israelites. So, after forty years, says the historian, meaning,
according to the usage of the language, after a few years,
Absalom asked leave of David to quit the city, under the
pretence of a vow to go to serve Jehovah at Hebron.
Hebron was then the chief city of the heads of the Levites,
and the most approved spot for the worship of Jehovah.
Accordingly, David's permission was granted. Had Absalom
asked leave to go northward, his intentions would have been
suspected, and he might have been refused. He took with
him two hundred men, and at Hebron **he** raised the standard
of rebellion, having previously sent trusty spies through the
northern tribes, to **let** his friends and the discontented
Israelites know what **he** was going to do, and to summon them
to meet him at Jerusalem. No sooner was the trumpet
blown, and the shout raised that Absalom was king in
Hebron, than his supporters increased rapidly. Absalom
was at once joined by Ahithophel, one of David's chief coun-
sellors, and David's power was on the wane.

With Absalom now marching against Jerusalem, David
                      * 2 Sam. xiv.

felt unsafe in the unfriendly city. The enemies by whom he was surrounded, and those who were likely to come in from **the** north, were far more to be feared than Absalom's little army, which was coming up from the south. So taking with him his body guard, the axe-bearers and runners, and his six hundred faithful Gathites, he left Jerusalem in mournful procession, and the city was soon entered by Absalom. David left behind him the two chief priests, Zadok and Abiathar, and also his friend Hushai, who was to feign himself a traitor, and with the priests was to act **as a** spy upon Absalom.* Saul's family, and the friends of Saul's family, remained in the city to welcome Absalom ; and among these was Mephibosheth, the **son** of Jonathan ; but whether he stayed behind, when David fled, in forgetfulness of David's kindness, or because he **was** lame, as he afterwards said, seems doubtful.†

At this time, when David left the city, if there had been any form of government, any civil authority, any council of elders, **or** any magistrate but himself and his servants, we must have been told. The only men who had any acknowledged power, independent of the king, were the priests. They alone are mentioned in this revolution. They alone can give to the throne any support or offer any control.

No sooner had Absalom entered Jerusalem than he made **his** cousin **Amasa**, one **of** David's nephews, his chief captain ; and **he** took counsel with his friends as to what he should do. Ahithophel advised sending a body of troops in pursuit of David that very night ; on the other hand, Hushai counselled some delay, under pretence of caution, but with the secret wish that David should have time to escape across the Jordan. The advice of Hushai, the traitor, was followed ; and Ahithophel, **after a** time, saw that the foolish Absalom had fallen among either false friends or bad advisers. So he left Jerusalem in despair **and went to** his own city near Hebron. In the meantime David and **his** followers crossed the Jordan, probably at a southern ford, and hastening northward, had reached the strong city of Mahanaim in northern Gilead in safety. There he was well received, and his men had time to refresh themselves as if at home, before it was necessary to march out and fight Absalom.‡ David had before placed there a body of twenty-seven hundred men from Hebron, the men in whom he had the greatest trust, to keep the eastern tribes

---

* 2 Sam. xv. † 2 Sam. xvi. 1-14.
‡ 2 Sam. xvi. 15—xvii.

in obedience.* These were the friends to whom he now fled, and to whom he looked for the recovery of his throne.

Absalom crossed the Jordan in pursuit of his father; and David proposed to march forward himself with his army against Absalom. But his friends, feeling how important his safety was to their cause, persuaded him to remain in Mahanaim; and he accordingly sent forth his troops under the command of his faithful nephews Joab and Abishai, and Ittai the leader of his Gathite mercenaries. Absalom had put his forces under the command of his cousin Amasa, who like Joab was a son of one of David's sisters, but whose father was a man of northern Israel. For this reason Absalom may have thought that Amasa would win the northern Israelites to his side. The two armies met in the forest of Ephraim, in the land of Gilead, where Absalom's troops were defeated, and Absalom himself slain. David had given charge to his captains that his favourite son, who had driven him from his throne, and was in arms against him, should not be hurt. But Joab here, as on other occasions, had his own opinion as to what was most for his uncle's advantage, and killed Absalom with his own hands, when he fell into his power in the flight. Absalom's soldiers then dispersed themselves, every man fled to his own home, and no body of troops remained to oppose themselves to David's return to his capital.

From the name of the forest in which the battle was fought, it might be argued that both the armies had crossed to the west side of the Jordan. But this is an unnecessary conjecture. The name of Ephraim is a corruption of Abarim, *the* beyond men; and though it is never elsewhere used except for the tribe which settled on the west side of the Jordan, yet here the Forest of Ephraim seems to mean a spot adjoining the well-known mountains of Abarim in the land of Gilead.

As soon as the victory was complete, the young Ahimaaz, the son of Zadok the priest, asked leave of Joab, the captain, to be allowed to carry the news to David, who was at Mahanaim. But Joab, well knowing how painful to David would be the first news of his son's death, would not send him; David in his displeasure might even do violence to the messenger. So he sent a Cushite, or negro, to carry the tidings to the indulgent father, and to bear the consequences. But some time after the Cushite had started, he allowed

* 1 Chron. xxvi. 32.

Ahimaaz to follow. The Cushite took the straight road where he may have met with hindrances; Ahimaaz, with perhaps more knowledge of the country, ran by the circle of the Jordan. By so doing, though he lengthened his journey, he **reached** the king before the other messenger who had started first. He told the king that he brought nothing but the good news of the victory, and when David asked if Absalom was safe, he assured him that he did not know. A little later the Cushite runner arrived, and when David repeated the question, Is Absalom safe? he answered, May all the king's enemies be as that young man is.*

David's grief for the death of his son Absalom was far from agreeable to his friends. They had fought for him, and regained for him his throne; and his mournful behaviour was but a reproachful return for their services. It was only at the request of his nephew and best friend Joab, that he consented to sit at the gate of the city of Mahanaim and receive the congratulations of the people.

As soon as the death of Absalom was known to tho northern tribes their resistance to David was at an end, and they began to talk about inviting him back to Jerusalem. David sent to his friends Zadok and Abiathar, the priests, to get them to call upon the men of Judah to rise in his favour; and, in order to win back the traitors, he promised that his nephew Amasa, who had commanded Absalom's troops, should not lose his post, but should for the future be his chief captain in place of his cousin the faithful Joab. He then came down from Mahanaim to the southern ford of the Jordan, while the men of Judah came down to Gilgal to meet him, and to conduct him over the river. They were followed by a large body of those who had lately been in arms against him, who came now to ask for his forgiveness. Ahithophel had before hanged himself in his despair. Amasa, Absalom's chief captain, had already received forgiveness and promotion.

Shimei, the leader of the Benjamites, who had insulted David on his fall, now placed his thousand men at David's service, and was also forgiven. Mephibosheth, Jonathan's lame son, who stayed behind in Jerusalem when David fled, was only deprived of half his property. Forgiveness was promised to all, though with what sincerity may be doubted. But David was far too weak in power to venture on punishing his enemies. On entering the ferry-boat on the river,

* 2 Sam. xviii.

while his little army crossed the ford, he bid farewell to his faithful Gileadite friends, and soon afterwards reached Jerusalem, where he was to meet with fresh difficulties from the divided state of the nation, and the angry feelings which never fail to rankle long after a civil war.*

Though the late rebellion bore the appearance of an attempt of the son to gain his father's throne, it **was** in reality an attempt of the northern tribes to separate **them-** selves from the tribe of Judah, with whom they had few feelings in common. David seems to have governed with reasonable impartiality, and perhaps meant to do the same on his regaining his capital. But he soon changed his policy, and threw himself wholly into the arms of the men of Judah, and the disappointed Israelites were again in rebellion.

Sheba, a Benjamite, now set himself up as the leader of Israel, and summoned his followers to join him in the north. David, on the other hand, summoned the south to his support, **and in this** task he employed his nephew, Amasa, whom he had allowed to remain his chief captain. But Joab was not so forgiving as David; he remembered Amasa's share in the late rebellion; he was also jealous of him as now holding the chief post in the army, which Joab thought belonged to him- self; so on meeting him alone he slew him, while pretending to salute him as a friend. Joab and his brother Abishai then led their men in pursuit of the rebel Sheba, who had not met with the support that he expected. He had retreated north- wards as far as Abel, near Beth-maachah at the foot of Mount Lebanon. There he was overtaken by Joab, who laid siege to the place; but before it could be taken, Sheba was slain by the people of the city, who did not wish to engage in an unequal war against the king's forces. Joab returned to Jerusalem having met with no resistance in his march to the very northern limit of the kingdom.

This second rebellion was now at an end, and David was again at leisure to appoint his officers of government, and regulate the civil and ecclesiastical affairs of the kingdom. Joab was again made chief captain, having, as we have seen, removed his cousin Amasa out of the way by basely murder- ing him.† Henceforth David probably trusted himself chiefly to the support of the men of Judah. But he at the same time tried to blot out the distinction which had existed between the Hebrews and the Canaanites and other conquered races who dwelt among them. **We** find among

* 2 Sam. xix.　　　　　† 2 Sam. xx.

his thirty chief and trusted captains a Hittite, an Ammonite, a Syrian of Maachah, a Syrian of Zobah, and an Edomite from the valley of Arabah.* From this we may suppose that in the lower ranks of his army all Canaanites were equally welcome; and though the Israelites were taught to shun their idolatry, we hear of no attempts at present to restrain the free exercise of their religious rites.

As David's life drew to a close, a not unusual **jealousy** arose among his sons as to who should be his successor on the throne. **As** they were children of different wives, the priority by age was not held to confer a very certain birthright. Adonijah, perhaps now the eldest son after Absalom was dead, began to form a party to secure it for himself. His boastful name, meaning *my lord Jehovah*, had no doubt been given him in order to mark him out as heir to the throne. But Bath-sheba, the favourite wife, hoped **to** gain it for her son Solomon. Joab, at all times David's most faithful but wilful adviser, and now the captain of his armies, supported the claim of Adonijah as being the elder, as did most of the king's sons, and Abiathar, one of the two high priests. But Zadok, the other high priest, Benaiah the captain of the body-guard, and Nathan the prophet, waited to hear the decision of David himself on this important question. David, yielding to the persuasions of Bath-sheba, declared the young Solomon his successor; and, moreover, the better to secure **his** will being acted on, he ordered him to be proclaimed king at once, as his own colleague **on the** throne. Solomon was set upon the king's mule, and led in state through the city, accompanied by the priest Zadok, and by the axe-bearers and runners under the command of Benaiah; and he was then taken to Gihon, a spot of rising ground on the west side of the city, where David seems to have been living in a tent; and there Zadok anointed him as king.† It was probably on Solomon's being appointed heir to the throne that the prophet Nathan gave him the name of Jedidiah, or *beloved of Jehovah,* as being suited to his sacred rank.‡ But this new name did not come into use; and in history he is only known by the name of Solomon. David died shortly afterwards, and Solomon was quietly acknowledged as the successor by the whole of the country. Joab, though captain of all the armies when they were called together, had no power when the troops were sent away to their homes. The captain of

* 2 Sam. **xxiii.**   † 1 Kings i.   ‡ 2 Sam. xii. 25.

the guard, on the other hand, was at all times master of
a small force. Hence Joab had no troops that he could
oppose to Benaiah's body-guard.

David died about the year B.C. 976, having reigned, first
seven years in Hebron over Judah, and then thirty-three
years in Jerusalem over Israel and Judah united.

In 1 Chron. xxii., David describes himself as a man of
violence and bloodshed. He gained the throne by rebellion
against Saul, and kept it only by force against the rebellion
of others. But he was the founder of a long line of kings.
He was the founder of Jerusalem the religious capital of
Judaism, which in its ruins is still regarded with reverence
by the most civilized portions of the world. He began the
collection of Hebrew Psalms, which in translations and
imitations are more read by all Christians than any of their
own poetry. Well may the Jews shut their eyes to what
he did wrong, and be proud of their great king David.

David's long reign was a time of some literary activity.
The warlike king himself has the credit given to him of
being the author of many Hebrew psalms. The only other
authors whom we are told of are the prophet Nathan and the
prophet Gad. But there may have been many more. The
books which the Chronicler quotes as his authorities for the
history of David's reign are the Book of Nathan, the Book
of Gad, and the Book of Samuel; and our history of Samuel
and Saul is also probably drawn out of those three books.*
The Books of Nathan and Gad may have been so named
because those prophets were the authors of them; but the
Book of Samuel was probably the more modern of the three,
and called so only because Samuel was the subject of it.
The reader of our First Book of Samuel may observe that
the lives of Samuel and Saul, and part of the life of David,
are therein told in two rather contradictory manners, as if
compiled out of two narratives by authors with wholly
different views, the one political and the more trustworthy,
and the other priestly and coloured with modern opinions.
The Books of Nathan and Gad, whose authors lived at the
time, may have furnished the authentic portion, respecting
which we may remark that we have fuller and more trustworthy particulars of David's reign than we have of any one
of his successors on the throne. The life of Samuel, his
childhood under Eli, with the less probable portion of Saul's
life and of David's early life, would seem to have been taken

* 1 Chron. xxix. 29.

out of the third Book, the Book of Samuel, which was a
more modern memoir of that prophet, and which may have
given to him a larger share of political importance than was
allotted to him in the two other books.

Of king David, in his character of author, it is not easy to
form an opinion. At the end of the histories from which we
have been quoting he is called the sweet Psalmist of **Israel**,
and two poems are put into his mouth. But these have a
modern character. The account of his playing on the harp
to amuse Saul seems also to belong to the more modern of
the above quoted books, and must give way to the other
account, which says that he first became known to Saul as a
warrior. But David may at the same time have been both
a poet and a musician. That the book of Psalms bears his
name is of course no proof that he wrote any one of them.
The Pandects of Justinian, King James's Bible, the Code
Napoleon, are so called because those monarchs ordered
them to be written. David, no doubt, gave directions that
a body **of** religious poems should be written for the worship
of Jehovah; but whether any of the Psalms which now
remain to us were written by the king himself must **of**
course be doubtful. The Book of Psalms which bears **his**
name is a collection of religious pieces of very various ages,
some written in David's reign and some more modern than
even **the** fall **of** the monarchy. **The** titles placed at their
head **are** of no authority. The **date of** each must be judged
of by the political circumstances **mentioned**. The style is a
less certain guide to a psalm's age. **It is only in** a few that
we note a difference in the language. A poem, which was
from time to time chanted aloud in the temple-service, by
priests and musicians walking **round the** altar, was naturally
altered from century to century **as** the popular language
slowly changed. Hence, those which are simply devotional
are less easily dated; **those** which contain portions of
history point more clearly to the time when they were
written. They all breathe an earnest religious spirit, and
show a firm belief that the writer and his countrymen are
under the care **of an** all-powerful and ever-watchful God;
though some are disfigured by bitter **and** revengeful wishes
against their oppressors. Their high merit is best shown by
the remark that they are used even **to** the present day as
the chief well-spring whence writers **of** devotional poetry
draw their thoughts.

The Book of Jasher, or *of right*, was a poetical work of
this reign; but **we now** possess **of it** only a fragment of

four lines, and a valuable but short poem of six-and-twenty
lines. The former contains the bold poetical figure of the
sun and moon standing still in the heavens to give the
Israelites time for the more complete slaughter of the
Amorites in the valley of Ajalon. It is quoted in our Book
of Joshua, chap. x. We thus learn that it contained a
history of the early wars of the nation on their first entering
Canaan ; and it is not unreasonable to conjecture that it is
the same work as that called the Book of the Wars from
which we have four lines, and then perhaps another piece of
four lines, quoted in Numbers, chap. xxi. 14 and 47. The
second quotation from the Book of Jasher, is the beautiful
lamentation over Saul and Jonathan, which is put into the
mouth of David. This poem is called the Bow, from the
Hebrew custom of naming a poem, or a piece of history,
from one of the chief words in it.*   Thus :—

> From the blood of the slain, from the fat of the warriors,
> The Bow of Jonathan turned not back,
> And the sword of Saul returned not empty,
> Saul and Jonathan were lovely and pleasant in their **lives,**
> And in their death they **were** not divided.

As the Book of Jasher was written after David was king,
it probably took more notice of the tribe of Judah than the
earlier books had done.

We have before spoken of the earlier narrative in the
Books of Exodus and Numbers as probably written in the
time of Samuel ; and we may now, for reasons such as then
guided us, assign other portions of the Pentateuch to the
reign of David. First among these is the history of Joseph
and of his family settling in Lower Egypt. This history
belongs to the beginning of this reign, though like every
other part of the Pentateuch it has been enlarged by after
additions. It is not possible to divide off very exactly and
satisfactorily these additions, and to say when each was
written, because the editor has mixed them up with the
original narrative. This narrative, contained in Genesis
xxxvii. 2 ; 1., is by an Elohistic writer, so called because he
used the word Elohim for God, and not the word Jehovah.
The few times that the word Jehovah is used may be in
some of the portions afterwards added. The reasons for
judging that this Life of Joseph belongs to the very
beginning of David's reign may be seen by an examination
of Jacob's prophecy relating to his sons, in Genesis xlix.

* 2 Sam. i. 17.

This prophecy must have been written when the tribe of Judah under David had already gained the sceptre. Thus :—

> The sceptre shall not depart from Judah,
> Nor the staff of power from between his feet,
> Until he come to Shiloh ;
> And unto him shall be the obedience of the people.

But it was written before Ephraim and Manasseh, here called Joseph, had lost their importance as the great tribes; perhaps before Shiloh, their religious capital, had acknowledged the superior rank of Jerusalem; after the tribe of Benjamin under Saul had earned its reputation for bravery, but before the Levites had gained their high rank in Jerusalem, and while they were yet scattered outcasts, like the Simeonites. Thus :—

> Simeon and Levi are brethren ;
> Instruments of cruelty are their swords.
> O my soul, come not thou into their friendship,
> Unto their assembly, mine honour, be not thou united.

It was written before Asher had been made into a tribe, as this poem at one time included it in the tribe of Zebulun, saying—

> Zebulun shall dwell on the coast of the ocean ;
> And he shall be on a coast fit for ships ;
> And his farthest boundary shall be unto Sidon.

The second description of Dan, in verses 17, 18, is an after addition which we shall speak of presently.

Other marks, in other portions of the life of Joseph, by which we may see that they were written at this time, are the giving to the tribes of Ephraim and Manasseh the high rank of being descended from the prime minister of Lower Egypt, and the using the name of Israel for Jacob, the father of all the tribes, neither of which could have been done after the division of the kingdom upon Solomon's death ; and again, the calling God by the name of Elohim rather than Jehovah ; which latter name came into use with the rise of the Levites.

But the writer so little conceals that he is writing after the Exodus, as to make Jacob on his death-bed tell Joseph that he had conquered for his family from the Amorites, with his sword and his bow, a mountain track above the share of land that he would receive with his brethren. This was the territory of the half-tribe of Manasseh, on the east of the Jordan. The writer is quoting from Numbers xxi.; and he mistakes Israel the nation for Israel the patriarch. The

5

history of Joseph's introducing a land-tax in Lower Egypt
may have been thought useful as a support **to** David's doing
the same.

What early materials the writer had **for his** history it is
impossible now to say. The name of Joseph, meaning *He
will gather up*, may have been given to him because he stored
up the Egyptian corn in the years of plenty. Much of the
dramatic narrative may have been added at a later time, by
some writer of the same political feelings as the original
author. The interesting picture of the ten brothers' jealousy
against their father's favourite son, of their selling him as a
slave, his rising to high rank by his good conduct, and his
then forgiving his brethren who had injured him, together
with the father's tenderness for his youngest son, seem
hardly to belong to this early time of lawless violence. The
comparison **of** Jacob's twelve sons to the twelve signs of
the zodiac would lead us to think that the last editor lived
after the Jews had gained an acquaintance with Babylonian
science in their captivity. But the knowledge of Egyptian
customs, of their embalming the dead, of their mourning
for seventy days, of their use of the divining cup, of their
hatred of the shepherd race, and of the tenure of the soil
in Lower Egypt, gives great truthfulness to the narrative.

Chapters xxv. 19,—xxxvi. 8, of Genesis, contain the **lives**
of Isaac, Jacob, and Esau, with the births of Jacob's sons.
These chapters are of a more mixed character, partly
Elohistic and partly Jehovistic, and were written later in
David's reign. Here the Almighty declares his name to be
El; and Shechem and Beth-el are called holy spots, and
Levi is spoken of in terms of blame. These are all of them
circumstances which join these chapters to the Elohistic life
of Joseph; the Jehovistic passages seem to be later additions.
In these chapters, together with the Life of Joseph, the
Levites and the twelve tribes that claimed the land of
Canaan, are all arranged into one family, as sons of Israel.
This is done by declaring that Jacob is Israel, and that two
of the tribes are sons of Jacob's son Joseph.

That the patriarchs are named from David's tribes, or
districts, not the tribes from the patriarchs, appears from
the names themselves, and may be gathered from the history.
The sons and grandsons of Jacob, who give their names to
the thirteen tribes, are the following :—

Reuben, Simeon, Levi, and Judah, sons of the first wife;

Issachar and Zebulun, sons of the same wife, but born later;

Dan, Naphtali, Gad, and Asher, sons of handmaids;

Benjamin, Ephraim, and Manasseh, son and grandsons of the favourite wife.

These, we shall show, were originally only two tribes. The first four we may call Judah, and the last three Manasseh. The others were only divisions of these. They may have been arranged into thirteen tribes in David's reign.

Of these, we have seen that the Levites were a religious body, forming part of Judah, as said in Judges xvii. 7.

Reuben was that part of the tribe of Judah which remained behind among the Moabites, when the others crossed into Canaan; and hence is called Judah's elder brother. It had not gained its independence. Heshbon, the chief city in the district, was usually held by Moabites.

Simeon was that part of Judah which remained subject to the Philistines, when in Saul's reign, the rest of the tribe made itself free. Thus Reuben, Simeon, Levi and Judah, were only one tribe.

The origin of Issachar and Zebulun is explained in Judges iii. 7-11, where we read of a body of men from Southern Judah joining the Israelites of the North, and wresting a portion of northern territory from the Syrians. This agrees with the family history which makes these two to be younger brothers of Judah, and it agrees with the later political history which shows that Judah never felt the same enmity to them that it felt to Ephraim and Manasseh. These two tribes worshipped Jehovah on Mount Tabor, a hill situated on the boundary which separated them.*

The tribes called Sons of the Handmaids are all of later creation. They were at first included within other tribes. Dan was that portion of Ephraim which, like Simeon, was under the Philistines. It had no separate existence, until it migrated northward, to seize a territory, as described in Judges xviii. Asher and Naphtali were at first part of Zebulun, whose boundary reached to Sidon (Gen. xlix. 13). It was probably in the course of David's reign that the northern part of Zebulun was made into those two districts, after he had conquered the Syrians, from whom Asher had its name. Gad, called Gilead in Deborah's song had been part of the eastern half of Manasseh; see Numbers xxvi. 29.

The Ephraimites were part of Manasseh, that part which

* Deut. xxxiii. 19.

5 *

crossed into Canaan at a later time, and probably under the lead, and with the higher knowledge, of those who had escaped from Egypt. Their name of Ephraim may possibly be a corruption of Abarim, Hebrews, or *Beyond men*, which would be given to them on crossing the Jordan. As Manasseh settled in the land first, Manasseh **is** called the elder brother; but, as Ephraim became the stronger, Jacob's blessing was put upon him.

The Benjamites, called also Jaminites, were part of the Ephraimites, and hence Benjamin is made the brother of Joseph, the father of Ephraim. They took their name from the children of Ammon, Beni-ammon, among whom they settled and whom they conquered. One of their towns was named the City of the Ammonites (Josh. xviii. 24).

There remain, then, the two original tribes; the one called Manasseh, and the other Judah. These may have brought their names from Chaldea, when the one settled in the middle of Canaan, as said in the Life of Jacob, and the other settled in the southern part of Canaan, as said in the Life of Abraham. Throughout our history we shall always find the nation composed of these two parts, though not always with the same names. Sometimes they are known as Israel and Judah, sometimes as Joseph and Judah, sometimes as Ephraim and Judah, and lastly as Samaritans and Jews.

Thus the hints which have been gained from history, when compared with the map of the country, show us upon what grounds the tribes of Israel, though at first only two in number, were afterwards, when spread over the land, described as the thirteen children and grandchildren of Jacob, when he received the name of Israel.

Jacob fixed his dwelling first at Shechem, and then at Beth-el; his visit to Hebron, where Abraham and Isaac had settled, may be an after addition to the narrative. The Tower of Edar, or *the flocks*, near which Jacob spread his tent, was the tower in Jerusalem close to the Sheep-gate, perhaps the same as that called Millo and Beth-Millo in the Book of Kings; and, from the writer's mention of it, we learn that this portion of the history was not written until after Jerusalem had become David's capital. But out of this portion we must except many Jehovistic sentences, some perhaps written only a few years later than the original narrative. Chapter xxviii. 10-22 in particular, must be a very late addition. Here Jehovah appears to Jacob in Beth-el; and thus **the** Jehovistic and the Elohistic thoughts are united

in a manner very unusual. We shall hereafter find a date
for these words from the circumstance that Jacob makes a
vow to pay his tithes in that city. Other Jehovistic **passages**
may be of the same date; but they do **not all carry any**
evidence when they were written.

In continuation of the Elohistic list of the early Genealogies, and introductory to the Elohistic Life of Joseph, there
was once an Elohistic history of Abraham, Isaac, and Jacob.
We have still some portions of it woven into our present
Jehovistic narrative. Such is Genesis xvii., where the covenant
of circumcision is enjoined upon Abraham. Here a child **is**
promised to Sarah by God, while in **the next** chapter the
same promise is made by Jehovah. But this earlier Life **is**
lost in the newer.

Exodus vi. 2-9, is clearly **a Jehovistic** addition to the
original narrative of the march, and made at last as early as
this time. First, these words must be considered an addition,
because God therein tells Moses that his name is Jehovah, a
name not used by the original writer of the march out of
Egypt. And secondly, it must have been added thus early
before our Jehovistic Life of Abraham was written, because
God in this passage says that he was known to Abraham,
Isaac, and Jacob, only by the name of El, and not by **that of**
Jehovah. At the same time by referring to the promise made
to Abraham in Genesis xvii., it tells us that of the two Lives
of Abraham the Elohistic Life was the older. Now, we
shall presently give reasons for placing our present Life of
Abraham near the end of David's reign; and therefore to the
middle of David's reign may be **given** this and perhaps other
additions to the Books of Exodus **and** Numbers, and also to
the Lives of Isaac, Jacob, and Joseph, which by the use of the
word Jehovah are known not to belong to the original
narrative.

To some time before Genesis i. was written, and before the
Life of Abraham was written, we must give Genesis ii. 4—iv.,
containing the history of the Creation by Jehovah, and of the
Garden of Eden, as this is mentioned in the Life of Abraham
in Genesis xiii. 10. This second Birth-book of the Heavens
and the Earth seems older, and is of a less scientific
character, than that in chapter i. Here a single man is first
created, not a pair or a race; and a single woman is formed
afterwards. Man is not the last and crowning work, but the
animals are a later creation. In the Garden of Eden, Adam
and Eve lived in happy ease and innocence, until they fell

therefrom by eating the forbidden fruit. After their disobedience they were driven out, and had to till the earth
with labour for their food. Their life in the Garden is not
unlike the Golden Age of the Greek mythology, and is out of
place in the Hebrew books, which describe the nation as
always looking forward with religious hope; and not backward with regret, to a time of goodness and happiness.
Many of the thoughts relating to the Garden of Eden are
borrowed from Egypt, such as the ground being watered
without rain, the sacred tree of knowledge, the serpent the
author of sin, which speaks and walks upright before it
does wrong, but creeps upon its belly when it is cursed.
Moreover, the whole allegory is foreign from the Hebrew
mind, which never inquired into the origin of evil. By the
forbidden fruit the author means marriage, which he thus
blames; and the first pair have no children till they have
fallen from their state of innocence. It was among the
Egyptians, not among the Israelites, that celibacy was thought
more holy than marriage. In these chapters, Cain, the
murderer, is a husbandman; and Abel, whose offering was
acceptable to Jehovah, is a herdsman, which agrees with the
former enmity between the Egyptians who tilled the soil,
and the Israelites who were owners of cattle. The Elohistic
writer, when introducing this older narrative into his own,
was not pleased with the descent of man from Cain, the
murderer of his brother; and hence Seth, a new son, is given
to Adam, and thus a new parentage to Lamech, more agreeable to northern feelings; and the few words about Seth in
Genesis iv. 25, 26, may have been added by the Elohistic
writer, in order to unite the two accounts.

It is, as we have said, to the end of David's reign, after
he had placed his altar to Jehovah on Mount Moriah, that
we must give another large portion of the Book of Genesis,
one which is for the most part Jehovistic, so styled from
the writer's use of the name Jehovah for God. It is chap.
xii.—xxv. 18, containing the Life of Abraham, with a list
of his descendants through Ishmael, but exclusive of chap.
xxv. 1-6, which gives to him a second wife and a further
list of descendants, and exclusive of several other passages
to be hereafter mentioned. It shows not only a far wider
knowledge of geography than the writings that we have
before considered, but in particular, a knowledge of the
southern parts of Judah, such as Hebron, and the cave of
Machpelah; of the town of Zoar and parts to the south of

the Dead Sea; and of the Hittites in the south of Judah; all which knowledge was beyond the writers in Samuel's time and neighbourhood, or even in the beginning of David's disturbed reign, up to which time the writers had mostly belonged to the northern tribes. The frequent mention of the camel is a marked peculiarity of this writer, who may perhaps have lived near Hebron, where that southern animal was more often seen than in Jerusalem. Again, these chapters were written by a worshipper of Jehovah, who had a wish to give to the new altar on Mount Moriah, which David had lately gained from the hands of the Jebusites, a character for holiness by fixing upon it as the spot where Abraham was ordered to sacrifice his son Isaac; and he proposes an etymology for Jerusalem, the new name of the capital, in Abraham's calling the place Jehovah-jireh, or *Jehovah will show*. Indeed, the writer lets us know that the altar on Mount Moriah was already built, and that it had become usual to inquire of Jehovah there, by his telling us of the proverbial saying, "On the mountain of Jehovah it will be shown." The making Abraham, as the representative of all Israel, pay tithes to Melchizedek, *the righteous king* of Jerusalem, seems meant to justify David's claim to a land-tax of a tithe of the produce. Melchizedek was both king and priest, and so was David. David we have seen wearing the Ephod, the mark of a priest.* David also made his sons priests in his lifetime;† and it was as a priest only that Solomon stood beside the altar in the Inner Court of the Temple, and made his prayers to God at the feast of Tabernacles.

That Abraham's being willing to put his son to death should have been thought innocent, may be explained from the opinion of the time, that there was no limit to a father's rights over his children; it was not till the latter days of the monarchy that the approval of the city elders was needed before a father might cause the death of a son. That Abraham's willingness should moreover have been thought praiseworthy, may be explained from a son's being at that time a valuable property, and not only, as at all times, an object of affection and of family pride.

But there are some parts of the Life of Abraham which are by Elohistic writers, parts of an earlier narrative. One of these is chapter xvii., already mentioned, in which the covenant of circumcision is enjoined upon Abraham.

* 2 Sam. vi. 14.　　† 2 Sam. viii. 18.

Thus we have given the larger part of Genesis, including the lives of Abraham, Isaac, Jacob, and that of Joseph, to David's reign. No part of these Lives could have been written before the time of Saul, or we should have found traces of it in the Book of Judges. The Life of Abraham, indeed, was evidently written by one of the tribe of Judah, by one who had lived in Hebron, and it furnishes us with some of the traditions of that tribe, a people of whom we learnt so little from the writer of the Book of Judges. The tribe of Judah claimed to be living in that part of the land where the nation's forefathers had first settled; not when they forcibly gained a settlement in Canaan on their flight out of Egypt, but at a yet earlier time, when Abraham the Chaldee migrated there from Syria. Hebron was their chief city. Near to it was a grove, called the Oaks of Mamre, within which grove was an altar to Jehovah. This altar was said to have been built by Abraham when he first settled in the land; and it was considered to be the spot most sacred to Jehovah, until Jerusalem gained that high rank. At a later time, we find Hebron the chief city of the Levites; and it thus connects the Levites to the worship of Jehovah, and both to the tribe of Judah. In the same neighbourhood was a sacred burial-place, the cave of Machpelah, which had been bought from the Hittites, the Canaanite tribe, among whom the Chaldees first settled. This tradition, belonging to the tribe of Judah, of a quiet settlement in the south, is joined to the other tradition of a **forcible** settlement in the east and north, by making the **whole** of the family in the south migrate into Egypt, and **thence come** out under Moses. Whereas it is more agreeable to what we have been able to learn of the early history of the tribes in Canaan, to suppose that the land of Judah was in part at least peopled by Hebrews, before those who escaped from Egypt crossed the Jordan.

Some more modern writer, zealous for the honour of the southern towns, may very possibly have added to the Life of Joseph those passages which speak of his burying his father Jacob in the cave of Machpelah, near Hebron; because what we suppose to be the earlier narrative says, that he promised to bury him in a cave which Jacob had digged for himself, that is, as it would seem, near the city of Shechem.* Those added passages are, Gen. xlix. 29-32, and l. 13; and as they relate to the southern town of Hebron, they are not

* Gen. xxxiii. 19.

likely to have formed part of the Elohistic Life of Joseph. Moreover, Abel-Mizraim, where the mourners rested, was on the route from Egypt to Shechem, and far beyond Hebron. The history quoted by the martyr Stephen, in Acts vii. 16, must have rejected these passages, as it places Jacob's burial place at Shechem.

Those passages in the Life of Abraham which seem to be later additions, and will be mentioned hereafter, are chap. xii. 6, 7, relating to the altar to Jehovah at Shechem; xii. 8, the altar to Jehovah at Beth-el; xii. 9; xiii. 4, the visit to Egypt; xiv. 1-16, the defeat of the four kings; and xx. and xxi. 22-34, relating to the South Country and the altar to Jehovah at Beer-sheba, and xxxviii., relating to the birth of Pharez and Zarah. The honour given to the three altars at Shechem, Beth-el and Beer-sheba, is in opposition to the old altars at Hebron and Gibeah of Judah, and the only allowed new altar on Mount Moriah. The Levitical worship had followed David from Hebron and Gibeah to Jerusalem, and the Life of Abraham gives Divine authority for its doing so. The sanction given to the rival altars was not by the original writer.

We may now mention one of the Psalms to which, by the help of the Life of Abraham, where Melchizedek is first mentioned, we can give a very exact date. Psalm cx. may be quoted as certainly written very near the end of David's lifetime. In this the poet advises him not to go out with his army and risk his valuable life in battle; and he mentions his capture of Rabbah the capital of the Ammonites. Moreover, he styles the king a priest, a title that would hardly have been given to any except himself, and Solomon; the king would not have been so styled after the full rise of the Levites.

> Jehovah hath said to my lord,
> " Sit thou at my right hand
> " Until I make thine enemies a stool for thy feet."
> Jehovah will send the sceptre of thy power out of Zion;
> Rule thou in the midst of thine enemies.
> Thy people will be of willing heart in thy day of battle,
> On the holy mountains.
> From the womb of the morning is the dew of thy youth.
>   [That is, thou art now no longer young.]
> Jehovah hath sworn, and will not repent,
> " Thou art a priest for ever of the order of Melchizedek."
> The Lord is at thy right hand,
> He smiteth kings in the day of his wrath.
> He will judge among the nations;

> He will fill them with dead bodies.
> He hath smitten the chief [city] of the land of Rabbah.
> [Israel] shall drink of the brook in the way;
> Therefore shall he lift up his head.

This must have been written after the conquest of Rabbah, after the king's life had become valuable to his friends, and after the writing of the Life of Abraham in the Book of Genesis, where we are first introduced to the notice of Melchizedek.

Before entering upon Solomon's reign, it will be as well to take a glance at the Phenicians on the coast, with whom the Hebrew monarchs are for the future often closely connected by trade and friendly intercourse. Homer[*] and Strabo[†] both mention a city of the name of Sidon on the Persian Gulf, from which trading caravans crossed the desert to Jerusalem and Egypt and the Syrian coast. This was probably the city called Dedan by the Hebrew writers. From the Persian Gulf these industrious people seem to have made a settlement on a barren part of the coast of Syria, at the foot of Mount Lebanon, to which they carried their own name; and the Sidon in Syria soon rose into such importance as a place of trade, as to make the original Sidon be forgotten. The Sidonians afterwards built a new city on a rock, a few miles to the south of Sidon, which was known by the name of Tyre, *the rock.* Tyre soon became a more important city than Sidon itself, from which it sprang; but nevertheless its inhabitants continued the use of the old national name, and they were still called Sidonians. In Tyre we find these ship-building and sea-faring Phenicians engaged in a most prosperous carrying trade, with their numerous little vessels on every neighbouring coast, having other important settlements or colonies at Gebal and at Arvad, at Tarsus or Tarshish in Cilicia, and at several ports on the island of Cyprus. The Egyptian trade was their great source of wealth. The Egyptians were not sailors, they shunned the sea; and the Sidonians carried away the Egyptian corn in exchange for such commodities as the timber of Mount Lebanon and Mount Taurus, and the copper and iron of the isle of Cyprus, and the silver of Greece. Tyre and Sidon, in the days of Solomon, may be compared to the city of Venice fifteen centuries later. The active part of the population lived as much on shipboard and in foreign parts as they did in their own homes.

At the time of David's death, Hiram king of Tyre and

---

[*] Lib. iv. 84, and the Scholiast.   [†] xvi.; iv. 27.

Sidon had been eight years upon the throne. He had succeeded his father Abi-baal. With the wealth of his trading subjects, and with the tribute levied upon other cities, he ornamented Tyre with new temples to Hercules and Astarte, cutting the timber for their roofs in the neighbouring forest on Mount Lebanon. He laid out the open square, or broad-place called the Eurychoron, and set up a golden column in his temple of Jupiter. He reigned twenty-six years more in friendship with Solomon.*

SOLOMON, KING OF ISRAEL AND JUDAH. B.C. 976—937.

Solomon, while his father was alive, had spared his elder brother Adonijah, though at the time a rival claimant of the throne; but after David's death, on Adonijah asking for Abishag to wife, a young woman who had been brought to David for a concubine, Solomon considered that he was still a rival, and had him put to death. He also had his cousin Joab killed, as having been one of Adonijah's friends; and for the same reason he removed Abiathar from the priesthood, and made Zadok sole high priest. At this time the priests evidently held their appointments from the king. He then found a reason for having Shimei slain, a Benjamite who had joined Absalom in his revolt against David. The historian in the wish to find an excuse for the death of Shimei, to whom David had promised that his life should be spared and of Joab, David's faithful friend, says that Solomon had received David's dying orders to kill them. This it is difficult to believe; nor would it relieve Solomon of the guilt. He may have fancied that the safety of his throne required their death, with that of his elder brother.†

As soon as Solomon was safely seated on the throne, he went with the chiefs of the people to Gibeon or Gibeah, of Judah, to return thanks to Jehovah, by means of a costly sacrifice of oxen and sheep.‡ There David had left the Tabernacle, and a body of priests, when he brought the ark to Jerusalem; and the High Place of Gibeon, notwithstanding its loss of the ark, still kept a character for holiness, which the newer altar at Jerusalem had not yet gained. In Solomon's reign it was not thought wrong to have more than one altar of sacrifice. It was more than a century later before the priests of Jerusalem ventured to declare all High Places but their own to be idolatrous, and to put such an opinion into

---

* Menander in Josephus, Apion, i. 18.   † 1 Kings ii. 12-46.
‡ 1 Kings iii. 4.

the books of the Law. The religious doings of both David and Solomon clearly tell us that the ceremonial law was not yet written.

Solomon, by his acts of severity, terrified everybody who might be against him; and the whole of the tribes accepted him as king. Even the Philistines, without being conquered quietly yielded submission to him; and the Amalekites on the desert coast, towards Egypt, were forced into obedience. He had sway, not only over his own subjects of Israel and Judah, but over all the little kingdoms from Tiphsah on the river Euphrates, to the land of the Philistines, and the boundary of Lower Egypt, including Tadmor or Palmyra in the desert. The Philistines remained independent but friendly. He levied an ample tribute on the country, not of money but of food for the maintenance of his court, and of a standing army. This army included a small body of horsemen and of war-chariots. If his subjects felt his strong arm and his heavy taxes press severely on them, they at any rate received in return the blessings of peace abroad and of quiet at home; and every man dwelt safely under his own vine and under his own fig-tree all the days of Solomon. He had the reputation also of being as wise as he was powerful, and of not only writing proverbs and songs, which were counted by thousands, but also of understanding the whole animal and vegetable creation.*

Solomon's long but peaceful reign has few events for the historian, but there are two which rise into great importance hereafter; one the building of the Temple at Jerusalem, and the other the establishing the Levites as a body of priests to offer up the burnt offerings, and to perform the other ceremonies required in the worship of Jehovah. Solomon's subjects had so little skill in the mechanical arts that for this building he sent to the Tyrians for help. Hiram, king of Tyre, undertook to furnish the skilled workmen required, on Solomon's sending him payment in corn and oil. Solomon was to supply the labourers, for which he made a levy of men through all Israel; and he had several thousand men employed for a month at a time till his work was finished. The cedar and fir-wood required was cut on Mount Lebanon, and carried to the sea near Tyre. From thence it was sent in floats to Joppa, and then carried to Jerusalem on men's shoulders, so few were the beasts of burden in Solomon's kingdom. Other timber was cut in

* 1.Kings iv. 21-34.

Solomon's own forests, in the hill country, probably near the City of Jearim. It was not necessary to go to any distance for the stone; the neighbourhood of Jerusalem offers a fine white limestone, nearly equal to marble. This important work was begun in the fourth year of Solomon's reign, and finished in the eleventh.

The Temple of Jerusalem, before the fall of the monarchy, was a large space inclosed by stone walls, on the top of Mount Moriah, a hill on the east side of the city. In order to make this space level, the rock had been cut away at the north end, and the ground was built up at the south end. In the middle of this space, which was the temple area, there is a raised rock, fifty feet across; this had been the threshing-floor of Araunah, and then David's altar, and it was now to remain the great altar for burnt offerings in Solomon's temple. Around this altar a large raised space, measuring about five hundred feet by four hundred, was by Solomon inclosed with cedar rails. This, when other courts were built, was called the inner court, the court of the priests, which all other persons were forbidden to enter, and it was called also the Great Terrace or Platform.

From a comparison of the several passages in the Bible with the plot of ground as described by travellers, it seems probable that the House of Jehovah, the covered building, was placed at the south side of the court of the priests, facing the north. That the historian says that its front was towards the east, must be explained by the Hebrew custom of considering the east side of the heavens as the front, and by a disregard to scientific exactness. Had there been room on the hill to have placed the House on the west side of the altar, Solomon would probably have there placed it; and then its front would have been to the east, as it is said to have been, and as the tabernacle in the desert is described in the Book of Exodus. The House was a small building, but in the inside richly covered with gold. It consisted of a Porch with two tall columns, a Great Hall, and a room behind, called the Holy of Holies, or the Place of the Oracle. The House was surrounded on each side and on the back with small chambers for the priests, built in three stories. Within the Holy of Holies was to be placed the Ark of the covenant of Jehovah, a wooden chest overlaid with gold, containing the Two Tables inscribed with the Ten Commandments. Within the Holy of Holies also stood a small altar, coated with gold, for burning incense before Jehovah. On

each side of the place for the Ark was the figure of a Cherub
with outstretched wings. Nothing was to be placed on the
Cover of the Ark; because in the open space above the
Cover, and between the two Cherubs, the Almighty was
supposed to be present when the priest burnt incense on the
small altar. From this space over the Cover of the Ark the
priest was thought to receive his answer from Jehovah.[*]

As soon as the 'temple was ready to receive the Ark,
Solomon and the heads of the people brought it with much
ceremony from the city on Mount Zion to its place in the
Holy of Holies on Mount Moriah. It was carried on the
shoulders of the priests, who afterwards bear the name of
the Sons of Aaron. Solomon then assembled the people in
the court of the temple to the great ceremony of the dedication; and standing himself as priest beside the altar of burnt
offerings, he addressed a prayer to Jehovah, asking blessings
on his work. He then slew a vast number of sheep and
oxen, burning some as a burnt offering on the altar, and
sacrificing the rest as a peace offering, that is, as a love-
feast, with which he feasted the crowds for fourteen days.

Solomon seems to have been discontented with David's
plan of using the bare rock for an altar, and to have
prepared one made of wood, coated with copper, perhaps
that described in Exodus xxvii. as three cubits high, and
five cubits square on the top. But on this occasion it was
not large enough for the burnt offerings; so it was put
aside, and the offerings burnt on the rock in the middle of
the court, the site of David's altar.

An altar for sacrifice on a High Place, in the neighbourhood of each town, was all that the people of Judah had
hitherto been used to. The covered building, or House of
God, which sometimes, as at Shiloh, Shechem, and Beth-el,
stood near the altar, had not been necessary for the worship
of Jehovah. These sacred buildings had been peculiar to the
northern tribes, and to the worship of El and Baal; as
Nathan assured David that the Ark of Jehovah had never
rested otherwise than under a tent.

The feast at the dedication of the Temple received the
name of the Feast of Tabernacles or Booths, because the
people came up in such crowds that they had to lodge in
booths in the streets. It was the Feast of Ingathering,
when the labours of the field are ended, and was kept at
the full moon of the seventh month, which, in our northern

* 1 Kings v. vi.

climate, we call the harvest moon.* The other feasts which
Solomon kept by burnt offerings on the great altar, and
burning incense on the small altar within the House of
Jehovah, were that of the Passover, or Unleavened Bread,
when the barley was ripe, near the spring equinox, and that
of the wheat harvest, seven weeks after the Passover, called
the Feast of Weeks.†

Before the end of his reign, Solomon built an altar on the
site of David's natural altar on the Mount Moriah.‡ He
built it probably of unhewn stones, as described in Exodus
xx. 26, and not so high as to require steps. Later kings
raised it higher; and its height is often spoken of in the
later laws.

This building of a grand temple to Jehovah, to be used
for a stately ceremonial form of worship, with clouds of
incense rising at the door, burnt offerings smoking on the
altar in front, and priests in various dresses purifying the
worshippers by sprinkling them with water, and chanting
hymns with the accompaniment of musical instruments,
as they walked in a troop round the altar, naturally led to a
great increase of the priestly influence. Hitherto it would
seem, at least among the northern tribes, that the head of
every family was its priest; and the father sometimes
appointed his eldest son to be his deputy in the office, as did
Micah the Ephraimite.§ David appointed several of his
sons, perhaps the eldest of each mother, to be priests;‖ and
we have seen him and Solomon both acting as priests before
the altar.¶ This custom seems to be sanctioned in Exod.
xix. 6, written as we suppose in the time of Samuel, when
the Israelites are told at the mountain of God, "Ye shall
be unto me a kingdom of priests, and a holy nation." And,
again, it seems more particularly pointed to when it had
gone out of use, when in Numb. iii. 11-13, written, as we
suppose, about a century after Solomon's time, Jehovah
says, "I have taken the Levites from among the children
of Israel instead of the firstborn among the children of
Israel. And the Levites shall be mine, because all the
firstborn are mine. On the day that I smote all the first-
born in the land of Lower Egypt, I hallowed unto me all the
firstborn in Israel, both man and beast; mine shall they be,
I am Jehovah."

These words have been thought to prove that at one time
human sacrifices had been required in the worship of
Jehovah; but by putting these laws, each in its own
century, we see that this law is not necessarily a redemption
of the eldest son from death, but a dismissal from the office
of family priest, to make way for a Levite.

Thus, soon after the establishment of the monarchy, the
priesthood became a separate profession, and hereditary in
particular families. We hardly met with the Levites while
our history was confined to the northern tribes, **but** now
that the sceptre is held by a king of the tribe of Judah, they
come forward into notice. At the beginning of this reign,
the Levite Zadok was made sole high-priest; and henceforth the high-priesthood became hereditary in his family.
To his family was assigned the care of the Ark, of which
the Hebrew name is Aron; and hence, perhaps, they gained
the name of the sons of Aaron, meaning Aronites, or ark-
bearers. But they also kept, even until the overthrow of
the monarchy, the name of Sons of **Zadok**. Their position
in the capital gave them a rank above the rest of their
tribe. They alone had the power of entering the Holy of
Holies and of coming forth and declaring to the people the
will· of Jehovah. We do not learn very exactly by what
steps this gigantic power was obtained. It was probably
the growth of several reigns. David introduced the
Levites into Jerusalem. Solomon built the temple, and
confirmed them in their rank. But Solomon did not raise
the priesthood above the throne. He himself dedicated the
Temple, and hallowed the court of the Altar, and acted as
priest at the sacrifices. But under his weaker successors the
priestly power grew stronger. Until they became too strong,
the Levites were a great support to the royal power, particularly within the tribe of Judah, by whom they were chiefly
respected; and partially also within the northern tribes,
though there their superior holiness was less cordially granted.
Even in the north they were in part successful in throwing
a slight on many of the High Places, the spots held sacred of
old, where God was worshipped under the name of Elohim;
and by so doing they added weight both to the priestly and to
the royal power in Jerusalem. The Levites' power was founded
on their usefulness, and on the **value** of the religion that they
taught, **and** they were supported by the free-will offerings of
the people, **the** heave offerings, as they were called; but
after a time this power was abused for selfish ends, and then

they got the civil power to help them to levy a tax for their maintenance.

While the temple was new, and Jerusalem had not that character for holiness which still belonged to Shiloh, the priests were anxious to be thought the descendants of Eli of that city, for the same reason that made them say that their ark of Jehovah had once had its lodging in Shiloh. This we see by the following table:—

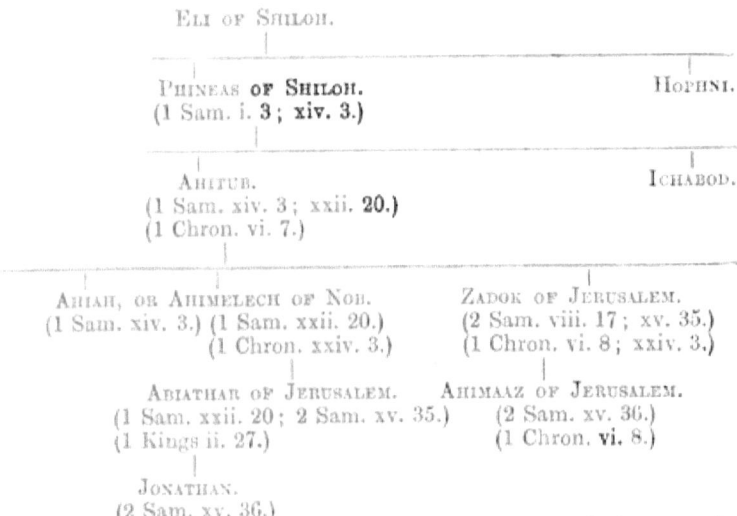

ELI OF SHILOH.

PHINEAS OF SHILOH.   HOPHNI.
(1 Sam. i. 3; xiv. 3.)

AHITUB.   ICHABOD.
(1 Sam. xiv. 3; xxii. 20.)
(1 Chron. vi. 7.)

AHIAH, OR AHIMELECH OF NOB.   ZADOK OF JERUSALEM.
(1 Sam. xiv. 3.) (1 Sam. xxii. 20.)   (2 Sam. viii. 17; xv. 35.)
(1 Chron. xxiv. 3.)   (1 Chron. vi. 8; xxiv. 3.)

ABIATHAR OF JERUSALEM.   AHIMAAZ OF JERUSALEM.
(1 Sam. xxii. 20; 2 Sam. xv. 35.)   (2 Sam. xv. 36.)
(1 Kings ii. 27.)   (1 Chron. vi. 8.)

JONATHAN.
(2 Sam. xv. 36.)

In 2 Sam. viii. 17, Ahimelech is called the son of Abiathar, not the father. This must be a mistake.

But, after a time, when Jerusalem and the priests in its temple held an undisputed rank for holiness, and could gain no glory from Shiloh, a city which had then become hateful for its people's rebellion, then a new pedigree was produced for Zadok and Ahimaaz, tracing their descent as sons of Aaron. This we have in 1 Chron. vi.

Before the time of David religious worship, or rather the means for religious worship, were provided for each man by himself. In the towns, when men were set apart as ministers of religion, they were maintained by those who valued them. So when David established the altar on Mount Moriah he did it for himself, rather than for the nation. But a king's doings are the nation's doings; and yet more when Solomon built the temple was it the nation's temple. Moreover, the king's money is the nation's money; and when Solomon maintained the temple-service and its priests at a great cost, it became the nation's service maintained at the nation's cost. So far, and so far only, was religion supported by the state. For the other towns throughout the land, when sacrifices were offered on a hill in the neighbourhood, and men were set apart to attend to them, they had no support but the offerings of the faithful; for as yet the Levites had not got the tithes. **Thus Jerusalem** gained an importance in religious matters over the other towns, for which it gave very little in return, and which was often to be a cause of jealousy and trouble.

When the temple was completed, Solomon spent thirteen years in building his own palace, which was situated on Mount Zion, within the city walls, and on the east side of the city, the side nearest to the temple. Another building of importance in the city was the House of the Forest of Lebanon, so called because it was little more than a roof upheld by a number of columns, each of which was a cedar tree. This was the royal armoury, holding not only weapons of war, but those ornamental arms which were used on state occasions. In this building were lodged the Runners, a body of men who attended the king wherever he moved, to carry his commands to the distant parts of the kingdom. Here were kept the golden shields which the runners carried before the king when he went in state into the house of Jehovah.* At the back of the royal palace, and separated from it by a court-yard, he built a portico, within which was placed a throne. This was called the Porch of the Throne, or the Porch of Judgment;† and the court-yard in front of it is mentioned in the New Testament under the names of the Pavement and Gabbatha, or *Back of the House.* Under this porch or portico Solomon sat to administer justice. We do not hear that he followed any known laws. He probably decided each case according to his own opinion of what was right.

Since David had made Jerusalem his capital, the population of the place had so far increased that a large suburb had grown up on the northern side of Mount Sion. This Solomon now inclosed within a wall, and at the same time he rebuilt or rather strengthened, the walls of the castle which David had built, namely Millo, or Beth-millo, over-hanging the brook Kidron.‡ This seems to have stood on the north end of Mount Moriah, on a part of the hill, which

---

* 1 Kings vii. 1-6; x. 17; xiv. 26-28.   † 1 Kings vii. 7, 8.
‡ 1 Kings ix. 15; 2 Kings xii. 20.

was now raised high above the temple-yard, because the ground of the temple-yard had been in part cut down to make the whole level. On this spot stood the Castle of Antonia in the time of Herod.

It was, perhaps, rather late in life that Solomon, to his other numerous wives and concubines, added the daughter of the Egyptian king. The name of this Pharaoh is not mentioned, but it was probably Shishak, who, while king of Bubastis, a little state forming the eastern part of Lower Egypt, was not too great a monarch to ally himself with Solomon. But he afterwards made himself king of both Upper and Lower Egypt, and displaced the family of Rameses from the throne at Thebes. This king was more powerful and wealthy than Solomon, whom he was now honouring with his daughter. The discipline of his soldiers, their arms, and military engines were far superior to any that Solomon had command of. The Israelites had never been able to take a hill fortress if tolerably well defended. Hence the Canaanite city of Gezer on the hills, within fifteen miles of Jerusalem, was able still to hold itself independent against the power of Solomon; and in order to oblige him, the Egyptian king sent an army to that distance from his country for the siege of the place. They took Gezer by storm, slew the Canaanites, burnt the town, and gave the ruins to Solomon as a dower with his daughter.* For his new wife, Solomon built a palace in the suburb lately inclosed,† and it seems to have stood close to Millo, the castle last described.

On this conquest of the city of Gezer, there remained no body of the original natives strong enough to offer any resistance to Solomon. Those who were left of the Amorites, Hittites, Perizites, Hivites, and Jebusites, were quietly reduced to the rank of bond-servants, or at least were required to pay a tribute of service to the king. These tribes lived under their own magistrates, who in some cases bore the title of king. Thus, when Solomon bought horses and chariots from Egypt, the kings of the Syrians and the Hittites bought them also for themselves, and at the same price.‡ The partial independence of these tribes is even proved by the historian's boast that Solomon had sway over all the kings on the west of the river Euphrates.§ The Philistines, at the south-western corner of the land, alone seemed to have

---

* 1 Kings ix. 16.   † 1 Kings iii. 1 ; and ix. 24.
‡ 1 Kings x. 29.   § 1 Kings iv. 24.

been treated as equals; they were neither conquered, nor
were they in arms as enemies. They seem to have been
allowed to keep their own lands as subjects; and hence the
tribe of Simeon, who claimed that territory, never gained any
lands of their own, but had their inheritance within the tribe
of Judah.*

The skill of the Tyrians was further useful to Solomon in
helping him to build a ship or ships on the Red Sea, to get a
share **of** the trade which had been so long profitable to the
Egyptian vessels on the Nile, and to the caravans of **the**
Arabs across the desert. Solomon's ships were built at
Ezion-geber in the land of Edom; and, with the help of
Hiram's Tyrian shipmen, they made a voyage once in three
years down the Red Sea. They brought back gold and
precious stones, a hard wood, probably ebony, tusks of ivory,
apes, and rare birds called Tak. These birds were probably
parrots, as we judge from their country and from the Greek
name of the parrot, Psit-tak-os. The gold, for the sake of
which the voyage was made, was brought **from a** port named
Ophir, which we may safely pronounce to have been near to
Souakin, on the coast of Nubia, and in the neighbourhood of
the Nubian gold-mines. Ptolemy Philadelphus gave to **the**
port the name of his mother, the queen Berenice; and to distinguish it from other cities of that name, it was called Berenice Panchrysos, or *all gold.*† These mines had for a long
time been a source of boundless wealth to Upper Egypt.‡
They furnished the money which ornamented Thebes with
its temples, statues, and obelisks, and as long as the Nile
was the easiest route by which the gold could reach the
Mediterranean Sea, Thebes was the richest city in the world.
But latterly civil war had closed the passage by the Nile;
new lines of trade had been opened first through Arabia, and
next by **the** Red Sea; and Thebes had lost its golden advantages, and its political rank, before Solomon's ships sailed
for a share of the profit. The three years occupied by this
short voyage are easily accounted for. The ships sailed
only with the trade wind, creeping along the shore, and
stopping occasionally for water. They then had to spend
some months at their place of destination, bartering with the
natives of the country for a cargo to carry back. They could
not be ready in time to return home by the return wind of

---

* **1 Kings ix.** 20-22; Joshua xix. 1.   † Pliny vi. 34.
     ‡ Agatharcides ap. Photium; Diod. Sic. i. 49.

the same year. Hence it was necessary for the crew to spend one year with the ships drawn on shore in Nubia or Abyssinia, waiting for the return wind of the next year; and, for the same reason, one year with the ships drawn on shore at Ezion-geber, while the cargo was being sent to Jerusalem and Tyre. The voyage out and the voyage home each occupied a half-year, whether the whole time was wanted for it or not. The gold which was brought to Jerusalem in one year was said to amount to six hundred and sixty-six kikars, a very doubtful sum; for, though a kikar of silver seems to have been about one hundredweight, yet, in the case of the more precious metal, the kikar, like the shekel, was of a far less weight.*

Solomon rewarded his friend Hiram, king of Tyre, for his valuable help in building and in navigation, by a present of twenty little towns in Galilee, on the Tyrian coast. These were of little worth, and Hiram was not well pleased with them.† But he had been paid in corn and oil for his builders, and had no doubt received his share of the profit from the voyages.

Though the gold of Ophir was the main object of Solomon's trading voyage down the Red Sea, yet his little vessels probably did not turn back at that port. In Isaiah xviii. we shall learn that there was a Jewish settlement in Abyssinia. We shall see in Genesis x. 26, written perhaps in the time of Hezekiah, by the mention of Hazramaveth, or Hadramout, the most southerly province in Arabia, that the Hebrew writer of that chapter had got some knowledge of that distant country. Ezekiel xxvii. 23, shows a knowledge of Eden or Aden, the well-known port in Southern Arabia. And in the fourth century of the Christian era, we find that there was a colony of Jews on both coasts at the southern end of the Red Sea, separated from their countrymen by the Arabs on one coast, and the Nubians on the other, and only to be reached by sea. These two Hebrew colonies probably both had their origin from Solomon's trading vessels. That Solomon's ships did not go to the East is known from the Greek authors, who some centuries later speak of the voyage from the Red Sea to India as then new. The winds forbade the vessels from passing along the southern coast of Arabia; but not until eight centuries after Solomon was it found out that by sailing southward as far as Zanzibar they would meet with a wind which would carry them to India.

* 1 Kings ix. 26-28; x. 11, 22.　　† 1 Kings ix. 10-14.

Solomon's marriage with an Egyptian princess, and his cultivation of trade and the arts of peace, brought him into close connection with Egypt. He bought his horses and his chariots, and probably many articles of state and luxury in Egypt. The price of a horse was a hundred and fifty shekels of silver, about fifteen pounds sterling; the price of a chariot was four times as much.* But for want of the art of shoeing the horses with metal they were of very little use to the Jews. It was not safe to make a horse run upon rocky ground,† and he had to be led with care in the desert for fear of the stones.‡ If the more luxurious Egypt did not furnish Solomon with any workmen or artists for his temples and palaces, it no doubt furnished his own artists with the taste and models from which they worked. His throne, with a golden lion on each side of the seat to support the arms, was after the Egyptian pattern.§

Of the new customs gained from abroad we are interested in noticing that the dress and ornaments of the priests were copied from Egypt. The breast-plate of the chief priest, though it had not the same ornaments as those of the Egyptian priests, was yet, like theirs, made in two halves, and called by its Egyptian name of Urim and Thummim, or *royalty* and *truth*, perhaps translated by the Hebrews as mercy and truth.‖ The priest's linen mitre, with the holy crown of bright gold put over it, were together the double crown of Egypt, which we now see upon the statues of the Theban kings.¶ And the cherubs that were placed within the Holy of Holies, with outstretched wings, one standing on each side of the sacred ark, had their originals on numerous stone chests in Egypt. But with all this we see no leaning towards the Egyptian opinions in religion. Egypt was the teacher of superstition to most of the nations around. The Assyrians, the Babylonians, and then the Greeks and the Romans, all made use of the Egyptian fertility of invention, and accepted its superstitious opinions as to the dead and their future state of existence. But the Hebrews drew back from every Egyptian superstition; and this may explain why we find in the Hebrew books so few passages relating to a life after death. Those few hints, however, go to show that belief in a future life was held by many, although it was not directly taught by the priests.

The great works, such as the buildings and walls of

* 1 Kings x. 29.   † Amos vi. 12.   ‡ Isaiah lxiii. 13.
§ 1 Kings x. 19.   ‖ Exod. xxviii. 15-30.   ¶ Levit. viii. 9.

defence which Solomon raised in Jerusalem **and in other** cities, together with the magnificence of his **court and the** army of footmen, horsemen, and chariots that **he kept up,** could not be supported without a large levy of taxes in **some** form or other. These taxes seem to have been taken **from** his subjects, not in money, but in produce. Of money **there** was but little in the country; the art of coining had not yet been invented; and when Hiram of Tyre was to be rewarded for his services, he was paid in corn and oil and towns. **The** gold from Ophir ma**y** have helped Solomon much to meet **his** great expenses. **The** tribute also from the Syrians **on this** side of the Euphrates, **and from** the Edomites, and **possibly** from the Philistines **and Moa**bites, gave him something more. The bond-service, **or** levy of labour, that he exacted from his Canaanite subjects did something for him. But, in addition to all this, there can be **no** doubt but he levied the land-tax of a tithe of the produce, which Samuel had warned the people would be required by the king. He had twelve officers over all Israel, who sent up to Jerusalem, every month, a large supply of fine flour, of other meal, of fowls, of sheep, of deer, of oxen from the field, and of fatted oxen.* This was probably the tithe taken in kind. The whole must have been very oppressive to the people, and may well account for the dis-content which was felt in his latter days, and which **burst** out into rebellion on his death.

The nine prince or great officers who dwelt in Jerusalem, and surrounded the throne and assisted Solomon in the government of his kingdom, were—

1. The hereditary chief priest, **the** head of the Levites; who may have been somewhat independent of the king;
2. A recorder or remembrancer; who probably assisted him when acting as a judge;
3. A captain **of** the guard, who may also have **had control** of the various garrisons;
4. A chief **of the** twelve officers who levied the tax **upon** produce throughout the country;
5. The king's friend, who being a priest may have helped him in governing the body of Levites;
6. A chamberlain, or officer "over the king's house;"
7. A chief of the numerous lower officers who directed the labour of the bondservants employed **on** the public

---

* 1 Kings iv. 17-23.

works. These lower officers **were** perhaps two hundred and fifty in number;*

8, 9. Two scribes **or** secretaries, who wrote his dispatches.†

With splendour and prosperity surrounding him at home, Solomon's fame spread far and wide; and many flocked from a distance **to** see the wonders **of** his capital. Chief among these **was the queen** of Sheba **in** Arabia, who **came with** a train **of camels in a** trading caravan, bringing a great weight of **gold and** spices and precious stones, which in courtly language she called a present to Solomon, but which she did not part with without receiving from him a suitable present in return. Before Solomon's trading voyage on the Red Sea, **Sheba** and the neighbourhood had been the route through **which** the gold reached Jerusalem; but, after the route by sea was understood, we hear of none but the gold of Ophir. Among other wonderful sights which were shown to the Arab queen **was** Solomon's ascent to **the** House of Jehovah, which can **have been** nothing else **than** a bridge, whether of wood or **stone, across** the valley **of** the Tyropœon, by which he was **able to** walk straight from his palace to the Temple without either going round **or** descending into the valley. This bridge, or rather one built in its place, was in use in the time of the Emperor Vespasian, nine centuries later.‡

The queen of Sheba probably lived at the Arab city now called Medina, from whence there is a well frequented route for caravans to Damascus. Strabo places the Sabæi, her people, on the middle of the eastern coast of the Arabian Gulf, saying that their country produced myrrh, frankincense, and cinnamon, with which they traded to Syria; and that their chief city was Mariaba.§ This name, when written in Hebrew, would be Ameh-rabah, *the great metropolis*, and was, no doubt, the same place as that afterwards called Medina, *the city*, when the language became less like Hebrew. For a short time, when Egypt was disturbed by the civil war which overthrew the power of Thebes, and before the trade on the Red Sea had begun, Sheba had the profit of carrying the Nubian gold to purchase such commodities as Damascus and Tyre supplied.

Solomon's numerous foreign wives, women of the

* **2 Chron. viii. 10.**   † 1 Kings iv. 1-6.   ‡ 1 Kings x. i. 10.
§ Strabo xvi. iv. 2 and 19.

Moabites, Ammonites, Edomites, Sidonians, and Hittites, very much turned his heart from the worship of Jehovah. On the hill in front of Jerusalem, well known as the Mount of Olives, he built for the use of these wives, altars to Ashtaroth, the goddess of the Sidonians, and to Milcom or Molech, the god of the Ammonites, and to Chemosh, the god of the Moabites. That hill was consequently long known by the name of the Mount of Corruption.* But the worship of these foreign gods was probably allowed for political reasons, in order to keep quiet the various tribes who lived under his sway, within his cities, and in daily intercourse with the Israelites, much more than from a wish to please his wives, or from any proneness in himself to idolatry. The safety of the throne required that these various tribes should be united into one nation; while, on the other hand, it was the aim of the Levites to bring them all to one religion. David had set the example of over-looking the distinctions of race among his subjects; and Solomon's following in this course is a better proof of his wisdom than any that the historian gives. Solomon valued the subject-tribes as useful bond-servants; and their condition may be understood from Genesis xv., written at the end of Solomon's reign, in which Jehovah gives to Abraham as his property the land of Canaan and all its inhabitants, except the Philistines.

In consequence of his acts of idolatry, says the historian, but perhaps also in consequence of the severity of his taxes, and his subjects' discontent thereat, Jehovah brought many troubles upon Solomon. The first was from Hadad king of Edom, who, when, David conquered that country, had escaped as a child into Lower Egypt, and there lived with king Shishak. He had latterly returned into his own land, and had succeeded in making it independent. This, of course, stopped not only the tribute, but also Solomon's trade on the Red Sea. A second trouble was from Syria, where Rezon of Damascus enabled that portion of the north to hold itself independent of Solomon, to withhold its tribute, and to harass Israel. But a yet more serious threatened danger was the unwilling obedience of the northern Israel-ites, who murmured at having to pay heavy taxes to a king of Judah. Solomon had appointed Jeroboam to the government of the great tribes of Ephraim and Manasseh,

* 1 Kings xi. 1-8 ; 2 Kings xxiii. 13.

a young man, very possibly a cousin, whom he had found
both useful and faithful as an overseer of his works in
building the walls of Jerusalem. But he saw reason to
distrust him in the more important post of governor of a
discontented province, and would have put him to death if
he could have seized him. But Jeroboam, when he learnt
that his life was in danger, fled for safety to Shishak king of
Egypt, and he remained in Egypt until Solomon's death.

Thus clouds were already gathering around Solomon's
throne. His wealth and power rested on no solid foundation; for his subjects were discontented. But fortunately
death removed him before the storm burst. He died about
the year B.C. 937, after a peaceable and prosperous reign of
forty years, leaving a great name for wisdom as a judge.
He was buried in Jerusalem, and his son Rehoboam reigned
in his stead.*

Solomon's reign was the most glorious time for the
Hebrew nation, being the only reign throughout which
the whole of the country that they called their own yielded
quiet obedience to one monarch. But for this the praise is
due less to himself than to David, who left him with all his
subjects united into one nation. He may, however, be praised
for knowing the value of foreign trade, for keeping his people
at peace, for his moderation in being contented with the
obedience of the little tribes around him, and for not aiming
at wider conquests. But the splendour of his court, his
buildings, and his costly doings, which have gained him
renown, oppressed his subjects and sowed the seeds of
discontent. That he governed with a shortsighted and
selfish policy is proved by the revolt of his northern and
eastern subjects, which followed immediately upon his death.

The authorities mentioned in the Chronicles as containing
the deeds of Solomon, are the Book of Nathan the Prophet,
before spoken of, the Prophecy of Ahijah, a priest at Shiloh,
and the Visions of Iddo the Seer. These two last-mentioned
writers lived into the next reign. Iddo is described as the
author of a Commentary, meaning, perhaps, the editor of
a compilation, and also as the author of a work on Genealogies.† Family genealogies were much valued by the
Hebrews; they seem, indeed, to have been among their
first attempts at history, as much as the song or ballad

---

* 1 Kings xi. 14-43.
† 1 Kings xiv. 2; 2 Chron. ix. 29; xii. 15; xiii. 22.

which in many nations gave rise to the graver form of narrative. A history was called a Book of Births; even the history of the Creation of the World is, in Genesis ii. 4, called the Birth-book of Heaven and Earth.

It is possible that Genesis i.—ii. 3, and v.—xi. may be Iddo's work on Genealogies above spoken of. These chapters begin with an account of the creation of the world by Elohim or *God*. This has a regular scientific aim. After the creation of shapeless matter six days are given to the after work. First, light is made, and day is known from night. Secondly, a solid firmament, or sky, is made to divide the **waters above** from the shapeless mass below. Thirdly, the waters below are gathered together into an ocean, leaving the land dry, which then bears trees and herbs. Fourthly, the sun, moon, and stars are placed in the firmament. Fifthly, fishes are created in the waters, and birds in the air. Sixthly, animals are created on the land, and mankind, male and female, to have dominion over them. The whole comes to pass because God orders it to be so; and writers on style, from Longinus downward, have admired the sublime simplicity with which we are told that God said, "Let there be light," and there was light.

Modern science does not wholly adopt the **order of events** as here set forth, and gives a far higher rank to the sun **and** stars, as compared to our earth. But we have in this first chapter a very remarkable attempt to group into one view all things that the eye of man can see; an attempt which appears the more remarkable when we remember that it is the only piece of Natural History which the Hebrews have left to us. This is accompanied with an acknowledgment that, as nothing comes into being without a cause, these things **had** a Creator. The Hebrew nation, indeed, did not rest a belief in a God on what they saw, or on the argument from design. They felt, more firmly **perhaps** than any others, a consciousness in their own breast that there was somewhere an unseen Power superior to themselves. Then looking around they found their feelings confirmed by what they saw. The created works which **we** can see prove the power **and wisdom of** the unseen Creator; and the devout historian of the nation, thinking that all our actions should be described as under the guiding power of God, naturally began his book, with what he supposed was the first time that God exercised that power.

The history of the creation is followed, in chapters v.—xi., by what may be more strictly called a genealogy, down to the time of Abraham. Here we trace an opinion common to many nations, that the life of man had at first been longer than afterwards; it becomes shorter as **we** approach more certain history. The first list of names is from Adam to Noah, and **then we** have the history of **the** Flood, which again brings down the human race to a single family, by destroying all the rest. The descent of all the then known nations in the world is afterwards traced from Noah's three sons, Shem, Ham, and Japheth; and the mountains of Ararat, or Armenia, the site of the Garden of Eden, are again made the cradle of the human race. The distant and less known nations of the world are traced from Japheth, whose name means *Spread abroad*. The Egyptians, Canaanites, Arabs, Assyrians, and Babylonians, the neighbours with whom the Israelites were chiefly at war, are traced from Ham, whose name **is** the **same as** Chem, the god of the Egyptians. **Abraham, the** father of the Israelites, Edomites, **and others whom they** owned as kindred tribes, is **traced from** Shem, a **name** which may be derived from **the** Egyptian **word** Shemmo, *a foreigner*, as their nation had been naturally called when in Egypt. All animals are here given to Noah and his sons for food. The later Levitical distinction between clean and unclean animals was unknown to the Elohistic writer. Chap. vii. 1-5, and viii. 20-22, in which the Levitical distinction is made **are** Jehovistic additions. That these Elohistic chapters were in the main written at this time, is probable, for two reasons; first, because, in giving the descent of the Arab tribes, they contain **a** correction of the views before given in the Jehovistic Life **of** Abraham; and, secondly, because we shall have to mention a further correction to the views here set forth, which was made when **a** more enlarged knowledge of geography had been gained. When this had made the Jews acquainted with southern Arabia, then Genesis x. 22—xi. 9, was added in explanation.

The intercourse between Judea and Greece did not begin till so long after the time of Iddo the Seer, that it is not safe to think that much can be learned about Iddo's Genealogies from the Greek writers. But in support of the opinion **that** this History of the World from the Creation to the birth **of** Abraham, written in the time of Iddo, may be called a **Genealogy, and that,** if not the work of Iddo, yet that Iddo's

Genealogies resembled it, we may quote the earliest Greek history of which any fragment remains to us. This is the work of Acusilaus, written about B.C. 600, called his Genealogies. It begins with Chaos, out of which came forth the earth, the rivers, the ocean, the winds, then the inferior gods of nature, and, lastly, men, described first by nations, and then singly by name. The Genealogies, also, of Hecatæus, a yet later writer, were, like those of Acusilaus, an attempt at prehistoric narrative, but they began, not with the creation or shaping of matter, but with Deucaleon, the Greek representative of Noah, in whose time the earth was again peopled with men, after the destruction of our race by the deluge.* With the same use of words the first book of the Bible was by the **Greek translators** named Genesis, or the Birth-book.

Solomon, **like his** father David, has himself **been** considered as an author. "He spake of trees, from **the** cedar tree which is in Lebanon even to the hyssop that springeth **out of** the wall. He spake also of beasts, and of fowl, and **of** creeping things, and of fishes."† But of this knowledge of Natural History we have no other remains than the first chapter of Genesis. He is said to have written or collected a large number of proverbs. Some of these may form part of our present Book of Proverbs, to which, however, additions have been afterwards made. The book was once limited **to** chapters x.—xxii. 16; and this may have been written at any time between Solomon and Hezekiah. The first nine chapters, a poetical Preface in praise of wisdom, are **no part** of the original work, and are of **a** more modern age. The Proverbs of Solomon, which follow the Preface, are **three** hundred and seventy-five in **number**, each consisting **of two** lines **of** poetry. These **mostly show** one of the chief peculiarities of Hebrew verse; **the** second line usually **repeats, or answers, or in** some such way is a fellow to the **first, as, for** example :—

> A false balance is an abomination to Jehovah ;
> But a just weight is his delight.
> When boasting cometh, then cometh **shame** ;
> But with **the** lowly is wisdom.—Prov. **xi. 1, 2.**

These proverbs, thus thrown **into** short pointed sentences **of** two lines each, give us the experience of many minds in a form in which advice can be best remembered. But, like those Psalms which are simply devotional, they contain

---

* **Muller's Fragm. Hist. Græc.**   † 1 Kings iv. 33.

nothing by which their age can be fixed with exactness. They teach the wisdom and power of God, and that it is our duty to fear and worship and trust Him. They praise wisdom, and the several virtues of temperance, chastity, meekness, friendship, truth, justice, and obedience to the king. Not a few are in favour of a rather worldly prudence, and dissuade from becoming surety, from quarrelling, from neglect of advice, and from an unbridled tongue. They never mention the priests. The other Hebrew books which bear Solomon's name, the Book of Ecclesiastes, and the Song of Songs, were not written until many centuries later.

After these three hundred and seventy-five couplets, we have in chap. xxii. 17—xxiv. 22, The words of the Wise men, which are a number of moral precepts in verse, but not written with the same regularity; and then in xxiv. 23-34, **a** further set of such precepts by the Wise men. Both these may perhaps be of a later date, as are the last seven chapters of the Book. Of these seven chapters the titles tell us that they were not written in Solomon's reign; but as they have the same purpose, and are of the same class, they have been very naturally added to the end of Solomon's Proverbs.

In Solomon's reign also many additions to the Book of Psalms are likely to have been made, as great attention was then paid to the service of the temple. We can at least recognize Psalm lxxii. as rightly attributed by the words at its head to this reign. It begins,—

> Give to the king thy judgments, O God,
> And thy righteousness to the king's son.

And again,—

> He shall bear rule from sea to sea,
> And from the river [Euphrates] to the ends of the land.
> The people of the desert [the Edomites] shall bow before him;
> And his enemies **shall** lick **the** dust.
> Kings of Tarshish and of the Isles shall bring presents.
> Kings of Sheba and Seba shall offer gifts.

Here we see described **the** extent of the kingdom in Solomon's reign, which **never** afterwards reached to the Euphrates. Here we also **have** his rule over Edom; the presents from the king of Tyre, who probably was ruler of the island of Cyprus and of Tarshish in Cilicia; and those from the queen of Sheba. Seba has been said to mean Meroë, but it more probably meant Nubia, the gold country, of which a capital city was Seboua.

Another Psalm of the time, and in honour of Solomon, is Ps. xlv., written on the occasion of his marriage with the Egyptian princess. After a preface of three lines the writer addresses the king and the young queen alternately, while perhaps a chorus breaks in with two lines addressed to God. To the king he says,—

> Thou fairest of the sons of Adam,
> Grace is poured on to thy lips,
> Because God hath blessed thee for **ever**.

And **again**,—

> King's daughters are among thy beloved women,
> On thy right hand standeth the queen in gold of Ophir.

To the queen, **who** has left her royal home, he says,—

> Hearken, O daughter, and look, and incline thine ear;
> Forget also thine own people, and thy father's house.
> So shall the king greatly desire thy beauty;
> For he is thy lord, and worship thou him.

And again,—

> Instead of thy forefathers will be thy children,
> Whom thou mayest make princes in **all the land**.

Or perhaps the preface, and the two lines to God, may have been sung by one voice, and the addresses to the king and queen may have been by two bands of singers.

Psalm ii. seems also to belong **to** the end of Solomon's reign, when the Syrians, Edomites, and even the Israelites of the north, were murmuring **in** rebellion. It is supposed to be spoken by **the** king, who **says**:

> Why do **the** nations rage,
> And the peoples imagine **a** vain thing?
> The kings of the earth set themselves up,
> And the rulers take counsel together,
> Against Jehovah and against his anointed one, [saying]
> "Let us break their bonds asunder,
> And cast away their cords from us."

In no reign but Solomon's have we the two circumstances, that there were subject nations **to** rebel against Jerusalem, and also that such rebellion should be thought a vain attempt.

As for what portions of the Books of Genesis and Exodus **were written** in this reign, as before remarked, the determination is conjectural and **uncertain**. The list of the princes

and kings of Edom who preceded the Hebrew monarchy, in
Genesis xxxvi. 9-43, cannot have been written earlier than
Solomon's reign; because it comes down to the reign of
Hadar, or rather Hadad, as the name is rightly written in
the Samaritan copy, and by the Chronicler.* This was the
boy who escaped into Lower Egypt towards the end of
David's reign, and returned home as a man in the course of
Solomon's reign to make his country again independent of
Jerusalem.

Probably at this time were added the last two lines to
Isaac's poetical blessing upon his son Esau, in Genesis xxvii.
40. The poem, written as we have supposed in the time of
David, may have ended with the words "and thou shalt
serve thy brother." But now on the successful revolt of the
Edomites there may have been added the following two lines,

> But it shall come to pass, when thou shalt get free,
> Thou shalt break his yoke from off thy neck.

Reign by reign, or century by century, from this time
forward, we must suppose that the early account of the
march out of Egypt, with the history of the nation's forefathers in yet earlier times, received its numerous additions,
till at last it grew into its present form, and became the
volume which we call the Pentateuch. The religious laws,
the enactments made by the priests of Jerusalem during the
five hundred years between Solomon and Nehemiah, are
here thrown into the form of speeches, usually spoken by
Jehovah, but sometimes by Moses. In this way the priests
claimed a divine origin for laws, which they believed to be
agreeable to the will of the Almighty, but which were often
made for their own benefit. It may be safely asserted that
no part of the ceremonial law was written before the reign
of Solomon. It was wholly unknown to David, Saul, and
the Judges; and we shall hereafter find reasons for thinking
that it began to take its present form about one hundred
years after Solomon's death.

These additions to the Book of Exodus are mostly
Jehovistic, but not always so. To some of them we shall
be able to give dates; but the time when the larger number
were written must be left uncertain. Among the earliest
of the ceremonial laws thus added may be that relating to
the Passover and Feast of Unleavened Bread, in Exodus xii.

* 1 Chron. i. 50.

1-28 and 43-51. The narrative had said in chap. xii. 39, that the Israelites eat unleavened **bread** because in their haste they had no time to prepare it properly; **and** the law that such bread is to be eaten every year at **the** return of the season, though it comes earlier in the narrative, **can** only have been added afterwards. Each family is to **slay a** Passover lamb for its **own** eating; **and** in the **command** to sprinkle the blood **upon** the doorposts to keep **off the** Destroyer, we have **traces of a** belief in **evil** spirits, and **of** an old superstitious practice. This **the** priests, instead **of** forbidding, adopted into **their own code**; and they gave **to** it a religious origin **to make it harmless.** If the earlier **account of the march out of Egypt under the** leadership of **Moses contained no mention of Aaron, at any** rate by this time **he had** a place **in the** narrative, **as he is** mentioned in 1 Samuel xii., which seems to have been **written before** the end of **Solomon's** reign. Hence **to** this **time we must** give Exodus iii.—vi., with the appointment of Aaron, **not** yet as chief priest, but as a help to Moses in his great work. In these Jehovistic additions Moses's father-in-law is named Jethro, *distinguished*; in the earlier Elohistic narrative his name is Reu-el, *the friend of God.*

In our lives of the prophet Samuel **and** of king **Saul,** taken from the first book of Samuel, we found that **they** were based on three **works, the Book of** Nathan **and the** Book of Gad, **both** written **in David's reign,** and **the Book of** Samuel, the **work** of a later **writer with a** more **priestly** and **a** Jehovistic spirit, who **says that there** was a **temple** to Jehovah at Shiloh. Of **this temple Eli** had **been the** priest; and one purpose of this **book is to say** that **Jehovah** had cast off the house of Eli, **from whom in David's reign** the priests of Jerusalem had eagerly claimed descent; **and** that he **had** appointed **a** faithful family, namely, **that of** Zadok in its place.* To this work, which **dwells more** on the doings of Samuel than of Saul, we **owe** the account of **the** ark at Shiloh and among the Philistines, of Samuel's choice of Saul **for a** king, of his being displeased with Saul's act of sacrifice, of his choice of David for Saul's successor, and of the voice of Samuel when dead, warning Saul of his overthrow.

The date of this part of our **First Book** of Samuel must be very uncertain; but its saying that the king will claim

---

* 1 Sam ii. 35

a tithe of the produce of the land very well agrees with
Solomon's tax on the produce; and at no time after the
reign of Solomon would a writer aim at giving sanctity to
the ark of Jehovah, by saying that it had been brought
from the city of Shiloh in the land of Ephraim, and
that Ahiah, a great-grandson of Eli, was the priest. Its
declaring that it was Jehovah's will that Saul should exter-
minate the Amalekites agrees with Solomon's claim to rule
over all the countries between the Euphrates and the Nile.
The offering brought to Jehovah by Samuel's mother, when
the child was weaned, is not that ordered in Leviticus xii.,
and tells us that that law had not yet been written. On
the other hand, in a speech in this part of the First Book
of Samuel, the prophet quotes history from the Book of
Exodus, and more largely from the Book of Judges,
showing the greater age of some parts of those books.[*]

The writer of this Life of Samuel tells us that the prophet,
when he appointed Saul to be king, wrote "The Manner of
the Kingdom" in a book, and laid it up before Jehovah.
Thus the priests even in Solomon's reign claimed to have
an opinion how the king ought to govern; and as the words
of this book, "The Manner of the Kingdom," whoever
wrote it, professed to be not the words of Jehovah, nor of
Moses, but of Samuel, we may suppose that this notice, and
the book itself, were both written before the custom had
arisen of putting the laws into the mouth of Jehovah, in
short, before the history of the march out of Egypt had
been made to contain the body of Jewish laws. If any part
of this book remains it has been adopted into the Pentateuch;
perhaps we have a part of it in Deuteronomy xvii. 14-20.
The blame of Saul for having sacrificed to Jehovah may
have been meant as a reproof to Solomon for having so acted
in the Temple of Jerusalem.

Another part of Deuteronomy, which is altogether un-
suited to the times when that book was written, or to any
later time, is chap xx. describing the rules which should
guide the Israelites when they proposed to conquer a neighbouring tribe, and to make it tributary. It fully recognizes
the right of the strong to attack, to plunder, and to kill the
weak; and the only tenderness shown is in the case of the
fruit trees, which are to be spared. Such a law does not
suit the latter days of the monarchy, when, after the rise

* 1 Sam. xii.

of Assyria, the chief thought of **the** Jews was how to avoid being made to pay tribute. As the policy here described was that which David followed **in** his wars of conquest, and which Solomon followed in keeping the conquered countries, it may very properly be mentioned here. We need find no difficulty in supposing that an ancient piece of writing may have **been** engrafted in that more modern book.

REHOBOAM KING OF JUDAH; B.C. **936—920.**

On Solomon's **death his** son Rehoboam was quietly acknowledged **as king of** Jerusalem; but the Israelites of the north rose in discontent, and claimed to be eased of the heavy burdens **which** Solomon had laid upon them for the support of his splendour. Jeroboam, who had fled from Solomon into Egypt, now hurried back to Shechem, to take advantage of the popularity that he had gained when he had been Solomon's governor of the tribes of Ephraim and Manasseh. When Rehoboam came to Shechem, the capital of Ephraim, to receive the submission of Israel, he **was met** by a demand for a redress of grievances, and a lessening of their taxes: but his answer was not satisfactory **to** them; **and** the northern tribes would not receive him as king. **When** the collector of the tribute attempted to enforce obedience the people stoned **him to** death, and Rehoboam had **to** escape in his chariot to Jerusalem. The blame for this sad misfortune, by which the once united kingdom **was** divided into **two,** with all the evils which followed, **must** be laid on Rehoboam's obstinacy. The people probably had a good ground for complaining, but he would not listen to them.

The assembled Israelites **then** made Jeroboam king in Shechem; and Rehoboam, says the historian, remained king of Judah **alone.** Simeon and Dan, in **the weakness** of the kingdom, remained under the Philistines. **The** tribe of Benjamin, situated in the middle between **the north** and **the** south, **had** always felt themselves part **of the** north; **but** Jerusalem, Rehoboam's capital and fortress being in their country, left them little choice, **and** Benjamin in part followed Judah. Issachar, **and Zebulun,** which included Asher and Naphtali, though **not unfriendly** to Judah, from whom **they** were separated by **Ephraim** and Manasseh, **naturally fell under** the rule of those **more** powerful **tribes.**

7 *

The tribes beyond the Jordan also joined Israel, to whom they were allied by blood. The little tribe of Reuben then ceased to exist. It had never been more than a handful of the men of Judah, and it then sank into Gad. The valley of the Arnon, which separated Israel from Moab, was after a time called the Valley of Gad (2 Sam. xxiv. 5).

Rehoboam's first wish on his return to Jerusalem was to gather together his troops, and enforce the obedience of his northern subjects; but wiser counsels prevailed. He was far from strong enough to conquer a people twice as numerous as his own, and he gave up the attempt.* He soon found, indeed, that he was unable even to defend his own country. In the fifth year of his reign, Shishak of Bubastis, now king of all Egypt, made a marauding inroad upon the land of Judah. This had the effect of making Rehoboam less able to assert his rights over the northern tribes, and it was probably intended to have that effect. Shishak gained possession of Jerusalem, and seized all the treasure that Solomon had collected, both that in the king's house and that in the temple of Jehovah, and the golden shields in the House of the Forest of Lebanon; and he then returned with them into Egypt. There in Thebes, now his capital, he boastfully recorded his conquest of Judah in sculpture, which remains there to this day. Before this time the Egyptian hieroglyphical records have given us no notice of the Israelites.

When Solomon built the House of Jehovah on Mount Moriah, an open hill on the east side of Jerusalem, we were told of no stronger fence around either that, or the altar in front of it, than a row of cedar rails. Shishak, therefore, can have had little difficulty in seizing the sacred treasures. But this misfortune no doubt led to fortifying the temple hill; and in later times we shall find the wall, which embraced Mount Moriah, and brought it within the fortified city, raised to such a height as to make Jerusalem stronger on the east than on the other sides. The wall thus guarding the altar and the temple was the work of various ages; but soon after this time we shall find the words Temple and House of Jehovah bearing a new meaning. They had meant the roofed building which Solomon raised, and so placed that it had the altar and the court of the priests in front of it; but within a century they mean a walled area including the

* 1 Kings xii.

House, the altar with **the** court of the priests, and the larger **court** of Israel.

This invasion by Shishak was only the **first** of a long series **of** misfortunes which were to fall upon Israel and Judah as the necessary punishment for their want of union. The states on all sides of them had been uniting themselves more and more into larger monarchies. The Hebrews, under David and Solomon, had felt the advantage of being thus united; but the union did not last beyond two generations, and henceforth they were, in **both** halves of the country, to feel the **evil of** being too **few in number to defend** themselves from **the** attacks of their neighbours. **Of all** the Hebrew tribes Judah, including as it did Simeon, was the most populous, and being a kingdom in itself, though holding a portion of Benjamin, it had not the weakness of a confederacy. **The** kingdom of Israel on the other hand, consisting of **several** tribes, some to the east and some to the **west** of the **Jordan, and with** Issachar and Zebulun friendly to Judah, though **more** populous was less united; and far **weaker for** self-defence. Thus, though the first misfortune fell upon **Judah,** we shall hereafter see that Israel was the greater **sufferer** from its successful rebellion against Rehoboam.

Moreover, the throne of Judah had a source of strength, which its northern sister wanted, **in its** close alliance with the priesthood. This was begun **by** David, who brought the Levites into Jerusalem, was **cemented** by Solomon in the arrangements of his new tem**ple, and** was continued by Solomon's successors until the growing power of the Sons of Aaron, as they soon began to style themselves, made the monarch weary of a partnership in which the advantages **were** not evenly divided. But in the meantime **the** Levites **claimed** for the **altar** at Jerusalem a superiority **over** all **other** High **Places** or **altars**; and, in doing so, they **threw** a character **for** holiness around the throne **on** which **sat the** anointed of Jehovah. The Psalmist in Solomon**'s reign had** styled **it God's** throne, saying,—

Thy throne, **O** God, is for ever and ever;
The sceptre of thy kingdom is a sceptre of Justice.*

And the king himself was styled, **in one of** the additions to the Book of Exodus, "The hand **upon** the throne of Jah." †

* Ps. xlv. 6. † Exod. xvii. 16.

Thus the priesthood gave great support to **the** king's power in Judah.

Among the cities which Rehoboam built or rebuilt, or fortified, was Hebron in southern Judah.* This is mentioned in Numbers xiii. 22, as having been done seven years before the building of Zoan. The city of Zoan, or Tanis, in Lower Egypt, rose about this time to be one of the chief cities in the country; and in the Hebrew poetry Egypt is called the Fields of Zoan. Tanis rose over Shishak's city Bubastis, and it held its rank against Thebes, until about the reign of Hezekiah.

Rehoboam followed the debasing example of David and Solomon in having a number of wives. He had eighteen wives and sixty concubines. Among these wives Maachah, the daughter of Absalom, was the favourite; and her son Abijam, or Abijah, was made ruler over his brethren, and pointed out as the **successor** to the throne. Rehoboam reigned seventeen years.†

ABIJAM **KING OF JUDAH**; B.C. **919—917.**

Abijam, the son of Rehoboam, reigned for two years, or rather for part of three years, dying in the third year of his reign. Like his fathers he had a large number of wives. And from this practice of the Hebrew kings it often followed that no one of the wives held the high rank of queen. That post of honour fell to the king's mother, or grandmother if she was yet living; she was naturally the greatest lady in the land, and had the place of first importance in the state, which would have been held by the king's wife if he had but one. The historian does not trouble himself with the names of all a king's wives, but he usually gives us the name of the queen-mother.

During this short reign the enmity between Judah and Israel broke out into open war. Israel was defeated in battle, and Abijam took from Jeroboam Beth-el, and some of the neighbouring towns, thus making himself master of a large part of the land of Benjamin, which, if it had been free to choose, would have all belonged to Israel rather than Judah, and of which the larger part did soon join itself to the northern kingdom. Had Jerusalem belonged to the northern kingdom the natural boundary between the two

---

* 2 Chron. xi. 10.   † **1 Kings xiv.** 21-31; 2 Chron. xi. xii.

would have been on the south side of that city; but as Judah held Jerusalem there was no natural line of boundary, and it changed with the changing strength of the two kingdoms.

For the history of Abijam's reign we are indebted to the Chronicles of the Kings of Judah, and the Commentary of Iddo the Seer.*

JEROBOAM KING OF ISRAEL; B.C. 936—916.

The **northern** and eastern tribes, on their revolt from Rehoboam, the **son of** Solomon, made Jeroboam king. He had, as we have seen, been appointed by Solomon governor of the land of Ephraim and Manasseh; and then had fallen into displeasure **and fled** into Egypt, and he returned, as the friend, and with the countenance, of the Egyptian king, to divide the Hebrew tribes, and to seize the sceptre of the northern half.

His mother was a widow named Zeruah, and he was the son of her second marriage with Nebat, a man of Ephraim. We are tempted to conjecture that she may **have** been **the** same person as Zeruiah, David's sister and Joab's mother. Zeruah may be translated *a Leper*, a very improbable name for any child; and it looks like a nick-name made from the real name by the change of a letter, and used to throw a reproach upon Jeroboam, the leader in the great revolt. If he were a younger half-brother of Joab, and thus Solomon's cousin, it would explain his rise, first to the government of a province, and then to a throne. He seems to have been raised to the throne for his good qualities, and by the free choice of the people. The charge against him of idolatry may have been exaggerated by southern hatred.

The southern writers often speak of the revolt of the northern tribes as the Sin of Jeroboam, whereby he made Israel to sin. But the revolt was the act of the people, not of their leader. Jeroboam was in Egypt when it began, and they sent for him to come and be their king. We must not lay upon him the blame for the misfortune of the kingdom being henceforth divided into two. The blame must be shared between Rehoboam and Solomon.

Jeroboam's kingdom, though the larger of the two, was less thickly peopled, and had a source of weakness in its

* 1 Kings xv. 1-8; 2 Chron. xiii.

want of union. The more northerly tribes of Issachar and Zebulun, as we have seen in the history of Jacob's family, were not unfriendly to Judah, and they probably joined in the revolt unwillingly. Jeroboam's kingdom, moreover, had no large cities. It had, however, Joppa, the one port on the Mediterranean, which gave it some little trading advantages.[*] For his capital Jeroboam fortified Shechem in the hill country of Ephraim, and Penuel on the river Jabbok, as a second capital, to secure the obedience of the tribes on the east of the Jordan. Mahanaim, the former capital of Gilead, may not have been in such a convenient situation. He also had a house at Tirzah, a village a few miles to the north of Shechem, which was a more pleasant spot for a dwelling than the walled city. The beauty of Tirzah, thus made the site of a royal palace, lay probably in its gardens; it was proverbial; and seven centuries later the writer of Solomon's Song says of the bride that she was beautiful as Tirzah.

Jeroboam made two golden calves, and set up one at Dan at the northern end of his kingdom, and one at Beth-el in the south; and many of the people may have fallen into the idolatry of worshipping them. But when the southern historians charge this guilt so freely upon the northern tribes, we are tempted to be rather distrustful. Jeroboam drove all the Levites out of his kingdom; they were supporters of Rehoboam's claim to the throne, they were perhaps natives of Judah; and Jeroboam gave their places to priests who were natives of Israel. He thus rebelled against the chief priests of Jerusalem as much as against the king of Jerusalem, and hence the charges against him of favouring idolatry may not all be true. For the next two hundred years the sin of Jeroboam, the son of Nebat, became a proverb with the writers in the kingdom of Judah; but whether they mean his rebellion against Solomon's son, or his driving the Levites out of his kingdom, or his idolatry, is often doubtful. His golden calves were no doubt copied from Egypt. It was the custom for a nation at this time, and indeed at many times, to force a conquered or dependent people to adopt its gods as an act of homage to its superior power; and when Shishak, king of Egypt, favoured Jeroboam's aim at the throne, and further strengthened him on it by his attack upon Jerusalem, he probably required Jeroboam to set up these Egyptian emblems in his new kingdom. In Judea the Feast of Ingathering, when

---

[*] Josh. xix. 46; Hos. xii. 7.

the figs and grapes had been housed, was celebrated on the fifteenth day of the seventh month, that is, at the first full moon after the autumnal equinox, which we call the harvest moon. But for northern Israel, where the seasons are later, Jeroboam very naturally fixed the Feast of Ingathering a month later, at the next full moon; and this was counted against him as a crime by the priests of Jerusalem.

Jeroboam had not leant more to idolatry than Solomon had. The driving the Levites out of the north was not done so much to change the religion as to get rid of a body of priests whose influence was used in favour of Judah's claim to superiority. As they were obedient servants to the chief priest in Jerusalem, they could not be good subjects to Jeroboam.

At the revolt, a part of Benjamin had given its obedience to Jeroboam, but towards the end of his reign he had been so far defeated by Abijam, king of Judah, that he lost the town of Beth-el, with the neighbouring villages, and very possibly the whole of Benjamin. No part of this tribe was more than twenty miles from Jerusalem; so it often had to fall under the power of that capital.

Jeroboam reigned twenty-one years, and was succeeded by his son Nadab.* We do not hear that he had more wives than one. Whether that arises from our having less information about the northern kings, or from their not following the debasing practice of the kings of Judah, is doubtful. But the same may be remarked of Jeroboam's successors, as also of his predecessor, king Saul.

To a time soon after Jeroboam had set up his golden calves we must give Exod. xxxii.—xxxiv. 9, wherein is described the slaughter by the hands of the Sons of Levi of the three thousand worshippers of Aaron's golden calf. We must put these chapters thus early while Aaron was considered as only a help to Moses, and before he and his sons had the higher rank given to them of hereditary chief priests, as in chap. xxviii. The approval given here and elsewhere to putting to death all idolatrous brethren is one of the sad features in the priestly portion of the Hebrew writings. It gives countenance to the opinion that the governing power does right to check errors in religion by punishment, and has thus provided the faggots by which Christians have burnt both Jews and heretics.

The rebuke by Moses of the worship of the Calf was a

* 1 Kings xii.—xiv. 20; 2 Chron. xi. 14; xiii. 20.

rebuke to the Northern Israelites, and was followed by his
breaking the two first Tables of the Law. These, perhaps,
had some Elohistic words, displeasing to the Jehovistic
writer, or at least not sufficiently Jehovistic and forbidding
of image worship. To this time, therefore, we must give
chap. xxxiv., with the making of the two new Tables of Stone,
and the present disordered state of the narrative, the rejection
of the original commandments from chap. xix. 6, and the
insertion of the Jehovistic Ten Commandments in their
present place. We must not suppose that **these** were now
new ; they may have been written long before **on** the Stone
Tables, which were within the Ark in the city of Jearim
before Saul was king.

NADAB KING OF ISRAEL ; B.C. 916—915.

Nadab, **the son** of Jeroboam, reigned for one year, dying
in the second year of his reign. He had entered upon the
war against Judah, in that part of the land of the Philistines
which the geographer had given to the tribe of Dan, a part
of the country that upon the quarrel between Israel and
Judah had no strong feelings towards one more than the
other. Nadab was engaged in besieging the Philistine city
of Gibbethon and the land of Dan, when he was slain by
Baasha, a native of Issachar, probably an officer in his army.
Baasha put to death every one of Jeroboam's family, and
then reigned in his stead. This, says the southern historian,
was in punishment for Jeroboam's sins against Jehovah,
meaning perhaps as much his rebellion against Judah and
its priests as his leaning towards idolatry. The lives of these
kings are said to be written in the Book of the Chronicles
of the Kings of Israel, a work about which we have no
further information than its title.*

BAASHA KING OF ISRAEL ; B.C. 915—892.

Baasha the usurper was of the tribe of Issachar, which
was not so unfriendly to Judah as were Ephraim and
Manasseh. His father bore the Jehovistic name of Ahijah,
and perhaps was the prophet of that name. So a difference
in religion may have been one cause for Baasha's rebellion,
as it continued to be a cause of weakness to the northern
kingdom.

* 1 Kings xv. 25-31.

In the reign of Baasha the **civil war continued** between Israel and Judah with various success. **Baasha** regained possession of part of the land of Benjamin, **and** he attempted to fortify Ramah near Beth-el, as a check upon the king of Judah. But he was defeated, and his work **was** stopped. He was recalled from his attack upon Judah by being himself invaded by Ben-hadad king of Damascus, who took from him the land of Naphtali and all **to** the north of it. And the prophet Jehu, the son of Hanani, rightly described **him** as bringing this trouble **upon** himself by his invasion **of** Judah. Baasha **removed his** dwelling from Shechem, his capital, to Tirzah, **a spot a few** miles to **the** north, celebrated for its pleasant **situation, where Jeroboam** had sometimes dwelt. But, besides **the pleasantness of the** place, Baasha may have had another **reason** for liking Tirzah **better than** Shechem, as it **was** nearer to his own friends in **the land of** Issachar. He died in the twenty-fourth year **of his reign,** and was succeeded by his son Elah.*

By this late Syrian invasion, if not before, the **second of** Jeroboam's golden calves must have been destroyed. **That** at Beth-el cannot have remained there after that **town** was captured by Abijah, nor that at Dan after Ben-hadad conquered Naphtali. But, though these northern idols were destroyed, they were not forgotten by **the** people **of** the south; and **two** centuries later, the **prophet** Hosea would wish us **to** believe that the men of Samaria were worshipping a calf.

ASA KING OF JUDAH ; B.C. **917—877.**

Abijam had died in the third year **of** his reign **over** Judah, leaving his son **Asa to** succeed him. Asa was young, perhaps only a child; **and he** at first fell to the care of his grandmother Maachah. But **we are** told that he did what was right in the **eyes of Jehovah ;** which means that **he** governed agreeably to **the will of the** priests, or rather, that **he** allowed himself **to be governed** by them. Under Asa **the** priests were able to strengthen their power **in** civil affairs, and year by year they became more important. One **of** the king's early acts was deposing his grandmother from her political rank as queen, because she had **made an** idol to Ashera, a Phenician goddess, usually worshipped **in** a grove ; but it is quite possible that he may have done this in order to give to his mother **the rank of** chief lady in the kingdom. Maachah's

* 1 Kings **xv.** 32—**xvi.** 7 ; 2 Chron. xvi. 1-6.

idol he burnt in the valley of Kidron, a dirty brook running along the east side of the city. Asa also added largely to the treasures in the temple, handing over to the priests both the treasures which his father had collected and those which he himself collected, of gold and silver and vessels. Thus a large part of the public treasure was placed in the hands of the priests. It was safer in the temple than in the palace. The holiness of the place gave it better protection than the royal guards could give it elsewhere. The king's heart was perfect with Jehovah, says the historian, with but one exception, namely, the High Places or altars in other parts of the land of Judah were not removed.* It was the tyrannical aim of the priests in Jerusalem, at the same time that they taught the duty of offering up burnt-offerings and bringing sacrifices to Jehovah, to stop such acts of worship from being performed in any place but Jerusalem. They may have justified this by saying that elsewhere such sacrifices were likely to be accompanied with idolatrous ceremonies; but it is impossible not to believe that their wish to bring all the offerings to Jehovah up to Jerusalem, arose mainly from a desire to increase their own importance.

For the first ten years of Asa's reign the land enjoyed quiet; but this prosperity was for a moment disturbed by another Egyptian marauding inroad. Zerah, an Ethiopian, by which we may understand a king of Thebes, not a native of Lower Egypt like Shishak, led a large army into southern Judah. He was probably called in as an ally by the king of Israel, whose war with Judah had only slumbered. But he was able to advance no further than Moreshah near Gath, in the valley of Zephathah. There the invaders were met by Asa, at the head of his army. The Ethiopians were routed and pursued as far as Gerar in the land of the Philistines; and Asa returned to Jerusalem laden with spoil, gained not only from the invaders, but from the Philistines, in whose country the battle had been fought. He smote all the cities round about Gerar, and found a large amount of booty, which he carried off, together with the sheep and camels of the herdsmen around. Zerah's army is said to have held a million men, and Asa's to have held more than half a million; but these numbers are so far beyond all probability that it is in vain to reason about them.†

The word Zerah is an Egyptian title, meaning "Son of the

---

* 1 Kings xv. 9-15.　　　　† 2 Chron. xiv.—xv.

Sun," a title used by all the Theban kings, and it gives us but little help in learning what king was meant. Shishak of Bubastis, who some forty years earlier had made himself king of Thebes, had been succeeded by a son; but there his line had ended. It is probable that, on the fall of his family, the family of Rameses again for a few years held the sceptre of all Egypt. But it was a time of civil war and disturbance, and we can only offer as a conjecture that Zerah, the Ethiopian, was Rameses VII of Thebes.

From this time forward for the next three hundred years we shall hear of no further attack upon Judea by Egypt. During the first half of that time Egypt was too busy in its civil struggles to attempt foreign conquest; and during the latter half it was glad to support Judea against the incroaching power of Assyria, a country which then rises against them both. Hence what little Jewish trade there was with Egypt met with no interruption; and that there was a little colony of prosperous Jewish traders living in the Delta we have curious evidence in the name of the Holy Mount in Sinai. Even before the reign of Hezekiah, it had gained the name of Sephar, or the *written* mountain, from the numerous votive inscriptions cut upon its rocks by Jews who made a pilgrimage from Egypt to visit the spot made so dear to them by the narrative in the Book of Exodus.

In the thirty-sixth year of Asa, which we must understand to mean the thirty-sixth year of Rehoboam, and therefore the seventeenth of Asa, according to our mode of reckoning, Baasha, king of Israel, as mentioned above, made a successful attack upon Asa, and seizing the town of Ramah, which was less than ten miles from Jerusalem, he fortified it in order to separate the northern half of Benjamin from the capital. Asa in his difficulty looked about for an ally, and he took the treasures of his own palace, and those of the temple of Jehovah, and sent them to Ben-hadad king of Damascus, with a request that he would invade the territory of Israel. Ben-hadad accepted the bribe, and overran with his troops the fertile province of Naphtali. This invasion in the north called back Baasha from his invasion in the south. It was no longer possible for him to hold Ramah; and Asa took possession of the timber and stones that he had prepared for the defence of that city, and made use of them to fortify Geba and Mizpah, two cities in the same neighbourhood which were better situated for defence. While fortifying the town of Mizpah, Asa made there a great pit which remained open for the next three centuries.* For what purpose it was made is doubtful ; perhaps as a tank for water, which is very necessary in a town without wells. His sending the treasures out of the Temple to purchase the Syrian help may have been wise, but it can hardly have been approved of by the priests; and Hanani, the seer, is said to have reproached him for relying upon the king of Syria, instead of relying upon Jehovah. The king in a rage sent the prophet to prison.

The last fifteen years of Asa's reign were a time of peace. The rival kingdom, after the death of Baasha, was torn to pieces by civil wars, in which Asa wisely took no part. He must be counted as one of the best of the kings of Judah, and he left his kingdom to his only son Jehoshaphat at peace with all around.

Asa repaired the great altar in front of the Temple-porch ;† and since we have reason to believe it was raised in height by some king in the course of this century, we may reasonably suppose that this was done on that occasion by Asa. Exodus xx. 24-26, written perhaps in approval of Solomon's altar, had said that it was not to be so lofty as to need steps. But Exodus xxviii. 42, and Leviticus vi. 10, which describe the priests' garments, and were written about the reign of Jehoash, let us understand that then the altar was so lofty as to require steps for the priests to mount by when laying upon it the wood and animals. Hence we have reason for supposing that its height was raised by Asa when he repaired it ; and probably with the approval of the priests, although it was done in neglect of Exodus xx. 24-26.

The plunder of the Temple by the Egyptians in Rehoboam's reign had no doubt left it deprived of much of its costly furniture ; and this loss also may have been in part repaired during Asa's long reign ; although his tribute to the Syrians had left the Temple with lessened wealth. Solomon had ornamented it with ten golden lampstands, and had placed ten handsome copper lavers, or basins, in the courtyard for the priests' use.‡ But portions of the Book of Exodus, written within the century following Asa's reign, tell us that the Sons of Aaron then had to be contented with one golden lampstand and one copper laver.§ Asa in his old age was diseased in his feet, and here again he offended the priests. For relief in his illness he sought help not from Jehovah, but from the physicians. He died in the forty-first

---

* Jerem. xli. 9.   † 2 Chron. xv. 8.
‡ 1 Kings vii.   § Exod. xxv. 31; xxx. 17·

year of his reign His body was then laid in spices, not to be embalmed, according to the custom of the Egyptians, but to be burnt with great ceremony. The ashes were probably then placed in the tomb; and this seems to have been the usual mode of burial for the Hebrew monarchs.*

The Levitical law gives no directions about the burial of the dead. Two modes of putting the body out of sight were in use in Judea. In the villages and country places a grave was probably more often dug, and the body returned to its parent, but in cities, and in particular in Jerusalem, where the whole neighbourhood is of stone, and a grave cannot be so easily dug, the body was usually burnt. In the case of the wealthy the bone ashes were then placed in a chest within a tomb; but with the larger number of persons this trouble was not taken. Hence, while in many countries tombs and monuments for the dead are among the chief architectural remains of antiquity, in Palestine they are almost unknown. The place appointed for burning those who died in Jerusalem, was at the south-west side of the city, in the Valley of Hinnom, a valley into which the rubbish and filth of all sorts was freely thrown. There at a separate part of the valley, called Tophet, funeral fires were always burning, as no day in the year was without many deaths. At times these fires at Tophet had taken the character of sacrifices to Molech, a Canaanite god; and many are the complaints that we meet with in the prophets against this piece of idolatry. The tombs of the kings were within the walls of the city; those of any other persons whose families went to the expense of a tomb, seem to have been on the other side of the valley.

The authority quoted for the history of this reign is the Chronicles of the Kings of Judah, a book now lost, which must not be mistaken for our present two Books of Chronicles, which are a compilation made several centuries later.†

Hanani, the seer of Asa's reign, is the last person we meet with bearing that title. Henceforward such men are called Prophets. The seer was so named because he gave his advice as received from God in a vision; the Prophet was so called from the poetic manner, or the ready utterance, with which he delivered such advice. The remark in our First Book of Samuel, that "he that is now called a Prophet was before time called a Seer," was of course written some generations after the time of Samuel. We have given it to the end of Solomon's reign.

* 2 Chron. xvi.   † 1 Kings xv.; 2 Chron. xvi.

ELAH KING OF ISRAEL ; B.C. 892—891.
ZIMRI KING OF ISRAEL ; B.C. 891.
OMRI AND TIBNI KINGS OF ISRAEL; B.C. 891—887.
OMRI KING OF ISRAEL ; B.C. 886—880.

Before the end of Asa's reign Elah, the son of the rebel Baasha, succeeded his father as king of Israel, and was himself to be slain by another rebel. He sent an army southward, hoping to gain the land of Dan, as Nadab the son of Jeroboam had attempted to gain it twenty-five years before. He gave himself up to luxurious living, and when drunk with wine at Tirzah he was killed by Zimri, one of the captains of his chariots. Zimri killed at the same time all the rest of the family of Baasha, and declared himself king of Israel.

Elah's troops were besieging Gibbethon in the land of Dan, when they heard of his murder by Zimri. Omri was at the head of that army; and his soldiers thought that he was at least as suitable a man for the crown as the murderer Zimri. They accordingly declared him king of Israel, and marched without loss of time against Zimri, who had shut himself up in Tirzah. Zimri, seeing that he had no chance of defending the place against Omri's army, set fire to the palace and killed himself, after having been king seven days. Thus the attempt to gain the land of Dan from Judah was sadly fatal to the kings of Israel.

Omri's claim to the throne was, however, not undisputed. He had no better right to be king than Zimri; and while one half of Israel obeyed him as king in Tirzah, another half set up Tibni as king. Though we are not told what tribes followed Tibni, we must suppose that they were not the northerly tribes of Asher, Issachar, Zebulun, and Naphtali, as their lands seem to have been the battle-field between Omri and Ben-hadad king of Syria, who held a number of cities there,* but rather the tribes on the east of the Jordan, of which country Penuel was the capital. The civil war between Omri and Tibni, of which we have no particulars, lasted for six years; Omri's people then gained the superiority, and Tibni was put to death.

Omri then reigned for six years more over the whole of the northern and eastern tribes, so far at least as he could hold the northern part of his kingdom against the Syrians. To strengthen himself against these dangerous neighbours,

* 1 Kings xx. 34.

he courted the alliance of the king of Tyre, as Solomon had
before done; and attained for his son Ahab as a wife Jezebel
the daughter of Ethbaal who was then on the throne of Tyre
and Sidon. He removed his residence from Tirzah to the
hill of Shemer in the same neighbourhood, and equally
within the land of Manasseh. Tirzah had been chosen for
the pleasantness of the situation, but the hill of Shemer was
chosen for its strength as a military position. There Omri
built his castle; and the town that grew up around it was
in later days known by the name of Samaria. Shechem, the
former capital, was perhaps thought too near to the unfriendly
country of Judah. Omri died in the twelfth year of his
reign, and was succeeded by his son Ahab.*

In Jacob's prophecy relating to his sons in Gen. xlix.,
which we have given to David's reign, Dan is mentioned
twice. The added words are—

> Dan shall be a serpent by the way,
> An adder in the path; he biteth the horse's heels,
> So that the rider falleth backward.
> I have waited for thy salvation, O Jehovah.

This may naturally have been written soon after this time,
when Judah gained its easy victory in the land of Dan. We
have seen two kings of Israel, Nadab and Zimri, put to death
to the relief of Judah by the troops which they employed in
an endeavour to conquer the land of Dan.

AHAB KING OF ISRAEL; B.C. 880—861.

Ahab, we are told by the historian, did evil in the sight of
Jehovah above all that were before him. He was very much
governed by his wife Jezebel the daughter of Ethbaal king
of Tyre, or rather of the Sidonians, as the king held sway
over all their cities on that coast. Ahab, falling into his
wife's religion, built a temple to Baal in his new city,
Samaria, and had an altar there, where he sacrificed to
that god. Here, then, we see why it was unwise in the
Israelites to speak of the Almighty, the one God, the Creator
of the world, by the name of Baal, or *Lord*. The use of the
word made it more easy for a worshipper of the Sidonian
idol Baal, to introduce his corrupting worship into the
country. It was perhaps not before this time that the name
of Baal was so much blamed by the Hebrew writers, when it

* 1 Kings xvi. 8-23.

8

was used as a name for God. It was not thought blamable
in David's time, when his son was named Baaliada.

Jeroboam, at the beginning of the revolt, had driven the
Levites out of the northern kingdom, and now Ahab, under
the advice of his foreign wife, put to death the prophets
or worshippers of Jehovah.* This irreligious conduct was
thought to have been the cause of a severe drought and
famine which afflicted the land for three years at the
beginning of this reign. Ahab also made a grove for Ashera,
who was perhaps the same as the Sidonian goddess Astarte.†

It is very probable that as Ahab married his Sidonian wife
in the reign of his father Omri, this attack upon the worship
of Jehovah may have been begun by Omri, the father, rather
than by Ahab, the son, though it is not mentioned in the
former reign. But when the prophet Micah, writing a
century and a **half later,** speaks of the wicked Decree **of**
Omri,‡ he clearly means this attack upon the worship of
Jehovah. So, when the prophet Hosea blames Ephraim for
walking after the Decree,§ he means a decree to the same
purpose, whether that issued by Jeroboam I., or this issued
by Omri and enforced by Ahab.

Ethbaal, the father of Ahab's queen, was a priest of
Astarte, in the city of Tyre. He was a usurper; he had
slain the Sidonian king Pheles, a descendant of Hiram, and
thus gained the throne. He reigned thirty-two years. The
Tyrian annals place seventy-two years between Solomon's
fourth year, when Hiram helped to build the Temple of
Jerusalem, and the accession of Ethbaal. If, then, we may
suppose that Ethbaal had reigned twenty-two years when
Ahab came to the throne of Israel, our chronology will agree
with the Tyrian records.‖

Ben-hadad, king of Damascus, had invaded Israel in the
reign of Baasha, and again in the reign of Omri, taking many
of the northern cities; he seems to have conquered and held
in subjection the three northern tribes, Asher, Naphtali, and
Zebulun, to the north of the valley of Jezreel; and now
Ben-hadad's son, a second of the same name, repeated the
attack upon Omri's son, Ahab. Ahab in his fright at once
owned himself to be Ben-hadad's servant, and that all he
had, his gold, his silver, his wives and his children, were at
Ben-hadad's service. But these mere words did not satisfy

* 1 Kings xviii. 4.   † 1 Kings xvi. 29-33.   ‡ Micah vi. 16.
§ Hosea v. 11.   ‖ Josephus, contr. Ap. 1. 18.

Ben-hadad, he said he should come with his army and fetch them. Accordingly he came as far south as the city of Samaria, in which Ahab had shut himself up. He brought with him, in his army, thirty-two kings, his allies, and laid siege to the city. But he was repulsed by Ahab, and his army was put to rout, and he himself fled with his horsemen.*

Ahab's courteous words, by which he promised to give all that he possessed to Ben-hadad, were a form of eastern politeness of which we have many examples in this history. When the Hittite offered to give to Abraham the Cave of Machpelah, when Araunah the Jebusite offered to give to David the Threshing-floor, when the Queen of Sheba brought her presents to Solomon; in all these cases they meant to be paid for what they called gifts, and like king Ahab they did not mean to be taken at their word.

The next year, Ben-hadad proposed again to attempt the conquest of Samaria. He mustered his army near the city of Aphek, in the land of Issachar, in the valley of Jezreel. This is a valley made interesting by the number of important battles that have been there fought. It runs across the country from the Jordan to the sea, dividing the hill country of Ephraim and Manasseh from the hill country of Naphtali and Zebulun. In the war between Ben-hadad and Ahab, either army would perhaps have been superior if it had waited the attack on its own hills; but Ben-hadad, trusting to his chariots and horsemen, went down into the valley; and the Israelites, encouraged by the belief that Jehovah was a God of the valleys as much as of the hills, went down to meet him. The Israelites were victorious, and Ben-hadad fled into the city of Aphek, to wait his fate from the conqueror.

Ahab was contented with his victory; perhaps he distrusted his own means of pursuing it further; so he made a treaty with Ben-hadad, who undertook to retire peaceably, and to withdraw his troops from those cities in the land of Israel which his father, the first Ben-hadad, had conquered from Baasha and Omri. Using the figurative language of the East to mean that his capital should no longer be a hostile city, he promised that Ahab should have leave to make such highways into Damascus as the first Ben-hadad had made into the town of Samaria.†

On this defeat of the Syrian invasion, king Ahab, relying

---

* 1 Kings xx. 1-21.   † 1 Kings xx. 22-34.

on the treaty of peace which he had generously granted to
Ben-hadad, moved his dwelling-place to the northern part of
his kingdom. He built for his Sidonian wife a new palace
at Jezreel, a small town in the fertile valley of the same
name.   Queen Jezebel may have wished for this move,
because it placed her nearer to the Phenician territory.
This palace was called his Ivory House,* perhaps from the
large quantity of ivory with which it was ornamented ; and
it was soon disgraced by the murder of Naboth, whose death
Jezebel caused that she might gain possession of an adjoining
vineyard which Ahab wished to add to his garden.† This
new palace took the place of the summer palace at Tirzah ;
but Samaria continued to be the capital of the kingdom.

In the reign of Ahab, Hiel of Beth-el built, or rather
fortified, Jericho, a village in the desert part of the land of
Benjamin, in a line between Beth-el and the southern ford
of the Jordan. This act, says the southern historian, was
displeasing to Jehovah, and it cost Hiel the lives of two of his
sons.‡ For the explanation of this, we are left to conjecture.
Beth-el, on the border between Benjamin and Ephraim, was
often in the hands of the king of Israel. This building of
Jericho was probably a hostile act on the part of the northern
king, and an attempt to cut off Jerusalem from the ford, or
rather to keep open a road through Beth-el and across the
southern ford from Ephraim to the eastern districts which
were under the king of Israel, and to the Moabites who paid
him a tribute. This was the more important, because, as we
shall learn presently, the Syrians now held so large a portion
of Israelite land on the east of the Jordan, that this was the
only ford by which one part of Ahab's dominions could hold
intercourse with the other part.

For the next three years there was no war between Israel
and Syria ; but it began again in the fourth year. The
king of Damascus had promised to restore to Ahab certain
conquered cities. What the promise included, or how far
it was performed, does not appear ; but we find that Ben-
hadad still kept possession of his conquests on the east of
the Jordan. These Ahab now proposed to recover, and
with this view he made an alliance with Jehoshaphat, the
next king of Judah. Israel and Judah had been at war
for seventy years, and this was the first time that a treaty
had been concluded between them since the death of Solomon and the revolt of Jeroboam.

* 1 Kings xxii. 39.   † 1 Kings xxi.   ‡ 1 Kings xvi. 34.

This treaty between the two kings took place in the tenth year of Ahab's reign, when he gave his daughter in marriage to Jehoshaphat's son Jehoram. But the treaty was not made on equal terms; it was more or less an act of submission on the part of Israel to the superior power of Judah, whose help was now needed against Syria. One article of the treaty certainly was the introduction of the Levites and the worship of Jehovah into the Northern kingdom. It was at this time probably that Ahab gave to his three children, who were all grown up, Jehovistic names. These names, Athaliah, Ahaziah, and Jehoram, two ending and the other beginning with the word Jah or Jehovah, show that though he had married a Phenician princess, and under her influence had at one time put the worshippers of Jehovah to death, yet during the latter part of his reign his leaning had been towards the religion, as well as the political friendship, of his southern neighbour. He, and perhaps his people, had halted between two opinions; and the northern nation, as we shall find, was seriously weakened by its division into two parties.

We may perhaps find another reason for Ahab's change in his religious policy, and for this friendship between Israel and Judah. We have already shown that Ethbaal, king of Tyre, Ahab's friend and father-in-law, had probably reigned twenty-two years when Ahab came to the throne, and Ethbaal's death in Ahab's tenth year must have lessened the influence of queen Jezebel, his daughter, over her husband Ahab, and may have made it necessary for Ahab to look for a new friend in Jehoshaphat, to help him against the Syrians. At least we know, from a comparison between the Tyrian annals and the Book of Kings, that Ethbaal died about the time that his granddaughter, Athaliah of Israel, married Jehoshaphat's son Jehoram.

In those days, a war was always supposed to pay for itself; a king went to battle in the belief that the booty gained would pay for the expenses of the preparation. So, when Ahab asked Jehoshaphat to join him in attempting to recover Gilead from the Syrians of Damascus, he was as much granting a favour as asking one. Jehoshaphat went to Samaria to consult with Ahab about the war. Before moving their armies Jehoshaphat proposed that they should consult the prophets; and Ahab gathered together four hundred of his prophets, who all promised him success. But Jehoshaphat wished for the opinion of one of his own prophets of

Jehovah; and Ahab rather unwillingly sent for Micaiah.
Micaiah assured them that Jehovah had sent a lying Spirit
on purpose to mislead Ahab and his prophets; and he
warned Ahab that he would not return in safety from the
battle.   But the more rash counsels prevailed, and the two
kings led their forces against the city of Ramoth in Gilead,
which was then held by the Syrians of **Damascus**.

Our Book of Kings, after the prophet's speech **to the** two
kings, adds, "And he said, *Hear, O ye peoples, every one of
you.*" These are the words with which the **Book** of Micah
now begins; and they have been added to the **Book** of Kings
by an editor, who meant to tell us that Micah, who wrote a
hundred and fifty years later in the reign of Hezekiah, **was**
the same person as this Micaiah of Jehoshaphat's time.

Before the battle the **two** kings had agreed that Ahab
should **be** disguised in dress like one of his own captains, and
not distinguishable in the crowd, but that Jehoshaphat should
wear his **robes**.   But the disguise did **not** save Ahab.   He
was shot by an arrow, which entered **between the** joints of
his armour, and **he was** propped up in his **chariot** while the
fight continued, **and** then he died in the evening.   With the
death **of** Ahab the fight **was at** an end.   Jehoshaphat seems
then **to** have retired **from this** invasion of Gilead, and the
Syrians did **not** pursue.   Ahab had reigned twenty-one or
twenty-two years.   His body was carried **to** Samaria, and
there buried.*

Our finding, during this half century, the same names
upon the throne of Judah, and upon that of Israel, leads to
some confusion, which can be best removed by a table.   This
also will further explain how the idolatrous queen Jezebel,
and her violent daughter, queen Athaliah, became so important during **these** reigns, the **one** in Israel, and the other
in Judah.

* 1 Kings xxii. 1-40.

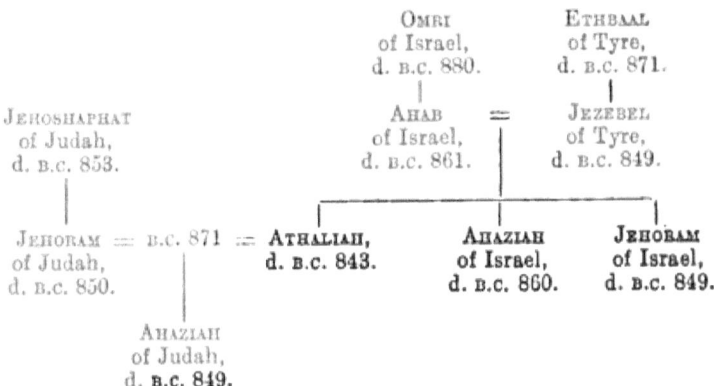

AHAZIAH KING OF ISRAEL; B.C. 861.

Ahaziah, who succeeded his father Ahab, or perhaps reigned jointly with him, reigned only parts of two years. He continued in the idolatrous practices of his mother, the Tyrian princess, and when laid on the sick bed, in consequence of a fall in Samaria, he sent to inquire of Baalzebub, the god of Ekron, a city of the Philistines, as to whether he should recover. Baal-zebub, *Baal the fly*, is not otherwise known to us. The name was perhaps a nickname, given by the Hebrew writer to Baal-zephon, or *Typhon*, an Egyptian god, who may have been worshipped at Ekron.

Ahaziah's reign, though short, was marked by serious misfortune. The Moabites had hitherto paid a tribute to the kings of Israel in lambs and wool; but, on the defeat of Ahab by the Syrians, the Israelite power on the east of the Jordan was very much weakened, and the Moabites revolted, and sent no further tribute.*

Ahaziah left no children, and he was succeeded by his brother Jehoram.

JEHORAM KING OF ISRAEL; B.C. 860—849.

Jehoram began his reign with an endeavour to reduce the rebellious Moabites to obedience, and to enforce the payment of the usual tribute. But as the Syrians of Damascus were masters of the east side of the Jordan, he could not easily reach Moab from the north; therefore, for this purpose, like his father, he asked for the help of Jehoshaphat, king of

---

* 1 Kings xxii. 51; 2 Kings iii. 5.

Judah. This was granted, and the **two** monarchs further agreed to ask the king of Edom to join them. He also consented. The three little armies united at the southern **end** of the Dead Sea, and laid waste the land of Moab far and wide. On reaching Kir-hareseth, the more southerly of the two chief cities of Moab, they laid siege to it, and seemed on the point of taking it. Their slingers pressed sorely on the defenders. Mesha, king of Moab, who was within the place, made **a fierce** sally at the head of seven hundred swordsmen. But he was driven back into the city. He was able, however, to **seize the** eldest son of the king of Edom, and **him he carried** with him into the city, and then burnt on **the wall, in** sight of the invading armies, as a burnt-offering to his **god. It** is from the prophet Amos that we learn that it was not **his own son** that he burnt, as has been usually thought, and as the passage might mean. The Edomites, with Israel and Judah, then withdrew from before the city, and returned to their own homes. The Edomites gained very little by this war, as during the next two centuries we usually find them subject to Moab.*

The Moabite Stone, a slab of basalt, now in Paris, contains a proclamation by Mesha, written in Hebrew but with Phenician characters, which declares that about this time Mesha conquered from the son of Omri the land between the town of Medeba and the River Arnon, and then dwelt in Dibon. But the authenticity of the Moabite stone is too doubtful for us to notice it otherwise than as a probable forgery of the third century.

Israel, during the reign of Jehoram, was reduced to a very low state. The kingdom was little more than the land of Ephraim and Manasseh, on the west of the Jordan. He had **lost the larger part of the** country on the east of the river. **The Syrians of Damascus** from the north had occupied all to the **north of Gilead. We** are not **told** that Jehoram had **made himself tributary to** Jehoshaphat, but it is impossible not to conjecture that **both he** and his father had done so, when we remember the help that Israel received from Judah during both their reigns, and that Jehoshaphat never took advantage of his neighbour's weakness to overrun the country. What remained to Jehoram of the former kingdom was sadly pressed by famine and the Syrians. Ben-hadad the Second again laid siege to the city of Samaria; and such

* **2 Kings iii.**; Amos ii. 1.

was the want of necessaries within the walls, that the very coarsest of food, such as the root of the herb dove's dung, was said to have been sold for almost its weight in silver. But out of this difficulty Jehoram was, in some strange way, unexpectedly relieved. We are not told of the battle in which the Syrians were routed and driven to retire from the siege, nor what forces they were that brought this deliverance to the besieged city. We only read of the plunder of the Syrian camp when it was learned that they had retreated northwards, and of the general belief that they had heard a noise in heaven of chariots and horses, and of a great army.* In our difficulty we are tempted to conjecture that the besieged city may have been relieved by the army of Jehoshaphat, and, indeed, that this may have been the battle fought against the Syrians in winter, on Mount Zalmon, in that neighbourhood, so poetically described in Psalm lxviii. 11-19, as a victory gained by the men of Judah.

That the people of Israel, under Ahab and Jehoram, were tributary to the king of Judah, or at least dependent on his good will, is further made probable by their consenting to receive his religion, together with his military aid. At this time, by the treaty with Jehoshaphat, the Hill country of Ephraim, that is, nearly all that remained to Jehoram of the revolting tribes, was in some degree brought back to the worship of Jehovah.† Though the queen-mother, the idolatrous and hated Jezebel, had still a large share of power in the kingdom, yet we have seen syllables borrowed from the name of Jehovah, in her two sons', or perhaps step-sons' names, and therefore can believe that some part of the north consented to receive the Levites as their priests. The Levites, it will be remembered, had been driven out of the northern kingdom by Jeroboam.

About this time, Ben-hadad II, king of Damascus, was murdered by Hazael, one of his servants, and Hazael succeeded in making himself king. His country was still at war with the kings of Israel and Judah. Israel had, it seems, still held against the Syrians the city of Ramoth in Gilead, and Jehoram had there been wounded, and had returned home to Jezreel to be healed, leaving his victorious army under the command of his captains. The Israelites had also, in the land of Manasseh, so far driven the Syrians back, that Israel now held the Hill country, as far as the valley of

* 2 Kings vi. 8—vii.   † 2 Chron. xix. 4.

Jezreel. While Jehoram remained wounded in the city of Jezreel, he was visited by his nephew Ahaziah, the young king of Judah. At that moment, while the two kings were together, Jehu, the son of Jehoshaphat, the son of Nimshi, one of the captains in command of the army in Gilead, raised the standard of rebellion, and proclaimed himself king of Israel. He crossed over the Jordan, and came upon the two kings in Jezreel, before they knew that they were in danger, and slew both Jehoram and Ahaziah when they came out of the city to meet him. He then entered the city, and slew queen Jezebel, Jehoram's mother, whose love of idolatry had done much to weaken her son's throne; and lastly, he sent to Samaria, and had every member of Ahab's family put to death; and he remained undisputed master of the northern kingdom. Jehoram had reigned eleven years.*

This violent revolution, which overthrew the family of Ahab in the northern kingdom, was a religious revolution, arising from the divided state of that nation. Jehu's name and his father's name Jehoshaphat, the son of Nimshi, tells us that he belonged to the Jehovistic party. On the other hand, Ahab's children, though they bore Jehovistic names, had probably taken them only for political reasons, when Ahab needed the help of Judah; and as Ahab's son Jehoram was governed by his Tyrian mother Jezebel, his friends were of the other party. Hence Jehu, coming upon Jehoram in Jezreel, at a distance from his friends in Ephraim and Manasseh, found less difficulty in overpowering him, and putting him to death. The young Ahaziah of Judah met with his death because he was on a visit to Jehoram.

JEHOSHAPHAT KING OF JUDAH ; B.C. 877—853.

We now return to where we left the history of Judah, thirty years earlier. Jehoshaphat, like his father, Asa, on coming to the throne, did what was pleasing to Jehovah, that is to the priests of Jehovah, but he did not obey their wishes so far as to forbid all sacrifice out of Jerusalem. The people still sacrificed and burned incense on the High Places in the other cities. He was the first successor of Solomon that made peace with the king of the revolted tribes. But, as we have seen, it was not quite on even terms; the king of Israel, more or less, owned himself a

* 2 Kings viii. ix. x.

vassal to his more powerful neighbour; **he** perhaps paid tribute **to** Judah; he certainly allowed **the** worship of Jehovah within his dominions, and in some degree re-established the Levites there.

The city-ditch, or valley on the east side of Jerusalem, has been named the Valley of Jehoshaphat.* This leads to **the** conjecture that Jehoshaphat strengthened the fortifications at the foot of the Temple, by deepening or widening **the** ditch, through which the brook Kidron flows.

Jehoshaphat's wars and doings in alliance with Israel have been already described. In the south he had at one time so far sway over Edom, **where he** had placed an officer to govern for him, that he attempted to revive Solomon's trade on the **Red Sea.** For that purpose, he built ships at Ezion-**geber.** But his ships were wrecked, and his purpose defeated. **Ahaziah, the** king of Israel, wished to be allowed to join him **in the** undertaking; but Jehoshaphat refused, and it was **never** again attempted. The wreck of Jehoshaphat's ships may have been caused by the Edomites who, in his reign or his son's, revolted from under the hand of Judah, and were never again brought into subjection.†

The modern Chronicler says that Jehoshaphat, in the **third** year of his reign, employed Levites to teach the Law through all the cities of Judah; and using words which belong to his **own** century, not to this, says that they taught the people out **of the** Book of **the** Law of Jehovah.‡ He also appointed some of the **Levites and** of the priests, jointly with the princes, to sit **as judges in** Jerusalem and the cities of Judah, **to** declare **the judgments** of Jehovah, and to decide in **all** civil and criminal **matters.** These judgments may have **been** those in Exodus xxi.—xxiii. afterwards added to the **volume.** Amariah was at this time chief priest, and he was perhaps **the** first who held the high rank which is claimed in Exodus xxviii.—xxix. for the eldest male descendant of Aaron. The Levites at this time were declared to be of a lower rank; they were to stand as officers **in the** presence of the priests.§

This is the **first time** in the history **that we** find the priests acting as judges since the days of Samuel. King David had sat as judge; his son Absalom had acted **as** judge; Solomon was famed for his wisdom as judge; **and** his royal throne

---

* Joel iii. 2. † 1 Kings xxii. 41-50.
‡ 2 Chron. xvii. 7-9. § 2 Chron. xix. 5-11.

was called the throne of judgment. But now jointly with
the princes, the chief of the fathers of Israel, the priests also
were judges, with a daily increasing power in civil matters.
This was naturally brought about by their education, and
also by the superstitious belief that they spoke in the name
of Jehovah. They spoke with an authority higher than that
of a judge, and could decide disputed cases without the help
of witnesses. A devout feeling made the nation reject the
notion that anything ever happened by chance, or that the
lot fell otherwise than as ordered by God. So, if a dispute arose, in which no evidence could be obtained, the two
parties came before the priest, who decided the question
by throwing lots. This was called bringing a cause before
God.* The religious trust which made both parties accept
such a decision is shown in the Proverbs—

> The lot is cast into the lap,
> But its whole deciding is from Jehovah (xvi. 33).

> Casting of lots causeth **contentions to cease** (xviii. 18).

The same religious trust, leading to the belief that nothing
ever happens by chance, may be the reason why the Hebrews
were not gamesters. Among all the vices which the prophets
blame, and against which the Proverbs give warning, we do
not read of gambling.

Jehoshaphat, as he grew old, four years before his death,
made his son Jehoram his partner on the throne. Jehoram
had married Athaliah, a daughter of Ahab, king of Israel, a
sister of Jehoram, afterwards king of Israel.† Jehoshaphat
died in the twenty-fifth year of his reign.

For the history of Jehoshaphat king of Judah, as also, we
must suppose, for the history of the kings of Israel who
reigned at **the** same time, we are indebted to the Book of
Jehu the **son of** Hanani.‡ This Jehu was a prophet of
Jehovah, in the **service of** the king of Judah. He may have
been one of the Levites placed in the northern kingdom
when they were re-established there by Jehoram, as he had
witnessed the posterity of Baasha overthrown there.§ If
so, this would explain the peculiarity of this half century,
namely, that we have the history of Israel written with far
greater detail than the history of Judah, and yet written in
a spirit friendly to Judah rather than to Israel.

* **Exod. xxii. 8, 9.**   † 2 Kings viii. 16-18.
‡ **2 Chron. xx. 34.**   § 1 Kings xvi. 1.

We have mentioned one of the most interesting of the Psalms, the 68th, as belonging to this time. The reader will observe that the battle there spoken of was fought on Mount Zalmon, near the city of Samaria, and in winter; and from the taunt against Mount Bashan, he will see that the enemies who were defeated were the Syrians of Damascus; and yet more exactly from the chariots of God fighting against the enemy, that it was the battle which relieved the city of Samaria from its state of siege when the Syrians were said to have been frightened by the noise of chariots in heaven; and from the hope that Ethiopia would stretch out hands to God, that it was written when Jehoshaphat **was** planning his voyage on the Red Sea. The enemy **to** be turned back at the depths of the sea may be the Edomites at Ezion-geber, and the Dogs, who are to have a **share of** the spoil, may be the Calebites of South Judah, whose name may be so translated. The bold figure of speech relating to the chariots in this poem was copied by the historian, and is thus in 2 Kings vii. 6, spoken of as a matter of fact. We add a portion of this beautiful Psalm:

The Lord gave the word,
Great was the company of those that brought the news;
[Saying] "Kings of armies have fled." They have fled;
And she that **tarried** at home is dividing the spoil.
Though ye [hills] be lying down among the cattle-stalls,
Ye were as the wings of a dove covered with silver,
And her feathers with yellow gold.
When the Almighty scattered kings **upon it,**
There was snow on Zalmon.
A hill of God is mount Bashan,
A hill with peaks is mount Bashan,
Why look ye enviously, ye hills with peaks,
At the hill which God desireth to dwell on?
Yea, Jehovah will dwell on it for ever,
The chariots **of** God were twenty thousand,
Even thousands of thousands;
The Lord was among them as on Sinai, at Kadesh.

＊   ＊   ＊   ＊   ＊

The Lord said, "I will turn them back at **Bashan,**
I will turn them back at the depths of the **sea,**
So that thy **foot** may be dipped in blood,
And the tongue of thy dogs have its share **of** thy foes."
They have seen thy train of walkers, **O** God,
The walkers of my God, my King, in the holy place.
The singers went before, the musicians followed;
Among them were the maidens striking timbrels.

The writer had perhaps read Jacob's blessing on his sons, in Genesis xlix., as he applies to Mount Zalmon in Ephraim the same figure of speech, for a cattle feeding district, that is there used for Mount Gilboa in Issachar, as lying down among the cattle-stalls.

From the lines quoted above from this Psalm, we are able to picture to ourselves the train of priests walking round the altar of Jerusalem with measured steps on the new moon days and solemn feasts, with musical instruments of various kinds, and accompanied by the singing men and singing women, chanting aloud the Psalms of David, while the crowd of people stood in the outer court around, separated from the priests by the cedar rails. A sacrifice on the altar had probably been performed before the Walkers were called in for their part of the ceremony.

But if we are right in placing this Psalm thus early, the mention of the wild beasts of the reeds, verse 30, if the Babylonians are thereby meant, must be a late addition to it; as up to this time the Jews had no dealings with Babylon.

To the eighty years **between** the time **of** Solomon and Jehoshaphat's death **we may** give the authorship of many large portions of the **Book of** Exodus. So large indeed are these additions that we may call this century the date of our present Book of Exodus, written by the help of the earlier narrative which we have spoken of in the time of Samuel, and to be afterwards enlarged by a few yet more modern additions. Chapters vii.-xi. contain the account of the **plagues** brought upon the Egyptians. They also contain **the request** made by Moses to Pharaoh that the Israelites might **make a** pilgrimage to the Mount of God in Horeb. They **tell** us that a pilgrimage from Egypt to the Holy Mount **was** already thought to be a religious duty among the Jews **in** Lower Egypt. Hence these chapters could not have been written until **after** chapters xix.-xx. were written, which describe the delivery of the Law, and give to that mountain its name of Mount of God.

In chap. xviii. Moses joins **with** himself rulers to help him, exactly as king Jehoshaphat appointed some of the rulers to assist the priests in their duty of deciding causes. **The** Judgments in Exodus xxi.-xxiii. 13, may be those according to which Jehoshaphat's priest Amariah decided **the** causes brought before him, when "he declared the judgments of Jehovah." Hitherto the judges had decided causes and punished crimes according to their own sense of what was right. We have heard of no laws to guide them. The Ten Commandments are rules to guide simply each man's own conscience; but these judgments are rules to guide the judge. Few and irregular as they are, they are interesting as the nation's first attempt to give to the judges' decisions the regularity which can alone make life and property secure. They are meant to soften the severity of an uncivilized age. If a Hebrew through poverty sells himself into bondage, he is to be released after six years' service. A thief found in the act of stealing, if in the day-time, may not be slain. For the most part justice was to be dealt out on the simple rule of an eye for an eye and a tooth for a tooth, a barbarous rule, but one which everybody could understand, and which was therefore the more likely to be accepted in the place of private revenge.

From Exod. xxiii. 20-33, we learn something of the subject Canaanites. There Jehovah promises to drive them out year by year, little by little; and the Israelites are ordered to break down their idolatrous images and at length to destroy them utterly. This is very unlike the treatment which these tribes received from David, who admitted them into his armies, or from Solomon, who made them bond-servants, while he allowed them their own religion. But from these words in Exod. xxiii., joined to what history tells, we trace the growth of the more priestly policy which now prevails. Under this treatment the Canaanites were more and more made to conform to the religious rites and usages of their better educated masters; and though they kept up their own places of sacrifice, idolatry was less practised. In matters of religion, if we may use a modern expression, their priestly rulers refused to them Toleration but offered them Comprehension, which they readily accepted. The two races, the conquering Israelites and the subject Canaanites, were thus becoming very much united into one nation, with no more difference between them than between the rich and the poor, the educated and the ignorant, the masters and the servants.

These chapters cannot have been written much earlier than this reign. They now, many of them, stand very in-conveniently between the Ten Commandments in chap. xx., the summons to Moses to come near and receive the Tables of stone in chap. xxiv. 12, and the delivering of the Tables to Moses in chap. xxxi. 18.

With these chapters, we may join the joyful song of

Moses in Exodus xv., which is very unlike the earlier
narrative, which makes the Israelites avoid the Philistines,
and turn back from the Edomites ; thus,

> The Peoples shall hear and tremble ;
> Sorrows shall take hold of the inhabitants of Philistia.
> Then the princes of Edom shall be amazed,
> The mighty men of Moab, trembling shall seize them.

But those chapters which give to Aaron and his sons a
high rank above the rest of the Levites, together with the
first part of Leviticus and Numbers, may have been written
a few years later.

JEHORAM KING OF JUDAH ; B.C. 856—849.
AHAZIAH KING OF JUDAH ; B.C. 849.
ATHALIAH QUEEN OF JUDAH ; B.C. 849—843.
JEHOASH KING OF JUDAH ; B.C. 843—804.

JEHORAM, the son of Jehoshaphat, was not contented with
his father's arrangements, and he began his reign by putting
to death his six brothers, whom Jehoshaphat had made in
some degree independent of him, by giving to each a fortified city in Judea for his residence. Such crimes were
unfortunately but too common ; David and Solomon had
both been guilty of such ; and this murder by king Jehoram
calls for no especial notice. Jehoram reigned for eight years
over Judah, four of which were during his father's lifetime.
Against him, the Edomites revolted ; and the kings of Judah
never again made themselves masters of that warlike,
unsettled people. At the same time Libnah revolted, and
the kings of Judah began to lose their hold upon the South
Country, around and to the south of Hebron, the land of the
Calebites. This was a district which, when Judah was
strong, belonged to the kings of Judah, and when Judah was
weak belonged to the Edomites.

We are not told the cause which made the town of Libnah
revolt ; perhaps it was in defence of one of the king's
brothers, to whom it may have been given by Jehoshaphat ;
but from what we shall afterwards meet with we may
suppose that it was part of the general discontent of the
country at being governed for the good of the capital,
including the discontent of the Levites of the villages at the
lordly conduct of the priests of Jerusalem. The disobedience
of Libnah did not continue long.

The Chronicler adds a yet more serious trouble to the
reign of Jehoram, namely that the Philistines and Arabians

so far defeated him that they plundered Jerusalem and slew all his sons except Jehoahaz, usually called Ahaziah, the youngest.*

Jehoram gave one of his daughters in marriage to the priest Jehoiada, whose after rise to the rank of chief priest may have been brought about by this union to the royal family. But such was now the importance of the family of the chief priest that the throne may have gained by the marriage as much strength as it gave.†

Ahaziah, the son of Jehoram and grandson of Jehoshaphat, then reigned for one year. His mother, Athaliah, was the daughter, or rather granddaughter, of Omri, king of Israel; and under her influence he joined his uncle Jehoram of Israel in his war against Hazael, king of Syria. The increasing power of Syria had healed the old jealousy between Judah and Israel. Ahaziah, like his father, was not so favourable to the priests as his grandfather, Jehoshaphat, had been. But the shortness of his reign made his opinions unimportant. He was killed, as we have seen, by Jehu, the grandson of Nimshi, at Jezreel, at the same time that Jehoram, king of Israel, was killed by that rebel.‡

When the news of king Ahaziah's death reached Jerusalem, his mother Athaliah seized the throne for herself. Neither Israel nor Judah had ever been governed by a woman since the establishment of the monarchy. But it does not appear that she was striving for any male in the family. She ordered all the royal family to be put to death, and she thought that her orders had been obeyed; but, as it was afterwards asserted, Jehoshebah, the sister of Ahaziah, and wife of one of the chief priests, succeeded in saving and hiding a child of one year old, one of Ahaziah's sons. Thus Jehu's successful violence, which in the northern kingdom overthrew Ahab's family, placed Ahab's daughter Athaliah on the throne of the southern kingdom. This double revolution placed the government of each kingdom for the time in the hands of the weaker party. Jehu in the north was a worshipper of Jehovah, and Athaliah in the south was unfriendly to that worship.

The usurping queen, Athaliah, was a native of Israel, and no friend to either priests or Levites. Mattan, the chief priest of Jerusalem during her reign, was after his death reproachfully called a priest of Baal, which may mean that

* 2 Chron. xxi.   † 2 Chron. xxii. 11.
‡ 2 Kings viii. 20—ix. 29.

9

he belonged to the northern kingdom, and was not a Levite. Under these circumstances the discontent throughout Judah must have been universal. While the whole weight of the Levites was against her, the more distant parts of the kingdom can have yielded no obedience to her orders. She was supported by a party that was opposed to the priests; and under such circumstances taxes would be badly paid, money would begin to fail in the treasury, and the power of the crown to grow weaker daily, until some one should arise bold enough to attempt its overthrow. During these years the holy vessels of the house of Jehovah seem to have been made use of by the queen, either for the support of her power, or of worship displeasing to the Levites.*

Queen Athaliah reigned in Jerusalem for six years, towards the end of which time a conspiracy was formed among the priests to dethrone her. Jehoiada the priest, the brother by marriage to the late king, gained the confidence of the royal body-guard, and after swearing them to secrecy in the Temple, brought out to them a boy of seven years old, who, he said, truly or falsely, was the son of their late king Ahaziah, and had been hidden by his aunt, Jehosheba, Jehoiada's wife, in one of the chambers adjoining the House of Jehovah. He arranged with them that, at the hour when the guard at the Temple was to be changed, the soldiers who were to quit should remain with those that then arrived, and that this double body of troops should proclaim the boy, whose name was Jehoash, as king.

They did so at the time appointed; and Queen Athaliah, who was brought into the Temple by the noise of the trumpets and the shouts, was led out between a file of soldiers, and slain as soon as she was beyond the walls of the Temple-yard. The young Jehoash was made to stand upon a pillar in the court of the Temple, in sight of the people, the crown was placed upon his head, and the Testimonials, or two stone Tables of the Law, were held up above him, while the priests anointed him as king. The conspiracy was wholly successful; Jehoash was made king; and as he was only seven years old, the sovereign power rested entirely in the hands of the high priest, Jehoiada. Mattan, the rival priest, was the only other person besides the queen who seems to have been put to death; and by way of justifying his death, he is described as a priest in the Temple of Baal.†

* 2 Chron. xxiv. 7.　　　　　† 2 Kings xi.

The coronation of the young JEHOASH is the only occasion in which the Tables of the Law are mentioned in the history since the Ark which contained them was first placed in the Holy of Holies by King Solomon.

King Jehoash did what was right in the sight of Jehovah all the days that he obeyed the instructions of his uncle Jehoiada the priest. Being a child, and placed upon the throne by him, he was, of course, entirely governed by him. Under the priest's orders, he levied a forced tax upon the people, in addition to the usual free-will offering, for the repair of the Temple. This was called a tax upon souls, or a poll-tax, and was probably at the rate of half a shekel a man, as ordered in Exodus xxx. 13, where it is described as a payment to make atonement for each man's sins. As it is not before mentioned in the history, we may suppose that it was a new tax. Jehoiada placed a chest by the side of the altar, and into that was put the money as it was brought into the House of Jehovah. Thus the whole country was taxed for the support of the priests and the sacrifices in Jerusalem. The Temple-service in the capital was considered of national importance; and indeed justly if the chief priest had the power to make atonement in the Holy of Holies for the sins of every man who sent up the half shekel.

The Book of Kings tells us that notwithstanding this supply of money, the repair of the Temple was not completed till after the twenty-third year of the king's reign. The priests had held it back for themselves, but in that year Jehoash felt strong enough to stop the abuse, and to require that the money should be spent upon repairing the Temple. But even when the repairs were finished, the priests did not then supply the Temple with the required gold and silver vessels. The Book of Chronicles, on the other hand, says that the surplus was used for the holy dishes, ladles, and vessels of gold and silver, such as are described in Numbers vii. From these contradictory accounts we learn that at least it ought to have been so employed. The money of the guilt-offerings, and of the sin-offerings, which are now mentioned for the first time, was not brought into the Temple, it was the property of the priests.

It is at this time, when the king was a child, and the power of the government, with the command of the troops, was in the hands of the priest, Jehoiada, that we must suppose that the tithe of the land's produce first fell into

9 *

the hands of the priesthood. During **the** seven years of
Athaliah's usurpation, there may have been no power strong
enough to collect this royal tax ; and now the king's power
had passed into the hands **of** the chief priest. This will
appear yet more probable when we show reasons for thinking that Leviticus i.—xi., and a large portion of the Book of
Numbers, including the laws relating to tithes, were written
at or soon after this time. But, great as was the power of
the priests of Jerusalem, they had not yet attempted the
policy **of** forbidding all sacrifices on the High Places in
favour **of** their own altar. That was not attempted until
about a century later.

In the twenty-third year of this reign the king of Israel,
Jehoahaz, the son of Jehu, in his distress besought the face
of Jehovah, that is, he sent to Jerusalem to beg for help
against the invading army **of** Syria. He no doubt sent
money to purchase that help, and Jehoash sent a force to
his relief.* That levy of troops **may** have had a double
effect ; it relieved Israel for a time **from** the oppression of
Syria, and it relieved Jehoash, king **of** Judah, from the
oppression of his own priests. A king **of** Judah had no
standing army ; he had not the means to support one. The
guards of his palace may not have been more numerous than
the guards of the Temple who were in the pay of the priests.
Hence when a gift from abroad, or the hope of plunder,
enabled him to call together an army, he was able to shake
off for a time the control of the priests and nobles, which he
usually had to yield to.

Jehoiada, the chief priest, died at a great age, and his
importance was shown by his being buried among the kings
of Judah. His **son**, Zechariah, succeeded him in the priesthood, and **perhaps** hoped to have the same power in the
state. But the **king was** now no longer a child, and he
wished to **be** independent, and to govern according to his
own judgment, **or perhaps** to be guided by the advice of his
princes rather **than by the** priests. His servants would not
listen to the remonstrances of tae high priest, Zechariah,
the son of Jehoiada. They conspired against him, and slew
him in the court of the Temple, by the command of the
king, who had forgotten the service done to him by the
father. Zechariah probably left no son, and the priesthood
may then have gone to a cousin, as he and his father are not

* 2 Kings xiii. 4, 5.

mentioned in the line of priests in **1 Chron.** vi., where they otherwise would have been, between Amariah and Hilkiah.

Jehoash was now independent of the priesthood, but he did not prosper after the death of his wise adviser. Hazael, king of Syria, after overrunning the kingdom of **Israel,** and taking the town of Gath, in the land of Dan, was **marching** upon Jerusalem. Jehoahaz, who was then king **of Israel,** could offer no resistance, and the kingdom of Judah seemed in danger. Jehoash, **in** his alarm, sent to offer a tribute **to** Hazael, to pay him **if** he would **return** home, or confine **his** ravages to the kingdom of Israel. **The terms** were accepted, and Jehoash sent **to him all the gold** and other treasures that **his** fathers had laid up in the palace and in the Temple. Satisfied with this **booty,** Hazael withdrew and left Jeru-**salem** unattacked.

After a long reign **of** thirty-seven or forty years, Jehoash **was slain** in Beth-millo, the castle near the north end of the **Temple** of Jerusalem, by conspirators of the priestly party **in** revenge for the blood of Jehoiada. **He** was succeeded **by** his son Amaziah, who may perhaps have been already **for** three years his father's partner on the throne.*

It would seem that this reign, when King Jehoash was **a** child, and the kingdom was governed in his name by **a** clever, bold priest, was the time **in which** the priesthood rose in Jerusalem to its greatest dignity. It then surrounded itself with all those circumstances of wealth and ceremony which we see **described in the Mosaic Law,** but which are wholly unknown in our history **until the time** of Solomon, and, indeed, only given to Solomon's reign by the partiality of the modern **writer** of the Book **of** Chronicles. To this reign, or a little later, **we must** give the authorship of a large number of passages in the Books of the Law ; beginning at Exodus xxv. The heave-offerings which the people are ordered to bring to Jehovah were the free-will gifts **by which** the Temple in Jerusalem was supported; and they **far sur-**pass in costliness any that can have been thought **of before** the time of Solomon. The shape of the Tabernacle **is copied** from Solomon's Temple, lessening its measurement **by one-**half. The description of the cherubs **over the ark is of** course borrowed from those made for Solomon.

Exodus xxx. 11-16, enacts that **the** heave-offering to the Temple shall be levied upon **the people as** a poll-tax of half a shekel on every male of **twenty years** old and upward.

* 2 Kings xii. ; 2 Chron. xxiv.

Before the time of the high priest Jehoiada, the heave-offering had been a free-will gift, as described in Exodus xxv. and xxxv. But, as the voluntary offerings were not sufficient for the needs of the Temple, recourse was now had to a forced tax. This was called the Atonement money, in return for which the chief priest made atonement for the nation's sins. Every man was to purchase this benefit at the price of half a shekel a year. Now, for the first time, the national standard weight is called the Holy Shekel, as the priests were the persons interested in receiving full payment. In the reign of David it had been called the King's Weight.*

Exodus xxvii. 20—xxix., with the costly garments for the chief priest, the ceremony of his consecration, the title of Sons of Aaron taken by the priests, and the higher rank given to the Sons of Aaron over the rest of the Levites, must be claimed for the time of the high priest Jehoiada.

Chapters xxxv. 4—xl., in which the Tabernacle is made, may be of the same date. Before this time we have only read of Aaron as the servant of Moses, and even as falling into idolatry and making a golden calf; but henceforth he is the head of the priesthood, and Moses is for the time forgotten. When the writer says that Moses made the laver, for the use of the priests of the Tabernacle in the desert, out of the copper mirrors of the women who crowded at the doorway of the Tent of Meeting, he seems to be blaming the luxurious habits of his own time.

The chief priest in Jerusalem, and his sons, styling themselves Sons of Aaron, declared that members of their family were the only priests, and that the rest of the Levites were the servants of the Sons of Aaron. The Sons of Aaron reserved to themselves the privilege of making atonement by burnt-offerings for the sins of the worshippers, an office which gave them ample sway over the minds of the people. But the chief priest alone had power to enter the Holy of Holies, and burn incense there before the Ark, and to come forth and tell the king, or the assembled congregation, that he had received a command from Jehovah, which he then delivered to them.

Among the longest of the passages inserted into the history of the march out of Egypt, are Leviticus i.—vii. These chapters offer to us a more systematic body of ceremonial laws than the other parts of the Pentateuch. They describe

* 2 Sam. xiv. 26.

the Burnt Offering, the Meal Offering, the Peace Offering, or love feast, the Sin Offering, the Guilt Offering, and the Consecration Offering. Thus the first attempt at giving to any laws the regularity of a code is in the case of those which regulate the gifts to the altar and the priests. Such a code of laws is never the lawgiver's creation. It is the result of his observation. He reduces into law usages which may have been of slow growth. He gives regularity to practices which may have been occasional, and he strengthens them or relaxes them as the case may be. The old customs relating to offerings and sacrifices had, no doubt, been enforced by the priests from time to time during the years which followed the building of the Temple; and now at length they are reduced into laws. Thus they are little connected with the history, not being written as the occasion required; and therefore they have few marks by which their date can be learnt. But they belong to the century now beginning, when the priesthood was at the height of its power. They cannot have been written before the days of Jehoiada, who introduced the poll-tax for the support of the Temple.

These laws, together with chapters viii.—x. on the consecration of priests, and xi. on clean and unclean animals, may be distinguished from the later parts of the book by having the commands for the most part addressed to Aaron and his sons, who hold the rank of priests, while the other Levites are their servants. They are also distinguished from the laws in Exodus by the new name for the free-will offering, which used to be called a heave-offering. But now that the heave-offering is made a forced poll-tax, the whole command to the people to bring up their pious offerings needs a new form. Hence a new command is put forth; and, in addition to the heave-offering, which is now a forced tax, they are exhorted to bring to the priests their free-will offering as a Corban, or *gift*. These gifts must therefore be rather more modern than Exodus xxxv. 4—xl., where the free-will offerings are called heave-offerings. Again, these chapters which describe Nadab and Abihu's death, show themselves older than the Books of Numbers and Joshua, as there Eleazer is Aaron's eldest son then living, and older than the prophet Amos, as they forbid leaven to be burnt with an offering to Jehovah; and older than Deuteronomy xii., where the various offerings are spoken of as having been already ordered. In chapter xi. the distinction is introduced between clean and unclean animals, both for food and for sacrifices, a distinction not attended to in the northern kingdom, where herds of swine were freely reared,* and where, at least, in a time of scarcity, asses' flesh was eaten by the poor.†

The tithes are not mentioned among the gifts and offerings in these, the early chapters of Leviticus. As yet they may have been considered as belonging to the king; and though at this time, in the weakness of the monarchy, if collected at all, they must have been collected by the priests, yet they may have been considered as a royal tax, as they were under Solomon.

We have before given the probable date of the original history of the March out of Egypt, under the leadership of Moses, and also of several additions which were made to that narrative. But now the narrative takes a new and more important form. By the addition of Jehovah's speeches addressed to Moses during the march, it becomes no longer the history of a journey, but a body of Jewish law. This important change, this creation, we may say, of the three middle books of the Pentateuch, seems to belong to the time of the high priest Jehoiada. They naturally, at some later time, received the Book of Genesis, with the history of the arrival in Egypt, as a suitable introduction, and from time to time during the two following centuries, a number of further speeches by Jehovah were added as the laws were called for. Then, when it was thought unbecoming to use the name of Jehovah so freely, we shall find the laws put into the mouth of Moses. These form the Fifth Book of the Pentateuch. At a later time was written the latter half of the Third Book. Thus though one part of this immortal work was written during the two centuries before this time, and other parts were added during the four centuries which follow, yet it may be said to have received its present religious character from the writer who, in the time of Jehoiada, first added to the history of the march out of Egypt, the national laws in the form of speeches spoken by Jehovah.

We have no reason to suppose that when the ceremonial laws were written, they were published to the people. When giving orders to the people, the priests would not wish to appeal to any book as an authority. They were themselves the only authority in matters of religion. They came forth out of the Temple saying that they had learnt the will of Jehovah from the space over the Cover of the Ark. A written law places a limit upon despotism ; and a

* Matt. viii. 30.   † 2 Kings vi. 25.

sacred book, when published, is a rival to the priesthood. The priests wrote these laws for their own guidance only.

If we could successfully disentangle the several parts of the Pentateuch, and give each to its own century, we **should** probably find that in the earlier account of the march out of Egypt and the delivery of the Law, the supremacy **of** Conscience was acknowledged more completely than in the present mixed writings. The God of Israel, when compared with the various gods of the Pagans, was He **who** speaks through the conscience, who puts a voice into every breast to say what is right and what is wrong in conduct, who said, as in Exod. xx., Thou shalt not steal, Thou shalt not speak falsely. But as **law-making** went forward the distinction between the **Moral Law and the** Civil Law got somewhat overlooked; and **when the** Judgments of Exodus xxi. were added **to** the Ten Commandments, the same divine sanction, which **had** been given to the Moral Law, was then given to the degrees of punishment proposed for a breach of that Law, and even for the amount of evidence required for guilt. But it was only when the power of the priests was at its height that Law and Morality were put so wholly on the same footing, that the voice of Jehovah was made use of to regulate the ceremonial of the altar, and to say what dresses should **be** worn by the priests of each rank. This confounding the eternal principles of right and wrong with the wise and even with the unwise enactments of the law-maker seems to have been the work of the priestly writers of this and the coming century, and sad would it have been for Hebrew literature if it had not soon afterwards called up the noble race of prophets to protest against it.

To the century and a half following this time, we must also give the authorship of a large part of the Book of Numbers, namely chapters i.—xxi., though we find scattered up and down these chapters a few passages already spoken of as belonging to the older narrative, and a few additions of **a** more modern date. Here the Israelites are described even on their flight out of Egypt, as a powerful and numerous body, possessed of ample wealth, and governed by an established order of priests. Thus in chapters i.—vi. the males of twenty years old and upwards are said to be six hundred thousand, a number which quite contradicts the older narrative, that they are unable to force a way through the scattered tribes of Edomites. This number is about one-half of that reported to David when he counted the people; and it may have been taken from that, in the same way that the measurements of the Tabernacle are half those of Solomon's Temple. That these high numbers are an afterthought and no part of the original narrative may be seen by their making the male Levites, who were all cousins and second cousins to Moses and Aaron, 22,000 in number (iii. 29).

Again, the description of manna in chap. xi. 4-15, as being ground in mills, or bruised in a mortar, before being cooked, contradicts Exodus xvi., where it is said to be so soft that it melts when the sun is hot. The author may have read Genesis vi. 1-8, as in chap. xiii. 33 he says that the sons of Anak were decended from the race of Giants, the offspring of the mixed marriages between the Sons of God and the Daughters of Men. He had also read Exodus xxxiv. 7, as in chap. xiv. he quotes a speech in which Jehovah is described as when forgiving iniquity not wholly acquitting, but visiting it on the children to the fourth generation. Chapter xv. makes a correction, or at least an addition, to the laws in Leviticus relating to the offerings ; and it orders that with every Gift to Jehovah of an animal for sacrifice, a suitable quantity of meal, of oil, and of wine, shall also be brought. In chapters xvi. xvii. the sacred rank of the Levites is asserted and is proved by miracles from heaven, when Dathan and Abiram, and their families, are swallowed up alive into the ground for having disputed it ; and Aaron's staff, the staff of the house of Levi, bears blossoms. In chapter xviii. the tithe is mentioned for the first time as a priestly tax. In that chapter, written later than Leviticus i.—xi., the tithe of the land's produce is **mentioned** as belonging to the Levites, and the Levites are ordered to give a tithe of the tithe to the priests. The tithes had been a royal tax, as we learned from 1 Sam. viii. 15-17, and they would seem to have passed for a time into the hands of the priests upon the decay of the king's power, when the Levites were the only body able to collect such a tax. That portion of the Book of Numbers of which we are now speaking, ends perhaps with chapter xxi.

These portions of Leviticus and Numbers introduce us to an organized moral code of sins and forms of guilt which are to be atoned for by offerings brought to the priest. Here we find ordered the manner and the occasion for bringing the Meal Offering, the Peace Offering, which is to be eaten as a love-feast, the Consecration Offering, when a priest is consecrated, the Sin Offering, and the Trespass or Guilt Offering, for sins of various kinds, and the Burnt Offering, to be wholly burnt. The several feasts, that of the Passover or Unleavened Bread at the barley harvest, the Pentecost at the wheat harvest, and the Blowing of Trumpets and Feast of Tabernacles in the autumn, together with the Fast-day between the last two, are ordered to be kept with due regularity. The law of vows explains how and when these must be kept, and when they need not be kept, and it regulates the Vow of the Nazarite.

The ceremonial laws, while attempting to regulate the religious practices then thought useful, show a strong priestly wish to bring the people into a state of ignorant obedience to their religious leaders. These books contain no advice that men should offer either prayer or praise to their Maker in any form but that of a holy gift to the priests. Even the moral laws are often directed to the same selfish end ; and there were few crimes from which a man might not fancy himself relieved by an offering to the priest and the altar. Every sin committed by a bad man, every blessing from God on a good man, was to bring some profit to the priests. Every ceremonial law, by the possible breach of it, introduced a new sin, with further profit to the priests ; for as the Apostle Paul remarks, without the law there would not have been the sin. Even a yet more refined and entangling sin was invented, as it would seem, on purpose to be atoned for by an offering brought to the priests. This was the Error or Sin of Ignorance of Leviticus iv., v., and Numb. xv. 22-31, which a person might fall into either by doing something unawares, or by doing it in ignorance of its being wrong. When after the deed he became aware of the sin, he then had to cleanse himself from it by his Sin Offering : as if a man could defile his conscience, as he may at any moment defile his skin, without knowing it, and then be able to purify his conscience as he purifies his skin, by washing. If he had sinned in ignorance, in the matter of holy things, then a Sin Offering will not be enough, but he shall cleanse himself with a Guilt Offering. This creation of an artificial sin often brought real sin with it. Instead of its introducing a stricter moral law, it tended to break down the distinction between right and wrong, between innocence and sin. A man who had really done wrong was led to excuse himself by pleading that it was a sin of ignorance. Thus at a yet later time it became necessary to make a new prohibition not to commit the real sin of making false excuses; "Say not before the preacher that it was a sin of ignorance," says Ecclesiastes v. 6.

The right understanding of the religion of Israel, and of the progress of that religion, very much depends upon our giving a correct date to the ceremonial laws which we have been describing. We give this date to them because, first, they seem to have been unknown to Samuel, David, and Solomon; and secondly, because, from numerous hints in Deuteronomy, and the prophets who slight these laws, and in Ezekiel, where they are highly valued, we judge that they were written before the reign of Hezekiah.

JEHU KING OF ISRAEL; B.C. 849—822.
JEHOAHAZ KING OF ISRAEL; B.C. 821—805.
JEHOASH KING OF ISRAEL; B.C. 807—792.
JEROBOAM II. KING OF ISRAEL; B.C. 804—764.
ZACHARIAH KING OF ISRAEL; B.C. 764.

We now return **to the** kingdom of Israel. Of the reigns of Jehu the grandson of Nimshi, and of his descendants to the fourth degree **who ruled** over Israel for eighty years, the historians have given us very few particulars. Jehu had been the captain of such forces as had remained to the king of Israel on the east side of the Jordan. He was a wicked bold man, and had been unable to resist the temptation, when he saw the path to a throne open to him. The idolatries of queen Jezebel, the wife of Ahab, and queen-mother to the **two next** kings, had made rebellion easy. The city of **Jezreel,** where king Jehoram was then living, was within the tribe of Issachar, among a people not wholly friendly to Ephraim; **and** there Jehu might hope to find supporters. He **accordingly** declared himself the friend of Jehovah's people. **After** killing king Jehoram, and queen Jezebel his mother, **at the town** of Jezreel, where they then were, and slaying all the king's family in the town of Samaria, he slaughtered the priests of Baal, having called them together into the house of Baal, which Ahab had lately built for them. This was probably on the hill near the town of Shechem, which town the historian may mean by "the city of the house of Baal." He then destroyed the idols and the building, and it was never again restored. Jehu, we are **told,** continued in the sins of Jeroboam, as to the golden **calves** at Beth-el and Dan. But these calves had probably **long** since been destroyed. If not, Jehu would have de-

stroyed them with the other idols. That reproach only
means that when he destroyed the idols of Baal, he did not
give to the Levites the power which they wished for. His
kingdom was in the greatest distress. Hazael, king of
Syria, overran it in his attack upon Jerusalem, and laid it
waste down to Gath, in the southern land of Dan, and
moreover soon held the whole of the country to the east
of the Jordan, down to the river Arnon, the boundary of
Moab.*

It was near the end of Jehu's reign that Dido, the great
niece of queen Jezebel, whom Jehu had slain, fled from
Tyre, and put herself at the head of a body of Tyrian
colonists who founded Carthage, on the Lybian coast,† in
the country called Phut by Jeremiah and Ezekiel. This
event connects the history of Israel, in a very interesting
manner, with the early history of Greece and Rome.

Jehu, with all his crimes, had shown ample zeal for the
name of Jehovah, and he gave to his son and successor a
Jehovistic name; hence to this time we may give the few
words in Genesis xii. 7, which say that Abram set up an
altar to Jehovah near the town of Shechem. These words
may have been introduced into the Life of Abraham to give
sanctity to an altar which had been built on a hill near that
town; and perhaps the building of the altar and the above
words may both belong to this time. Neither can the altar
itself have been built, nor these words about it have been
written, under a king of Judah, because the priests at
Jerusalem allowed no altar to Jehovah but their own. Nor
can they have belonged to a much earlier time, because
Jehovistic names have been only lately met with on the
throne of Israel. Again, as to which of the two hills this
altar was built on, it is not likely that such an altar to
Jehovah should be built on a hill already dedicated to Baal;
therefore, of the two hills between which the town of
Shechem stood, we must suppose that the altar to Jehovah
was on Mount Gerizim. The altar to El, spoken of in the
life of Jacob, was probably the same as that to Baal, since
in the northern kingdom God was worshipped under both
those names. It must have existed from the time of
Abimelech; and when it went to decay, gave to the hill on
which it stood the name of Ebal, the Baal-ruins. We shall
have occasion more than once to speak of these two hills
and their altars.

* 2 Kings x. xii.   † Josephus, Apion, I. 18.

The above remarks will fix the date of a part of Judges
vi. There Gideon, who may be known to have worshipped
God under the name of Baal, because he was named
Jerubbaal, is described as destroying the altar of Baal, and
as building one to Jehovah, at Ophrah. This can hardly
have been written before Jehu destroyed the altar **to** Baal,
at Shechem.

We may here also mention two other Jehovistic additions
of very uncertain date, made to the **life** of Noah. The
Elohistic writer had said that God commanded **Noah to** take
with him into the Ark two of every living creature, **in** order
to keep the race alive. But the later writer, in **vii.** 1-5.
adds that Jehovah ordered him to take in with him seven
of every clean animal; and in **viii.** 20-22, he says that Noah
sacrificed some of these clean animals on the altar to Jehovah,
an act which would have destroyed the race, if he had not
saved more than a pair of each. The distinction between
clean and unclean animals which is **here** introduced, proves
the modern date of the passage, **and** agrees with its Jehovistic character.

In the reign of JEHOHAZ, **Jehu's son, Israel** again suffered
from the Syrian inroads, under **Hazael,** and then under
Ben-hadad the Third, the son of **Hazael.** Jehoahaz in his
distress called upon Jehovah; that is, he applied to Jehoash
king of Judah for help. He gave to his son the name of
Jehoash, in compliment to the king of Judah, and no doubt
paid a tribute to Judah; and with Judah's help, before the
end of his reign, he defeated the Syrians and gained a little
relief.*

JEHOASH, Jehu's grandson, the next king of Israel, was
even able to recover some little of the territory from Ben-
hadad the Third, the son of Hazael, the new king of Syria.
He defeated him three times in battle, recovering the cities
which his father **had** lost.† Such indeed was the recovery
of Israel, **from the low** state to which the rebel Jehu had
brought it, that **Jehoash** then renewed the war with Judah
after a peace of half **a** century. From this we learn that
Jehoash was not now governing **his** kingdom with the help
of the party to which his grandfather Jehu belonged. He
had, as was natural, fallen in with the wishes of the majority,
the stronger party in the state; and the strength gained
thereby urged him to this war against Judah. Accordingly,
he did not **give to** his son a Jehovistic name. Jehoash

* **2 Kings** xiii. 5.   † 2 Kings xiii. 25.

marched against Jerusalem, and defeated Amaziah in battle and took him prisoner. He entered and plundered the city and the Temple, and took hostages for peace on releasing the captured king, and he returned home, after breaking down the wall for the length of four hundred cubits, between the gate of Ephraim at the northern side of the city and the Corner Gate which was near to the Temple.* Jehoash was succeeded by his son Jeroboam.

JEROBOAM II, the next king of Israel, was yet more successful than his father. He wisely made peace with Judah; and when the two halves of the nation were not at war with one another, they were usually both prosperous. This peace gave Jeroboam leisure to free his kingdom from the Syrians; and he regained the whole of his northern territory to the south of Hamath and Damascus, and was king over all the land of Israel on both sides of the Jordan. That portion of the land of Hamath which Jeroboam recovered was called Hamath of Judah. This may perhaps be explained by the migration of a body from Judah to settle in that spot, perhaps the migratiom mentioned in Judges iii. 9. The southern historian says that Jeroboam continued in all the sins of the former Jeroboam the son of Nebat; but he lets us understand that the northern kingdom was never so prosperous as during this long reign of forty-one years.† Jeroboam had lived at peace with Judah without being tributary to it. His independence is shown by his not having a Jehovistic name.

The Chronicles tell us of a register of all the families on the east of the Jordan, made in this reign; when the males of a military age, belonging to the three eastern tribes, were found to be forty-four thousand seven hundred and sixty.‡ If we multiply this by five and a half, to obtain the number of souls of both sexes, and again by five, as those tribes may be supposed to be about one-fifth of the whole, we should obtain about a million and a quarter for the population of the two kingdoms. This is quite as large a population as the country is likely to have held at this time.

ZACHARIAH, the son of Jeroboam, was murdered by Shallum, after a reign of six months.§ With him the family of Jehu came to an end. Such are the annals of the kings of Israel during a space of eighty-five years. That these kings had for the most part given their support to the

---

* 2 Kings xiv. 8-14. † 2 Kings xiv. 23-29.
‡ 1 Chron. v. 17, 18. § 2 Kings xv. 8-10.

worship of Jehovah, may be supposed from their bearing names containing the syllable Jah.

In the reign of Jeroboam II the prophet Jonah, the son of Amittai, lived. He was a worshipper of Jehovah, and a native of the town of Gath-hepher in the land of Zebulun.* It is as well to remark here that our present Book of Jonah was not written till perhaps four centuries later.

During the forty years before Jehu's family gained the throne of Israel, the history of the two kingdoms seems to have been found for the most part in the northern writers; but during the eighty-five years that Jehu's family held possession, the northern annals have been very scanty. But in place of any information about the kingdom, we find scattered among the few facts mentioned an account of the lives of two prophets, Elijah and his successor Elisha, full of improbable events, and probably of a very modern age.

AMAZIAH KING OF JUDAH; 806—778.

JEHOASH the late **king of Judah had been** put to death by conspirators of the priestly party; **and** his son Amaziah began his reign by putting to death his father's murderers; and the historian mentions as a proof of the humanity of the age that the children of the murderers were spared. He attacked the Edomites and took the city of Petra, a place so strong by nature, that on being taken it got the name of Joktheel, or *captured by God*. Before this attack upon Edom he had hired a large army from the northern tribes to help **him.** But, upon the advice of one of his prophets, he sent **them back,** and went to the attack and plunder of Edom **without them.** The Israelite soldiers in disappointment **overran** and plundered the cities of Judah on their way home. This led **to** a quarrel with Jehoash, and then began again the **war with** Israel, which had ceased for the last half century. **During part of** this time Israel had probably bought the truce by **a tribute.** But Jehoash had defeated the Syrians and regained strength, and now thought it his turn to gain the mastery over Judah. Amaziah met him in battle at Beth-shemesh, situated between Judah and Dan, but was wholly defeated and taken prisoner. The conqueror, with **more** humanity than usual, did not put him to death, but contented himself with breaking down four hundred cubits **of** the wall of Jerusalem, between the Gate of Ephraim and

* 2 Kings xiv. 25.

the Corner Gate, with carrying off the treasures of the palace and the Temple, and with taking hostages from Amaziah for his future submission, making Judah for the moment tributary to Israel.

Such was at this time the rank of the chief priest that there was no family more suitable than his from which the heir to the throne could take a wife; and Amaziah married his son Uzziah to the daughter of the chief priest Zadok.* But even this did not allow Amaziah to act independently of the priesthood. He gave them some offence; and on a conspiracy being formed against him in Jerusalem, he fled to Lachish, where he was overtaken and put to death, because he turned aside from following Jehovah; that is because he was not obedient to the priests.† Thus, if we may trust the Chronicles, not only queen Athaliah but Jehoash and Amaziah, three sovereigns in succession, were put to death for opposing the will of the priests.

AZARIAH OR UZZIAH KING OF JUDAH; B.C. 801 OR 778—750.

The contradictory dates given in the Book of Kings for these reigns make it necessary to suppose that Uzziah, before he was made king, had in name reigned twenty-three years jointly with his father; and this is made probable by finding fifty-two years given to his reign. He was at first guided by the advice of the prophet Zechariah, and during that time he prospered in his undertakings. He was at peace with Jeroboam king of Israel, and thus at leisure to check disobedience at home, and inroads from neighbours on the south, while Jeroboam stood between him and all other unfriendly neighbours. He defeated the Philistines and destroyed the fortifications of Gath, and Jabneh, and Ashdod. He routed the Arabs and Maonites in the south. He strengthened the walls of Jerusalem by towers at the Valley Gate, at the Corner Gate, and at the Turning of the Wall. These last two were probably at the two ends of the east side of the Temple. In these towers he placed engines of war to throw stones and arrows, engines before unknown in Jerusalem.

In the reign of Uzziah's father the city of Jerusalem had been entered by the enemy, and its outer northern wall had been broken down. Hence Uzziah's attention to the fortifications was quite natural. They were further strengthened

* 2 Kings xv. 33.   † 2 Kings xiv.; 2 Chron. xxv.

10

by his son Jotham, **and again** by Manasseh; but many of the large stones which **are** yet admired for their size were no doubt laid in the reign of Uzziah.

Uzziah paid great attention to the cultivation of **the** crown lands and **to** his herds of cattle, which **were an** important source of **revenue.** He had **ploughmen and** vine-dressers in the mountains and in Carmel; and in the desert he dug wells for his cattle, and built towers for the herdsmen who had the charge of them. **He** had also other herds **of** cattle in the Low country and **on the** Table land. Perhaps the account of the crown lands, of the store-houses **for** their produce, and of herds of cattle, in 1 Chron. xxvii., **which** the writer gives to David's troubled reign, belongs **to this** quiet time. So large a part of the country was uninclosed that **a** great source **of wealth** was always open to **any king** who, like Uzziah, should turn his attention to **husbandry.** The **other** landowners were, no doubt, doing the **same. The** wealth **of the country** was greater than at any **former** time. **The arts of production** must **have** been much improved since **Solomon's peaceable and** prosperous reign; and now that **they were not checked by** foolish wars they bore full fruit.

But Uzziah, strong as he was, was not strong enough to quarrel with the priesthood. He rashly chose to act as priest himself, as Saul, David and Solomon had done; and he presumed to burn incense within the House of Jehovah. This **was** an attempt to overthrow the power which the priests had been for two centuries building up against the throne. Thereupon the chief priest Azariah collected a body **of** eighty priests, and went in after him, and had him seized and put in confinement as a leper for the rest of his life. The king was, perhaps, in part bald, he may have lost some of the hair off his forehead, enough to give a cloak to the priest's assertion. **The** priest, as we see in Leviticus xiii., a chapter written about this **time,** had the sole power of declaring who was **a** leper; **and in the** exercise of this arbitrary power Azariah dethroned **the king** and put him in a leper-house. His son Jotham was then **allowed** to dwell in the palace and to sit as judge till his father's death, when he succeeded him. But the priests were again lords over the throne of Jerusalem. For the history of Uzziah's reign the Chronicler quotes the writings of the prophet Isaiah.* This portion of the prophet's writings is now lost.

* 2 Kings xv. 1-7; 2 Chron. xxvi.

To the reign of Uzziah we may give Leviticus **xii.—xv.** These chapters contain the law of leprosy, and authorize the priests to put a leper into solitary confinement. This may have been written to justify the deposition **of the** king by the chief priest. These chapters show how low was the state of physical science in the nation. They altogether overlook the art of healing, which **the** priests treated as irreligious, and as an attempt to oppose the will **of Jehovah.***

The law in chapter **xiv.** about the damp **on** the **plastered** walls of a house **built of rough stones, there called the** leprosy in **a house, reminds us that** such **houses were not** in very general **use, though now** becoming less uncommon. In the cities the wealthy had houses, but many of the people dwelt wholly in tents made of skins, or in booths made of branches of trees; and when we read of the Israelites refusing **to** fight and fleeing to their tents, it means that they left **the** camp and withdrew each man to his own place of abode.

SHALLUM KING OF ISRAEL; B.C. 763.

On the murder of Zechariah, the son of Jeroboam II, Shallum seized the throne of Israel for himself. He reigned, however, only one month, when he was slain in the city of Samaria by Menahem, who had raised **a** body of followers at Tirzah, the former capital. Menahem made himself king of the unhappy, distracted kingdom **of** Israel. Usurper succeeded usurper, each preparing **the northern** kingdom for its final overthrow.†

MENAHEM KING OF ISRAEL; B.C. 763—753.

The death of three kings within seven months, of whom the last two were murdered, brought the kingdom of Israel to the very brink **of ruin.** Menahem, who slew Shallum, **the last** of **the** three, **did not** gain a quiet throne. In Tirzah he was king, but before he was obeyed he **had** to treat the neighbourhood with all the inhumanity with **which** he would have treated a foreign country. With his accession the peace **between** Israel **and** Judah **came to an end,** and the priests of Jehovah were no longer **welcome** in the northern kingdom. The writer of Zechariah **xi. then** returned to the south, at the same time breaking **his** staff in token of the brotherhood of Israel and Judah being broken.

* 2 **Chron.** xvi. 12. † 2 Kings xv. 10-15.

In Menahem's reign came a new trouble over the land, from a nation that we have not before heard of. The Assyrians, whose capital city Nineveh lay on the east bank of the Tigris, in the fork between that river and the Great Zab, had latterly become a powerful monarchy. Their kings held sway over all the country watered by the Tigris and Euphrates, to the south of their capital. Their massive palaces prove their wealth; while the sculpture and the writing on the walls show the civilization of the people. The Assyrian language was allied to that of Israel. Assyria as a kingdom was second only to Egypt. Pul, the king, had lately conquered Syria of the Rivers, or at least a large part of it. He had then overrun Cœle-Syria, and was now entering on the land of Israel. But he retired on Menahem offering to give him in silver the booty that he hoped to gain by fighting. Menahem gave him a large sum, said to be one thousand kikars' weight, which would amount to the improbable value of half-a-million sterling. In order to raise this sum he made every man of wealth pay him fifty shekels, or five pounds sterling. This is a credible sum, but it quite contradicts the former. The king of Assyria returned home with his booty, and with a knowledge that at a future time more might be obtained in the same manner.

Pul also was probably the Assyrian king who about this time conquered Chaldea.* If, according to the Assyrian custom, he removed the unhappy people from that fertile country, in the neighbourhood of Armenia, and placed them at the southern end of his kingdom, at the head of the Persian Gulf, to cultivate that barren district bordering on the Arabian desert, it will explain how Chaldees are afterwards to be met with so far to the south of Chaldea.† There we find them two centuries later as a seafaring race, glad to be released from the Babylonian rule, even at a time when a Chaldee family was seated on the throne of Babylon.‡

Menahem helped to ruin the kingdom of Israel by the way that he gained his throne, and by the way that he kept it, but he reigned for ten years, and was succeeded by his son Pekahiah.§

We now enter upon the earliest of those valuable writings, the Books of the Hebrew Prophets. Isaiah was born in the reign of Uzziah, but his writings belong to a later time.

* Isaiah xxiii. 13.   † Strabo xii. iii. 28, and 2 Kings xxv.
‡ Isaiah xliii. 14.   § 2 Kings xv. 16-22.

We have, however, a fragment of another prophet, which seems to belong to this time. It has been joined by an injudicious editor to the writings of Zechariah, the son of Berechiah, who lived three hundred years later, in the reign of Darius. It is called chapter xi. of that author. In the Gospel of Matthew it is quoted as the work of Jeremiah, to whom we can by no means give it.* It may be claimed for this time by its mention of the breaking off of the treaty between Israel and Judah, which had lasted during the reign of Jeroboam, and it may possibly be the work of Uzziah's wise adviser Zechariah, who had understanding in the visions of God.

It begins as an oration, and ironically as if welcoming the northern invaders: "Open thy doors, O Lebanon, that the fire may devour thy cedars." But it soon turns to narrative: "There is a sound of the howling of the shepherds, for their glory is spoiled; a sound of the roaring of young lions [the Assyrians], for the pride of the Jordan is laid waste." The three shepherds, or kings, cut off in one month, are Jeroboam II, Zachariah, and Shallum. The wicked shepherd who succeeds them is Menahem; and the young lions who overrun both Mount Lebanon and Mount Bashan, are the Assyrians, who in his reign conquered Syria, and Israel on both sides of the Jordan. The prophet speaks as if he had at one time lived in the service of the king of Israel, perhaps Jeroboam, and on that king's death, and the war breaking out between Israel and Judah, had claimed his hire, and withdrawn into the latter country on the death of Jeroboam. He breaks two staves, one figurative of the peace between the two kingdoms, and the other figurative of Jehovah's covenant with them, which was broken in the north by the dismissal of Jehovah's priests, and in the south perhaps by Uzziah's conduct in claiming the right to enter the Holy of Holies.

This fragment, bearing the name of Zechariah, does not rise to the high flight of eloquence that is reached by some of his immediate successors; but it is interesting as being the oldest that we now possess and can give a date to.

PEKAHIAH KING OF ISRAEL; B.C. 752—751.
PEKAH KING OF ISRAEL; B.C. 750—731.

Pekahiah, the son of Menahem, reigned over Israel for two

* Matth. xxvii. 9.

years, when he was dethroned by Pekah, one of his captains, who slew him in the city of Samaria, and then reigned in his stead. Pekah's force, by which he gained the throne, was a body of fifty men of Gilead; hence it would seem that, like the former usurper Jehu, he had been in command of the troops on the east side of the Jordan.

The kingdom of Israel, on the accession of the usurper Pekah, was reduced to a very low ebb, not so much by loss of territory as by its internal weakness and disordered state. We learn from the prophet Amos,* however, that it held sway over Beth-el, and perhaps Gilgal in Benjamin, two towns which were on the route from Samaria to the southern ford of the Jordan, and were thus important to the northern king, as long as he had any subjects on the east side of the river. He still held part of Gilead. Beth-el, moreover, was the religious capital for those who worshipped Jehovah in the southern part of the northern kingdom.

Pekah, in the tenth year of his reign, most unwisely formed an alliance with Rezin, king of Syria, for the invasion of Judah. The kingdom of Israel had been at peace with Judah for fifty years, at first while rising in prosperity under **Jeroboam II,** and then while going to ruin under Menahem. **The two** kingdoms had once before been at peace for sixty years; and peace with Judah was now more necessary than ever to Israel, in consequence of the growing powers of its northern neighbours. But Pekah madly proposed to Rezin, king of Syria, to join him in a wanton and unnecessary war, to attempt the overthrow of Ahaz, king of Judah, and to place a creature of their own on the throne at Jerusalem.† The Syrians, however, did as much harm to Israel their friends, as to Judah their enemies. They marched on the east side of the Jordan; and while they drove Judah out of Elath on the Red Sea, they trod down poor Gilead as a threshing-floor.

This invasion of Judah by the Syrians was soon stopped by the Assyrians, who, as might have been expected, came down upon Syria and Israel for plunder. This was under Pul's successor, Tiglath-pileser, who was called in by Judah. The Assyrians, after taking Damascus, which was a convenient resting-place for their soldiers, conquered all Naphtali and Galilee, that is to say, all the land to the north of Manasseh. Tiglath-pileser carried off the people, or such of them as he thought would be useful to him, and placed

* Amos iv. 4.   † Isaiah vii. 6.

them as colonists and slaves in some districts of Assyria where skilled labourers were wanted. He also overran the land of Gilead; and many of the Israelites on the east side of the Jordan, who were yet more open to the attack, were carried off at the same time.* This is the first of the two captivities that came upon the northern kingdom of Israel. The prophet Amos describes the tribes of Ephraim and Manasseh, with those in Gilead who were left behind, as the two legs of a sheep and the piece of an ear, saved out of the lion's mouth.†

At this early stage of the world's progress towards civilization, History had not yet taught by examples, nor had Foreign Travel gleaned facts upon which to reason. But we can now see the mistake made by Israel and Judah in regard to Assyria. Had they known, first, the vast power of the Assyrians, and the cruelty with which they treated those whom they conquered; and secondly, that the place in which the advance of the Assyrians could be most easily checked was at the passage from the valley of the Orontes to Damascus, they would have united their forces to defend the Syrians, and would have known that, as soon as the Assyrians had gained Damascus, Israel and Judah were both at their mercy.

In the twentieth year of his reign, Pekah met with the fate of so many of his predecessors. He was slain by Hoshea, who seized the throne of Israel for himself.‡

We may here conjecturally mention Gen. xix. 29-38, a few verses written in reproach of the Moabites and Ammonites. They are Elohistic, and by a northern writer. They belong to a time when the northern Israelites were weak enough to be sorely vexed on their eastern boundary by those little neighbouring tribes, and wished to revenge by the pen injuries which they had suffered from the sword. They were written before Israel finally fell under the Assyrians, at least before Psalm lxxxiii. was written, as they are there referred to. We may remark that the art of writing must have been possessed by very few, for such a worthless piece to have been preserved to the time when the books were collected after the captivity.

JOTHAM KING OF JUDAH; B.C. 749—734.
AHAZ KING OF JUDAH; B.C. 741—726.

Jotham began to reign over Judah in the second year

* 1 Chron. v. 26.   † Amos iii. 12.   ‡ 2 Kings xv. 23-31.

of Pekah's reign over Israel, after having governed the
kingdom for several years during his father's confinement
as a leper.   His mother was the daughter of Zadok, probably
the chief priest, and he governed agreeably to the wishes of
the priesthood.   Under him the kingdom continued to be
prosperous.   He was careful not to copy his father Uzziah
in entering the House of Jehovah.   He built for the Temple-
yard a new gate called the Upper Gate.   And he added to
the wall near Ophel the suburb to Jerusalem, at the south
end of the Temple and on the east side of Zion.   He did
much to strengthen the whole country by building cities on
the hills, or rather putting walls to the hill-top villages, and
by putting castles or towers to the thicket-camps in which
the country people often dwelt.   He fought successfully
against the Children of Ammon, and he made them pay him
for three years together a large tribute in silver, wheat, and
barley; greediness for booty was the cause of this war, as
of almost all the wars.*

The kingdom of Judah had now been at peace with that
of Israel for fifty years.   The wealth of Jerusalem was
greater than at any former time, and so unhappily was its
luxury.   The country was full of silver and gold, says
Isaiah, there was no end of treasures.   The country was
full of horses, there was no end of chariots.   And pride
rose with wealth.   The new fashioned dresses and costly
ornaments worn by the women of Jerusalem were proofs
how steadily wealth had increased during these years of
peace.   But the wealth did not fall to the share of all alike.
The poor in their ignorance sold themselves to the rich;
they then felt crushed and plundered, while the nobles
rioted in ease.   We remark upon the nation's prosperity at
this time, because it was soon to receive a check.   Jotham's
kingdom was not half the size of Solomon's, but its wealth
was far greater.   The united Hebrew nation was at its
highest state under Solomon; but the southern half reached
to its greatest prosperity under Jotham.

A time of wealth is naturally a time when the ceremonies
of the Temple service were carried on with the greatest
splendour, for priestly ritualism is a costly luxury.   Isaiah's
indignation was moved at the wasteful sacrifices, and burnt-
offerings of rams, and of the fat of fed beasts, the blood of
bullocks, lambs, and he-goats.   The meal-offerings seemed
vanity to him, the incense an abomination.   The attention

* 2 Kings xv.; 2 Chron. xxvii.

to the new-moon days, the sabbaths, the convocations, the days of restraint from work, and the appointed feasts, all added to the importance of the priests, but were very little helpful to religion. The moral law was neglected while the Levitical law received full attention.*

Jotham in the ninth year of his reign made his son **Ahaz** his partner on the throne.† His prosperity was soon **after**-wards threatened **by an invasion** of the Syrians united **with** northern Israel. **In order to defeat this** danger he bou**ght** the help of the **Assyrians; and** not seeing that they came rather as his **masters than** as **his** servants, he thereby **for a** moment seemed yet **more prosperous**.

Jotham's name is **shortened** from Jehotham, *upright in the sight* **of Jehovah,** and Psalm xviii. **seems to** have been written, **as if to be spoken** by him, thus :—

> 23. I have also been *upright* before him,
>   And have kept myself from mine iniquity.
> **25.** With the merciful Thou showest thyself merciful ;
>   With the *upright man* Thou showest thyself upright.

This is a Psalm of thanksgiving for deliverance from enemies, perhaps the Syrians and northern Israel ; and the Assyrians, whose help he had bought, who have hitherto been unknown to the Jews, seem to be here pointed to as his servants :—

> Thou deliverest me from the strivings of the people,
> And Thou makest me the head of nations.
> A people [the Assyrians] whom I did not know shall **serve me,**
> When the ear heareth, they shall be obedient to me.
> The sons of foreigners [the Syrians] shall fawn before me.
> The sons of foreigners shall fade away,
> And shall tremble within their border fastnesses.

The contempt which mingled with the hatred **of** the foreigners was one of the Hebrew failings. The feeling of their own superiority in the worship of one God and in the moral benefits which followed thereon, closed their eyes to the foreigners' superiority in other matters. David had employed Philistine Gathites as **soldiers,** Solomon had employed the Tyrians as house builders **and as** ship builders, and the Egyptian engineers in a siege ; **but** these kings had failed to make their own people learn from their allies. Thus **the** Jews **were** sadly behind in the art of war ; and

---

* **Isaiah i. ; iv.**   † Comp. 2 Kings xv. 30, and xvii. **1.**

they were in a few years to be conquered by the very people
of whom the Psalmist speaks so contemptuously.

AHAZ continued his father's unwise policy of quarrelling
with northern Israel and Syria, and looking to Assyria for
help. He not only sent a large amount of treasure to
Tiglath-pileser, king of Assyria, to invite him to come down
upon the northern invaders, but went to Damascus to meet
him, and he promised to remain his tributary servant.
Jotham may have been dead, for Ahaz did not take this
unfortunate step before his misfortunes had deeply humbled
him. Pekah and Rezin had defeated his army, had come up
to the walls of Jerusalem, and had slain one of his sons and
two of his chief officers. They had retired, carrying away
a large booty, and a number of prisoners to Samaria.
Moreover, the Edomites had made incursions on the South
Country, some part of whose population was never very
unfriendly to them, and had carried away such booty and
captives as they could lay their hands upon. The Philistines
also had overrun the Low Country up to the Valley of
Ajalon, within ten miles of Jerusalem. What Judah suffered
at this time from his "brother" Edom is described in the
first chapter of Amos.

Tiglath-pileser readily accepted the treasure and the
invitation, and he came down upon Damascus and took that
city. He slew Rezin the king, and carried off the people to
Kir in Georgia, on the western shore of the Caspian Sea.
Then after plundering Naphtali, Zebulun, and the rest of
Galilee, he sent two armies southward; one on the east of
Jordan as far as Moab, and one along the coast of the
Mediterranean as far as the land of the Philistines.* This
latter army probably did as much injury to the kingdom of
Judah as to its enemies.

When Ahaz went to meet the Assyrian king at Damascus,
according to the usual mode of doing homage to a conqueror,
he copied his altar, and probably his form of worship, and
introduced them into the Temple of Jerusalem. Ahaz
received very little help from his new ally. He plundered
the Temple and his own people to gratify the king of
Assyria; and at this the people were probably more displeased with him than if he had been defeated in battle, and
they had been plundered in the more usual way. He reigned
a tributary to the king of Assyria.

Ahaz, unlike his father, was in no wise obedient to the

* Isaiah ix. 1, and xiv. 29—xv.

priests. If there was any struggle between them, Ahaz was the master; for the priests usually opposed the Assyrian alliance, which had to be purchased with money which they perhaps claimed. Moreover, not being frightened by Uzziah's failure in his attempts to check the power of the priesthood, he followed Solomon's example in himself acting as a priest and sacrificing on his new altar. He had the copper altar removed from the place where it had stood, between the Great Altar and the House of Jehovah, to the north side of the Great Altar, meaning to use that smaller altar himself, when he chose to inquire of Jehovah by his own hands, instead of employing a priest. The high priest **Urijah** was a willing instrument in his hand for the changes thus made in the Temple service.

The great **altar** which king Ahaz built in the middle of the Temple-yard was probably of the size and shape of that described in Ezekiel xliii. 13-17, as built of stone, and ten cubits high. The lower portion of it, six cubits high, called the Harel, or *Mount of God*, may have been built by Asa, in neglect of the command in Exodus xx. 26, that it should not be so high as to require steps, and may have called forth Exod. xxviii. 42, and Lev. vi. 10, which regulate the priests' clothing when they mount the steps. The upper portion, called the Ariel, or *Hearth of God*, which raised it to the height of ten cubits, was in further breach of that command. That this addition, the Ariel, **was now** made to **it,** we learn **from** its being spoken of in **Isaiah** xxix. Ahaz also, in compliment to the king of Assyria, carried round the whole Temple the shelter, or portico, which before had been built at the king's entrance, and there only. This may have been the original of that which Herod built seven hundred years later. It **was** useful when the people were gathered into the courts on **the** sabbaths during the rainy seasons.

Ahaz copied many of the superstitious practices of the neighbouring **nations,** and like them he made his **son** pass through the **fire.** This was probably meant **as** a ceremonial purification, **either** to make the boy holy, or to prove that he was so. It was a custom at a later time blamed by the Hebrew prophets, as a cloak for infanticide, a crime from which few nations have been wholly free; it may have been a religious ceremony used to cover the guilt. But the pride which a king feels in leaving **an** heir, makes us sure that, however much the father **may have** been wanting in natural affection, the king's son **was not** put to death by this ceremony.* Deut. xii. 31 tells us that some of the neighbouring nations did so destroy their children in superstition ; but Deut. xviii. 10 only forbids the ceremony as a superstitious charm, and as leading to idolatry. Hence we judge that it was not until a yet later time, after Deuteronomy was written, that this superstitious practice was used to cover the most unnatural crime of infanticide.

To the reign of Ahaz belongs the erection of a sun-dial in Jerusalem.† This may have introduced more exactness in measuring time than had been hitherto customary with the Hebrews; but as yet there was no Hebrew word for an Hour. The day was only divided by Day-break, Sunrise, Noon, Sunset, and Dark. And we must not suppose that the gnomon which threw the shadow sloped in the line of the earth's pole. It was no doubt placed horizontally like many ancient sun-dials now remaining, which thus divided the time of daylight between sunrise and sunset, into twelve hours, which of necessity varied in length with the time of year.

Nor were the longer portions of time measured more accurately. The beginning of every month, like the beginning of the day, was known by observation, by seeing when the new moon rose. The first month in the year was the lunar month in which the barley was in ear, hence called the month of Abib.‡ And from that full moon the others were counted until the full moon when the barley was again ripe in the following spring ; and it was then found that a year had sometimes twelve and sometimes thirteen months. The three great feasts were fixed by the seasons ; the Passover at the full moon of the barley harvest; the First fruits at the wheat harvest; and the In-gathering when the grapes and figs were ripe.§ Towards the end of the monarchy, however, a little more exactness in fixing the feast days is shown in Numbers xxviii. and yet more in Leviticus xxiii., written after the Captivity.

To the foreign tastes of Ahaz we must give the great copper Seraph, or fiery serpent, which was said to have been made by Moses, and was set up on a pole, like a military standard, in the Temple-yard, and was removed in the next reign, when the rest of this king's impurities were removed. This serpent was very probably of Egyptian workmanship, and leads us to think that Ahaz, when he found his Assyrian alliance was

* 2 Kings xvi. ; 2 Chron. xxviii.   † 2 Kings xx. 11.
‡ Exod. ix. 31 ; xii. 2 ; xiii. 4.   § Exod. xxxiv.

likely to be his ruin, and asked for help from Egypt, and, like Hoshea, offered homage to the Egyptian king. This copper serpent was called the Nehushtan, and is described in Numbers xxi. 5-9. To this time therefore we may safely give the authorship of that portion of writing which gives the **sanction of** Moses to this image, which in the next **reign** was removed from the Temple-yard as idolatrous. These words in Numbers contain the nearest approach to the approval of idolatry of any met with in the Bible. Such was the unpopularity of Ahaz with the priests, that when he died **he was** not buried in the royal burial place. He was **succeeded by** his son Hezekiah.*

The **carrying** off **captives by the Assyrians and** Edomites in the late wars brings to our notice a new **feature** in the his-**tory of** the world's civilization. Hitherto wars had usually **ended** with the slaughter of the conquered, at least, of all the **males**; and their mutilated limbs were often **sent** home by **the** victorious general **as a** present to his sovereign. Such trophies of cruelty were sent by David as a present to king Saul, and such were the presents which Rameses II received from his generals, as we see on the Egyptian sculptured monuments. But henceforth captivity rather than death was to be the fate of the conquered. If we may not say that the cruelty of the conquerors was softened by their humanity, at least their angry passions were restrained by their cold selfishness. The Assyrians made use of their prisoners on the waste lands of their wide dominions; **but** such conquerors as could not use their prisoners sold them **to** those that could.

The misery caused by **the invaders of** Judah fell, of course, chiefly upon the inhabitants **of the** open country, and less upon the rulers within the strong walls of Zion. This divided the state **into two** political parties; and of this we shall see more hereafter, as the invasions become more serious. It made the country less **obedient to** the capital; **and** it lessened the power of the ruling priests.

It is to **the** reign of Ahaz that we must give one of the most beautiful pieces of writing among the Hebrew prophets, that of Joel. It is a noble patriotic outburst **of** anger against the king's doings, and of encouragement to the people on witnessing their troubles. **It** begins in a manner which was afterwards followed **by** most of the prophets, " Hear this, ye old men, and give ear all ye inhabitants of the land." The invasion of the Edomites had been followed by that of the Philistines, then by that of the Syrians jointly

* 2 Kings xvi.; 2 Chron. xxviii.

with Israel, and lastly, **to** crown the misfortunes, the
Assyrians had been unwisely called in by the king, and had
added to the troubles which he fancied they would have
removed.   The prophet compares these nations to so many
flights of locusts, each worse than the **former**; "What the
grasshopper hath left the cricket hath eaten; what the
cricket hath left the locust hath eaten, **and what** the locust
hath left the great locust hath eaten.   Be ye ashamed. **O**
husbandmen;" it was your own doing.   Some critics **are** of
opinion that Joel is speaking of real locusts, **and** not using
them **as a** cover to describe enemies whom it was unsafe to
name openly.   But the danger was such as fully **to** justify
his caution.   Moreover, the Assyrian invader is very clearly
pointed to when **the** prophet asks, "Who knoweth but he
will turn back **and** repent, **and** will leave a blessing behind
him, even **a** meal-offering and a drink-offering unto Jehovah
your God?"   While thus treating of religious matters, and
quoting from Exodus xxxiv. 6, the words "Jehovah is
gracious and merciful, slow **to** anger **and** abundant in kindness," we find no evidence that Joel had **read** the ceremonial
laws of Leviticus and Numbers.   They had been written for
the use of the priests alone.

Joel admires the regular order which was kept by the
Assyrian soldiers, and which gave them such force in battle:
"They march every one on his ways, they vary not in their
ranks, neither doth one thrust another; they walk every
warrior in his own path; and when they fall upon the sword
they **are** not wounded."   His description of an army's march
is admirable: "A fire devoureth before them; and behind
them **a** flame burneth.   The land is as the garden of Eden
before **them, and** behind them a wasted desert."   Equally
fine is his **call to arms,** which has been copied by the later
prophets; **"Consecrate** the war, wake up the warriors,
let all the men **of war draw near;** let them come up.   Beat
your plough-shares **into swords,** and your pruning-hooks
into spears; let **the weak man** say, I am strong."   But
though writing **in such a** time of distress, he trusts in
Jehovah; and he promises, like **all** the prophets, a future of
happiness and prosperity for Judah, when Jehovah will
judge the nations in the valley of Jehoshaphat, immediately
outside the walls of Jerusalem.   He thus plays upon the
name of the valley, which may be translated *Jehovah judgeth.*
He also gives to that valley another name with a double
meaning, which may be rendered either the Valley of
Decision, or of the *Ditch* of the city wall.

We may learn from the style of Joel's writing that his book was written to be read aloud to a circle of listeners. Indeed that was the only way in which it could be made much known when the readers were not many. Some few of those who heard it read, may have asked for copies for themselves. The Book of Joel is rather an oration than an essay for a quiet reader; and it marks a new era in the history of learning, when the orator became also a writer, and thus made a regular attempt to have his voice heard by a wider circle. Before this the poet alone had been able to send his words from one end of the land to the other. Though we have already mentioned a chapter in Zechariah, by a writer who had understanding in visions of God; yet the Book of Joel, as being of far higher value, may be said to introduce us to the age of the prophets, to the golden age of Hebrew literature.

The Hebrew prophet was a man who had the power of writing and of speaking in public, and that poetic genius and earnestness that give persuasiveness and force to the words uttered. He was not a priest, or Levite, or a man appointed to the office; but he stepped forward of his own accord to the task of warning the nation and its rulers. He was usually opposed to the priests. He was moved by a noble hatred of what he, wisely or unwisely, thought evil. Speaking from his conscience he declared that his words were the words of Jehovah. His voice was against sin of all kinds, against injustice, against idolatry, against distrusting Jehovah and looking for Egyptian or Assyrian help. His wish was to preserve to the people their nationality, and to check foreign customs and the introduction of foreign gods. He called upon the people to trust in themselves and in their God. His words were warm with earnestness, with piety, with hope. When the nation was overrun with foreign armies and plundered, he saw in all the hand of a just God punishing them for their sins. He assured them that the day of punishment would be followed by a day of prosperity. He taught them to look forward to that day, the day of Jehovah, as a time when peace would be upon earth, and Jerusalem perhaps give laws to the surrounding nations, and Jehovah be acknowledged as the only God. Writings such as these are sometimes hard to be understood. Earnest feelings poured forth 2500 years ago in a poetic torrent by an Asiatic may easily be misunderstood by a Western reader. While writing sometimes about the future, to a people who were familiar with the past and present, the prophets do not always describe even history clearly. Sometimes they had a reason of prudence for not naming the persons whom they speak about. But by comparing their writings with the Books of Kings and Chronicles, we can for the **most** part learn the time when each wrote, and the events **which** gave rise to his feelings.

From **out** of the Book of **Joel** it seems necessary to except two small portions as later additions made by some writers who lived after the tribe of Judah had been carried into captivity. One is chapter ii. 28—iii. 8, in which the writer says **that** the captives of Judah and Jerusalem will be brought **back** home. The expressions in this passage will **not** apply **to** any but the great captivity in Babylon. There are very **few** writings in the Bible from which criticism does not require us to **remove** passages that have been improperly added by the **later** editor. Of course it is very possible that when Tiglath Pileser carried captive the men of Israel, as above described, there may have been men of Judah among them. We have also been reading of many defeats and unfortunate **wars, in** which **men** of Judah may have been carried off into **distant** lands, while the monarchy remained yet standing, but none in which Jerusalem was made captive, before the monarchy was overthrown. The other addition to Joel is chapter iii. 18-21, written in anger against Egypt and Edom, who were to be punished about the time of the return from captivity.

Psalms lxi. and lxiii. are Elohistic, and seem both to belong to this time, and to have been written by captives, perhaps of Israel, living away from home while the king was safe upon the throne, and therefore before one or other of the great captivities which put down the kings. The writer of lxi. says—

> **Hear my** cry, O God ; attend unto my prayer.
> **From the end** of the earth I cry unto thee.

But he also **says,** showing that the monarchy is not yet destroyed—

> Thou wilt add **years to** the king's days ;
> His years will **be as** generations and generations.

The writer of lxiii. says—

> O God, thou art my God ; early will I seek thee ;
> My soul thirsteth for thee, my flesh longeth for thee,
> In a dry and thirsty land where no water is.

Yet he adds—

> But the king will rejoice in God ;
> Every one that sweareth by him will glory.

These two Psalms are obviously both written by captives living abroad, but before the time of the great Babylonian captivity.

The prophet Isaiah began his life in Uzziah's reign, and he describes in chapter vi. a Vision that he had on Uzziah's death; and the Lord as sending him to warn the people of their danger; but at the same time to promise them that the invasion by Pekah king of Israel, and Rezin king of Syria, shall not be successful. Their real danger is from Egypt and Assyria. The writings of Isaiah, though a later editor has called them "The Vision of Isaiah," have much the character of speeches. The earliest portion belongs to the reign of Ahaz and the very beginning of Hezekiah's reign. This portion ends with chapter x. 4, and we must except from it several short sentences, namely, ii. 1-4, iv., v. 13-17, and part of vii. 8 and 21-25, which a later editor has taken the liberty to insert in the middle of it, and chapter vi. which the prophet wrote at a later time as an introduction to the book.

Isaiah's work opens with a mournful remonstrance to the nation for their attention to sacrifices, days, and feasts, and for their neglect of righteousness and justice, and for their running after soothsayers and idols. The Levitical priesthood, which rose into importance by its usefulness, had, as we have seen, used that importance for its own selfish purposes. It had cumbered religion with its ceremonies, and the people had gone astray under these blind guides. Isaiah does not attack the priests, but in the name of Jehovah he threatens the people with the ruin which is coming on them for their sins and vanities; he says that they had every spiritual advantage, but to no purpose. He blames Ahaz's government, saying, " As for my peoples, babes are their taskmasters, women rule over them." He mentions the expected birth of a child who is to be called Emmanuel or *God with us.* This was said when Hezekiah, the king's son, was about twenty years old, and he may perhaps at that time have taken a wife. In the next chapter Isaiah gives to this child, which proves to be male, and therefore heir to the throne, a series of remarkable titles, such as Wonderful Counsellor, Mighty God, Everlasting Father, Prince of Peace, titles which seem so very unsuitable to Ahaz's grandchild, that they have been held to point to a spiritual Messiah. But these titles are hardly more flattering than the names of many kings of Judah would appear, if translated into English; and, far less so than that of Adonijah, one of David's sons, which means *My lord Jehovah.*

11

From the writings of the prophets we may learn that the
Hebrew preachers often allowed their language to pass into
metrical prose, marked like the **poetry by the** parallelism of
the classes, and very probably **accompanied** by a musical
intonation of voice. As an example **take Isaiah** v. 5-7, where
he compares Judea to a vineyard :—

> And now let me tell you what I will do to my vineyard ;
> I will take away its hedge, and it shall be wasted ;
> I will break down its wall, and it shall be trodden down,
> And I will make it a waste, and it shall not be pruned nor digged ;
> But there shall come up briars and thorns ;
> And I will command the clouds that they rain no rain on it ;
> For the vineyard of Jehovah of hosts is the house of Israel,
> And the men of Judah were the plant of his delight ;
> And he looked for justice, but behold bloodshed,
> For righteousness, but behold a cry.

Chapters ix. 12—x. 4, belong to a time a little later than the
foregoing, when the northern kingdom was to be punished
for its alliance with Rezin king of Syria, and was to be overrun by the Assyrians, the adversaries of their friend Rezin.
The later portions of Isaiah's writings **must** be left to the
next reign.

Numbers xxxi., with the destruction of Midian and
the division of the booty would agree well with this
time, when Isaiah ix. 4 had mentioned " the day of
Midian ;" and at no time after the reign of Ahaz were the
people interested in the division of the booty taken from an
enemy in battle. The mention of the alloy, which we may
render mixed metal, joins this passage to the early writings
of **Isaiah.**

The writings of Joel, which we lately noticed, those of
Isaiah, which we have now come upon, and which are soon
to be followed by those of Amos, Micah, and Hosea, all published within one generation, show a great awakening of the
Jewish mind, and an increase of spiritual religion, while
Isaiah and Amos show yet further a revolt against the burnt-
offerings, and sin-offerings, and freewill-offerings, which the
priests had too much placed at the head of religion. The
progress of time, and a wider acquaintance with the neighbouring nations, had brought an increase of knowledge. The
idolatries, which the Jews were ordered to shun, may have
taught them that their own ceremonies were not more valuable. The Assyrian armies had given a severe but useful
lesson. The fast day, which Joel had called for, the priests
weeping between the porch and the altar, had not checked
the march of Tiglath-pileser. Ceremonial religion flourishes

only in a time of prosperity; in a time of **distress** spiritual religion alone is valued. Such a time of suffering from foreign invasion, and of spiritual improvement within themselves, the Jews were now entering upon, **as** we shall have to note in the writings of the next century.

The increase of literature, which we meet with about this time, leads to an inquiry **as to the** materials used for writing. In the earliest ages poetry asked for **no** help but the memory. The poem called the Book of the Wars, and Deborah's song, and at a later **time the** Psalms, may have been composed centuries before **they** were written down. But laws **need** a lasting **record which can be** referred **to, and** the Ten Commandments **were engraved on** Tables **of Stone.** For other writings **we are left to our** conjectures. **Messages may** have been **written on pieces of** pottery, as in **Egypt even at a** later time. **Money** accounts may also have **been so kept.** The neighbouring Assyrians wrote on clay, **which they** then **hardened** in the fire. As in modern days **the Books of** the **Law** have always been written on rolls of **leather, very possibly** they may by the priests have been **so written.** Indeed, writing by the priests upon leather **seems to have been** spoken of in Numbers v. 23, which **we have given to the** century after queen Athaliah's **reign; as a** book from which writing was to be washed by water **was** probably of leather. But leather is costly, and writings **can have** had a **very** small circulation, and very few facts or **thoughts** can have been committed to writing, until a cheaper material was found. This was the Egyptian papyrus, **w**hich probably came into use in Judea gradually; but **when and** how far we are not told until the burst of prophetic writing at this time assures us that it was now becoming **common.** This is confirmed to us a little later by Jeremiah, **who** tells us that his works were written **down** by Baruch by **means** of ink upon **rolls which** were readily burnt when put into the fire.

The prophets wrote for the public at large, **but the number of** those who **could** read was very small. Hence **the way** in which their **thoughts were** made known was mostly by their writings being **read** aloud to an assembled body of listeners.[*] This indeed appears from the language itself, **as** the only Hebrew word for Reading means to Call out, or Read aloud. This brought no small advantage **to** the writer's style; as the best style in all languages is that **w**hich is fitted for the ears of a listener, equally with **the eyes of** the reader.

---

[*] Jerem. xxxvi. **10 and 22.**

HOSHEA KING OF ISRAEL; B.C. 730—722.

Hoshea was the twentieth and last **king** of Israel since the revolt of the tribes against Solomon's son. Of these, so many had gained the throne by violence that the murder of a predecessor seemed almost to establish **a** right to it. Under such circumstances we need not wonder that the kingdom was hastening to its ruin. Hoshea began his reign with a fruitless attempt to resist the invading army of Shalmaneser, king of Assyria, which, after conquering Sidon and attacking Tyre, overran Zebulun **and** Naphtali, and then dividing itself into two bodies, crushed yet more severely the country on the **coast** of the Mediterranean and that on the east of the Jordan.* Upon this, Hoshea submitted, and became the tributary servant of Shalmaneser. After a time, however, he thought he could gain **a** little more independence if he put himself under the care of a more distant master. He therefore sent his tribute **to** Seve, or So, an Ethiopian king who had become king of **all** Egypt, and he left off sending his tribute to Assyria. But his Egyptian alliance was of no use to him; and in the sixth **year** of his reign Shalmaneser's troops came down **a** second **time** to the **conquest** of the country.

Hoshea went forward to meet the invaders in the land of Zebulun, the place where what remained of his kingdom could be best defended; and there his army was routed. "The bow of Israel was broken in the valley of Jezreel," between the hill-country of Samaria and the hill-country of Galilee.† Hoshea never recovered from this defeat. For three years the city of Samaria was besieged by the Assyrians, not, we must suppose, so closely but that it had free intercourse with the surrounding country for supplies of men and food. The severe treatment which the village of Beth-arbel, in Galilee, had received from the invaders, who slaughtered the women and children equally with the soldiers, was a warning to the Israelites, and encouraged them to a brave resistance.‡ But in the third year Shalmaneser gained possession of the place; he made Hoshea prisoner, and put an end to the kingdom of Israel. It had lasted two hundred and fifteen years, during which time it had been always a simple despotism. It had never been a united people. It had no established priesthood like that in Judea, which, by claiming a share of power for itself, very

---

* Isaiah ix. 1.   Menander in Josephus, Antiq. IX. xiv. 2.
  † Hosea i. 5.   ‡ Hosea x. 14.

much supported the throne like a body of nobles, and at the same time checked its irregular action.

Some few of the northern Israelites may have fled southward as far as Beer-sheba; since Amos blames as idolatrous the worship which was established there.*

The southern historian, while saying of Hoshea, as of all the kings of Israel, that he did evil in the sight of Jehovah, adds in his favour "but not as the kings of Israel that were before him." From these words we may suppose that he had been in alliance with Judah, and that the young Hezekiah may have wisely thought him a valuable friend in his brave attempt to resist the encroaching power of Assyria.

The king of Assyria, in order to establish his power over the country, removed a large part of the population to a distant part of his own dominions, treating them as his predecessor had treated the Chaldees; and he brought in a new population, on whom he could rely, to keep the rest of the Israelites in obedience. He placed the rulers and landowners of Israel in Halah and Habor, by the river Gozan, as it falls into the Caspian Sea, and also in some of the cities of Media; where many of the Israelites had already been placed by his predecessors, Pul and Tiglath-pileser. On the other hand, he sent down into the land of Israel men from Babylon and Syria, and Cuthah in Elam, who brought in their own customs and their own religion. Some of these strangers wished to worship the God of the country in which they had settled, holding the very common opinion, that in every place the God of that place is the true God; and at their request the king of Assyria sent back one of the captive Israelite priests to introduce or to continue the sacrifices to Jehovah in Beth-el. This worship at Beth-el we may see justified in two passages in the Book of Genesis, namely, xii. 8, and xxviii. 10-22; and also denounced as idolatrous by the prophets Amos and Hosea. As the prophets join Gilgal to Beth-el in their blame, we may suppose that at this time sacrifices were offered at both places, under the protection of the Assyrians; and what is yet more important, that the Assyrians by holding Gilgal had cut off Judea from the fords of the Jordan and from the east. For the future, our history of the Hebrew nation is almost confined to Judah and Jerusalem.†

We have so little information about the population of the northern country before its conquest, that we can by no

---

* Amos viii. 14. † 2 Kings xvii.

means determine what it was after the change made by
Shalmaneser. It, no doubt, had consisted of a mixed body
of Israelites and Canaanites, the former being for the most
part landowners and soldiers, and the latter labourers. But
in what proportion these two races lived together, or how
far they had intermarried and become one, it is in vain to
ask. Shalmaneser wished to remove those only ·who, by
their rank and education, could be troublesome to his
government, and those whom he could make use of for their
skill. These were the Israelities. But it is reasonable to
suppose that many of pure Hebrew blood, and a still
greater number of mixed blood, were left behind. Hence
we can by no means believe the opinion of the later writers,
that from this time the northern tribes wholly ceased to
exist in their own country, and that those who remained
there were all of Gentile origin. The Samaritans and
Galileans of the following centuries were, of course, not
Jews, because they were not of the tribe of Judah; but
many of them must have been as truly Israelites as some
of those who denied them that title, notwithstanding the
reproachful name of Cuthæans, by which, as Josephus says,
the Samaritans were henceforth called by the Jews.*

The writings of the prophet Amos belong to this time.
They carry internal evidence of a very exact date, and we
must reject the introductory verse, which gives them to the
reign of Jeroboam II as of no authority. Jeroboam's long
reign was the time of the northern kingdom's greatest
prosperity, a time very different from that described by
Amos. These prophecies were written while the Syrians
were being carried off into captivity to Kir by Tiglath-
pileser, in the reign of Ahaz, and after Galilee and Naphtali
had been carried away captive by the same conqueror, but
before the final captivity of Israel in the reign of Hezekiah.
Thus Amos wrote thirty years at least after the death of
Jeroboam II ; and therefore, when he says that Jeroboam
shall die by the sword, we must understand him as speaking
covertly of king Pekah, to whom he gives the most
reproachful of names when he calls him Jeroboam, after
the hated son of Nebat, whose rebellion divided the kingdom. In the same guarded way, Amos avoids naming their
dangerous enemies, the Assyrians; and, copying Joel, he
calls them locusts, but such unnatural locusts as came up in
the rainy season, before the latter grass crop. He calls the
Syrians, who are overrunning Samaria, Cows of Bashan,

* Antiq. IX. xiv. 3.

refusing to them the name of Bulls, which is so often given to them in the Hebrew writings. Amos lived for some time in the land of Israel, when he reproached the people for their idolatry. And he was ordered by the priest of Beth-el to leave the country, and to return into the land of Judah, as the writer of Zechariah xi. had been before sent away from the northern kingdom in the reign of Menahem.

Amos foresees the ruin of northern Israel from the Assyrians. The being carried into captivity, the usual fate of the conquered, was awaiting them. He reproaches the Israelites with taking up their tithes every third year to Beth-el, which he considers an idolatrous city. Thus it would seem that, in the northern kingdom, the tithes were to some extent claimed by the priests, though only on the third year. We shall hereafter see, in Judah also, the priests claiming the tithes only on two years out of three, and, later still, only on one year in three. But at what time this tax passed into the hands of the priests, is not clearly shown. The last five verses in the Book of Amos are by a later writer, who lived after the overthrow of Jerusalem and of the Temple. Following a custom so common with the Hebrew editors, he has added these few words to say that a day will come when the Temple shall be again raised up and the breaches in the city walls repaired.

Amos had read the history of the march out of Egypt, and of the destruction of the Amorites in Numbers xxi.; and the lives of Jacob and Joseph in Genesis, as he names the tribes after those patriarchs; and also the law in Leviticus ii. 11, which forbids burning leaven with the incense. Thus we see that much of the Pentateuch was already written; but the first portions of Numbers, which we lately described, may not have been known to Amos who lived at a distance from Jerusalem, as he speaks of sacrifices and meal-offerings being unused during the wanderings of forty years in the desert (Amos v. 25).

The few words in addition to the Life of Jacob, in Genesis xxviii. 10-22, which support the priests of Beth-el in their claim to the tithes, must belong to this century. Jacob there vows to pay tithes to Jehovah in that city. The addition, also, to the Life of Abraham, in Genesis xii. 8, which gives countenance to the altar at Beth-el, by saying that the patriarch set it up to Jehovah, belongs to the same time. These two additions to Genesis, written in opposition to the priests at Jerusalem, and as we must suppose by priests at Beth-el, cannot at the time, nor indeed for many generations after, have formed any part of the Jerusalem copies. They must have been written into the northern copies, and only adopted into the others after the time of the Captivity, when the jealousy between the tribes had ceased. The prophet Hosea quotes these and other passages relating to the Life of Jacob as if he were the patriarch of the northern tribes only.

Whatever feelings of prudence led Joel and Amos to avoid naming the Assyrian invaders, and to speak of them guardedly as a swarm of devouring locusts, made it still more necessary for their successors to write with like care. And hence arose a custom with the Hebrew writers of speaking of their invading enemies, their oppressors, as they usually style them, under cover of some poetical figure or characteristic emblem. Thus, as we have seen, the Syrians, who dwelt in a rich grazing country, are called Bulls, and the smaller Syrian kingdoms Bullocks and Calves; so the Egyptians are called Buffaloes,* and the king of Egypt a Dragon or Crocodile;† the Babylonians were called the Wild Beasts of the Reeds, from the reed beds with which their city was surrounded;‡ the Edomites are called Dogs, a translation of the name Calebites;§ and the Arabs are called the Men shorn on the Cheek, because they had not the same strength of beard as the Israelites;‖ Nahum calls the king of Nineveh and his family the Lion with several Lionesses and young Lions;¶ Job calls Assyria the Lion, Babylon the Black Lion, and Egypt the Panther;** the writer of a short paragraph in Jeremiah calls Babylon the city of Sheshak, by writing its name Babel by means of a reversed alphabet;†† and lastly, Ezekiel xxxviii. denounces Antiochus Epiphanes under the name of Gog of the land of Magog. In most of these cases it was a wise fear of the danger that might arise from speaking openly that led the writer to use a dark poetical expression. He had every wish to be understood by those for whom he wrote; and such examples by no means justify us in looking for a secondary or hidden meaning, except in cases where such meaning could not have been expressed without risk of punishment.

In the earlier portion of our history, the land held by the Israelites seemed to be most favourably situated for national

---

* Psalm xxii. 21; Num. xxiii. 22.   † Isaiah li. 9; Ezek. xxix. 3.
‡ Psalm lxviii. 30.   § Psalm xxii. 16.   ‖ Jerem. xxv. 23.
¶ Nahum ii. 11, 12.   ** Job iv. 10, 11.   †† Jerem. xxv. 26; li. 41.

independence and prosperity. Their various tribes being united into one monarchy, were stronger than any of the tribes by which they were surrounded. Safely might the psalmist of Solomon's reign speak of all attempts against his power as vain.* Even after Solomon's death, when the nation was divided into two monarchies, they were yet both for some time able to hold their ground against their neighbours. But latterly other tribes had learned to unite, or rather, had been forced by conquest to act as if willingly united; kingdoms had grown greater; and henceforth we shall find Palestine most unfortunately placed between two powerful nations; that on the banks of the Tigris and Euphrates, and that on the banks of the Nile. It was the highway by which **armies** marched backwards and forwards between western Asia and Egypt. We have seen northern Israel conquered and destroyed by Assyria; and now we shall note Judah's struggles for a century and a half to uphold **its** independence, until it sinks in the same way, crushed between its rival neighbours.

Hitherto, on the throne of Nineveh, we have met with the names of Pul, the conqueror of Armenia and Chaldæa; of Tiglath-pileser, the conqueror of Syria and part of Israel; and then of Shalmanezer, who completed the captivity of Israel and made Babylon and Judea pay tribute. Thus Nineveh had become the capital of the most powerful kingdom in the world. Its kings, flushed with conquest, and the wealth which their conquests brought, employed that wealth in supporting armies to make further conquests, and in building palaces at home. The kingdom of Babylon, and then Elam, on the south-east, and that of Judea, and then Tyre, the Island of Cyprus, and Egypt, on the south-west, were the prizes which the Assyrians now looked forward to as their own. Such may have been among the dreams of Shalmanezer; he died at the very moment of conquering Israel; and his generals sent the captive Israelites to Nineveh **as a** present to his successor Sennacherib.†

HEZEKIAH KING OF JUDAH; FIRST PERIOD, B.C. 727—712.

When Hezekiah came to the throne, the country of Judea had reached to its greatest wealth and prosperity, from which it was soon to fall. The produce of the soil, which at first barely supported those **that** tilled it, had increased,

* Psalm ii.   † Hosea x. 6.

first to be able to support a king and **his** army, and then a
wealthy priesthood. The overthrow of northern Israel may
for the moment have added to the wealth of Judah. Hezekiah
hoped to receive from Moab the tribute in lambs which it
used to pay to Israel.* It was at this time such that the
larger land-owners became a body of nobles, whom we shall
find struggling against the priests of Jerusalem for political
power.

Hezekiah did not follow in the footsteps of his father Ahaz.
His mother was a daughter of Zechariah, probably of that
Zechariah who had been the wise adviser of his grandfather
Uzziah. She perhaps had more influence over her son than
over her husband. Hezekiah governed entirely to the satis-
faction of the priesthood, and some time before his fourteenth
year he discontinued the tribute to Assyria, which it would
seem that **he** had been forced to pay. He cut down the
groves at Ashera, and broke in pieces a copper serpent
called the Nehushtan, which was said to have been made
by Moses, **but** which was probably set up in Jerusalem by
Ahaz, and had incense there burnt before it.

The ecclesiastical changes made in this reign were indeed
most important, so much so that the scantiness of particulars is very much to be regretted. One of these changes
was the removal of the High Places, that is, the forbidding sacrifices to be made in any place out of Jerusalem.
Hitherto many cities throughout Judah, as throughout
Israel, had each its own High Place, or altar, upon which
the Levites of the neighbourhood had offered up their
burnt-offerings. These, the priests in Jerusalem, had long
wished to have abolished; and in the history of those kings
who governed agreeably to the priests, the historian has
usually added, as one of the king's shortcomings, that the
High Places were not removed. This change, so gratifying
to the selfish priests **of** Jerusalem, was at last brought about
by Hezekiah.†

Hezekiah **made a** great ceremonial purification of the
Temple-yard and of the House of Jehovah, to cleanse it
from the sin of idolatry with which it had been polluted in
the last reign. This occupied fifteen days of the first month
in the year, during which time bullocks and rams were slain
and burnt, and their blood sprinkled on the altar. The
he-goats had the priest's hands laid upon their heads before

---

* Isaiah xvi. 1.   † 2 Kings xviii. 1-8.

they were slain as a sin-offering. The Levites raised the music with cymbals, psalteries, and harps, while the priests sounded with the trumpets; and psalms were sung to Jehovah in the words of David and Asaph the seer.*

Before this ceremony was ended, it was already time to keep the Passover, which Hezekiah had proposed to do in an equally costly manner. But the preparations could not be made without some little further delay, so he appointed that it should be on the full moon of the second month, instead of the first month. In the meantime, he sent runners, not only through Judah, but also through the northern country, inviting everybody up to Jerusalem to the feast. The men of Judah came in large numbers, with some few from Asher, Zebulun, and Manasseh, while the larger part of the northern tribes, and Ephraim in particular, laughed at the invitation. There had been no such celebration of the Passover since the days of Solomon.† But, for its being kept on the second month, we shall find a new enactment introduced into the Law in justification. As soon as the celebration of the Passover was ended, those who had joined in it undertook in a spirit of religious enthusiasm to break the altars, whether idolatrous or not, of those who did not come up to the feast. And this was not limited to Judea. In the weakness of the kingdom of Israel, the men of Judah thought fit to punish the men of Ephraim and Manasseh for having any altar other than that in Jerusalem.‡

We take the account of this grand national celebration of the Passover by Hezekiah from the Chronicles; the Book of Kings, the more trustworthy of the two histories does not mention it. But that the Passover was so kept as a national festival by Hezekiah is probable from our finding it ordered in Deuteronomy, which was written before Josiah had so kept the Passover at Jerusalem.§

Thus Hezekiah proposed that the Passover, which had hitherto been a family feast celebrated by each family at home, should for that year at least be a national feast to be celebrated at the capital. Solomon at the dedication of his Temple at the Feast of Ingathering had proposed that the autumnal feast should be kept by a pilgrimage of all males to Jerusalem; and now Hezekiah proposes a second such pilgrimage at the time of the Passover. Hence to no time before Hezekiah's can we give Exod. xxiii. 14-17 and

---

* 2 Chron. xxix.   † 2 Chron. xxx.
‡ 2 Chron. xxxi.   § Deut. xv

xxxiv. 23, 24, which direct that there should be three such pilgrimages to Jerusalem every year, adding the Feast of Weeks to the two feasts mentioned above.

In this reign, we are told of two marauding attacks by some men from the southern kingdom upon their weaker neighbours. One body of Simeonites, in search of pasture for their flocks, slew the Maonites on the east side of the valley of Arabah, and seized their lands; while a second body, to the number of five hundred, went to Mount Seir, and there gained a settlement by slaying the Amalekites of that neighbourhood.*

Hezekiah, in his wars against the Philistines, routed **their** forces, and drove them back as far as Gaza. And this is the **last** time for many years that we hear of these troublesome neighbours. Not that they were henceforth subject to Judea; but with the larger armies of the great kingdoms which now come upon the stage, this little tribe, which had once been so important, now falls out of notice.†

We have usually in this history delayed all mention of the writings of each reign until we have reached the end of it. But in the case of Hezekiah's reign the break in the course of events caused by the Assyrian invasion is **so** important, that it is as well to treat his reign as **of two periods** of time; and here to mention those writings which were written before the fourteenth year.

To the beginning of his reign, when the priests made atonement for the Temple, and purified it from his father's transgressions, we must give Leviticus xvi. which describes the ceremony, and then orders that it shall for the future be a yearly ceremony. One remarkable custom, which is to be used on such **an** occasion, is the releasing a goat, called the Scapegoat, into the desert to carry off the sins which are to be atoned **for.** **This** may be compared to the custom mentioned in chapter xiv., of releasing a bird to carry off with it the remains of **the leprosy,** when the disease seems healed. From the name of the scapegoat, Azazel, we learn that it had been originally a female, though the priests, for reasons of their own, now ordered that it should be a he-goat. The custom was most likely not an invention by the priests. They merely adopted an old superstition into their religious **code.** In after centuries the superstition was again somewhat changed, and the goat Azazel became a wicked demon

* 1 Chron. iv. 39-43.   † 2 Kings xviii. 8.

haunting the desert. The Satyrs which were thought to be living in the desert may have grown out of this superstition.* In the Book of Enoch one of the wicked angels is named Azazel.

To the same time we may give Leviticus xvii., which forbids all sacrifices elsewhere than before the tabernacle of Jehovah, agreeably to Hezekiah's command to stop the sacrifices on the High Places. This law, if strictly interpreted, would have forbidden all eating of animal food at a distance from Jerusalem. The mistake is carefully corrected in Deut. xii. 15 and 21.

Psalm lxxxiii. may perhaps be given to the beginning of Hezekiah's reign, before he had been invaded by the Assyrians, as it enumerates the several enemies that about the same time attacked the land of Judah, such as the Edomites, the Philistines, and the Tyrians, while the Assyrians also gave their help to the children of Lot, as it styles the Moabites and the Ammonites. The writer thus shows his acquaintance with the life of Abraham in the Book of Genesis, where Lot's parentage of Moab and Ammon is described. He had also read the Book of Judges, as we see by his knowledge of Deborah's and Gideon's wars. This Psalm seems to belong to a time when there was no warfare between Judah and Israel, and when Assyria having been the ally of Judah had not yet become its open and formidable enemy. This date for our Psalm is also made probable by its agreement with Isaiah xvii. 12-14, which the Psalmist had, perhaps, read.

The prophecy of Hosea is of this time. It is a continual reproach against both halves of the Hebrew nation, but more particularly against Israel, for Jehu's murders at Jezreel, for forsaking Jehovah, and for looking to Assyria and Egypt for help. But it also contains promises that when the nation again seeks Jehovah she shall be forgiven. It opens with quiet narrative. The speech begins only in chapter iv. "Hear the word of Jehovah, O ye children of Israel." The people are blamed for sending tribute or bribes to Jareb, that is, to Sennacherib, king of Assyria; and they are warned not to worship at Beth-el, now nicknamed Beth-aven, or *house of idolatry*; "Go ye not up to Gilgal, or to Beth-aven, nor swear as Jehovah liveth." We have seen in the Book of Amos the same reproach thrown upon Gilgal and

* Isaiah xiii. 21 ; xxxiv. 14.

Beth-el, where some of the priests of Jehovah had settled, having been sent there from the captivity by the king of Assyria. When Hosea reproaches Ephraim as idolatrous, saying, "Thy Calf, O Samaria, hath cast thee off;" and when he quotes the southern proverbial reproach against the north, "Let them that sacrifice, being men, kiss the Calves;" we merely notice that the priests of Jerusalem thought all the northern priests idolatrous.

If we may understand Hosea iii. 2, as meaning that fifteen shekels of silver were equal to a homer and a half of barley, we should have barley worth about two shillings and a half the bushel. But the meaning of the passage is too doubtful for us to obtain the value of silver.

Hosea wrote after the captivity of Israel; because he asks in chapter xiii. 10, "Where is now thy king?" He is the only Hebrew writer that shows a knowledge of the pyramids of Egypt. Those wonderful tombs near Memphis seem to have been in his mind when he says, in chapter ix. 6, that if the people go down into Egypt they will die there, and Memphis will bury them. His references to the early books of the Bible are numerous and important, as they tell us that such were already written, and in circulation. He quotes the Book of Exodus for history, and also the Book of Judges, the first Book of Samuel, and the Book of Kings. And he had read the account of Adam's disobedience in the beginning of Genesis. He advises the nation to call God not my Baal, *lord or master*, but my husband, a name meant to express the same feelings which Christians cultivate when they address the Almighty as Our Father.

Hosea, speaking of the nation in its childhood, says, in chapter xi. 1, "I called my son out of Egypt." These words have been taken prophetically; and critics are of opinion that they led to the belief that Jesus Christ had been brought out of Egypt, and that they were the cause for the narrative in the second chapter of Matthew's Gospel being written. By the same mode of reasoning we may suppose that these words made some editor of the Life of Abraham think it necessary to bring that patriarch out of Egypt; and it was probably not till after the time of Hosea that Genesis xii. 10 —xiii. 4, was written, in which Abraham is carried into Egypt, and then brought back again to Beth-el and Ai, from whence he went thither. The narrative is copied out of chapter xx., and it thus makes him a second time declare his wife to be his sister. The writers who added these chapters to the Life of Abraham have done much to injure his character.

Hosea speaks of the destruction of Admah and Zebrim, two small towns or villages on the shores of the Dead Sea (xi. 8). They seem a little before this time to have met with the fate which at an earlier time had befallen Sodom and Gomorrah, and probably from the same agency, but whether volcanic or not, is uncertain.

Of Isaiah's writings, many belong to the latter part of this reign, but here we may mention, chapters v. 1-12 and 18, end; and ix. 12—x. 4, against Judah for luxury and injustice to the poor; also chapters xiv. 28—xvii. 3, which are a threat against the Philistines; against Moab; against Petra the capital of Edom, then under the rule of Moab, which shall again send its tribute of rams and wool; against Damascus, which shall be ruined together with Ephraim; and against the rabble of smaller tribes. Chapter xxiii. 1-14 is a lament, with some little boast, over Tyre, the Fortress of the Sea, whose revenue is the corn seed of the Sihor, or Nile; and over Sidon, which is to be ruined by the Assyrians, as Chaldea has been ruined by them; while Tarsus is henceforth to be free, and to spread abroad like the Nile when it overflows.

Numbers ix. 1-14 also seems to belong to the reign of Hezekiah. It contains an answer to the question which arose when that king wished to celebrate the Passover, and when the preparations were not completed in time for the ceremony to take place in the month of Abib, at the spring equinox. This passage repeats the directions for keeping the Passover which had been first given in Exodus xii.; but it adds the further command that if at any time a man shall have been hindered from purifying himself for the occasion by the fourteenth day of the first month, then he shall keep the feast on the fourteenth day of the second month. To these chapters are naturally joined chapters vii. and viii., which describe the same gifts to the altar, and which, moreover, lower the age at which a Levite is to enter upon his duties, from his thirtieth year, at which it had been fixed in Numbers iv., to his twenty-fifth year.

To an early part of Hezekiah's reign, when the northern Israelites fled from their homes, and some took refuge in the southern desert, we must give Genesis xx. and xxi., which describes Abraham as living in that neighbourhood, at Beer-sheba. It was written to support the right of the

Israelites to the wells in that desert, a right which was
denied to them by the herdsmen of the place. These
chapters describe Abraham's falsehood in saying that his
wife Sarah was his sister, and thus injure a character which
the original writer held up for us to admire. But the
Elohistic writer did not accept Abraham as his hero; and
chapter xxi. 33, which is Jehovistic, is probably a rather
later addition.

But to return to our history, and **to** the great event
which changed in such a marked manner the social condition of the kingdom. In the sixth year **of** this reign,
Shalmanezer had conquered the kingdom of Israel, and had
carried its chief men into captivity on the eastern side
of Assyria; and had placed in the land of Israel, among
other colonists, some brought from Babylon. Hence we
learn that Babylon was then tributary to Assyria. But
Babylon was now rising in importance. The very next
year B.C. 721, Mardoc-empadus came to the throne of that
kingdom, and he would seem **to** have claimed to be independent of Assyria. Perhaps Hezekiah may have had the
encouragement of his example in refusing to send his tribute
to Nineveh. The death of Shalmanezer may also have been
a further encouragement. **Be** this as **it may,** at any rate
Hezekiah took that bold step and rebelled against Assyria.
This, however, was soon to be followed by its punishment.
Sennacherib, the new king of Assyria, invaded Judea to
bring Hezekiah to obedience, and to enforce the payment
of the usual tribute. Sennacherib's aim, however, was by
no means limited to any task so easy; he proposed at the
same time to pass through the country to Egypt. of course
meaning to levy tribute and plunder as he passed. The
route by which he came, and the particulars of his march,
are doubtful. We may reasonably suppose that the head-
quarters of the Assyrians in that neigbourhood were at
Damascus. Isaiah* mentions the Assyrian army on its way
to Egypt as arriving at Aiath, perhaps the same place as Ai,
on the east of the Jordan, as crossing over to Migron. as
passing through the defile to Michmash, and then threatening
Jerusalem. It thence passed on to Nob, a few miles to the
west of Jerusalem, and at the head of the fertile valley of
Ajalon, where it would find plenty of food, and an easy route
southwards, towards Egypt. If this was Sennacherib's own
army he quickly passed on towards the greater object that

* Isaiah x. 28-32.

he had in view. A little later Jerusalem was a second time vigorously besieged. A line of forts was erected against it; breaches were made in its walls, and we must believe, though we are not told, that the conquered Jews had to yield to the demands of the conquerors.*

There are two or three passages in the prophets which tell us that king Hezekiah had fled for safety from Jerusalem during some part of the Assyrian invasion. Isaiah in chapter xxii. 3, mentions the flight of the rulers, but does not speak of the king. He addresses the city—" All thy rulers are fled together. They are taken captive by the [Assyrian] archers; all of thee that are found are taken captive." The prophet Micah, in chapter i. 15, says, " The glory of Israel shall go to Adullam," meaning that the king, like David, shall flee to some hiding place. And he more expressly says in chapter ii. 13, that the flight took place during the siege ; " He that breaketh down is come up before them. They have broken down ; and they [the Israelites] pass through the city gate and go out by it, and their king passeth before them, and Jehovah at the head of them." Thus the priests had at the same time carried out the Ark to some place of safety. This was written, as we learn from Jeremiah,† in the reign of Hezekiah.

Psalm xi. may be supposed to have been written at this time, by one who refused to leave the city when the rulers fled, as he thought there was greater danger outside than in. He says—

> In Jehovah I put my trust; how say ye to my soul,
> " Flee as a bird to your mountain? "
> For, lo, the wicked aim with their bow,
> They make ready their arrow on the string,
> To shoot in the dark at the upright in heart.
> When the pillars [or princes] are broken down,   •
> What can a righteous man do ?

Isaiah in chapter xix. 10, had in the same way called the princes the pillars.

Hezekiah may have been in danger of being taken, and he may have escaped from the enemy with difficulty ; as what seems to be the return of this king is described in Zechariah ix. 9, " Rejoice greatly, O daughter of Zion ; shout, O daughter of Jerusalem. Behold, thy king cometh to thee ; he is just, and hath been saved, lowly, and riding upon an ass, even upon a colt, the foal of a she-ass." These

* Isaiah xxii.   † Jerem. xxvi. 18.

several passages, which all relate to this time, can hardly be explained without supposing that Hezekiah had for a time quitted the city to avoid the threatened danger.

This siege of Jerusalem was probably followed by submission, and by the payment of the required tribute. But if so, the tribute was after a time again refused; as we meet with a third invasion of Judea, or at least a third approach of the Assyrian army to Jerusalem in the fourteenth year of Hezekiah. This is the only attack on the city of which we have many particulars. We first hear of Sennacherib at Lachish, five-and-twenty miles to the south-west of Jerusalem, on the direct road to Egypt. There Hezekiah sent an embassy to him with a large amount of gold and silver, of which he had stripped his palace and the Temple.

This gift, it seems, did not satisfy Sennacherib. He then sent part of his army, under the command of his generals, from Lachish, where he seems to have had a permanent camp, to the siege of Jerusalem. The Assyrian army encamped on the high ground near Gihon, at the north side of the city. Sennacherib's generals were well aware that there was a division in the councils within the city; and, before beginning the attack, they addressed themselves to the guards on the walls, and made good use of the arguments which were likely to increase that division. The landowners, the men of Judah, and the country Levites, who had fled for safety within the walls, were highly displeased with Hezekiah and his priestly advisers for closing the High **Places and** forbidding all sacrifices out of Jerusalem; and **the** Assyrian generals reminded them of this, and promised **that, if they** would make peace with Sennacherib they should **be well treated,** and live every man under his own fig-tree, **and beside his own cistern.** But they made no secret of **Sennacherib's intention to** carry the heads of the nation **into captivity. Had the** tribute been regularly paid, the **Assyrians would have left the Jews** alone; it was only after **the** tribute had been **withheld** that captivity was threatened, and that with a promise of good treatment. All this is to be considered when we attempt to judge between the two parties in the state—the men of Judah, who wished to pay the tribute, and the inhabitants of Jerusalem, who refused to pay it.

The guards on the walls, however, did not listen to the Assyrian offers. Moreover, Hezekiah was then prepared to **defend** his capital, and was not moved by the threats of the

Assyrian general, who soon withdrew, and returned towards Sennacherib, whom he now found besieging the city of Libnah, five or six miles nearer to Jerusalem than Lachish, where he had left him.* Sennacherib was on the retreat slowly, because he heard that Tirhakah, king of Egypt, was marching against him, but he took time enough to plunder the towns as he passed. He did not, however, again attack Jerusalem. He probably returned home by the southern ford of the Jordan and by Damascus, the route by which we supposed him to have arrived.

Hezekiah, in preparation for an attack upon Jerusalem, had strengthened the wall that had been broken down eighty years before by the king of Israel, and built a second, or rather a third, on the outside to inclose a second suburb, He also repaired Millo, the castle, and dug a new pool, or tank, within the city for a supply of water. This was known by the name of Hezekiah's Pool. Hitherto the city had been supplied with water from two sources, Solomon's Pool on the south, and the Upper and Lower Pools of the Gihon on the west. Hezekiah turned the water from the Lower Pool of the Gihon, and brought it into his new tank direct from the Upper Pool of the Gihon, as it would seem by an underground pipe ; and knowing that he should not be able to guard Solomon's Pool from the Assyrians, he broke down the bank and let the water run to waste, lest the enemy should make use of it. The city was wholly supplied with water from the pools which caught the rain in the rainy seasons ; there were few springs in the neighbourhood, and no army could live on the outside of the walls in the dry season when the artificial pools were broken down.†

In more important matters Hezekiah had been very badly prepared to meet an invasion. His subjects were divided. Some towns even hoped to profit by the nation's misfortunes.‡ The people of the country were against the inhabitants of the cities, the poor against the rich, the thoughtless debtors against their exacting creditors. The unfeeling selfishness of the educated had led them to seek their profit in keeping the poor in the bonds of debt rather than in raising them to be their friends and helpers.§ Such a nation may appear prosperous until danger approaches from without, and then its weakness becomes evident.

---

* 2 Kings xix. ; Isaiah xxxvi., xxxvii.
† 2 Kings xx. 20 ; 2 Chron. xxxii. 3-30.   ‡ Micah i. 12.
§ Micah iii.—vi. ; Amos viii. 4-7 ; Isaiah iii. 12 ; v. 8.

The lofty and massive **stone** walls of Jerusalem yet remain **as a** proof of the selfish policy which had usually guided the nation's rulers.   No other city had walls equally strong against an invading army.   The wealth of the whole country had been employed in defending the capital.   The men of Judah might be plundered and slaughtered provided the inhabitants of Jerusalem were safe.   Moreover it was on the side of the Temple, where the priests dwelt, that the wall was most lofty.   On the Assyrians entering the country, Hezekiah instead of attempting to guard the frontier had shut himself up in Jerusalem and left the open country to **its** fate.

Hezekiah hoped to receive some help from Egypt on payment **of** a proper tribute; but Egypt was in no condition to help him.   It had been weakened by civil war.   The city of Bubastis, **which in** Solomon's reign had risen over Thebes, in the next generation sank under Tanis.   Memphis and Sais had then claimed to share the power **with** Tanis; and all three had sunk under **the** Ethiopians **about the** time that Hezekiah came to **the** throne.   **Hence when** Hezekiah's messengers came to Taphanes they met with nothing but disappointment[*] and did not go on to Tanis where the Egyptian princes were waiting for them.

The inhabitants of Jerusalem were not all heroes in the face of this overwhelming danger.   Many rushed into violent excesses in very despair.   The times called for weeping and mourning, and girding with sackcloth; but behold there was joy and gladness, eating flesh and drinking wine, with the sad excuses, Let us eat and drink for to-morrow we die.[†]

The **history of** the Assyrian attack or attacks upon Hezekiah is full **of** difficulties.   We are, however, a little helped by **what we learn** from Herodotus[‡]—namely, that Sennacherib had **reached** Pelusium, the frontier town of Egypt, and sat down to the siege **of it.**   We gain another hint from the Assyrian sculptures,[§] **and** from Psalm xlviii., that in this distant undertaking he trusted for his supplies to the Tyrian ships, and that these were scattered in a storm.   This and the Babylonian rebellion may have been the cause of his hastily breaking up his camp before Pelusium, and of his hurrying away without waiting to give battle to the Egyptian **army** that Tirhakah, the king, had sent against him.   So unexpected **was** this move, that the Hebrew historian describes

* **Isaiah xxx. 4.**   † Isaiah xxii. 12.   ‡ Lib. ii. 141.
§ "**Bonomi's** Nineveh," 3rd Edit. Fig. 53.

it as caused by the stroke **of an** angel, which **slew a** large part of **his** army. He withdrew in the night; and when the Egyptians, in the morning, entered his camp, they found the ground strewed with dead bodies.

Thus the kingdom of Judah was saved by no **act of its own.** It was saved by what a Pagan might call a lucky accident; as the Hebrew prophet says, it was not saved by bow, nor by sword, nor by battle, nor by horses, nor by horsemen; it was saved by **Jehovah their** God.* Of the state in **which** it was left we **gain a** few important hints. The male population had by **the slaughter** been halved, or perhaps reduced to one quarter **of the** former number. The women had been spared to gratify **the** passions of the brutal conquerors. The **prophet** looking forward **to the** return of the scattered few to **their homes, says, that** "In that day **seven** women shall take hold **of one** man, saying we will eat our own bread, and wear **our own** apparel, only let us be called **by** thy name to take away our reproach."†

While the main body of the Assyrians had been trampling down Judea on the route to Egypt, a part of the army turned aside to plunder the fertile valleys of northern Moab. On the overthrow of Israel by Shalmanezer the Moabites had been able to **take** possession of the land of Reuben; but they did not hold it long. One of Sennacherib's armies entered Moab from the south, destroyed Ar-Moab and Kir-Moab, the two capitals, **marched** northward, slaughtering **on** their route, while the frightened Moabites found no safety by running northwards, as they **then came** upon the Assyrian line of march from Damascus, through Bashan, **to** Jerusalem. Nor did this happen once only. After an interval of three years **the same** calamity came upon Moab a **second** time.‡ This **seems to** place an interval **of** three years between Sennacherib's **first and** second invasion of Judea. But **the** order of events in Hezekiah's reign **is** sadly confused. Now **and** during the coming century Edom was subject to **Moab;** and the **capital of** Edom, **whether called** Sela,§ **or** Mibzar,‖ **is** spoken **of** as a city **of** Moab.

In these years of trouble to the inhabitants of the open villages, not a few of the people sought safety by flight from their homes. Beer-sheba, on the edge of the southern desert, on the road towards Egypt, received many, as we judge from the frequent mention of that place in the Hebrew writings

* Hosea i. 7.　　　† Isaiah iv. **1.**　　　‡ Isaiah xv.—xvi.
§ Isaiah xvi. **1.**　　‖ Isaiah xxv. **12.**

at this time.   The prophet Amos in the beginning of Hezekiah's reign, blames the northern Israelites for rushing to Beer-sheba,* and afterwards **blames the** men of Judah for rushing to that spot and raising an altar to Jehovah in that town.†

But Beer-sheba and the neighbourhood **were not far** enough removed from the danger; and **as the** Assyrians moved southward the people of southern Judea, putting their wealth on the backs of their camels and asses, had taken refuge in Egypt.‡ There, on the eastern bank **of** the Nile, they may have found many of their own race; and thither in after centuries they were followed by others who, **like** themselves, fled from invading armies.   Thus was at **last** formed the important colony of Jews in the Delta.

Hezekiah's change of policy in favour of a brave resistance. seems to have been accompanied with a change of advisers. His favourite **Shebna,** who had made himself unpopular by his boastful **style of** living, **and** had been ruler of the royal household, or **prime** minister, **was** for a **short** time removed **from** his high **post; and** Eliakim the **son of** Hilkiah was appointed to **his place.**   This **was** done **with** the warm approval of the **prophet Isaiah, who had counselled** resistance and promised success.§

The retreat of the Assyrians from the land of Judah was soon followed by the serious illness of Hezekiah, which brought him to the point of death.   This is memorable from the king's conversation with the prophet Isaiah, who promised him that he should recover.|| The statement that Isaiah, to convince him that he had power to promise him his recovery, **made the** shadow on the sundial go backwards, seems to have been created out of the not uncommon figure of poetry by which the decline of life is compared to the lengthening **shadow.**

HEZEKIAH'S **REIGN, SECOND PERIOD; B.C.** 712—699.

Partial writers do not **always** record a nation's misfortunes. But hereafter it will be seen that from the time when king Ahaz sent his first tribute to the king of Assyria, the Jews lost their full independence.   They had been their own masters for three hundred years since Saul released them **from** Philistine bondage.   But henceforth we shall usually

* Amos v. 5.   † Amos viii. 14.   ‡ Isaiah xxx. 6.
§ Isaiah xxii. 15-24. || 2 Kings xx. 1-11.

find them paying tribute, or even in worse bondage, to one
or other of the great nations around. Their efforts at resistance were few and never successful. This must not be
forgotten when we judge their writings. The Book of Joel,
and some few of the Psalms were written in brave defiance
of the enemy; but the prophets usually wrote about foreign
matters in fear and trembling.

The historians do not tell us of any after invasion of
Hezekiah's kingdom by the Assyrians. But we may be
sure that Sennacherib did not leave the ruined little kingdom
of Judah independent. Eliakim, who may have advised
resistance, and the withholding of the tribute, was shortly
afterwards removed from his post in the government,* and
the later policy of Hezekiah, with the policy of his successor,
both make it probable that Hezekiah ended his reign as a
tributary to Sennacherib, and followed a line of policy which
was more agreeable to the men of the country than to the
priests and nobles of Jerusalem.

Hezekiah had begun his reign by stopping the High Places
to please the priests of the capital; but before the end of his
reign he made another change, which would seem as if made
in the very opposite direction. This was the raising the
Levites of the whole kingdom almost to an equality with
the priests, the sons of Aaron, who had the care of the
Ark. These latter, ever since the establishment of the
priesthood in Jerusalem, had been claiming a superiority
over their brethren in the smaller towns, till, in the reign
of Jehoash, by the power of the chief priest Jehoiada,
their claim was fully established, and the Levites were
declared to be their servants. But, under Hezekiah, the
Levites of other towns claimed, and were allowed, to join
the priests on equal terms in offering up burnt-offerings
on the altar in Jerusalem.† The law had ordered that the
half shekel or atonement money from all the country and a
tenth part of the tithes should be brought up to the capital;
hence the Levites of the other towns naturally wished to be
allowed to come up to Jerusalem themselves and to have a
share of these advantages. This is very clearly granted
to them in Deut. xviii. Hezekiah also made a new appointment of the courses of the priests and Levites in the service
of the Temple. He lowered the age at which the Levites
entered upon the duties and profits of their office from the
thirtieth year, at which it had been fixed in Numbers iv.,

* Isaiah xxii. 25.   † 2 Chron. xxix.—xxxi.

to the twentieth year. But this change was not wholly
approved of by the priests; and the new law of Numbers
viii. fixes it at the twenty-fifth year. He placed a Levite,
not a son of Aaron, in one of the most important posts,
that of receiver of the tithes. This, indeed, is the first
time that **we have** heard of the tithes in the kingdom of
Judah since **we** were told in the Book of Samuel that they
would be levied by the king for the expenses of his government. Under Hezekiah's new arrangements they may have
been collected with greater regularity than before. It would
seem as if the tithe, having been at first a royal tax, **was**
become a priestly tax, as we have seen it in the kingdom **of**
Israel, from the simple circumstance that the influence of the
priests was made use of in its collection. Any supply in
money that the throne needed beyond the produce of the
royal estates required the help of the Levites for its collection; and the Levites of the provinces may have been more
willing that the tax should be gathered in, now that the
produce **was** carried **to** the Temple for safe custody, and
their own order **was** allowed, with the priests, to have a
control over its **expenditure.*** We shall hereafter see a
number of new **enactments** introduced into the Mosaic Law,
agreeably to the **changes spoken** of **above.** They seem to
have been made to **meet the lessened wealth of** the people,
which followed upon **the Assyrian ruinous** occupation of
the country.

Hezekiah died after a troubled reign of twenty-nine year,
leaving his throne to a child, probably a grandson, who had
no choice but to be an obedient servant to Sennacherib.

The rebellion of Hezekiah against Assyria may have been
encouraged, as we have said, by the revolt of Babylon, a
city which now rises into notice. It has not left to us such
noble ruins to prove its high civilization as Egyptian Thebes
and Assyrian Nineveh; but in some sciences it was before
them both. Its records of accurately observed eclipses are
even now the foundation on which our ancient chronology
rests. The earliest of these is an eclipse of the moon in
Hezekiah's reign, in the first year of Mardoc-empadus, who,
in the latter years of Shalmanezer's reign, held the tributary
throne of Babylon. He is called Berodach Baladan in the
Bible. In the reign of Sennacherib this king declared
himself independent, and instead of sending his tribute to
Nineveh, sent a present to Hezekiah at Jerusalem, hoping

* 2 Chron. xxxi.

that the weaker and more distant power might **be a less** troublesome friend than the Great King of Assyria. **Babylon** was becoming independent of Nineveh during **the same** centuries that Lower Egypt was becoming independent of Thebes ; and probably from the same causes. The changes **in** the arts of life, in the art of war, and in the course **of** trade, were now giving to the fertile plains nearer to the **river's** mouth those advantages which had belonged to the more inaccessible city nearer to the mountains. In Hezekiah's reign the Assyrians were the formidable enemies of the Jews ; but in one hundred years later **the** Babylonians will be their worse oppressors. Mardoc-empadus, or Berodach Baladan, king of Babylon, who, in the year B.C. **714,** the eighth **of** his **reign,** had thrown off the Assyrian yoke, reigned only for **six months** after he had gained his independence. He was **then** slain by Elibus. Elibus, or Belibus, reigned for three years, while Sennacherib's armies were overrunning Judea with a view to the conquest of Egypt. At the end of that time Sennacherib had withdrawn his forces from Judea, and returned home to grapple with the Babylonian difficulty. He then conquered Elibus, and left his son Esarhaddon in Babylon to secure its obedience.[*] When Babylon was conquered he was at leisure to require payment of the Jewish tribute ; and though the historians have not mentioned Hezekiah's return to obedience, we may notice it in his changed policy.

The ruinous occupation of the country by the Assyrians brought with it great political changes. Some of these are told by the historians, and others we may safely imagine. The invaders had carried off all the cattle and all the movable wealth that they could seize. As Isaiah **says,** they had come upon the riches of the people as on a **bird's** nest ; and as one gathereth up eggs that are left, **so they** gathered up the land. For three years the fields had been untilled. The population had been lessened ; and when the Assyrians withdrew they left the cultivators of the soil **miserable, and the** priests and nobles in the cities reduced **to** poverty. **Before the** end of Hezekiah's **reign the great** power of the priesthood was gone.

The priests first became of political importance when David took the Ark and its keepers under his care ; and their power was strengthened by Solomon when he built the Temple, and gave them wealth to support its costly cere-

* Alex. Polyhistor, in Armin. Chron. of Eusebius.

monies. In Asa's reign they were able to put aside the
queen-mother, and to take the young king for a time into
their own hands. Under Jehoshaphat they sat as judges,
and their decisions were law. A little later they dethroned
a usurping queen, and governed the kingdom in the name
of a child, until foreign war put Jehoash in possession of **an**
army, and he gained his independence. Their power grew
with the wealth of the country. When king Uzziah displeased them they dethroned him as a leper. Under Ahaz
their power received a check, when danger from foreign
invasion made the throne more dependent on **those who** fight
for it. Hezekiah began his reign in obedience **to** the priests;
and their power over men's minds, and over the nation's
councils was for a time unshaken.

During those reigns was written the greater part of **the**
Levitical Law in the middle Books of the Pentateuch, laws
which gave to the priests the offerings, the tithes, and the
poll-tax, or atonement money. But this well-built ecclesiastical fabric received a rude shock from the Assyrian
invasion. In a time **of** poverty there is no surplus wealth
for those who do not work. **In** a long-continued famine there
is no food for any but those who help to produce it. A well-
paid priesthood is a luxury which a nation in distress must
for a time do without.

There are several of the Psalms which belong to a late
time in this reign, and were written on the occasion of
Sennacherib's invasion and retreat. Psalm xlvi. rejoices in
Hezekiah's new pool which supplied the city with water
from the spring of the Gihon by means of pipes underground
and therefore safe from being cut by the enemy :—

> **A river** and its streams make glad the city of God
> And **the** holy place of the tabernacle of the Most High.
> God **is in the** midst of her, she will not be disturbed.

On the retreat **of the** Assyrians the people are invited to
come out and **note the** tokens of disorder, which they had
left behind on **their** hurried **march** :—

> Come, behold the doings of Jehovah,
> What an overthrow [of the enemy] he hath wrought in the land,
> Making wars to cease unto the end of the land.
> He breaketh the bow, and cutteth the spear in sunder,
> He burneth the chariots in the fire.

Psalm xlviii. exults in the strength of the city, in the
retreat of the threatening army, and in the destruction of

the Tyrian vessels, which, as we learn from the Assyrian sculptures, were employed to carry supplies to the army of Sennacherib at the siege of Pelusium :—

> Great is Jehovah, and greatly to be praised
> In the city of our God, on his holy mountain.
> Beautiful in height, the joy of all the land is mount Zion ;
> On the north side is the city of the great King.
> God is known in its palaces as a tower of defence.
> For lo, the kings were assembled, they passed by at once.
> They saw it and so they marvelled ;
> They were troubled and fled away hastily.
> Fear took hold **of them there.**
> Pain as **of a woman in childbirth.**
> Thou breakest **the** ships of Tarshish with an east wind.

Psalm **lxxvi. describes** the destruction of Sennacherib's army **at the** siege of Pelusium, and the appearance of the camp when the Egyptians entered it in the morning :—

> The stout-hearted had become a booty,
> They were dozing in their sleep.
> And none of the men of might found their hands :
> At thy rebuke, O God of Jacob,
> Both the rider and the horse were cast into a deep sleep.

In this Psalm Jerusalem is called Salem, a name by which it is nowhere else called except in a part of the life of Abraham, which we shall come to presently. This Psalm also gives us an early example of the word Adam being used for the Israelites as opposed to the rest of mankind. Thus, with a threat against the retreating Assyrians, it adds :—

> **Surely the wrath** of [the sons of] Adam will bring thee praise,
> With **the remainder** of wrath thou wilt gird thyself.

In the writings of Isaiah it may be doubted whether Adam and men mean two classes of men, or only two names for all mankind.

Psalm lxxviii. was written after the northern kingdom was destroyed ; as God

> Forsook the tabernacle of Shiloh,
> The tent in which he had dwelt among men,
> And delivered its strength into captivity.

It was written after the **High Places** had been declared blameable ;

> For they provoked him to anger by their high places,
> And moved him to jealousy by their graven images ;

but before the captivity of Judah, and the destruction of the
Temple of Jerusalem ; as

> He chose the tribe of Judah,
> Mount Zion which he loved ;
> And he built his sanctuary like a citadel,
> Like the earth which he hath established for ever.

It may **be** compared to the Book of Hosea, which it is **like**
in its blame of Ephraim, and in its use of early history.   **In**
this Psalm Zoan or Tanis is spoken of as the capital **of**
Egypt, **as it** was when Homer's Odyssey was written, **and as**
it was until about the time when Hezekiah came to **the**
throne.

Psalm xxi. may be on Hezekiah's recovery from sickness,
when he asked for life and it was given to him ; and when his
enemies had intended evil against him from which he escaped.

For the history of Hezekiah's reign we are in part indebted
to the writings of the prophet Isaiah.   He began writing in
the reign of Ahaz ; and we have already had to notice the
first nine chapters of the Book bearing his name.   The
remainder of Isaiah's writings begin **at** chapter x. 5, and end
with chapter xxxix.   The chapters that follow these are by
various later authors ; **and even** out of those which we are
now giving to Isaiah **we** must except large portions which
are easily recognized as relating to the Babylonians and the
later centuries.

Of Isaiah's writings, chapter xxviii. is a reproach to the
northern tribes for their not following Jehovah, with a warning that they will be over-run by a great conqueror, and also
a warning to the rulers in Jerusalem, who think that they
shall escape the destruction by a treaty made with Death and
Hell, probably that with Egypt.   But Jehovah will destroy
the invaders as David destroyed the Philistines.   Chapter
xxix. contains **a** lament for Jerusalem : "Woe to Ariel,
Ariel [or the **Lion** of God], the city where David
dwelt, it shall be **to me** an Ariel [or hearth of God] ; " but
it also contains a promise **that the** invading enemy shall not
be successful.   Chapter **x. 5-34,** is an eloquent threat of woe
against the Assyrian king Sennacherib, who is described as
a rod **in the** hand of Jehovah to punish the Israelites, but
who is rising in rebellion against God, with as little reason as
if the axe should boast itself against the hand that holds it.
It describes him as smiting Judea on his way to attack
Egypt : but it threatens that Jehovah will smite him on the
way to Egypt.   It describes his route ; having come from

Damascus, " **He** is come to Aiath [the Ai or Aim of the Hebrews], he hath crossed over the [the Jordan] to Migron; at Michmash **he** hath **laid** up his baggage; they have passed through the passage; . . . he shaketh his hand against the Mount of the daughter of Zion, the hill of Jerusalem." At that time Sennacherib may not have stayed to besiege the city. But on another occasion, whether earlier or later is doubtful, the siege of Jerusalem was pushed forward to the breaking down the walls, if not to the capture of the city; and chapter xxii. mentions the flight of the rulers out of Jerusalem at the time of the siege; the king was no doubt among the fugitives. It contains a warning to the inhabitants of Jerusalem that while preparing for the siege of their city they should also look for help to Jehovah who made it; and a threat that Hezekiah's favourite minister Shebna shall be put aside for Eliakim, who is to keep his power in the palace like a nail fastened in a sure place. But it would seem that Eliakim's power did not last long. A later writer added **a** verse to say that "the nail in a sure place" shall be removed. Eliakim's power may have ceased when Hezekiah ceased to follow the wishes of the priestly party. Lastly, chapters xxx. and xxxi. contain a threat against those who desert their country and go down into Egypt as a place of safety, particularly against the inhabitants of the southern parts of Judea, the Beasts of the South Country, as they are called, who on many occasions showed themselves little zealous for the nation's welfare. Here the nickname of Rahab, *the Boaster*, is given to Egypt for its holding out false hopes of help against the Assyrians, " For Egypt is vanity, and will help to no purpose; therefore have I named it the Boaster that sitteth still." The Egyptian little horned serpent, and the fabulous flying serpent are both here mentioned, together with the African lion and the panther.

Isaiah xviii. gives **us** a knowledge of **an** important settlement of **Jews in** Abyssinia. This country he addresses whimsically as the land of the winged Tsaltsal, or *spear fly*, which sends its ambassadors by sea on rafts made of the paper-reed. The Tsaltsal is an insect now well-known to naturalists. It is a small fly, but a dreadful scourge, which kills all the domestic cattle that may be brought into that country. To Abyssinia the Jews may have fled as a place of safety when their own nation had been " scattered and made bare, measured out and trodden down, and plundered by the rivers [Tigris and Euphrates]."

The last verse of this chapter may be more modern; it foretells that hereafter the Jews living there will send their tribute to the Temple in Jerusalem.

Isaiah xvii. 4-11 describes a sad time when the glory of Jacob is made thin, and when his strong cities are like the abandoned thicket-camps and hill-camps of the Amorites, which the Israelites found in the land when they first conquered it. Such was the state of Judea when the Assyrians left it; and as for the population, the males had been so far killed off that chapter iv. 1 says that there remained seven women for every man.

Chapter xxxvi—xxxix. are a portion of history relating to what was perhaps the second Assyrian invasion, and to Hezekiah's illness. It is the same as what we read in our Book of Kings, but it adds a poetical prayer written after the captivity of Babylon in the name of king Hezekiah; and it omits all mention of the first invasion and of Hezekiah's sending his treasures as a tribute to the king of Assyria, an act of humiliation particularly painful to every man of patriotic feelings. Isaiah had written a history of his own times, embracing about a half a century. An earlier portion relating to the reign of Uzziah is spoken of in the Chronicles; but this latter portion relating to Hezekiah is all that now remains to us. To this, however, has been added a part of xxxix. in the form of prophecy relating to the captivity in Babylon. Isaiah had read the Book of Judges, and mentions out of it the slaughter of the Midianites at the rock of Oreb.

Other large parts of the Book of Isaiah we put aside for the present, as having been written by other authors and at various later times. If we except a few inserted sentences, these later writings seem to have been added to the Book by the blunder of the scribes; it does not appear that the authors meant to pass off their writings as the work of the prophet Isaiah.

Difficult as it is to form an opinion of when the several large parts of the Pentateuch were written, still more difficult is it to see when the later additions in the middle of the narrative were made. But in numerous cases it is extremely easy to see that such sentences are after additions.

One of the most remarkable additions to an early narrative is Genesis xiv. 1-16, which was written after Sennacherib's retreat from Judea, and was then woven into that part of the Life of Abraham, which was written in David's reign. Sennacherib had retreated hastily, as described in the above-quoted Psalms, and, as it seemed, without a cause. He had probably been recalled by troubles in Babylon. The Jews followed his retreat even beyond Damascus, picking up the spoil which he had left behind. And as though to laugh **at** the Assyrians, when the danger was over, the kings of Elam, of Ellassar or Assyria, of Shinar or Babylonia, and the king of Nations, are described, first, as attacking five little villages on the shores of the Dead Sea, and then as being defeated by Abraham's three hundred and eighteen servants, who pursue them beyond Damascus and pick up the spoil. One of these kings receives the name of Chedorlaomer, *the binder of the sheaves*, from the work of carrying off the harvests of Judea, which the Assyrians **did for** three years together. The original **narrative had described** Abraham as defeating some enemies; **but who those** enemies **were does not** now appear, as the description of them has been removed to make way for the Assyrians. From this fanciful narrative we should **suppose** that Hezekiah after paying his tribute to Assyria, **had** withheld it on the thirteenth year of his reign, and was attacked by Sennacherib in his fourteenth year as **is said** in the Book of Kings.

A part of Numbers xvi., in which Korah the **Levite is** punished for claiming the rank of a priest, seems to have **been** written in blame **of** Hezekiah's giving to Kore, a Levite, **the** high post of having the charge of the holy things of the temple. "Ye take too much upon you, ye sons of Levi," said Moses. All **that is woven** very **incon**veniently into the blame of certain Israelites who claimed the rank of Levites.

The writings of the prophets Amos and Isaiah, which teach the little value of offerings and sacrifices, compared with moral duties, cannot have been pleasing to the priests, although they did not go so far as to teach that it was unwise to make any offerings to the altar. Perhaps those prophets had not themselves arrived at such an opinion. They were proposing **a** religious reformation, but they were **not pro**posing to quarrel with the priesthood. They **may be** compared to Luther at the beginning of his career, **before** he had written against the Papal authority. Whether, if the country had been left at peace, they would have had any followers who would have gone a step further, it is now in vain to conjecture; but in the meantime came the Assyrian invasion under Sennacherib. This so lessened the wealth of the country, and the people's power to send up offerings to Jerusalem, that when these offerings came up in lessened quantities, the priests could hardly have thrown the blame on Amos and Isaiah.

The history of Balaam being asked to curse Israel, in Numbers xxii. and xxiii., cannot be much more modern than this time, because it is quoted in Micah and in Joshua; and there are several words in it which forbid us to place it much earlier; such as Jacob and Israel as joint names of the nation, as in Isaiah ix.; and the Buffalo as a figurative name for Egypt. The imaginary town of Pethor on the Euphrates, from which Balaam the soothsayer was fetched, means the place of *interpretations;* and the intercourse with the Babylonians, which had lately begun with Berodach Baladan's embassy, may have led the writer to look to that country for a soothsayer.

Psalm lxxxvii., which uses Isaiah's name for Egypt, and calls it **the** Boaster, was probably of this time, while the poet could yet sing with pride of his country and its capital city. The writer of this last psalm says:—

> I will allow mention **of** the boaster [or Egypt],
> And of Babylon, to those that know me;
> Behold Philistia, and Tyre, **and** Ethiopia;
> [They may say] "This man **was** born there."
> But of Zion it will be said,
> "This and that man was born in her,
> And her the Most High himself establisheth."
> Jehovah will count, when he writeth up the peoples,
> "This man was born there."

The writings of Isaiah make frequent use of a poetical name for the Hebrew nation, calling it the house of Jacob; and the Psalms of Hezekiah's reign and later sometimes call the Almighty the God of Jacob. This name seems to have been made use of in order to avoid the confusion that often arose from the word Israel having two meanings, sometimes meaning the whole Hebrew nation, and sometimes the northern tribes only. Thus Isaiah says, in chapter ix. 8, "The Lord sent a word unto Jacob (the twelve tribes), and it hath fallen upon Israel" (the northern tribes). But this attempt to escape from a misunderstanding was not very successful. Being introduced in opposition to the word Israel, **some** writers used it to mean Judah. Psalm lxxvii. describes **the** two halves of the nation as "Sons of Jacob and Joseph;" and Obadiah calls them "the house of Jacob and **the** house of Joseph." These Jehovistic writers seem by **Jacob to mean** Judah. Indeed it was soon found that the new name would bear a double meaning, quite as readily as the old name. Thus Hosea, a little later, calls the northern tribes Jacob, saying in chapter x. 11, "I will make Ephraim to carry a rider; Judah shall plow, and Jacob shall break the clods for him." **So also** does Micah, saying, **in** chapter i. 5, "What is the transgression of Jacob, is it **not** Samaria? And **what are the** High **Places** of Judah, are they not Jerusalem?" **But** later still, on the return from the captivity, **when the wish** arose among **some to** cancel the distinction between the **two halves** of the nation, the writer of **Isaiah xliv. 5, shows** his wish that the names of Jacob and **Israel should no longer have** different meanings; he says, "**One shall say, I am Jehovah's,** and he shall call himself **by the name of Jacob; and** another shall subscribe with **his hand unto Jehovah, and** surname himself by the name **of Israel.**" And yet later in Numbers xxiv. 17, and Psalm **xxii. 23, the** double name of Jacob and Israel is used **with a** careful wish to wipe out **the** distinction between the **two** halves of the nation. The only passages in which we find the two nations clearly and distinctly named are Zechariah x. 6, and Ezekiel xxxvii. 16, where they are called the house of Judah and the house of Joseph.

Chapters xxv.—xxix. of the Book of Proverbs are **said** in the first verse to have been written in the reign of Hezekiah. They have not **the** regularity **of** the older parts of that book, **and many of** them show **a more** humane and less selfish spirit. **They show that the moral** feelings of the nation had been not a little softened in the last three centuries. Thus, we have not before met with such advice as, "If thine enemy be hungry, give him bread to eat; and if he be thirsty give him water **to** drink;" or as, "Thine own friend and thy father's friend forsake not;" **or as,** "He that hasteneth to be rich, **will not** be guiltless;" or as, "He that **giveth** to the poor will **not** lack."

We know by the authority of Jeremiah in chapter xxvi. 18, that the prophet Micah wrote in the reign of Hezekiah; but from Micah's own writings **we** could hardly **learn it,** as the tenor of his argument is very obscure. Thus **Micah** wrote at the same time as **Isaiah;** but Isaiah **lived in** Jerusalem, and was one of king Hezekiah's advisers, **while** Micah lived at a distance. Hence while Isaiah tells the nation of its faults, Micah reproaches the rulers **in** Jerusalem; and he blames its priests, its prophets, and its judges alike:—

Hear this I pray you, ye, heads of the house of Jacob, and princes

13

of the house of Israel, that abhor judgment, and pervert all equity, that build up Zion with bloodshed and Jerusalem with iniquity. Her heads judge for bribes and her teachers teach for hire, and her prophets divine for money; **yet** they lean upon Jehovah, and say, "Is it not Jehovah among us? No evil can come upon us." Therefore shall Zion for your sake **be** plowed as a field, and Jerusalem become heaps of ruins, and the Mountain of the House, **as the** High Places in the forest.

The tribute sent to Lachish, which Isaiah does not mention, Micah seems to point to when he says that in the chariot sent from that city were the transgressions **of Israel,** and that was the beginning of sin to Zion. The payment **of** the tribute brought no peace, and it was followed by the **flight** of the king and nobles from Jerusalem, "they pass through the city gate, and go out by it; and their king passeth before them, and Jehovah at the head of them." The Book of Micah shows a knowledge of the Books of Exodus and Numbers, quoting, in chapter vi., the doings of Moses, Aaron, Miriam, Balak, and Balaam. But short as is the work of Micah, even from this **we** must except some passages as by **later** hands. Such are chapters iv.—v., which were probably written after the people had returned from Babylon under Zerubbabel, and such is chapter vii. 1-10, written perhaps during the discomfort **on** the death of Zerubbabel; and verses 11-13, written at a yet later time, when the walls of Jerusalem were soon to be rebuilt by the permission of the king of Persia.

We must claim also for the reign of Hezekiah, chapters ix. 1-10 and x. of the prophecy of Zechariah. They were **written** against the land of Hadrach, perhaps Assyria, and against Damascus, its resting-place, from whence its armies entered **Canaan.** The **writer,** who closely resembles Isaiah, boasts **that Jehovah** "will encamp about his Temple, against the **army of the** enemy, against it when it passeth by, and against **it when it** returneth." He thus describes Sennacherib's double march through **the** land of Judea. The pride of Assyria is to be brought **low, and** the sceptre of Egypt to depart. No tribute collector is to remain in Judea, and Ephraim is to be brought home from captivity. Hence these chapters were written after the captivity of northern Israel, and after the Assyrians had retreated from Judea, and when the kingdom of Judea was again free from the invader. The historian, indeed, in the life of Hezekiah, does **not tell us** of that king having fled from Jerusalem on either occasion of Sennacherib's approach, but such a flight here seems spoken of, as the king is described as returning to Jerusalem, "just, having been saved, lowly, and riding upon an ass, even upon a colt the foal of a she-ass."

These two chapters of Zechariah tell us that at the moment of Sennacherib's retreat the rulers in Jerusalem hoped that they might again be masters of what was lately the northern kingdom; and the prophet says that Jehovah will whistle for captive Israel and bring them home again. Out of these chapters, however, we must except ix. 11-17, the work of a very late time.

In Genesis xxvi., Isaac is told by Jehovah not to go down into Egypt. Hence that would seem to have been written after chapter xii., which describes Abraham's journey into that country, and after Isaiah xxx. 6, had blamed the flight of the Jews into Egypt. This chapter xxvi. gives the sanction of the patriarch Isaac to the Altar to Jehovah at Beer-sheba, in opposition to the priests of Jerusalem. The few words in chapter xxi. 33, which give Abraham's sanction to the same Altar to Jehovah may also have been added at the same time to that Elohistic chapter. Beer-sheba at the very southern limit of Judea, in the desert between Judea and Egypt, had probably sheltered many Jews who had fled thither from Assyrian cruelty. This chapter was probably written by one of them, as we have supposed that chapters xx., xxi. had been written a little earlier by a man of northern Israel who had lived there.

MANASSEH KING OF JUDAH ; B.C. 698—644.

Manasseh, the next king, called the son of Hezekiah, was only twelve years old when he came to the throne. The child mentioned in Isaiah ix., as heir to the kingdom, would by this time, had he lived, have been about thirty-five years old; and hence he may have been the father of Manasseh; and Manasseh the grandson of Hezekiah. Unlike some of the other kings who began their reigns in childhood, Manasseh seems to have fallen into hands strongly opposed to the priests. His name must have been highly displeasing to them, being that of the oldest of the northern tribes He must have taken it with a view to please the northern Israelites; and it is quite possible that the Assyrian king may have made him his vice-roy over that country as well as over Judea. Manasseh allowed the worship on the High Places which Hezekiah had at one time stopped. This would

13 *

seem a praiseworthy act in favour of the inhabitants who dwelt at a distance from Jerusalem. It left every person at liberty to carry his religious offerings to the priests in his own neighbourhood; but it thus lessened the income of the chief priests. In the struggle for wealth and power between the capital and the country at large, Hezekiah had in this matter at first taken the side of the priests and of the capital, but he had been forced to change, and had latterly governed according to the wish of the country party and the Levites. So **the** young Manasseh's advisers took the side of the country with its mixed races of people. For doing this the king was charged with encouraging idolatry of various kinds, and with copying the worship which had been introduced into Israel by Jezebel the Tyrian princess, the wife of Ahab, and with causing his son to **pass** through the fire. This last was a superstitious ceremony, first introduced by king Ahaz, which in this **case can** only have meant the making the boy jump, or perhaps **even** ride **on horseback**, through the flames, as a ceremonial **purification, or to** prove his sacred character.*

Manasseh's reign was quiet but not prosperous. **He was**, no doubt, wholly at the mercy of the king **of** Assyria, **and** paying such tribute to him as could be raised out of the ruined country. On failure of the tribute, or **on** some signs of disobedience, the king of Assyria, a successor of Sennacherib, probably Esarhaddon, sent an army against Jerusalem, and carried off Manasseh a prisoner to Babylon. This must have **been after** the conquest of Babylon by Esarhaddon, B.C. 680. **After** a **time** Manasseh was released, and allowed to return **to** his kingdom, but **of** course to remain tributary to the king of Assyria. This is the third or fourth time that Jerusalem had been entered by a foreign army, and its Temple plundered, since Solomon placed **in** it the golden Ark containing the Tables of **Stone on** which **the** Law **was** written. These misfortunes **may** explain **how** it was possible for the Ten Commandments, when hereafter copied into the Book of Deuteronomy, to **be in** part changed from those which we have seen in the Book **of** Exodus.

Manasseh was released and **sent** home to govern Judea, of course in the belief that he **would** be an obedient servant **to the** king of Assyria. But if we are right **in our** dates, his return was very soon followed by the death of Esarhaddon. This may have released Judea from its bondage ; for we find

* 2 Kings xxi. 1-18.

that Manasseh was so far his own master that he very much strengthened the wall of Jerusalem on the north and east sides, from the north-west corner of the city, near the valley of the Gihon, to the Fishgate at the north-east corner, and thence round to the suburb Ophel, on the south side of the Temple-yard. There he raised it to a very great height. Thus he would seem to be the finisher of that gigantic piece of stone-work, which at the south-east corner of the Temple-yard, rose out of the ditch to the height of one hundred and forty feet, built of stones as remarkable, even in the time of the apostles, for their size as the wall was for its height. Jotham had begun this part of the wall near Ophel, three reigns earlier; and no doubt Ahaz and Hezekiah, while living in fear of the Assyrians, had also carried this great work forward; but the Chronicler gives the chief share of it to Manasseh.

Manasseh, after his return from Babylon, changed his policy; he put away the idolatry which he had before encouraged, and repaired the altar in front of the House of Jehovah. But he did not stop the sacrificing on the High Places. The priests of Jerusalem had evidently lost that power which in the reign of Hezekiah had for a time allowed them to require all burnt-offerings to be sent up to Jerusalem.

During the latter half of Manasseh's reign Necho I and then Psammetichus I were kings of Egypt; and Assurbanipal, the effeminate Sardanapalus, the son of Esarhaddon was king of Nineveh.*

Manasseh reigned fifty-five years, a longer period than that of any other of the kings. But he held his power with difficulty against frequent attempts at rebellion, made by the priestly party in Jerusalem. These were not crushed without the city being filled with blood from one end to the other. It is a reign of which we have very few particulars. This may in part be explained by supposing that for the greatest part of his life he continued, against the will of the priests, an obedient vassal of the king of Assyria.† The Hebrew writers are agreed in blaming those kings who bought peace by paying a tribute, and in praising those who refused. But when we consider the overwhelming superiority of the invaders in men, in horses, and in weapons, and the certain misery which they brought on all the country, except Jerusalem and possibly a few strong places, we see that resistance was rather an act of madness than of wise patriotism.

* G. Smith's History of Assurbanipal.   † 2 Chron. xxxiii. 1 20.

In the reigns of Ahaz and Hezekiah, when danger from
the Assyrians was overhanging Judea, the prophets uttered
many noble words of trust and encouragement; and when
the Assyrians withdrew and the danger was over for a time,
the poets wrote many Psalms of triumph and thankfulness.
But afterwards when it was found by sad experience that all
resistance to the overwhelming power of Sennacherib and
Esarhaddon was useless, and the people had no choice but to
yield their liberty, and to purchase their lives and peace by
paying a tribute, the prophets were silent; and if the poets
yet wrote any Psalms they are free from all mention of public
events. Hence we can point to no writings as certainly
belonging to Manasseh's long reign.

A few **words** inserted into the middle of a prophecy by
Isaiah, chapter vii. 8, speak of a final destruction of Ephraim,
a little less than sixty-five years after the death of Ahaz, or
in the middle of Manasseh's reign, about B.C. 670. Perhaps
at this time Esarhaddon, King of Assyria, carried off a
further body of captives **from** Northern Israel, as we hear
that he sent into the scantily peopled country some more
Assyrian colonists. These new comers seem readily to have
adopted the customs and even the religion of the country;
and two centuries later we find their children asking to be
considered as Jews.*

The words in Isaiah vii. 8, spoken of above, foretelling a
further misfortune to Ephraim are our earliest example of
the corruption of the prophetic writings by a pretended
prophecy written after the event. They spoil the sense of
the passage. Unfortunately we shall meet with many more
such before the end of our history. It may seem an un-
gracious task to discover such a blot in writings which we
value **so highly**. But by its discovery the blot is removed.
When the **alloy is** taken away the pure metal shines the
brighter.

We may **here** mention, as being later than the Assyrian
invasion in Hezekiah's reign, Genesis x. 22—xi. 9, a correction of the history of **the** descent of nations from Noah. The
original writer had made the Arabs, Assyrians, and Babylonians, children of Ham ;† and perhaps brought from Shem
only the Chaldees, Hebrews, and children of Abraham.‡ It
is in contradiction to this that a later writer, in Genesis x.
22—xi. 9, makes Shem to be the father of the Elamites, the

* Ezra iv. 2.   † Gen. x. 7-12.   ‡ Gen. xi. 10-27.

Assyrians, and of the Arabs, even to Hazramaveth or Hadramout in Southern Arabia, and to Ophir on the Nubian coast, places that could hardly have been known to a Hebrew writer before the time of Solomon's voyage down the Red Sea. To this the writer was led by the study of language, by observing that most of these people spoke dialects of one common tongue, which might be called Arabic or Shemitic. He may have been led to class the Elamites in the same family of nations, by knowing that they formed part of the Assyrian army during Sennacherib's invasion of Judea.* Had he lived when they formed part of the Persian army under Cyrus, he might have classed them differently. This same study of language led him to find a reason or an occasion for the introduction of so many different languages into the world, or dialects into the Shemitic race; and this he did in the building of the tower of Babel. As the confusion of the tower of Babel does not reach to the "words" or language but only to the "lip," or pronunciation, we must suppose that the writer is only treating of the children of Shem. He derives his own nation not from Chesed, the Chaldees, as that name had lately followed a forced migration of the people to the neighbourhood of Babylon, but from Arep-cheshed, a name which had not been carried southward.

In this account of the descent of nations, the Arabian coast of the Red Sea is well described; the Arab races are said to dwell between Mesha, a town near the southern point of Arabia, and the holy mountain in Sinai, called "Sephar, the mountain which was of old." It is by the help of this name, Sephar, or *written*, called Shephar in Numbers xxxiii. 23, that travellers may now recognize Mount Serbal as the Mount of God spoken of in Exodus xix. Wady Mucatteb, the *sculptured valley*, is full of inscriptions cut on the face of the rocks; and similar inscriptions mark the pathway to the very peak of Serbal, cut there by pious Jews, pilgrims from Egypt who visited that holy spot.

But again, these Arab tribes, which one writer had made so distant from the Israelites as to call them children of Ham, and a second had brought nearer by calling them childrem of Shem, a third writer in Genesis xxv. 1-6 and 12-18, brought still nearer to the family of Israel by ranking them as children of Abraham. This later passage must be held to be contradictory to the original life of Abraham,

* Isaiah xxii. 6.

which certainly meant **us** to understand that he had only two sons.

The name of Mount " Sephar, the mountain which was of old," in this addition to Genesis x., leads to the opinion that the pious custom of visiting the holy spot, where the Law was said to have been delivered by Jehovah to Moses, was not new even in the time of Hezekiah. It was already called "the mountain which was of old." The Hebrew prayers, which we now read sculptured on the rocks, may have been cut many centuries after this reign; but the Jewish pilgrims who cut them were only following the custom of earlier pilgrims, Israelites who had fled from Shalmanezer, and Jews who had escaped from Sennacherib, and those who had settled in Egypt for the purposes of trade. By the time of Hezekiah the mount of God was already called Mount Sephar, or *written.*

AMON KING OF JUDAH; B.C. 643—642.

Amon, the son of Manasseh, reigned but two years, when he was slain by his servants, who had conspired against him. It would appear as if the cause of this revolution was the king's not walking in the way of Jehovah, or in other words, not according to the will of the priests; for his death, which was cause by the people of the capital, was immediately revenged by the people of the country, who put the conspirators to death, and gave the crown to Josiah, Amon's son, a child of eight years old.*

Amon and his father Manasseh did not bear Jehovistic names; they were both opposed to the policy of the priests. Neither in the history does king Ahaz, who like them governed the kingdom in a spirit opposed to the priests of Jerusalem, bear a Jehovistic name. Had he been less unpopular, the historians would probably have given to him the full name of Ahaz-iah. But with those three exceptions every king of Judah, since the rise of the priestly power in Jehosaphat's reign, bore a name either beginning with the syllables Jeho-, or ending with -jah.

JOSIAH KING OF JUDAH; B.C. 641—611.

For the first eight years of Josiah's reign we have no **events** recorded; we may suppose that he was tributary

2 Kings xxi. 19—26.

to the king of Assyria, and that he was governed by the
country party which had put him on the throne, the party
opposed to the high priests and nobles in Jerusalem. The
country people who dwelt in the open villages, were naturally those who most dreaded invasion, and were most
willing to purchase peace by a tribute. But in the eight
year of his reign Josiah changed his policy, and put himself
into the hands of the priests. This change was made at
a time when the Assyrian power was weakened by a war
with Babylon. In his twelfth year Josiah began to stop
the sacrifices on the High Places in favour of the Temple
of Jerusalem.* But in so doing he seems to have acted
with moderation. The inhabitants of Jerusalem and the
men of Judah had lost their chief cause of quarrel when the
fear of invasion was over. And Josiah perhaps limited his
attack to those High Places where the worship had been
idolatrous. The priests of the other High Places continued
to serve and be served at their own altars.†

Josiah at the same time defiled Topheth in the Valley
of Hinnom, on the south side of Jerusalem.‡ This was
a spot where the inhabitants of Jerusalem burnt the dead.
It had been lately treated as an altar, on which children
were made to pass through the flames, perhaps originally
as a ceremonial purification, but sometimes to cause their
death. The superstitious ceremony had been introduced
by Ahaz, and had been practised by Manasseh, perhaps
only for sons. Those two kings did not thereby kill their
sons. But when the common people adopted the superstition, it seems to have been used as a cloak for child-murder,
for sons and daughters alike. In Deuteronomy, written
in Josiah's reign, it is forbidden only as a superstition,
together with divination and serpent-charming.§ But
Josiah did not succeed in stopping it ; and Jeremiah, writing
only a few years later than the publication of Deuteronomy,
says that the children were really burnt to death.‖ This
shocking practice tells us of the misery of the people who
could be driven to such an unnatural crime ; and the manner
in which it was spoken of, when the word " fire " was dropt,
and it was called " passing the children through to Moloch,"
leads us to fear that it had become sadly common.¶

* 2 Chron. xxxiv. 1-5.   † 2 Kings xxiii. 1-9.
‡ 2 Kings xxiii. 10.   § Deut. xviii. 10.
‖ Jerem. vii. 31.   ¶ Jerem. xxxii. 35.

The High Place at Beth-el was a particular object of **Josiah's** attack. He destroyed it, and in order to defile the **spot** most thoroughly he had the tombs of the priests opened, and burnt their **bones** on the altar. He did the same through Samaria, burning the priests' bones on their own altars.*

In the eighteenth year Josiah set himself to repair the House of Jehovah, which the priests seem **to** have neglected although they had received money for the purpose.

From the words of the prophet Jeremiah, we learn that the Holy of Holies no longer held the Ark which had been called the seat of Jehovah ; as he tells the people to forget it altogether, and he does not wish that a new Ark should be made ; for not the Ark but the city of Jerusalem is Jehovah's throne.† As it was necessary for this sacred chest to have a golden cover, it was naturally carried off every time that Jerusalem was plundered ; and there may have been no Ark in **the** Temple since Manasseh was carried prisoner to Babylon. The Chronicler says that Josiah again placed an Ark in the Holy of Holies.‡ From Jeremiah's words we should think this doubtful : but if true the priests can have had no difficulty in copying from the Book of Exodus on to new stones the Ten Commandments, **in the old** words so far as they wished.

At that time the king was very much governed by men of remarkable intelligence and liberality ; Hilkiah, the high-priest, the father of Jeremiah, and Achbor, as it would seem the **head** of the Zarhites, and Shaphan, the king's scribe, or secretary of state, perhaps the head of the Pharezites, of which **two** families we shall hear more hereafter. When the workmen were repairing the Temple of Jehovah, Hilkiah sent **word to** the king by Shaphan that he had there found a Book of the Law. To Hilkiah and Shaphan we seem to owe chapters iv. 44—xviii. 8, and chapters xxviii.—xxx. of Deuteronomy. These chapters support Hezekiah's policy of forbidding all sacrifices, except at one only place ; but on the other hand they declare the little value of all such sacrifices ; and they enact that when the Levites of the country come up to the capital they shall share equally with the priests, and they thus overthrow the power of the one family which had hitherto held that rank. Rivalry and jealousy **may have** had some share in writing these laws ; but **they were for** the most part an improvement on the old

* **2 Kings xxiii.**   † Jerem. iii. 16, 17.   ‡ 2 Chron. xxxv. 3.

laws. Shaphan carried the book to the king, and read some
sentences to him out of it. These were passages which
threatened God's wrath upon the nation for their **sins** and
idolatries, probably chapter xxviii.; and they caused **great**
alarm in the king's mind. The book was called the **Book**
of the Covenant, and the words which are either quoted or
referred to are contained in our Book of Deuteronomy. We
thus learn when part **at least** of the Book of Deuteronomy
was **first made** known, and **we may** say, when it was
written.

The king then commanded the priests to inquire of
Jehovah what was to **be** done : and strange to say they
went **to take** the advice of Huldah, a prophetess : and **she**
repeated **the threats** contained in **the** newly found book
against the people for their forsaking Jehovah.* They may
have chosen her as their adviser because of her ignorance,
as it has been often thought by the superstitious that
the utterances of those who have no human knowledge are
most likely words from heaven. Josiah then summoned the
people to meet him in the courts of the Temple, where he
stood upon his pillar and read to them out of the book ;
and the people all undertook to obey the laws therein
written, and to walk after Jehovah. Josiah **had all the**
idolatrous vessels and altars removed **out of the** Temple,
with the image **of the** Goddess Ashera, **and** the statues of
horses to the chariot of the sun which **stood** at one of the
gates to the Temple-yard. All **the** High Places which
Solomon had allowed for the Abominations of the conquered
tribes did king Josiah defile.

Thus whatever changes Josiah **aimed** at were in the
priestly direction of making a separation between the Jews
and the mixed people of the country ; and it is probable
that Josiah's so-called reforms, by keeping up the division
of the nation into two classes, hastened not a **little its** loss
of independence

Josiah then celebrated **the** Passover in **Jerusalem with**
great splendour and ceremony ; such **a Passover,** says the
historian, had never before been kept in **all the** days of the
kings of Israel and Judah. This, however, may not have
stopped the celebration of the feast in the various cities
throughout the country.†

The publication **of** Deuteronomy, **however,** marks a decline
of the priests' power. When the priests were most powerful

---

* 2 Kings xxii.   † 2 Kings xxiii. 1-23.

it is true that they wrote the ceremonial laws in Exodus,
Leviticus and Numbers; but they wrote them only for their
own use. Those laws had not been written for the people;
and but few of the people could have been able to read
them if they had been made public. The priests never
quoted the laws as an authority; they were themselves the
only authority in religious matters. But latterly the prophets
also had undertaken to declare the will of Jehovah, by simply
appealing to every man's conscience and good sense. The
speeches and writings of the prophets had **made** more in-
quirers and more readers; and a people who spoke the same
language as Joel, Amos, and Isaiah could not remain wholly
satisfied with sacrifices and ceremonies in religion. The priests
therefore, perhaps unwillingly, had to make the same appeal
to the people. For this the laws in the older books were
unsuitable; and though referred to in Deuteronomy, they are
now put forward in a new and amended form, a form written
for the people. The publication of this new book looks like
an attempt by the priests to regain from the prophets some
of the weight which they had been slowly losing. Here the
very style of the prophets is imitated.

We have seen how the elder Zechariah and Joel begin as
speakers with words of irony and reproach. Others, who
may not all have been speakers, usually begin their writings
after a short preface, as if they were; thus—

Isaiah, "Hear, O heavens, and give ear, O earth, for
Jehovah speaketh."

Amos, " Hear the word which Jehovah hath spoken against
you, O children of Israel."

Michah, "Hear, O ye peoples, every one of you, O land and
all that is therein."

Hosea, **"Hear** the word of Jehovah, ye children of
Israel."

Jeremiah, **"Hear ye the word of** Jehovah, O house of
Jacob."

Nahum, who was more **of an** orator than most of the
prophets, begins more quietly, but he soon rises to the warmth
and eloquence which was the mark of a prophet as long as
the nation enjoyed its freedom.

The Book of Deuteronomy copies the prophets with its
fine burst of " Hear, O Israel, Jehovah is our God, Jehovah
alone."

Before this time the laws would seem to have been for the
use of the priests **alone;** but now the priests think that they

can strengthen their declining power by appealing to a written sacred volume. When Deuteronomy was brought out of the Temple, the other books of the law, though not mentioned, were probably not kept back, but simply thought less suitable to be read to the king and the public. Indeed Jeremiah tells us that the Law of Jehovah, meaning probably the older books, was already being circulated by the pen of the scribes, and that the people boasted of it as a national possession.[*]

When Josiah's servants were repairing the Temple they paid the workmen's wages in silver; and in order to do so they melted the metal, to divide it into small sums.[†] This is the nearest approach to modern money that we have yet met with; but we must not suppose that the silver was made into real coins, each marked with figures or characters by which its value was shown. That was a convenience not known to the world till some time later, and not known to Judea till the time of the Maccabee princes. Hitherto, and for some time longer, the precious metals were paid away and received by weight; the shekel was a weight not a coin, but yet it might be convenient to melt the silver into small lumps before paying it away. For this purpose there was a melting-place in one of the courts of the Temple, adjoining the treasury.[‡] The lumps into which the silver was melted were probably meant for shekels, and half shekels; but when Jeremiah makes a payment by weight we find that ten pieces of silver were needed to equal seven shekels.[§]

It was in the year B.C. 625, the year before that of which we have been speaking, that Babylon again threw off the yoke of Nineveh. It had before done so in the reign of Hezekiah, when Berodach Baladan refused to send up his tribute; but it had afterwards sunk before the stronger power; and Esarhaddon in the middle of Manasseh's reign pushed aside its king, and united it to the Assyrian crown. But now by some revolution, about which history gives us no hint, the Chaldees, who, as we have supposed, had been brought by the Assyrians from the north, and placed as colonists and bond servants in the neighbourhood of Babylon, rise into rank and power. We find a Chaldee dynasty seated on the throne of Babylon; and Nabopulassar, a Chaldean, again makes Babylon independent, and aims at the conquest of Nineveh.

An eclipse of the moon, observed at Babylon in the fifth

---

[*] Jerem. viii. 8.
[†] 2 Kings xxii. 9.
[‡] Zech. xi. 13, comp. Greek.
[§] Jerem. xxxii. 9.

year of Nabopulassar, when compared with the calculations
of modern astronomers, tells us that year was B.C. 621. The
record was brought from Babylon by Alexander the Great,
and is preserved in the writings of Claudius Ptolemy. Upon
that eclipse the chronology of the early Jewish history rests.

The war between Babylon and Nineveh for a few years
left King Josiah without a master. But it was only for a
few years. Assyria and Egypt had each for a century past
thought themselves equally entitled to receive a tribute from
the Hebrew nation, and we shall presently see that as soon
as Jerusalem had nothing to fear from Assyria, it was in
equal danger of being conquered by Egypt.

And here we remark on the changed use of the word
Chaldean in the Bible. It had been the name of a tribe
placed by Strabo the geographer at the sources of the
Euphrates, between Armenia and Syria,* from which country
tradition had brought Abraham southward. But from the
time of Nabopulassar, a Chaldean is another name for a
Babylonian; and by a second change, before the end of our
history, after the Greek conquest of the country, the Soothsayers of Babylon are the only people known to us as
Chaldeans.

In the meantime a new and unexpected trouble burst over
Judea. This was an inroad of Scythians, who coming down
from Tartary, from the northern and eastern sides of the
Caspian Sea, had some of them poured over Media, and
some turned upon Asia Minor, while a third body had
marched through Josiah's kingdom on their way to Egypt.
These last plundered and laid waste the open country, while
the frightened inhabitants flew to the walled cities, which
the invaders had neither time nor skill to attack. They
were turned back by the Egyptian king Psammetichus
before they reached his country.† The desolation brought
upon Judea by the Scythians seems described by Jeremiah.
The description of these barbarians, and of the alarm which
they occasioned, is among the most striking parts of
Jeremiah's writings :—

Declare ye in Judah, and publish in Jerusalem, and say, "Blow ye the
trumpet in the land." Cry with a full voice, and say, "Assemble your-
selves, and let us go into the fenced cities." Set up the standard toward
Zion; flee in haste, stay not; for I will bring evil from the north, and a
great breaking up. The lion is come up from his thicket, and the des-

---

* Strabo. XII, iii. 28, 29; **Xenop.** Anab. IV, iii. 4.
† Herodotus, **I. 104.**

troyer of nations has moved his camp. He is gone forth from his place to make thy land desolate ; and thy cities shall be laid waste without an inhabitant.*

And again :—

Lo, I will bring upon you a nation from far, O house of Israel; **Jehovah** hath said it. It is a mighty nation, it is an ancient nation, a nation whose language thou knowest not, neither understandest thou what they say. Their quiver is as an open sepulchre, they are all warriors. And **they** shall eat up thy harvest and thy bread, which thy sons and daughters should eat ; they shall eat up thy flocks and thy herds ; they shall eat up thy vines and thy fig trees ; they shall break down thy fenced cities, wherein thou trustest, with the sword.†

These **invaders are again** described **in** Deuteronomy, in nearly **the same words** :—

Jehovah will bring up against thee a **nation from** far, from the ends of **the earth** flying as an eagle, a nation whose tongue thou shalt not understand, **a** nation of fierce countenance, which will not regard the person of the old, or show favour to the young.‡

The historians of this reign do not mention these enemies by name. But we learn from Ezekiel, chapter xxxix., that these barbarians, whom he speaks of under the name of Gog of the land of Magog, on reaching the southern end of the country, not attempting to cross the desert into Egypt, turned northward along the shores of the Mediterranean Sea, and there perished **on the** road, **no doubt** because supplies and plunder both failed them.

Together with the Scythians another distant nation now comes forward to our notice, namely the Medes, whose capital city was Ecbatana, situated between the river Tigris and the Caspian Sea. They were invited by the Babylonians to join in a revolt against their common enemies the Assyrians **of** Nineveh. With the Medes came also the Persians; and even the distant Bactrians, who may have been a **race** of Scythians, rushed to the overthrow of the last king **of** Assyria. The history of the Medes and their **rise** is obscure. From the Greek historian, however, joined to the Assyrian inscriptions in the cuneiform character, we glean that this king of Assyria was Assurbanipal the son of Esarhaddon, the Sardanapalus of the Greeks, whose luxurious effeminate character readily explains his overthrow.§ But the Babylonian annals are more accurate; and from them

* Jerem. iv. 5-7.   † Jerem. v. 15-17.   ‡ Deut. xxviii. 49, 50.
§ Diod. Sic. ii. 23-27.   Smith's History of Assurbanipal.

and the Hebrew writings we learn that in the thirtieth year
of Josiah's reign, B.C. 612, Nineveh was conquered by
Nabopulassar, the Chaldee king of Babylon.

Great was the joy of the Jews. For more than one
hundred years their sufferings had come from the Assyrians.
The northern tribes had been carried into captivity by them.
The southern tribes had been repeatedly invaded by them,
and had suffered severely from their cruelty and their
exactions; and the woe with which Isaiah and the other
Hebrew prophets had threatened them had now fallen upon
them. Nineveh was conquered, and Judea was free from
all foreign tribute, and the northern tribes had now no
master. Josiah was able to enforce the wishes of his priests,
so far as to stop the sacrifices at the High Places throughout
Samaria. The altar at Beth-el, the particular object of
their dislike, was then destroyed, and its priests put to
death. Josiah for the moment may have had dreams of
making his kingdom, like Solomon's, reach from the Euphrates to the southern desert, as the northern and eastern
tribes had now no master. But he had neither strength nor
time for such a conquest. Short was the relief even to his
own subjects. In the very next year the Egyptian army
entered the country, to take possession of such portion of
territory and of such plunder as the Assyrians had left for
them.

Egypt had latterly undergone many changes, and at this
time the city of Sais, on the west side of the Delta, was the
seat of government. Sais was a city as much Greek as
Egyptian; Greek traders had settled in large numbers on
that side of the Delta; the kings of Sais had introduced
not only Greek letters but Greek arms and discipline, and
they usually had a body of Greek mercenaries in their pay.
These Greek soldiers were far superior to any soldiers of the
surrounding nations, and they gave a superiority to every
king that engaged their services. At present we hear of
them only in the Egyptian army, but within a century we
shall find them holding the front post even in the Persian
armies.

Psammetichus, who was king of Egypt at the time of the
late inroad of the Scythians, was succeeded by Necho II,
shortly before the overthrow of Assyria; and the ruin
brought upon that country by Babylon was probably the
cause of his now venturing upon such a great undertaking
as his march to the river Euphrates. His aim was not to

attack Jerusalem, but perhaps to make himself master of the ruined, and now deserted northern half of Canaan. At the moment he meant no injury to Josiah's kingdom. He probably brought his army by sea, and he was on his route from the coast to Carchemish on the Euphrates, and had reached Megiddo, sixty miles to the north of Jerusalem, when Josiah rashly led his forces against him, thinking that the northern half of Canaan belonged to himself rather than to the king of Egypt. But the Jews were defeated in the battle, Josiah was slain by an archer, and his body carried back to Jerusalem to be buried. Josiah, during the larger part of his reign, had been governed by the priests; and they said that Jehovah overthrew him for the sins of his father, Manasseh, whose opposite line of policy had saved his country from ruin during his long reign.*

The quiet reign of Josiah was as eventful in Hebrew literature as in the politics of the neighbouring nations. A large part of the Book of Deuteronomy as we have said was then written; beginning at chapter iv. 44. It is a new and corrected edition of the Mosaic law. The changes which may be noted in it, when we compare it with the older form of the law, mark the nation's advance in civilization, and its better views of religion. It begins with a slight mention of the former narrative of the march, and thus it does not need the four introductory chapters which have been added to it. In what we must consider the original portion of the book no mention is made of Joshua and Caleb; their names had not yet been introduced into the narrative.

The speeches in this more modern book of the law are put into the mouth of Moses, and Jehovah no longer appears as himself uttering the commands. In the Ten Commandments the Sabbath is to be kept, not because God created the world in seven days, but because he brought the nation out of the land of Egypt. The people are ordered to love Jehovah, their God, with all their heart, and with all their soul (vi. 5); a command more nearly approaching Christianity than any we have before met with. God's punishments are looked upon as a father's chastisement for our amendment (viii. 5). The threats against the Canaanites are repeated from Exodus xxiii.; but now that the conquered race has been partially woven into that of their masters, the threats are

---

* 2 Kings xxiii. 26-30; 2 Chron. xxxv. 20-27.

14

made more violent because they hurt nobody; the Canaanites are not, as before, to be driven out year by year, and
little by little, but they are to be wholly destroyed, together
with their images and groves of Ashera (vii.).

The attempt made by Hezekiah and Josiah to put down
the worship on the High Places is strongly enforced, and all
offerings are to be made and feasts to be observed in The
Place which Jehovah shall choose for the dwelling-place of
his name, that is in Jerusalem. The distinction between Sons
of Aaron and Levites is denied; all the tribe of Levi are
called priests; and when they come up to The Place which
Jehovah shall choose, they are to have like duties and like
portions with those who dwell there (xviii. 1-8). When the
punishment of Dathan and Abiram for claiming to act as
Levites is mentioned (xi. 6), no mention is made of Korah
the Levite, who was punished for acting as a priest. This
act was perhaps not thought blamable.

The three great feasts, namely, the Passover or Unleavened
Bread, the Feast of Weeks or First Fruits, the Feast of
Ingathering, which is now called the Feast of Tabernacles,
are to be kept at The **Place,** and not in any other city
(xvi. 1-17). The **laws** in Exodus xxiii. and xxxiv., which
order the three yearly pilgrimages to Jerusalem for the celebration of these feasts, had not forbidden the family celebration. But this command in Deuteronomy goes further, and
is in direct contradiction of the old law, that every family
should keep the Passover at home. Many passages in this
book tell us· of the lessened wealth of the people since the
Assyrian occupation of the country. The classes which do
not themselves produce wealth were the chief sufferers; and
the Levites are now counted among the poor who need
relief. The Levites are no longer able to claim the tithe as
their own. It is to be eaten as a peace-offering or love-feast
by the owner and his household and the poor Levite; not at
home, but at The Place (xii. 17-19). And even this command is afterwards made yet lighter to the owner, when it is
ordered that the tithe of the first and second year only is to
be brought up to The Place to be eaten there before Jehovah
by its owner, his household, and the Levite (xiv. 22-29). The
tithe of the third year may be eaten at home, but like that of
the other years it is to be shared with the Levite, the
stranger, the fatherless, and the widow (xiv. 28, 29). Hence
it is evident that the rulers, whether king or priests, had not
been able to levy this land-tax, which had at first been

claimed by the king, and then by king and priests jointly. The collecting of the tithe would seem to have wholly ceased before it was ordered to be brought up to Jerusalem in this very unoppressive way.

A slight is thrown on some of the laws which in the Book of Exodus follow the Ten Commandments, by the writer's saying that when Jehovah delivered the Commandments "he added no more" (v. 22). The Gifts to the altar, the Burnt Offerings, Sacrifices, Tithes, Heave Offerings, Vows, Free-will Offerings, and Firstlings, though not described, are ordered to be duly paid (xii. 6). This shows a full acquaint-ance with the Book of Leviticus. Permission is given to eat animal food in any city (xii. 21). This permission was needed, because Leviticus xvii. seemed to have forbidden it.

The law about clean and unclean animals, which in Leviticus is laid down in general terms, is here made more clear by the animals being named (xiv.). And a doubt seems to have arisen about the hart and the roebuck, or gazelle, which as being wild could not have been seen to chew the cud, and thus were thought not wholly clean. Hence it was ordered that, like a lame animal, they might be eaten, but might not be sacrificed to Jehovah (xv.).

Chapters xviii. 9—xxvii. seem to be of a later date. Chapters xxviii.—xxx. contain the threats read to king Josiah.

Deuteronomy xxix. 23 mentions the overthrow of four villages, Sodom and Gomorrah, Admah and Zebiim, as if all overthrown at one time by Jehovah's wrath. But the early tradition in Genesis xix. only speaks of Sodom and Gomorrah as so destroyed; and from Hosea xi. 8 it would seem as if Admah and Zebiim had been destroyed at a much later time. Whatever physical agency brought about the early destruction of the first two cities, probably brought about the later destruction of the two others.

There are two passages in this book which seem much better fitted for an earlier part of the monarchy than either for the reign of Josiah, or for any later time. Thus chapter xvii. 14-20, after telling the people not to choose a foreigner for their king, gives some advice how he should govern, that he should not multiply his horses and wives, and silver and gold, and that he should write for himself a copy of this law out of the book which is laid up with the priests. This advice seems as if meant for Solomon, and may have been copied from the book which we have spoken of in his reign,

14 *

and which was said to have been written by Samuel, containing "the manner of the kingdom." The other passage is chapter xx., which contains advice about foreign conquests, and the siege of cities at a distance. This may well have been borrowed from a book written when David's wars were fresh in the writer's memory; but is very unsuitable for the nation in its weakness.

The few works containing part of the march of the Israelites, in Deuteronomy x. 6, 7, are clearly out of place. They belong to the earlier narrative; and by the help of Numbers xxxiii. we may conclude that they should stand somewhere between Exodus xxxii. and Numbers xiii.

The Book of Deuteronomy was a most praiseworthy attempt on the part of a few of the priests to stem the downward rush of the nation into follies and vices which never fail to break up all civil society. The established priesthood, with its Levitical law, its rites and ceremonies, had hitherto offered a very deceptive remedy to such evils. The prophets, Isaiah and others, had ventured, against the priests, to point out the worthlessness of religious ceremonies as a check to vice; but now the chief priest himself (may all honour be given to him) seems to be the proposer of a priestly reformation. Hilkiah was a statesman as well as a priest; and with the assistance probably of his son Jeremiah, who may at that time have been twenty-five years of age, he undertook to rewrite the Mosaic Law in a popular form, dropping or laying no stress on what was worthless, and adding to what was valuable. This new Book of the Covenant enacts no new ceremonial Statutes, though it says that the old Statutes are to be obeyed.

This attempt at reform met with but little success. The priesthood remained, though it was enlarged, the altar and its ceremonies remained. The remedy was far too gentle to meet the evil. But if it failed for the moment, it has remained for all time as an improved summary of Jewish law; and when the hostile critic of the Pentateuch points to the littleness of the enactments in Leviticus, the Jew may defend himself by the Book of Deuteronomy.

To the reign of Josiah, after the Book of Deuteronomy had been written, rather than to the reign of Hezekiah, we must give Numbers xxviii., xxix., which describe the offerings which ought to be brought to the altar, and the national celebration of the several feasts. The Book of Deuteronomy had, for the first time, ordered a national celebration of the Passover, forbidding its celebration in other cities; and it had also for the first time told us of the Feast of Weeks, when it was to be celebrated, and why it received that name; and these chapters' give directions about that feast, and the national celebration of the other feasts, as though the reader was well acquainted with such a national celebration. They also fix the fast to the tenth day of the seventh month. This was nearly the same as fixing it to a given day of the week. Since the first day and the fifteenth day were always sabbaths, the tenth day never could be so. This arrangement was brought about by allowing some weeks to have eight days. The fourth week in the month must always have had eight days; and the first week seven days on one month, and eight days on the next month, a month which had two new moon days.*

From the command that the fifteenth day and the twenty-second day of the tenth month, the Sabbaths with which the Feast of Tabernacles begins and ends, should be days of restraint from work, we learn how little the more general command to keep the Sabbath holy was at this time attended to, except in the matter of sending the required gifts to the priests.

Here we seem to have bid farewell to the ceremonial additions to the Mosaic Laws in Exodus, Leviticus, and Numbers. These laws were for the guidance of the priests and Levites, and were not addressed to the people at large. They were meant to uphold and increase the importance of the priests of Jerusalem, and often at the cost of the Levites throughout the rest of Judea; and they lessened the comfort of the scattered flocks of worshippers. After the Assyrian invasion in Hezekiah's reign, the strength of both parties was changed; and the laws in Deuteronomy, and the latter chapters of Leviticus, favour the equality between the priests and Levites, and are mostly moral and social. The Mosaic laws teach us that an established body of priests is by no means an unmixed good. The Jews were a very religious people; and their religious earnestness was the creator of the priesthood, not the priesthood of the religious earnestness. The Psalms are full of devotional feeling, and full also of encouragement to offer prayer and thanks to God. The writings of the prophets also give encouragement to the same religious duties. But the priests were too eager

---

* 1 Sam. xx. 27; Luke vi. 1; Mishna, Erubin, iii. 9.

for their own importance and power to advise any man to
address his Maker except through their hands. From the
first to the last of the Mosaic laws there is no encouragement whatever given either to prayer for blessings desired,
or to thanks for blessings received, except through the
sacrifices at the altar on Mount Moriah. This is shown
even in the language. " To fill a man's hands," that is to
give him something to carry to the altar, of which a part
would be his own, are the words used for " to consecrate
him as a priest."

In the reign of Josiah, when he may for a year or two
have thought himself king of both halves of the nation, was
probably written Numbers xxvi. 4-62, containing a second
register of the twelve tribes. It seems to be compiled by
the help of the former register in chapter i. That it was not
written much before this time appears from its speaking of
the death of Nadab and Abihu, which is described in
Leviticus x. It differs from the former register by giving
the names of the families which came out of Egypt ; and
thus like the so-called Roll of Battle Abbey, it sheds honour
upon those living when it was written. These families, or
rather clans, are about sixty in number ; the chiefs are the
nobles of the nation. The power of each chief depended on
the size of his estates, and on the number of his servants,
tenants, and labourers, who ranked themselves as of his
family. What the number in each family may have been we
do not learn ; but as the sixty families or clans included the
whole of the 601,730 men mentioned, we see that it averaged
about ten thousand each, being males of an age to bear arms.

But the writer can have had but poor authority for the
names in most of the tribes ; as at no time after Solomon's
death can a joint survey of both halves of the nation have
been made, and we have no trace in it of those families which
were of importance in David's and Solomon's reigns. Half
a century after Josiah's reign all knowledge of most of these
families was swept away by the Captivity. Two of them
only, the Pharezites and the Zarhites, are then known to us.
In this register neither Joshua nor Caleb are mentioned.
Joshua's name had not yet been brought into the narrative
of the march out of Egypt. This forbids our placing this
register of the families much later.

The Book of Nahum also is of this time, and its noble
heart-stirring eloquence, not even falling below that of Joel,
well declares the excitement of the time, the hopes and fears

raised in Jerusalem, when the news reached that city, of Nabopulassar's successful attack on **Nineveh.** Unlike Joel, Nahum begins more coolly, with a threat against the enemy,

Jehovah is a God jealous and vengeful. Jehovah is slow to anger, and great in power, and he will not wholly acquit. Jehovah hath his way in the whirlwind and in the storm, and the clouds are the dust of his **feet.**

Then like a master of his art his words **rise into warmth** as his matter rouses him. They must **be read as an impas-**sioned speech, spoken **with** action and change of voice, so that the hearers should **know who** was spoken of even when not named. Thus **pointing as if to the** Assyrians, **he says,**

With an overflowing torrent he will make an **utter end** of the place thereof, **and darkness shall pursue his** enemies. . . . Thus saith Jehovah; **Though they be prosperous, and** likewise **many,** yet *thus* **shall** they **be carried off and pass away.**

Here a contemptuous action of the hand may explain the **word "**thus." Then a change to a tender tone may let us understand that he is speaking to Judah :—

Though I have afflicted thee, I will afflict thee no more. For now I will break his yoke from **off** thee, and I will break thy bonds asunder.

He then turns again to Nineveh, and **with angry tone and action declares :** –

Jehovah hath given a command against thee, that no more of thy name be sown. Out of the house of thy gods will I cut off the graven image and the molten image. I will make thy grave, for thou art vile.

Then turning again his **eager** looks, he gives **a** hint of the good news which is coming ; and he points to a distance, **saying,**

Behold **upon** the mountains the feet of him that bringeth good tidings, **that publisheth** peace. O Judah, keep thy solemn feasts, perform thy **vows ; for the** wicked one shall no more pass through thee. He is utterly cut off.

Then by an ironical tone, and by turning to **the other side, he for** the third time lets us understand that he **is addressing** Nineveh :—

The destroyer is come up against thee. Guard **the** fortress, watch the road, make thy loins strong, fortify thy power mightily.—The shield of the warriors is made red, the valiant men are dyed in scarlet.—The chariots rage in the streets, they run to and fro in the broad ways ; they seem like torches ; they run like the lightenings ; . . . And [queen] Huzzab shall be taken captive ; and her maidens shall sigh as with the voice of doves, beating upon their breasts.

The following passage is a fine example of the sublime in oratory, rising step by step from quiet to awful violence. Longinus would have admired it, and Quintilian would have thought it perfect. The speaker doubtless first by his action called upon his hearers to listen to the slight sounds at a distance, becoming louder **as** they grew nearer, until the noise of war-chariots was recognized. Then by a change of look he bade them strain their eyes and they would **see** the flash of the soldiers' polished weapons. Lastly he shudders with exultation over the slaughter of the Assyrians. It can hardly be understood without the help of action and change of tone; thus,

Woe to the city of bloodshed, it is wholly false and full of robbery; **it** letteth not the prey to escape.

Then the speaker, perhaps holding his hand to his ear as if listening, adopts a low tone,

There is the noise of a whip, and the noise of the rattling of wheels, and of prancing horses, and of jolting chariots.

He then points eagerly **to** what **is coming into** sight, and becomes excited,

The horseman lifteth up both the bright sword and the glittering spear.—And there is a multitude of slain, and a great number of carcases, and no end of corpses. They stumble over their corpses.

Well might the nation rejoice over the city which for four generations had overrun their country and slaughtered the inhabitants without mercy. Well might the prophet say, " Nineveh is laid waste, who will bemoan her ? " It remains uncertain whether Elkosh, the village in which Nahum lived, **was in Galilee, or on** the banks of the Tigris. If it was in the latter **district, then** the prophet was there in captivity, and he must **have felt a** double interest in watching the overthrow **of his country's** great **enemy,** and his own taskmasters.

JEHOAHAZ **KING OF JUDAH;** B.C. 610.

Great was the grief **in** Jerusalem **for** the death of Josiah and the defeat of the army by the Egyptians, heightened no doubt by disappointment. The people had enjoyed a few years of independence while Nineveh was being overthrown; and Babylon had not yet risen to take its place as their **oppressor,** when this new danger burst upon them.

Shallum, the fourth **and** youngest son of Josiah, was at once declared king. He took the name of Jehoahaz, or *helped by Jehovah*. But his reign only lasted for three months. He had been chosen by the country party, called the men of the land, to the exclusion of his elder brothers, probably for political reasons. He was set up by those who had wished to be friendly to the Assyrians. But resistance, whether attempted or not, was in vain against the Egyptian army. Necho came down to Jerusalem, deposed Jehoahaz, **and** carried him off **as** prisoner, first to Hamath, in Syria, and thence to Egypt.

The Greek historian of Jehoahaz's fall calls Jerusalem, Kadytis, meaning Kedesh, the *holy* city, a name often given to it. **Necho set up** in Jehoahaz's place his brother Eliakim as king, on Eliakim's consenting to govern as an obedient servant. Jehoahaz, or Shallum, remained a prisoner in Egypt till **his** death.* He was carried to Egypt by sea, from some **port on** the Syrian coast to the mouth of the Nile; and this voyage seems spoken of in Deuteronomy xxviii. 68.

We have no reason to suppose that the Egyptians carried on warfare in the same cruel and destructive spirit as the Assyrians did. The Jews never speak against them with the same bitterness. They fought for tribute rather than for plunder. They did not wish to carry away the people as captives. But the soldiers of course lived upon what they could seize; and each invading army left the country poorer and weaker than before.

JEHOIAKIM KING OF JUDAH; B.C. 610—600.

Eliakim, when made king in his brother's stead by Pharaoh Necho, followed his brother's example, and changed his name to Jehoinkim. He changed it from *Supported by God*, to *Supported by Jehovah*. This was no doubt done to please the priestly party in the state. He was in everything **a** servant **of** the Egyptian king, and at his command he raised a hea**vy** tribute from his people.†

The king of Egypt was not strong enough long **to** keep possession of Judea and its tribute. In the third year of Jehoiakim's reign, Nebuchadnezzar, king of Babylon, or, if not yet king, acting as general for his father, Nabopulassar, came out to struggle for that unhappy country. The march of the Babylonians was heard of by the Jews with the greatest alarm.

---

* 2 Kings xxiii. 30-34; **2 Chron. xxxvi. 1-4**; Jeremiah xxii. 11; Herodotus ii. 159.

† 2 Kings xxiii. 35.

It was an invasion by their old cruel enemies the Assyrians under a new name. Though the capital of the invaders was now Babylon, not Nineveh, it was the capital of the same kingdom, and with better means of warfare; with cavalry not of chariots, but of men riding on horses,[*] with infantry of the same mixed races of soldiers, from whom the same cruelty was to be expected. Necho sent an army to meet them, hoping to stop their advance between the Euphrates and Damascus. But the Egyptians were defeated by the Babylonians at Carchemish on the Euphrates, and Jehoiakim then bought off the plunder of his unhappy country by promising to become the tributary servant of Nebuchadnezzar. The Egyptians were wholly driven out of Canaan.[†]

Judea was being torn to pieces and ruined as much by the two quarrelling parties within, as by the two invading nations without. The one party, in the hope of quiet and safety, were willing to pay tribute to their stronger neighbours the Babylonians; while the other party hoped for a seeming independence by paying the tribute to their weaker neighbours the Egyptians. The country was powerless against either invader; as each found friends among the Jews, who, if they did not welcome, would at least not join in resisting the invasion.

Nebuchadnezzar, when carrying off home the Jewish tribute, carried away also several Jewish children to be educated in Babylon, and to remain as slaves in his palace. Among these was Daniel.[‡] Of the after life of these young Jews we know nothing, as what we now read about them seems to be fable. All that we know is that Daniel, while in Babylon made for himself a name, which, like that of Solomon, became proverbial for wisdom, and like that of Noah proverbial for righteousness. Seven years after they had been taken to Babylon, king Jehoiakim was put to death by the Babylonians, and his son and the Jewish nobles carried into captivity; and it is highly probable that Daniel, a trusted inmate of the palace, may have been able to do such services to his unfortunate fellow-countrymen that they may have looked upon him as the king of Babylon's chief adviser.

In the meanwhile, with these dangers hanging over the nation, with the grave doubt how they could be best avoided, whether by quiet submission to the Babylonians, or by a

---

[*] Jerem. vi. 23; Ezek. xxiii. 6.
[†] Josephus, Ant. X. vi. 1; 2 Kings xxiv. 1-7.   [‡] Daniel 1.

brave resistance, the quarrel between the two parties, the priestly party and the country party, became very violent. A prophet, or any one who ventured publicly to give advice, did so at the risk of his life. Each party might naturally think that the other was bringing on the nation's ruin. Religion added earnestness to the struggle, for each party claimed to know the will **of** Jehovah; and the religious teachers put themselves forward as the political advisers.

Sometimes a political orator would wear a garment of hair in order to gain credit with the common people as **a prophet**; and then the priestly writer naturally wishes that "the prophets and the spirit of uncleanness" may be got rid **of** from the land. He thinks that father and mother should be willing to kill a man if his prophecying, and thus raising a disturbance, could not be otherwise stopped. These prophets were often of the class of labourers, and the war between the classes was such that a labourer, if he had shown himself for**ward in** giving an opinion about matters of state, had to save himself from persecution by showing the palms of his hands and pleading that he was no prophet but a tiller of **the** ground, a bondservant from his youth.*

Josephus says in Ant. X. vi., that some of Ezekiel's writings are of the reign of Josiah; but if so, they are lost. We may, however, safely give to this time his "Woe to the foolish prophets" in chapters xiii. xiv., who will not go **up** into the breaches, or make up the wall of Jerusalem, **but ask for peace**, when there can be **no peace**. He **threatens the** prophets that they shall be destroyed **from the midst** of the people; and adds that as is the iniquity **of** the prophets, so is the iniquity of him that inquireth of him. This reproach of the prophets was no doubt levelled against Jeremiah quite as much **as against those of lower rank**; his being born a priest **would only make** him the more blamable in Ezekiel's eyes.

In the reign of Josiah the prophet Jeremiah had begun rebuking the people and the rulers for their sins, but in the **fourth** year **of** this reign he comes still more forward, warning them, at the risk of his life from the priestly party, that they had forsaken Jehovah their God, and that their misfortunes **were** all brought upon them as a punishment. He advised submission to Babylon. Urijah was another prophet who was equally bold in blaming **the** rulers. He seems to have advised resistance **to** Babylon and friendship with Egypt;

* **Zech.** xiii.

and his words gave such offence to the king and the princes
of the other party that he had to flee into Egypt. There,
however, he was by no means safe. Jehoiakim sent after
him; Necho gave him up to the messengers, and he was
brought back to Jerusalem and put to death. Jeremiah's
words on the other hand offended chiefly the priests, and
though his death was called for by his enemies, he was protected by the princes. Ahikam the son of Shaphan one of
the nobles, whose family belonged to the party which advised
quiet submission to the overwhelming power of Babylon,
was on this occasion Jeremiah's good friend.* On another
occasion Jeremiah was put in the stocks by the priest Pashur
for advising submission to the Babylonians.† But nothing
daunted by this violence, he employed the hand of Baruch,
his friend and scribe, who wrote down his words; and under
the protection of one of the sons of Shaphan, Baruch read
them to the people from a chamber of the Temple which
overlooked the public court.‡

Jeremiah lets us understand that at this time there was no
Ark in the Temple; it may have been carried off in one of
the late plundering invasions. He tells the people not to
think of it or remember it; for not the Ark of the priests,
but the city of Jerusalem is Jehovah's throne.§

Jehoiakim remained for three years obedient to Nebuchadnezzar, but in his seventh year he broke his promises, he was
rash enough to rebel, and his falsehood and his rashness led
to his ruin. Nebuchadnezzar again brought up an army
against Jerusalem, and made himself master of the city.
Jehoiakim had probably been encouraged to rebel against the
Babylonians by the priestly party, who may have reckoned
on receiving help from Egypt; but no help came from
Psammeticus II, who was then on the throne of Sais.
Jehoiakim was deposed in the eleventh year of his reign, so
he may have been able to resist the Babylonians for two or
three years. The first change in Jehoiakim's counsels, from
being tributary to the Egyptians who put him on the throne,
to being tributary to the Babylonians who defeated the
Egyptians, was brought about by the chances of war. But
his second change, his breaking his promise and attempting
to be independent of the Babylonians, was his own unwise
act, or the act of the priestly party around him; and it caused

* **Jeremiah xxvi.**   † Jeremiah xx.
‡ **Jeremiah xxxvi.**   § Jeremiah iii. 16.

violent struggles, which, says the historian, filled Jerusalem
with innocent blood, which Jehovah would not pardon. The
Book of Chronicles tells us that Jehoiakim was carried off to
Babylon; but this is contradicted by Jeremiah, who says that
he was buried with the burial of an ass, after being dragged
along and cast forth beyond the walls of Jerusalem.* The
Book of Kings also, the more trustworthy of our **two**
authorities, does **not** mention Jehoiakim's being carried
captive to Babylon, but says that he slept with his fathers.

During the several a**ttacks of** the Babylonians upon Judea
in the reign **of** Jehoiakim, **the** neighbouring peoples, the
Moabites, the children **of** Ammon, and the Edomites, **were**
all overrun; **and the** cities of Moab, which had been at rest
since **the** invasion by Sennacherib, were plundered and
destroyed. Their conquest by the Babylonians is described
in Jeremiah xlviii. and xlix., but without order of events.

From the title of Pasha of Moab, which we meet with soon
after this time as a name for the head of one of the chief
families of Jerusalem,† we learn that Nebuchadnezzar, either
when **he** dethroned Jehoiakim, and placed Jehoiachin on the
throne as his servant, or yet earlier, when he left Jehoiakim
on the throne as his obedient tributary, had appointed one of
the Jews to be governor of Moab, as a province of his kingdom;
and the person chosen seems to have been the head of the
great family **of the** Zarhites. **To accept such** a post from the
enemy, and to wear **the** Babylonian **robe** of office when so
many of his countrymen were **clothed in** affliction, was **of**
course in the highest **degree** unpopular; and we shall see him
very clearly pointed **to in** Josh. vii. where we have the history
of a mean thief **who** had **stolen** a goodly Babylonian garment,
and who was **of** the family of Zarah. He was perhaps
Achbor, whom we have met with as one of the nobles of
Jerusalem at the end of Josiah's reign;‡ and by a play upon
words he is named Achor, *the troubler.*§

The prophet Zephaniah also at the same time blames **those**
who wear the apparel of foreigners. Such a dress was **very**
insulting to their countrymen, who had fought against **the**
Babylonians, and had been conquered.

The Pharezites and the Zarhites were, **at the** fall of the
monarchy, the two greatest families in Jerusalem. As they

---

* 2 Kings xxiii. 34—xxiv. 6; 2 Chron. xxxvi. 5-8; Jeremiah xxii. 19.
† Ezra viii. 4. ‡ 2 Kings xxii. 12.
§ Josh. vii. in the **Greek; and** 1 Chron. ii. 7.

both returned home seventy years afterwards in large
numbers, we judge that they had counselled submission, and
had gone quietly into captivity. They were probably among
those whom Ezekiel blames as refusing to go up into the
breaches, to make up the wall, and to stand in the battle in
the day of Jehovah. They had perhaps gone out of the city
into the Babylonian camp before the last fatal day. Such
men were traitors in the eyes of those who stayed in the city;
and Genesis xxxviii. may have been written at this time, with
strong political feelings, by one of the priestly party, in
order to give a base origin to Pharez and Zarah, the supposed
founders of those powerful but now unpopular families. A
piece of writing so worthless to us can only have been saved
from the fire for important political reasons.

During the reign of Jehoiakim, when the Chaldees of
Babylon, after having delighted the Jews by destroying the
Assyrian power, were now in their turn moving down upon
Judea to its plunder and ruin, the prophet Habakkuk wrote
his short work. He describes the enemy as a terrible and
dreadful nation, who will laugh at every fortress, and take
it by heaping a mound against it, and will gather up captives
as sand, or rather "as fishes of the sea." For it was the
cruel custom for a conqueror to spread his army into a line
reaching across the whole country and to drive all the inhabitants before it; and this was called "taking them in drag
nets."* Habakkuk's beautiful hymn gives to him a high place
among the Hebrew poets. The bold description of the
Almighty, as a warrior riding in a chariot to victory over the
Assyrians, may be compared to the figure of the Pagan
Jupiter on a Greek vase; but we shall in vain look round for a
poet of any nation who can have given him a hint for his grand
picture of the world's awe and alarm, when the power of
Nineveh **was** overthrown by Nebuchadnezzar :—

> The mountains saw thee and they trembled,
> The overflowing of the water passed by;
> The deep uttered his voice, lifting up his hands on high.
> The sun and moon stood still in their dwellings.
>   By the light of thine arrows they [the Chaldeans] moved on
> By the shining of thy glittering spear.
> Thou didst march through the land in indignation,
> Thou didst trample on nations [the Assyrians] in anger.
> Thou wentest forth for the salvation of thy people.
>
> [But now] I have heard; my bowels tremble,
> My lips quiver at the sound [of the Chaldeans].

* Herodotus vi. 31.

Not less to be admired is the poet's more quiet expression
of devout religious trust, notwithstanding the ruin and
misery with which his country seems to be threatened :—

> Although the fig-tree shall not blossom,
> Neither shall fruit be on the vines ;
> Though the labour of the olive-tree shall fail,
> And the fields shall yield no food ;
> Though the flock shall be cut off from the fold,
> And there shall be no herd in the stalls ;
> Yet will I rejoice in Jehovah.
> I will joy in the God of my salvation.

Ezekiel xix. is a lament for the princes, Jehoahaz who was
a prisoner in Egypt, and Jehoiakim, who was taken captive
by the Babylonians ; and thus the matter tells us that it was
written at this time.

To this time we may give the prophecy of Zephaniah,
limited, however, to chapters i. and ii. It is said in the
Introductory verse to be of the reign of Josiah ; but it seems
to belong to a time about ten years later ; as the ruin coming
on the country is not that brought by the invasion of the
Scythians in Josiah's reign, but the more serious invasion by
the Babylonians, which embraced the whole of the country,
with Moab and Ammon on the east, and the Philistines on
the west. Nineveh is also a desolation. Punishment is to
come on the princes and on the king's children, and on those
who wear the apparel of the foreigners, meaning those who
have taken office under the Babylonians.

A priest of the name of Zephaniah is mentioned in the
Book of Kings, as being among the captives, who, soon after
this time, were carried to Riblah on the Orontes, and were
there put to death. He may possibly have been our prophet,
the son of Cushi. We must distinguish him from Zephaniah
the son of Maaseiah, of Jeremiah xxix. 25, who was recommended by the captives to the rank of chief priest at the
beginning of the Captivity.

JEHOIACHIN KING OF JUDAH ; B.C. 600.

Jehoiachin, the son of Jehoiakim, was eighteen years old
when he was allowed by Nebuchadnezzar, the conqueror, to
mount his father's throne. But, at the end of three months,
Nebuchadnezzar changed his purpose, and determined to
crush to the very ground the kingdom of Judah. He came
himself with his army. The route from Babylon is up the

Euphrates to Tiphsah; then westward to Helbon, the modern Aleppo; and then southward to Damascus. From Damascus, the army might march on either side of the Jordan. Nebuchadnezzar came on the east side of the river, and leaving Rabbah, the city of the Ammonites, on his left hand, he crossed the Jordan at the southern ford. He met with no serious resistance. The young king, with his mother and a body of the nobles, went out to meet him and gave themselves up to him. Nebuchadnezzar entered Jerusalem with his army, and then carried into captivity the king and his nobles, taking with them the treasures of the palace and of the Temple. He, at the same time, carried off from Jerusalem every priest, every soldier, and every skilled workman, to the number of ten thousand men, not counting, as we shall learn from later history, their wives and children who went with them, to find homes in an unknown country. None were left behind but the poorest sort of people, including the larger body of the Levites. Many of those who were left were as willing to serve under the Babylonians as under their Jewish masters.[*]

The captivity of Jehoiachin took place in the year B.C. 600, the eighth of Nebuchadnezzar's reign; and for the future this year, instead of being called the first of Jehoiachin, was called the first of the Captivity, and this date was for some time used as the era from which the years were counted.

It was during Jehoiachin's short reign of eleven months, and at its unhappy close, that chapters xii.—xiii. of Zechariah were written. In them Jerusalem is spoken of as the prize for which the nations were struggling, but as " a burdensome stone for all the peoples, and all that burden themselves with it will be cut to pieces, though all the people of the earth be gathered against it." The two parties in the state, whose want of agreement sadly weakened their power of resisting the invader, are here spoken of, the country party which usually counselled submission, and the city party which attempted resistance. The prophets are blamed for their false visions and bad advice. The writer belongs to the priestly party, to the Jerusalem party; and he says that the men of Judah should own that their strength for safety lies in the inhabitants of Jerusalem. But he is not violent in that matter, and thinks that his friends the inhabitants of Jerusalem should not boast over the men of Judah. Against

* 2 Kings xxiv. 8-17.

the prophets he is not so moderate. He classes them with the spirit of uncleanness, and says that Jehovah will get rid of them both out of the land. He accuses them of reporting false visions, and of giving bad advice; and such was Jeremiah's public character at the time that this writer cannot but have included Jeremiah in his accusation.

The grief for king Jehoiakim is compared to that for king Josiah, called "the mourning of Hadadrimmon in the valley of Megiddon," where Josiah was slain. The mourning families of Nathan and Shemei, we may recognize as those of Elnathan and Shemeiah in Jeremiah xxxvi. 12. Jehoiachin is called the man of Jehovah's friendship, who is to be smitten, the city is to be taken, and one half to go into captivity.

ZEDEKIAH KING OF JUDAH; B.C. 599—589.

Nebuchadnezzar on the conquest of Jerusalem placed on the throne, if it then could be called a throne, Mattaniah, the young king's uncle, still holding the lawful king a prisoner in Babylon, as the best means of keeping the wrongful king and his people obedient. Mattaniah, on being made king, followed the example of his predecessors, and changed his name to Zedekiah.

There are only two or three of the nobles whose names are known to us, and whose fate calls for notice, at this time of misfortune. Ishmael the son of Nethaniah, of the great family of Elishama, escaped to the children of Ammon on the eastern side of the country.* Of those families which had advised submission to Nebuchadnezzar, and were allowed to remain in Jerusalem, that of the sons of Shaphan, the friends of Jeremiah, was the most important. We may conjecture that they were at the head of the great families of the Pharezites, who with the Zarhites saved their lives by yielding on seeing that resistance was useless, and who at the close of the Captivity returned home to be the chiefs of the nation. Jaazaniah, one of Shaphan's family, and therefore not even a Levite, acted as chief priest during the reign of Zedekiah, while Jehozadak, called also Jehoiada, the hereditary chief priest, was in captivity. This was no longer the important office that it used to be; but it gave some dignity if not much power to the holder. The great body of priests in the Captivity were not pleased that it should be

* Jerem. xl. 14.

held by one who had been opposed to their views, and who
was not of a priestly family; they claimed that their voice
should be heard in the appointment; and they wrote word
from Babylon, that they wished Zephaniah, the son of Maaseiah, a priest and one of a less powerful family, to have that
post.* Ezekiel, writing in captivity with all the spiritual
pride of a martyr, accuses Jaazaniah, the son of Shaphan,
and the seventy elders who were joined with him, as pol-
luting the Temple with idolatry and burning incense in their
unlawful censers.† The elders thus acting as priests were
not of priestly families, probably few or none of them were
of Levitical families; and hence Ezekiel's displeasure.

This appointment of seventy elders, which followed upon
the removal of the priests, may have laid the foundation for
that governing body, which we shall hereafter meet with
under the name of the Sanhedrim, or High Council; and at
a later time we shall find passages added to the Pentateuch
to support that Council's authority.‡

Zedekiah remained obedient and tributary to Babylon for
nine years, but perhaps never without a hope that the
Egyptians might one day relieve him. In the beginning of
his reign he sent an embassy to Babylon, choosing for that
duty Elasah the son of Shaphan and Gemariah the son of
Hilkiah. They were both of the party favourable to submission to Nebuchadnezzar; and by them Jeremiah sent a
letter to the captives, advising them to live quietly as good
subjects to the conqueror.§

In his fourth year Zedekiah went to Babylon himself,
probably summoned there by his master, Nebuchadnezzar. He
was accompanied by his chief chamberlain, Seraiah, and therefore probably went with his wives and some degree of state;
but we cannot believe in the genuineness of the letter from
Jeremiah, which a late writer says that Seraiah carried to
the captives.‖

Jeremiah seems to have thought that there was some
danger of the Babylonian worship of the heavenly bodies
being followed by the king and nobles, as he reproaches them
with it;¶ but this probably only means that they were too
fond of the foreign manners.

In his ninth year, perhaps relying upon a promise of help

---

* Jerem. xxix. 25.   † Ezek. viii.
‡ Numb. xi. 16-30; Exod. xxiv. 1-11.   § Jerem. xxix. 3.
‖ Jerem. li. 59.   ¶ Jerem. viii. 2; Jerem. vii. 18.

from Hophra, king of Egypt, Zedekiah ventured to rebel, though against the earnest remonstrance of the prophet Jeremiah, who warned him that the Egyptian army would not be able to save him. He had also been encouraged by messengers who came to him from the Jews who had escaped to Tyre and Sidon, Edom, Moab, and the children of Ammon.* These men were in distress, and being led by their wishes, may have fancied that these little peoples among whom they were living would make an effort to help Zedekiah against the Babylonian tyranny, under which they all trembled. But they gave Zedekiah no help; and Nebuchadnezzar again sent an army to besiege Jerusalem, and to reduce the Jews to obedience.

The prophet Ezekiel, who was among the captives, was placed on the bank of the river Chaboras, in Syria. He describes the route by which Nebuchadnezzar came.† Thus, if we draw a line from Damascus, the invader's headquarters, to the Dead Sea, it will pass through a spot where a road turns off eastward to Rabbah of Ammon. This spot must be " the parting of the two ways," of which one led to Rabbah, and the other to Jerusalem. From thence Nebuchadnezzar came southward to Ai, which town he plundered, as we learn from Jeremiah xlix. 3, to the alarm of the two neighbouring towns of Heshbon and Rabbah. From Ai he crossed the Jordan to Jerusalem. By the help of this march we may place Ai, by guess, at about fifteen miles from the Jordan, and at an equal distance from Heshbon and Rabbah; and may safely say that it is the town called Aiath, on Sennacherib's march, already described, and also that called Aim, on the route of the Israelites out of Egypt. Both these words are merely plural forms of Ai, and mean *the mounds*.

Zedekiah, in his alarm at the danger, put forth a proclamation that all Hebrew bondservants should be allowed to go free, in the hope of gaining, as a support to his throne, a large body of men whose oppressed condition made foreign conquest no matter of alarm to them. They were paupers, who, when in want of food and clothing, had sold themselves and their children to their wealthy neighbours; and they had lost all care for the welfare of their country. The Jewish Law, in order to stem this growing evil, had ordered that the power of sale should be limited to six years, and that after seven years of servitude every bondservant should be let

* Jerem. xxvii. 3.   † Ezek. xxi. 19-21.

15 *

free,* that the foreign servants alone should be kept in
bondage for life.   But the rich had very little regarded that
law, and the Hebrew bondservants rarely found the release
ordered by the Law.   Now, however, the nobles promised to
obey the proclamation of Zedekiah; and to mark the solemnity
of their promise, they cut a calf in twain and walked between
its two halves.   This, in the Hebrew language, is called
Cutting a Covenant.   But the siege of Jerusalem was for a
short time interrupted by the arrival of an Egyptian army,
and then the proclamation of freedom to the bondservants,
and the solemn covenant were at once forgotten.

The Chaldees, however, shortly returned in greater force;
the Egyptians retired, and left the country; and when they
were gone, the Chaldees spread themselves over the land, in
search of food and plunder.   While Jerusalem was strongly
fortified, the selfish policy of its rulers had left the other
towns for the most part open and helpless.   Lachish in the
south, and Azekah, a small hill fortress about fifteen miles
to the north-west of Jerusalem, alone could for the moment
save themselves by their walls.   But the main body of the
invaders gathered around Jerusalem.   There they renewed
the siege, and built forts around the city to starve it into
surrender.

During this reign, as during the former reigns, Jeremiah
had warned the people that they could not resist the Babylonians.   Zedekiah had no army to send into the field; and
the country people's only chance of safety lay in flight to the
desert.   But flight had not saved them from the Assyrian
foot soldiers, and would yet less avail against the Babylonian
cavalry.   "If thou hast run with men on foot," says Jeremiah,†
"and they have wearied thee, how canst thou rival horses?"
But the prophet's warning gave great offence to the rulers;
and at this time Zedekiah had shut Jeremiah up in the
watchhouse to forbid his advising the people to submit, and
very possibly in order to save him from worse treatment; and
he directed him to pray to Jehovah for him.   But the priests
and nobles of the other party, taking him out of the watch-
house, threw him into a loathsome dungeon-pit, where he
certainly would have died if the king had not sent to have
him drawn out and released.   Zedekiah had great trust in
Jeremiah, and under his advice, would probably then have
made his submission to the Chaldees; but while he hesitated

* Exod. xxi. 2.   † Jerem. xii. 5

how to act, some of his nobles would not allow him to yield; while those who saw that all resistance was useless against such an overwhelming force, had already gone out of the city, and saved their lives by giving themselves up to the enemy. A little later Zedekiah would have done the same, had he not feared the taunts of these men even more than ill-treatment from the conqueror. In a short time famine prevailed, and further resistance was impossible. Zedekiah, at the head of his soldiers, fled by night, by the way of the gate by the king's garden between the two walls, the east wall of Zion and the west wall of Ophel. He was overtaken by the Chaldees at Jericho, on his way to the southern ford of the Jordan, and brought as a prisoner to Nebuchadnezzar at Riblah, near Hamath, in Syria. There Zedekiah's eyes were put out, his sons were slain, and, in the eleventh year of his reign, he was sent in chains to Babylon, where his nephew Jehoiachin was already a prisoner.*

From this year Ezekiel counts the years as from a new era; and the year B.C. 589, the twelfth of the captivity, the eleventh of Zedekiah, is called the year when the city was destroyed.

Thus ended the Jewish monarchy, if it may not be said to have ended eleven years earlier, with the captivity of Jehoiachin. Ezekiel, living in captivity, does not give to Zedekiah the title of king, but styles him a rebellious prince. He had made a treaty with the Babylonians and bound himself by an oath; and he broke his oath. The falsehood of the two brothers, Jehoiakim and Zedekiah, did much to ruin the country. They suffered by their own fault; the younger brother Jehoahaz, and Jehoiachin the son of Jehoiakim, had suffered in innocence.

Judea was in size not one-tenth part of the Babylonian empire, which it had vainly attempted to resist. Had the Jews submitted and paid tribute, as Jeremiah advised, though they would have lost their independence, they would have kept their self-government and their national character; and their taxes would perhaps not have been heavier than those of the other provinces. We have not heard of any attempt to force idolatry upon them. Hence we cannot but blame the want of wisdom in their rulers; and when to this we add their breach of every treaty and every promise made with the conquerors, we must acknowledge that the severe punishment

* 2 Kings xxiv. 17—xxv. 7; Jerem. xxxii.—xxxviii.

of the Captivity was brought upon them by themselves.
Their prophets were right when they said that it was a
punishment for the nation's sins.

The Hebrews had been a marauding people from their
infancy, and had given too little attention to the means of
defence. Their severe sufferings from the Assyrians, and the
late alarm caused by the Scythians, should have taught them
that courage alone will not protect a nation against ambitious
and unscrupulous neighbours. They should have given more
attention to the art of war, without which as a guard, the
arts of peace unfortunately are never allowed to flourish.
The days were gone by when Joshua's shout and trumpet-
blast, or David's pebble and sling, were of much avail in
battle. They should have learnt new weapons and new
methods from the nations around; the cavalry and the war-
chariots might have been usefully copied from the idolaters.
The Psalmist says,

> Some trust in chariots and some in horses:
> But we will celebrate the name of Jehovah our God (xx. 7).

But this pious trust should not have stopped their learning
the improved methods of warfare. They should have
strengthened themselves by an alliance with their brethren
the Syrians; but above all they should have made their own
little nation one by peace between Israel and Judah, and one
in a yet more important case by friendship between the rich
and the poor, between the educated and the ignorant, and
between the capital and the villagers.

Jeremiah describes in various chapters the misery of the
unhappy Jews during these last years, when the Babylonians,
like ravenous wild beasts gathered from all sides, not content
with killing all who resisted and ill-treating the helpless, had
devoured, destroyed, and trodden under foot the pastures,
leaving those whom the sword had spared to perish by famine.
The young men went in vain to the tanks for water, the
mothers had no food for their babes. The superstitious
practice of passing children through the fire, which king
Josiah and the Book of Deuteronomy had wisely endeavoured
to check, was then used as a cloak for child murder.* Such
was the sad state of the country, that its final conquest, the
carrying off the upper class into captivity, and the reducing

* Jerem. vii. 31; xxxii. 35.

the lower class to the state of bondservants, brought no increase, and in many cases a relief to this misery.

During the last seventeen years of the monarchy, and the repeated cruel invasions by the Babylonians, there had been a continual flight of the population southward, as in the **time** of Assyrian invasions a hundred years earlier. Many Jews then found refuge in Kedar, a part of Arabia on the south of Edom, now called Akhdar, a country partially known **to** them by the caravans which passed through it to the Persian Gulf.* Of their condition in Kedar history is silent; we do not hear of them until they were driven out of the country by the Moslems above **a** thousand **years** after this time; but that they prospered there we may judge from the strength of Khaibar, their chief city, and from their inscriptions on the rocks near Tema **and Salah.**

The last days of the monarchy are rich in literature. The **Book of** Joshua now appears in the form of a continuation to the Book of Deuteronomy; and like Deuteronomy it teaches the more modern view of its being our duty to love Jehovah. It contains the history of the tribes crossing the Jordan, and of their conquest of the land of Canaan, a list of the kings conquered, with a minute account of the boundaries between the tribes, such as they existed when the whole country was **in** a **settled** state. Its history, written so long after the events, is of little value. It is contradicted by the more trustworthy Book of Judges, **and** First **Book** of Samuel. From **its** mention of the Zarhite in chapter **vii.** who stole the Babylonian garment, we **see** that it was **not** written till after a member of that family had been made Pasha of Moab by Nebuchadnezzar. The only ancient writing quoted is the Book of Jasher, a poetical work of David's reign, which says that the sun stood still while the Israelites completed the slaughter of **their enemies. But** as a geographical description of the land of **Canaan** chapters xiii.—xix. are most valuable. The writer, however, **or rather a** later editor, was not without the political feelings of his **own times;** for in the tribes of Ephraim and Manasseh he **mentions no** towns except **those** necessary for the description of the boundaries, but in **all the other** tribes he gives full lists of the towns and villages. The list of boundary towns may have been taken out of one ancient document, and that probably of David's or Solomon's reign, before the kingdom was divided by Israel's rebellion; the

* Isaiah xxi. 13-17; Pliny V. 12.

list of the other towns may be out of another document.
From the Book of Joshua, as we now have it, we must except
chapter viii. 30-35, which belongs to the time of the dispute
about Ebal and Gerizim; and chapters xx.—xxii., containing
the list of Levitical cities, because in chapter xiii. 14 and 33,
the writer, like all the writers before the Return from Captivity, had said that the Levites are to have no inheritance
but the offerings to Jehovah. We must except also chapters
xiv. and **xv.** 13-19, relating to Caleb the **son of** Jephunneh
and the town of Hebron; and also chapter **xv.** 2-4, which
gives wider southern limits to the land and contradicts **the**
foregoing verse.

Having thus put aside the additions afterwards made to the
Book of Joshua, there remains a Jehovistic account of the conquest of all Canaan, by which it was reduced to such a state as
we do not find there before the end of David's reign. Moreover,
this is founded on a survey of the land made probably in the
time of David or Solomon. And apart from these wide conquests, related in a rather contradictory manner, we trace a
slight line of march, by which the invaders, crossing over the
Jordan with the priests and the Ark of Jehovah, come to
Gilgal, Jericho, Beth-el, and Ai, and set up the Tent of
Meeting at Shiloh; and lastly, all the tribes are assembled at
Shechem. At Shechem they leave, not the Jehovistic Tables
of the Law, they are in the Ark at Shiloh, but the book of
the Law of God, possibly the Law which once stood between
Exodus xix. 6 and 7. Joshua is then buried in the land of
Ephraim, as are Joseph's bones, and as is Eleazar the son of
Aaron, the last on the hill of Phinehas, Aaron's grandson.
That Phinehas the son of Eli should have given his name to
a hill in **the** land of Ephraim is not improbable; but that
Phinehas **the grandson of** Aaron should have done so, and that
before the **death of his father** Eleazar, is highly improbable.
The name **of Phinehas seems to have** been taken from one
family and given to **the other.**

The Book of Joshua, **though** written in continuation of
Deuteronomy, is not **in** the same spirit. It has no preference
for Jerusalem, "the Place which Jehovah shall choose" as it
is called in Deuteronomy. Our Book shows traces of an
earlier Elohistic narrative, in which possibly, as in the original history of the march out of Egypt, the name of the
hero, the son of Nun, was not Jehoshua, but Oshea, as it yet
is in **Numbers xiii.** 8.

Deuteronomy xxviii.—xxx. present difficulties which make it necessary to mention them again here. These chapters **were** part of the original work. They contain the curses which frightened King Josiah when they were read to him. They contain words which seem to be quoted in 2 Kings xxii.* But then on the other hand they seem to mention the captivity of Jehoahaz in Egypt,† and that of Jehoiachin in Babylon.‡ Hence we are led to conjecture that after having been written before the captivity of those two kings, they had alterations made in them about **twelve years later.** Of Jeremiah's friends who brought the book out of the Temple to Josiah, some who were yet alive were allowed to remain **in** Jerusalem, and they may have made these slight alterations.

Deuteronomy xiv. 22-29 is a correction of chapter xii. 18, **made** thus early, or perhaps in Jehoiakim's reign. It makes **the payment** of tithes yet more easy, by saying that they **need be** taken up to the capital only on two years, but on the third year they may be eaten in the city where the owner lives. Chapter xv. 1-18 is of Zedekiah's reign, containing his proposal that the rich should release their poor debtors who had sold themselves into bondage. It renews the law of Exodus xxi. 1-6, which had said that every bondservant ought to be released on the seventh year, counting from when his service began. But in Zedekiah's reign, when the evil of bond-service reached to all the poor, he proposed that they should be all released at once; and this law, in order to check the evil for the future, proposes that there should be such **a** release every seventh year.

At the same time the few words, in chapters xxxi. 9-15 and 23-29, may have been added to close the book. They direct that every seventh year, at the feast of Tabernacles, the book of **the** Law shall be read to the assembled people **in** The Place which Jehovah shall choose; and that it shall **be** laid **up by** the side of the Ark of the Covenant, the place where **we may suppose** that it was found. In the closing words mention is **made of** Joshua, as the Book of Joshua had lately been added to the Pentateuch. Thus the Book of Deuteronomy at the fall of the monarchy may have **been limited** to chapters iv. 44—xviii. 8, containing a correction of the Levitical law; chapters xxviii.—xxx., containing threats and promises which enforce the law; and chapter xxxi. 9-15 and 23-29, the closing words, which agree with the opening words in chapter iv. 44. The original book had contained no mention of Joshua, nor of Moses's death.

* **Deut. xxix.** 25.   † Deut. xxviii. 68.   ‡ Deut. xxviii. 36.

From these last few words in Deuteronomy we judge that
the laws of Hezekiah's and Josiah's reigns, ordering three
pilgrimages a year to Jerusalem, had been very little obeyed.
This writer thinks that such a journey once in seven years is
as much as can be hoped for.

No two men could be more unlike than Ezekiel and Jeremiah, the two chief writers of Zedekiah's reign. They were
both priests, and had both from their youth seen ruin
hanging over their country; but they had learned different
lessons from the same misfortune. Ezekiel had encouraged
resistance against the invading Babylonians, and was carried
into captivity; Jeremiah had advised submission, and was
left in Judea. And their religious writings were as unlike as
their fates. They both acknowledged that the Temple was
no longer the one place where Jehovah could be fitly worshipped. But Ezekiel, when ruin came, still clung to the
value of sacrifices and incense, and the rest of the ceremonial
law, to the superior holiness of the priests, and to the belief
that the worship of Jehovah through the hands of the priests
was the only acceptable worship. Jeremiah, on the other
hand, had at an early time thrown off these narrow views; he
looked for personal righteousness, he reproached priests and
people alike with their sins, and endeavoured to draw a lesson
from the nation's misfortunes, which might lead to its moral
improvement. Jeremiah, though a priest, may properly be
called one of the prophets. Ezekiel would have scorned the
title, as meaning nothing but rebellion and mischief.

While Zedekiah was yet upon the throne the priest
Ezekiel, living in captivity in Syria, on the river Chaboras, a
tributary branch of the Euphrates, was there writing his
visions. He had been carried off by Nebuchadnezzar in the
captivity of Jehoiachin, and left there while other prisoners
were sent on to Babylon. He describes his receiving power
to utter the word of God, which he had first swallowed in the
form of a book-roll. This had been given to him by Jehovah,
who came to him in a storm of lightning and wind from the
north, seated on a slab of crystal, carried by four cherubs.
In the sixth year he has a vision of the elders in Jerusalem
burning incense before a number of unclean idols; whereupon
Jehovah, carried upon the wings of the cherubs, leaves the
city in displeasure to make his Sanctuary for a time among
the men of the Captivity (i.—xii.). Here Ezekiel shows us
his political, or rather ecclesiastical, feelings; he supposes
that all the Jews who were left behind in Jerusalem were

given up to idolatry, and that the elders in the Temple were worshipping every form of creeping thing and abominable beasts; thus showing us also to what lengths a heated imagination may carry a religious controversialist.

Chapters xv. xvi. are against Jerusalem and Judea. Judea is compared to a lewd woman, as again in chapters xxii. xxiii. Chapter xx. 1, 44 is against the Elders, against the neglect of the command that the Sabbath should be kept holy; but Ezekiel shows his trust in God's goodness, by promising that the whole house of Israel shall be brought back from captivity. In chapter xx. 45-49 he sets his face against the men of the South Country, whom Isaiah had before denounced for their desertion of the rest of the nation. In chapter xxi. he sets his face against Israel, and describes the route by which Nebuchadnezzar marches against that wicked prince Zedekiah, whom he does not style a king. In chapters xxii. xxiii. he reproaches Jerusalem, and then the two halves of the nation under the figure of two lewd women, one named " Her own tent," and the other " My tent in her," who are described in coarse disagreeable terms as falling in love with the Assyrians and Babylonians. In chapter xxiv. Nebuchadnezzar besieges Jerusalem.

Of the several denunciations against Egypt, chapters xxix. 1-12, and xxxii. 17-32, may perhaps be by Ezekiel. In neither is Babylon mentioned. It would have been unsafe for a captive to have spoken openly. In the former Egypt is blamed for not helping the Jews when such help was needed. In the latter, namely chapter xxxii. 17-32, Ezekiel describes the under-world, the abode of the wicked, in a manner which shows that intercourse with Babylon and the east had brought some new views into the Jewish religion. At the back of the pit of destruction, the Assyrians and Elam and Edom, and other unfriendly nations, are there laid in their graves, but able to speak and think, and bearing their shame. Pharaoh, when he goes down to them with his rabble, will be comforted at meeting them. We shall find this view of the world below further enlarged in some of the later chapters added to the Book of Isaiah. In the other chapters against Egypt that country is blamed and Babylon is not blamed; and hence they could not have been written by Ezekiel.

In chapter xxxiii. 21, 22, the writer while in captivity is told that Jerusalem is destroyed. Ezekiel was a priest, but he is usually counted among the prophets. Those writings

which alone we can give to him **have** very little of the lofty
inspiring tone which entitles a writer to that honoured
name.

Chapters xl.—xliv. of the Book of Ezekiel describe a vision
seen in the twenty-fifth year of the Captivity, when he was
carried into Judea and saw the Temple, or rather the new
Temple which was hereafter to be built. He describes its
several parts, the courtyard, the gates, the House of Jehovah,
with the Buildings on each side of the House. He then sees
the glory of Jehovah, the same appearance which he saw
quitting the Temple when the priests left it, now returning
from the east, where we must suppose it had hitherto been
dwelling with the priests in Captivity. He gives very
exactly the measures of the altar of burnt-offerings which
stood in front of the House. The altar had a ditch or drain
round it, of which traces may yet be **seen** in the rock under
the dome **of** the Mosque of Omar. **His** description of an
imaginary temple agrees **in so** many parts with what we
know of Solomon's Temple, that it is evident that he was
proposing that it should be rebuilt with the former measurements. In one **passage only have we any** difficulty, that is
in chapter xlii. **16-19,** where he **gives to the** great court a
measure of five hundred reeds on each **side.** But the Greek
translation here helps us. From this we understand that he
may have said Cubits. In chapter xli. 22, the Altar of
Wood, called also the Presence Table, seems, when compared
with the furniture in Solomon's Temple, to **be at** the same
time the Altar of Incense, and the Table on which the
Presence Bread was set in order before Jehovah.

In **these latter** chapters of Ezekiel the priests of the capital
are called, not Sons of Aaron, as in the early part of Leviticus,
but Sons of Zadok, after Solomon's high priest, from whom
they claimed descent. By the use of this name he certainly
meant to claim for the priests that higher rank over the rest
of the Levites, of which the Book of Deuteronomy deprives
them. This gives us also the origin of the name of Zadokites,
or Sadducees, the **name** afterwards borne by the more
wealthy religious party in Jerusalem. The word Pharisee,
the name of the party opposed to them, means *a Villager.*

In chapter viii., Ezekiel had blamed the elders who continued the Temple-service in Jerusalem while the priests
were absent and in captivity; and Exodus xxiv. 1-11 seems
to have been then written to defend the elders whom Ezekiel
blamed. Jehovah there directs Moses to come up with

seventy elders, who see the God of Israel with a paved work of sapphire stone under his feet, as described in Ezekiel's vision; and though they see God they do not die. The people promise to obey the words of the Book of the Covenant, meaning the Book of Deuteronomy. Thus the removal of the priests to Babylon had left the laity at liberty to make their own additions to the sacred books.

The writings of the prophet Jeremiah have come down to us in a sadly confused state, some parts of them having had additions made to them by after writers, and many parts being put in their wrong places. They have less of the character of speeches than the writings of the earlier prophets; but scattered among them are several portions which may have been written to be spoken. They are dated in the reigns of Josiah, Jehoiakim, and Zedekiah, and seem to have been written in the following order.

Chapters ii.—xvii. 18, may have been of the reigns of Josiah and Jehoiakim. After a preface, the first speech begins at chapter ii. 4, " Hear the word of Jehovah, O house of Israel." They contain the prophet's warnings to his countrymen against their sins, against their fondness for foreign customs, and against their looking to Egypt for help, and a threat of the ruin which was coming on the land, first perhaps from the Scythians, a people whose language they do not understand, and then from the Babylonians. They will come like fishermen, and carry off all the people in a drag-net, and then like hunters they will hunt for those that have escaped, chasing them upon every mountain and out of the holes in the rocks. These writings are in a melancholy tone, with very little of poetic fire. Jeremiah often uses the words of Deuteronomy, calling Egypt "the iron furnace," and speaking of the "words of the covenant;" and like Deuteronomy he shows a lessened value for ceremonies, and in particular he contradicts Exodus and Numbers by saying that God, when he brought the people out of Egypt, gave no commands about sacrifices and burnt-offerings. From this portion we must accept a few verses, which look like after additions, namely, x. 1-16, and xvi. 14, 15. Moreover, chapter xiii. 1-11, which describes the prophet as taking his girdle to the river Euphrates, seems to belong to the Book of Ezekiel, who lived upon its banks, rather than to the writings of Jeremiah.

Chapters xxxv. and xxxvi. are also of the reign of

Jehoiakim.   The Rechabites, the Arab drivers of the
chariots, are praised for their obedience to their law of not
drinking wine, obedience which **the** Jews would do well to
imitate.   As Judea and **Jerusalem have** not been obedient,
God will bring upon them the evil pronounced against them
(in Deuteronomy xxviii.).   The prophet makes use of the
hand of his friend Baruch the scribe to write his warnings
that the Babylonians would conquer and destroy the country;
and being himself not free, Baruch reads them to the people
on the day of a public fast from the chamber of Jeremiah's
friend, **one** of the sons of Shaphan, which overlooked the
northern court of the Temple.   Jeremiah and Baruch **have**
to hide themselves from the displeasure of the king.

Chapter xxvi. contains a narrative of the prophet's
warning the people in the reign of Jehoiakim that Jerusalem
will soon **be** overthrown as the city of Shiloh was.   By this
freedom of speech he gave great offence to the priests, as
discouraging resistance **to** the Chaldees, and they would
have put him to death **if he** had not been protected by
Ahikam the **son** of Shaphan, who **was one of** the heads of
the country party.   In verse 18 we find a quotation from the
prophet Micah.

In chapters xviii.—xx. Pashur **the priest,** who was the
chief officer in the Temple, puts **Jeremiah in the** stocks for
advising submission, and for saying **that the** city will be
destroyed by Nebuchadnezzar in punishment for the king's
rebellion.   Jeremiah calls him not Pashur, **or** *Safety around,*
but "Terror on all sides."

This last portion, though dated in Jehoiakim's reign,
seems to belong to Zedekiah's reign, as Zedekiah is therein
mentioned as a king.   So also chapter xxvi., though dated in
Jehoiakim's reign, may be of Zedekiah's reign, narrating
however what happened to Urijah in Jehoiakim's reign.

We then have six portions of the history of Zedekiah's
reign, **each more or** less dated, so that they can be placed in
order, **but not** so written **that** they will follow one another
as parts of a whole.

Chapter xxii. is of **the** reign of Zedekiah.   Jeremiah
tells the people not to weep for the dead, meaning king
Jehoiakim, but for Shallum, or Jehoahaz, who is gone into
captivity in Egypt, and will return no **more.**   Jehoiakim
they are not to mourn for, he is to have the burial of an ass.
Coniah, or Jehoiachin, has been cast off like **a** despised idol,
and is **to be** conquered by the Babylonians.   Here the

prophet clearly declares his political opinions. He has no regard for the king who rebelled against Babylon, and was carried into captivity there; he reserves his pity for Shallum, the king who resisted the Egyptians and was conquered. Zedekiah, who is not named, but called This Man, is not to prosper but is to die childless.

Chapters xxvii.—xxix. relate to the **fourth year** of Zedekiah's reign, **if we** except xxvii. **1, a** verse not in the LXX., and **xxvii. 7,** and xxix. 10-14, two after insertions. Jeremiah exhorts the people to submit quietly to Nebuchadnezzar. He assures **them that** Judah, Edom, Moab, the Children of **Ammon,** Tyre, and Sidon, have no choice but to be the **servants of** Nebuchadnezzar ; **and he** rebukes the prophet **Ananiah, who** advises **resistance. He writes** to the captives **in Babylon** advising **them** to live as good citizens, **and he** rebukes **them** for claiming the right to fix upon Zephaniah the **son** of Masseiah, **as a** proper person to **succeed to the** office of high priest in Jerusalem. Throughout **these** three chapters Jeremiah's name is spelt with **one** letter **fewer** than in the other parts of the book.

Chapters xxiii. 9—xxiv. contain a warning against **false** prophets, who profess to have a Burden, or **message from** Jehovah. If **they** have a dream let them **tell the dream,** but **the use of the word** "Burden" in such **a sense is to be** blamed. Jeremiah compares the Jews of **the Captivity who** live quietly in Babylon to good figs, while **Zedekiah and all** those who resist the Chaldees are like bad figs.

Chapter **xxxiv.** relates that Zedekiah had rebelled **against** Nebuchadnezzar ; Nebuchadnezzar had sent his army against Jerusalem to **reduce** it to **obedience.** Jeremiah threatens Zedekiah that he will be **taken** prisoner and carried to Babylon. **But** at this time the prophet seems **to** have **thought that** Zedekiah would afterwards be allowed to **return** to Jerusalem and die at **home** and be buried with due **honour.** Zedekiah, in his alarm, had taken the wise step of declaring all the bondservants free, in the hopes of finding **them more** willing **to** fight for him. But **as soon** as the danger was less pressing the promise of freedom was forgotten ; and Jeremiah foretells that the city **will** be taken and burnt.

Chapter xxi. Zedekiah sends Pashur **the priest** to inquire of Jehovah ; and Jeremiah again tells him **that in** submission to the Chaldees is his only chance of life.

Chapter xxxii. 1-35. In the tenth **year of** Zedekiah,

Jeremiah is shut up in the watch-house by the king; and while there he buys of his cousin a field in Anathoth, in the land of Benjamin, while it was within the power of the Chaldees' army, thus showing his opinion that the land would soon be quiet and prosperous.

Chapters xxxvii., xxxviii. **Zedekiah** had rebelled against Nebuchadnezzar; Nebuchadnezzar **had sent** his army against Jerusalem to reduce it to obedience; **Pharaoh** Hophra had sent an Egyptian army to the relief of Zedekiah; and the Chaldees had retreated from before **the city.** Jeremiah was going out of the city to take possession **of his** field in the land of Benjamin; but he was put in prison as one wishing to desert to the Chaldees, and he remains **in the** watch-house till the city is taken. He would probably have been put to death by the nobles if the king had not befriended him. He warns the king that his only chance **of** life is to quit the city, **and** give himself up to the Babylonian generals; and Zedekiah would have done so, but that he feared being laughed at by those Jews who had from the first been prudent **enough to** join the Chaldees.

Chapters xxxix.—xliii. **contain the history** of the taking of the city. Nebuchadnezzar comes up against **it in** the ninth year of Zedekiah's reign, and his army takes it in the eleventh year, when Zedekiah flees away, but is overtaken, has his eyes put out, **and** is carried captive **to** Babylon. Nebuchadnezzar gives orders that Jeremiah shall not be hurt; and the prophet is released from the watch-house by Nebuzar-adan, the Chaldee general, and he withdraws from **the** ruins of the city to Mizpah, where Gedaliah, the Jewish governor of the province under the Chaldees, fixes his residence. After Gedaliah is killed, Jeremiah is carried off against his will by Johanan and his followers into Egypt. From **his** threat that Jehovah will break the pillars of Beth-shemish, we learn that the two obelisks were then both standing in front of the temple of Heliopolis. One of these was afterwards removed by one of the foreign conquerors of Egypt to ornament his own capital.

Chapter lii. is a short history of Zedekiah's whole reign, in nearly the same words as 2 Kings xxiv. 18—xxv.

Chapters i. 4—ii. 3, like chapter vi. of Isaiah, is an introduction to the Book, and it contains Jeremiah's appointment to the office of warning his countrymen. It was not written **until** after Nebuchadnezzar's captains had " set every one **his** throne at the entering of the gates of Jerusalem."

Verses **i.** 1-3, containing the Title, are by **a** later editor, who has taken the date, "the thirteenth year of Josiah," from chapter xxv. 3, which was written after Jeremiah's death.

Thus Jeremiah's writings contain many particulars of his own life; but the confused state in which we now have them makes it difficult to follow the narrative.

Some part of Jeremiah's prophecies may have been written in Egypt; but it is more probable that he did not dwell long on the banks of the Nile, and ill treatment may soon have brought his life to a close. None of his writings **show** any great acquaintance with Egypt, or prove a lengthened residence in that country.

There **is not** a little resemblance between Jeremiah's writings and the **Book of** Deuteronomy. He was the son of Hilkiah, and very probably of that Hilkiah who in Josiah's **reign** found the Book of the Law in the Temple, and who **was** perhaps the author of Deuteronomy. Thus Jeremiah was by birth and education a priest, in which respect he differs from the elder prophets, whose glowing words and inspiring thoughts roused their hearers into action, **and often** in opposition to the priests. The priests, while the monarchy flourished, were men **in** authority; they had their modes of usefulness, and the unpaid, self-appointed prophets **had** theirs. But now, **in Jeremiah's time,** that the priesthood is overthrown **with the** monarchy, **and the** priests are outcasts, they are led to make themselves useful and important, by addressing themselves **to the** people **as** the prophets did of old. It was not till the priesthood had lost its wealth and power that the priests rose up to be prophets.

There **is so** close an agreement between Psalm xxxi. and the writings of Jeremiah, that he has been thought **to be** author of it. The writer says :—

> I was the reproach of all mine oppressors,
> But mostly among my neighbours,
> And a fear to mine acquaintance.
> They that saw me in the street fled from me.
> I was forgotten as a dead man out of mind;
> I became like a broken vessel.
> For I heard the evil report of many, [saying]
> "Terror is on all sides."

These last two lines are from Jeremiah **xx.** 10. In two other lines the Psalmist speaks as if he had been in Jerusalem when **it** was attacked by Nebuchadnezzar, saying :—

16

> Blessed be Jehovah, for he wrought marvellously
> His loving kindness to me in the besieged city.

Moreover, like Jeremiah, the writer calls the false gods "Vanities."

Jeremiah, says the Chronicler, lamented **for** king Josiah; and the singing men, and singing women also, repeated Lamentations for that king, which were probably committed to writing. It is upon the strength of this remark that the Book of Lamentations has been called the work of Jeremiah. It contains five melancholy poems mourning over the ruin of the city, and the misery of the inhabitants, and devoutly acknowledging that they were brought upon them for their **sins**; "the Lord hath cast off his altar, he abhorreth **his** sanctuary, he hath given up into the hand of the enemy the walls of her palaces." The first four of these poems are alphabetic, each verse beginning with a letter of the alphabet in its due order. **They** were so written in order to assist the memory of **the singers.** The same artificial arrangement is used in **several of the Psalms.** The **first** two may be by Jeremiah. **The second** contains his favourite words "Terrors on all **sides,**" and says that the king and princes are among the **nations.** The third is probably not Jeremiah's, but it contains no **marks** by which **we** can put a date to it. The fourth and fifth **are** much more modern, and will be mentioned hereafter.

JUDEA UNDER THE BABYLONIANS; B.C. 589—538.

Nebuzar-adan, the Babylonian captain who was sent by Nebuchadnezzar to the command of Jerusalem, then began his work of destruction. He broke down the walls of Jerusalem, he burnt the Temple and the king's palace, and the houses of the **chief men.** He broke in pieces all the metal **work and** vessels of the Temple, whether gold, silver, or copper, **and** sent it off to Babylon. Seraiah, the chief priest, the grandson of Hilkiah, with several men of rank, and sixty others, who were found in the city, he took to his master at Riblah, in the land of Hamath, where Nebuchad-**nezzar had** them put **to** death. Another body of prisoners, including those who **in** the beginning of Zedekiah's reign had promised obedience, **were** sent off to Babylon as bond-servants, and none but the poor of the land were left in the city. This was in the nineteenth year of Nebuchadnezzar, B.C. 589.

Nebuchadnezzar then appointed Gedaliah, a Hebrew of rank, who had not entered into Zedekiah's rebellion, to be the governor of the land. He was of the family of Shaphan, which had taken part with Jeremiah in the endeavour to persuade Zedekiah to submit quietly to Nebuchadnezzar, the family which had given a high priest to the Temple in Zedekiah's reign, when the priests who counselled resistance were in captivity. Gedaliah fixed his residence at Mizpah, a town in the neighbourhood of Jerusalem, as the city itself was too much in ruins to be a suitable spot to live in. He exhorted the people to live quietly and industriously as servants of the Chaldees.* There Jeremiah also came to live in as a place of safety; he had throughout advised the people to submit quietly to a fate from which they could not escape, and he had therefore been spared by the Chaldees.

But there were two leaders yet in arms against the Chaldees, though with no power to resist them. One was Ishmael, of the family of Elishama, who had fled across the Jordan to the Ammonites. He soon afterwards returned, and slew Gedaliah the governor as being a traitor to his country, and again escaped to the Ammonites in safety. The other was Johanan, who, having quarrelled with Ishmael, and obtained the leadership of such forces as had belonged to both, withdrew slowly towards Egypt as a place of safety; since his little body of men was quite unable to resist the troops that Nebuchadnezzar might send against him.

Johanan on his retreat carried the prophet Jeremiah with him, for the double reason that, as a friend of the Chaldees, he could intercede for him with Nebuchadnezzar, and that, as a priest, he could tell him the will of Jehovah. Jeremiah gave him the advice that he had given throughout, to submit to the conquerors. But Johanan would not trust his advice, but continued his retreat, and carried Jeremiah and his friend Baruch with him into Egypt. This brave little band of patriots, the remnant of Judah as they called themselves, settled at Tahpanhes, a town on the east side of the Delta,† where a century earlier a former body of their countrymen had found safety from the armies of Assyria.

Four years later Nebuzar-adan sent off a third body of captives to Babylon, making with those before sent off by Nebuchadnezzar and himself four thousand six hundred men,‡ exclusive of the soldiers taken in battle.

While the Babylonians were carrying off the inhabitants

* 2 Kings xxv. 8-26.   † Jerem. xl.—xliii.   ‡ Jerem. lii. 30.

of Jerusalem, and the treasures of the Temple, there were other enemies plundering the villages, and adding largely to the misery of the country. Of these the Edomites were the **most** hostile and the most important. They overran Judea, even to the walls of Jerusalem, calling upon the Chaldees to "Raze it, raze it, even to its foundations."* The Philistines, the Moabites, and **the** Ammonites, each **on** their own side, now that **the** Jewish superiority was destroyed, rushed **in** for their share of such plunder as had escaped **the** Chaldees.† So dreadfully had the Israelites on the east of the **Jordan** been slaughtered by the Assyrians and Babylonians **on their** marches through them, that their country was left almost empty of people; and the wandering tribes of the eastern highlands, the Children of Ammon, now came down into **the** plain, and dwelt in the cities of Gad, on the very spot from which they had been driven by Sihon, king of the Amorites, before the Israelities arrived there from Egypt.‡ **The** Tyrians, still keeping to their own calling as merchants, found their profit in carrying away the Jewish children, which the others had seized, and selling them as slaves to **the** Ionians, or **Greeks of** Asia Minor, and to the Tibareni and Muscovites on the shores **of** the Black Sea.§ The lawless inroads of these little tribes were more insulting, **if** not more cruel, than that of the conquering Babylonian army ; and it is very possible **that** the captives carried to Babylon suffered a fate by no means worse than that of many who were left at home.

Of the condition of Judea under the Babylonians we have very few hints. We have to imagine what may have been the state **of** the remaining population, when the country **became** quiet, **under** conquerors whose cruelty was somewhat checked by their wish to levy a tribute off the soil. Nebuchadnezzar's general had given the ploughed lands and vineyards to the bondservants of those whom he carried into captivity.‖ These they were to cultivate for their new masters ; and many thus found themselves better off than under their old masters.¶ Land within the cities was not so given to the labouring class. But the conquerors could neither occupy nor carry away the houses; and hence they naturally fell to the lot of those who ventured to seize them.**

---

* Psalm cxxxvii. ; Obadiah.　　† Ezek. xxv.
‡ Jerem. xlix. 1.　　§ Ezek. xxvii. 13 ; Joel iii. 6.
‖ Jer. xxxix. 10.　　¶ **Isaiah** v. 17 ; **vii. 22.**　　** Jer. xl. 10.

The attempt to employ a Jew as governor of the province was not successful in the case of Gedaliah, who was assassinated. Other Jews who accepted lower offices under the Babylonians were naturally despised by their countrymen. "The sinners in Zion," they are called, who accepted "the gain of oppression."* Some of them bore the title of Sagins, or Babylonian deputies, and were perhaps tribute collectors.†

The Jews who at this time escaped to Lower Egypt, and again made a settlement on the east bank of the Nile, must have much of the credit given to them for the school of philosophy which then rose in Heliopolis. In that city Jews, Greeks, and Egyptians met on equal terms, under the rule of the kings of Sais. The three languages were there all spoken; and the union of the three streams of thought in one channel produced at Heliopolis a school which was looked up to by the neighbouring nations for the next three centuries. It was from Heliopolis that the Greek philosophers Pythagoras and Solon drew their opinions; they both were in Egypt a few years later than Jeremiah; as was Xenophanes, the first Greek who was known to teach the Unity of God; and to Heliopolis Plato afterwards came to study. When this school arose, Homer and Hesiod, of the Greek writers that now remain to us, had alone been written. It is, therefore, far from improbable that the latter Greek writers may have profited much by the Jewish thoughts which then reached Athens from Heliopolis. From thence Acusilaus, whose history of the Creation, under the name of his Genealogies, we have already spoken of, may have borrowed his views, which so closely resemble the beginning of the Book of Genesis; and what is yet more important to remark, from thence Æschylus may have gained his higher notions of the Greek gods, so superior to those of Homer and Hesiod.

Chapters xlv.—xlix. 33 of Jeremiah should rather be called the writings of his friend Baruch, who was carried with him into Egypt, and may there have written them. They are denunciations against some of their nation's enemies; and they cannot have been the words which Baruch wrote down from Jeremiah's mouth, as mentioned in chapter xxxvi. 32, since those were against Zedekiah and Jerusalem.

---

* Isaiah xxxiii. 14, 15. † Isaiah xli. 25.

These writings by the scribe Baruch are mostly borrowed **from** those of other prophets. They describe the ruin brought by Nebuchadnezzar's armies upon the countries through which they passed. That against Egypt describes Jehovah coming up and overwhelming the country like the inundation of the Nile, and is in part borrowed from Amos ix. 5. The Egyptian soldiers in their **defeat are** taunted with the flight of their mighty bull Apis (xlvi. 15). The Jews who had fled to Egypt fear that they shall **not be safe** there from the Babylonians. The mercenary soldiers **whom** Necho had hired, probably Greeks, will not fight **for him.** The writing against Moab is in part borrowed from Isaiah xv., and in part from Numbers xxi. 28, 29, where the early wars of the Amorites are described. It tells us that between the invasion by Sennacherib **and that** by Nebuchadnezzar **the** Moabites had obtained full possession **of** the cities in the land of Reuben.

THE JEWS IN CAPTIVITY.

Of the suffering of those **Jews who** were **sent** off to Babylon as captives, **we** have no account. Whatever these were at first, they **were** probably lessened after **a** time. The captives were treated as colonists, and were required to pay some large proportion of the produce of their labour to their masters. But in addition to what they may have suffered from hard labour, with scarcity of food and raiment, **a** body of high-minded and educated men, many of noble birth, smarted severely under the insults of their task-master, and groaned **over** the recollection of their homes, their gardens, **and their** fields, which they had left, of their capital city and Temple which had been burnt, and of their religious ceremonies which had been brought to a close. As their troubles forbad their keeping the feast days, they very naturally added **to** the number **of** their fast days. The law had ordered a fast to be kept on the tenth day of the seventh month, **that** is, in our October; but now they appointed fast days on the ninth day of **the** fourth month, on the seventh day of the fifth month, and on the tenth day of the tenth month.* That in the tenth month was for the beginning of the siege of Jerusalem; that in the fourth for the day when the Chaldees entered the city; and that in the fifth for when the Temple and palace were burnt to the

---

* Zech. viii. 19.

ground. Of these the last was naturally the fast thought the **most** solemn. They were all fixed on such days of the month **as** were not sabbaths. The first day, the eighth, **the** fifteenth, and the twenty-second, were sabbaths; **an** arrangement which can only have **been kept by giving to** some weeks eight days each.

While in captivity the Jews wrote no history of their sufferings; but some of the **most valuable of** their religious writings are by men living at this time at a distance from home. In the Book of Psalms there are many which were written in this **sad** time by captives pining to return, and mourning over their country's woes. Psalms xiv. and liii., which **differ** in **little more than** in the use of the words God and Jehovah, both **begin with blame** for **those** whose **trust** in God was failing **under their disappointment**; thus—

> **The fool saith in** his heart there **is no God,**

And they end with a prayer for a return home; thus:—

> O that the salvation of Israel were come out of Zion !
> When Jehovah bringeth home the captivity of his people,
> Jacob will rejoice and Israel will be glad.

Psalm lxxxix. may **be** of this time, as it points to the defeat of the Egyptian army by Nebuchadnezzar, and then to the overthrow of the Jewish king, who is spoken of as if yet alive. Thus:—

> O Jehovah, **God** of hosts, who is like unto thee?
> Strong art thou, O Jah, and thy truth is round about thee.
> Thou rulest the pride of the sea;
> When the waves thereof arise thou stillest them.
> Thou hast broken the Boaster [or Egypt] as one slain.
> **Thou scatterest** thine enemies **with** thy strong arm.

It cannot, **therefore, be** from any **want of power that the** Jews are **allowed to** be overthrown :—

> **But thou hast** cast off and abhorrest;
> **Thou hast been** wroth with thine anointed one;
> **Thou hast set** aside the covenant made with thy servant;
> **Thou** hast profaned **his crown** to the ground;
> Thou hast broken down all his fences;
> Thou hast brought his strongholds to ruin.

The new opinions which **the** Jews learnt in Babylon about the inhabitants of heaven, and which we shall meet with **in** the Book of Job, are shown in the following lines :—

> The heavens do praise thy wonders, O Jehovah,
> Thy truth also in the assembly of the Holy Ones;
> For who in the skies can be compared to Jehovah?
> Who of the sons of the gods can be likened to Jehovah?
> God is very terrible in the council of his Holy Ones.

The Psalm, **divided into xlii. and xliii., is** one of the most interesting specimens of Hebrew poetry, **both** for the beauty of the thoughts, and for the judicious use **of** pauses and repetitions. Here an unhappy captive, a native of a northern tribe, asks in a melancholy recurring burden :—

> Why art thou cast down, O my soul?
> And why art thou disquieted within me?
> Hope thou in God; I will yet praise him;
> He is the health of my countenance and my God.

And he answers :—

> My soul is cast down within me; for I remember thee,
> Far from the land of the Jordan, and the peaks of Hermon.
> Far from the little hill [of Sacrifice].

The "little hill" is probably Mount Tabor on the boundary between Zebulun and Issachar, where those two tribes had an altar in common, as said in Deut. xxxiii. 18, 19.

Psalm lxxx. also seems to be the work of a captive poet, whose feelings were with the northern tribes; he does not mention Judah :—

> Give ear, O shepherd of Israel,
> Thou that leadest Joseph like a flock;
> Thou that dwellest between the cherubs, shine forth.
> Before Ephraim and Benjamin and Manasseh
> Stir up thy strength and come for our salvation.
>   Bring us home again, O God,
>   And cause thy face to shine, and we shall be saved.

This last couplet is used three times as a recurring burden. This peculiarity here, and in the last-mentioned Psalm, shows that a greater attention was at this time being given to versification in the poetry. This Psalmist prays for the captive Jehoiachin :—

> Let thy hand be on the man of thy right hand,
> On the son of Adam, whom thou didst fix on for thyself.

Living among their conquerors and task-masters, as the **Jews now** were, in whatever spot a writer might be dwelling, the caution required of him would naturally show itself in his writings. Thus in Psalm xxxix. an unhappy poet says :—

> I will guard my ways lest I offend by my tongue,
> I will keep a muzzle on my mouth,
> While the wicked man is before me.

Equally cautious **is the writer** of Psalm xxxviii., who says :—

> They that seek my hurt speak mischief,
> And imagine deceits all the day long.
> But I am as a deaf man, and will not hear,
> And as a dumb man that cannot open his mouth.
> Thus I am as a man that heareth not,
> **And** in whose mouth are no arguments.

These two Psalms remind **us in a** melancholy manner of the change which is henceforth to come over the national character. The Jews are for the future to have a country, a religion, a language, and a literature of their own, but they are for at least four centuries to be dead politically. Such a change cannot but show itself in their writings. Their writers may yet have many fine qualities ; but the bold fire of genius can hardly dwell with caution. It is said as praise of the Servant of Jehovah in Isaiah liii., meaning prince Zerubbabel in captivity, that "as a sheep before her shearers is dumb, so he opened not his mouth."

Chapters xxvi., xxvii., and xxix.—xxxii. 16, of **the** Book **of** Ezekiel, though for their date they might perhaps have been written by the prophet, yet in the larger portions prove themselves to be by another writer, since they show greater enmity to Tyre and Egypt than to Nebuchadnezzar. This could not have been Ezekiel's feeling. They begin with a threat against Tyre, which Nebuchadnezzar attacks. Then follows an interesting account of the trade of Tyre. The **writer**, living abroad, but not in captivity, may have dwelt at **Tyre,** but more probably at some place once dependent on Tyre, such as the island of Cyprus, or Tarsus in Cilicia. There he could have gained both his knowledge of the Tyrian trade, and his hatred of the Tyrians. He threatens Egypt, and promises to Nebuchadnezzar that the conquest of that country shall be the wages of his army for serving against Tyre. From these chapters we must set aside one or two passages to be mentioned a little later.

From the trade of the city of Tyre, which this writer describes at some length in chapter xxvii, we may learn

from whence the Israelites had been receiving many of those
articles of trade which their own country did not furnish
for them. Egypt was at all times famous for its linen, and,
indeed, was almost the only country in which flax was
grown. Tarshish, or Tarsus, is said to have furnished
silver, but this we may suppose these Cilician traders
brought from Greece, the only known seat of the silver
mines. It was customary with the merchants, in order to
keep the trade to themselves, to conceal as far as possible from
whence they brought their goods. Tarshish also furnished
iron, perhaps from Cyprus, and lead, and another white
metal, by some translators thought to be tin, but more
probably a mixed metal, the refuse of the silver mines, as, in
chapter xxii. 18, 20, Ezekiel classes it with the dross of
silver, as of little worth. Tin, when it first became known
to the ancients, was as valuable as silver. Ivory and ebony
came from Dedan, on the Persian Gulf; the seafaring men
of that town probably brought them both from Zanzibar, on
the coast of Africa. Horses and mules came from Togarmah,
or Armenia. The Arabs to the east of Canaan sent sheep
and goats, and the Arabs to the south of Canaan sent spices
and gold. Arabia had been thought to be the seat of the
gold mines before Solomon sent his ships down the Red
Sea to Ophir, on the Nubian coast; and when the trade on
the Red Sea was discontinued, the Nubian gold again, as
before, came through Arabia. Arabia sent also the sweet-
scented cane and cassia. From this chapter we also learn
how far the geographical knowledge of the Hebrew writers
reached. The town of Aden, on the coast of Arabia, was
perhaps the most southerly spot known to them, the Greek
isles, and Phut, the north coast of Africa, perhaps including
Carthage, the most westerly; while the most northerly was
Meshech, a district on the northern side of the Black Sea,
which has given its name to Muscovy. Towards the east
it is through this writer, for the first time, that we hear
of any country so distant as Persia. The caravan routes,
which ran to the Persian Gulf and the Red Sea, may have
brought the Persians and Arabs to stand beside the Africans
in the motley garrison of Tyre. If a circle be drawn upon
the map at about one thousand miles from Jerusalem as its
centre, it will include all that was known of the world in the
time of Solomon. For the time of the Captivity, the circle
must be drawn at fifteen hundred miles from the same
centre. During these centuries the Jews were not without

some reason when they compared Jerusalem to **the navel** of the **human** body, as **being** the very middle spot **of the** earth.*

EVIL-MERODACH KING OF BABYLON; **B.C.** 564—562.

In the thirty-seventh year of the Captivity, Evil-Merodach came to the throne of Babylon as successor to Nebuchadnezzar; and the treatment which the conquered Jews received from their masters was at once changed for the better. Jehoiachin, who had been in prison, and **wearing the dress** of a prisoner, **was** then brought into the **royal** palace, **and** treated **with the** respect due to his **rank.†** There can be no **doubt but his** countrymen, whether in Judea or in **captivity, all felt their** chains lighter. Evil-Merodach reigned **only three** years, but the **better** treatment of **the** captives continued until their release, about a quarter of a **century** afterwards.

Psalm cvi. was written at this time, when the writer, praying for a return from the Captivity, had by no means foreseen the manner in which the return home was to be brought about. That it was written after the accession of Evil-Merodach to the throne of Babylon, appears from the Psalmist's thankfulness **for the** milder treatment which the Jews then received **from their conquerors.** He says that God:—

> . . . . . remembered for **them his covenant,**
> And repented according to his **great kindness.**
> He made them to be pitied
> In the sight of those that carried **them** captives.

He **runs over** a few of the chief **events** of the march out of Egypt, as **told in the** Books of Exodus and Numbers. But he seems to **have read** those books before the chapters were put in their present geographical disorder; as his **events** follow according **to** the list of stations in Numbers **xxxiii.** rather than as we **have it in** the history.

This Psalm cvi., by quoting so largely **from the historical** portions of Exodus and Numbers, is an important **witness** for the age of those writings; and since one quotation relates to the death of Dathan and Abiram, which took place when Eleazar was Aaron's eldest surviving son, the Psalm further bears witness **that** Leviticus x., with the

---

* Ezek. xxxviii. 12.　　　† Kings xxv. 27.

narrative of the death of Eleazar's elder brothers, was also written before the Captivity.

Though the captives **were not yet** released, those Jews who had fled to other countries were at liberty to return to Judea, as appears by Jeremiah xliv., which belongs to this time. It was written after the **death** of Hophra, king of Egypt, which happened about the time that Evil-Merodach came to the throne of Babylon. The **writer,** who may have been Baruch, using Jeremiah's name, reproaches the Jews with remaining in Egypt, where they had **now** spread themselves, not only in the east of the Delta, but in Noph **or** Memphis, and Pathros or the Thebaid. His charge against them of idolatry may not have been deserved; the real cause of his displeasure was their want of patriotism.

Isaiah v. 13-17 contains a moralizing remark that the luxurious habits and unjust conduct of the rich, which Isaiah describes, brought upon the nation its punishment. The writer is one of the poor who were left behind by Nebuchadnezzar. He is not discontented with his condition. He calls the labourers Lambs who are now feeding in their own pasture, while those in captivity are the Fat Ones whose deserted harvests strangers are eating. Another writer in chapter vii. 21, 22, in the same spirit tells us that the evils of the Captivity did not fall on the poor, and that those who were left behind lived on curds and honey. These few words most clearly explain how the divided state of the nation brought about its ruin. The poor, who are the bone and muscle of the nation, had been so unfriendly to the rich, **that they** would not join them in its defence.

THE WAR OF THE MEDES AND PERSIANS AGAINST BABYLON.

The better treatment **of** the Jews may have been a simple **act of** humanity; but **it** probably was an act of policy, brought about by the rise of the Median power, the union of the Median and Persian forces under the command of Cyrus, king of Persia, and the war which Cyrus was then carrying on against Babylon. The history of Cyrus is very obscure, but it is probable that he was engaged in war with the Babylonian power for the greatest **part** of his life, and for many years before the conquest **of that** country.

We have a passage in the Book **of** Jeremiah, chapter xxv. 15-38, written at this time, when the storm was rising, and the nations of the East, which had hitherto oppressed

the Jews, were beginning to quarrel among themselves, and
to be overwhelmed in their turn :—

Take this cup of the wine of my wrath, says Jehovah, from my
hand, and cause all the nations, to whom I shall send thee, to drink
of it. And they shall drink and shall totter to and fro, and become
mad, because of the sword which I shall send among them. . . . . .
For lo, I begin by sending evil on the city which is called by
my name, and should ye be utterly unpunished? Ye shall not be
unpunished.

When the writer thus threatens a punishment from Jehovah
on the nations of the earth, he fearlessly mentions Pharaoh,
king of Egypt, with the rest, but he avoids any open mention
of the Babylonians, whom it might be dangerous to affront.
In the most guarded way he says that " the king of Sheshak "
shall drink the cup of punishment with the others. Sheshak
is the word Babel, or Babylon, written by beginning at the
wrong end of the alphabet; and the use of such a method of
concealing his meaning is a proof that the writer was not
beyond the reach of the Babylonian power.

The writer includes the Medes and Elamites among the
nations which he wishes to be punished; and he is not aware
that in a few years, or a few months later, they will be
among the saviours of the Jews. After a time, however, the
Jews felt that every defeat of the Babylonians was followed by
better treatment of themselves, and even before they heard the
name of Cyrus, they began to look forward to the success of the
Medes and Persians as their best chance of relief.

Chapter xxv. of Ezekiel threatens punishment on the small
states of Ammon, Moab, Edom, and the Philistines, because
they had attacked Judah in the day of misfortune. It belongs
to a time when the return home was expected.

During some of these years the great province of Elam,
which was situated between Media, Babylonia, and Persia,
was conquered by Cyrus; and after having been part of the
great kingdom of Babylon, it was now part of the kingdom
of Persia. When the Assyrians under Sennacherib besieged
Jerusalem, the Elamites had formed a part of the army; * and
in Genesis x. 22, the Elamites are classed with the Assyrians
and Chaldees, as children of Shem. But we must believe that
they were much more allied in language to the Persians or
Medes than to the Semitic races, and thus their conquest at
this time by Cyrus may have been an easy task. It is mentioned in Jeremiah xlix. 34; and we shall soon find them
forming part of the Persian army in its attack upon Babylon.

* Isaiah xxii. 6.

According to the historian Berosus Evil-Merodach the son of Nebuchadnezzar was succeeded by his brother-in-law Nergal-shorezer, or Neriglissar, and then by his nephew Laborosoarchod. This last was slain before the end of the year by Nabonned, who then seized the crown; and it was under him that Babylon was overthrown. As Cyrus approached the city, Nabonned marched out to meet him, and being defeated in battle fled southward to the town of Borsippa. Cyrus then pushed forward the siege of Babylon, which he soon captured. He gave orders that the outer walls of it should be destroyed, and he led his army in pursuit of king Nabonned, whom he took prisoner at Borsippa.* From that time began the reign of Cyrus as king of Babylon, perhaps jointly with the king of the Medes; and two years later, on the death of the Median king, Cyrus became king of the great empire of Persia, Media, Babylonia, and Assyria. Henceforth the kings of Persia dwelt chiefly at Susa in Elam, as being a spot better situated for the seat of government of their enlarged kingdom than Persepolis the old capital of Persia.

To some part of this quarter of a century we must give chapter xiii.—xiv. 23, of the Book of Isaiah. Here the writer summons the Medes from the mountains, calls them warriors consecrated by Jehovah for his purpose, and promises that Babylon, the glory of kingdoms, the beauty of the Chaldees' excellence, shall be overthrown like Sodom and Gomorrah. The king of Babylon will be cast down into the underground world, the abode of the dead, of which the writer gives a picture, not very unlike that of the Greek Mythology. He addresses the king of Babylon: "Hell from beneath is moved for thee to meet thy coming. It stirreth up the departed spirits for thee, even all the leader-goats of the earth. It hath raised up from their thrones all the kings of the nations. All they shall speak and say unto thee, 'Art thou also become weak as we? Art thou become like unto us?' Thy pomp is brought down unto hell, and the noise of thy psalteries. The maggot is spread under thee, and the worms cover thee. How art thou fallen from the heavens, O Daystar, son of the morning! How art thou cut down to the ground, thou who didst crush the nations! For thou hast said in thy heart, 'I will go up to heaven; I will exalt my throne above the stars of God; I will sit also upon the mountain of the assembly in the recesses of the north;'" that is, upon

* Josephus, Apion, i. 20.

Mount Olympus, or some such hill where the Pagan gods dwelt. The satyrs mentioned among the wild animals who are to dance over the ruins of Babylon, may have been borrowed from the scape-goats. This writer, who lived one hundred years later than the prophet Isaiah, we may call the Isaiah of the Captivity, or rather the First Isaiah of the Captivity, as other chapters, written at this time, seem to be by other authors.

The Isaiah of chapters xxxii.—xxxv. also rejoices over the expected destruction of Babylon, and using the words of Isaiah xiii. declares that it shall be made a dwelling-place for ostriches, and jackals, and satyrs. The author of these chapters distinguishes himself from the former author, by calling his writings, which he quotes, "the Book of Jehovah," and thus gives us a remarkable proof of the reverence in which these prophetic writings were held even by those who lived at the time; for these writings, the one quoting and the other quoted, were both written within a few years of one another, during the short time that the overthrow of Babylon was being brought about by the Medes and Persians. This writer we may call the Second Isaiah of the Captivity. He looks forward to the return of the ransomed captives to Zion, and to his country being again governed by a king who shall rule in righteousness. But he does not mention the Babylonians by name. And the same caution led him, when threatening the Egyptians and Syrians, to speak of the former as Buffaloes, and the latter as Bulls and Bullocks, saying, "There shall be a great slaughter in Edom; and the Buffaloes shall be cast down with them, and the Bullocks with the Bulls, and their lands shall be bathed with blood, and their dust made fat with fatness."

He reproaches those of his countrymen who had taken part with the Babylonians in the government of the country, or as he would say, in oppressing it; and who are now alarmed at their overthrow, thus—

The sinners in Zion are afraid; fear hath seized the ungodly [saying] "Who of us shall dwell when the fire devoureth? Who of us shall dwell through everlasting burning?" He that hath walked in righteousness, and spoken uprightly; he that hath refused the gain of oppression, that hath shaken his hands from taking bribes, that hath stopped his ears from hearing of blood shed, and shut his eyes from looking on evil. He shall dwell on high; his place of defence shall be castles upon rocks; bread shall be given to him; his waters shall be unfailing.

The attack upon Babylon by the Medes had for the time released Egypt from all danger on that side; and Ezek. xxix. 13-16 is now added to correct the earlier part of that chapter in which Ezekiel fifty years before had threatened complete ruin on the Egyptians because they had been a broken staff to the house of Israel.

To the same time belongs the last chapter **of the** Book of Zephaniah. It is historical, but obscure, because no names are given. Jehovah reproaches Jerusalem **as** a rebellious city, whose princes are roaring lions and evening wolves. He had cut off the nations by making their towers desolate, and their streets waste; but yet Jerusalem did not receive instruction. So he gathers nations to pour his indignation on them, and to devour their land. He carries off from Jerusalem the proud nobles, **and** leaves only the poor behind. This writer, unlike Ezekiel, thinks that the poor who were left behind at the time of the Captivity were those who trusted in Jehovah, rather than the proud captives, who had **been in** Babylon. Lastly, Jehovah has pardoned the people, **and** will call home the dispersed ones, who are in captivity, grieving at a distance from the Place of Meeting. This is the name now given to the Temple, as in Psalm lxxiv. 4, and Lamentations ii. 6.

In the year B.C. 538, Cyrus, king of Persia, commanding the joint armies of Persia and Media, conquered Babylon. The Hebrew writings tell us of the interest with which the Jews had watched the war, well knowing that any misfortune **to the** Babylonians must be an advantage to them. The event forms an epoch by which we fix the date of many **parts** of **the** Hebrew Prophets. The Book of Daniel[*] tells **us that the** Babylonian king Belshazzar was feasting with his nobles within the city on the night that it was taken by the Medes, and that he then perished in the ruins. But from the additions to Isaiah and to Jeremiah, as from Berosus already quoted, we learn that the king was away from his capital at the time, and that the fatal news was brought to him by swift messengers, while he was feasting in safety at a distance. The contradiction may be in part explained by the very probable conjecture that Belshazzar, who perished in the city, was reigning jointly with his

[*] Daniel v.

father Nabonned, who had escaped to Borsippa. Claudius Ptolemy, the astronomer, omits the name of Laborosoarchod from the list given above from Berosus, because his few months call for no notice in a table of years. A similar reason might lead him to omit Belshazzar, if he reigned jointly with his father Nabonned, and also to omit the king of the Medes, in whose name Babylon was conquered by Cyrus; because the Mede, whether named Darius or Cyaxares II, though now king of Babylon, jointly with Cyrus the Persian, calls for no notice in a table of Babylonian years, since the years of Cyrus were also counted as following immediately upon those of Nabonned.

To this time belongs a joyful passage of more than usual eloquence. Chapters xlix. 34—li. of Jeremiah, which are put into that prophet's mouth, as if written in the reign of Zedekiah, and in the lifetime of Nebuchadnezzar. But they belong to a time when Nebuchadnezzar had been dead twenty-seven years. "Declare ye among the nations," says the writer, whoever he may have been, "and publish, and lift up a standard; publish, and conceal not. Say, Babylon is taken, Bel is confounded." "Out of the north there is come up a nation," the Medes, "against her, who shall make her land desolate." When the garrison could hold out no longer, runner is sent to meet runner, and messenger to meet messenger, to tell the king, who is at a distance, "That his city is taken from end to end, and that the fords are seized, and the reed-beds they have burned with fire." The reed-beds in the waters around the city of Babylon are shown in a slab in the British Museum, where we see the armed men in boats fighting in the midst of them. In Psalm lxviii. 30 the Babylonians are called Wild Beasts of the Reeds.

This chapter of Jeremiah also gives to Babylon the enigmatic name of Sheshak, which had been used in an earlier chapter of Jeremiah; but he does not now use it to conceal his meaning, indeed, he carefully explains the enigma: "How is Sheshak taken! and how is the praise of the whole earth seized! how is Babylon become an astonishment among the nations." And the very words which in Jeremiah xlix. 19, had been used when speaking of Nebuchadnezzar, this writer employs rather incorrectly for Cyrus, saying, "Behold he shall come up like a lion from the pride [or head springs] of the Jordan, against the abode of the strong. . . . . At the noise of the taking of

17

Babylon the earth is moved and the cry is heard among the nations." When borrowing these words the writer forgot that the Medes **did** not come against Babylon from the sources of the Jordan. Verses li. 15-19, are out of place. They are repeated from chapter x. 12-16. They are of a yet later date. Verse 58 borrows the words of Habakkuk, ii. 13, of the peoples labouring for nought, and **the** nations for the fire. In verses 59-64 we have a letter said to have been sent by Jeremiah to the captives in Babylon in the fourth year of Zedekiah's reign, very unlike the real **letter** which he sent in that year, as related in chapter xxix.

To the same time, when the prospect of a return from captivity was in sight, and hopes were indulged that the nation would be restored, and again have a king of the line **of** David, we must give chapter xxx. of Jeremiah. It cannot have been written by Jeremiah himself, as he had begun to prophesy twenty years before the Captivity. It promises that the nation's nobles shall be some **of** themselves, and their governor shall proceed **from among** them. They shall yet have a David **for** their **king.** **The** same hope of a king of their own is expressed in **Isaiah xxxii.** 1, already spoken of, and written about the same **time.**

Chapter xxi. of Isaiah, On the desert by the Persian Gulf, describes the arrival of a messenger to tell the king [Nabonned] who is feasting at Borsippa, whither he had fled, at a distance from his capital, the great news " Babylon is fallen, is fallen ; and all the graven images of her gods are broken to the ground." Here the Medes and Persians are spoken of as united for the conquest of Babylon : " Go up, O Elam, besiege, O Media." Elam was a province between Persia and Babylonia, sometimes belonging to one, and sometimes to the other. Here it is used as a name for Persia, though **it had not belonged** to Persia before the union of that kingdom **with the Medes.**

If the whole **of the chapter** was by one writer, it was written by one **of those, or by** the son of one of those, who had fled from Judea to escape Nebuchadnezzar's army, and had found safety in the desert between Judea and the Persian Gulf. There, like a watchman in the night looking eagerly for day-break, he had watched for the first news of the fall of Babylon, while his friends in the neighbourhood of Mount Seir were in their turn anxiously waiting for his **report.**

Isaiah, chapters xxiv.——xxvii., though written in a more

guarded manner, clearly declare **that Babylon has** been
conquered :—

> O Jehovah, thou art my God, I will exalt thee ;
> I will praise thy name, for thou hast done wonders ;
> Thy counsels of old are faithfulness and truth.
> For thou hast made of the city [Babylon] a heap of stones.
> Of the fenced city, a ruin, a citadel of strangers,
> Of a city for ever, one not to be built up.

Here we note **a change in the** prophetic style, marking the
greater refinement and polish of the people. We have less
of the orator's fire, and more of poetic sweetness. While
much **was** lost, something was also gained during the **life in**
Babylon. **In** these chapters, which were perhaps written **by
one who had lived there,** we first meet with the opinion,
which **we see more** of in the Book **of** Daniel, **that** every
nation **had** its own guardian angel in heaven, as **it** had its
king upon earth, a good angel for a good nation, and a
wicked angel for a wicked nation; and the writer says of the
Babylonians and their allies, "In that day I will punish the
host of High Ones that are on high, and the kings of the
earth that are upon earth."

Chapters xi. and xii. of Isaiah **belong to about** the same
time, or at least a little later **than chapter** xiii. Here a
highly poetical description of **a** future **time,** not of victory
over enemies, but of peaceful prosperity, **is** followed by a
promise that the **despised** Israelites, **both** of Ephraim and
Judah, shall return **home** and lay **aside** their old quarrels.
The nation is **again to be** governed **by a** ruler of the family
of Jesse ; and **the earth** shall **be full** of the knowledge of
Jehovah as the **waters** cover the **sea.** These beautiful lines,
full of religious **hope,** may well **be** the writing of him who we
shall speak **of** presently as the Isaiah of the return home.

The beautiful Psalm cxxxvii. was written when the success
of Cyrus seemed certain, and the destruction of Babylon was
looked **for as** likely to follow. The writer speaks of his
captivity **as already past** :—

> By the rivers of Babylon, there we sat down,
> Yea, we wept when we remembered Zion.
> We hanged our harps on the willows in the midst of it.
> For there they that carried us captive asked of us a song ;
> And they that made us mourn asked for mirth,
> [Saying,] "Sing us one of the songs of Zion."
> How can we sing a song of Jehovah in a foreign land ?
> If I forget thee, O Jerusalem, let my right hand forget [its cunning].

17 *

Let **my** tongue cleave to the roof of my mouth,
If I do not remember thee,
If I prefer not Jerusalem **above my chief joy.**

As the writer had been living in captivity, and had suffered
the taunts of the Babylonians, and remembered the ruin that
they had brought upon his country, and also how the neighbouring little nations had come in to share the plunder, we
must not judge him too severely for the bitter curse with
which he ends his poem :—

> Remember, O Jehovah, the children of Edom.
> Who said in the day of Jerusalem.
> "Raze it, raze it, even to its foundations."
> O daughter of Babylon, who art to be destroyed,
> Happy he that repayeth thee as thou hast served us ;
> Happy shall he be that taketh
> And dasheth thy little ones against **the rock.**

The short prophecy of Obadiah was written while the Jews
were yet smarting under the mortification and humiliation
of not having been able to defend themselves from their
despised neighbours, the Edomites ; and it is a threat of
punishment that **was** coming upon that nation from the
Persians.　The Edomites had overrun Judea, and, as it seems,
had come up to the very walls of Jerusalem—had "drunk
upon the holy mountain," as the prophet says, when the
Chaldees were in possession of the country ; and they shall
hereafter be made to drink the cup of bitterness in their
turn.　Many of Obadiah's words may be found in chapter
xlix. of Jeremiah, or rather in Baruch's addition to Jeremiah,
in the threat against Edom.　It is in vain to inquire where
Obadiah was living when he wrote these few words.　He was
perhaps one of those who had escaped southward from the
invading armies of Nebuchadnezzar ; but as he does not
mention the Babylonians he was probably not wholly safe out
of reach of their power.　The words "saviours shall come
upon Mount Zion to judge the mountains of Esau" point to
the Persians.

In Edom the Persian troops may **have met** with some little
resistance, **as** we learn from the Fourth Lamentation, which
seems to **have been** written on the occasion of Cyrus's troops
overrunning the country of the Edomites.　The writer tells
us that the Captivity is at an end ; "Thy punishment is
accomplished, O daughter of Zion."　And he rejoices in the
thought that Edom's turn for punishment is now come ;
"Rejoice, and be glad [O Zion].　O daughter of Edom, that

dwellest in the land of Uz, the cup shall pass over unto thee ; thou shalt be drunken, and shalt make thyself naked." The writer speaks of the captivity of king Jehoiachin, "The breath of our nostrils, the anointed of Jehovah, was taken in their pitfalls." And he speaks of the disappointment at not being relieved by the Egyptians ; " We watched for a nation that could not save us." These last words could not have been written by Jeremiah, who suffered no such disappointment, and never looked for help from Egypt.

Isaiah xxi. 16, 17, tells us that Kedar, on the south of Edom, suffered at the same time from the Persians. The caravans from Kedar to the Persian Gulf may have been a source of jealousy and have led to occasional quarrels.

JUDEA UNDER THE PERSIANS.

We have no particulars of how the Persians gained possession of Palestine, nor of their entrance into Judea, to which country our history is very much limited. The Babylonian forces had been for the most part withdrawn for the defence of the capital ; and when Babylon and its king were overthrown, its subject provinces could offer no resistance to the Persians. The Persians copied the Babylonians in making Damascus their head-quarters for the government of all the country beyond the River Euphrates. Samaria and Jerusalem were each the seat of government for its own province, but more or less in obedience to Damascus. Troops in small bodies were probably stationed in the other towns whose duty was to guard and support a number of tribute-collectors named Sagins, who were scattered over the land and were often Jews. Such was the ill-treatment that the Jews had received from the Babylonians, that the Persians were welcomed as deliverers. The Jews who accepted the office of Sagin under the Babylonians was hated and despised, but under the Persians the Jewish Sagin was respected. The Persians were not idolaters ; and thus they gave no offence to the Jews in religious matters. During the two centuries that Judea was under their rule, we do not once hear of any rebellion or attempt to regain the national independence.

We know from the after events that when Cyrus had made himself king of Babylon, he adopted the aim of the former kings of that country, and proposed to himself the conquest of Egypt, as sooner or later to be attempted.

Xenophon, in the Cyropædia,* says that Cyrus dwelt seven months in Babylon, and that from that city he sent forward an army for the invasion of Egypt. The Persian invasion, however, of Egypt was **not** seriously begun until the next reign.

In the very first year that Cyrus king **of** Persia was master of Babylon, he issued his celebrated decree that the Jewish captives might return home, and rebuild their Temple in Jerusalem. This was in the sixty-third year from the accession of Jehoiachin, and was called, according to their usual mode of reckoning, the sixty-third of the Captivity, though the Captivity did not begin till the end **of** Jehoiachin's first year. This decree of Cyrus was **not wholly** dictated by humanity. With the conquest of **one kingdom** he immediately had visions of the conquest **of** other kingdoms; and we shall meet with very good evidence that as soon as he had made himself king of Babylon, he proposed to himself the conquest of Egypt, as what was sooner or later to be attempted. But with this view he followed a wiser policy than his Chaldee predecessors, and began by making the Jews his friends. He was master of Syria, and all Palestine, as well as of Babylon; and therefore in sending the Jews home, he was only moving a body of his subjects from one province of his kingdom into another province, in which they could be more useful to him.

Among the captives in Babylon the man of highest rank was the young Zerubbabel, called also Sheshbazzar, the grandson of king Jehoiachin, who had died in Babylon. Him Cyrus appointed to the office of viceroy of Judea, with the Persian title of the Tirshatha. The Hebrew writers style him Prince Zerubbabel, and sometimes the Pacha. Of this modest heir to the throne of David, to whom the Jews were so much indebted, we learn very little from the historians. We are left to picture to ourselves his character by the help of his situation. His quiet submission to the Babylonian tyrants, his prudent dealing with the Persian conqueror, his successful intercession for his countrymen, are nowhere described, unless we accept the Servant of Jehovah, in Isaiah lii. 13—liii., as meant for him. He was young; in Ezekiel xvii. 22, he is called a tender twig. But he was married, and had several sons whom he left behind him in Babylon, probably detained by the Persian king as hostages.

* **Lib. VIII.** vi. **20.**

With the permission of Cyrus, Zerubbabel gathered together in the neighbourhood of Babylon nearly fifty thousand Jews, beside their male and female servants; among them was Jeshua, the representative of the family of the high priests, with above three thousand other priests, but only twenty-seven Levites. Cyrus gave into their hands more than five thousand gold and silver dishes which had been carried away from Jerusalem by Nebuchadnezzar, and had been kept in the Temples of the Babylonian gods. This caravan, with their wealth and their cattle, Zerubbabel led in safety to Jerusalem. They reached their wished-for home probably in the second year of Cyrus's reign, B.C. 537.

These people were for the most part the grandchildren of those that had been carried into captivity, and they came back men, women, and children. While in Babylon they had carefully kept records of the births, so that every family could prove to what tribe it belonged, or at least that it was part of the great family of Israel. They were for the most part those who had given themselves up willingly to Nebuchadnezzar, and had not brought upon themselves his vengeance by resisting. The leaders were the sons of Pharez and the sons of Zarah, the latter called the sons of the Pasha of Moab. The captives in Syria, on the banks of the Chaboras, had not been so careful of their genealogies; and about six hundred of these, who returned home at the same time, were not immediately allowed by their brethren to be true Jews. Such of these as claimed to be priests did not at once have their claims allowed. They were not permitted to eat from the Holy of Holies, and were told to wait until a chief priest, properly robed with the Urim and Thummim, could decide the question. They probably had not to wait long, because Jeshua, the son or grandson of Josadak, was acknowledged by Prince Zerubbabel and the whole assembly to be the chief of the priests.[*]

While living in captivity, more or less as slaves, in spots where they had been placed, the northern and southern tribes may have in some degree continued separate; but when freedom to move was granted to them by Cyrus, the distinction began to be lost, particularly among those who remained abroad. They were all at liberty to return, and some of Ephraim and Manasseh followed Zerubbabel to Judea, as the best chance of finding a comfortable home.

---

[*] Ezra i. ii.

Others of Israel, but as it would seem not many, returned to Samaria, and to their old enmity to Judah. But among those who remained scattered abroad, "in the dispersion" as it was called, such jealousy fortunately died out. The foreigners among whom they dwelt looked upon them all as one people. The name of Jew covered them all; and as the government in Jerusalem gave rank to those who when at a distance were willing to be thought its subjects, they were all glad to be thought Jews. They thus left to our eastern travellers the interesting but hopeless inquiry, where the tribes of Northern Israelites are to be found, since so small a number returned from captivity to Samaria. The want of population in Samaria the Persian king in part supplied by sending a number of colonists from Elam, Media, and Persia, to enjoy the lands in Samaria, and to trample on what remained there of the old inhabitants.*

The captives who followed Zerubbabel soon scattered themselves over Judea, every family going to its own city. These cities were far from being without inhabitants. The peasants and labourers had been left behind in them when their masters had been carried off by the Chaldees. Many of the Assyrians whom Sennacherib and Esarhaddon had placed in Samaria had spread themselves over Judea. Such of the Jewish families as had been able to escape the danger, and had found safety as exiles in Egypt or in the neighbourhood of the Ammonites and Moabites, or among the ruined cities of the Philistines, after Nebuchadnezzar's armies had plundered Gaza, Askalon, and Ashdod, must have reached their old homes before the captives had travelled their longer journey.† Hebron, and all the country to the south of it, was now in the hands of the Edomites. Such was the population of Judea, some friendly, and some unfriendly, when the captives returned home to repair the waste places.

Among those who returned from captivity, we find two new bodies of men mentioned with the priests and Levites. These are the Nethins and the sons of Solomon's servants. In Numbers iii., written in the middle of the monarchy, the priests are a single family, while the Levites are counted by thousands. But before the close of the monarchy Deuteronomy declared that all the Levites were priests. But a law cannot make those equal who in education and habits are unequal. The distinction between the upper and lower class

* Ezra iv. 9, 10.   † Zephan. ii. 7, 9.

was not wholly abolished ; the line which divided them was, however, removed a few steps lower down ; and now, on the return from Babylon, the priests are the more numerous body, and the numbers in the classes are as follows:— Priests, 4289 ; Levites, 74 ; Singers, 128 ; Gatekeepers, 139 ; Nethins and sons of Solomon's servants, 392.* The Nethins were a lower class of Levites, who are said to be Nethun, or *given* to the priests as servants, as the name **may** be explained from Numb. iii. 9.

They lodged in the suburb Ophel, outside the south end of the Temple-yard.† Of the duties of the sons of Solomon's servants we have no account ; but they were ranked with the Nethins. They were very possibly the Temple servants, called **Gibeonites** in Joshua ix. 27. Those men were called Gibeonites **after the** town from which the ark was brought into **Jerusalem** ; and the reason for their being servants, which **is given** in the Book of Joshua, we may safely disregard.

The large number of priests mentioned above explains why they no longer bore the name of Sons of Aaron. Such a name would have revived the narrow enactments of the Levitical law, which had been widened by the Book of Deuteronomy ; it would have limited the priesthood, as before, to a **single** family, the sons of Zadok, and shut out from it that **large** body of the Levites whose claim to the higher rank **was** now admitted. The chief priest at this time was **of** such lessened importance, that the latter chapters of Ezekiel, when describing the Temple and its ordinances, do not mention such a **person**.

In Jerusalem the prince Zerub**babel** and the chief priest **Jeshua** immediately set up the altar and took steps for the repair **of the** Temple and the renewal of the worship there. They ga**thered in** the freewill offerings, and sent for timber from Lebanon, which was again brought by sea to **Joppa**, **as in** Solomon's **time**; and in the second year after **their** arrival they laid the foundation of the House of **Jehovah**, which was **to** be built on the same spot on Mount **Moriah** as that where Solomon had before built it.

Now began to show itself the jealousy which might easily have been foreseen between the men of the Captivity and those whom they found living in and around Jerusalem, whom they styled their adversaries. The grounds for a

* Ezra ii.　　† Nehemiah iii. 26.

separation between them can have been very slight, except that these had **been** in captivity **and** those had not. The conduct of the captives seems to have been both unwise and unkind, and probably very unjust. The new Assyrian settlers were only a handful, and need not be taken into account. Whatever difference there had been at first between the Israelites and the conquered Canaanites, it had been blotted **out** during the four centuries **of** the monarchy, They **had** during that long time intermarried, at least, so far as the rich and the poor are in the habit **of** intermarrying. They were the same in religion and language, at least, so far as the rich and the poor are ever the same in religion **and** language. When Nebuchadnezzar invaded Judea, he found no other division among the people than that between the educated rich who owned the land, and the uneducated poor who tilled it. The men while in captivity could have as little obeyed the **law** against foreign marriages, as the women **who** were left behind. **The** required purity of blood was lost to both parties alike. But on the return home the separation between the children of **the** Captivity and the others was very clearly marked. The foreign manners, foreign opinions, and foreign accent **in** the Captives, was accompanied with a better education, and **a** proud assertion that they alone were the true Jews who had followed the old traditions. But education was not wholly in the hands of those who had been in captivity; and we shall find among the later writings some which seem to be the product of the despised class. Thus each party might naturally claim to be **the** old inhabitants, and might style the others the new **comers.** Even those who acknowledged that they were **colonists,** brought in by the Assyrians, asked leave to join **the men** of the Captivity in their pious work of rebuilding **the** Temple, pleading that they had worshipped Jehovah **there ever** since their arrival. But their request was **haughtily** refused. They were all alike told that they **should have** no part in building the House for the God of the **Jews.** A careful jealous line was in every thing drawn between **the** handful of men who had come up from the Captivity and the great mass of the people. The former said that they alone were the true Jews, the children of Judah and Benjamin, and that all but themselves were Gentiles and Assyrian colonists.

The feelings which led men to oppose the rebuilding of **the** Temple may have been those which led the Scotch reformers under John Knox to destroy the cathedrals. They feared that the religious services were to be used to mark the difference between the children of the Captivity and the rest of the nation, who were often called foreigners, and always treated as inferiors. The latter accordingly took every step in their power to weaken the hands of Zerubbabel; and though he had come up bearing the royal letter of Cyrus, yet they were able, with the help of the Persian officers in the country, to stop his work during the whole of that reign.*

The return of the captive Jews from Babylon called forth a burst of religious poetry expressive of the people's thankfulness to Jehovah. But they rejoiced with trembling. They had for a moment hoped for a restoration of their monarchy; but Zerubbabel was not to be a king. To speak of him in any lofty terms might rouse the Persian jealousy. And this may explain why the Jewish writers when praising him usually avoid the use of his name. He is called by the prophets the Offshoot from the root of Jesse; the Righteous Branch raised up to David; the Righteous Man; the Tender Twig from the highest cedar; and the Servant of Jehovah. These names were no doubt all well understood at the time. But in later days, and particularly when the Hebrew books had got thrown into their present confused state, it became by no means clear what person the prophets were looking for so hopefully; and hence many passages relating to Zerubbabel have been thought to point to a spiritual Messiah.

The writings are now expressive of the change which sixty years of suffering in a foreign land had made in their religious feelings. The prophets now taught the nation to look forward less to a time of worldly greatness, which had become hopeless, and more to a time of spiritual blessings, which might be helped on by their own efforts. First among the writers now to be mentioned is the Isaiah of the Return Home, called the Later Isaiah by those critics who divide the Book of Isaiah into two portions, and give each portion to a single writer. But we have already mentioned the first Isaiah's own writings, about the year B.C. 700, and we then gave reasons for placing a second portion of this book about B.C. 550, and now we have a third portion about B.C. 538. So we shall have occasion to divide further portions of the

* Ezra iii. iv. 5.

book between an equal number of different centuries. To the writer who lived under Zerubbabel we can only give chapters xi., xii., already mentioned, and xl.—lv., written while the captives were on their journey home; as the following chapters differ from these in purpose, and also by many years in the time that they were written.

The writer of these beautiful chapters begins—"Comfort ye, comfort ye my people, saith your God. Speak ye to the heart of Jerusalem, and cry unto her that her warfare is accomplished, that her iniquity is pardoned." Cyrus has released the captives; there is "the voice of one that crieth, Prepare ye in the desert the way of Jehovah," for their return; "make straight in the barren valley a highway for our God."

Respecting Cyrus he asks, "Who hath raised up the righteous man from the east, hath called him to be His follower, hath given up the nations before him, and made him rule over kings?" And he answers, it was "I, Jehovah, who am the first and with the last; I am he" (xli. 4). Cyrus "will come upon the Sagins, or *deputies*, as upon mortar, and as the potter treadeth the clay." These men are the Jews who had taken office under the Babylonian conquerors of their country.

Jehovah declares his trust in Prince Zerubbabel, who is to lead the Jews home from Babylon :—

"Behold my Servant, whom I will uphold, my chosen one in whom my soul delighteth. I have put my spirit upon him; he shall bring forth judgment upon the nations. He shall not cry, nor lift up, nor cause his voice to be heard abroad. A bruised reed he shall not break, and the dimly burning flax he shall not quench; he shall bring forth judgment unto truth. He shall not fail nor be discouraged, till he have set up judgment on the land; and the isles shall wait for his law." (xlii. 1-4).

But the writer also blames the want of action both in Zerubbabel, the Servant of Jehovah, who seems to have been a well-meaning but weak man, and in the high priest Jeshua, whom he calls Jehovah's messenger, giving him a title which was now coming into use for a preacher :—

"Hear ye deaf, and look ye blind, that ye may see. Who is so blind as my Servant? or so deaf as my Messenger, whom I am sending? Who is so blind as he that has been recompensed, even so blind as Jehovah's Servant?" (xlii. 19).

Then we are told of Cyrus's future intentions, that in

releasing the Jews, he **was preparing for the invasion of** Egypt :—

" I have given Egypt for thy ransom, Ethiopia and Seba [or Nubia,] in place of thee. Since thou art precious in my sight, thou hast been honourable, and I have loved thee. Therefore will I give men for thee, and peoples for thy life " (xliii. 3, 4).

But he gently reminds the people of their transgressions :—

" Thou hast bought for me no sweet cane with money, neither hast thou moistened me with the fat of thy sacrifices; but thou hast burdened me with thy sins, thou hast wearied me with thine iniquities. I, even I, am He that blotteth out thy transgressions for mine own sake, and I will not remember thy sins " (xliii. 24, 25).

In chapter xlvii. **he tells Babylon that her knowledge of** astronomy will **not save her** :—

Let now those who divide out the heavens, those who gaze on the stars, those who understand the moon's changes, let them stand up and save thee from the things that are coming on thee. Behold, they are as stubble; the fire shall burn them; they shall not deliver themselves from the power of the flame. It shall not be a coal only to warm at, nor a light to sit before it.

In chapter xlix. the **writer makes Zerubbabel the** speaker, and he says:—

Jehovah formed me to be a Servant **to him, to raise** up the tribes of Jacob, and **to** bring back **the preserved** of Israel; and, " behold, some shall come **from far**; and lo, some from the north, and from the west, and some from the land of the Sinites," perhaps India. He quotes the words of the prophet Nahum, which were written on the destruction of Nineveh seventy-four years **earlier**:—" How beautiful upon the mountains are the feet of him that bringeth good tidings, that publisheth peace " (lii. 7). **He** calls to Zerubbabel and **his companions,** who are yet in Babylon :—

Get ye out, get ye out, go ye out thence. Touch no unclean thing. Go **out of the** midst of her. Be ye clean, ye who carry **the vessels of** Jehovah. **For** ye shall not go out with haste, nor go **in** flight; **for** Jehovah **will go** before you, and the God of Israel will be **your rearguard** (lii. 12).

He again **in** chapter lii., 13—liii. describes **the** Servant **of** Jehovah in words very suitable to Zerubbabel, as " Despised and rejected by men, a man of sorrows and acquainted with grief." He borrows thoughts from Jeremiah xi. 19, when he describes **Jehovah's** servant as " brought like a lamb to the slaughter, and as kept apart from the land of the living." Again "He prepared his grave with the wicked, and with the rich **one** among his dead **men**." Yet "he shall see his seed, he shall prolong his days, and the pleasure of Jehovah shall prosper **in** his hand." And again, "Behold, I have given him for **a** witness to the peoples, a leader and commander **to the** tribes."

Aben Ezra in his commentary on Isaiah rightly considers the Servant of Jehovah in chapter xlii. **l, xlix.** 3, and lii. 13, —liii. 12, as one and the same person.

In the words quoted above, "He prepared his grave with **the** wicked men, and with the rich one among his dead men," **it is** very possible that "the rich one" may have been meant **for** "the Assyrian," as the two words are not very unlike, **and we** have many cases of writers thus concealing their **meaning** in prudence. There may also here be a reference **to Ezekiel** xxxii. 22, where Assyria and her company, with the other tyrants of the earth, are described as lying in their graves.

This writer shows his acquaintance with the Babylonians by the mention of their soothsayers, of the gods Bel and Nebo, **and** of these gods being carried off by their owners in flight on the backs of their cattle. His more exact knowledge of the fugitives from Babylon escaping as far as the head of the Persian Gulf, where dwelt "the Chaldeans whose shout is in ships," and of their not being safe there, leads us to think that like the writer of chapter xxi. he had dwelt in that southerly spot. Joel, Nahum, and sometimes Isaiah, write with more vigour and energy than this unknown author, but no Hebrew writer whatever has the same religious sweetness.

There are several of the Psalms that belong to this time of rejoicing and hope. Thus Psalm lxxxiv. may have been **written** by one **of** the captives of the journey before he had reached the city of his forefathers :—

> How lovely is thy tabernacle, O Jehovah of hosts!
> My soul longeth, yea, fainteth for the courts of Jehovah.

And again :—

> Blessed is the man whose strength is in thee;
> In whose heart are the highways [to Zion].
> On passing through the valley of Baca [or tears],
> They make it a spring, yea the early rain covereth it with blessings.
> They go from strength to strength,
> Every one of them appeareth before God in Zion.

Psalm cxxvi. says:—

> When Jehovah brought home **the captivity of Zion**,
> We were like them that dream.
> Then was our mouth filled with laughter,
> And our tongue with singing.

This latter Psalm is called a Song of **the** Steps, or **of** Going Up; and there **are** fourteen others with the same title. The reason **for their** being so styled **is** very doubtful. It might mean that **they** were sung by worshippers on their route up to Jerusalem; or, sung by the priests on the steps of the Temple; **or** again, written, as some of them are, with returning catch words, **to** help the memory by leading it from sentence to sentence. But as no one of these reasons will apply to all of them, **no one** can **be** taken to **be** the **true** reason. These Psalms seem **to be** of **various** dates.

Psalm cvii. is of this time, or at least not earlier; for it quotes from Isaiah xlv. **2**, the description **of** the release of the captives from Babylon,

> For He brake the doors of copper,
> And cut the bars of iron asunder.

The writer may have been born and lived all **his** life as a captive in Susiana beyond Babylon, with sea on **the** south side of him, as he **so** places it in verse 3; while the Hebrew writers generally **speak** of **the** sea as in the **west**.

In the history **of literature** there has been in every country a time when it has **flourished** and a time of decay; a time of original genius and a **time of** imitation and even of forgery. So in Judea soon **after** the return from the Captivity, when men began to inquire after the old and valued books, they began also **to** make unauthorized additions to them, **in** the form of prophecies written **after the** events. The Books of Jeremiah **and** Ezekiel are the **two** which have received the largest additions **in** this improper manner. The Book of Isaiah received **fewer** of these unauthorized additions. The newer parts **of that** Book seem for the most part to have been joined to that prophet's writings only in carelessness; and as for the Pentateuch and the Book of Psalms, it was always the custom to add **new** laws to **the one** and **new poems to** the other as they were written. But some **of** the **additions** to Jeremiah and Ezekiel were added very **im**properly. Thus it is upon some of the scribes of this time that we must fix the blame of adding to the writings of Jeremiah words prophetic of the Return, which were certainly written after the event,

and which are mostly very much **out** of place where they now stand.

Jeremiah xii. 14-17 promises to **the** house of Judah a return from captivity every man to his own heritage.

Chapter xvi. 14, 15, promises the Israelites a return, and stands between two sentences threatening **them** with punishment. Chapter xxvii. 7 is dated in the reign of Jehoiakim, and it prophesies not only that the future king Zedekiah shall serve Nebuchadnezzar, but that **all** nations shall continue to serve him, and his son, and his grandson; and that then great kings, meaning the Median king and Cyrus, shall require service of Babylon. The exactness in all these prophecies makes us think that they were written after the events had happened. Chapters xxxii. 36—xxxiii. promise a return home from Captivity; and the latter verses, 14-26, of this last chapter, which are not in the Greek copies, add that a righteous Branch shall be raised up to David, meaning **prince** Zerubbabel, **who is** afterwards described by that name **in the writings** of **the prophet Zechariah. Chapter** xxiii. **1-8 has** the **same promise of a righteous Branch raised up** to David. Yet more exact are chapters **xxv. 1-14,** and xxix. 10-14, which threaten that Babylon is **to** be overthrown in the seventieth year from the accession **of** Nebuchadnezzar. The words beginning at xxxii. 36, could never have been written by Jeremiah, they quite misstate his opinions. It was himself, not his opponents, who said that the city would be delivered up into the hands of the king **of** Babylon.

Ezekiel xxviii. 25, 26, was also most proba**bly** written after the return from Captivity, as also xxix. 21, saying that the Horn of the house of Israel shall branch forth. Other large portions of Ezekiel we shall meet with presently.

There are in some of the other Prophets similar passages which declare themselves plainly to be insertions of this or a later time. Such is Joel ii. 28—iii. 8, which promises to Judah and Jerusalem a return from captivity, and speaks of the Jewish children being sold by the Tyrians to the Greeks, as slaves. Such is Amos. ix. 11-15, which promises that the fallen Temple shall be rebuilt, and the captives brought home to build up their ruined cities, and be masters over every nation that worships Jehovah; a description which we are particularly told included the Edomites. Such also is Micah iv. v., which first threatens that Jerusalem shall be carried captive to Babylon, and then promises that the captives shall be set free, and that a ruler shall rise up out of Beth-lehem to govern Judah. This, of course, is prince Zerubbabel, of the family of David. Such is Isaiah xxiii. 15, 18, foretelling that the sufferings of Tyre from the Babylonians shall come to an end after seventy years, dating from the first year of Nebuchadnezzar. Such again is Isaiah ii. 1-4, which is wholly taken from the passage of Micah above spoken of; and iv. 2-6, which is in praise of the Branch of Jehovah, the title often given to Zerubbabel. This latter passage is noteworthy as declaring that those who at the time escaped the Captivity, and were left in Jerusalem, were all holy, not limiting, like Ezekiel, that character to the captives. That no such prophecies of a return from the Captivity in Babylon had ever been published, is again and again declared by the Isaiah of the Return, in chapters xli. 26-29; xliii. 9; also xlviii. 6-8.

The wish to know what will happen to-morrow, or on any more distant day, is a wish so natural, that men have not been content with asking the opinion of those who by a study of the past can in some degree make a guess at the future; but they have often run to ignorant pretenders, as did king Saul on the eve of his last fatal battle, and as king Josiah did when frightened by the threats in Deuteronomy. It was in Babylon that this silly art of fortune-telling was most cultivated. There the Chaldee astronomers had proved their right to be believed by foretelling eclipses; and building upon the credit thus gained they had ventured to foretell the fate of men and nations. A Chaldean had become a name for a fortune-teller. The Jews, when in captivity, may have yielded a belief to these pretensions. Some had learned to think that such powers were the one great proof of wisdom, or at least of the possession of knowledge from heaven. Hence on the return from Babylon the scribes thought that they could add to the authority of their great writers by grafting into the text prophecies written after the events. In this spirit were made the additions to the Books of Jeremiah and the other prophets as pointed out above. The meaning of the name of Prophet became changed. It had meant a wise adviser of the people, one who warned from sin and encouraged goodness; but they lowered it to mean one who, like a fortune-teller, could foretell the future. From such blots on the Prophets' writings it is now the business of the critic to clear them.

Psalm cii. was written after the return home, but while the city was yet in ruins. The writer, an old man whose days

18

were like a lengthened shadow, whose prayers had been the groanings of a prisoner appointed to death, and whose strength had been weakened **on the** journey home, now says,

> Thou wilt arise, and have pity on Zion,
> For the time to favour her, yea, the set **time is** come.
> For thy servants take pleasure in her stones,
> They look with favour even on the dust thereof.
> Then will the nations fear the name of Jehovah,
> And all the kings of the earth thy glory,
> When Jehovah buildeth up Zion, appearing in his glory.

The "**set** time" here spoken of is that mentioned **in** Jeremiah xxv. 11, and xxix. 10, as declared beforehand **by** the Almighty.

Psalm lxix. also declares **the** writer's trust that God will **save Zion** and build up again the cities of Judah. He complains sorely of the enemies by whom he is surrounded. It may belong to this time of distress and hope.

While in captivity the Jews had clung with pious zeal to their old customs and traditions, but at the same time they had gained many new and some wiser opinions. They had become more enlightened by mixing with men of other faiths. They gave up their old opinion that a man's sufferings were always a punishment for his sins ; that opinion their own bitter experience had disproved. They gave up also the opinion that he was punished for his forefathers' sins (Ezekiel xviii. Jeremiah xxxi. 30). Rather than that they thought that he might sometimes be punished for his children's sins (Job viii. 4).

Henceforth also we meet with not a little of fable, which **we** may call Eastern Mythology mixed with the pure theology of **the** prophets. Thus we now read of Jehovah sitting in a council of holy angels (Psalm lxxxix. 5-7), and of these angels presenting themselves before him on stated days. One of the angels, named Satan, or *the Accuser*, has the duty of pointing out who among men is deserving of punishment (Job i.). Other angels are appointed as watchers, or guardians, to watch over the welfare of men (Daniel iv. 17). To these Holy Ones some persons would address prayer in times of distress, like the Romish invocation of saints (Job v. 1). Each nation was thought to have a High One, or prince, in heaven, as it had a king on earth ; and when **the** earthly king was overthrown and punished, the High **One** in heaven was punished also (Isaiah xxiv. 21 ; Daniel **x. 13-20).** Another opinion gave to each nation its god ; and as Jehovah and his angels met in assembly in heaven, the gods of the nations met on a mountain in the recesses of the north, which may be compared to the mount Olympus of the Greeks (Isaiah xiv. 13). The wicked kings of the nations who carried the Jews into captivity are described as cast down into hell, with all their pomp and their glory. This is a pit under the ground, where the maggot is spread under them, and the worms cover them, where they are met by the other departed spirits (Isaiah xiv. 9-18). The good and bad alike when dead go down into this dreary pit called **hell.** Before or **after** entering it, they have to pass through the Valley of the Shadow of Death, a valley divided by several doors, to **each of which** there was a doorkeeper (Job xxxviii. 17). Whatever were the dangers to be met with in this valley, the good man was able to walk past **them** unhurt (Psalm xxiii. 4). His soul was not left to corrupt in hell (Psalm xvi. 10; xlix. 15). While the wicked of the Gentiles were thrust into the back of this pit of destruction, others who had been less unfriendly to the Jews **were** allowed to lie by themselves, with their weapons of war and their swords under their heads (Ezekiel xxxii. 23-27). The Mighty One of the nations was a cruel being to whom Jehovah handed up **his** enemies, knowing that he would surely deal with them, and force them down into this pit (Ezekiel xxxi. 11-14). Such were the new opinions about the under-world which **now** crept into Judea **from Babylon.**

The Jews also brought with **them from Babylon the** custom of counting their months **for civil** purposes **from the** autumn instead of from the spring; **but** they continued to use the old beginning of the year **for** religious purposes. They also brought home new names **for** the months. These **are used in** the Books of Esther, Zechariah, and Nehemiah. **But these new** months did not at **once** give greater exactness to **the measure of time.** They were still lunar months, some of twenty-nine **days** each, and some of thirty days. It also seems probable **that** the weeks were of the same varying length, **and that** every lunar month, **as** perhaps in Egypt, was divided into four weeks, with the full moon always a sabbath. Thus some **weeks** must have had eight days. From a comparison between 2 Kings xxv. and Zechariah viii., **we** see that the law had fixed the fast days for the seventh, ninth, and tenth days of the month, so they never fell on the first, eighth, fifteenth, or twenty-second day, which were sabbaths. Up to this time all events have been dated by the day of the month only.   It was not necessary to mention the day of the week, if the week was a known portion of the month.   The change to make the week to be always of seven days exactly, as proposed in Leviticus xxiii. 15, 16, may have come to pass in the course of the following century.

Babylon was not the only country with which the Jews in their misfortunes had become better acquainted.   Some of the captives had been placed in Elam, which had become a part of Persia.   Some had been sold as slaves to the Tyrians, who had again sold them to the Greeks.   Egypt has often been mentioned as a place to which many of the outcasts had fled.   Hence the later writers not only teach a wider geography, but let us understand that they had visited and brought home some little knowledge of Greece, Nubia, and Abyssinia.   Isaiah xlix. even speaks of the land of the Sinites, perhaps India.   But that country was known only by name.   The winds forbad the little vessels from passing eastward along the southern coast of Arabia; and no one knew that the Red Sea and the Persian Gulf opened into the same ocean, an ocean which separates India from Africa.

There was a caravan route from Damascus southward to Arabia, by which the Queen of Sheba had visited Solomon, and by which the writer of Job travelled in his way to Nubia.   By this route many Israelites had settled in Kedar in Arabia; others gained a knowledge of Hadramout, and Mesha, and Aden, in south Arabia.   By the help of this route Judea now hoped to receive tribute from Abyssinia, as said in Isaiah xviii. 7, which foretells that a time will come when "presents will be brought to Jehovah of hosts from a people scattered and made bare, who are some of the people terrible from the beginning and hitherto, the nation measured out and trodden down, whose land the Rivers [Tigris and Euphrates] have plundered."

Psalm xl. quotes Isaiah i. 11, for Jehovah not requiring burnt-offerings and sacrifices, saying, "In the roll of the Book it is written."   It probably belongs to this century, but carries with it no very exact date.   It closely resembles Psalm xxxv.   They both belong to a time of distress after the Captivity.   Psalm lxx. is taken out of Psalm xl.

There are also many other Psalms which are known by modern peculiarities to belong to the time after the Captivity; and they may be mentioned here as well as at any other place.   Such are the Alphabetic Psalms, in which each letter of the alphabet in its turn is the first letter of the verse. These are Ps. xxv., xxxiv., xxxvii., cxi., cxii., cxix., and cxlv. Every one of these consists of a string of moral and religious thoughts; and like all poems in which the writer is cramped by the too artificial structure, they are wholly wanting in fire and energy. The attention given to versification has not in this case been given wisely. The same alphabetic arrangement is used in the first four of the Lamentations, and also in the poem in Praise of a Virtuous Woman at the end of the Proverbs.

Of these Alphabetic Psalms, number **xxv.** ends with the prayer so descriptive of these sad times :—

> Redeem Israel, O God, out of all his troubles.

Psalm xxxvii. contains many traces of the sad state of affairs after the return from Captivity. Some men may have wished to quit a country in which they found it difficult to obtain food. The Psalmist dissuades such from forsaking the land of their fathers, saying :—

> Trust in Jehovah, and do good ;
> Dwell in the land, and thou wilt assuredly be fed.
> Delight thyself also in Jehovah,
> And he will give thee the requests of thy heart.

And looks forward to a time when they shall be relieved from the oppression of wicked men, that is, of the foreign conquerors of his country :—

> For yet a little while and the wicked shall not be ;
> Yea, thou shalt consider his place and it shall not be.
> But the afflicted will inherit the land.

Psalm cxix. speaks repeatedly of the entangling Sins of Ignorance, which had been created by the law of Numbers xv. 22-31, and treats every such profession of ignorance as a quibble, saying :—

> Thou despisest all that sin in ignorance of thy laws ;
> For their pretence [of ignorance] is false. (verse 118.)
> Thou hast rebuked the proud that are cursed,
> Who [say they] sin in ignorance of thy commands. (verse 21.)

At the same time the writer himself humbly prays to be saved from such sins, saying :—

> With my whole heart have I sought thee ;
> Let me not sin in ignorance of thy commands. (verse 10.)

This writer is one of the humbler class, who suffers less from the foreigners than from his countrymen ; and he ventures to hint that those who are in power are neglectful of the religious laws which they profess to teach :—

> I have more understanding than **all my** teachers,
> For thy Testimonies are my meditation.
> I understand more than the elders,
> Because I have **kept** thy Precepts.

This Psalm is not only artificial in its alphabetical arrangement, in having every stanza consist of eight verses, each beginning with the same letter, but, moreover, every stanza repeats, in its eight verses, nearly the same eight words, **as** Law, Testimonies, Ways, Precepts, Statutes, Commands, Judgments, and Word.

The latter half of Psalm xix., verses 7-14, may here be mentioned, as it resembles the above, not only in its running over the words Law, Testimony, Precepts, Command, Fear, Judgments, but also in its prayer against falling into Sins of Ignorance, saying :—

> **Who can** understand his Sins of Ignorance?
> Cleanse thou me from hidden faults;
> **Keep** back thy servant also from presumptuous sins.

The introduction to the Book **of** Proverbs in praise of Wisdom, contained in chapters i.—ix. bears but few marks by which we can fix its age. But its modern character forbids us to place it before this time; and as it seems to have been known to the writer of Job, we cannot place it **later.** It is in the form of a speech spoken by Solomon to his son; and he relates the advice which Wisdom gives to her children.

Thus Wisdom **speaks as a person, saying** :—

> **I was** poured **out** [**or** begotten] from everlasting,
> From the beginning, before the earth was.
> When there were no waters below; I was brought forth,
> When there were no fountains abounding with water.
> Ere yet the mountains were settled,
> Before the hills, was I brought forth;
> While yet He had not made the earth nor the plains
> Nor the highest part of the dust of the world.
> When he prepared the heavens I was there;
> When he fixed the arch upon the face of the deep
> When he made firm the skies above;
> When he stopped up the fountains of the deep;
> When he gave to the sea his decree,
> That the waters should not pass its shore;
> When he fixed the foundations of the earth;

> Then I was with him as a nursling;
> And I have been a daily delight, sporting ever before him,
> Sporting in the habitable parts of his earth;
> And my delights are with the sons of Adam.

Of the Jewish writings which remain to us, this furnishes the earliest example of God's Wisdom being made a person, begotten before all worlds, a thought which is carried further in the Greek Apocryphal work of the Wisdom of the Son of Sirach, and again in the Wisdom of Solomon, a yet more modern Apocryphal work. The writer may, perhaps, have visited the Jewish colony in Lower Egypt, and thence have learnt this figure of speech. But his Wisdom is not the speculative wisdom of the Greeks, which sought for a reason why one action was to be thought right and another wrong; but it is the practical wisdom of obeying the commands of conscience or the moral sense.

First in importance among the Hebrew books is the Book of Job, which, by its quotations out of the Isaiah of the Return, cannot have been written earlier than this time. It is a poem in the form of a dialogue between Job and his friends, in which the writer's aim is to justify the ways of God to man. Job, a righteous man, has the misfortune to lose his wealth, and then his children, and lastly to be broken down by a loathsome and painful disease. His friends follow the arguments of the Hebrew prophets, and tell him that these sufferings are a punishment for his sins. But Job does not acknowledge himself wicked, and he denies that the good are always prosperous. The friends repeat their opinion in eight speeches, to which he makes eight replies, which are supposed to be so far convincing that the third friend does not venture on his third speech. Then a new speaker is introduced, who may be compared to the chorus in a Greek play. He reproves them all. And lastly the Almighty speaks, and gives the only answer that can be given to the inquiry why evil is allowed; he shows, by recounting the wonders of nature which are beyond man's knowledge, how far any man is from being able to solve the yet greater difficulties of this moral inquiry :—

> Hast thou gone to the springs of the sea?
> Or hast thou walked about in search of the deep?
> Have the gates of death been opened unto thee?
> Or hast thou seen the doorkeepers of the shadow of death?
> Hast thou considered the breadth of the earth?
> Declare if thou knowest it all.

Which is the way to where light dwelleth?
And darkness where is the place thereof,
That thou mayest take each to its own bounds,
And that thou shouldest know the paths to its house?
Knowest thou this because thou wast then born?
Or because the number of thy days is great?

We cannot venture to say that the writer meant Job in
his sufferings to be a representative of the Israelites in their
Captivity; but the poem runs upon the very thoughts that
must have been in the minds of many at the time. They
had suffered a heavy affliction, and they naturally asked
themselves, Did we deserve it? Is it true, as our teachers
have often said, like Job's friends, that such afflictions are
always sent as a punishment for sins? The Isaiah of the
Return had met all such doubts about God's dealings shortly
and with authority, making the Almighty say, "My thoughts
are not as your thoughts, neither are your ways as my ways."
But the writer of Job meets them with more of argument;
and he reminds us at some length of our ignorance of God's
ways and purposes. He also shows how little he is satisfied
with his own treatment of the subject; for he thinks it
necessary to restore the righteous Job to his former prosperity, as the safest way of making the Almighty appear to
act towards him with justice. He does not, like so many
Hebrew writers at this time, enlarge with bitterness against
the Edomites; he had probably lived among them and
received shelter from them; and though the three Edomite
friends argue that Job has been wicked and thus deserved
his sufferings, yet he makes Job obtain forgiveness for them
by his prayers.

Such part of the scenery of the poem as is in heaven is
borrowed from the East, and it could hardly have been
written before the Jews became acquainted with the Babylonians. The angels, here called the Sons of God, present
themselves from time to time before Jehovah as before their
sovereign. On one such day Satan, *the accuser*, tells the
Almighty that Job's piety arises from his prosperity, and
that if that should leave him he would curse God to his face.
Upon this Satan has permission given to him to afflict Job
as before mentioned, and the result is the dialogue which
we have described, in which Job defends himself from the
accusation of being wicked, without charging the Almighty
with injustice. Such part of the scenery as is on earth
belongs to the Arabs of the desert. Job's wealth is in asses,

sheep, oxen, and camels. He lives in the land of Uz, to the east of the Israelites, away from all cities and agriculture.

The simple manners of the speakers, which may be compared with those of Abraham and his family, have made some critics consider this poem as of a very early date. But these simple manners are due to the place chosen for the narrative, not to the time of the writer; they may be found in the desert as well now as in the time of Abraham, and they by no means give us a date to the poem. On the other hand the writer's acquaintance with the numerous modern arts of civilization, forbids our placing it earlier than the Captivity. He mentions gold of Ophir, silver, iron, copper, and the art of mining (xxviii. 1-11), writing and sculptured writing on stones (xix. 23); the sapphire stone had gained its present name (xxviii. 6); land-marks were used to divide estates (xxiv. 2); wheat and barley were cultivated (xxxi. 40); oil and wine were made (xxiv. 11); fields were ploughed and harrowed (xxxix. 10); cattle were pledged for debt (xxiv. 3); swift couriers and ships were in use (ix. 25); kings and judges, and priestly rulers are mentioned (xii. 17-19), and it was the custom for an accusation to be made in writing (xxxi. 35); mirrors were made of polished metal (xxxvii. 18); music was produced by harps and pipes (xxx. 31), and in war by trumpets (xxxix. 24); soldiers carried shields made with bosses (xv. 26), and when their ranks were closed held them lapping one over the other like the scales of a crocodile (xli. 15); many of the constellations had received names, and the zodiac was divided into parts, called, as by the Alexandrian astrologers, the chambers of the planets (ix. 9. and xxxvii. 9).

His acquaintance with Egypt is shown in his mention of the crocodile, and river-horse, and the paper-reed, and of the Egyptian conjurors, who could in safety play with the crocodile, and distinguish between a lucky and an unlucky day (iii. 4-8). As a knowledge of foreign countries was only to be gained by travelling, we must suppose that the writer had dwelt chiefly in the desert on the east of the Jordan, but also in Egypt, during the time of the Captivity, and that he afterwards wrote his poem when he could return to Judea in safety. He describes himself as working on the Egyptian side of the head of the Red Sea, and as gathering the mineral oil, the Petroleum which there flows from the Oil-mountains (xxix. 6).

He had probably visited the Nubian gold mines, for the

purposes of trade ; and there only can he have seen the workman sitting upon a stick and thus let down by a cord into the
cavern below, as described in chapter xxviii. 4 :—

> He breaketh a shaft through the lime stone ;
> Not helped by the feet, they hang down,
> They swing to and fro, far away from men.

He notes the success of the miners in finding the metal
they are in search for; and then he asks and answers the
question :—

> But where shall wisdom be found,
> And where is the place of understanding ?
> Behold the fear of Jehovah that is wisdom,
> And to depart from evil is understanding. (xxviii. 12, 28.)

In the Nubian desert he may also have seen the ostrich
sailing over the sands :—

> What time she lifteth up herself on high
> She scorneth the horse and its rider. (xxxix. 18.)

But he did not go to Nubia through Upper Egypt, and by
the cataracts; as when he describes a rush of water he
mentions not the Nile but the Jordan. He took the easier
but longer route. We can track him in his poem.

The valley near the foot of Mount Sinai is interesting to
travellers, from the Hebrew inscriptions cut upon the rocks
by pious pilgrims from Egypt to the Holy Mount. It bears
the name of Wady Mocatteb, or *the sculptured valley.* They
are written in large letters each three inches high. Every
inscription contains a short prayer to Jehovah on behalf of
the afflicted Jerusalem. They are of various ages. Some
may have been written during the Captivity, some even
earlier by men who had fled from the Assyrian conquerors
of their country. The great age of these inscriptions is
made probable by the name of Sephar, or *written,* being
given to the Holy Mount in Genesis x. 30, perhaps about the
end of Hezekiah's reign. Hence it is by no means unreasonable to suppose that they may be the letters which the writer
of Job had in his mind when says, in xix. 23, 24 :—

> Oh, that my words were now written !
> Oh, that they were imprinted on [Mount] Sephar !
> That with an iron pen and a leaden hammer
> They were chiselled into the rock for ever.

From the peninsula of Sinai he may have joined the
caravan going from Damascus to Medina, "the travelling

companies of Sheba," and on the route have fallen in with
"the travelling companies of Tema" (vi. 19). Like other
travellers through the desert he may have felt the disappointment on coming to a known water-course and finding
the waters are not there, "When it is hot they are consumed
out of their place" (vi. 17). He may then have crossed the
Red Sea to the mines near Ophir in "a ship of reeds" (ix.
26). The description of what he saw teaches us his route,
and we judge that though a poet he was also a merchant.

After his return to Judea, he had seen the rulers of his
country, the Persians, kiss their hands to the sun and moon
in worship (xxxi. 27); for we cannot trace his steps further
eastward than the desert of Uz, which may at one time have
been his home.

Though he has no intention of describing his own country,
he now and then lets us see very clearly its unhappy state
under its foreign masters, as when he speaks of the fathers :—

> To whom for themselves the land was given
> And no stranger passed among them. (xv. 19.)

And again, when he describes the grave as a place where

> The prisoners are at ease together,
> They hear not the voice of the taskmaster. (iii. 18.)

And again, when he wishes for the wicked man, that

> He shall dwell in desolated cities,
> In houses which no man inhabiteth,
> Which are ready to become heaps of ruins. (xv. 28.)

He seems to be describing quarrels that must have arisen
on the return from Captivity about the claim to estates by
men who could not show their genealogy, when he speaks
of worthless persons as

> Sons of fools, yea, sons of men without a name;
> They were driven out of the land. (xxx. 8.)

When arguing that the wicked always come to ruin, he
gives as an example the destruction of the lion, the black
lion, and the panther, meaning the Assyrians, the Babylonians, and the Egyptians, the former oppressors of his
country; describing each by its own animal :—

> By the blast of God they perish,
> And by the breath of his nostrils they are consumed.
> There is a roar of the Lion and a voice of the Black Lion,

> And the teeth of the young lions are broken ;
> The Panther perisheth for lack of prey,
> And the whelps of the African Lion are scattered abroad.

No Hebrew writer has borrowed more lines from those that went before him than this author.   He wrote as a quiet moralist in a time of peace, not like **the** prophets with a wish to rouse men to action in the hurry of a political revolution ; and he was therefore at leisure to study and to make use of the words of others.   He shows a knowledge of the Book of Genesis and of the Garden of Eden when he says, in chapter xxxi. 33 :—

> If I had covered my transgressions as Adam.

He borrows from **Jeremiah xx.** 14-18, his despairing words in chapter iii. 3 :—

> Let the day perish wherein I was born,
> And the night which said, A man child is conceived.

He shows acquaintance with Psalm lxxxix., and with **Isaiah xxvii.,** when, in chapter xxvi. 12, he says of God :—

> **He** stilleth the sea with his power,
> And by his understanding he smote the **Boaster,**
> By his spirit he garnished the heavens,
> And his hand pierced the cowardly serpent.

He borrows from the Introduction to the Book of Proverbs, iii. 11, and ix. 10, when he says in chapters v. 17, and xxviii. 28 :—

> Despise not thou the chastening of the Almighty,—
> Behold the fear of Jehovah that is wisdom,
> And to depart from evil is understanding.

He makes use of words which we find in Hosea x. 12, 13, **when he says, chapter iv. 8** :—

> But as I have seen, they that plow iniquity,
> **And they** that sow trouble, reap the same.

He borrows words from chapter xxxv. 3, of the writer **whom we** have called the **second** Isaiah of the Captivity, **when** in chapter iv. 3, 4, he says :—

> Behold, thou hast instructed many,
> And thou hast strengthened the weak hands ;
> Thy words have upholden him that was stumbling,
> And thou hast confirmed the feeble knees.

He shows that he had read the Isaiah of the Return, xli. 20, when in chapter xii. 9, he says :—

> Who among all these knoweth not
> That the hand of Jehovah hath done this?

And again, when in chapter iv. 18, he says :—

> Behold, he putteth no trust in his servants,
> And his messengers he chargeth with folly;

he is clearly referring to the words of the same writer, who, in chapter xlii. 19, had said, " Who is so blind as my servant, or so deaf as my messenger whom I am sending ? "

His use of the word "Messenger" for a religious teacher, in chapter xxxiii. 23, also brings this book down towards the time of Haggai and Malachi; while his calling this teacher an interpreter, shows that the Hebrew language, in which the Law was written, had already so far gone out of common use, that it was necessary, as in the time of Ezra, to translate its commands into the Syriac or Aramaic spoken by the people.

The writer must be considered as Elohistic rather than Jehovistic. For although in his prose he always uses the name of Jehovah, he never does so in his poetry, where he speaks more directly from the heart, except in two of the lines given above as quotations from other authors.

Though the scenery of the poem is Arabic and Eastern, the philosophy is for the most part Jewish. Had the writer not been a Hebrew, the inquiry would have turned upon the origin of evil, whether the devil had caused Job's sufferings, or whether they had come by chance. But such thoughts never enter the Hebrew mind; the history of the fall of man in the Book of Genesis, which approaches such an inquiry, is not of Hebrew origin. Satan, in the Book of Job, is not an opposing devil, as the Serpent in the garden of Eden has sometimes been thought to be; but an obedient servant of God, like the lying spirit that was sent to earth to deceive the king of Israel, in 1 Kings xxii.

In a philosophical treatise like the Book of Job, we must not look for the fire and energy and warmth of feeling, which we admire in Joel, Nahum, Isaiah, and the Isaiah of chapter xl. It is one of the most carefully finished pieces of writing in the Bible. The writer, in his poem of more than two thousand lines, is sometimes tedious; and though, in the original language, his sentences are often obscure through their shortness, yet his reasoning is as often darkened by its lengthiness.   But his descriptions **of** the various animals are admirable; and his richness of illustration enlivens, in a very remarkable manner, a subject which, in the hands of an ordinary writer, would be most **dull.**   The poetry is in couplets, with a third line added at **times to** give weight to an argument at its close.   **The speeches in** this way often end with a triplet.

In this book we meet for the first time **with a** belief **in** the sinfulness of human nature, even in the case **of** one who does not feel himself a sinner; and Job says, in xv. **14:—**

> What is man that he should be pure?
> And one born of woman that he should be righteous?

We have the same thought in Psalm li., which, with the exception of the last two verses, may be of this time :—

> Behold, I was begotten in iniquity,
> And in sin my mother conceived me.

The belief **in Satan, an** evil angel, **was** brought home by the Jews from the Captivity in Babylon.   It may have come from Persia, though in the Hebrew writings Satan hardly appears in the Persian form of a second god.   In the Book of Zechariah, where he stands at the right hand of Jehovah to oppose the welfare of the high priest Jeshua, he is, as in the Book of Job, a servant of the Almighty.   But in the Book of Chronicles, when the blame of David's numbering the people is laid upon Satan, to relieve Jehovah from being the author of that act, he becomes an independent agent, like the serpent, the tempter in the garden of Eden.   But there is an abundance of passages in the Bible to show that the Jews did not adopt this opinion of the world being governed by two opposing gods, one good and one evil.

Isaiah had spoken of the Pagan gods as dwelling in the recesses **of** the north,* a place like the fabled mount Olympus of the Greeks; and Ezekiel describes Jehovah as coming on the wings of the cherubs with a storm of lightning from the north.†   The same thought that God dwells more particularly in the north appears also in Psalm lxxv. 6.   So in the Book of Job we find the Almighty working with the stormy elements in the north.   Thus in chapter xxiii. 9:—

---

* Isaiah xiv. 13.   † Ezek. i. 4.

> Behold, I go to the east but he is not there ;
> And to the west but I cannot perceive him ;
> To the north, where he worketh, but I behold him **not** ;
> He covereth up the south, that I see him not.

Moreover, in the course of the drama, when Jehovah would answer for Job, he comes in a storm of lightning from the north :—

> A golden brightness cometh out of the north,
> With God is terrible majesty.
> It is the Almighty. (xxxvii. 22.)

These last and other words by Elihu in this chapter show that Elihu's speech is an original part of the book, introducing the speech **of** Jehovah, and by no means an after addition ; and moreover they show that the **poem was** written to be **read** aloud. The reader by his action was to call upon his hearers to listen to the thunder and to notice the lightning in the sky which give warning of Jehovah's speech.

When Job says, in chapter xix. 26, " From my flesh I shall see God," the use of the preposition, in chapter xxxv. 3, leads us to understand this as meaning " when free from my flesh," and as asserting a belief that after death the soul of man would live free from the body. The writer's visit to Egypt had not led him to adopt the coarser opinion of the Egyptian priests, **that** the embalmed body would be wanted for life after death. The same preposition has this force also in Isaac's speech to Esau, **Gen.** xxxvii. 39, where **we must** render it "apart from." **As the Book of Job quotes the** Isaiah of the return home, and **Job is** himself mentioned in Ezekiel xiv., the time when it was written is very well fixed.

As soon as Cyrus gave the captives **leave to** return home, they **felt** that Persia was also **open to** them, **and,** led by the spirit of trade, some few of them settled in that country, or if **not in** Persia proper, at least in the city of Susa, which **the** Persian kings henceforth made their capital. It was at no great **distance from** those spots in Media, and on the eastern side of **Babylon,** where many of the captive Israelites had been **placed by the** Assyrians, and where some remained, through **choice or** poverty, when the others returned to Judea. We shall **find** proof that some of the Hebrew writings were written in Persia.

The first chapter in Daniel seems to have been written soon after the return from Captivity ; and its use of Persian words for *nobles, delicate food,* and *steward,* makes it probable that **it was** written in **Persia. It contains only a** bald notice

of Nebuchadnezzar, in the reign of Jehoiakim, taking Daniel
and three other Jewish children to Babylon to be educated
as slaves in the king's palace, and taught the writing and
language of the Chaldees. These young Jews, when they
grew up, gained **more wisdom** and understanding than all
the magicians and soothsayers in Nebuchadnezzar's kingdom,
while Daniel **had** understanding **in visions** and dreams. He
lived to a great age, to see the beginning of Cyrus's reign.
The other chapters **in** this book were written more than three
hundred years later; but as Noah, Daniel, and Job are
mentioned in Ezekiel xiv. as proverbially righteous, and
Daniel in Ezekiel xxviii. as proverbially wise, we give Daniel i.
to this time. The later chapters are wholly different in
matter as in date. If this one chapter is not enough to have
gained for Daniel the high character given to him in Ezekiel,
we must suppose that there had once been a longer Life of
him, or some writings by him, which have been lost with so
many other Hebrew books.

We may reasonably suppose that Daniel, a favourite slave,
who was about the Babylonian king's person, and had become
in some degree his adviser, was able to befriend the Jewish
captives in Babylon. **They** may thus have thought him the
chief governor **of the wide** provinces, and hence may have
arisen his high renown.

Cyrus died in the year B.C. 529, and **under** CAMBYSES, the
next king of Persia, the Jews were equally unable to proceed
with the building of the Temple, and were painfully reminded
that Jerusalem was now subject to the despised Samaria,
which **was the** Persian capital of the province. The Persians
and **others who** had been brought from their own country,
and placed in the cities of Samaria, wrote by the hand of the
Persian officers to the king, who in the narrative is called
first Ahasuerus and then Artaxerxes; and they obtained an
order that the building of the Temple should be stopped.*

The reign of Cambyses over Persia chiefly deserves
mention here because of his invasion and conquest of Egypt.
This may be taken as a proof that his father Cyrus had that
end in view when he released the Jewish captives in Babylon,
in exchange for whom chapter xliii. of Isaiah promises that
Egypt shall be given to him as their ransom. In the fourth
year of his reign B.C. 524, Cambyses moved his army along
the coast from Judea to Egypt. Psammenitus the son of

---

* Ezra iv.

Amasis, who had been only six months on the Egyptian throne, led his forces to meet him. The two armies met near Tahpenes, on the Pelusiac branch of the Nile, and there, after a hard battle, the Egyptians were routed. At Tahpenes the sceptre of Egypt was broken; Psammenitus was soon put to death, and henceforth Egypt was a province of Persia. Cambyses then **sent** messengers up the Nile to invite the submission of the Ethiopians; and on their refusal sent an army against them.* By this conquest of Egypt, the condition **of** Judea was a good deal changed. It was no longer **a bone of** contention, a prize to be struggled **for** by two hostile **monarchs**; it was a province in the middle **of the** great **Persian empire.**

The rejoicing and pleasing hopes which accompanied the captives on their return had very soon faded away, and left the Jews to the sad reality of their situation. They had returned to poverty and want, to discomfort of every kind. Though a prince of their own nation was appointed to be their ruler, they were still harassed by Persian tax-gatherers, who enforced their demands by the help of Assyrian or Babylonian soldiers.

The burdens under which the Jews laboured were a tax on produce, a poll-tax, and the road service.† The first two **were** levied with cruelty, and probably with irregularity, by overseers throughout the fields, and by tribute gatherers in the towns. Equally galling was the road service, or the duty of helping forward on their journey, with labourers and beasts of burden, all troops and officers who were moving about the country on the public service.

Zerubbabel was a prince only in name. He had no troops under his command; he could collect no taxes; but he had a small allowance from the Persian tribute to support his state, and possibly the produce of such lands as he may have held as a family estate. The unhappy country was no longer a kingdom, it was a province of Persia, receiving orders from Susa, through a Pacha, or governor, who was ruler over all the lands to the west of the river Euphrates, and probably dwelt in Damascus.

This makes itself seen in the very language. After this time the Jews are spoken of as living beyond the river Euphrates, meaning to the west of it, because distances were measured from Babylon; in the same way that Gilead used

---

* Herodotus iii. 10-20   † Ezra iv. 13.

to be called beyond the Jordan, meaning to the east of it, when distances were measured from Jerusalem. Not the least among the troubles was the quarrel between the two parties in the state, arising from the narrow jealousy by which the men of the Captivity denied the rest of the nation the rank of being Jews. Many of the melancholy complaining Psalms seem to belong to this time. The writer of Psalm cxx. compares Jerusalem, first to the unknown country on the northern shore of the Black Sea, and then to the desert on the northern part of Arabia :—

> Woe is me that I sojourn in Mesech,
> That I dwell among the tents of Kedar.
> My soul hath long dwelt with him that hateth peace :
> I am for peace ; but when I speak they are for war.

Ezekiel xxx. 9 and 13-19 may be safely given to the reign of Cambyses, as it mentions the overthrow of the Egyptian monarch at the great battle of Tahpenes, the conquest of all Egypt from Magdolon to Syene, and the messengers sent by galleys up the Nile to require the submission of the Ethiopians. In these sentences the knowledge of Egyptian cities is remarkable. Sais, called Sin, is at this time the capital of Egypt. The galley, or rowing vessel of war, as distinguished from the ship, is mentioned as in Isaiah xxxiii. 21, which is also of this date.

When DARIUS HYSTASPES came to the throne of Persia B.C. 521, the whole of his wide dominions, from the Caspian Sea to the Nile, felt a relief from wanton tyranny. He had the good sense to know that he could raise a larger tribute **from the** subject provinces by good government than by cruelty. Accordingly the Jews found their condition much improved ; and in the second year of his reign, moved by a reverence for the number seventy, as it was the seventieth year since the city and Temple had been destroyed by the Babylonians, they again began to rebuild the Temple. The work had been stopped during the reign of the mad and violent Cambyses. Prince Zerubbabel and the high priest Jeshua were encouraged in this renewed attempt by the arrival of three of their countrymen from Babylon, who brought with them a supply of money, and probably were able to assure them of the goodwill of Darius.* They were also assured that " the time was come " by the prophets Haggai and Zechariah. But the Pacha or Persian governor

---

* Zech. vi. 10.

of all the provinces to the west of the Euphrates, wished
them to stop till he had learnt the pleasure of King Darius
on the matter. He wrote to Darius, and in answer received
a Decree, giving to Zerubbabel the title of Pacha of the
Jews, and reciting the former Decree by Cyrus, and ordering
that the expense of the building should be paid out of the
Persian tribute that was levied in the country. The
favourable answer arrived in the fourth year of Darius, by
the hands of Sherezer and Regem-melech, two Persian
officers of rank, who further gratified the Jews by going
with their attendants to worship in the courts of the
Temple.* From that year forward the Jews discontinued
their **fasts** for the destruction of the city.† With **this** permission and help, the Temple of Jerusalem was rebuilt, and
the **work** was finished in the sixth year of Darius. This
was about 450 years since it was first built by Solomon, and
74 years since it was destroyed by Nebuchadnezzar. It was
rebuilt on the old foundations, and if not with equal splendour of gold and cedar, yet in all probability with the same
raised terrace for the court of the priests, the same natural
rock for the place of the altar, and, so far as the poverty of
the times would allow, in all respects the same as the former
Temple, according to the description given in the latter
chapters of Ezekiel. Those who had returned from Captivity, to the exclusion of all others, then dedicated the
Temple with such burnt-offerings as their means allowed ;
and, when the first month of the year came round, celebrated
the Passover there.‡

The lessened number of the priests of necessity lessened
the grandeur of the ceremonies in the Temple. An important
part of the service was the recital of psalms by the priests
as they walked with musical instruments in procession round
the altar. Thus in Psalm xxvi. the writer says :—

> And I will walk around thine altar, O Jehovah,
> To publish with the voice of thanksgiving,
> And to relate all thy wondrous works.

But after the return from Babylon the high priest Jeshua
had to make up his processions by taking his walkers from
the bystanders who were not priests.§

The Persian decree had not only directed that the Jews
should be supplied with what was needed for building the

---

* Zech. vii. 2.   † Zech. vii. 3 ; viii. 19.   ‡ Ezra v. vi.
§ Zech. iii. 7.

Temple, but also with bullocks, rams, lambs, wheat, salt, wine and oil, day by day without fail. These were for the burnt-offerings on the altar, and also for support of the priests who served in the Temple. They were to be supplied out of the Persian tribute. Thus the Persian king and his advisers considered the support of the Temple-worship a matter of national importance. No such support was given to religious worship in any other of the Jewish towns.

When we remember the lofty claim for power made by the priests under the monarchy, and confirmed to them in the Books of the Law, we might look for some little rivalry between prince Zerubbabel the pacha and Jeshua the chief-priest. But we hear of none; their Persian rulers left them little of wealth or power to struggle for. The prophet Zechariah leads us to think that they had no disputes, saying, "This one shall build the Temple of Jehovah, and that one shall bear honour; and the one shall sit and rule upon his throne, and the other shall be a priest upon his throne; and the counsel of peace shall be between the two.*

In the same year that Darius gave the Jews leave to rebuild their Temple, he relieved them from a harassing uncertainty by a decree fixing the tribute which he required of them.† He divided his vast empire into twenty Satrapies. Of these the fourth reached from the river Orontes to the Nile, and included Syria, the Phenicians, the island of Cyprus, Palestine and Arabia Nabatœa. From the Nabatœans no tribute could be levied, but the rest of this Satrapy was required to pay three hundred and fifty Babylonian talents of silver yearly.‡

This was perhaps equal to £90,000 sterling. Of this, if we look to the mineral wealth of Cyprus, the trading wealth of the Phenicians, the size of Syria, and the small size of Judea, it is not probable that one-sixth part fell upon the Jews. This small sum, for which the Greek historian is our authority, stands in strange contrast to the large sums, of which we have been reading in the books of Kings and Chronicles, in times when silver was less common than in the reign of Darius.

Whatever may have been the methods by which the mad Cambyses governed Judea, it is probable that Darius found no difficulty in employing Jews as his officers of government. Under the Babylonians any Jew who accepted the post of

---

* Zech. vi. 13.   † Paschal Chron.   ‡ Herodotus iii. 89-91.

Sagin or *deputy*, became an object of hatred to his country-men; but under the Persians, this office brought no ill-will upon the Jews who accepted it.* They bore the same title of Sagin, but we have no account of what their duties were.

There were two marked features in the popular religion of the Persians which the Jews may have become acquainted with from those of their rulers who lived in Judea, and which are noticed in the Hebrew writings of this time, but noticed only to be rejected. One was the worship, or **seeming** worship, of the sun, moon, and **stars**. Of this Job says in chapter xxxi. 26 :—

> If I looked on the sun when it shined,
> Or the moon walking in its brightness ;
> And my heart hath been secretly enticed,
> Or my mouth hath kissed my hand [in worship] ;
> This also were an iniquity for the judge ;
> For I should have denied the God that is above.

The other peculiarity in the Persian religion was its dualism, or the belief in two principles throughout nature, and in a good God and in a bad God. This is pointed to by the Isaiah of the return home, who in chapter xlv. 7 makes Jehovah say :—

> I am Jehovah, and there is none else,
> I form light, and I create darkness ;
> I make safety, and I create misfortune.
> I Jehovah do all these things.

The same thought appears in the Song of Moses, in Deuteronomy xxxii. 39, which **we** shall come upon presently :—

> See now that I, even I, am He,
> And there is no god beside me.
> I kill and I make alive.
> I wound and I will heal ;
> Neither is there anyone that can deliver out of my hand.

So in Hannah's prayer, 1 Samuel ii. 6 :—

> Jehovah killeth and maketh alive ;
> He bringeth down to the grave, and bringeth up,
> Jehovah maketh poor, and maketh rich ;
> He bringeth low, and he also lifteth up.

These three writers seem to be all carefully contradicting the Dualism of the Persians ; and their opinions so far confirm the date which on other grounds must be given to them.

* Isaiah xli. 25 ; Ezra ix. 2 ; Nehem. vii. 5.

We may now mention further portions of the Book of
Ezekiel, which belong to a time later than when the priest
Ezekiel lived. They are not easily distinguished from the
others, because the writer adopts Ezekiel's manner, and often
styles himself Son of Adam. Some are written in a spirit
very much opposed to that of Ezekiel. Chapter xiv. 12-23,
speaks of Daniel and Job, jointly with Noah, as righteous
men, and also speaks of the returning captives finding a
comfort in the few inhabitants of Jerusalem, who have been
saved, and who come forth to meet them. Chapter xvii.
relates a riddle about Jehoiachin and Zedekiah, who are
carried to Babylon; and then a tender twig is taken from
the highest branch of the cedar, and is planted on the loftiest
mountain of Israel. This is Zerubbabel, and it gives us
a date to the writing. Chapter xviii. shows the modern
improved views of God's government, when saying that
every man is to be punished only for his own sins. Even
the Book of Deuteronomy, which made a great advance over
the older books of the law, and had ordered, in respect to
human punishments, that the children should not be put to
death for their fathers' sins, had yet repeated, as part of
God's law in the Ten Commandments, that the iniquity of
the fathers should be visited on the children to the fourth
generation. In answer to this seeming injustice, the people
had scoffed at their religious teachers by quoting the proverb,
"The fathers have eaten sour grapes, and the children's teeth
are set on edge." The writer of this chapter, instead of
rebuking this, acknowledges the strength of the reply, and
answers that every man will have to bear his own guilt only.
For thus contradicting the Mosaic Law, some of the later
Rabbis wished to remove this book from the canon of
Scripture. They blamed Ezekiel for those very chapters
which are here set apart as being too good for him. Ezekiel
belonged to the order of priests; but this writer's opinions
are opposed to those of the priests.

Chapter xxviii., ending with a few words which mention
the return from Captivity, is against Tyre and Sidon, which
are to be conquered, not by Nebuchadnezzar, but by strangers, the terrible of the nations, meaning perhaps the Medes
and Persians. Tyre was once an outstretched over-shadow-
ing cherub on the mountain of God, possibly in Solomon's
reign, when Hiram helped to build the Temple, but since
then, with Sidon, it has been a pricking briar in Israel's
side.

Chapters xxxiii.—xxxvii. contain warnings by a writer who has not Ezekiel's priestly bias. Chapter xxxiii. says that Jehovah has no pleasure in the death of the wicked, but wishes the wicked man to turn from his evil ways and live. Chapter xxxiv. blames the rulers, under the name of shepherds who do not feed the flock, and have not yet brought them back from the countries where they are scattered ; and **he** recognizes the unhappy quarrel between the two parties in the state, saying, "I will distinguish between small cattle and small cattle." It promises to the nation a David as a prince, a plant of renown, meaning Zerubbabel. In chapter xxxv. the Edomites, who had spread themselves over southern Judea, are threatened for having attacked Israel in the day of their calamity. In chapter xxxvi. the desolate cities of Israel are again to be inhabited. Men are to become as numerous as the flocks of holy animals which are brought up to **Jerusalem on** the days of the solemn feasts. In chapter xxxvii. the writer, using a highly poetical figure, looks forward to the revival of his country in the vision of a valley full of dry bones, which, when commanded by Jehovah, came together bone to its bone, and then flesh and skin came upon them, and lastly the wind breathed upon them, and they lived. They are no more to be two nations. Jehovah will take one stick for the house of Joseph, and another stick for the house of Judah, and the two will become one stick in his hand : and a David shall be king over them both. This writer has much of the power of the old prophets.

The writings which we have here glanced at, since the overthrow of the monarchy, are some of the most valuable in the collection. Dangers, misfortunes, and sufferings had strengthened the spirit of devotion and the spirit of poetry. In the foregoing centuries, the Assyrian and the Babylonian invasions had called forth the passionate eloquence of Joel, Isaiah, and Nahum, with many grand Psalms of triumph and thanksgiving; which were followed by Habakkuk's highly figurative hymn of religious trust. And on the return home from Captivity, after seventy years of suffering, we find that while the nation had been in its lowest state, poetic genius had been by no means crushed. Hebrew versification was always very slight; but as it becomes more regular we find it still chiefly marked by the arrangement of the thoughts into two or more parts, the so-called Parallelism of Hebrew verse, so that the latter clauses repeat in new words or in some **way answer** the former clause. The poetry has very little of artificial diction; its words are those which were in every-day use. It could only gain attention by its real excellence, its lofty aim, and its soul-stirring thoughts. From this description it follows that there is no certain boundary dividing poetry from prose; and therefore the chapters added to the Book of Isaiah on the return home with their inspiring burst of joy and hope, and chapter xxxvii. of Ezekiel with its promise of the nation's increase in a vision of the dry bones in the valley coming to life again, though not in verse, must be counted as poetry, equally with the exhortations to practical wisdom in the Introduction of Proverbs, the rich illustrations to the argument in the Book of Job, and the sorrowful but hopeful Psalms with their regular versification. These all mark the time of the Captivity, and the beginning of Zerubbabel's viceregal government, as a highly poetic age. Hezekiah's reign was rather the age of eloquence.

The conquest of Egypt by Cambyses, and the bringing under one government provinces which had been at war, allowed trade to revive, and the Tyrians in particular regained much of their former prosperity. Then the corn and linen of Egypt again reached Jerusalem by their vessels to the coast. This is mentioned in Isaiah xxiii. 15-18, where, however, the writers seem to confound the seventy years which came to an end on the overthrow of Babylon, with the seventy years which came to an end in the second year of Darius; for the produce of Egypt could scarcely have reached Judea until the wars of Cambyses were over.

The lofty spiritual writings which we **have** seen written since the return from Captivity, have shown us how greatly in some minds the Jewish religion had become improved by being released from the priestly bonds which had pulled towards the Ark in the Holy of Holies. But there were other minds which knew of no religion but that in the Mosaic Law. These were the priestly nobles to whom Darius now gave leave to re-build the Temple, and who thereby gained the opportunity of again enslaving the people in the bondage of ritual and ceremony. They had returned home with the pride of martyrs. Their sufferings had made them not more charitable, but more bigoted, and more eager to enforce the observance of the Sabbath and the Temple-service, and to make a separation of the nation into two classes, rather than to unite it in the bonds of friendship. Thus during the following century we shall meet with writings of very opposite views; some with the improved moral tone which comes with wider knowledge, and some wholly looking back to the past, and urging the duty of not allowing the pure Jews to marry with the large mass of the population who may have been of mixed blood. We shall see that the re-building of the Temple brought by no means a certain gain to **the** nation. The new Temple brought with it the old thoughts, the old ceremonies, the old superstitious value of sacrifices, and the old claim of the priests for power; while the teachings of the prophets, and the lessons learnt through so much suffering during the Captivity, were in some measure forgotten. The reverence for the Temple, though **it gave** political steadiness to the nation, was of doubtful value **for** religion. The thought **that** Jehovah was more present in Jerusalem than elsewhere, was a mistake not wholly corrected as long as the sacrifices there were continued.

When the old jealousies between Jerusalem and the country again appear, they appear in a new form. We no longer hear of forbidding sacrifices on the High Places. The custom of making such sacrifices was gone by; those in Jerusalem had become less costly, and probably less frequent. We must suppose that already the praiseworthy custom had begun for the people, at a distance from Jerusalem, to meet together for worship without sacrifices, although it is three centuries later before **any such** places of meeting, or synagogues are mentioned.

Chapters xlv.-xlviii. **of Ezekiel we must** distinguish from the last-mentioned portion of that book, because here the writer gives large portions of land to the priests and Levites. To them also, in the place of tithes, he would give a sixtieth part of the wheat and barley, a hundredth part of the oil, and one in two hundred of the lambs. He supposes the **land** of Canaan divided afresh among the tribes, by lines drawn straight across from east to west, leaving a portion in the middle, which he again divides between the Priests, the Levites, the City, and the Prince. The Prince here spoken of is Zerubbabel; and the proposal to give to him a large portion of territory for his maintenance was naturally called for by his evident want of means. The author writes in the belief that the soil had no owners, or from the scantiness **of** the population had no value; as he allows the strangers who settle among them to share with the Israelites. This whimsical proposal for a division of the land is nowhere else mentioned.

This writer while thus giving a portion of land to the Prince for himself and his sons, does not allow him to alienate it. If he should give any part to one of his servants it should return to his family in the Year of Liberty (xlvi. 17). We shall meet with a second mention of such a year, written about fifty years later, and at the same time with a law fixing the Jubilee or Year of Liberty at every fiftieth year. Hence it seems probable that our author was looking forward to the year B.C. 487, the fiftieth year from the return home from Babylon, that is from "the year of recompences for the controversy of Zion," as it is called in Isaiah xxxiv. 8. But history does not tell us that any such Year of Liberty was observed, although much wished for on behalf of the bondservants and debtors.

In Ezekiel xlv. 18-25 directions are given as to the manner in which the Prince is to celebrate the Passover and the Feast of Tabernacles or Ingathering at Jerusalem. No mention is made of the Feast of Weeks, showing that there had not been the same reason for ordering a third pilgrimage to Jerusalem, and a national celebration of that feast, as there had been for the other two. Solomon had made the Ingathering a national feast, and Hezekiah had done the same for the Passover; but we have never heard of a national celebration at Jerusalem of the Feast of Weeks.

The vision in Ezekiel xlvii. is of streams flowing from the altar in Jerusalem in such abundance as to make the waters of the Dead Sea fresh. The valley through which the water flows is to be made fertile, and trees are to grow on both sides of the river, whose fruit is to be for food and for medicine. This tells us of two works carried on by the Persian government; one the supplying Jerusalem with water, and the other the irrigating the valley of Jericho for the growth of palm-trees and balsam-trees.

The conduit-pipe which brought water to Jerusalem had probably been lately repaired after its destruction by the Babylonians. From the Temple the water flows by the brook Kidron towards the Dead Sea. For the other work we must look to a valley which runs in the same direction a little to the north of the former. It brings from the hills of Ephraim the rain torrents which had been allowed to run to waste. By a little care this water may be made useful; and this is the first notice that we get of the plantation of palm-trees and balsam-trees near Jericho, which afterwards grew luxuriantly in a valley naturally barren. We shall meet with further hints about the palm-plantation at Jericho, when we come to the Chronicles and the Life of Elisha.

Joel iii. 18-21 was written at the same time with a similar prophecy. The pools of Jerusalem are to flow with **water.** The fountain going forth from the Temple is **to be** so abundant that when the waters reach the Jordan, **the** Valley of Shittim on its east bank will be watered by them. Such was the promise of prosperity to Judea in the reign **of** Darius.

To this time we may give **Psalm cxxvii.**, written on the rebuilding of the Temple :—

> Except Jehovah build the House,
> They toil in vain that build it ;
> Except Jehovah guard the city, **the guard waketh in vain.**

Psalm xcvi. is said in the Title to the Greek translation to **have** been used on the building of Zerubbabel's Temple, and it **is** perhaps of this date, though in 1 Chron. xvi. 23-33 we find it given to David as sung when he brought the Ark into Jerusalem.

Psalm cxxxii. also seems to have been written for this second Temple, upon the occasion of placing a new Ark in the Holy of Holies, in imitation of the Ark in Solomon's Temple. That a new Ark had been placed in the Temple after the return from Captivity, we may learn from the Chronicles.* Of the former Ark the Psalmist says,

> Lo, we **heard of** it at Ephratah,
> We found **it in the** fields of the **forest** [or Jearim].

And turning to the new Ark, he says,

> Arise, O Jehovah, into thy resting **place,**
> Thou and the Ark of thy strength.
> Let thy priests be clothed with righteousness,
> And let thy godly ones shout for joy.

He makes **use** of a figure of speech common among the Jews, who fancied that a family remained in prosperity as long as its lamp, or star, was hanging up in heaven ; but when its lamp was put out, then the family came to an end. He says,

> I will also clothe her priests with salvation,
> And her godly ones shall shout aloud for joy.
> There will I make the horn of David to branch forth
> I have established the lamp for mine anointed.

---

* 2 Chron. v. 9.

Verses 7-10 of Psalm xxiv., which should be separated from the beginning of the Psalm, may have been written to be sung on the same occasion:—

> Lift up your heads, O ye gates,
> And be ye lifted up, ye everlasting doorways,
> And the King of Glory will come in.
> " Who is this King of Glory ? "
> Jehovah strong and mighty, Jehovah mighty in battle.

That **part** of **the** prophecy of Zechariah which belongs to this time must be limited to the first eight chapters and perhaps chapter xiv. of the book bearing his name; the other **chapters we have** already spoken of as written at **various times, but all** much earlier. It contains a variety **of** visions; one, of an angel, who tells us of the mildness **of** Darius's government by saying, "We have walked to and fro upon the earth, and behold, all the earth sitteth still, and is at rest." He promises that the Temple shall be rebuilt, and the cities of Judah again overflow with prosperity. Other visions are of the four horns of the nations that had scattered Judah; of a man with a measuring line measuring the city in order that it may be rebuilt; of Jeshua, the high priest, standing before Jehovah, and Satan accusing him, and Jehovah ordering him to be clothed with the garments of a chief priest; of two olive trees standing by a golden lamp-stand, who are Jeshua the priest, and Zerubbabel the prince; of seven angels who are the eyes of Jehovah; of a book-roll flying through the air containing a curse upon stealing and false swearing; of an Ephah, or bushel measure, in which sits a woman, the figure of wickedness, who is carried through **the air** to Babylon; and lastly, of four chariots that go forth, **one to each** corner of the earth. Jehovah then tells him to **make golden** crowns for Jeshua and the other priests; **and he lets** us clearly understand how unimportant **a** person Zerubbabel the prince was, by saying that "the one [Zerubbabel] shall build the Temple of Jehovah, and the other [Jeshua] shall bear honour, and one shall shall sit and rule upon his throne, and the other shall be a priest upon his throne. And the council of peace shall be between the two." Those of the captives who have not yet returned from Babylon are invited back.

The mildness of the Persian government under Darius is shown by the lessened severity of the road-service, and by the remark that now, if a man's services are wanted, hire is **paid to** him for his work, and for the **use of his** beast. The writer is **fully** assured of the value of the Jewish religion, and, moreover, had observed that foreigners, at least the Persians, had begun to acknowledge its value; and he asserts that hereafter men of all nations will take hold of the skirts of the Jew, saying, "We will go with you, for we have heard that God is with you." Zechariah was the son of Berechiah, and **we are** told **in** the New Testament that he was slain in the Temple-yard, between the altar and the House.* But **in** this there seems to be a mistake; as it was the high priest Zechariah, the son of Jehoiada, who was so slain in the reign of Jehoash.

Chapter xiv. **may** be of the same time as the above, whether by the **same** author or not. It foretells like Ezek. **xlvii.** that living waters shall flow out of Jerusalem, half **towards** the east, and half towards the west in all seasons alike. It says Jehovah will smite the people that have fought against Jerusalem, and that then the wealth of all countries shall flow thither, and that the nations shall come up there to worship Jehovah at the Feast of Tabernacles. That three such yearly pilgrimages should be made to Jerusalem, as were ordered towards the close of the monarchy, was not to be expected. Lastly, it is foretold that the dealers shall be turned out of the Temple, agreeably to the promise made in Ezekiel xliii. 12, that the whole of mount Moriah shall be most holy.

It is at all times interesting **to trace the growth of a** thought, when **it** shows itself **in** an unusual expression; **and** this can be done very satisfactorily in the case of **the name** which Zechariah gives to Zerubbabel, of the Branch. First, a writer in the Book of Ezekiel who lived during the Captivity, foretelling the prosperity of the nation, had said in chapter **xxix.** 21, "I will cause the horn of the house of Israel to branch forth." When that prosperity did arrive, a writer adding **to the Book** of Isaiah, in chapter xi. 1, promises to the nation **as a ruler**, an Offshoot from the roots of Jesse. A later **writer also**, in the Book of Isaiah, says in chapter iv. 2, "In that **day** shall the Branch of Jehovah be beautiful and glorious." **In the** additions to Jeremiah, in chapters xxiii. 5, and xxxiii. **15**, the coming ruler is called "a righteous Branch," raised up unto David. Psalm cxxxii. then says, "I will cause the horn of David to branch forth," and lastly, when the expressions had been so often

* Matt. xxiii. 25.

applied to Zerubbabel that they could not be misunderstood, Zechariah calls him " the man whose name is the Branch." Some of these passages have been also applied to Jesus, and that in Isaiah xi. 1, which promises a Nazar, or *Offshoot*, gave rise to the words of Matthew ii. 23, "He will be called a Nazarite," meaning, as it would **seem, a** Nazarene, or native of Nazareth.

The prophecy of Haggai also belongs **to this** time. It is little more than a few words of encouragement to the people to rebuild the Temple under Zerubbabel the prince and Jeshua the high priest. Haggai styles himself Jehovah's messenger, using a title which in the early writings had been given only to heavenly messengers or angels, but had latterly been used to mean a religious teacher or preacher. This word is thus used in Job xxxiii. 23, and in Ecclesiastes v. 6. So in the New Testament the Greek word of the same meaning, Angel, is often used for a preacher, as in Revelation ii.—iii.; and we still keep it in our word Evangelist.

Psalm cix. may be given to this time, or soon after, as it borrows a thought from Zechariah, who had seen in a vision Satan standing at the right hand of the high priest to accuse him to Jehovah. The Psalmist complains of his enemies, who, like himself, were bond-servants under the foreigner, that they encompass him with words of hatred. He repeats in verses 6-19, their uncharitable wishes against himself.

> Let a wicked man be overseer over him,
> And let an accuser [or Satan] stand at his right hand.

The two last-mentioned writers, Zechariah and Haggai, are the only prophets living after the Return from Captivity whose names have reached us. The writings of any others, who after the Return, addressed their countrymen in words of advice or reproach, were either published as the works of those who lived during the monarchy, or perhaps published without a name. Of the first class are the prophecy of Jonah, Ecclesiastes given to Solomon, and many Psalms given to David. Of the latter class are the anonymous prophecy bearing the name of Malachi, and large additions to Isaiah, Jeremiah, and Ezekiel.

The forty years which followed the building of the Temple are wholly without events in our history. Historians write about kingdoms and armies, and take little notice of a pro-**vince.** During this time Jeshua **had** died, as also had

Zerubbabel at a great age. History does not tell us how long Zerubbabel lived; but if we read Daniel ix. 25, as "From the going forth of the command to lead back home [B.C. 538] while there is an anointed prince shall be seven weeks [or 49 years]," we have his death in the year B.C. 489. We do not hear that Darius had appointed any one of Zerubbabel's family to succeed him as prince of Judea, although there were many living who might have had a claim to that post. It was a post with very little profit, very little honour, but with some power of usefulness to his countrymen; and we see in Micah vii. 2, Isaiah lvii. 1, and Psalm xii. 1, traces of his death being lamented.

Micah vii. 1-10, describes the discomfort in which the people were now living. The godly man who has perished, like the righteous man in Isaiah lvii. 1, may perhaps be Zerubbabel. The writer complains of the sad state of distrust in which he was living, when no man can open his mouth in safety to a friend; a man's enemies are the men of his own house. He is suffering under oppression from his countrymen; but he also complains of the taunts of their rivals in Samaria, under the name of a woman his enemy.

Psalm xii., like this passage in Micah, complains of those of his countrymen among whom he is living,

> Help, O Jehovah, for the Godly Man hath passed away,
> For the truthful fail from among the children of Adam,
> They speak falsehood every one with his neighbour,
> They speak with flattering lips, but with a double heart.
> The wicked walk about on every side,
> Vileness is as dignity among the children of Adam.

The Godly man here spoken of was probably Zerubbabel. To a time soon after Zerubbabel's death we may perhaps give Isaiah lvi. 9—lviii. containing a melancholy complaint about the disordered state of the country. It begins with sad irony, "All ye wild beasts of the field come to devour, yea, all ye wild beasts in the forest." The writer thus tells us of the alarm felt at the government of Jerusalem falling into the hands of their enemies the Samaritans. This alarm was probably well founded, though it hardly justified the foolish exaggeration of the same in the Book of Esther which relates to the same time.

As usual, Zerubbabel is not mentioned by name:—

> The righteous man hath perished, and no man layeth it to heart: and merciful men are taken away, while none consider that the righteous man is taken away from misfortune.

It was perhaps on his death, when the government of Jerusalem fell to the governor of Samaria, that the Samaritans sent messengers, with presents of ointment and perfumes, to the king of Persia. Josephus mentions a former embassy of the Jews to Darius, and says that it was to beg for relief against the governor of Samaria, who hindered the Jews in the service of the Temple, and did not supply them out of the tribute with the allowed sum which was necessary for their sacrifices.* The remark that Jehovah wondereth that the people have now no one to plead for them, or to intercede for them, points to the death of Zerubbabel who had gone on the former embassy on their behalf. The writer tells the nobles "to loosen the fetters of injustice, to undo the fastenings of the yoke, and to let the oppressed go free." He feels for the poor, whom the rich held in bondage, and lets us understand that if there had been any proposal to celebrate at that time the jubilee or Year of Liberty for the bondservants "an acceptable year of Jehovah," it had been very badly kept. These words, however, lead to the belief that the fiftieth year since the return home was already past, and thus that Darius was dead and Xerxes I was already king of Persia.

Though no son of Zerubbabel was appointed to succeed him as Pacha of Judea, the case was otherwise with the hereditary priesthood, and the return of Ezra which happened a few years later, with a second body of those who had been captives, seems to be pointed to by some words, borrowed in part from Isaiah xxxv. 8, which were written for the return of the first body of captives, thus :—

Build ye up the road, build ye up, prepare the way, take up the stumbling-blocks out of the way of my people (lvii. 14).

According to an Arabic historian, it was in the thirtieth year of Darius that Zoroaster, the Persian sage, proposed his reform of the religion of the Magi. The popular religion of the Persians was founded on the belief of two principles in nature ; a good principle or good god, named Ormuzd, in whose honour they worshipped Fire, and the Sun, Moon, and Stars ; and a bad principle, or bad god, named Ahriman. The Persians had no idols in their Temples, and so far their Temple-worship did not offend the Jews. The Isaiah of the return home had, in chapter xli. 25, even counted Cyrus

* Antiq. XI. vi. 9.

among the worshippers of Jehovah. And Zoroaster advocated a further approach to pure religion, and said that the world was governed by One God, who had no equal and no companion; and as he had been a hearer of Ozeir or Ezra, and he professed that this was the religion of Abraham, he was probably led to it by his intercourse with the Jews. His writings were called the Book of Abraham.* They were perhaps the original of the Zend-Avesta.

XERXES I succeeded to Darius on the throne of Persia, in B.C. 485, and the Jews found themselves equally well treated by the son as by the father.† The first years of his reign were made memorable by his gigantic preparations for the invasion of Greece, and then by the defeat of his large army at Thermopylæ, and of his fleet at Salamis. The Jews had no friendly feelings towards the Greeks, who had been known to them as purchasers of the stolen children whom the Tyrians had seized for slaves on the ruin of the country by Nebuchadnezzar.‡ Hence they had hoped for the success of Xerxes in his invasion. Many of them may have been soldiers in his army. The prophet is most hopeful, saying, Jehovah "will repay wrath to his adversaries, like doings to his enemies; to the [Greek] islands he will repay like doings. And they of the west shall fear the name of Jehovah, and they at the rising of the sun [shall reverence] his glory; when he [Xerxes] shall come like a pent up flood, which the breath of Jehovah driveth forward."§

The Jews hoped that on his journey towards Europe he might pass through Judea, might "come as a redeemer to Zion," and relieve them, perhaps, from the pain of receiving orders from Samaria. But Xerxes was too busy to visit or think about Jerusalem.

It was, however, at that time that Isaiah lix. was written on the hoped for conquest of Greece. This portion of Isaiah ends with a promise to the writer, who was an hereditary priest, that Jehovah's spirit will continue with his family after him.

It was at the end of the year B.C. 480, that Xerxes recrossed the Hellespont on his hasty retreat from Europe into Asia,‖ and in the beginning of the next year he reached Babylon on his way to Susa.¶ It was perhaps then that, in his zeal against idolatry, he plundered the Temple of Bel of

---

* Hyde, Vet. Persarum Hist., ch. 24. † Antiq. XI. v. 1.
‡ Joel iii. 6.   § Isaiah lix. 18-20.
‖ Diod. Sic. XI. 19 and 36.   ¶ Ctesias in Photius.

its sacred treasures, which his father Darius had spared,[*]
and there he may have met the Jewish scribe and priest
Ezra, and have given to him the appointment of governor
of Judea. The vessels which Ezra carried to the Temple of
Jerusalem may have been some of those which Xerxes took
from the Temple of Bel. Xerxes, though he was returning
to Persia defeated, had left a large army behind to carry on
the war against the Greeks ; and the example of Cyrus may
have taught him that, while engaged in a war in the distant
west, it was a wise policy to make the Jews his friends, and
to encourage the return home of those who still remained
near Babylon.

Ezra, indeed, calls the Persian king, who gave him his
high post, Artaxerxes, thus placing the appointment twenty-
one years later; and this is supported by Nehem. viii. 9,
which makes Ezra the contemporary of Nehemiah. But the
name of the king presents no difficulty. Ezra places him
next after Darius. The Greek, 1 Esdras ix., let us understand that Nehem. viii. is a quotation from the Book of Ezra,
though not now in the Hebrew, and that the name of Nehemiah should be removed from verse 9. Hence we follow
Josephus in thinking that Ezra received his appointment
from Xerxes I, while Joiakim, the son of Jeshua, was
hereditary chief priest.[†] The Paschal Chronicle also says
that Ezra was the chief priest in the reign of Xerxes I, and
it satisfies the requirements of Nehem. xii. 36, by making
Ezra, the scribe, yet alive with Nehemiah in the reign of
Artaxerxes Longimanus.

EZRA GOVERNOR OF JUDEA ; B.C. 479—.

When Ezra, the priest and scribe, arrived in Jerusalem,
in the year B.C. 479, with the rank of Persian governor, we
hear of no chief priest then living there. Perhaps his
cousin Joiakim, the son of Jeshua, had died at the time of
Ezra's appointment. Ezra had already gained a great name
in Babylon as a Jewish scribe, and on arriving in Jerusalem
he seems to have entered upon the double office of governor
and chief priest. The Persian king is said to have given to
him a decree directed to the treasurers who collected the
tribute in Judea, ordering them to help him with a fixed
sum of money and a supply of food for the service of the
Temple, and an order that the priests and servants of the
Temple should be free from all taxes. But the royal letter,

---

[*] Herodotus I. 183.   [†] Antiq. XI. v. 1.

as we now have it, gives him authority over all the country beyond or to the west of the river Euphrates, even unto death, banishment, confiscation of goods, or imprisonment. This throws a great doubt upon the genuineness of the letter, although it limits Ezra's authority to the Jews, or "such as know the Law of thy God."

Armed, however, with this or some such royal letter, Ezra went up to Jerusalem in the seventh year of Xerxes I, B.C. 479. It gave to him all the power held by Zerubbabel, together with which he had of himself such authority as the Jews yielded willingly to the office of chief priest. He had gathered together a body of Jews who were willing to accompany him, to the number of fifteen hundred males, including Hattush of the line of David, a child, a great grandson of Zerubbabel, who had no official rank given to him. These men were part of the families that had before chosen to remain in Babylon rather than accompany Prince Zerubbabel when Cyrus gave them leave to return; and their staying behind shows that they were not very badly treated in the spots where they had been placed as colonists. In the list of those who followed Ezra, the families of Pharezites and Zarhites are, as in the case of those who followed Zerubbabel, the two mentioned first. Ezra, moreover, had received from the king and the Babylonian nobles, and from the Jews of Babylonia, a large amount of gold and silver, together with twenty golden cups, and two cups of yellow brass, a metal then new, and thought precious as gold. He arrived in safety, but not without having felt some fears on the journey; for he had been ashamed to ask the king for a guard, as he had boasted to him that the hand of God would protect them on the journey.

Ezra, like Jeshua, the former high priest, arrived in Jerusalem with the full determination to keep up the strict line of separation between the Jews of pure blood, who could show their pedigrees, those, in short, who had been in captivity, and those humbler inhabitants of the city who had been left behind unnoticed, and whom the captives on their return found there. Instead of trying to unite the two halves of the people into one, he insisted on widening the breach. He called upon all the true Israelites to put away their foreign wives and the children born of them, quoting the Book of Deuteronomy, which forbade them to marry with the people of the country that they were coming into. He forgot that Deuteronomy did not order them to put away

20 *

the foreign wives whom they might have already married, still less did it order them to neglect their children. But the treasure which he brought may have given him weight; and when he summoned all the children of the Captivity to appear before him in Jerusalem, he threatened the disobedient with loss of property, and with being put out of the assembly. He claimed to have power over Judea as well as Jerusalem; but this authority probably did not reach far south of the capital.* Within these limits, however, Ezra seems to have been very generally obeyed, and his narrow policy must now be looked upon as one of the great causes which led to the weakness and fall of the nation. It saved the family of Israel from the reproach of idolatry, by declaring that more than one half of the people were foreigners. While the Jewish monarchy lasted, while they had a country to struggle for, the prophets had endeavoured to win the mixed population, as being their countrymen, to the pure worship of Jehovah. But when Judea became only one out of the one hundred and twenty-seven provinces of the Persian monarchy, Jewish patriotism took narrower limits, and the priests only recognized those as belonging to the nation who worshipped God under their law. This may have been good policy as regards the Jewish religion, but was not good for the nation. When the time came round for celebrating the Feast of Tabernacles, and living for seven days under booths, none seem to have been allowed to join in the religious celebration but those who had themselves or their forefathers come home from Captivity.

At this time, as under Zerubbabel, the priesthood was not limited to the sons of Aaron; we find Levites counted among the chief priests.† The body called Levites when Leviticus and Numbers were written, was on the return from Captivity divided into three classes; some were raised to be priests, some remained Levites, and some were lowered to be Nethins. On what principle the division was made does not appear.

At this Feast of Tabernacles Ezra read to the assembled people out of the Book of the Law of Moses, while some of the priests and Levites explained its meaning in the language of the day to such of his hearers as could not understand the Biblical Hebrew. This he did for each of the seven days of the feast, reading from daybreak to noon. The people

---

* Ezra vii.—x.   † Ezra viii.

stood in the Broad Place of the Water Gate, being the space
better known as the Court of the Gentiles; while Ezra stood
on a tower of wood, probably within the court of the priests.[*]
Such was now the difference between the Biblical Hebrew
and the language spoken and understood by the common
people, that the priests who read the law to them were
sometimes called Interpreters, as we see in the Isaiah of the
Return, chapter xliii. 27, and in the Book of Job, xxxiii. 23.
Thus, when the living priests have lost their gigantic power
over men's minds, the old books are brought out and
appealed to as the highest authority. We have not heard
of such public instructions being given to the people before
the Captivity, although it was proposed in Deuteronomy
xxxi. 11, written, as we suppose, at the very close of
Zedekiah's reign.

When the Book of the Law was thus read to the people
of Jerusalem, and Ezra preached to them in the Court of
the Temple, we may safely suppose that those who lived at
a distance from Jerusalem received the same instruction.
This would naturally bring into being other Places of Meeting
or Synagogues, as they were afterwards called. The growth
of such an institution is usually gradual, its beginning is
unnoticed, and its origin can only be traced by conjecture.
We do not hear of Synagogues until they were closed
by Antiochus Epiphanes,[†] and we can only conjecture
that they began with the reading of the Law to the people
after the Return from Captivity. The Book of the Law
spoken of above as read by Ezra, was of course the Book of
Deuteronomy, which is so named at its beginning, and at its
end.[‡] It was written for the people. The ceremonial law
in Leviticus and Numbers was written for the priests, and
was less suitable for public reading. The Books of the
Prophets may also have been sometimes read; and we
reasonably suppose that such readings, led to further
writings of a popular character, such as the latter chapters
of Leviticus, and the additions to Deuteronomy, which we
shall meet with presently. In these Synagogues we have
the origin of that valuable institution the Christian Congregation.

With this spread of religious knowledge among the people,
when all men "from the least of them to the greatest of

---

[*] Nehem. viii. 1-8.   [†] Psalm lxxiv.
[‡] Deut. iv. 44; xxxi. 9.

them " were made to know Jehovah, doubts arose in some
minds about the justice of the old threat that children were
to be punished for the sins of their fathers, or " to have
their teeth set on **edge** because their fathers had eaten sour
grapes." In order to quiet these doubts, the prophets now
taught that God would make a New Covenant with Israel
and Judah, and that henceforth every man should die for his
own sins only.*

Soon after this time we find that the scribe is a person of
little less importance than the priest ; and much as we may
disapprove of making the words of the past a model for all
future ages, yet it was a step towards mental freedom.
The appeal to the Book of the Law made the priest at once
give up half his power over men's minds, and the scribe's
superiority consisted in little more than his being able to
read and write.

The Sagins, the Jews who acted as Persian officers,
perhaps tribute collectors, were at this time reckoned among
the nobles of Jerusalem. Under the Babylonians they had
been hated by their countrymen; but under the mild government of the Persians such men were less unpopular. We
are not surprised, however, to find that the Sagins were
chief among the Jews who had disregarded the law against
foreign marriages.†

Notwithstanding Ezra's disapproval of foreign marriages,
it seems that his son Mered had married Bithiah, the
daughter of a Pharaoh. Egypt, when it rebelled against
the Persians, had for a short time been governed by two
native kings, Inarus and Amyrtæus. When these were
conquered their sons were allowed to govern the country,
as satraps, under the Persian monarch ; and Mered, the
son of the Pasha of Judea, may have married the sister of
one of the satraps of Egypt. Mered had a second wife, who
was a Jewess; hence he may possibly have been forced to
put away the foreigner.‡ Ezra may have become less
important after B.C. 468; as then Eliashib entered upon the
office of chief priest, and held it for the long period of forty
years.§ During Ezra's time we heard nothing of Joiakim,
the son of Jeshua, and the father of Eliashib.

It is probable that Ezra, acting as editor, for the first
time gathered together the scattered laws into one work,

---

* Jerem. xxxi. 27-40.   † Ezra ix. 2.
‡ 1 Chron. iv. 17, 18.   § Paschal Chronicle.

and joined them on to the Book of Genesis; and thus gave an appearance of unity to what, when closely looked into, is evidently a confused mass of writing. The Pentateuch, as we have seen, is the work of very many authors; but in its present form it is the work of some one mind; it is a connected History of Israel until the time when they entered Canaan; and to no one so safely as to Ezra can conjecture give the credit of having put the scattered materials into their present form. He is usually called Ezra the Scribe, which means that he was better known as an editor than as an author. A few years later we shall hear of Nehemiah gathering together the other parts of the Bible, without any mention of the Pentateuch, showing that the Book of the Law had been before collected. It was not, as now, divided into five books; that was done by the Greek translators from whom it gained its name of the Pentateuch. Nor could Ezra have been the latest editor of the Mosaic Law, and have left it to us in its present state; as we shall presently meet with reasons for thinking that about half of Leviticus, and some few passages in Numbers and Deuteronomy, are yet more modern.

One of the features, which we may suppose was introduced into the early books by Ezra, was the rejection of the numeral letters, and the writing all numbers by words. We must believe that the improbable numbers which we find in the Pentateuch and historical books arose from the use of numerals in the early documents; as in the Books of Ezra and Nehemiah the numbers call for no such distrust.

We have seen that parts of the Book of Genesis were written in behalf of northern feelings and prejudices, such as those which make Beth-el a holy place. At the time when written they could have formed no portion of Jerusalem literature. It can have been only at some time after the return from the Captivity when the jealousy between Israel and Judah was in part forgotten, that these have been woven into one whole with writings in defence of Jerusalem's claim to superiority. So also of Genesis xxxvii—l, although the history of Jacob's sons belongs to David's reign, yet Joseph's Dream, in which he saw the sun, moon, and eleven stars bow down to the twelfth star, shows a knowledge of the Zodiac and its twelve signs, which was probably gained from Babylon during the Captivity. Hence these and other modern thoughts may have crept into the Life of Joseph in Ezra's time, when it may have received its present colouring.

To this time, when Ezra was stretching the Levitical law which forbade marriages with foreigners, so far as to make it mean dissolving such marriages when made, we will give Numbers xii. 1-15, which seems to have been written in defence of the foreign wives whom Ezra required the husbands to put away. Moses's foreign wife had been called a Midianite ; but here, in order to make the case stronger, she is called by the more general name of Cushite, which may even mean a negress ; and yet Aaron and Miriam are reproved by Jehovah for blaming the marriage.

Of the historical Book of Ezra little description is needed **beyond** saying that it contains the history of the two caravans of captives, as above described : the first brought from Babylon by Zerubbabel, and the second brought by himself ; together with the letters of the Persian king, at first forbidding and then allowing the Temple to be rebuilt, and the letter appointing Ezra to his high post. The greater part of the book is in Hebrew, but two small portions **are in** the Chaldee language. A later editor has introduced each with a few words of Hebrew. The first of these, chapter iv. 7—vi. 18, rather interrupts the narrative which had brought us to the reign of Darius. It tells us of hindrances to the work of rebuilding the Temple, which the Jews met with in the reign of Cambyses, whom it names Artaxerxes. The second of these additions, chapter vii. 12-26, contains the letter in which the Persian king gives to Ezra his high appointment. These were added after the time **of** Nehemiah. Chapter iv. 6 had been added, probably before that time, by a different editor, who gives to Cambyses the name **of** Ahasuerus.

It is doubtful how much of this book is the work of Ezra. **In** only a small portion of it does he speak in the first person. In the Greek translation of the Bible, known by the name of the Septuagint, there is at the end of this book a small addition, not now found in the Hebrew, but quoted in Nehemiah viii. In the Book of Ezra, iv. 6, the successor of Cyrus is named Ahasuerus, who can only be Cambyses. The decree in chapter iv. 7—vi. 18, by Artaxerxes, is thought by some critics to be by Smerdis, who reigned for seven months after Cambyses ; but he is more probably the **same** Cambyses, with his name written according to the **Chaldee** custom. He is followed by Darius ; and he again by Artaxerxes, who can only be Xerxes I. The letter from this last king to Ezra gives to him not only a claim upon the royal treasurers for money and materials for rebuilding the Temple, but authority to appoint magistrates and judges over all the people beyond or to the west of the river Euphrates. Such a wide authority we can by no means believe that he ever possessed, and it throws a doubt upon the genuineness of the letter from Artaxerxes to Ezra.

We gave to the reign of Josiah the ill-natured attack upon the great family of the Pharezites in Genesis xxxviii.; and here, in the Book of Ezra, we find the same want of popularity following them, and they are called, not the Sons of Pharez, but the Sons of Pharosh, *a flea*.

The two Books of Samuel and the two Books of Kings were compiled at about this time. In the Greek translation they are called the four Books of Kings. A better division of them would be, the one Book of Samuel and the three Books of Kings; as the first book begins with the birth of Samuel and ends with the woman at Endor pretending to raise him from the dead. They have very much the appearance of being all four the work of one editor, who has woven them out of the materials that were before him impartially and carefully, with very little colouring from his own mind. The varieties in style seem to belong to the original materials from which he composed his work; and these materials are woven together with very little skill. Thus, in the lives of Samuel and Saul the most careless reader can see that we have more than one history; and the editor has not used his judgment so as to choose the most trustworthy of his authorities, but he has given us both, though they sometimes contradict one another. Hannah's poetical prayer in 1 Samuel ii., and David's song in 2 Samuel xxii., are both of a later time. The latter is nearly the same as Psalm xviii., which we have given to Jotham's reign.

The editor's calling Solomon's kingdom "beyond the river Euphrates"* shows that he had lived in the neighbourhood of Babylon, or perhaps was living there at the time that he so wrote. This would allow us to think Ezra the writer, for he was known as a scribe or author while yet in Babylon. The giving the name of prophets to the singers and musicians whom Saul meets with belongs to this late time. The evil spirit from Jehovah which caused Saul's madness in

* 1 Kings iv. 24.

1 Samuel xvi. 14, and the lying spirit which offered to go to earth, and mislead kings Jehoshaphat and Ahab in 1 Kings xxii., are both, like Satan in the Book of Job, importations from the Captivity. The Books of Job and Kings are, moreover, alike in a peculiarity that can hardly have lasted many generations, that of using the word "bless" for "curse," without a hint that it is to be understood ironically. Of course, a speaker would have no difficulty in showing, by the tone of his voice, that he meant the **words** to be taken in a bad sense, as explained in one of the latter Proverbs, thus:—

> He that blesseth his neighbour with a loud voice,
> Rising early in the morning,
> It shall be counted a curse to him (xxvii. 14).

Compared with the histories of Greece, Rome, and modern Europe, the Books of Samuel and Kings are little more than bald annals; but as the original authors all lived before the time that Herodotus began to write, they rather oppose his claim to be called the Father of History.

The lives of Elijah and Elisha, full of marvellous and yet often trifling events, are woven into the bald annals of the Kings with very little regard to uniformity, and belong rather to the time of Nehemiah than to that of Ezra. They will be spoken of hereafter. In smaller matters also we trace the variety of dates. Thus Hiram king of Tyre helps Solomon to build his Temple; and a later sentence gives the name of Hiram to the workman. Again, after Solomon had built this small roofed building, called the House of Jehovah, the more modern prayer, then spoken by Solomon, gives to the whole courtyard the name of the House, a name it did not deserve until at **a** later time it was enclosed within its own walls.

The beautiful prayer **put** into the mouth of Solomon at the dedication of the Temple is the editor's addition, and cannot have been written before the carrying into captivity, as that national misfortune is there mentioned. Solomon prays that on the people's turning to Jehovah He will cause them to be pitied in the sight of those who should carry them captive, using the words of Psalm cvi., which was written in the reign of Evil-merodach, who treated the captives more kindly. But the prayer does not speak of a return from captivity, as if the writer, living in Babylon, had **felt the better** treatment, but thought that the return home had not yet been brought about. This beautiful prayer has the merits and the faults which we notice in the best writers after the Captivity, such as the Isaiah of the Return home, when compared with the Books of Joel and Nahum. It shows kindness towards strangers, and a value for devotional feelings rather than for sacrifices; but in style it shows smoothness rather than force, and its best thoughts are weakened by repetition.

The editor of the Books of Kings had read the Book of Joshua, from which he quotes, though without naming it, on the building of Jericho in Ahab's reign; and also Deuteronomy, from which he quotes, though without naming it, in Amaziah's reign, and again in Josiah's reign. He quotes for his authorities the Acts of Solomon, the Chronicles of the Kings of Israel, and the Chronicles of the Kings of Judah, of which the language may have been of an older form, now going out of use; and we can see that he made use of the Books of Isaiah and Jeremiah for the times when these prophets lived. He composed his work after the death of the captive king Jehoiachin, and before the time of Nehemiah, when the Books of Chronicles were written, as the author of those books had probably seen these. In this way the editor tells us pretty exactly when he lived; and Ezra's reputation as a scribe would lead us to conjecture that we own these four books, or at least the two Books of Kings, to him, and that he wrote them while living in Babylon, before he entered on his high political duties. When he tells us the days of the month on which the last great misfortunes fell upon Jerusalem, with an exactness nowhere else met with in his history, he perhaps takes those days from a law which fixed the fast days for the nation's grief, rather than from a certain knowledge of the fact.

These scanty annals give us very little insight into the characters of the kings, and very few other actors appear upon the scene. They rarely show the motives which may have led to a line of policy, or the causes for the nation's wellbeing or for its misfortunes, other than a foreign invasion. In the prosperous reigns the history is nearly blank. The interest centres in Jerusalem; the rest of the kingdom is forgotten. But in one matter we must give full praise to the compiler—namely, in his careful chronology, which is of itself an evidence of his accuracy in other matters. Here, by a skilful use of the two lines of kings, those of Judah and those of Israel, he has well supplied the want of a fixed era to reckon his years from.* If this skill in chronology is due to Ezra, he may have learned it in Babylon, where eclipses had been recorded by means of a fixed era as early as Hezekiah's reign.

The last words of king David, in 2 Samuel xxiii. 1-7, are called a Naham, or *inspired speech* using in a new sense this word, which, throughout the Prophets, had been used only for speeches spoken by the Almighty. The thoughts also in that speech suit the time of the nation's ruin rather than that of its strength. Its enemies are **spoken of as** too strong **to be** easily opposed :—

> They shall all be thrust away as thorns,
> Because they cannot be taken hold of by the hands ;
> But the man that shall touch them
> Must be fenced with iron and the staff of a spear,
> And they shall be utterly burned with fire in their place.

The only other places in which this word Naham, *inspired speech*, if used otherwise than for God's words, may as well be here mentioned as being all of a late date.

Balaam's third poetical speech, in Numbers xxiii. 27—xxiv. 13, in which, while in a trance, he blesses the Israelites, is called a Naham. Here two lines are borrowed from Balaam's former speech, in Numbers xxiii. 22 ; two lines from Jacob's description of Judah, in Genesis xlix. 9 ; and two lines from Isaac's blessing on Jacob, in Genesis xxvii. 29.

Balaam's fourth poetical speech, in Numbers xxiv. 15-19, which is also called a Naham, we shall hereafter have to speak of as being yet more modern.

The words of Agur, which, with those of king Lemuel, have been added to the Book of Proverbs, are another Naham. Who Agur was is unknown. He reproves the habit, which **we** have already had to notice, of writers adding portions to the written law, and calling their own opinions the words of God. He says, " Every word of God is pure ; he is a shield to those who trust in him. Add not thou to his words lest he reprove thee, and thou be found a liar." When he says, " The horseleach hath two daughters [who cry] Give, give," we are tempted to think that he means the Persian monarchy, which, though mild in its despotism, it would not be safe to complain of openly, and which was ever hungry for tribute. The land-tax and the poll-tax may be the two daughters. The burden of the

---

* See the Table of Chronology at the end of this volume.

road-service had been removed, or, at **least**, very much lightened by Darius.

King Lemuel, whose words accompany these in the Book of Proverbs, is equally unknown. His name seems to have been created by the mere change of a letter ; and Prov. xxxi. should perhaps begin with " The words *of his mother to* the king [meaning Solomon] the burden which his mother taught him."

The next place in which this word **Naham** is used is in Psalm xxxvi. 1, where it is **no** longer an inspired speech, but the **profane oath** of a wicked man ; thus :—

> The profane oath of the wicked man is in my heart ;
> There is no fear of God before his eyes.

This Psalm may **well** be of a modern date ; but there is nothing in it to fix very certainly when it was written.

Psalm l. is also of uncertain date ; but it contains a severe rebuke upon those, who like Ezra, divided the nation into two parties, by stretching the priestly law of the Statutes, to the neglect of the moral law of the Words or Ten Commandments. They claimed of Jehovah that he should remember his promised Covenant, while they forgot to perform the conditions required of them. Thus :—

> Unto the wicked man God saith,
> What hast thou to do to declare my Statutes ?
> And thou takest my covenant in thy mouth,
> While thou hatest instruction,
> And casteth my Words behind thee.
> Thou sittest [as judge] and speaketh against thy brother ;
> Thou utterest slanders against thy mother's son.

The writer makes a clear distinction between the eternal Moral Law and the Statute Law, a distinction very much overlooked in the Pentateuch.

Much of Deuteronomy xviii. 9—xxvi. is of very uncertain date; but it belongs to a time after the Captivity, and **its** humane laws agree very well with the time of good government which began with the reign of Darius. It begins with the important promise that at a future time a prophet, a second Moses, shall be raised up to guide the people. **As** we must look for this unnamed person among those who have given laws to the nation, the words seem to point to Ezra. The new laws are very valuable. Thus, no **man** is now to be found guilty of any sin by the evidence of only **one** witness (xix. 15) ; while in **chapter** xvii. 6, it was for

murder only that two witnesses were needed. New houses
are to have battlements to the roofs, lest any man should
fall therefrom (xxii. 8). A hand-mill or an upper mill-stone,
by' which a man supports his life, may not be taken in
pledge for debt (xxiv. 6). The creditor may not enter
the debtor's house to fetch a pledge ; he must wait on the
outside till it is brought out to him (xxiv. 10). If a poor
man pledges his outer garment, his thick coat, it must be
returned to him at night that he may sleep in it (xxiv. 13).
No man shall be punished with more than forty stripes
(**xxv.** 3). Protection is offered to the poor Israelite who
had sold himself into bondage to his richer neighbour. **And
the** inhumanity to which these bondservants were yet **liable,
is** amply shown by the new law which allows them to escape
when they can; "thou shalt not deliver up into bondage to
his master the servant who has escaped from his master unto
thee. He shall dwell with thee, even among you, in that
place which he shall choose, within any of thy city gates,
where it liketh him best " (xxiii. 15, 16). By such words
the humane lawgiver acknowledges the existence of the
cruelty which he has no power to put an end to. Cities for
refuge are to be appointed, where the manslayer may flee
from hasty vengeance (xix.). The division of the land of
Canaan for this purpose into three parts, described in Joshua
xx. as Galilee, Ephraim, and Judah, gives a modern date to
this chapter, and to Numbers **xxxv.** as well as to Joshua
xxi. where these cities are mentioned. The tithes are to be
paid only on the third year, called the year of tithing (xxvi.
12), while in chapter xiv. 22 they were to be brought forth
year by year.

These late chapters of the Book of Deuteronomy show
some little improvement in the treatment of women. No
formal contract or ceremony was needed to make a marriage.
A young woman was the property of **her** father, and when
he gave her in marriage he received a sum of money as the
purchase money. She then became her husband's property,
and may sometime have been treated as his slave, since his
was the stronger arm. But when husband and wife both
have to work for a livelihood, they are not far from equal ;
they neither have any education but what is gained from
such work. After the Captivity the Jews were not so
wealthy that women could be degraded and kept in idleness.

Such was the state of society to which the laws were to
be fitted. By the former law in Exodus xxii. 16, 17, if a

man took a woman to himself to bear children without her
father's leave, whether with her consent or by force, he was
required to pay to the father the usual purchase money, and
that whether the father allowed her to remain with him or
not. If the husband wished to take a second wife he was at
liberty to do so, provided he continued to treat the first as a
wife also. If he did not so treat her, she was at liberty, by
Exodus xxi. 10, 11, to leave him, and go out free, without
returning to him the purchase money. The only rights
secured to a woman, the only rights she wished for, were the
right to leave her husband, and go out free, if ill-treated.
Such was the law laid down in the Judgments, which we
have supposed written in the reign of Jehoshaphat. It **was**
only when a wife became too old to work that the law gave
her protection; and then her legal claim had been upon her
children, not upon her husband. "Honour thy father and
thy mother," in the fifth Commandment, means maintain
them in their old age; and so it was interpreted by the
judge. And the Proverb xix. 26, justly remarks that :—

> He who robbeth his father, and chaseth away his mother,
> Is a son that causeth shame, and bringeth reproach.

But as the state of society improved, a wife became less
a piece of property. She was even supposed to have feelings of her own; she had rights even against her husband;
and these the Book of Deuteronomy in some degree protects.
It enacts that if the man use force, and took her against her
will, he shall not only pay to her father fifty shekels, as
purchase money, but she shall be his wife; he shall not at
any time be allowed to put her away.* So also if he should
bring against his wife a false charge of previous misconduct,
he shall **not only** forfeit one hundred shekels to her father,
but he shall lose the power of ever putting her away.†
And if she were a captive taken in war, though he shall
have **power to** put her away at his pleasure, he shall **not**
have power **to** sell her.‡

These chapters in Deuteronomy, with the latter chapters
of Leviticus which we shall soon speak of, like the Judgments in Exodus xxi.—xxiii. mentioned in Jehoshaphat's
reign, contain laws to guide the judge, the criminal and
civil laws by which society is held together. The irregular
manner in which these few laws are scattered through the

---

* Deut. xxii. 28, 29.   † Deut. xxii. 13-19.   ‡ Deut. xxi. 10-14.

Pentateuch, teaches how little importance was as yet given
to the science of law-making. But we do not know that
any other nation had as yet advanced further in this matter.
The Pentateuch is named the Five Books of the Law; but
the only laws to which clearness and exactness are given are
those which relate to the priests and the sacrifices.

Deuteronomy xxvii. must be a late addition to that book,
and it may be mentioned now, when Mount Ebal and
Mount Gerizim are no longer in an unfriendly country.
The command given by Moses and the elders in this
chapter, which gives a sanction to the altar to Jehovah
near the town of Shechem, whether on Mount Ebal, as in
the Hebrew, or on Mount Gerizim, as in the Samaritan
copies, is strongly opposed to the older parts of Deuteronomy,
which were written in support of the claim made for
Jerusalem to be the only spot where an altar to Jehovah
was allowed ; but it agrees with Joshua xxi. 21, which we
must suppose to be written soon after this time, and which
makes Shechem a Levitical city. It agrees also with the
Life of Elijah, which we shall come to presently, which says
that Elijah built an altar to Jehovah on Mount Carmel, and
thus overlooked the command that there should be only
one such altar. Chapter xi. 29—31, may have been written
at the same time, directing the blessings to be put on mount
Gerizim and the curses on mount Ebal, as in chapter xxvii.

To this time perhaps belongs Deuteronomy xxxiii. which
contains the poetical Blessings in which Moses describes the
tribes under the names of the Sons of Jacob. This shows
the nation in a very different state from that described in
Jacob's Blessing of his sons in Genesis xlix., which was
written some centuries earlier. Levi is not now blamed, as
then ; but the prayer for him is :—

> Let thy Urim and thy Thummim be with thy godly man.
> Bless, O Jehovah, his inheritance,
> And accept the work of his hands.

Benjamin is no longer known for its bravery, but for the
Temple which stood within its boundaries :—

> Beloved of Jehovah, may he dwell in safety by Him,
> May He cover him all the day long.
> And may He dwell between his shoulders.

Another peculiarity in this poem, is that **it** is Jehovistic,
and yet gives the superiority among the sons to Ephraim

and Manasseh. Judah is spoken of in a very slight manner. Simeon is not mentioned, it was swallowed up in Judah. Dan is known only as a northern portion of territory bordering on Bashan. Zebulun and Issachar together worship Jehovah on a mount situated between the two, probably Mount Tabor, and they are both enriched by the "secret hidden in the sand," namely the Murex, the shellfish from which the valuable Tyrian purple dye was obtained.

The song of Moses which he spoke shortly before his death, and the words which introduce it, in Deut. **xxxi.** 16-22, and 30—xxxii. 44, are inserted passages which interrupt **the narrative** ; and they may be mentioned here, because they seem of the same age as Hannah's Prayer, and David's Song mentioned above. The name of Jeshurun for Israel, of Vanities for false gods, of **the Rock for God,** belong **to** a late time. Moreover, God is here styled the Nation's Father, a title not given to him in the earlier parts of the Pentateuch. But the date of these additions to Deuteronomy cannot be fixed with any exactness.

With the portions of the Book of Proverbs lately spoken of, we may mention the last portion of that book, which is an Alphabetic poem, and of about the same age as the Alphabetic Psalms lately described. It is in praise of a virtuous woman, and it belongs to some time, such perhaps as the reign of Darius or Xerxes, when it was possible to describe a happy home without adding a complaint against oppression. The wife's condition is now very much improved. She employs her maids in making linen and woollen clothing for sale ; and she buys land for her husband with the produce of her trade. If for the support of the family an undue share of work is thrown upon her, while her husband is sitting among the elders at the city gate, at **least** she gains the importance and honour arising from her **usefulness.**

The Book **of** Esther may have been written shortly after the time **of** Ezra, **but** its date cannot be **fixed** with any certainty. It is the history of a young Jewess, belonging to one of the Jewish families at this time living in Persia. She is raised by her beauty to be the favourite wife in place of the former queen of Ahasuerus, king of Persia, who seems to be Xerxes **I.** While in the palace at Susa, she hears through her **uncle** Mordecai, of an intention to cause a massacre of **the** Jews throughout the Persian empire, which she is able **to** defeat in consequence of her influence with the king. She obtains for her brethren in the faith a royal letter, granting them protection from all ill-treatment, with leave to defend themselves from their oppressors. The author of the intended cruelty, a super-stitious man, had been casting Purim, or divining lots, to learn when and how his design could be best carried into execution; and the Jews throughout the kingdom, by the advice of the Persian queen, their protector, ever after kept two days in the year, as days of rejoicing for their escape from the threatened danger. These days are called the Feast of Purim, and are even yet kept sacred by the Jews throughout the world. In the second Book of Maccabees, xv. 36, they are named Mordecai's days from the name of the queen's uncle, who informed her of the plot. The Book of Esther is written with great knowledge of Persian manners and customs. The author, no doubt, lived at Susa, and for his authority he refers to the Chronicles of the kings of Media and Persia. The story is told with a strong political feeling towards the writer's countrymen, the Jews, but without the religious tone which makes the other Hebrew books so valuable. It has also a poetical and eastern colouring, which lessens its appearance of truth; but the favour obtained by Esther from Xerxes, in Susa, agrees very closely with the royal commission granted by that king to Ezra; and the name of Xerxes's queen Ames-tris, as spelt by Herodotus,* is not very unlike Am-Esther, or Mother-Esther; and again Hegias, an Ephesian by birth, who was in the service of Xerxes shortly before the battle of Thermopylæ,† may be the same person as Hegia the king's chamberlain, the keeper of the women at Susa, who brought Esther to Ahasuerus. Though the particulars may have been exaggerated by Jewish partiality, or *Mother-Esther;* the story had no doubt some foundation in fact. The Jews had been made uncomfortable for the ten years which followed the death of Zerubbabel by finding themselves under a Samaritan governor, and their wishes opposed by the Samaritans and other enemies. They perhaps feared a kind of servile war, a rising of their own bondservants, the poor whom they had not been treating well, and to whom they denied the name of Jews.

From this discomfort, which is here spoken of as a danger of being slaughtered throughout the Persian king-

* Lib. ix. 109.   † Ctesias in Photius.

dom, the influence of a Jewish queen on the Persian throne
may have helped to relieve them.

As long as the Persian monarchy lasted Tyre and **Sidon**
continued to prosper and to some year within these **three**
centuries we may give the sarcophagus of Eshmonezer, **king**
of the Sidonians, now at Paris, bearing a Phenician inscription, which speaks of a Sidonian queen, Am-ashtoreth. As
it was usual for the kings of smaller states to copy their
great neighbours, we mention this sarcophagus now, as the
name of queen Am-ashtoreth may **have** been copied from
that of the Persian queen Am-esther.

To about this time, also, we may perhaps give chapter xxxi.
of Jeremiah, but it must be divided into three parts, written
by more than one author, and perhaps at more than one
period. Verses 1-26 contain a promise given to the **writer
when** asleep, that Jehovah will be the God of all the families
of Israel, and that Ephraim, his first-born, or the northern
tribe, shall now seek Jehovah on Mount Sion. The writer
was an Israelite of the tribe of Ephraim; and Ephraim is
invited to return again to his cities, thus reminding us that
when Judah returned home from the captivity in Babylon,
the northern tribes did **not** return in **any** large numbers.
The writer gives **as a reason for their** return home, **that**
Jehovah had **created a** new thing, that **a** woman shall come
round or lead about **a** man; by which ambiguous words **he**
seems to point to the share that Esther, the Jewish maiden,
had in persuading the Persian king to appoint her country-
man Ezra, to the government of Judea. Verses 27-37 point
to the smallness of the population in both halves of the
country, and, like Ezekiel xviii., quote the scoffing proverb
that the fathers have eaten sour grapes, and the children's
teeth are set on edge, in order to contradict the old law, and
to promise that every man shall suffer only for **his own**
iniquity. **The** writer considers the Old Covenant of
Exodus **xix. 5, that** Jehovah would be the nation's God,
provided that **they** consented to be his people, as **forfeited**
by their disobedience, and thus followed by the **Captivity;**
but now on their return home he promises that **they shall**
have a New Covenant, **to be** written not on tables **of** stone,
but on their hearts, and that on their keeping the Law they
shall be again prosperous as a nation. The readiness with
which the Northern Israelites had latterly been willing to
own themselves Jews, and to worship Jehovah at Jerusalem,
is shown by its being no longer necessary for each man **to**

teach his neighbour, the Jews to teach the Israelites, saying
"Know ye Jehovah," for then they will all worship Jehovah.

The thoughts in verses 35-37 are borrowed from Jeremiah
xxxiii. 20-22. Verses 38-40 are on the rebuilding of the city.
The writer, when declaring that the fields around Jerusalem
are to be measured and made holy to Jehovah, seems to refer
to Ezekiel xlii. 16-20, as it now stands in the Hebrew, and
so far disproves our conjecture in page 236, that the space
measured was smaller, being measured in cubits not in reeds
of ten cubits each.

When we part with the Book of Ezra, we again **meet** with
a blank of twenty or more years in our history. During
this time Xerxes I had been murdered and his younger son
Artaxerxes Longimanus had made himself king of Persia;
Egypt had rebelled and made itself independent; and Judea
may have then suffered, if not from the distrust of its conquerors, yet from the armies which in the year B.C. 460,
marched through it to the conquest of Egypt.[*] The revolt
of Megabyzus in Syria, and his war against Artaxerxes, may
yet further have brought trouble upon Judea. During this
time Eliashib was chief priest, but without civil authority.

NEHEMIAH GOVERNOR OF JUDEA; B.C. 445—433.

We have spoken of Jews settling in Persia in the reign
of Cyrus, then of the Persian ambassadors worshipping in
the Temple of Jerusalem, in the reign of Darius, and then of
a Jewish queen of Persia, the wife of Xerxes I, and now our
history again leads us to the same country, when in the
twentieth year of Artaxerxes Longimanus, B.C. 445, Nehemiah, a Jew of Susa, the capital of Persia, a cup-bearer in
the king's **service,** obtained from him the appointment of
Governor **of Judea,** with permission **to** rebuild the walls of
Jerusalem, **as a** necessary step to protect the unhappy
inhabitants **from robbery** and illtreatment. He had perhaps
never seen **Jerusalem; but** though living in the palace, as the
chief favourite **of the** great king, his thoughts ran upon the
city of his fathers, **on** the Temple in which they had worshipped, and on the sepulchres in the neighbourhood. On
the arrival of some of his countrymen at Susa, which had
been the chief city of Elam, but was now the capital of the
Persian empire, they told him of the ruined state of Jerusalem,
and he ventured to ask of Artaxerxes to be allowed to rebuild

* Diod. Sic. xi. 77.

it The king granted his request, and sent him away with
the rank of Tirshatha, or governor, of Judea. He also gave
him a guard of horsemen to accompany him, as far as was
necessary, on the journey, and an order, directed to the
keeper of the royal forests, that he should be supplied with
the necessary timber.

After crossing the Euphrates, before going to Jerusalem,
Nehemiah carried the Royal Letter which he had obtained
in his favour **to the** Persian governors of the provinces to the
west of the Euphrates, and also to Sanballat, a Samaritan,
who was governor of Samaria. Sanballat received him very
coldly, showing a natural jealousy against Jerusalem's wish
for independence; and Nehemiah saw that the Letter would
obtain for him very little help. A governor at a distance of
perhaps a thousand miles from his sovereign, need not be
very obedient to orders in matters of small moment.

On reaching Jerusalem, Nehemiah at first told nobody
what he came about. He even took his survey of the
ruined walls in the dark. When he had formed his plans,
and got acquainted with the chief Jews in the city, he then
told them of his purpose, and asked their help in rebuilding the walls. Eliashib, the grandson of Jeshua, had
succeeded Ezra, and was at the time the chief priest; and he
and his brethren warmly entered into the plan, well knowing, however, that if the Samaritan governor did not
venture to stop them by force and in defiance of the Royal
Letter, he would do all he could to hinder them. Sanballat,
when he heard that they had begun, laughed at their
trifling attempts, and asked mockingly if they were going to
rebel against the king. The Jews of the city divided the work
among themselves, each undertaking, with such materials
as were at hand among the ruins, to build that portion of the
wall which was nearest to his own house. In this way about
one half of the wall was rebuilt, when Sanballat and their
enemies began to think the work important. He had at first
laughed at it as such a weak wall that a fox would knock it
down if he came near it; but now he threatened to bring
down his troops to stop any further progress.

Nehemiah, however, did not much fear that Sanballat, in
direct disobedience to the Royal Letter, would openly try
to stop the work. What he more feared was that their
numerous enemies, Arabs, Ammonites, and Philistines, as
he styled those who were not of the Captivity, might
attempt, **with** Sanballat's encouragement, to do what he

would not venture to do himself: for the old jealousy of
the people of the country, against the selfish policy of the
rulers in Jerusalem, was not dead.   But against these
enemies he hoped that they should be able to defend themselves. So he divided the Jews into two parties; appointing
one to continue the work of building, while the other half
rested with their arms in their hands to guard the builders
from any attack.   In this way the wall was finished in fifty-
two days.

While this was going on there was not a little murmuring
of the humbler labourers against their more wealthy nobles
and rulers, the Jews. Now that they were invited to work
for the general good they claimed to be relieved from the
heavy burden of usury which they had foolishly taken upon
themselves, and from the bond-service to which many had
sold themselves.   This demand was enforced by Nehemiah;
and supported as it was by the Mosaic law, the wealthy could
not resist it.   They promised to restore the lands taken in
pledge and to give up the interest upon their mortgages,
which seems to have been at the rate of one *per cent.* per
month.*

Since the return from Captivity, we have seen no more of
the struggle between the city and the country, about the
High Places.   Jerusalem and its priests had not the power
to give laws to the nation. But with the building of the
walls, the old fears again arose among the country party;
and many of the nobles of Judah now joined the Samaritans
in weakening Nehemiah's hands.

We note not a little difference between the policy of Ezra
the priest and that of Nehemiah the cup-bearer. The Book
of Ezra treats Judah and Benjamin as the nation, and the
rest of the people as "their adversaries."   But Nehemiah
endeavoured to befriend the mixed population, "the people
and their wives," against the unkind treatment of "their
brethren the Jews;" and he finds himself opposed by the
nobles of Judah.   Ezra had sprung from the Jewish captives
in Babylon, and Nehemiah very probably from the Israelite
captives in Media.   But Nehemiah had accepted the Mosaic
law, which forbids marriage with women of Ashdod and
Ammon and Moab, and so far he followed Ezra's policy.
Whether he followed Ezra so far as to declare that such
marriages, when they had been made, were void and should

* Nehem. i.—vi.

be broken, is doubtful. But it is to be feared that his command not to marry a foreigner, included the command to put her away if already married.

When the wall was finished Nehemiah appointed gate-keepers, who were to keep the city gates shut from sunset to sunrise. He then examined the registers of the genealogies of those who claimed to be true Jews, taking out of the Book of Ezra the list of those who had come up from captivity, as containing the names of all the families who were entitled to be so considered.[*] With a view to keep up the separation between the true Jews and the other people of the land, the Levites summoned them to meet in the **courts** of the Temple ; and after they had listened to the **reading of** the law for a quarter of the day, and prayed **and publicly** confessed their sins for a quarter of the day, they made a solemn covenant that their families should not **marry** with any but true Jews. Nehemiah and the priests, and the Levites, and the nobles, set their seals to a written promise to walk in the law of Moses ; and the rest of the Jews bound themselves with a curse to hold to the agreement, and at the same time to keep the Sabbath holy, and to release all debts on the Sabbath year. The former title for the priests of **the** Sons of Aaron now again comes into use.

The new moon days, the Sabbaths, and solemn feasts, were now to be kept with strictness unknown during the last century of the monarchy. Burnt-offerings, which, towards the close of the monarchy, had been less esteemed, were again treated as of importance. The Book of Deuteronomy, with the writings of Isaiah and Jeremiah, had pressed upon the people the superior value of spiritual worship over ceremony ; but since the rebuilding of the Temple there had arisen, with an increase of patriotism, an increase of narrow zeal for the letter of the law ; and hence for a time the Jewish mind was turned back into a more priestly direction. It was the aim of the rulers to carry out the commands of the ceremonial laws with a strictness which had **not** been possible during the Captivity, and the first years of their return home. They made a number of enactments about the maintenance of the Levites throughout the country, and the service of the Temple in Jerusalem. The Levites were to have the tithes, each in his own city ; and the Temple was **to** have a tithe of the tithe, and the first fruits, and the redemp-

* Nehem. vii. 6—viii. 18.

tion money for the first-born, and the heave offerings, and the yearly poll-tax of one-third of a shekel, in place of the half-shekel ordered in the law. This proposal tells us that the people were in a far more comfortable condition than they had hitherto been since the return from captivity. But as Nehemiah and the priests had no power to enforce the collection of the payments here ordered, the enactments had no force, except upon those who thought it their duty to obey the priests. The only taxes levied by the civil government were those required to make up the tribute to Persia, and of these no mention is here made.*

The well-known laws of political economy will teach us that in the depressed state of the country, with trade ruined, and industry discouraged, land can have yielded very little produce beyond that required for the maintenance of the cultivator. Hence very little rent or surplus profit reached the cities. Jerusalem, in particular, was very much deserted; and the rulers who settled there called upon the people as a duty to come up and live there also. They proposed that at least one in ten of the Jews should fix his residence in Jerusalem. They drew lots to determine upon whom this burden should fall; and those who were chosen, and complied, received the blessing of the others for their dutiful obedience.

The Jews in Jerusalem, the heads of families, the chiefs of the fathers, as they are styled, were at this time not quite fourteen hundred, most of them belonging to the tribes of Benjamin and Judah. These men, acting with the priests, were lords over the mixed population, and masters of the city, so long as the Persian tribute was regularly paid. If there was a Persian garrison in the castle, it left the government of the city, even to the execution of justice, wholly in the hands of the Jews. The priests, who did the service of the Temple, and garrisoned it as a fortress, were twelve hundred, with one hundred and seventy gate-keepers. Many of these lived within the Temple-yard. The Nethins, or Temple-servants, lived in Ophel, a suburb, at the south side of the Temple, while two hundred and eighty Levites dwelt in the city.†

The mildness of the Persian government was shown in the appointment of Pethahiah, a Jew of the great family of Zarah, to one of the chief offices. He was "at the king's

---

* Nehemiah ix., x.   † Nehemiah xi.

hand" for all matters concerning the people.* From this we must not understand that he dwelt at Susa near Artaxerxes, but that, while living in Jerusalem, he had power to decide, like a chancellor, a variety of causes which the ordinary judges were not allowed to decide, causes which were said to be referred to the king's own hearing.

The eighty chief persons in the city who with Nehemiah set their seals to the promise, or rather to the law relating to marriage, are described as priests, Levites, and nobles. They formed the Sanhedrim or High Council, who in the Gospels are described as High-priests, Elders and Scribes. This oligarchical body now wielded the spiritual power which before the Captivity had been in the hands of the high priest. With them, and Nehemiah, the Pasha, the government of the city rested. But how far Nehemiah had the power of enforcing his laws is doubtful. The penalty attached to the laws added to the Book of Leviticus, that he who is guilty "shall be cut off from among his people," is of doubtful meaning. It may mean, "he shall be put to death," but it more probably means "he shall be declared not to be a Jew."

Ezra's name is not among those of the eighty chief men above mentioned. But when at the dedication of the wall, Nehemiah divided the princes of Judah into two companies, and he went with one company, Ezra the scribe went with the other.†

Nehemiah, as the Pasha, fed one hundred and fifty of the chief men every day at his table. The Jewish inhabitants of the city may have been about fifteen thousand souls; but what was the number of the others, the larger part of the population, to whom the honourable name of Jews was denied, we have no means of knowing. The ruined state of the city was such that the Persian governor, the Pasha of the provinces to the west of the Euphrates, when he came to Jerusalem, fixed his quarters in the northern and newer part of the city. His throne stood not in Zion, where Solomon's Porch of Judgment stood, but near the Damascus gate, at the furthest end of the new suburb.‡

The returning prosperity of Judea under the Persians may be imagined from a few hints which tell us that the cultivation of palm trees and balsam trees at Jericho, which

---

* Nehemiah xi. 24. † Nehemiah xii. 36.
‡ Nehemiah iii. 7.

in a later century was very profitable, had already been
begun. The valley is naturally almost as barren as the
neighbouring hills, and could only be watered by tanks,
which were filled in the rainy season by the torrents from
the mountains of Ephraim. But in the Life of Elisha,
which was added at this time to the Book of Kings, that
prophet is said to have brought fertility into the valley by
a miracle, and it continued "unto this day."* We find,
however, no notice of such cultivation there before the
Captivity, when Jericho was only important as being on the
military route from Beth-el to the fords of the Jordan, and
when it was cursed in Joshua vi., written in the reign of
Zedekiah. In Ezekiel xlvii. the fertility of the valley is
promised as a thing of the future. Strabo describes this
valuable plantation in his time, as being ten miles in length
and bringing in a great revenue,† and as having a palace or
castle for the keeper. In the Chronicles, Jericho is called
the City of the Palm Trees."‡ If in the earlier books that
name is given to Jericho, it may have crept in at a later
time.

Under the despotism **of the** Persians the **Jews** were now
living in peace, if not in comfort. Their late sufferings
under the Babylonians made them grateful for their present
lot. The growth of the great monarchies around was such
that, as Jeremiah had long ago told them, the Jews were
too few and too weak to hope for independence. To have
attempted to throw off the Persian yoke would have been
madness. The line of David's family had by no means
come to an end. The stem of Jesse was still flourishing
with many branches. Three grandsons of Hattush were
living and not unknown, and Elioenai, the eldest, had seven
sons ; § but the wiser part of the nation was well contented
to forget the promise that the throne should never be with-
out one of David's family to sit upon it. The writings of
these two centuries are no longer filled with politics, and
are without the fire and patriotic energy of the older
prophets. The few more quiet words of prophecy that
we now meet with promise not so much national glory as
moral and religious improvement, with the happiness of
seeing the old waste places built up again, and the desolations
of many generations repaired.

* 2 Kings ii. 22.   † Strabo, XVI. ii. 41.
‡ 2 Chronicles xxviii. 15.   § 1 Chronicles iii. 24.

There can, however, never have been wanting other men
of a more hasty temper, ignorant perhaps of the gigantic
force which could be sent against them from Persia, who
would have been glad to have risen in rebellion and to have
attempted to make a revolutionary *change* in the government.
Against all such rash doings the Proverb warns, saying
(xxiv. 21) :—

> " My son, fear thou Jehovah and the king,
>   And meddle not with them that are given to change."

When the nation had been independent and the people
wealthy, the priests and Levites had claimed in laws of their
own making to be released from agriculture, to have no
inheritance in land, and to be maintained by the tithes
and offerings of the faithful. In the Captivity they
had no doubt all alike been required to work as labourers,
and to give up to their masters a share of the produce. So
on the return from captivity the poverty of the people was
such that the offerings to the altar, and the atonement money,
would fall far short of keeping a body of clergy without the
labour of their own hands. Hence, we now find new passages
added to the old laws, allowing the Levites to hold lands.
As they were no longer able to live without work, they
wished to rise above the rank of labourers.

Chapters xviii.—xxvii. of Leviticus seem to belong to the
time of Nehemiah. They are distinguished from the former
chapters by having the commands addressed, not to Aaron
and his sons, but to the children of Israel. They speak of
the return from captivity; they support Nehemiah's order
that the wealthy shall not require interest for money lent
to a Jew, or hold a Jew in bond-service for his debts; and
they declare that the tithe of the produce of the land is to
be given to Jehovah. They strictly enforce the law of the
Sabbath, so far that even the land is to have rest on the
seventh year; and after seven such Sabbatical years, that
is on the fiftieth year, there is to be a jubilee, when bond-
servants are to be set free, and the land that has been sold
is to return to its former owner. An oppressed people's
opinion of a man's duty to his fellow-man is likely to be
kinder and more tender than that held by a conquering
nation. And accordingly justice is to be even-handed; a
man is not to be favoured because he is poor, nor because
he is powerful (xix. 15). Riches shall not save a guilty
man from punishment; no one when condemned to death

shall be ransomed by money (xxvii. 29). These chapters
are in every respect more modern in character, and show
a morality more humane, than the earlier parts of the
Mosaic law. They give us the original of the great Christian
precept, "Thou shalt love thy neighbour as thyself" (xix. 18),
a command which would seem not to have been written till
centuries after that out of which it **grew,** "Thou shalt love
Jehovah thy God."

These repeated laws about releasing debtors who **had** sold
themselves into bond-service mark the sad condition of the
poor. The humane law of Exodus xxi. orders that every
such bondservant shall be set free on the seventh year of his
service. But this was much neglected, and the evil had
grown so great, that king Zedekiah, when the nation was in
trouble, had declared them all free on one day; and then
Deuteronomy xv. 1-18 directs that from that time forward
every seventh year shall be a year of release from all debtors.
But this law was as much neglected as the former. After
the return from Babylon, as we learn from Ezekiel xlvi. 17,
a Year of Liberty had been appointed to be kept in the next
generation, probably on the fiftieth year from the **return.**
This year of acceptance by Jehovah we find mentioned in
Isaiah lviii. 5, written probably at that time. Yet later
Nehemiah again directs a general release; and Leviticus xxv.
orders that on the Year of Jubilee which was to return every
fiftieth year all mortgages on land shall be cancelled. This
law may have been meant for the year B.C. 437, the hundredth
year from the return of the captives, when also Isaiah lxi. 1
may have been written. These few hints are all that is
known of the year of release, a year often looked forward to,
which perhaps never arrived.

Leviticus xxi. and xxii. which relate to the Sons of Aaron,
are not like the earlier chapter's directions as to what offerings they are to claim from the people, but are for the most
part regulations as to their own conduct under the new
circumstances, when many irregularities had crept in.

Leviticus xxiii. gives several new orders about the great
feasts. Deuteronomy xvi. had said that the Feast of Weeks
was to be kept seven weeks after the first putting the sickle
into the standing corn, thus making the day vary with the
forwardness of the season. But the new law is that the
seven weeks are to be reckoned from the morrow after the
Sabbath in the Week of Unleavened Bread. At these feasts
the **gifts** to the altar are to be on a very moderate scale, very

different from those of Numbers xxviii. xxix., written when the nation was more prosperous. Here the directions for keeping the feast of Tabernacles or Booths are given twice. In the second, perhaps the later of the two, the people are to rejoice before Jehovah, with palm-branches and willows; and a fanciful reason is given for the crowds who come to the feast dwelling in booths, because when they came out of Egypt they rested in the town of Succoth, or *booths*. Chapter xxiii. further enforces the observance of the day of Atonement as before ordered. But no chief priest is now mentioned. He had become a less important person since the Captivity.

In this chapter of Leviticus we for the first time find a number of weeks counted as of seven days each; they are called perfect or regular weeks, as though to distinguish them from the weeks hitherto spoken of, of which four made a lunar month. Seven of these regular weeks are contained within fifty days. This more exact arrangement of the week may have enabled Nehemiah to require that the Sabbath should be kept with greater strictness.

This change of separating the days of the week from the days of the moon was probably brought about by the civil months being first separated from the lunations in Babylon. The Egyptians from a very early time had disregarded the moon, and counted time by months of thirty days each, with five additional days at the end of the year. The Babylonian astronomers had adopted these exact Egyptian months in the reign of Mardoc Empadus, the friend of king Hezekiah; and very possibly these months were now coming into use in Judea, although we cannot show that to be the case until one hundred and fifty years later.

Leviticus xxv. mentions the Levitical cities, which are also mentioned in the chapters of Joshua and Numbers, which we give to this time. From chapter xxvii. 16, we learn something of the value of silver. In the bargain with the priest for the redemption of a field which had been vowed to Jehovah, barley was to be reckoned at fifty shekels the homer, that is, about eleven shillings the bushel. At the time of the prophet Hosea silver would seem to have been far more valuable.* The reasons given in this chapter of Leviticus against oppressing the poor Israelite are the same as those used by Nehemiah in chapter v. of his book.

* See page 174.

With these chapters of Leviticus we may mention three inserted passages in the Book of Exodus, chapters xvi. 16-30, xxxi. 12-17, and chapter xxxv. 1-3. They are all out of place where they now stand. They contain commands to keep the sabbath, and they give to it a name used only here and in the above mentioned chapters of Leviticus, namely, a Sabbath of rest.

The list of places at which the Israelites encamped on their route out of Egypt in Numbers xxxiii., is of a late date, and may here be mentioned. It seems to be more correct in its geography than the account in the earlier books, which by the map we may learn had been thrown into disorder. It shows that the encampment of the Israelites at the well-known burial place of Taavah and then at Hazeroth, the *Village* of Paran, in Numbers xi. 34, 35, should be placed before the fall of Manna in the fertile valley of Paran in Exodus xvi. 13; and before the arrival at the Mountain of God, in Exodus xix. That this chapter was written by the help of our present books, which it enables us to correct, is shown from the fanciful names given to some of the stations. Thus Rissah, *dew*, is the place where "the dew lay around the camp," Exodus xvi. 13; Haradah, *tremblings*, is where "the people trembled," Exodus xix. 16; Makeheloth, *assemblings*, is where "they assembled themselves," Exodus xxxii. 1; and Tahath, *the bottom*, is "the bottom of the mountain," where Moses broke the Tables of the Law, Exodus xxxii. 19.

This geographical chapter tells us plainly that Serbal was the Mount of God, the Holy Mount of the Book of Exodus. From the numerous inscriptions which the Jewish pilgrims from Egypt had cut upon it, it had gained the name of Sephar, *written*, as in Genesis x. 30, and Job xix. 23. But this later writer calls it Mount Sephar. He was very probably one of those pilgrims; as Numbers xxxiii. 1-49 was certainly written by a traveller, who had walked over the ground from Egypt to the Holy Mount, with the narrative of the Exodus in his hand, to which by his own observation as far as the mountain, and by the help of his imagination afterwards, he added the names of stations which are not in the older narrative.

For a time after the lately-mentioned chapters of Leviticus were written we must claim part at least of Numbers xxxiv. —xxxvi.; because, when the permission to inherit land, given to Zelophehad's daughters, is repeated from Numbers

xxvii. and from Joshua xvii., mention is made of the Jubilee year; and because the daughters with land are now required to marry each within her own tribe, and also because the writer proposes to give to the Levites forty-eight cities, with the pasture lands around them, for their inheritance. The earlier books had **said** that the Levites were to have **no** inheritance in land; and this new proposal, like the proposed **new** division of the **country** among the tribes in Ezekiel xlviii., belongs to a time when the land was thought to have no legal owners. Among these Levitical cities are **to be** counted the six cities of refuge set apart of old that **the** manslayer might flee there for safety from the avenging **next** of kin. These are first mentioned in Deuteronomy xix.

As long as the nation was independent, the writers **had** described its boundaries **very** much **as** they found them. Thus Genesis xv. 18, written in David's reign, after he had **defeated the** Amalekites, claimed their desert coast for Abraham's children, and placed the boundary of the Promised Land at the valley of the Nile. Exodus xxiii. 31, written in Jehoshaphat's reign, and Deuteronomy xi. 24, Joshua i. 4, and xv. 1, of the last days of the monarchy, are more moderate, and do not claim the desert; which so far as it had a master belonged to the king of Egypt. But now that Palestine, Egypt, and the desert between them, are all under the sway of the Persian king, the Jewish writers are **at** liberty to say that the southern desert belongs **to** their country; and Numbers xxxiv. claims for Israel the country of the Amalekites to the valley of Lower Egypt, as does Joshua xv. 2-4, which may have been added to that book at **this** time. In this last passage we may understand Azmon, *force*, Karkaa, *the floor*, Adar, *the area*, to be the same places as Dophkah, Alush, and Rephidim, of Numbers xxxiii. 12-14. Both sets of names may belong to the copper mines of Sinai.

Numbers xi. 16-30, appoints a body of seventy elders to assist Moses in governing the people, and it seems to belong to Nehemiah's time. Ezekiel in a vision had seen seventy elders unlawfully burning incense before the altar, thus letting us know that such was the number of attending priests in the Temple in the reign of Zedekiah; and in Exodus xxiv. 1-11, when Moses reads to the people out of **the** Book of the Covenant, their appointment seems to be defended against Ezekiel's blame. But neither in Ezekiel nor **in** that chapter of Exodus are these elders a body sharing authority with king **or** chief priest; nor have we under **the** monarchy met with any such council. Ezra, however, governed with the help of princes and rulers; and Nehemiah associated with himself the priests, the Levites, and the chiefs of the people, and thus laid the foundation of the High Council of seventy, which we hear of in after centuries by its Greek name of Sanhedrim. This body seems to be more particularly shadowed forth in Numbers xi. 16-30, wherein Jehovah orders Moses to appoint such a body of seventy rulers, who are at the same time prophets on whom the spirit of Jehovah **rested**. The passage in Exodus may have been written at any time after Deuteronomy or the Book of the Covenant **was** written; but the passage in Numbers belongs to the time of Nehemiah, and is further remarkable for its allowing the liberty of prophesying to all who claimed to have the spirit of Jehovah; and this suits better with the governorship of Nehemiah the cup-bearer than with that of Ezra the high priest.

Numbers xv. 32-36, which relates how **a** man was stoned to death for picking up sticks upon the Sabbath, may be given to this time when Nehemiah was endeavouring to enforce the observance of that **day**.

From the laws which we have lately mentioned, we note how far opinions about criminal justice had changed for the better since the time of David and Solomon. In David's reign a crime committed was looked at chiefly, if not wholly, as an injury done to a fellow man, and to him it was to be recompensed. If he were slain, his death was to be avenged by his next of kin, the avenger of blood, whose rights and duties were both acknowledged.* The state itself took little notice of the quarrel. From the avenger of blood, a man who had slain another, might sometimes escape by flight to **the** altar.† But the **priests at** the altar could not always **save** him. The Judgments, however, which we have given **to** Jehoshaphat's reign, declare that no man shall be taken from the altar by the avenger, except for wilful murder.‡ But the line between murder and manslaughter was not very clearly drawn. From the revenge of the next-of-kin a rich man could often escape by the payment of money.§ A sum of money would clear him of the crime; but then as the crime was also an offence against God, the man-slayer, by a law which we have given to Jehoash's reign, was not only to recompense the injured family, but to bring a ram of atone-

* 2 Sam. xiv. 11.   † 1 Kings i. 51.   ‡ Exod. xxi. 12-14.
§ Prov. xiii. 8.

ment to the priest; and if the man slain had no kindred, then the recompense also was to be paid to the priest.* After the Captivity, in order to lessen the evils of revenge, six Levitical cities of refuge were appointed, beside the altar at Jerusalem; and to **these** also the man-slayer might **run to** save himself **from the** next-of-kin.† Society then began to feel that it **had to** bear **its share of** guilt for the crime committed; and **when** a **dead body is** found, and the murderer is not discovered, the **nearest** city is to make its offering to the altar, as an atonement.‡ Hence as society felt injured by the crime, then at length **it** was ordered that no ransom should be allowed to save a murderer **from** death.§ The Persians **seem** to have taken very little part in the administration of justice, confining their care to the collection of the tribute.

Joshua xx. and xxi. give the names of the Levitical cities, and **quote** the above-mentioned chapters of Numbers, namely xxxiv.—xxxvi. as Joshua's authority for giving them to the Levites. An earlier chapter, Joshua xiii. 33, had said that the Levites were to have no inheritance in land. These two chapters were added a little later than the passages relating to Caleb's right to Hebron, because they give the town of Hebron to the priests, the Sons of Aaron, and leave to Caleb only the fields in **the** neighbourhood.

Joshua xxii. describes the Eastern Israelites as building **an** altar to Jehovah near Gilgal, within the land of Canaan, near the southern ford of the Jordan, and at **the same** time promising not to be so rebellious against the one allowed altar as to offer sacrifices upon it. They say that they only meant it as a pattern of the true altar to Jehovah. This **is** an acknowledgment of the importance of the one altar in Jerusalem, such as does not appear in the original Book of Joshua.

After the **Book** of Joshua had been written, the **Book of** Judges **was** adapted as a continuation to it. Thus **Judges** ii. 6—iii. 6, followed upon Joshua xxiv. 28. The **inter**mediate sentences, part in one book, and part in the other, are yet later additions. The writer who thus united the two books may also have introduced the name of Jehovah into the older parts of the Book of Judges; since we now find it

---

* Numb. v. 5-8.
† Deut. xix. 1-13; Numb. xxxv. 9-24; Josh. xx.
‡ Deut. xxi. 1-9.   § Lev. xxiv. 17; Numb. xxxv. 31.

there more frequently than it is likely to have been in the
original work.   The governorship of Nehemiah was a time
in which much was done in editing the various Books, and
putting them into their present shape ; hence the few words
at the beginning and end of these **Books** may be **of** his
time.

Here we may mention chapters i.—iv. 43 of Deuteronomy,
which a **late** editor placed at the **beginning** of that book
as **an** introduction.   They formed no part **of** the Book of
the Covenant brought to king Josiah.   They rehearse the
events in Exodus and Numbers.   The writer had not got
before him the list of journeys made by the Israelites in
Numbers xxxiii. ; as he says in chapter i. 2, that there were
only eleven days' journeys between Horeb and Kadesh,
whereas that list contains several more.   Again he sends
the Israelites along the coast by the town of Dizahab, a
place not mentioned in that list.

The editors, or psssibly the one editor, who wrote the
Introduction to Judges, the Introduction to Deuteronomy,
and added several passages to Numbers and Joshua, had a
strong partiality for the towns of Hebron and Debir ; and
his great hero, whom he even classes with Joshua the conqueror of Canaan, is Caleb the son of Jephunneh, who, we
are told, "wholly followed Jehovah."   The writer meant to
do honour to some living Calebite family, owners of property
around Hebron ; but who they were does not now appear.

We are familiar with the words Rock and Fortress as
names, or rather titles, of God ; but less so with the word
Portion.   Several of the Psalms say of Jehovah, "Thou
art my portion," an expression which is scarcely figurative.[*]
In a late addition to the Book of Jeremiah, however, the
word is used as a title ; and he says, "The portion of Jacob
is **not** like these [idols] ; **for** He is the former of all things ;
Jehovah of hosts is his name."[†]   Again, in the last-mentioned **part of** the Book of Isaiah, the word Portion is used
for "god," and the idolater is told, "Among the smooth
stones of the valley is thy Portion [or god].   These, these
are thy lot, and to them hast thou poured a drink-offering,
thou hast offered a meal-offering."[‡]   So, lastly, in the
Introduction to Deuteronomy, we find that the word had by
this time gained a fixed meaning ; and when the Jews are for-

---

[*] Psalm xvi. 5; lxxiii. 26; cxix. 57; cxlii. 5.   Lam. iii. 24.
[†] Jerem. x. 16; li. 19.   [‡] Isaiah lvii. 6.

bidden to worship the sun, moon, and stars, they are told that Jehovah had "portioned out" them to the other peoples.*

To the time of Nehemiah we may give the two Books of Chronicles, and the book which bears his own name. The Books of Chronicles contain fewer marks of having been altered or added to after they were first written than most books in the Bible. They seem to be the work of one writer, with the exception of the genealogies, which have received both alterations and additions. The genealogy of David's family is continued through the kings of Judah to Zerubbabel, who came up from captivity in the reign of Cyrus, to Hattush, who afterwards came up from Babylon with Ezra, and it ends with the great nephews of Hattush.† The descendants of Ezra are mentioned down to his great grand-children.‡ It is possible that Nehemiah may have been the author of these two books, as he wrote a volume of Commentaries in addition to his History ; and these Books of Chronicles may be that volume.§ Nehemiah, though not a priest, had a strong leaning to the Levitical law ; and the priestly bias of these books is most certain. The writer seems to have had in his hand the Book of Genesis, the Books of Samuel, and the Books of Kings, and also other original authorities, such as

The Book of Samuel the Seer,
The Book of Nathan the Prophet,
The Book of Gad the Seer,
The Book of Ahijah the Shilonite.   [Nebat,
The Visions of Iddo the Seer against Jeroboam the Son of
The Book of Iddo the Seer concerning Genealogies,
The Commentary of the Prophet Iddo,
The Book of Shemaiah the Prophet,
The Book of Jehu the Son of Hanani,
The Sayings of the Seers,
The Book of the Kings of Israel,
The Acts of the Kings of Israel,
The Commentary of the Book of Kings,
A History by Isaiah the Prophet, containing Uzziah's reign,
The Vision of Isaiah the Prophet, and
The Books of the Kings of Judah and Israel.
These last two may be the books that we now possess.

The Books of Chronicles are confined almost exclusively

---

* Deut. iv. 19.   † 1 Chron. iii. 24.
‡ 1 Chron. iv. 19.   § 2 Maccab. ii. 13.

22 *

to the tribe of Judah. Though they begin with Adam they
do not mention the Israelites' residence in Egypt, nor the
Exodus, nor the Judges, nor Eli's nor Samuel's rule. They
slightly mention Saul's death, and then give the history of
the reigns of David and his successors on the throne of
Judah, omitting the history of the northern tribes. These
books, though often using the very words of the Books of
Kings, differ from them in the spirit in which they are
written. They are evidently less impartial and less trustworthy; they strongly favour the priests, whom they style
Sons of Aaron, and they omit to mention the faults of the
favourite kings. But they add some few valuable facts not
mentioned in the other books, such as the invasion of Judea
by Zerah the Ethiopian, in the reign of Asa, and the
conquest of king Manasseh by the king of Assyria, and his
captivity in Babylon, and his release. They introduce
many modern thoughts into the older parts of the history,
making Solomon, when dedicating the Temple, speak of the
return from Captivity, and quote two lines from Psalm
cxxxvi., and four lines from Psalm cxxxii.

David's priests, Zadok and Abiathar, whose genealogies
in Solomon's time were carefully traced up to Eli, as we
have shown in page 81, are now in the Chronicles both
brought from Aaron; and Eli is never mentioned. Thus
Zadok, in 1 Chronicles vi. 8, is made a son of Aaron through
Eleazar; and Ahimelech, the father of Abiathar, is, in 1
Chronicles xxiv. 3, a son of Aaron through Ithamar. Again,
the prophet Samuel in the earlier history is an Ephraimite,
and his name is not there made use of to give rank to any
of the priesthood; but in 1 Chronicles vi. 33, he is a Levite;
and the names of himself, his son Joel, and his five forefathers, are brought into the pedigree of Heman the singer,
which through them is traced up to Kohath the son of Levi.
Again, in the earlier history, in the Books of Samuel,
David's faithful body-guard were foreign mercenaries, men
of Gath; but in 1 Chronicles xii. 8 they are his countrymen,
sons of Gad; and that the change is not made by the mere
carelessness of the scribe is shown by the first body of men
being friends of the Philistines, and by the second having
come from the other side of the Jordan. From these and
many other places in which the Chronicles differ from the
earlier history, it may be easily shown that these later books
are written with a strong national and priestly bias, and
that they cannot be relied upon when they contradict the

more impartial Books of Kings. On comparing the list of
Levitical cities in 1 Chronicles vi. with that in Joshua xx.
xxi., we find reason to think that the list in Joshua is the
original, and that the list in Chronicles is an incomplete
and perhaps incorrect copy. The Chronicles speak of the
prophet Elijah as living in Jehoram's reign, but do not
mention the marvellous events of his life which we now
read of in the Books of Kings. Nor do they mention the
prophet Elisha. The last two verses in the Chronicles are
borrowed from the beginning of Ezra.

It is only in a few cases that we know enough of the
Jewish families to understand the genealogies at the
beginning of the Chronicles. At the time of the Captivity,
and after the return, the Pharezites were the chief people in
Jesusalem next to the priests;* and hence when, for the
first time, a pedigree was to be found for king David, he
was said to have come from Pharez the son of Judah,†
notwithstanding the slight thrown upon Pharez in Genesis
xxxviii. The history of David's rise, and his birth at
Bethlehem, would, on the other hand, have led us to
consider him a Calebite. At the time of the Captivity,
Ishmael the son of Elishama was one of the most determined
enemies to any peace with Babylon;‡ and now Elishama
has a pedigree given to him equal to that of the kings and
chief priests. He is said to be descended from Jerameel,
the supposed father of the Jerameelites, a tribe in the South
Country.§ Another family belonging to the Calebites of
the South Country, which was lately important enough to
add a number of passages to the Pentateuch and the Book
of Joshua, in praise of Caleb the son of Jephunneh, who
" wholly followed Jehovah," is now lost sight of, and Caleb
the son of Jephunneh is mentioned at the beginning of the
Chronicles, but without forefathers, and without descendants.‖ Another Caleb seems to have robbed him of his
importance.¶

The genealogy of the chief priests seems to be in the early
part imaginary, and in the later part both incorrect and
incomplete. Thus Hilkiah the son of Shallum, is made the
same person as Hilkiah the father of Azariah, while two
generations should be placed between them; and again we

---

* 1 Chron. ix. 4. † 1 Chron. ii. 15.
‡ Jerem. xli. § 1 Chron. ii. 41.
‖ 1 Chron. iv. 15. ¶ 1 Chron. ii. 42, and 50.

have no mention of Jehoida and his son Zechariah, the priests in the reign of Jehoash.

The Chronicles were written before the Book of Nehemiah, as we learn from finding 2 Chronicles viii. 14 quoted in Nehemiah xii. 45.

The Book of Nehemiah is one of the most interesting of the historical Books of the Bible. It contains that good man's account of his attempts to serve his unhappy countrymen. We admire his patient zeal, his disinterestedness, his good judgment, his simple manner of telling his story; we regret nothing but his strong prejudices. His obtaining for the citizens of Jerusalem permission to rebuild the city walls, though it was no step towards national independence, was a great comfort to them, and a protection against lawless marauders. The walls were not built as a defence against an army, but they allowed the inhabitants to sleep more quietly, and with less fear of robbery.

But this book is in a sadly confused state. The first part is written by Nehemiah; then, in chapter vii. 6-73, we have a quotation from the Book of Ezra relating to Zerubbabel's doings. This is continued in chapter viii., by a quotation relating to Ezra's doings, of which verses 1-12 are to be found in the Greek, 1 Esdras, and for the rest of the chapter we have no original. Of this we remark that the word "Nehemiah," in verse 9, is not in 1 Esdras; and it has been added by a scribe who thought the chapter related to Nehemiah's doings. The rest of the book relates to Nehemiah's time, except that in chapter xii. 1-26 we have a list of the priests and Levites who came up to Jerusalem with Zerubbabel, but continued by additions down to the time of Alexander the Great. Chapter xiii. 7 to the end, relates to when Nehemiah came to Jerusalem a second time.

In the Book of Nehemiah we for the first time meet with the word " Jew," with the limited meaning which it bears in the New Testament. " There was a cry," says Nehemiah, " of the people and their wives against their brethren, the Jews." Nine-tenths of the population, on the return of the captives from Babylon, were in religious matters declared not to be Jews. They were indeed called upon to bear their share of the cost of the priesthood, as being " strangers within thy city gates;" but the full religious privileges were denied them. Fortunately in civil matters their Persian masters knew little of this jealous division, except so far as it insured the nation's quiet servitude.

In Jeremiah xvii. 19-27, which forbids burdens being brought through the gates of Jerusalem on the Sabbath day, we find words put into the prophet's mouth, which agree so exactly with the command of Nehemiah to the same purpose, and which so little agree with Jeremiah's own views, that we may give them to this time.

The few words in the prophecy of Micah vii. 11-13, which speak of the walls of Jerusalem being rebuilt, may also have been added to that prophet's writings at this time.

It is to this half century, to the time of Nehemiah, that we must give another portion of the Book of Isaiah, written by an author whom, for distinction's sake, we may call the Isaiah of the Rebuilding, who for the beauty of his style and breadth of his religion deserves to be classed with the Isaiah of the Return Home. These are chapters lx.—lxii., which are expressive of delight at the mildness of the foreign despots, and at the permission given to build up the walls of Jerusalem. " Arise [O Jerusalem], shine, for thy light is come ; and the glory of Jehovah is risen upon thee." . . . "The sons of foreigners shall build up thy walls, and their kings shall minister unto thee. . . . I will make thine overseers peace, and thy tribute-gatherers righteousness. Violence shall no more be heard in thy land, wasting nor destruction within thy borders ; but thou shalt call thy walls Salvation, and thy city gates Praise." The people are promised not national glory, but that the year of acceptance by Jehovah is at hand. He may be supposed to point to the Year of Liberty ordered at this time in Leviticus **xxv. 10. The** prophet's words are :—

" Jehovah hath sent me to bind up the broken-hearted, to proclaim liberty to the captives, and the opening of the prison to them that are bound ; to proclaim the Year of Acceptance by Jehovah, and the day of our God's vengeance " (lxi. 1).

This may have been written shortly before B.C. 438, the hundredth year after the return from Babylon. We do not hear that such a year of release was ever kept for the benefit of the poor who had sold themselves to the rich, though we found it mentioned fifty years earlier in Ezek. xlvi. 17, and perhaps in Isaiah lviii. 6.

In these chapters of Isaiah the priesthood is forgotten, and the people are to be called priests of Jehovah, and ministers of our God ; and Zion's righteousness is to go forth as brightness, and its salvation as a lamp that burneth.

Isaiah lvi. 1-8, may be by the same writer. It uses the same thought, that salvation is near to come, and righteousness to be revealed. It also belongs to the time of Nehemiah, when the Sabbath is to be kept more strictly; and it may be compared to Jeremiah xvii. 19-27, which we have given to this time. The permission for eunuchs to enter the Temple seems to have been written in favour of Nehemiah himself, who had been chamberlain to the Persian king. This permission, though it was limited to "an appointed place" in the Temple-yard, as we know that Nehemiah would have understood it, yet is in direct contradiction to Deuteronomy xxiii. 1.

To the time of Nehemiah, but after the Chronicles were written, and before the Book of Malachi, we must give the history of Elijah, and that of his servant and successor, Elisha. The name of Elijah is quoted by no writer earlier than Malachi and the Chronicler; and that of Elisha seems to have been unknown even to the Chronicler. These two lives very much interrupt the narrative at the end of the First Book of Kings, and at the beginning of the Second, into which they have been woven very awkwardly.

Elijah is a native of Gilead, a prophet of Jehovah, who reproves Ahab, king of Israel, for his worship of Baal, and threatens him with a famine for three years. During that time he makes a widow's pitcher of meal and cruse of oil furnish her with an unfailing supply of food, and he heals her sick son by his prayers.* He challenges four hundred and fifty prophets of Baal to a trial of whose god is the true god, by every one preparing an ox upon an altar for a burnt-offering on Mount Carmel, and praying to heaven for the fire. The priests of Baal try in vain to burn their offerings; but Elijah obtains the fire that he prays for. It consumes his offering, and then he slays the prophets of Baal.† Queen Jezebel then tries to kill Elijah, but he escapes to Beer-sheba in the south of Judah, and goes on a pilgrimage to the Mount of God in Horeb, where he hides himself in a cave. Then we have that grandest of descriptions, an example of the sublime in writing, which surpasses that which we have admired in the Book of Nahum. In that the description rises from a state of quiet to one of noise and action. In this, on the other hand, it rises from noise and action, to rest and silence. Perhaps no other example can be

---

* 1 **Kings xvii.**   † 1 Kings xviii.

shown of a writer venturing so slowly and so boldly to raise our expectations, and then wholly satisfying them :—

> " Jehovah passed by, and a great and strong wind rent the mountains and brake in pieces the rocks before Jehovah ; but Jehovah was not in the wind.—And after the wind there was an earthquake ; but Jehovah was not in the earthquake.—And after the earthquake there was a fire, but Jehovah was not in the fire.—And after the fire there was a still small voice.—And it was so when Elijah heard it, that he wrapped his face in his mantle and went out and stood at the entrance of the cave."

In this remarkable passage we see the softer view of the Almighty now taken by the Israelites. We see, also, that poetic genius was not dead among the Hebrew writers. The language contains no finer piece of writing than the above. But it was like the glow in the western sky shortly before sunset. **Whatever** literary excellence we meet with after this time is of another character.

Elijah on departing from Horeb meets with Elisha, whom he takes as his servant.* Elijah afterwards reproves Ahab and Jezebel for their crime in causing the death of Naboth, that they might obtain his vineyard.† When the next king of Israel, Ahaziah, sends a captain with fifty men to seize Elijah, perhaps to punish him for his bold reproofs, Elijah calls down fire from heaven, which consumes them. He does the same with the second troop that is sent for him ; but he spares the third troop, and goes with them to the king. When he has occasion to cross the Jordan he divides the waters by a stroke of his mantle, and he and his servant Elisha pass over on dry ground. He is soon afterwards taken up to heaven in a chariot of fire, without dying naturally ; and the sons of the prophets send fifty men who seek for him during three days in vain.

The history of Elijah being taken up to heaven alive is not mentioned in the Chronicles; we therefore place it between the time of the Chronicles and the time of Malachi. It led to a belief that he would some day return to earth again. This belief was either created or strengthened by the prophecy of Malachi ; it continued to be held for many centuries, and by no means died out among the Jews when the Christians said that it had been fulfilled in the person of John the Baptist.

When Elijah is taken up to heaven his spirit then rests on **his** servant Elisha, and Elisha's doings are related as equally

---

* 1 Kings xix.   † 1 Kings xxi.

miraculous. He makes Jericho an oasis in the desert, and its spring of water sweet, which had been bad. He curses forty-two children who had mocked him, and they are devoured by two she-bears.* His other doings are equally improbable, and equally foreign from the history of the times. He dies in the reign of Jehoash, the grandson of Jehu.†

The fertilizing the valley of Jericho, which is here given to the miraculous power of Elisha in Ahab's reign, was probably due to the Persian government in hopes of profit from the plantation of palm trees, which then gave a new name to Jericho, "the city of the palm trees." Moreover, the fragrance of the trees made a slight change in the old name. Jericho, as usually spelt, may have meant the *hamlet-city*, but by the insertion of a letter it was made to mean *they scatter scent*.

Another part of Elisha's life seems very particularly to belong to this time. When Elisha gives Naaman permission to accompany his master into the Temple of Rimmon, and there to bow down before the idol, we read of the only case in which a Hebrew writer has shown the least willingness to excuse the yielding to the pressure put upon them by their conquerors.‡ The good Nehemiah, while living in the palace at Susa as the cup-bearer and favourite of king Artaxerxes, had no doubt often bowed his head in seeming worship in the Persian Temple; and the writer may have added to the Book of Kings this story of Naaman, to comfort Nehemiah in his doubts as to whether he had done right, or to apologize to others for his conduct. But the Persians were not idolaters, and there may have been nothing to offend Nehemiah's conscience when he accompanied Artaxerxes to his devotions.

When in the life of Elijah we read of four hundred prophets prophesying from noon to sunset, and in the Chronicles, of men who prophesied on the harp, we see that the word prophet had gained a new meaning. Before the Captivity it had meant a *ready speaker*, who gave religious and political advice to the people. After the return from Babylon it further meant one who *foretold the future*. And now in the time of Nehemiah it also means a *singer* who sang the praise of Jehovah. In Numbers xi. 16-30 also, which we have already given to this time, we see that this act of prophesy-

---

* 2 Kings i., ii.   † 2 Kings xiii. **20.**
‡ **2 Kings v.** 18, 19.

ing or praising God was not to be limited to the priests;
but Moses wishes that every one should so prophesy. Thus
when the custom of sacrificing on the High Places was gone
by, the custom of meeting to worship God by singing his
praise, had taken its place; and as we may suppose that this
was often done at the same time that the people met to hear
the Law read and explained, we gain by conjecture a further
picture of the synagogues, of which as yet we have had no
mention in history.

Chapter xiii. of the First Book of Kings with its history
of the Man of God, who prophesied in the reign of Jeroboam
that the altar at Bethel should be destroyed by king Josiah,
might be written at any time after Josiah came to the
throne. But the character of the narrative, with the mention
of "the cities of Samaria," as a name for the cities of the
northern kingdom, place it at some time after the return
from captivity. This old altar at Beth-el, at first dedicated
to El, or *God*, had been defiled by king Jeroboam with one
of his golden calves; it had been changed into an altar to
Jehovah by permission of the Assyrians, when Israel was
taken into captivity; then, being a rival to that on mount
Moriah, it had been denounced by the prophets Amos and
Hosea; it had been supported by a sentence added to the
Life of Abraham, and by another added to the Life of
Jacob; it had been destroyed by king Josiah; and lastly, its
destruction was justified, and said to have been foretold in
this chapter of the Book of Kings.

From the Lives of Elijah and Elisha, and the doings of
other men of God, which have been added to the Books of
Kings, we see that a new view of the religious life had
lately reached Judea, perhaps from India, or perhaps from
the Thebaid; teaching that a man who would be perfect
should separate himself from the affairs of this world, and
give himself up to solitude, to meditation, and to the
practice of self-denial. The holy man of God is not to be
a priest, nor is he to be an eloquent writer and a cultivated
man, like the great prophets who lived under the monarchy.
He is to shun the cities, to live in a cave, to drink water
from the brook, and to eat such bread as the ravens or the
angels should bring to him. He will be known by sight as
a hairy man, having no clothing but a leathern apron about
his loins. He will sit upon the ground in silent prayer, with
his face between his knees. He will defend himself in his
solitude by calling down fire from heaven against those who

would hurt him, or a bear from the woods against children
who should laugh at him. When he travels he lives on
charity, and he repays kindness by working miraculous
cures. He refuses all wealth when offered; and if he is
not, before he dies, carried up to heaven in a whirlwind, his
body, when he is dead, works miracles. Such at a later age
were the Essenes, and such was John the Baptist.

The prophecy of Malachi is of the time of Nehemiah.
Like Isaiah lxiii. 1-6, the writer tells us that the mountains
of Edom have been made a waste, and his heritage been
given to the jackals of the desert. He complains that the
priests and the people bring worthless animals to the Temple
for their offerings, such as they would not think of offering
to their Pasha; and that no one will open or shut the Temple
doors without pay. He may have approved of Nehemiah's
command that they should not marry foreigners, but he does
not approve of this being understood to mean that they
should put away the foreign wives whom they have married.
He blames, indeed, Judah, for having married the daughter
of a foreign god; but then he warns every man not to deal
treacherously against the wife of his youth, and says that
she is the wife of his covenant, and that the putter away is
hateful to Jehovah, and yet further, that putting away their
wives in the name of religion has covered the altar of Jehovah
with tears, with weeping, and with groans. He charges the
people to remember the law of Moses, with the statutes and
judgments, thus describing the Pentateuch. He is the only
one of the prophets that does so. He threatens the people
with a coming day of punishment upon the wicked, but
when, to those who fear the name of Jehovah, the sun of
righteousness shall arise with healing on its wings; and he
promises that, before that time, the prophet Elijah shall
return to earth to bring them back to their duty. He thus
puts forth a promise quite new to the Hebrew writings.
The former prophets had taught the people to look for a
prince of the line of David who should again raise up the
nation to its former glory. But in the face of the great
empires by which the Jews were now surrounded, national
independence was hardly to be hoped for. Hence the
wished-for help is to come in the form of a spiritual teacher
sent from heaven.

In Malachi iii. 1, Elijah is "the messenger of the
Covenant which ye delight in;" a title borrowed from
1 Kings xix. 10-14, where he complains that the Children of

Israel had forsaken Jehovah's Covenant. **He** is also called "the master whom ye are seeking," from 2 Kings ii. 16, 17, where after he is carried up to heaven he is sought **for** in vain for three days in the neighbourhood of Jericho.

He seems also to be the "messenger whom I am sending" of Isaiah xlii. 19, and he is to "prepare the way of Jehovah," **as** in Isaiah xl. 3. His Temple, or palace, to which he is to come suddenly, may be the castle in the palm-plantation lately mentioned, near to Jericho, where he had been sought for.

Whether Malachi, *my messenger*, is the author's name is doubtful. Perhaps the **book** received its name from its relating to "my messenger," as Elijah is called in chapter iii. The writer was a priest. He complains that God is cheated in the matter of tithes, which were very little paid when the people were poor, and there was no power to enforce their payment. The Persian tax-gatherer claimed all that could be spared.

And here we may take a review of the history of the tithes, founded upon our attempted chronological arrangement of the books which mention them. They are first mentioned in David's reign, when Abraham, the representative **of** the nation, is said to have paid tithes to Melchizedek, the representative of David. That they were a royal tax, and at that time a new tax, is explained in the Book of Samuel, which was written in Solomon's reign. This book, speaking about Saul's election as king, makes the prophet Samuel warn the people that, if they appoint a king, he will **claim** for himself a tithe of the produce of their fields, **of the sheep** as well as of the corn. The victuals which Solomon's officers gathered for him were probably the produce of the tithe. After this **we** do not again hear of the tithes for several centuries. They are not mentioned in the Book of Exodus. While that was being written they were probably being paid very regularly as a royal tax. Nor are they mentioned in the early part of the Book of Leviticus. When that was being written the power of the king was very much lessened; the taxes could **not** be collected without the help of the Levites; they were passing out of the king's hands; and after a time the Levites claimed the tithes as their own property. Numbers xviii., written between the reigns of Jehoash and Hezekiah, gives the tithe of the corn and grape juice to the Levites for their maintenance, in addition to the offerings of the worshippers, upon which they had hitherto lived; and it

gives the tithe of the tithe for the support of the priests; and
the Chronicler tells us that the tithes were then in the hands
of the Levites. Moreover, in the reign of Hezekiah, when
the northern kingdom had been carried into captivity, the
prophet Amos informs us that some of those who were left
behind, and had their own priests, paid their tithe every
third year at the town of Bethel. This was only paid in
good will. When Deuteronomy xii. was written, in the reign
of Josiah, the power of the priests and Levites was very
much lessened. They could no longer claim the tithes as
their own. They only hoped for a share of them; and the
new law advises, rather than commands, the owner to
consume them as a peace-offering or love-feast with his
friends and the Levites at the national altar. But it was
soon found necessary to make this demand upon the people
lighter; and Deuteronomy xiv., added, perhaps, in the next
reign, directs that this love-feast is to be for two years only
at the national altar, and on the third year at the owner's
own city. During the Captivity, and after the return home,
the poverty of the country made the Levites turn to cultivate
the soil for themselves; there was no power to enforce the
payment of tithes, and very few were then paid. The
chapters added to the Book of Ezekiel under Zerubbabel
only propose that a sixtieth part of the corn, a hundredth
part of the oil, and one in two hundred of the lambs should
be given to the Temple as a heave-offering. When we come
to Ezra's time, Deuteronomy xxvi. limits the payment of
tithes to every third year, which is called the year of tithing;
and then the owner is only asked to share them with his
friends and the strangers and the Levites in his own city—
he is not told to carry them up to Jerusalem. This makes
the payment quite as light as that proposed in Ezekiel xlv.
Nehemiah, however, in better times, boldly attempted to
revive the old law of Numbers xviii., and called upon the
people to give the tithe of the corn, the grape-juice, and the
oil to the Levites, who were to give the tithe of the tithe, as
before, to the priests. Then we have a law, which may be
of Nehemiah's time, in Leviticus xxvii., which explains how
the tithe on produce may be redeemed for money, while the
tithe on calves and lambs, now mentioned for the first time
since Solomon's reign, may not be so redeemed. But Malachi
lets us understand that the old laws and the new laws had
alike fallen into disuse. A few zealous persons may have

paid tithes in one or other of the above forms; but by the people at large that duty was neglected.

The concluding lines of Psalm li. declare their date as belonging to the time of Nehemiah, by speaking of the city walls as likely to be rebuilt :—

> Do good in thy **good** pleasure unto **Zion,**
> Build thou the walls of Jerusalem.
> Then shalt thou be pleased with sacrifices of righteousness,
> With burnt-offerings and whole burnt-offerings;
> Then shall bullocks be offered up on thine altar.

These words remind us that **the** wish for the ceremonial in religion had revived since the time of Isaiah, Jeremiah, and Deuteronomy. But the greater **part** of the Psalm is probably by a different writer, and of **a** rather earlier time, and of a very different opinion about the value of burnt-offerings; as, like Isaiah, he considers that repentance, not sacrifice, is what God requires of the sinner.

Psalm cxlvii. speaks of the walls of Jerusalem as having been rebuilt :—

> Praise Jehovah, O Jerusalem,
> Praise thy God, O Zion.
> For he strengtheneth the bars of thy gates;
> He blesseth thy children within thee.

This Psalm begins and ends with the words Hallelu-Jah, or *praise ye Jehovah*, as also do many of these later Psalms.

Another class of Psalms, which belong to a time later than the return from Captivity, is known by their drawing a distinction between the Israelites and those that fear Jehovah. By these latter words are meant all those who worshipped with the Jews, who would have called themselves Jews if they had been allowed, but who were pushed aside by their proud superiors and masters as Gentiles, as Samaritans, as the strangers who sojourned among them.

Of this class is Psalm cxviii., which was written to be sung in parts at one of the national feasts :—

> Let Israel now say
>   that His kindness endureth for ever.
> Let the house of Aaron now say
>   that His kindness endureth for ever.
> Let them that fear Jehovah now say
>   that His kindness endureth for ever.

So is Psalm cxv., which was also sung in parts :—

> Let Israel trust in Jehovah,
>> He is their help and their shield.
> Let the house of Aaron trust in Jehovah,
>> He is their help and their shield.
> Let them that fear Jehovah trust in Jehovah,
>> He is their help and their shield.

Here the Levites are not distinguished from the priests; but in **Psalm** cxxxv. **we** have four classes of men :—

> O house of Israel, bless ye Jehovah,
> O house of Aaron, bless ye Jehovah,
> O house of Levi, bless ye Jehovah,
> Ye that fear Jehovah, bless ye Jehovah.

It was the feeling here described which led to the forbidding a large part of the population of Jerusalem from entering the courts of the Temple on the east and west of the Altar. The space on the north of the Altar, to which alone strangers were admitted, was, after a time, called the **Court of** the Gentiles. It is "the appointed place" of Isaiah **lvi. 5. It** was used as a market-place; and though it was part **of** Mount Moriah, some of the **more** prejudiced Jews at times declared **that** it was no part **of the** Holy Place. It was in contradiction **to** this opinion that chapter xliii. 12 of Ezekiel, written before the Temple had been rebuilt, **but** when its restoration was hoped for, had promised that the whole top of the hill should be most holy. The **time** of Ezra and Nehemiah is strongly marked by the revival of the priesthood, as shown in these Psalms. The priests had been called the Sons of Aaron in the early chapters of Leviticus; but since the religious changes which followed the Assyrian invasion **in** Hezekiah's reign, we have not met with that title until we come to these Psalms and the Books of Chronicles and of Nehemiah.

When the Jews had become acquainted with a larger portion of our globe, with nations not mentioned in Genesis x., **a** new opinion shows itself in their writings about the races of men. We have traces of this as early as the reign of Hezekiah. They had discovered that the Book of Genesis gave too narrow a view of the origin of mankind; and some writers began to make a division between the Sons of Adam, meaning themselves, and the Sons of Men, meaning the rest of the human family. Psalm lxii. clearly distinguishes between Sons of Adam and Sons of Men, saying :—

> Truly the Sons of Adam are vanity,
> The Sons of Men are falsehood.
> In the balance they are together lighter than vanity.

Here, however, we are not told to what race either name belongs. In Psalm iv. the writer reproachfully calls his enemies "Sons of men," as if he were a Son of Adam. So Wisdom, speaking in the Introduction to Proverbs, chapter viii. 31, says, "My delights are with the Sons of Adam." The Elohistic Psalm lxvi., written after the return home, says :—

> Come ye, and consider the works of God ;
> He was terrible in his doings for the Sons of **Adam**.
> He turned **the sea** into dry land ;
> They passed **over** the river on foot.

Again, Psalm xxxvi., **which we have given to the time of Ezra, or later,** says:—

> **How** excellent is thy loving kindness, O God ;
> And the Sons of Adam trust in the shade of thy wings ;
> They are watered with the fatness of thy House.

In both these cases this name of Sons of Adam is strictly limited to the Israelites ; it cannot even be allowed to include the whole of the Semitic race. In the Song of Moses we ought probably to give the same limited meaning to the name of Sons of Adam ; thus :—

> When the Most High gave inheritance to the Nations,
> When he separated the Sons of Adam,
> He set the boundaries of the peoples
> According to the number of the Children of Israel.*

In Psalm xlix., also, the name of Sons of Adam is used very distinctly for a part, and a part only, of the human family. But here, as in Psalm lxii., it does not appear to what races it is limited, though it includes the upper and more favoured ; thus :—

> Give ear, all ye inhabitants of the world,
> **Sons** of Adam, and Sons of Men, rich and poor together.

The Talmud agrees with this, and says in the treatise Baba Mezia,† that the Israelites alone are to be called Sons of Adam. The poor of the land, nine-tenths of the population of Palestine, were thus after the Return from the Captivity denied that more honourable title ; and this may explain how Jesus in humility took upon himself the name of the Son of Man, perhaps even in contrast to the prophet Ezekiel, who calls himself Son of Adam.

---

* Deut. xxxii.   † Fo. 14, col. 2.

The writer of this last Psalm, No. xlix., shows very clearly his hopes of a future life after death, thus, speaking of the wicked :—

> Like sheep they are laid in the **grave**;
> Death will be their shepherd,
> And the upright will tread over them in the morning;
> And their form will waste away in hell,
> Every one away from his dwelling.
> But God will redeem my soul from the power **of** hell;
> For he will receive me.

With this **we** may mention Psalm xvi., though **there** is no reason for placing it at this late date, except that it points to a future life after death. With us the liver is usually called the seat **of** jealousy and ill-temper; but it is otherwise with the Hebrew writers; thus:—

> My heart is glad and my liver rejoiceth,
> My flesh also will dwell in hope;
> For thou wilt not leave my soul in hell,
> Nor suffer thy Godly one to see corruption.
> Thou wilt make known to me the path of life.
> In thy presence is fulness of joy;
> At thy right hand are pleasures for evermore.

We have no clear account of the Schools of Learning at this time in Judea; but we have many scattered hints which tell us that since the Return from Captivity learning had been very much cultivated. A nation which produced new writings in every generation since the time of the prophet Samuel, can never have been without schools; and the change in the language which took place in Judea, while the priests were in captivity, made such schools more particularly necessary, when the captives returned home, and again called **the** people's attention to the written Law. The language **at** that time in use approached the Syriac **and** Chaldee; and when Ezra read the Law to the assembled people, some of the Levites who understood both the Biblical Hebrew and the spoken language, then explained it to those who understood the spoken language only.* Those of the Levites who could do this were called Interpreters.† The need for such a class of men naturally gave encouragement to the schools.

Moreover, among the people at large who listened eagerly to hear the Law read to them by Ezra, a wish must have

---

* **Nehem. viii. 7, 8.**   † Job xxxiii. 23; Isaiah xliii. 27.

arisen in many to be able to read it for themselves. A nation whose religion is to be found in a Book is thus likely to have more readers than other nations. An uneducated man among the Jews would feel a stronger wish to read the Law and the Prophets, than a Greek could feel to read Homer and Hesiod, the only two of their great writers that had yet arisen. The march of the Israelites out of Egypt would be more deeply interesting to the one, than Achilles' wrath during the siege of Troy to the other.

The schools did not limit their instruction to language. Religious wisdom and the Books of the Law received their first attention. Under what heads the other branches of human knowledge were grouped we do not know. But as the **Greeks** divided all knowledge among the nine Muses, **so in Judea** Wisdom built her house with seven pillars, and **placed** it beside the public paths, and called upon the simple **to come** in and learn.* Even **yet** the old opinion lingers among us, that all knowledge is embraced within seven sciences. The short proverbs and pithy sentences which float about from mouth to mouth, had under the monarchy, when collected been given to Solomon; but such sayings at this later time are called the Words of the Wise Men. We have two such collections added to the Proverbs of Solomon. They are chapters xxii. 17—xxiv. 22, and xxiv. 23-34. They show their late date by teaching a life hereafter for the good, but for the good only; thus :—

> Be in the fear of Jehovah all the day long;
> For surely there will be an hereafter;
> And thine expectation will **not be cut off.**
> Be not envious of the wicked;
> For there will be no hereafter to the evil man;
> The lamp of the wicked will be put out.

The Introduction to the Proverbs, which we have already mentioned, belongs to **the same** class of Wise Men. Their name **may** have been borrowed from Babylon; in Greece they **would have been** called Philosophers. The writer of Psalm **xlix.**, just mentioned, claims to belong to the class of Wise Men, saying :—

> My mouth shall speak of Wisdom,
> And the thoughts of my heart shall be of understanding.
> I will incline mine ear to a Proverb,
> I will open my dark sayings upon the harp.

---

* **Prov. viii ix.**

He then moralizes on the little value of wealth and rank without Wisdom. Some of the thoughts are borrowed from the Introduction to Proverbs; and again we shall meet with some in the Book of Ecclesiastes, though accompanied with a very different philosophy.

The Son of Sirach tells us that there was a class of learned men, whose life was devoted to study and teaching. Unlike the carpenter, the smith, and the potter, whose useful but humble employments engaged their whole time, the learned man was at leisure to study the Law of God, and the sayings of the famous men of old, and even to gain wisdom by foreign travel. Such a man, when filled with the spirit of understanding, could pour out wise sentences, and give thanks unto the Lord in prayer.*

We get a hint of their method of teaching by question and answer from Malachi ii. 12, where "he that wakeneth up, and he that answereth," probably mean the teacher and the learner. The learners in these schools no doubt paid a fee to the teacher; as they are earnestly advised to buy the truth, and are assured that the trade of wisdom is better than the trade of silver.†

Out of these schools came not only the Teachers of the Law, but also the Scribes, whose careful penmanship was laboriously employed in copying the sacred books on sheets of leather prepared for the purpose.

Nehemiah, as we have said, left behind him a volume of history, probably the book which we now possess with his name; and also a volume of Commentaries, possibly the two Books of Chronicles. But he did more than that for the literature of his country; he gathered together into a library, perhaps in one of the chambers of the Temple, those sacred treasures, the writings of the learned men who had gone before him. These are described as four classes :—

First, the Acts of the Kings: these may be most of our historic books;

Secondly, the writings of the Prophets;

Thirdly, the writings of David, being, of course, such Psalms as were already written; and

Fourthly, the Epistles of the Kings concerning the holy gifts.‡ These may be the letters contained in the Book

---

of Ezra. These letters, which are in the Chaldee language, and indeed all the Chaldee portions of the Book of Ezra, namely, iv. 7—vi. 18, and vii. 12-26, were added to that book after this time. Chapter iv. 6, which is in Hebrew, is also an addition made at a different time; it is not found in 1 Esdras ii.

The Book of the Law, or the Pentateuch, is not mentioned among Nehemiah's books, probably because it had been before collected by Ezra, whom we have seen reading it to the assembled people in the courts of the Temple. The Hebrew Scriptures are at present in the original text divided into the Law, the Histories, the Prophets, and a miscellaneous volume, called the Writings. Of this last volume Nehemiah only collected some Psalms and part of Ezra; and there remain unmentioned, Job, the Proverbs, Solomon's Song, Ruth, Lamentations, Ecclesiastes, Daniel, and Esther, together with his own writings, the Book of Nehemiah, and the Chronicles. Of these some were unwritten, and others had not yet obtained that sacred character that now gives to them a place among the books of the Bible.

Nehemiah had only received leave of absence from Susa for a limited time, and in the year B.C. 433, he returned to the duties of his office of cup-bearer to the king, after he had been twelve years in Jerusalem. During these years he had devoted himself to the good of his countrymen. He had refused to receive from them the pay of a Pasha, of forty shekels, or eighty shillings, a month, not wishing to be a burden to them; and he had contented himself with a daily supply of food for himself and his officers of government. This was an ox and six sheep, with some fowls and wine; and it fed one hundred and fifty of the rulers who dwelt with him, beside those who came up to him from a distance on business. Such was the establishment of the Pasha of the Jews.* The former Pashas had received the supply of food together with their pay.

When in the year B.C. 433, Nehemiah returned to his former office in Susa, the government of Jerusalem fell to Sanballat, the governor of Samaria. He carried it on by means of Tobiah, one of his officers, who often dwelt at Jerusalem. Eliashib, the chief priest, then became of more importance than he had before been. Nehemiah had thrown him into the shade. Nehemiah had been more zealous for

* Nehem. v. 14-18.

the Levitical law than the chief priest himself. But
Nehemiah had not been able to enforce his own orders.
He had seen with pain two nobles of Jerusalem give their
daughters in marriage to Samaritans. One of these was
married to Tobiah, and the other to Tobiah's son.* When
Nehemiah left Jerusalem this disobedience still further
increased. He had attempted too much ; he had attempted
to draw a line of separation where nature had not made one.
In a short time one of Eliashib's grandsons, who might one
day by the law of blood be himself the chief priest, married
Sanballat's daughter.† This took place with Eliashib's
approval. And further, Eliashib, who as chief priest was
the governor of the Temple and of the chambers around the
Great Hall, gave up one of these chambers for the use of
Tobiah, Sanballat's officer, whose frequent presence in Jerusalem is explained by his acting in the government of
Jerusalem for Sanballat, governor of Samaria.

The beautiful story of Ruth is one of those which have
no certain place in the history of Hebrew literature. It is
placed early in our Bibles, but by the Jews has always
been considered one of the later books. Indeed the peaceable
life of the reapers and gleaners there described, with the
quiet purchase of the mortgaged estate in the presence of the
elders of Beth-lehem seated at the city gate, is wholly unlike
the lawless times of the Judges, in which Ruth was supposed
to live. At that time Beth-lehem, with the larger part of
Judah, was in servitude under the Philistines, or if not,
every man was doing what was right in his own eyes. Ruth,
the heroine of the story, is a young Moabite woman, who, in
devotedness to her late husband's mother, follows her out of
the land of Moab into Judea to Beth-lehem, the place of her
husband's family. There she lives in poverty ; but her good
conduct gains for her the notice of a wealthy member of her
husband's family, who marries her; and her son Obed
becomes the grandfather of king David. The moral that we
may draw from the story is, that no Jew is the worse for being
born of a Moabite mother ; and when Nehemiah quotes from
the Book of Moses that a Moabite shall not come into the
assembly of God for ever, it looks as if this history of Ruth
were written to throw a doubt upon the value or wisdom of
that law.

The Book of Jonah, like the Book of Ruth, does not bear
upon its face a very exact date. The prophet, the subject

* Nehem. vi. 18.　　† Nehem. xiii. 28.

of the story, lived in the time of Jeroboam II; but as his poetical prayer, spoken when he was in the fish's belly, is made of lines borrowed from perhaps six Psalms; one, Psalm xlii. written during the captivity; one, Psalm cxx. written after the return, it belongs to a very late period. It has very little literary merit; but no Hebrew book shows a kinder feeling towards the nation's enemies. The direct aim of the writer is to justify God in not wholly destroying the city of Nineveh, the old capital of Assyria. The Jews now felt grateful to the mild government of the present king of Assyria, as the Persian monarch was usually styled by them. The writer had perhaps dwelt at Nineveh himself. He describes it as a city of three days' journey, with much cattle; thus including within the one name the three towns of Nineveh, Resen, and Calah, all within the fork made by the Tigris and the Great Zab. He counts its population at a hundred and twenty thousand persons, living in heathen ignorance, which he describes as not knowing the right hand from the left. But the indirect purport of the book, like that of the Book of Ruth, is to lessen the separation between the Jews, and the strangers who were living among them, a separation which Ezra and Nehemiah had taken pains to widen.

NEHEMIAH AGAIN GOVERNOR OF JUDEA, B.C. 420?

Nehemiah returned to Jerusalem as governor a second time, after some years' absence. Eliashib the chief priest was dead. Joiada had succeeded him. It was therefore after the year B.C. 428, the year in which Eliashib died.[*] Artaxerxes Longimanus was dead; and it was probably in the reign of Darius Ochus, called also Nothus, that Nehemiah again obtained leave to return to Jerusalem, with the same authority as before. But on his arrival he found to his disappointment that his regulations had been very much neglected. Joiada the high priest had allowed his son to marry a daughter of Sanballat the Samaritan, the governor of Samaria, and he had granted to Tobiah, who was related to Sanballat, the use of a chamber within the courts of the Temple. Tobiah probably claimed to govern the city for Sanballat, whose servant he was. But the quarrel between Jews and Samaritans was already too strong for this to be allowed if it could be stopped. So Nehemiah had Tobiah's

[*] Paschal Chronicle.

furniture at once removed, and had the chamber cleansed from the impurity. Nehemiah reproachfully calls Tobiah an Ammonite; but his name, *The goodness of Jehovah*, and his alliance to the chief priest, disprove this.

The neglect of the people to send **up** to Jerusalem the appointed tithes had made it necessary **for** some of the Levites and singers in the service of the Temple to leave the city and take themselves to the fields, where they could support themselves by their labour. **This** irregularity Nehemiah corrected, and the service of **the** Temple was again performed more as he wished it to be. Moreover, the holiness of the Sabbath had been sadly neglected : the wine-presses were trodden on the Sabbath, and the market people brought in their burdens of food for sale on that day as on the others. This Nehemiah stopped by having the city gates shut for the twenty-four hours of the Sabbath ; and when the dealers, Tyrians and others, travelling on that day, lodged on the outside, waiting for the first day of the week, he threatened that if they came up again on the Sabbath he would have them punished.

Lastly, Nehemiah again strictly enforced his former orders, that the Jews should not marry foreign wives; and when Manasseh, **the son of Joiada the** chief priest, the grandson of Eliashib, the late high priest, disobeyed, **he** was forced to leave Judea.*

We are not told how long Nehemiah remained governor this second time. We have supposed that the chief part of his own Book was written before ; but now must have been added chapter xiii. 7 to the end, which relates to this time. At a yet later time several other passages were added by later editors.

Though we shall hereafter have to mention a few later additions to the Hebrew Books, yet we have reason to think that no great alterations were made in them after this time. As within a very few years after Nehemiah's death the Samaritan transcript of the Pentateuch was made, and only a century later copies of all the Books were sent to Alexandria, and from them the Greek translation was made; we judge that the Books which have been saved out of Nehemiah's library were, in all that is important, the same as those which we now have.

If we look carefully into the several books, having a

---

* Nehem. xiii. 28.

regard to their dates, with a view to study the growth of the language, we soon find that we have not got materials for such a study. We are driven to the conclusion that the scribes of Ezra's and Nehemiah's time have given to the older books a more modern dress; probably not by any rule, but from the simple wish that each new copy should be in such a form as it could be best understood. We have noticed the generation which followed the return from captivity as one of high poetical merit; but we must go back to the century before the Captivity for the greatest purity of language. The age of Joel, Isaiah, Nahum, and Habakkuk, we may call the age of orators, when the spoken and the written languages were yet in agreement. After the Captivity they were no longer so. If Ezra's and Nehemiah's scribes, in revising the text, in making the spelling of the older books modern, in removing forgotten words, if they had any standard of excellence, it was probably the Book of Isaiah. From this none of the books written before the Captivity now depart very widely. To bring this agreement about, the prophets, the great writers who were themselves the standard, needed no alteration; but we must believe that the Books of Judges, Samuel, Kings, the Pentateuch, and the Psalms, if given to us in their original form would show more obsolete **words** and expressions than we now find in them.

For the books written after the Captivity the case is different; they needed no such correction. Though the spoken language continued to change, the written language ceased to follow, and remained fixed, as far at least as any thing is fixed in this changing world. A few of the later writers, men of real genius, may be supposed to show in their works each his own peculiar style and choice of words, as in Job and Ecclesiastes; but in most of the late writings we find the quiet regularity, and tame, weak uniformity, of men who were writing in a dead language. This is particularly shown in Moses's Song and Blessing at the end of Deuteronomy, and in the Alphabetic and Hallelujah Psalms.

Origen and later Christian writers had a tradition that the Jews, on their return from captivity, changed the characters in which their books had been written, and then introduced the Hebrew square letters; and that before the Captivity the letters in use had been nearly the same as the Samaritan letters. But neither Ezra nor Nehemiah give us any hint of such a change having been made. Nor is it probable that any change was ever made, other than that which time always brings in, that slight change in the form of the letters, as in the way of spelling the words, by which each generation thinks that it is improving upon the former, while careful not to depart from it.

We observe that the scribes have left very many glaring contradictions, both in the Laws and in the History; and as they did not remove these we judge that they executed their task with great modesty and reverence, changing nothing that was important, but making the books more easy to be understood.

On parting with Nehemiah, as Hebrew literature is drawing to a close, we are tempted to look around upon the neighbouring nations; and on turning to Greece, at this time the most cultivated, we remark that Nehemiah lived at the same time as Æschylus and Pindar. These were followed by Sophocles, Herodotus, Thucydides, and a crowd of other great authors; but of those who lived before this time Homer and Hesiod alone can be put in comparison with the best Hebrew writers. The Books of Joel, Isaiah, Nahum, Habakkuk, the Isaiah of the Return Home, and Job, were all written before Greece could show as much literary excellence. Had a traveller, after surveying the known world in the reign of Xerxes I. been asked what country furnished the best models of good writing, the most inspiring examples for a writer to study, he would have named not Greece but Judea.

One of the last acts mentioned in the life of Nehemiah, was his driving away from Jerusalem and from the priesthood a son of Joiada, a grandson of Eliashib, because he married a Samaritan wife, the daughter of Sanballat the governor of Samaria, in disobedience to the general order issued by Nehemiah. Manasseh, the young man who had thus offended, withdrew from Jerusalem and came to his father-in-law Sanballat, at Samaria; and Sanballat, to console him for the loss of his rank as high priest, promised to obtain leave from Darius, the Persian king, to build for him a Temple on Mount Gerizim like that at Jerusalem, and to make him the chief priest there. The request was granted, and the Samaritan Temple to Jehovah was accordingly built on Mount Gerizim, overlooking the city of Shechem. Josephus places this in the reign of Darius Codomanus, the last of the Persian kings, B.C. 334; but the **name** of Sanballat fixes it to the time of Nehemiah and the reign of Darius Nothus, perhaps about B.C. 408.* Moreover, Josephus contradicts himself by making Sanballat a general in Alexander the Great's army, and Manasseh the son-in-law to Jaddua.†

As we know nothing of either half of the nation **since** the return from captivity, except through southern historians, we have but slender notices of the Samaritans, and those probably rather unfair. We are never indeed told of the return of any number of the northern captives. The Jewish historian says that they were a very mixed race, with idols copied from those of the surrounding nations, who now dwelt among them; but he acknowledges many of them **as** Israelites, by saying that they forsook the ordinances and statutes which Jehovah had commanded them. Some feared Jehovah, but yet made for themselves, **out** of the lowest of the people, priests to sacrifice on the High Places; while others, worse still, sacrificed for themselves within the houses on the High Places.‡ In short, they had no Levites among them, and never came up with their free-will offerings to worship in Jerusalem. The unfavourable picture of them is no doubt overcoloured, as the nations had never been friends since the revolt on the death of Solomon, which was always spoken of as the Sin of Jeroboam the son of Nebat, wherein he made Israel to sin.

The building by the Samaritans of a Temple to Jehovah on Mount Gerizim, in rivalry to that of Jerusalem, was a new cause of jealousy between the two nations. There had been an altar there centuries ago, but now they built a Temple. Hitherto the northern tribes, the Samaritans, as we must now call them, had sacrificed on a variety of High Places; but now, like the Jews, they professed that there was one only place for the worship of Jehovah; but in opposition to the Jews they said that that place was not Mount **Moriah but** Mount Gerizim. In support of this opinion they quoted Deuteronomy xxvii. 4, where, however, our present Hebrew copies have the name of the hill not Gerizim but Ebal. Many were the disputes which arose about this Temple; and one or other of the nations must have falsified its copies of the Bible in order to justify or to blame the choice of the spot for the building. The settlement of this disputed point of criticism depends upon the age assigned to the Samaritan version of the Pentateuch, and also

---

* Josephus Ant. XI. viii. 2.   † Ant. XIII. ix. 1.   ‡ 2 Kings xvii.

upon the relative age of the Samaritan alphabet and of the square characters in which the Hebrew Bible is written. The author will content himself with stating his own view of the matter.

The Samaritan Pentateuch is not a version into a language different from the Hebrew. It is merely a transcript, which professes to make no change in the words, but to give the Hebrew words in the Samaritan letters. It is very improbable **that** the Jews, reverencing their books so highly, should have ever ventured to change the characters in which they were first written, otherwise than by gradual improvement. The Samaritans on the other hand, now for the first time building a Temple to Jehovah, and proposing to have **a** priesthood of the line of Aaron, would wish for a transcript of the sacred books, only because the characters in which the Jews had written them were not so well understood on Mount Gerizim. The argument that the Samaritan letters are the older of the two, because no Hebrew monuments can now be shown that are as old as the Samaritan letters on the Maccabee coins, would be of little weight, if true, since those coins are too modern to have much bearing on the controversy. But that argument is shown to be unfounded by the greater age of the Hebrew inscriptions on the rocks near to Mount Serbal.

Upon the whole it seems probable that the Hebrew Scriptures were in Jerusalem always written in rude characters, allied to those in which we now read them, and that the Samaritan transcript of the Pentateuch was made from the square characters into the northern characters soon after the time of Nehemiah. The Samaritan Bible does not reach beyond the Pentateuch, which circumstance alone should settle that it is a transcript, having no claim to be the original. The Samaritans seem never to have taken the trouble to complete the task.

The city of Shechem stood in a very narrow valley between Mount Ebal and Mount Gerizim, but close to the foot of Mount Gerizim, as is shown on a coin of the Emperor Titus. On this latter hill the Samaritan Temple was built, no doubt near the site of an ancient altar. As soon as it was built, the Jews said that the Samaritans were acting in disobedience to the Law, and quoted their Bible, which, in Deuteronomy xxvii. 4, says that Moses had fixed upon Mount Ebal and not on Mount Gerizim for Joshua's altar. The Samaritans on the other hand, quoted from their own Bible

the same command of Moses to Joshua, to build an altar
to Jehovah at Mount Gerizim, as a proof that Gerizim
was the proper spot, as opposed to Mount Moriah, near
Jerusalem. From that time to this the controversy has
continued as to which was the truth. One nation or the
other must have falsified their Bible. In support of the
Samaritan claim to have acted honestly, we may remark
that when Sanballat and the high priest Manasseh began
to build, they had no wish but to follow the Mosaic law.
Moreover, it is the Samaritan reading which makes the
Bible consistent with itself. Deuteronomy xi. 29 and xxvii.
12, in the Hebrew copies, as in the Samaritan, both place the
blessings of the Law on Mount Gerizim and the curses on
Mount Ebal, which passages seem to support the Samaritans,
and to prove that the Jews had altered their Hebrew Bible,
in the passage quoted above, on purpose to throw blame
on the Samaritans. The same spirit of hostility to the
Samaritans led the Jews to call the city not Shechem but
Sychar, *falsehood*, which is the name used in John's gospel,
iv. 5; and in the same manner they gave to Beth-el, *the
house of God*, the reproachful name of Beth-aven, *the house of
Idolatry*. Moreover, there are other passages which throw
a light on the controversy. There had been a High Place
or Altar in the neighbourhood of Shechem from the earliest
times; and so important had this High Place been held by
those who lived in the neighbourhood, that an Elohistic
writer of the life of Jacob says, in Genesis xxxiii. 17-20,
that Jacob built an altar there to El, the God of Israel (see
pages 10 and 66); and a Jehovistic writer has added a
passage in the life of Abraham, in Genesis xii. 6-8, to say
that Abram built an altar there to Jehovah (see page 141).
Each writer claimed a High Place near Shechem for his own
religion, but they do not say of which of the two hills they
are speaking. There had, without doubt, been an altar on
each of these hills, that on Ebal dedicated to Baal, at a very
early time, and that on Gerizim dedicated to Jehovah, built
when the other was allowed to go to ruin. And as Deuteronomy xi. and xxvii. place the curses on Mount Ebal and
the blessings on Mount Gerizim, we may conclude that the
altar to Jehovah stood on Mount Gerizim, and hence that it
was by the side of that ancient altar that the Samaritans
built their new Temple to Jehovah, in the same way that
Solomon built his House for Jehovah by the side of David's
altar. Before this Temple was built by Sanballat, Deutero-

nomy xxvii. 4 would be written with impartiality as respects
the two hills; and in all probability at first the Hebrew
Bible placed the altar on Mount Gerizim, agreeably with the
Samaritan copy. It was only after the Samaritan Temple
had been built, and had gained importance for the hill by
its rivalry with Mount Moriah, that any controversy about
it arose; and thus the Jews seem to be convicted out of
their own Bible of having made the alteration in the disputed
passage.

Joshua viii. 30-35, is a sentence clearly out of place. In
the foregoing verses Joshua was fighting at Ai, near Beth-el;
and in the verses which follow them he is again at Ai;
while in these verses he is described as at a distance, and
building an altar to Jehovah on Mount Ebal. The writer
quotes Deuteronomy xxvii., the passage with the doubtful
reading Ebal or Gerizim, as a reason for Joshua's doing so.
Now as that chapter of Deuteronomy was written after the
return from captivity, this whole sentence must be new;
and it seems probable that it was at this time written to
support the falsification in the name of the mountain on
which the altar stood.

The Samaritans, however, seem not to have been wholly
blameless in this literary quarrel; for while the Jews altered
a word in Deuteronomy, and added the above quoted
sentence to the Book of Joshua, in order to rob Mount
Gerizim of its honour, the Samaritans added two passages
to their Bible in order to defend the situation of their altar
and new Temple. In the Samaritan Bible, immediately
following the Ten Commandments, both in Exodus and
Deuteronomy, is a command to build an altar of unhewn
stones on Mount Gerizim, and to write upon it the words of
that Law. In other respects the departure of the Samaritan
text from the Hebrew original is not important, except that
by its adding to the age of each patriarch at the birth of his
son, in Genesis xi., it lengthens the early chronology.

The high-priest Eliashib had been succeeded by his son
Joiada or Judas, and he was succeeded by his son Jonathan
or John,* the brother of Manasseh, the high-priest of
Samaria. Jonathan had another brother, named Joshua or
Jesus, whom he slew within the walls of the Temple, because
Bagoses, the Persian general and governor of the province,
had promised to give him the office of chief-priest. Bagoses
came up to Jerusalem to punish this crime and disobedience;

* Nehem. xii. 10.

and he laid upon the Jews the heavy fine of fifty drachmæ for every lamb that they offered in the Temple in their daily sacrifices. This may not have amounted to a very large sum, as the sacrifices were very much lessened in frequency since the Captivity. Bagoses moreover went himself into the Temple, remarking that a foreigner entering the Holy Place could not pollute it so much as did the murder.* Bagoses was the governor under Artaxerxes Mnemon; and this murder may have taken place about the year B.C. 372.

The century between the time of Nehemiah and the overthrow of the Persians by the Greeks under Alexander the Great, is nearly a blank in our history. It was during those years that the Greek philosopher Plato visited Heliopolis in Lower Egypt. The course of trade had taken him to Egypt, but the love of learning took him to Heliopolis. That he there gained knowledge from the Jews who had settled in that school of learning we have evidence in his Timæus, where he describes God as making the world out of shapeless matter, with the sun and moon to mark the seasons, and his being pleased with his work when he had finished. The thoughts rather than the **words seem** borrowed from the first chapter of Genesis.

JUDEA UNDER THE GREEKS; B.C. 332.

In the year B.C. 332, Alexander the Great defeated the Persians under the last Darius; and after spending seven months on the siege of Tyre, and two months on the siege of Gaza, hastened on to the conquest of Egypt. The Jews had lived quietly for two hundred and six years under the kings of Persia, from the time when the Babylonian monarchy was overthrown by Cyrus; it had been a time of good government, and prosperity, **never** once disturbed by rebellion or struggles for independence; and they now waited with anxiety to know what their fate would be under the Greek conqueror. Josephus says that he came to Jerusalem, and that as he approached the **city** the priests went out to meet him in their robes of office; the chief-priest in purple and scarlet with the **mitre** and golden plate on his head, the other priests in **white** linen dresses. Alexander received th**em** favourably, **and** promised them kind treatment, and released them **from** tribute on the seventh year, the Sabbath year, claiming **on** the other years

* Josephus Antiq. XI. viii.

the same tribute that they had paid to the Persians. Jaddua was at that time high-priest; he is the last in the line of high-priests recorded in the Hebrew Books of the Bible. Alexander then, says Josephus, went to Shechem, where the Samaritan priests asked the same favour of him, as being under the same law, and equally bound, like the Jews, not to cultivate their fields on the seventh year; but Alexander did not grant their request. But these visits of Alexander to Jerusalem and Shechem are not mentioned by the Greek historians, and are probably an invention by Josephus. Alexander, when besieging Tyre, had had a body of seven thousand Samaritans in his army; these he took on with him into Egypt, whither he was then going, and he gave them lands in the upper part of that country, in order to help to keep the Egyptians in obedience.*

The genealogy of the high-priests in chapter xii. 1-26, of Nehemiah, was at this time added to that book. It is in continuation of the genealogy in 1 Chron. vi. 1-15, which ends with the Captivity. Like that, it is not a list of the chief priests; it contains those names only through which the male line was **continued.** Thus it does not mention Ezra, **since on his death the** priesthood returned to the elder branch **of the** family. The latest name mentioned is **that of** Jaddua, the son of Jonathan, who was at Jerusalem when Alexander came to Palestine as a conqueror.

Hitherto the countries over which the Jews had spread, and with whose civilization they were acquainted, all, except Egypt, lay to the east. The Babylonian Captivity, and the spirit of trade, had scattered them through all the large cities of Syria, Assyria, Babylonia, Egypt, Arabia, and Persia. But as yet the western half of what we call the World as known to the Ancients, was very little known to the Jews. Some few had been sold by the Tyrians as slaves to the Greeks; some few may have followed the Tyrians to their African colonies. But it was in Lower Egypt alone that they could have gained any knowledge of European civilization. Europe, however, was now open to them, a new world with Greek literature and Greek arts, with civilization and thoughts wholly foreign to the Hebrew mind. So foreign were the Greeks to the Jews, so little aware were they how much each might learn from the other, that small was the advantage that either at first gained except

* Josephus Antiq. XI. viii.

in the way of trade. In Judea some few of the rich and educated may have tasted the forbidden fruit of Greek knowledge, and thereby, though of priestly rank, may have lost somewhat of their priestly narrowness, and have been looked upon with jealousy for so doing. But of **the poor,** many were led in the search for a livelihood to leave **their** country and wander westward; and **in** the course of the **next** century or two we shall find that there were few great towns on the Mediterranean coasts, whether in Greece, Italy, Gaul, or Spain, in which Jews were not to be found enriching themselves, and **those** among whom they had settled, by their industry and skill in trade. In this way was brought about the wide spread of Jews westward of Judea, which afterwards very much helped the spread of Christianity in Greece and Italy, and has since made all Europe, and every colony from Europe, to be Christian.

Alexander of Macedon, by his defeat of Darius, had **brough**t the whole Persian monarchy under the Greek power. Egypt, Asia Minor, Assyria, including Syria and Babylonia, were henceforth to be governed by Greeks; and on his death these vast kingdoms were divided among his generals. Egypt fell to Ptolemy, who fixed his seat of government at Alexandria, the city lately founded by Alexander. Seleucus, after various struggles with his rivals, made himself master of the great country formerly held by Sennacherib and then by Nebuchadnezzar. He built Antioch, on the river Orontes, as his capital of the Greco-Syrian kingdom, still called **Assyria** by the Jews. Antioch on the Orontes soon became **as** celebrated for its luxury and licentiousness as Alexandria for its schools of learning. In these two wealthy capitals and mercantile ports, many Jews found a field for their industry, which the unsettled state of their own country denied them. Of these two kingdoms bordering on Palestine, Egypt **was** the first to be settled in quiet, and therefore Ptolemy was **able** to claim Palestine as belonging to Egypt. His mild government very much attached the Jews to him, and as long as he and his son were too strong to be attacked by the rival Greco-Syrian kings, the Jews were satisfied with their condition.

From the death of Alexander the Great, in the year B.C. 323, the Jews were governed for one hundred and fifty-five years by Greek kings, the successors of his generals, sometimes by a Ptolemy, king of Egypt, and sometimes by an Antigonus or a Seleucus, king of Syria.

24

The second speech of Noah, in Genesis ix. 26, 27, relates to this time, when the Greeks, called the Sons of Japheth, though fighting among themselves, held safe possession of the land of Canaan. Noah there **says** :—

> God will enlarge Japheth,
> And he shall dwell in the tents of Shem.
> And Canaan shall be his servant.

The very late character of this prophecy **is** seen in its marking the accusative case in the first line by **a** preposition meaning in olden Hebrew "unto."

The Jews often suffered severely in the wars between the rival kings ; but they were not usually treated with cruelty. From the year B.C. 301, when these kings made peace, and shared the empire among them, the Jews lived quietly under the rule of the kings of Egypt until the year B.C. 222, when Ptolemy Euergetes died. During this time they had been usually governed by their own chief priest, who had almost the rank of viceroy. Jaddua, the chief priest in the time of Alexander, had been succeeded by his son Onias I.* Onias I was followed by his son Simeon, whose knowledge of the Levitical Law and of his duties in the Temple, gained for him the name of Simeon the Righteous, or as he is less correctly but more usually styled, Simon the Just.

Under Simon the service of the Temple was conducted with great attention to the old forms, so far as the poverty of the time allowed. Simon himself, clothed in the robes of chief priest, stood aloft at the hearth of the altar, and received the offering which was to be burnt from the hands of the priests, who now bore the former name of the Sons of Aaron. He then poured out at the foot of the altar wine, the **blood** of the grape, perhaps to supply the place of the blood **of** the animals, which in a time of greater wealth would have flowed into the trench around. The Sons of Aaron shouted and sounded the trumpets. The people bowed their faces towards the ground in worship. The singers sang the Psalms of praise ; and when the solemnity was ended, Simon came down from the altar, and stretching his hands over the people around, gave them the blessing from Jehovah.

Simon repaired the House of God, and strengthened the walls of the Temple area, and again coated with copper the great water cistern.† Simon had a son, Onias II ; but as

---

* **Josephus Antiq.** XI. viii. 7.   † Ecclesiasticus l.

he was too young for the office of chief priest, it was, on Simon's death, B.C. 292, held by Simon's brother Eleazer. This was in the time of Ptolemy Philadelphus, king of Egypt.*

The high priest Simon the Just had lived wholly in the past, which he vainly attempted to recall by his attention to the Temple services and other ceremonial observances. The Mishna calls him the last of the Great Synagogue. He had known those **who** had known Nehemiah. He had been educated before Greek arts and learning had **been** known **to** the Jews.

The arrival of the Greeks in Judea during the lifetime of Simon marks **a** second great break in the stream of Hebrew thought. The first such break was made by the Babylonian Captivity. On the return from Babylon a halo of reverence was thrown around the old books which was dangerous to **the** future intelligence of **the** people. But fortunately literary genius was not dead, and new writers arose, though under less favourable circumstances. Their rank was rarely acknowledged; but when their writings were admired, it was thought necessary to ornament them with the name of some one who had lived before the Captivity. The Books of Isaiah, Jeremiah, and Ezekiel in this way became more bulky. But as the language of the people changed yet further from the Hebrew of the prophets, Hebrew writing became less common; and when, in addition, Hebrew thought was becoming changed by noting the great superiority of the Greeks in the art of war, in the arts of life, and, perhaps, in everything except religion, a second and **a** yet greater break was made in the stream of Hebrew thought; and thus the chief priest Simon was declared to **be the last** of **the** Great Synagogue.

Hitherto Traditional Wisdom, it was allowed by all, had dwelt **with** the chief priest; but on the death of Simon the Just, traditional Wisdom and the chief-priesthood were thought **by the** zealots for the Tradition to have parted company. **The** priesthood was hereditary and continued in the hands of the wealthy and the cultivated of the capital, who will be afterwards called the Sadducees, while the Traditional Wisdom was claimed by the country party and the humbler class, who will be afterwards called the Pharisees.

* Josephus Antiq. XII. ii. 4.

Simon's successor in the office of chief priest was his brother Eleazer, and with him the office lost much of its favour with zealous Jews. This is explained by his being made farmer of the taxes of Judea by the king of Egypt.* This civil employment, when joined to the office of chief priest, gave to him great political power, but lessened his character for holiness.

Eleazer was favourable to Greek learning; and he assisted the Jews in Egypt in their wish to have a Greek translation of the Bible. The Jews who had fled to Egypt from their conquerors, **and** some of the captives whom the Persians had placed there, had chiefly settled on the east side of the Delta. But the first Ptolemy invited them to the new city of Alexandria; and by granting to them the privileges of citizenship enabled them to take their share of the profitable **trade** between Egypt and Greece. This led to their culti-**vating** the Greek language; and some had so much lost the use **of** the Hebrew language, that they wished for a Greek translation of their sacred books. This was begun in the reign of Ptolemy Philadelphus, an enlightened patron of all learning, about the year B.C. 270; but it was not completed till one or two centuries later. It has received the name of the Septuagint, not perhaps because seventy translators were employed upon it, as some have supposed, but more probably because it received the approval of a Sanhedrim or council of that number of elders. It is a very incorrect translation, but valuable when it agrees with the Hebrew, **as it** sometimes explains words that are not understood in **the** original; and valuable when it differs from the Hebrew, **as it** then shows us some of the opinions which led the Greeks **to** make what they thought improvements in the Bible.

These translators did not venture to write the sacred **name of** Jehovah in Greek letters; in place of it they always wrote Kyrios, *Lord*, thus following a Jewish custom of **not** uttering the written name Jehovah. The Jews when speaking changed it into Adoni, *Lord*. This custom introduced into the Greek Bible the very ambiguity which their forefathers tried to avoid by forbidding the use of the ambiguous word Baal, *Lord*, as a name for God. It was followed, unfortunately, by the writers of the New Testament.

---

* Josephus Antiq. XII. iv. 1.

The Greek Jews, from their acquaintance with the very ancient monuments of Egypt, were of opinion that the world was far older than it is said to be in the Hebrew Bible. We learn from the Hebrew, by adding up the ages of the patriarchs at the birth of their sons, that man was thought to have lived upon earth 2023 years when Abraham left Chaldæa. But the Septuagint alters the age of each father at the time of the son's birth, and thus makes the world older by 1466 years. That this was done on purpose may be judged from the time added, as 1460 years is an Egyptian cycle of four times 365 years.

On the other hand, the Septuagint **shortens** the **time of** the Israelites' sojourn in Egypt. In the Hebrew, in **Exodus** xii. 40, there are said to have been 430 years between **Jacob's** entering Egypt **and** Moses leaving it; but the Septuagint says that this period of 430 years reaches from Abraham's leaving Chaldæa to Moses's leaving Egypt, thus making the residence in Egypt only 215 years.

The Hebrew, in Exodus xxx. 13, commands every male of twenty years of age to pay the sum of half a shekel yearly to the service of the Temple; Nehemiah had only called upon them for the third of a shekel, and the Septuagint again lessens the sum to half a didrachm, or a quarter of a shekel. The translators perhaps excused this alteration to themselves by finding that the tax was seized upon **by their** foreign masters.

The Greek translation shows us some of **the subtle** and refined speculations which had lately arisen about the nature of spiritual and angelic beings. In Psalm civ. 4, we read in the Hebrew, as a figurative description of the power of God :—

He maketh the winds his messengers and the flames of fire his **servants.**

To these words the Septuagint gives a new meaning, **and** says :—

He maketh his angels into spirit, and his ministers into **a flame of** fire.

Again Isaiah, in chapter xi. 2, when saying that the spirit of the Lord will rest upon the expected son of Jesse, explains that spirit to be "the spirit of wisdom and of understanding, the spirit of counsel and of might, and the spirit of knowledge and of the fear of Jehovah." But the Septuagint adds a seventh to these six spiritual gifts, namely, "the spirit of piety," and thus completes the mystical number of seven Spirits, or spiritual beings. These are mentioned in the Book of Revelation, chapter iv. 5, as standing before the throne of **God** ; and in the second century of our era, some Alexandrian Christians worshipped these seven spirits, jointly with the Creator, under the name of the blessed Ogdoad, eight persons forming one God.

To the Cover of **the** Ark which stood **within** the Holy of Holies the Septuagint gives the name of the Propitiatory, or in **the** English translation, the Mercy Seat, above which the Almighty was supposed to be present when the priest inquired **of** him. It gained this name, not only from that cause, **but** also from the play upon the Hebrew word "the **Cover,**" which was used not only for covering the sacred **Ark or** any other box, but also for covering our sins when forgiveness is granted.

The several books in this version are translated with very unequal skill, and some of the writers show a sad want of knowledge of one or both the languages. Moreover it had additions made to it at various times by various Alexandrian **editors.** Whatever later additions were made in the Hebrew books, were also made in the Greek Translation ; and hence we arrive at the important conclusion, that our finding any particular passage in the Septuagint, is no proof that the Hebrew original of it was written before this time. It is with the Septuagint that the quotations in the New Testament are chiefly found to agree ; but it is possible that this may have been brought about by the care of the later editors ; as certainly in one place, namely, in the Greek of Psalm xiv. 3, there are several lines borrowed from Paul's Epistle to the Romans iii. 13-18, which never formed part of that Psalm in the Hebrew. **The** Apostle had quoted **them,** not from one, but **from several** parts of the Old Testament.

Antioch on the Orontes, the new Greek capital of Syria, like **Alexandria in** Egypt, held out strong attractions to such **Jews and Israelites** as were uncomfortable at home ; and very many now settled there. They were probably natives of **northern** Israel, though when they settled abroad they all passed under the name of Jews. The Jewish influence on Greek civilization may not have been less in Syria than in Lower Egypt, since the Jews seem to have been the most moral and thoughtful of the mixed population of the new Syrian capital. The Greco-Syrians knew no difference between a Jew and a philosopher ;* and if, as there seems

* Josephus, Apion, i. 22.

reason to believe, the Stoical opinions reached Athens from the dissolute Antioch, it must have been from the Jews of that city.

During the reign of Ptolemy Euergetes, the chief priest Eleazer had been succeeded by Manasseh, one of his family, and then by Onias II, who had before been too young for the office. He, and perhaps two of his predecessors, had been allowed to farm the taxes for the Egyptian king. This post, being added to that of his priesthood, gave him viceregal rank. As farmer of the taxes he was assisted, and afterwards succeeded by his nephew Joseph ; while the priesthood descended to his son, Simon II.* Thus the Jews had something like self-government granted to them. Under a **chief** priest who was allowed to collect the tribute for the foreigner, they had as much independence as when, under the kings Jehoiakim and Zedekiah, they paid tribute to Nebuchadnezzar.

During these years the Jews were not unwilling to copy Greek manners and customs. When the high priest Simon the Just was succeeded in the priesthood by his brother Eleazer, the mantle of his wisdom, according to the Mishna, fell upon Antigonus of Socho, whose Greek name tells us of the change which was coming over the nation's mind. The time of their own Hebrew literature was going by. Indeed, their language was changing from what it had been when their sacred books had been collected together **and** had taken a fixed form. But it was rather in Jerusalem than in the villages that Greek thoughts gained admission into the Jewish mind ; and when the two parties, the **city** party and the country party, which had been divided on political grounds, become religious sects, it is among the city party that we find traces of Greek scepticism. The Hebrew mind had been contented to obey the commands of **conscience, as** being the voice of God speaking from within ; but Greek philosophy taught its followers to ask for a reason why one line of conduct was wise and another foolish. Among the Hebrew books the earliest trace of this moral inquiry is in the Book of Ecclesiastes. The Book of Job had been an inquiry into the wisdom and justice of God in his dealings with man ; the Book of Ecclesiastes is an inquiry into the line **of** conduct which it is wise for a man to follow.

It was near the end of the reign of Ptolemy Euergetes in Egypt, and at the beginning of the reign of Antiochus the

* Josephus Antiq. XII. iv. 1, 2.

Great in Syria, about the year B.C. 220, when Epicurus, the
founder of the Epicurean sect, had been dead about fifty
years, that the Book of Ecclesiastes was written, at a time
when, as the writer says, "Of making many books there
is no end, and in much study is a weariness of the flesh."
In this philosophical treatise on the ends which are worth
our pursuit in life, the writer sums up his experience with
saying, "Vanity of vanities, all is vanity." He sees the
sun arise only to go down, and the rivers run into the sea
without filling it. He says, "I have gotten more wisdom
than all they that have been before me in Jerusalem;" but
this also is vexation of spirit; "for in much wisdom is much
grief, and he that increaseth knowledge increaseth sorrow."
He indulges in wines, builds houses, plants gardens, makes
pools to water them, buys slaves, gathers gold and silver;
but finds it all vanity. The Book of Job, and the Isaiah of
the Return Home, had both made our ignorance of God's
dealings with man a reason for humble trust; but this
writer views the matter less religiously. He observes that
the fool and the wise man both die together, and concludes
with the Epicureans that there is nothing better for a man
than to eat and drink and enjoy himself. Nevertheless
actions are followed by their natural consequences, and
"Whoso breaketh a hedge a serpent will bite him."—
"Whoso removeth a boundary stone will be hurt therewith."
He sees no deviations from the usual course of nature, "The
thing that hath been is what will be, and there is nothing
new under the sun." He knows of nothing beyond the
grave, and a living dog is better than a dead lion. But he
wavers backward and forward, mingling with these sad
thoughts many wise proverbs and much good advice, for
which, however, he can give little reason, since "the race is
not to the swift nor the battle to the strong; but time and
chance happeneth to them all." Upon such a painful view
of life does our author build his philosophical system. Yet
true to the religion of his nation he advises trust in God,
"Cast thy bread-seed on the waters, and thou shall find it
after many days;" "Remember thy Creator in the days of
thy youth;" and lastly, "Let us hear the conclusion of the
whole matter; fear God and keep his commandments, for
this is the whole duty of man."

The book begins, "The words of Koheleth, the son of
David, King of Jerusalem." Koheleth is a feminine noun
meaning an *Assembly*, perhaps a *School*. In the Greek

version it is translated *The Preacher.* We **may** perhaps understand it as philosophy, and say in verse **12,** "I Philosophy was king over Israel in Jerusalem." Thus, the unknown writer puts his remarks on the vanity of riches, of pleasure, and of wisdom, into the mouth of Solomon ; since no one could be more fitted to pronounce such an opinion than that most prosperous of monarchs. This is the only work that we possess which teaches the opinions of the Sadducees ; the only Hebrew writing in which God's watchful care is so far forgotten as that chance **should** be allowed to have any power over our lives. The belief in a future state is here denied in a manner which shows that disputes about that opinion had already begun.

Our author is a philosopher rather than a moralist, and we naturally compare his work with our other two books of **the** same class. The Proverbs of Solomon is a philosophical **work,** but on practical every-day wisdom, thoroughly native to the Jewish mind. The Book of Job is another philosophical work in justification of God's dealings with man, and is Jewish in its devout feeling, though written by one who had probably lived a great part of his life abroad. But this Book **of** Ecclesiastes is wholly foreign to any thoughts which we have before met with in Hebrew literature.

Antioch on the Orontes was at that time the wealthy and dissolute capital of the Greek kingdom of Syria, Assyria, and Babylonia ; and there the writer may have lived, and gained his knowledge of Greek philosophy, and his low opinion of his fellow-creatures. If he made any search for honest men, he met with little success, and still less in the case of women ; saying, "one man among a thousand have I found, but a woman among all those have I not found." This we hope was said not of Judea, but of Syria. There in the court of Seleucus Callinicus he may have witnessed the costly luxuries which he describes as tasted but not enjoyed by Solomon. He shows some knowledge of the Greco-Syrian monarchy ; and from his not using the name of Jehovah, we judge that he belonged to northern Israel. In the following passage he dates the book very exactly to the beginning of the reign of Antiochus the Great ; thus :—

Better is one born poor and wise, than a king old and foolish, who can no more be warned. For from a prison he may come to reign, even though in the other's kingdom he was born poor. I considered all the living who walk about under the sun, with the second son that shall rise up in his stead (iv. 13-15).

The foolish king is Seleucus Callinicus, who, after being defeated in all his battles, at last died a prisoner. The wise **man** may be his minister **Achæus, to** whom, after the elder son's death, the crown was offered; but he wisely refused it. The elder son Seleucus Ceraunus reigned for three years; and Antiochus his younger brother, who then came to the throne, is the second son here mentioned. Our writer remarks upon his youth, as he was then under fifteen years of age, saying "Alas for thee, O land, when thy king is a child, and thy princes eat in the morning" (x. 16).

When the writer of Ecclesiastes advises the sinner to confess his sins frankly, "say not to the preacher that it **was a** sin of ignorance," we have to notice that the priest acted, not only **as** a sacrificer, but as a spiritual adviser. So in the penitential Psalm xxxii., we have first the sinner acknowledging the comfort of confessing his sin, saying :—

> When I kept silence my bones wasted away

and then the priest answering :—

> I will instruct thee, and teach thee
> In the way that thou shalt go.

Jeremiah x. 1-16 was written when Greek influence was beginning to be felt in Jerusalem, and was alarming those who feared that the heathen religion might follow upon the heathen civilization. They had lived for more than two hundred years under the Persians, who were as much opposed as the Jews were to idol-worship. But their new masters, the Greeks, whether Greeks of Egypt or Greeks of Syria, brought not their idols but their opinions with them into Judea. The Jews were neither scientific nor artistic; hence Babylonian science and Egyptian art had **not much** seducing power. But Greek philosophy was far more dangerous, and the writer taunts the philosophers, "the wise men of the Nations," with their gross theology, **as a** "Doctrine of Vanities." He says "Learn not the way of the Nations—the customs of the people are vain, they cut a tree out of the forest and made a god of it;" and then follow some noble words, declaring that Jehovah alone **is** the true God, the maker of all things. The idol is described as made of wood, clothed with blue and purple cloth, and coated in parts with plates of gold and silver. Such was the colossal statue of Serapis in Alexandria, of which this may be **a** description. This passage has several very modern peculiarities. Such is the calling God, "King of the nations;" such is the spelling Ophir, as in Daniel x. 5, "Ophaz;" and such is the comparing an idol to a scarecrow, called "a pillar in a cucumber garden;" as does the Apocryphal Epistle of Jeremiah. Some of these words are repeated in chapter li. 15-19. Yet more modern is verse 11, which is not Hebrew but Chaldee.

Psalm cxliv. may now be mentioned. It is by an unhappy musician, whose hands itched for war, and his fingers for fighting. He prays God for the relief from the oppression; and he would have put aside his psaltery of ten strings, and rebelled against the foreigners, if there had been any chance of success. His psalm is made up of borrowed thoughts, taken chiefly from Psalms viii. and xviii. He plays upon words with two meanings, saying :—

> O Jehovah, what is man [or Adam] that thou knowest him!
> The son of man [or of Enosh] that thou thinkest of him!
> Man [or Adam] is like to vanity [or Abel];
> His days are as a shadow that passeth away.

He had perhaps travelled in Greece; he shows an acquaintance with the Greek style of architecture, when he compares the young women to the marble statues used in Athens as columns to support a roof, praying :—

> That our sons may be as plants grown up in their youth,
> Our daughters as columns cut on the model of a palace.

On the death of Ptolemy Euergetes and the accession of Ptolemy Philopator, the gentle treatment of the Jews by their Greek rulers ceased. They were frequently roused into rebellion; and the willingness to learn from the higher civilization of the Greeks then ceased also.

In B.C. 202 Judea fell under the more powerful empire of Syria, of which Antiochus the Great was then king. During the wars which led to this change of rulers, the country suffered severely. But that upon the whole, Antiochus the Great treated the Jews well may be known from the trust which he placed in them. When the provinces of Phrygia and Lydia, in Asia Minor, showed signs of rebellion, he moved two thousand Jewish families from Mesopotamia and Babylon, and placed them in the discontented provinces. He gave to these Jews lands to cultivate, and food until their own labour could feed them, and ordered that they should be released from all taxes for the next ten years.* From

---

* Josephus Antiq. XII. iii. 4.

those spots the Jews spread after a time to the more busy
cities on the Ionian coast of Asia Minor, mixing with the
Greeks, learning the Greek language to the disuse of
Hebrew, and, we may safely say, largely modifying Greek
opinions by their monotheism.

About this time the chief priest Onias II died. He was
succeeded by his son Simón II, who, however, had far less
power than his father, because the office of farmer of the
taxes went to Onias's nephew, Joseph. Joseph, rather than
the chief priest, was viceroy of Judea under the kings,
Antiochus the Great of Syria, Ptolemy Epiphanes of Egypt,
and Seleucus Soter, called also Philopator, of Syria. He held
this office for twenty-two years.*

Seleucus Philopator is chiefly known to us for his sending
his treasurer Heliodorus to seize upon the treasures in the
Temple of Jerusalem.†

On the death of Joseph about the year B.C. 176, began a
series of troubles, arising from struggles for power among
the Jews themselves, which yet further ruined this unhappy
country. The elder sons of Joseph, the farmer of the taxes,
were afraid of being deprived of the office by their younger
brother Hyrcanus, and they raised a body of troops to
defend themselves. Hyrcanus did the same; but he was
defeated, and he left Judea to them, while he retreated to
the east of the Jordan. There, in the land of Heshbon, he
built for himself a strong castle with stone walls, ornamented
with sculptures. He called it Tyre, after the Phenician city
of that name. He ornamented it with pools of water, the
great luxury of that climate, and surrounded it with a canal
for strength. There he reigned for seven years, collecting
the taxes of that part of the country in the name of Seleucus
Philopator, but keeping them for his own use.‡

The Wisdom of Jesus the son of Sirach was written after
the death of the chief-priest Simon the Just, the son of
Onias I. The original author Jesus, the father of Sirach,
lived in Jerusalem. His book was perhaps never published
in Hebrew. It may have been written about B.C. 180, as
the author's grandson, whose name it now bears, met with
it in Egypt after the thirty-eighth year of Ptolemy
Euergetes II, that is after B.C. 132. There he translated
it into Greek; and it has been added to the Greek Bible.
A second preface by an unknown writer tells us that the

---

* Josephus Antiq. XII. iv. 2.   † 2 Macc. iii. ; Dan. xi. 20.
‡ Josephus Antiq. XII. iv. 11.

grandson also wrote part of it; and this is borne out by the Alexandrian opinions which we trace in the book. It begins like the Proverbs of Solomon with the praise of wisdom. Then **follow a** number of wise proverbs and moral rules. In chapter xxiv. Wisdom speaks as a person, as in the Introduction to the Book of Proverbs. She was created before time began; she performed the Service in the holy Tabernacle, and was afterwards established in Zion. The most famous of the holy men in the Bible are mentioned with due praise, together with Isaiah, Jeremiah, Ezekiel, and the twelve minor prophets. From the character given to Isaiah that he comforted the mourners in **Zion,** we learn that the larger part of the various writings which are now called by his name **had been** already classed as his. The omission of the Book **of Daniel from** this list tells us that as yet that **book** formed no part of the Bible. Zerubbabel is mentioned with praise, as also Nehemiah who built the wall. But Ezra **is** omitted. Possibly his division **of** the nation into two **classes,** the Children of the Captivity, and the others, may have been remembered against him. The writer has a strong dislike to the Samaritans of Shechem, and to the Jews who dwell among the Philistines, meaning the men of Beersheba, and the other Idumeans (1. 26). He looks forward to the second coming of Elijah, who is to appease God's anger, and to turn the heart of the Father to the child, and to restore the tribes of Jacob (xlviii. 10). He thus misquotes the last verse of Malachi, and takes a stern view of God's character, and joins to the Jewish religion the Pagan opinion that God would not look favourably on his children unless persuaded **by a** mediator. This book is an important link in the chain **which** joins the Hebrew writers to the Alexandrian Platonists. **The** following are some thoughts which we have not met with **in the** earlier books.

Almsgiving maketh an atonement for sins (iii. 30). Concerning the making atonement be not without fear to add sin to sin (v. 5). The greater thou art, the more humble thyself, and thou shalt find favour with the Lord (iii. 18). Strive for truth unto death, and the Lord God will fight for thee (iv. 28). Hate not laborious work, neither husbandry which the Most High hath ordained (vii. 15). Fear the Lord and honour the priest; and give him his portion as it is commanded thee (vii. 31). Blessed is he whose conscience doth **not** condemn him **(xiv. 2).** Say not, " It was through the **Lord** that I went astray " **(xv. 11).** Forgive thy neigh-

bour his injustice, and then when thou prayest thy sins will
be forgiven (xxviii. 2). He that keepeth the Law bringeth
offerings enough ; he that obeyeth the commandments sacri-
ficeth a peace-offering (xxxii. or xxxv. 1).

Among the thoughts which are not Jewish, and which had
been brought from the East, and thence carried to Egypt, is
the attempt to explain the origin of evil by the Gnostic
doctrine of Antitheses, or Oppositions, against which we have
already quoted the Isaiah of the return home, and the Song of
Moses, and against which the Apostle Paul warns Timothy.*
Thus the Son of Sirach says :—

> Good is the opposite of evil, and life is the opposite of death, so is the
> sinner the opposite of the godly man. And in the same way look upon
> all the works of the Most High ; they are two and two, one the opposite of
> the other (xxxiii. 14, 15).

ANTIOCHUS EPIPHANES KING OF SYRIA; B.C. 175.

During the hundred and forty-eight years since Alexander's death, our history has been very nearly a blank ; but
with the accession of Antiochus Epiphanes to the throne
of Syria, in the year B.C. 175, new troubles came upon the
Jews, and new struggles were called for ; and fortunately
historians at the same time arose to tell of them. The chief
priest Simon II was dead and had been succeeded by his son
Onias III, but his brother, who took the Greek name of
Jason, bought the favour of Antiochus with a large sum of
money, and procured that place for himself, with the avowed
aim of converting his nation to the Greek fashions and
religion. He established a gymnasium for Greek sports in
the outer court of the Temple, at the foot of the Castle, and
he very much neglected the sacrifices in the Temple. When
King Antiochus visited Jerusalem, Jason received him in
great state by torchlight. Jason was, however, three years
afterwards supplanted in his office by another ; for Menelaus,
whom he had sent to Antioch to carry his money to the king,
treacherously offered a yet larger bribe on his own account,
and obtained an order from Antiochus that he should have
the office of chief priest. But the pillage of the Temple, that
was committed by Menelaus and by his order, raised the
inhabitants of the city in rebellion ; and Lysimachus, the
brother of Menelaus, who brought three thousand armed men
against the rioters, was slain in the court of the Temple called
the treasury.†

* 1 Tim. vi. 20.   † 2 Maccab. iv.

About this time Antiochus twice invaded Egypt, on the first occasion defeating the army of Ptolemy Philometor, and remaining master of the country for nearly three years. By this the Jews lost all hope of succour from the Egyptians, **and they** also lost their place of refuge. But while he was absent **on** his second invasion of that country, a report reached Judea that he was dead. Whereupon Jason, the deposed high priest, raised a body of a thousand armed men and made an assault upon Jerusalem, and gained possession of the city, while Menelaus, his rival, fled to the Castle. Jason slew, without **mercy**, the citizens who opposed him, and gained full possession of the government, but he was not able **to** dislodge Menelaus from the Castle. Upon this King Antiochus hastened back from Egypt to quell what had become an insurrection of the Jews, having its beginning in this quarrel of two wicked men for the priesthood. He took Jerusalem by storm, and gave orders that nobody should be spared. For three whole days the slaughter continued; and the number slain was said to be eighty thousand persons, while an equal number were carried away to be sold as slaves. This was in the year B.C. 169.

Antiochus then, to the great dismay of the Jews, went into the Holy of Holies, or inner room of the Temple, under the guidance of Menelaus the apostate, whom he again established in the priesthood. He took up the Holy vessels in his own polluted hands, and had the treasures which were there deposited removed to his own capital, Antioch on the Orontes. The golden altar of incense, **the** lamp-stand, the table for the ceremonial bread, the **censers,** the sprinkling vessels—indeed, all the **gold and** silver dedicated to the service of the Temple, were carried away by profane hands, to **the** grief and dismay of the whole land.* Greek arts and civilization would have been welcomed on their own merits, had they entered the country peaceably; but they were now hated by every good Jew. The teacher, who a century earlier had been thought the best able to hand down the wisdom of the Law from Simon the Just to later ages, had borne a Greek name, Antigonus of Socho; but in this reign a Greek name is the mark of a faithless Jew. Henceforward, more than ever, patriotism takes the form of bigotry, while more enlightened views are spoiled by scepticism.

We have already mentioned the work which Jesus the

---

* 1 Maccab. i. 18-28 ; 2 Maccab. v. 5-21.

384 ANTIOCHUS EPIPHANES KING OF SYRIA; B.C. 175—.

father of Sirach wrote, and which his grandson published;
but chapter xxxvi. (or xxxiii.) 1-17, a prayer against the
oppressors of his country, interrupts the moral advice,
and may have been added by the grandson during this
persecution.

> Have mercy upon us, O Lord God of all, and behold us . . . Raise up
> indignation, and pour out wrath, take away the adversary, and destroy
> the enemy. . . . Smite asunder the heads of the rulers of the Nations,
> who say " There is none other but we." . . . Gather together all the
> tribes of Jacob. . . . Be merciful unto Jerusalem, thy holy city, the
> place of thy rest.

Isaiah xx. is on the conquest of Egypt by Antiochus
Epiphanes in the year B.C. 170, and the writer says that
as Judah in the time of Isaiah walked barefoot and naked
for three years, when their country was occupied by the
Assyrians, so long shall the king of Assyria, meaning
Antiochus Epiphanes, crush the Egyptians. The writer
gives to this short chapter the appearance of being the
words of Isaiah, by telling us the very year in which this
fore-knowledge came to him from Jehovah. Chapter xix. is
on the same subject, but written a little later.

The wars of Antiochus were carried on for the sake of
plunder; and this may have been the reason why Edom,
Moab, and Rabbah of Ammon, were spared by his wasting
armies.* Their poverty may have saved them from the
misfortune which fell so heavily upon Egypt and Judea.

In the year B.C. 167, Antiochus sent Apollonius, his chief
collector of tribute, with a force of twenty-two thousand
men, to further punish the inhabitants of Jerusalem.
Apollonius plundered the city and massacred the people,
and set fire to the houses. But he strengthened the walls of
the castle which the historian calls the city of David; and
from that stronghold, which overhung the courts of the
Temple, he was able to forbid the Jews to enter the holy
place. From this time the daily sacrifices in the Temple
ceased.

Antiochus then issued a decree from Antioch, that the
Jews throughout the country should discontinue all their
religious practices, their circumcision, their sacrifices, and
their keeping the Sabbath. He set up Pagan idols for them
to worship, and made them eat swine's flesh, and punished
those who disobeyed this order with death. Lastly, on

---

* Daniel xi. 41.

the fifteenth day of the month Casleu, a day ever to be remembered, he set up an idol, called the Abomination of Desolation, probably his military standards, on the altar in front of the Temple. All the Books of the Law that could be found were burnt in the fire; his purpose was that the Jewish religion should be wholly forgotten.*

When Antiochus made his attack upon the Jewish religion, he naturally did not allow the Synagogues to escape. These places of worship had grown up gradually during the three centuries which followed the Return from Captivity; but we hear of them for the first time when Antiochus destroyed them.† They had risen as the sacrifices at the High Places lost their value. The service in the Synagogues, as we shall learn in later centuries, was the Temple service, without its sacrifices, its ceremonies, its incense, and often with readers in the place of priests. It consisted of reading the scriptures, with hymns of prayer and praise, and when any one was qualified to teach the rest he was invited to speak. The title of Messenger given to Jeshua in Isaiah xlii. 19 tells us that immediately on the Return from Captivity preaching had become a duty for the priests. Synagogues were the forerunners of the Christian churches, those organized societies for the cultivation of religion and for moral improvement which have been found so well fitted to meet the wants of the human mind. Such societies were unknown in Greece and Rome. There the philosophers when opposing vice and superstition in their schools trusted to pure reason, which they thought needed no help from the moral feelings; and they have shown us how little power pure reason has, even when accompanied with high civilization, in restraining and guiding the human passions. In Greece superstition and immorality have often flourished side by side with philosophy, science, literature and the fine arts. The Jews, on the other hand, were less polished and less logical, but more true to human nature. They appealed less to reason and more to conscience, as the voice of God speaking from within. " The fear of Jehovah is the highest of wisdom," is the Hebrew expression for advising every man to obey his own moral sense of right and wrong. Such was the teaching of the Synagogues, which Antiochus for the time destroyed. The methods employed therein we may suppose were somewhat the same as those

---

* 1 Maccab. i. 29-57.   † Psalm lxxiv. 8.

25

which the Apostle Paul adopted for the Christian churches two centuries later, as described in his Epistles.

When Antiochus introduced **the** athletic sports of the Greeks into Jerusalem, the Greek **drama** was not likely to be omitted; and the Song of Solomon may perhaps be of this time. But its date can be judged of only from its style, as it contains no history by which we can fix it with exactness. The language has many peculiarities in common with that of Ecclesiastes. It is a nuptial poem, a drama in dialogue; the speakers are necessarily six in number, and they need not be more. These are Solomon, with a company of attendant youths, and the bride with her attendant damsels, and two brothers. The bride is called a Shulamite, which may mean a female Solomon. Throughout much of the poem she is speaking in her sleep, and she tells us herself, with the simplicity which is a mark of the early drama, "I am asleep, but my heart waketh." Solomon standing by admires and describes her beauty, and then addresses her maidens saying, "I charge you, O ye daughters of Jerusalem, that ye stir not, nor awaken my Love till she please." Thus it seems to have been written to be acted on the stage. The dialogue is occasionally broken off in a manner that makes it necessary to divide the drama into about ten acts. The writer was acquainted with the language of polished society. Thus he uses the complimentary style of Alexandria when he makes Solomon call his bride his sister, though as the poem shows she was a young woman of humble rank; and he calls his chariot a Pharaoh-chariot, because those brought from Egypt were better than those of the Jewish chariot-makers. The king's litter-bed was a luxury perhaps first known through the Persians. The writer, for a poetic simile, points to David's Tower in Jerusalem, "built for a fortress, on which hang a thousand bucklers," a simile which was just only when the castle had been fortified by Antiochus Epiphanes to overawe the city and the temple. If the pools in the land of Heshbon, by the gate of Beth-rabbim, to which the bride's eyes are compared, are those made by Hyrcanus the son of Joseph, who ruled over that district for seven years in the reign of Seleucus Philopator, the date of the poem is in some degree fixed.

The versification of this poem is more artificial than that of the earlier poetry. The lines answering one another are not simple couplets, but often like the chorus in a Greek **play,** in Strophe and Antistrophe, of several lines each, and then, perhaps, followed by an Epode of two or three lines. As a short specimen, see chapter v. 5-8 :—

STROPHE.

I rose up to open to my Beloved,
And my hands dropped myrrh,
And my fingers liquid myrrh on the handles of the lock.
I opened to my Beloved, but my Beloved was gone ;
He had passed by; my soul failed when **he** had spoken.

ANTISTROPHE.

I sought him, but I could not find him ;
I called him, but he gave me no answer.
The guards that went about the city found me;
They smote me ; they wounded me;
The keepers of the wall took my veil from me.

EPODE.

I charge you, O daughters of Jerusalem, **if ye find my Beloved,**
That ye tell him that I am sick for **love.**

From the unwillingness of commentators to grant a place in the canon of Scripture to a marriage poem, they have usually endeavoured to find in it some mystical allegory or religious argument hidden under the surface; but with very little success. We should consider it less as an example of Hebrew literature than of the corrupt taste of the city **of** Antioch, from which Antiochus was bringing Greek customs and forcing them **on** the Jews. Its sensual character declares its heathen **origin.**

Antiochus at this **time was not master** of Egypt, and there **was a** fresh flight **of Jews into that** country, where they **hoped** to find safety. **Among these was** Dositheus to whom **we** must give the blame **of adding some** worthless chapters to the Book of Esther. **They were** in Greek, and as he said, translated from the **Hebrew in** Jerusalem. But since the Hebrew has not been **found they** remain **as** part of the Apocrypha.[*]

It is to **the** reign **of** this mad and cruel **king, or of** his successors, that we must give the authorship **of the** greater part of the Book of Daniel; chapter i. **we** have supposed written three centuries earlier. Chapters ii.—vi. are a narrative of Daniel's life in Babylon, first under Nebuchadnezzar, then under his son Belshazzar, then under Darius the Mede who overthrew the Babylonian power, and lastly

[*] Esther xi. 1.

under Cyrus the Persian. In chapter ii. Daniel explains to
Nebuchadnezzar his dream about a statue made of gold, and
silver, and copper, and iron mixed with pottery, as meaning
his own kingdom and three kingdoms that were to follow—
namely, the Median, the Persian, and the Greek. This last
is to be divided into many parts, some of which are to be
united by marriages. In chapter iii. Daniel's three friends
are thrown into a fiery furnace, because they will not
worship the king's statue; but they are unhurt by the
flames. In chapter iv. Daniel explains another of the king's
dreams as meaning that Nebuchadnezzar will be changed
into a winged ox for seven years; and this came to pass
accordingly. This chapter is in the form of a proclamation
by Nebuchadnezzar in the king's own words. Here we
meet with a class of angels, called Watchers, or Guardians,
who are often spoken of in the Book of Enoch, a mystical
book of the next century. Chapter v. relates to a time
twenty-five years after the death of Nebuchadnezzar. At
the desire of king Belshazzar, Daniel reads certain mysterious
words written by part of a hand upon the wall, which
declare that the kingdom of Babylon is to be taken from
him, and given to the Medes and Persians. And this
also comes to pass. In chapter vi. Darius the Mede, who
conquers Babylon, throws Daniel into the lion's den because
he disobeys the king's command and continues to worship
God. But the lions do not hurt him; and the king orders
everybody to worship Daniel's God. Daniel lives to see
Cyrus on the throne of Babylon.

The writer of these five chapters uses Greek words for a
"herald" and for the musical instruments. He follows the
Greek custom of calling the fortune-tellers Chaldeans, which
no one living in Babylon under Nebuchadnezzar the Chaldee
could possibly have done. He follows Xenophon's Cyropædia in saying that the king of Babylon was living in his
capital at the time of the siege, and perished when it was
taken. This is in contradiction to the contemporary accounts
in Isaiah xxi. and Jeremiah li., which describe the messengers
as carrying the news of the fall of Babylon to the king,
who was at a distance; and in contradiction to Berosus,
who says that Nabonned, king of Babylon, fled in safety
before Babylon was shut up. The two accounts, however,
may be reconciled by supposing that Belshazzar had been
reigning jointly with his father.* This writer also follows

* Josephus, Apion i. 20.

the Cyropædia in making the king of the Medes ruler of the conquered Babylon for a short time, before he was succeeded by Cyrus; and this is contradicted by Claudius Ptolemy, who makes Cyrus the successor of the Babylonian king. Of these chapters three verses at the beginning are written in Hebrew; but as soon as the Chaldeans begin to speak, the writer uses their language, and then continues to use it for his own narrative to the end.

Secondly, chapter vii. is also written in Chaldee. This returns to an earlier time in Daniel's life, and describes a vision, which Daniel saw in the reign of Belshazzar, of four beasts, meaning **four** kingdoms, probably the same **four as** in the **former** vision. The first beast, a lion with **eagle's** wings, walking on its hind legs, is Babylon; the second, a bear, **is** Media; the third, like a leopard, is Persia, with four heads, namely, Nineveh, Babylon, Egbatana, Susa; the **fourth, the** Greeks, has ten horns, **or** successive kings, and then one a mean horn, which we may recognize as Antiochus Epiphanes. His kingdom is to be destroyed and is to be given to the holy people of the Most High, who are to have everlasting dominion.

Verses 9-14 of this chapter break the narrative and are a late addition, probably after the Christian Era. Here the writer sees one like a Son of Man coming on the clouds of Heaven, the expected Messiah; and to him God gives an everlasting kingdom, not of the Jews only but of all nations of the earth. This closely resembles the second vision in the Book of Enoch.

Thirdly, chapter viii. **is written in** Hebrew, as is also the remainder of the Book **of Daniel. It** describes another vision which Daniel saw in the reign of Belshazzar, not as before in Babylon, but **in** Susa, the capital of Persia. He saw **a ram** with two horns, namely, Media and Persia, and a he-goat, Greece, with a great horn between his eyes, namely, Alexander the Great, who smites the ram. When this great horn is broken four others rise in its place, the kings of Macedonia, Asia Minor, Syria, and Egypt. Out of one of these comes a mean horn, Antiochus Epiphanes, who stops the daily sacrifice in the Temple for two thousand three hundred days. He is to be broken, but not by any hand. That is to say, he is to die a natural death. The vision is explained to Daniel by the angel Gabriel. This is the first time that we have had any heavenly messenger, other than Satan, mentioned by name.

Fourthly, chapters x. and xi. contain a yet more descriptive vision, which Daniel saw in the third year of Cyrus's reign, when living on the banks of the Tigris. We here have the history of Alexander the Great and the wars and marriages between the kings of Egypt and the kings of Syria, till the time of a vile person, Antiochus Epiphanes. His three years of war against Egypt are mentioned in chapter xi. 25, 29, and 40, thus agreeing with Isaiah xx.; and then his being called away by tidings out of the east and the north, where he dies. We now meet with a second angel with a name, Michael, who is described as a great prince which standeth up for the children of Israel; and also with similar angels, or princes, for the kingdoms of Persia and Greece, as each nation was thought to have its own guardian-angel. In the Book of Tobit there are said to be seven angels who carry up the prayers of the saints to God.

The writer of this last mentioned portion of the Book of Daniel had probably lived in Egypt, as appears from his minute knowledge of the history of the first five Ptolemies.

The four portions of the book above described seem to be by three, or perhaps four authors, but all of one date. In these chapters the name of Jehovah is never used. Daniel's God is called the Most High, the God of Heaven, God of gods, and Lord of kings, the Ancient of days, but never Jehovah. In chapter ix., which is of yet later date and to be spoken of hereafter, the name of Jehovah is used.

The Book of Daniel is classed with the Prophets because, like the chapters improperly added to Jeremiah and Isaiah, it professes to foretell future events; but it does not aim like the old Prophets at the orator's style, nor does it make any approach to their persuasive eloquence.

If we compare the Book of Daniel with two Greek translations, the older one, which originally formed part of the Septuagint, and the newer made by Theodotion in the second century, which is now always printed as part of the Septuagint, we shall see reasons for thinking that, for chapters ii.—vi., the Greek is the original. These were written by an Alexandrian Jew, at this time, as an addition to the Greek Bible. The Jew of Palestine who added them to the Hebrew Bible began his translation in Hebrew, but, being more familiar with Chaldee, soon turned to that language. He did not aim at being quite literal. He rejected some sentences, such as that Nebuchadnezzar ruled over one hundred and twenty provinces from India to Ethiopia—words borrowed from Esther i. 1—and the hymn of the three men in the fiery furnace. He added others, such as the complimentary words, "O king! live for ever," and that Belshazzar, after reading the fatal words on the wall, was slain "that very night." For the seventh chapter, the Chaldee is probably the original, written, perhaps, by the translator of the former five chapters. For all chapters after the seventh, the Hebrew is, no doubt, the original.

Psalm lxxiv. is of this time, and describes the destruction of the Temple by order of Antiochus Epiphanes, in terms which will not suit the former destruction by Nebuchadnezzar, when the people were carried into captivity :—

> O God, why hast thou wholly cast us off?
> Thine anger smoketh against the sheep of thy pasture.
> Remember thy congregation, thou purchasedst it of old,
> The staff of thine inheritance, which thou didst redeem,
> This mount Zion, wherein thou didst dwell.
> Lift up thy steps toward the thorough desolations,
> All the wickedness of the enemy in the Holy Place.
> Thine enemies roar within thy Place of meeting [or temple];
> They set up their ensigns for signs.
> A man [of Tyre] was famous for bringing to the hill-side
> Axes against the thick branches of the trees ;
> But now the whole carved work thereof at once
> They break down with axes and hammers.
> They have cast fire into thy Sanctuary,
> They have crushed the Tabernacle of thy name to the ground.
> They said in their hearts, "Let us destroy them at once."
> They have burnt every Synagogue of God in the land.

In this Psalm, in the last of the lines here quoted, we remark that there are now throughout the land other places of worship than those before mentioned. We thus note the change in religious customs which has come over the people. In the earlier parts of this history the only public worship was the sacrifice on the Altar, or High place, accompanied with a Psalm sung, and sometimes with a feast made off part of the animal slain. After the return from captivity, we meet with a new religious act, the listening to the public reading and explanation of the Law, which was added to the confession of sins, as part of the worship of Jehovah. But now we find that there were buildings, or places of meeting, in every part of the land set apart for these religious acts; and the gradual way in which these came into use is shown by our finding the word "meeting or congregation" used for the building or place in which the congregation

met; this we must, in translating, call a Synagogue. In
Lamentations ii. 6, as in verse 4 of this Psalm, the Temple
had received the same name, place of meeting.

Psalm lxxix. also mourns over **the ruin** brought upon the
city by Antiochus in terms which do not suit with its former
overthrow by Nebuchadnezzar, **when** the people were carried
into captivity :—

> O God, the nations are come into thine **inheritance ;**
> Thy holy Temple have they defiled ;
> They have laid Jerusalem in ruins ;
> The dead bodies of thy servants have they given
> To be food to the fowls of the heavens,
> The flesh of thy saints to the wild beasts of the earth.

Psalm lxxxv. speaks of the Return from Captivity as a
forgiveness of sins, and as an event long since past; and it
mourns **over the** renewed anger of Jehovah, as shown in the
renewed misery of the country, and prays for a similar relief
from the enemy. It seems **to** belong to this time of Syrian
oppression.

Psalm xciv. may **be of this sad time of** suffering under
tyranny. The writer prays :—

> God of vengeance, Jehovah,
> God of vengeance shine forth.
> Lift thyself up, thou judge of the earth,
> Render back a reward to the proud.
> They crush thy people, O Jehovah,
> And afflict thy heritage.

He seems to point to the apostate priests who made agree-
ments with the foreign king, **and** even helped him in his
attack on their religion ; thus,—

> Shall a wicked throne have fellowship with Thee,
> One which frameth mischief against the Law ?

The fifth chapter of Lamentations seems to belong to this
later time of the city lying in ruins rather than to the time
of Nebuchadnezzar's conquest of the country, to which the
other Lamentations belong. In this chapter, though the
sufferings of the people are described at length, we have no
mention of any captivity. Nor is this an alphabetic poem
like the other Lamentations, and yet its couplets are twenty-
two in number, as if one for each letter of the alphabet.
The writer is troubled with the old national opinion that
misfortunes **are** always a punishment for sins ; and he complains,—

> Our fathers sinned, and they are not ;
> And we have borne their iniquities. (v. 7.)

Chapters xxxviii. xxxix. of Ezekiel relate to this time. The writer prophesies at some length the destruction of Gog of the land of Magog, a name for the Scythians, or rather the unknown barbarians, beyond the knowledge of the geographer. Gog is to perish miserably in the land of Judea, which he has conquered. The writer seems to be foretelling with minute description an event which took place at the time of Ezekiel's birth—namely, the invasion and destruction of the Scythians; but he is in reality concealing his denunciation of a king under whose tyranny the Israelites were suffering four centuries after the death of Ezekiel in whose name this is written. The invasion is spoken of as to take place " in the latter days," after Israel had been " brought back from the sword, and gathered out of many peoples," after " the mountains of Israel had been a long time waste," but when " the desolate homes were now inhabited " and the people " dwelling as if in safety, as if in villages, having neither bars nor doors " to their cities. The invader is to come from the north, and to be allied to " those who dwell securely in the isles," namely, the Greeks. He is the person foretold " by the prophets of Israel," perhaps in Daniel vii. viii. and xi., and the attempt to resist him will be the cause of civil war, when " every man's sword will be against his brother." This can be no other than Antiochus Epiphanes king of Syria.

Isaiah lxiii. 1-6 is not without its difficulty; for neither the Greek historians, nor the historical books of the Bible, have mentioned the conquest of Edom here spoken of. It is, however, described in Numbers xxiv. 21, 22. It has been conjectured that it was by the Persians, in one of their many wars with Egypt. But it was by Antiochus Epiphanes, perhaps, that Edom was thus severely treated, when his armies for three years together were marching to Egypt through the southern part of Judea. This date also receives some little confirmation from the agreement in expression between the opening words, and those of Solomon's Song viii. 5, which we give to this time.

Isaiah lxiii 7—lxvi., also belongs to this sad time. It begins with a prayer to Jehovah that he would remember the days of old, when he sent a Moses to raise up his people. The oppressors have trodden down the sanctuary, Zion is a desert, Jerusalem is a desolation ; the Holy House is burnt with fire. The writer encourages the people with the hope of again being masters of their own country, and threatens

punishment on the apostates who had worshipped in groves
and eaten the swine's flesh. The Book of Maccabees, in
relating the discreditable struggles between rival priests,
and how Antiochus endeavoured to force Greek manners
on the people, does not tell us how far the opposing parties
were the old parties whom we have seen dividing the State.
This is in some degree explained by these chapters of Isaiah.
The writer is evidently one of the lower class, to whom the
upper class denied the name of Jew. He says to Jehovah,
"Doubtless Thou art our Father, though Abraham should
be ignorant of us, and Israel should not acknowledge us."
At the same time, he strongly blames those who desert the
Law, and sacrifice in gardens, burn incense on altars of
brick, eat swine's flesh, and commit unnatural crimes. From
this we learn that it was the ruling party, perhaps we may
say the Sadducees, who were most willing to surrender their
Law to the will of Antiochus; and who hated their neighbours, and cast them out for Jehovah's name, and who,
while eating swine's flesh, would say to a more scrupulous
brother, "Come not near to me; for I am holier than
thou;" and that it was the humbler class—those who were
told that they were **not real** Jews—that struggled manfully
for their religion.

When the writer accuses these apostate Jews of preparing
a table unto Good Fortune, and filling up drink offerings
unto Fate, he may be blaming the Sadducees, or at least
the writer of Ecclesiastes, who taught that we were in some
degree governed by chance or Good Fortune. The writer
styles God the nation's Father, a title not used in the earlier
writings bearing the name of Isaiah. He then promises that
the seed of Judah shall again possess the holy mountain;
in chapter lxv. he quotes the words "Behold it is I," from
chapter lii. 6, and then the words "I will not keep silence,"
from chapter lxii. 1. He also, when promising the coming
prosperity, uses the words of Amos ix. 14:—"They shall
build houses, and inhabit them; and they shall plant vineyards, and **eat** the fruit thereof;" and the words of Isaiah
xi. 6, 7:—"The wolf and the lamb shall feed together, and
the lion shall eat straw like the ox." With this bold figure
of speech had Isaiah promised the return of peace upon
earth. The appearance of Judas the Maccabee, leader of
the revolt, is announced in the words, "the land was delivered
of a man child."

At such a time of distress, when every man had to work

with his own hands, there could have been but few ministers
of religion, even if the national worship had been allowed.
Our writer remarks their absence, and sets it down to the
scantiness of the population, saying that, when the scattered
children of Israel are recalled home, some will be taken for
priests and Levites (lxvi. 21).

THE REVOLT; JUDAS THE MACCABEE; B.C. 166.

The cruelty **with** which the order of Antiochus against
the Jewish religion were executed at last roused the people
into rebellion. The revolt is called a rising of the Jews,
but was not limited to Judea; nor did it begin in Judea.
Israel and Judah were for a time united by their common
sufferings. It was only when the revolt became successful
that it naturally took the form of a Jewish revolt; because
it was only in Judea that there remained any feelings of
union upon which it was possible to build up a nation. It
began in the city of Modin, a town near Lydda, perhaps
ten miles from Joppa, on the road to Jerusalem. At Modin,
Mattathias, an old priest with five sons, refused to break the
laws of their religion, and they fled to the mountains **to**
escape from the king's officers. There they were joined by
many others, and they were able to resist the troops sent
against them. Judas, one of the five sons, became general
of this little band of patriots. He defeated in battle, **first**
Apollonius, and afterwards Seron, who **came** against him
with a second army.*

This revolt was altogether **a popular** movement. It was
not encouraged by the chiefs **of the** nation in Jerusalem.
In all the struggles for independence during the monarchy,
the inhabitants of Jerusalem were always the party favourable
to **resistance** against the invader; the people of the country
wished **to pay** a tribute and live at peace. But at this time
the case **was** otherwise. The ruined city had no walls which
could protect its inhabitants against an army, while many
of them held office under Antiochus and were zealous in his
service. The nobles left the country people to fight the battle
by themselves, or rather took part against them.

Antiochus, if he had been at leisure, would have led his
army in person against the rebels, but he was called away by
news from Persia. So he led his principal army into that

* 1 Maccab. ii.—iii. 24.

country to enforce the collection of the Persian tribute, leaving Lysias in command on the west of the Euphrates, with orders to reduce the Jews to obedience.* Though the force of Syria was thus weakened by the two rebellions which at the same time called for the attention of Antiochus, yet the troops which were sent against the Jews were far more numerous than any that Judas could bring against them. But the Jews fought in despair, led on by religious patriotism. At Emmaus, near Jerusalem, they defeated a Syrian army commanded by Gorgias; and the next year they routed a second army under the command of Lysias, who then thought it wise to withdraw to Antioch.

The neighbourhood of Jerusalem was now free from the Syrians; and Judas proposed to attack Jerusalem itself, and to gain possession of the capital of the country for his seat of government. The Syrian garrison withdrew into the castle. His troops entered the ruined city without difficulty, and mourned over the desolation in the courts of the Temple. He was now in some degree at leisure; and, as a first step towards re-establishing the nation, he began to restore the service of the Temple.

The Syrian garrison, joined by such of the Jews as were on the side of the Syrians, kept themselves within the castle, while Judas repaired the altar and the Holy of Holies, and celebrated afresh the ceremony of dedication for eight days upon cleansing the Temple from the Gentiles. But as he was by no means strong enough to assault the castle, he contented himself with building strong walls against it, to protect the city and the Temple-yard from any attacks from the garrison of the castle. One of these walls divided the Great Court from the Court of the Gentiles. For the ceremony of dedication Judas chose the twenty-fifth day of Chisleu, the day on which Zerubbabel had laid the foundation of the second Temple, three hundred and fifty-six years before. On that day the priests, whom he had appointed, while he himself acted as high priest, offered their first sacrifice on the altar, and did the same on each of the following seven days.† From that time forward the Jews have kept that week, in mid-winter, holy, under the name of the Feast of Dedication.

Another important work which Judas then began was to bring together copies of the Hebrew religious books.

---

* 1 Maccab. iii. 27-37.   † 1 Maccab. iv.

The library in the Chambers of the Temple had been destroyed by order of Antiochus; and Judas now restored it so far as he was able.* He probably recovered copies of all the more important books—of all those, indeed, which had been sent, a century before, to Alexandria, to be translated into Greek; and the later writings which he was now able to add to the Hebrew volumes, were in due time added to the Greek copies by the Jews in Alexandria. The Greek Jews, while adding to their Bible several books which the Hebrews did not accept, omitted none to which the Hebrews from time to time had given authority. But there must have been many other valuable works which we have lost through the violence of Antiochus Epiphanes—in particular, we may suppose, the original authors from which the Books of Chronicles were compiled in the time of Nehemiah. The scribes to whom was intrusted the task of editing the sacred books no doubt had before them copies from various cities, some written by northern scribes and some by southern, each with passages more or less favourable to its own part of the country. Many of these contradictory passages we now find embodied in the Bible, with a praiseworthy impartiality; the Books of Kings and Chronicles are allowed to contradict one another with David's crimes and David's piety, with Solomon's idolatry and Solomon's devotion to the priests; and while a large part of the Bible condemns as blameable all altars but that at Jerusalem, we yet find the passages not excluded which give the authority of Abraham, Jacob, and Moses to the altar near Shechem, and the authority of Abraham and Jacob to that Beth-el.

Judas then carried the war against the Edomites, who held Hebron, and into the country of the Ammonites on the west of the Jordan. The Edomites had latterly spread themselves over the South Country, the district between Hebron and the desert, and had carried the name of Edom, or Idumea as it is now written, as far northward as Mareshah in the Low Country.† The Calebites, the Beasts of the South Country as they are called in Isaiah xxx., had never been wholly Jews, and had readily joined the Edomites. The sway of Judas over Judea did not reach beyond twenty miles to the south of Jerusalem; and there he fortified Beth-zur, as a protection against the encroaching Edomites.‡ He was nearly in the position of Saul with

* 2 Maccab. ii. 14.　† Joseph. Antiq. XIII. ix. 1.　‡ 1 Maccab. iv. 61.

David's country in arms against him. Now that the name
of Edom had travelled northward, the Arabs, or Ishmaelites,
who held the rocky fastness of Petra, are called Kenites.*

While this war against the Edomites was going on, Judas
received a considerable increase of strength from the people
of Galilee, where the tyranny of their Syrian neighbours
made them look to him as their deliverer. He accordingly
sent his brother Simon with a body of troops into Galilee,
where Simon defeated the enemy, and brought back with
him into Judea many families who were friendly to their
cause. In Gilead, also, Judas was equally successful; and
as he was not strong enough to hold any part of that
country on the east of the Jordan, he brought back with
him from thence a large number of Israelite families who
were glad to seek a refuge with him in Judea. In this
way, the struggle carried on by Judas was an Israelite as
much as a Jewish struggle. Though his sway did not
reach far, his army was composed of men of all the tribes;
and very possibly the men who held the castle of Jerusalem
against him, the party who counselled submission to the
Syrians, may have called themselves the Jewish party. In
the days of Jeremiah the party for resistance to the invader
was defeated, and we accordingly heard very little about
them; now the resisting party is successful, and those who,
like Jeremiah, advised submission, are called apostates and
deserters, as he was. In this miserable and distracted
condition did Judea and Jerusalem remain during the reign
of Antiochus Epiphanes.† He died in B.C. 164, and was
succeeded by his young son Antiochus Eupator.

After the death of Antiochus Epiphanes, the party of
Judas for a moment gained a truce from their enemies.‡
Encouraged by this success, Judas laid siege to the castle of
Jerusalem, which was held not by the Syrian troops, but
by the party opposed to him, the party who advised
submission to Syria, as the only way to obtain peace for
their distracted country. These were called the apostate
Jews, who preferred the Greco-Syrian government to the
independence of their country. The historian, who is
friendly to Judas, says nothing about any large party in
the country being on the side of those who held the castle;
but we may be sure that without such a party they could
not have held that fortress for years against those who held
the ruined city and temple.

* Numbers xxiv. 21.   † 1 Maccab. v.   ‡ 2 Maccab. xi.

Several centuries earlier, during the Assyrian and Babylonian invasions of Judea, the people had been divided, as now, into two parties. The country party, called the Men of the Land and Men of Judah, wished to buy off invasion by paying a tribute ; the priests and inhabitants of Jerusalem wished to resist. The more wealthy, the more educated, were then the patriots, or, as some would say, the fanatics, who struggled for independence. **But** since the Captivity, and during these Greco-Syrian troubles, the politics of the two parties seemed to have been changed. The country party, headed by Judas, were now the patriots or fanatics ; while the nobles and the wealthy were willing to yield to the new king, the young Antiochus Eupator, and were holding the castle of Jerusalem for the Greco-Syrians.

The attempt of Judas to gain the castle of Jerusalem brought down upon him king Antiochus Eupator, at the head of a large army, which included thirty-two elephants. The Syrians not only saved the castle from Judas, but drove him out of Jerusalem. Antiochus then entered the city under promise that it should not be hurt ; but he broke his oath, and destroyed the fortifications. The historian of the Maccabee revolt says that this capture of Jerusalem was made easy **to** the Syrians by reason of the scarcity of food, for it was **a seventh, or** sabbath year.* This was the year B.C. 164, and was perhaps the only time when such a year **is** mentioned in history. Though it was ordered in the Law, we have not before heard of its being observed.

Antiochus Eupator was soon afterwards **slain** ; but his death brought no relief to the Jews. Demetrius, the next king, sent an army under command of Nicanor into Judea. He came to Jerusalem, and from thence marched out against Judas. In the battle that followed, Nicanor's army was defeated, and he himself slain. This obtained for the country a short time of rest.

Judas then appointed the 13th of the month Adar, the twelfth month, to be a feast for ever in memory of the nation's deliverance, and he wrote a letter to the Jews of Egypt asking them to join in returning thanks to God for the purification of the Temple. The letter was addressed **to** Aristobulus, who had been king Ptolemy's tutor, and is dated forty years later, as we may suppose, by a mistake of the historian.† Judas also sent to the Romans, and made

---

* 1 Maccab. vi. 53.　　　　　† 2 Maccab. i. 10-18.

a treaty with that rising people, who now for the first time
are heard of in the East. In the next invasion by the Syrians,
the Jews were unsuccessful, and the brave Judas, the
liberator of his country, was slain.*

Judas, and afterwards his family, bore the name of Maccabee. The meaning and etymology of the word is uncertain.
It may possibly come from the Hebrew word Cocab, *a star*,
in Syriac, Cocaba; which derivation seems probable, because
some of his successors, when allowed to coin money, placed
a star upon their coins. The word is akin to the Arabic
Cocaba, *to shine;* and hence the word Macocaba might
mean *illustrious*, and his friends may have given that name
to Judas as a copy of the name of the Syrian king against
whom he was fighting, namely, Antiochus Epiphanes, *or the
illustrious*.

Part of Balaam's prophecy, in Numbers xxiv. 14-18, seems
meant for Judas, who would very naturally be described as a
Star, if that be the word upon which his name of Maccabee
was founded :—

> There shall come a Star out of Jacob,
> And a Sceptre shall arise out of Israel.
> And he will smite the sides of Moab,
> And destroy all the children of tumult.
> And Edom will be a possession,
> Seir also will be the possession of its enemies;
> And Israel will do valiantly.
> One sprung from Jacob will have dominion,
> And will destroy those that remain of the city.

"Those that remain of the city" are the so-called apostates
who held the castle of Jerusalem, who recommended submission to the king of Syria, and whom Judas had not yet been
able to dislodge. In all former prophecies, even in Isaiah lxv.,
written only a year or two before the revolt, the expected
deliverer was looked for in the tribe of Judah, he was to be
of the seed of David; but now the northern name of Israel is
used. This agrees with our seeing that Judas's army was
gathered out of all the tribes, and that the princes of Judah
held the castle of Jerusalem against him.

The destruction of Edom, in Numbers xxiv. 21, 22, is one
of several prophecies there put into Balaam's mouth, and it
was written perhaps at this time. It relates to Antiochus
Epiphanes :—

* 1 Maccab. vi.-ix.

And he looked on the Kenites [a tribe of Edomites], and took up his parable and said,

> Strong is thy dwelling-place,
> And thou puttest thy nest in the Rock [or Petra],
> Nevertheless the Kenite will be wasted.
> Till when will Asshur [or Syria] carry thee captive?

In explanation of this, we remark that, at this time, the name of Edom covered, not only the country to the south of the Dead Sea, but that part of Judea below Hebron which has been called the South Country; and the inhabitants of the city of Sela, or Petra, *the rock*, were now called Kenites.

In another inserted passage in the Book of Numbers, which seems to belong to this time, chapter xxiv. 23, 24, Balaam is made to say :—

> Alas, who shall be alive when God doeth this?
> And galleys from the coast of Chittim [or the Romans],
> Will even afflict Asshur [or the Syrians];
> And they [the Syrians] will afflict Eber [or the Hebrews].
> Then he also [Antiochus Epiphanes] will perish for ever.

The name of Chittim, properly Cyprians, is used for either Greeks or Romans; Asshur, properly Assyria, is several times used for the Syrians; and Eber, of course, is the Hebrew nation. The person who is to perish for ever is Antiochus Epiphanes, the king of Syria, whom the writer did not venture to name. Verses 21, 22, may perhaps be of the same date.

The few words of 1 Chronicles v. 1, 2, which say that when the birthright was taken away from Reuben it was given to the sons of Joseph, and which thus treat David and his family as usurpers, may perhaps have been added to that book at this time. The birthplace of the Maccabees was on the border between Dan and Ephraim, and not within the land of Judah.

Many of the Psalms were written at this time, among others the Elohistic Psalm lxxv. This, like Psalm lxxiv., calls the Temple the place of meeting or Synagogue. But this Psalm, written at the beginning of the revolt, is in a more hopeful strain. The Jews are in hopes of regaining possession of Jerusalem and their Temple. The writer looks forward to the near re-establishment of their religious worship, and says to God :—

> That thy Name is near thy wonders declare, [saying]
> When I take the place of Meeting I will judge aright;
> When the earth and all its inhabitants are dissolved,
> I will establish the pillars of it.

This writer follows Ezekiel and the Book of **Job** in making the north more particularly the dwelling-place of the Almighty; thus:—

> Lift not up your horn on high, speaking with a stiff neck;
> For lifting up cometh not from the east,
> Nor from the west, nor from the [southern] desert.
> But God is the judge;
> He putteth down one, and lifteth up another.

The last two lines in this Psalm may perhaps point to Judas the Maccabee:—

> All the horns of the wicked will I cut off,
> But the horns of a righteous man shall be lifted up.

Psalm cxxxvi. was probably written at this time. It **gives** praise to Jehovah:—

> For he is good, for his kindness endureth for ever
> He hath rescued us from our oppressors, for his kindness endureth
> for ever.

In 1 Chron. xvi. 34 this burden is said to have been sung when David brought the Ark into Jerusalem; and in 2 Chron. vii. 3-6, this burden is quoted as sung by the priests in the reign of Solomon, when he dedicated the first Temple to Jehovah.

Another of the Psalms which was written at this time is the Elohistic Psalm lx., which begins like Psalm lxxiv., already spoken of, but is far more hopeful. Judas has perhaps in part regained Jerusalem, but not the castle:—

> O God, thou hast cast us off, thou hast scattered us;
> Thou hast been **angry**; O turn thyself to us again.

God answers:—

> I will triumph, I will divide up Shechem into portions,
> And will measure out the valley of Succoth.
> Gilead is mine, and Manasseh is mine,
> Ephraim also is the strong covering of my head;
> Judah is my staff of power.
> Moab is my wash-pot; over Edom I will empty my shoe.
> Shout aloud [O Jerusalem] over the Philistines.

At this time Judas had been fighting successfully in Gilead, while his brother Simon, after passing through Ephraim and Manasseh, was attempting to reduce Galilee. He was not wholly master of Shechem and the neighbouring valley of Succoth, against which the Psalmist directs his threats. For the watery Moab, and the sandy **Edom,** he has nothing but hatred and contempt.

The writer asks :—

> Who will bring me into the besieged **city?**
> Who will lead me into Edom?
> Wilt not thou, O God, who hadst cast us off?
> And wilt not thou, O God, go out with our armies?

And here we are tempted to conjecture that by the Besieged City the Psalmist means the Castle of Jerusalem, which Judas had not yet been able to capture; and that to this **castle** he gives the name of Edom. Judas, though defending himself against the Edomites, was not proposing **to invade** Edom. Nearly the same as this is Psalm cviii.

Psalm xliv., another Elohistic Psalm, has many of the same thoughts **as** Psalm lx., the last mentioned. After recording God's **former** kindness, it complains :—

> But thou hast cast us off, and put us to shame,
> And goest not forth with our armies.
> Thou makest us to turn back from the enemy;
> And they that hate us plunder us for themselves.

Psalm xxii. belongs to some time after the Captivity, as it separates "those **that fear** Jehovah" from the seed of Jacob and Israel; and also to **a** time when the nation's enemies were the Syrians and Edomites. This seems to fix it to the time of the Maccabee struggle. The Syrians are called Bulls and Bullocks, as in Isaiah xxxiv.; thus :—

> Many Bullocks have encompassed me,
> Strong Bulls of Bashan have beset me round.
> They gape upon me with their mouths,
> As a ravening and roaring lion.

The Edom**ites of** the south are called Dogs, which indeed is simply their name, Calebites; thus :—

> For the Dogs have encompassed me;
> The assembly of the wicked have gone round me;
> Like a lion [they tear] my hands and my feet.

In the same figurative way the writer speaks of their old enemies, whom they have now no more occasion to fear;

the Assyrians he calls Lions, and the Egyptians he calls
Buffaloes, as other writers have done before him; thus:—

> Thou savedst me from the mouth of the Lion,
> And didst answer me from the horns of the Buffaloes.

He thus prays **for** relief from the present troubles. The
latter third **part of the** Psalm may have been added in thankfulness when the troubles were lessened.

Psalm lxxxi. belongs to a time of oppression under foreign
enemies, when, however, the people are yet able to celebrate
the solemn feasts, and when sufferings had in some minds
healed the jealousy which once divided northern Israel **from**
Judah. The writer, who belonged to Ephraim or Manasseh,
professes that those tribes also were under the care of
Jehovah, or rather makes Joseph enter the land of Egypt as
representative of the whole nation, saying,—

> The testimony was in his name Jeho-seph,
> When he went through the land of Egypt [saying]
> "I shall hear a language that I understand not."

He thus spells the name **of Joseph as if** it were a Jehovistic
name.

The few lines **of** Zechariah ix. 11-17, which tell us that
both the northern and the southern tribes were united against
the Greeks, can belong to no earlier time in our history.
Jehovah is there made to say, " I have guided the aim of
Judah for me; I have prepared the bow of Ephraim and have
raised up thy sons, O Zion, against thy sons, O Greece, and
made thee as the sword of a warrior." It was on the revolt
of the Maccabees against the Greek kings of Syria that the
Jews for the first time fought against Greeks. The Greeks
have already been known to us in Ezekiel xxvii., and in Joel
ii. 28—iii. 8, written about the time of Ezekiel, as people at a
distance to whom the Tyrians sold the Jewish children as
slaves; but not till the time of Alexander **the** Great do they
play any **part in** Jewish history.

Together with the other writings of this time we may also
mention the Inscriptions in Wady Mocatteb, *the sculptured
valley* **near** Mount Serbal, which the pilgrims from Egypt
to the Holy Mount continued to cut upon the rocks. While
Antiochus was master of Egypt, the pilgrims record their
hatred of their country's oppressors in a guarded manner
without naming them. One had prayed, " Utterly destroy
the rich men," meaning, probably, the Syrians, and trusting

that the near resemblance of the words "rich men" to "Assyrians" may lead the reader here, as in Isaiah liii. 9, to guess the meaning. But now the Jews in Egypt can speak without fear. One pilgrim, as his memorial offering to Jehovah, writes on the rock the prayer, "Slaughter, O Jehovah, the Syrians." He is followed by others who pray for the city which has broken free from a wicked people. One prays for the plundered city on the outside of the castle; while another, who may have been opposed to the Maccabee revolt, seems to pray for those who are in the castle.

On the death of Judas the Maccabee, his brother Jonathan took the chief command in Judea, and a few years afterwards the civil war between two claimants for the crown of Syria, Demetrius Soter and Alexander Balas, gave a short truce to this unhappy country. In the year B.C. 155, the Jews were able again to offer sacrifices on the altar of Jerusalem, to light the lamps in the Temple, and to set out the presence-bread on the table before Jehovah. On this occasion they wrote to the Jews in Egypt, inviting them to join in returning thanks at the Feast of Tabernacles for this relief. The letter was dated in the 169th year, thus using the Greek era of Alexander's death, not the era of the Seleucidæ, their enemies.*

In the year B.C. 152, the two kings both made offers to Jonathan, with a view to purchasing his friendship. Demetrius promised to add to Judea three portions of Samaria and Galilee which Jonathan already held, and also a district round Ptolemais on the Phenician coast, and to remit all tribute; and gave consent for a body of thirty thousand Jews to be enlisted in his army, who were to be paid by him, and to be under the command of their own officers. Demetrius at the same time sent orders to the hostile party in the castle of Jerusalem to cease from any act of war, and to deliver up the hostages whom they had in their possession, which they accordingly did.

Jonathan then removed his seat of government from Michmash into Jerusalem, though the castle was still held by his enemies. He took upon himself the office of high priest, to the disappointment of Onias IV, the son of Onias III. It is probable that Onias had belonged to the political party which had been opposed to the revolt; and Jonathan may have found it necessary to establish a new priesthood of men

* 2 Maccab. i. 7.

more friendly to himself. This **new** body of priests were of
the party afterwards called the Pharisees ; and the old hereditary party, who claimed to be lineal descendants of Zadok,
the priest in Solomon's reign, were put aside. This was
like a religious revolution ; and we may perhaps understand
the words of Isaiah lxv. as addressed to the rejected priests,
" Ye shall leave your name for a curse unto my chosen ones.
For the Lord Jehovah will slay thee, and will call his
servants by another name ; so that he who blesseth himself
on the earth shall bless himself by the God of truth. . . .
For behold, I will create new heavens, and a new earth."
And "they did evil before mine eyes, and chose that **in**
which I delighted not."

Upon this revolution Onias withdrew into Egypt ; and
there Ptolemy Philometor gave him permission to build a
Temple to Jehovah. Onias thereupon became the high
priest of the Jews living in lower Egypt, with a Temple in
rivalry to that in Jerusalem, in the same manner and for the
same reason that Manasseh had before made a rival Temple
in Samaria, because he had been deposed from the post of
high priest in Jerusalem. Of the Jews in Egypt those
who had settled among the Greeks in Alexandria, had very
much adopted the Greek language. But there remained the
old Jewish colony on the east of the Delta, where five cities,
between the Pelusiac branch of the Nile and the desert, yet
spoke the language of Canaan. There, in the city of Onion,
Onias was allowed to build his Temple.* This was, perhaps,
the city before called On. It is Vicus Judæorum in the
Roman Itinerary, and since it was ruined has been known as
Tel Yahoud, *the mounds of the Jews.*

Jonathan put no trust in the promises made to him by
Demetrius, and he made a treaty with Alexander Balas,
the rival claimant.† This struggle for the throne of Syria
between these kings was continued after their death by
their successors. On the death of Demetrius Soter, his son
Demetrius Nicator **succeeded to** his claim, and after a time
gained the throne of Syria from Alexander Balas. Which
ever family reigned in Antioch the Jews' sufferings were the
same.

In that same year Antiochus Theos II, the son of Alexander
Balas, gained the throne, though Demetrius Nicator was still
in arms, as was Jonathan the Maccabee in Jerusalem. But

---

* Joseph. **Antiq.** XIII. iii. 1; Isaiah xix   † 1 Maccab. x.

the next year, perhaps B.C. 144, the young Antiochus and Jonathan were both slain by a new claimant for the Syrian throne, a rebel named Trypho.

Simon, Jonathan's brother, was then chosen by the people as their leader, and shortly afterwards, in the year B.C. 142, Demetrius Nicator made peace with him, and confirmed to him the privileges which the former Demetrius had before granted to Jonathan. He remitted as before all arrears of tribute. Simon was henceforth to be treated as an independent though tributary prince ; and on that year the people of Israel dated their legal instruments and contracts, "In the first year of Simon the high priest, the governor and leader of the Jews."

Simon accepted these high offices only for the present, waiting "until a faithful prophet should arise." * In the same spirit, his late brother Judas left the stones of the **ruined** Temple "until a prophet **should arise to** show what **should** be done with them." † **The hope** for this prophet was probably founded on Deuteronomy xviii. 18, or was part of the expectation raised by the last words of Malachi, that Elijah the prophet should come before the dreadful day of Jehovah.

Psalms x. and ix. cannot be dated with any certainty, since our history has shown so many occasions for mournful and for thankful strains ; but they belong to a time after the Return from Captivity, and probably to this late time. Psalm x., written before the revolt, complains :—

> Why standest thou afar off, O Jehovah ?
> Thou hidest thyself in times of trouble.

The wicked man **in** the lurking places of the villages, **who** lieth in wait to catch the poor, is probably the foreign **tribute** collector. After praising the Almighty, it ends with the prayer :—

> May the nations be destroyed out of His land.

Psalm ix., on the other hand, having perhaps been written a little **later, is in** thankfulness for relief from the oppressor; saying:—

> Thou hast rebuked the nations and destroyed the wicked;
> Thou hast blotted out their name for ever and ever.
> The destruction of the enemy is wholly completed,
> And thou hast destroyed their cities.
> The memory of them is perished.

* 1 Maccab. xiv. 41.   † 1 Maccab. iv. 46.

It was then, perhaps, that the Second Book of Maccabees was written; and also the Letter of the Jews of Jerusalem to the Jews in Egypt which forms the introduction to that **Book**. The Letter asks them to join in celebrating the purification of the Temple, and it needs a few words of explanation. After the greetings it quotes a former Letter, written in 169 of Alexander's Death, or B.C. 155, in the time of Demetrius Soter and Jonathan, to the same purpose (i. 7-9); and then (in i. 10-18) an earlier letter, written when Judas was alive, also to the same purpose, dated in 188 of the Seleucidæ, which, however, Josephus, in Ant. XIII. vii. 6, corrects to 148, and the 154th Olympiad, B.C. 164. The introductory Letter ends in ii. 18, and then to the end of the Book we have the history of Judas's early struggles until he had defeated his enemies in B.C. 164 and had ordered his new fast day of rejoicing, the day before the Feast of Purim.

THE JEWS INDEPENDENT; B.C. 142.—SIMON CHIEF PRIEST; B.C. 141.

Now that danger **from** abroad was **for the** time removed, Simon was able to turn his forces against those who yet resisted his power at home. The hostile party in the castle of Jerusalem were then pressed with a close siege, and in the next year the want of food forced them to open the **gates.** They had held the fortress against Judas, Jonathan, **and Simon** for three-and-twenty years, during **the** time **that the** struggle against Syria had lasted; but now, at length, as they had lost the Greco-Syrian help, **the** castle that overhangs the Temple is taken, and Jerusalem again becomes the capital of Judea.*

The strong wall, **which** Judas built against his enemies **in the** castle, had **a sad** religious effect which he certainly never intended. It cut off the court **of** the Gentiles in a yet more marked manner from the rest **of the** Temple. The separation between the courts had been hitherto slight; henceforth it was **most** solid and real. Well might the Apostle Paul call it the Middle Wall of Partition. At a later time, when the castle was no longer a cause of fear, doors **were** made in this wall. By one door the cattle could be brought to **the altar**; by two others the true Jews might

* 1 Maccab. xiii. 51.

enter to witness the sacrifices; by another the women might enter their court; but the larger part of the population were shut out with jealous strictness from Temple-services, which they were yet taught to think the only worship acceptable to their Maker. How far the outer court on the Temple-hill had always been used as a market is unknown; but we may be sure that from the first day that any part of the population were told that it **was** the place of worship appointed for their use, they must have been displeased at seeing it so defiled.

There are coins now remaining which tell us that Simon in the first year of his reign as chief priest of the Jews, began to coin money in his own name as an independent prince. These are silver shekels and half shekels, the former weighing about two hundred and twenty grains, or nearly half an ounce. On one side is a cup, with the words " Shekel of Israel," and the letter A " for the year one," and on the other side is a flower with three heads, and the words " Jerusalem the holy." Others are for the years two, three, and four. The copper coins are of " the fourth year of the redemption of Israel." Copper, the harder metal, was not struck so early as silver. The words are written, not in the Hebrew square letters, but in the Samaritan or Phenician letters.* This has given rise to the opinion that the Samaritan alphabet is the older of the two, because we now possess no Hebrew writing so old as these Maccabee coins. We cannot now produce Hebrew inscriptions, except, indeed, those at the foot of Mount Sinai, **to** support the square letters in their claim to be equally old, or to be those used at all times by the Jews in writing their **holy** books. The oldest manuscript of the Hebrew Bible **was not** written before the year A.D. 900. But this argument carries very little weight. The two alphabets may both **have** been in use at the same time. The square characters **in** Judea, and the Samaritan characters in the northern provinces. The Syrian king, indeed, gave to Simon the limited title of High Priest of the Jews; to have called him High Priest of Israel would have been **to** surrender much of his own dominion. But Simon, we have seen, did really hold a part of Galilee and a part of Samaria; his subjects were many of them not Jews, but Israelites, whom we now call Samaritans; he was born, not

---

* Madden's Jewish Coinage.

in Judea, but on the boundary between Dan and Ephraim ; and the southern half of Judea including Hebron its capital, under the name of Idumæa, was in arms against him ; hence we may imagine that he had very good reasons for making use of the Samaritan characters rather than of the Jewish. Moreover, Simon styled his coin a Shekel of Israel, not of Judah. When he began to coin he was not even master of Jerusalem. We need not, therefore, from these coins alone, suppose that the square Jewish characters had not yet come into use, while there are so many good reasons for thinking that the Jews have at no time made a change in the letters in which their scriptures were first written, other than that gradual and unnoticed change which everything human undergoes from day to day.

For the history of these struggles of the brave Maccabees against the Greek kings of Syria, we are indebted, not to Hebrew writers, but to Greek Jews living in Alexandria, where some of them held high political rank. Josephus says that Onias the priest, and Dositheus, whom we have before mentioned, commanded the army for Ptolemy Philometor against his brother Ptolemy Euergetes II ; and he claims for the Jews the honour of bringing the civil war to an end, and saving the kingdom.* But that credit is rather due to the Roman name. For though the Romans had no forces in the country, yet when Antiochus was marching upon Alexandria, C. Popilius, the Roman ambassador, went forward to meet him, and ordered him out of the country. On Antiochus hesitating, Popilius drew a line round him on the sand with his stick, and told him that if he crossed that line, without promising to withdraw his army from Egypt, he would be declared the enemy of Rome.†

To this time of the nation's independence we may give Isaiah xviii. 7, in which it is said that the Jews of Abyssinia, who have been blamed, perhaps, for deserting their country, are to send their presents to the Temple of Jerusalem.

To this time we must give Isaiah xix., written against Egypt. Here we read of an altar to Jehovah in Egypt, which may have been that built by Onias in the reign of Ptolemy Philometor ; of the Egyptians crying to Jehovah for help from their oppressors, and his sending them a saviour who shall rebuke and deliver them, meaning

---

* Against Apion, II. 5.   † Livy, xlv. 12.

C. Popilius, whose threats saved them from the Syrian invasion under Antiochus ; of the Egyptians sending offerings to Jehovah, or courting the Jewish alliance, as they did in those reigns ; of the Assyrians coming into Egypt, and the Egyptians going into Assyria, thus describing the wars between the Ptolemies and the kings of Syria, as in Daniel xi. ; and lastly, of Israel being a third with Egypt and Assyria, as it was for a short time when independent under the Maccabees. For the moment, thanks to the Roman power, the Jews are at peace with both their powerful neighbours ; and Jehovah blesses them both, saying, " Blessed be Egypt my people, and Assyria the work of my hands, and Israel mine inheritance."

The pillar to Jehovah at the boundary of Egypt, which is here mentioned, may perhaps be the one remaining obelisk at Heliopolis, which can yet be seen by our travellers. The two were both standing when Jeremiah was in the Delta ; one may have been carried off by the Persian conquerors.

This chapter, relating to Egypt and the Jewish altar there, seems to be the last of the additions made to the Book of Isaiah. It contains a sprinkling of modern words. Much of it may have been written by Onias, or by one of the Jews frequenting his Temple. But the Altar and Temple on the banks of the Nile were naturally very displeasing to the Jews of Jerusalem ; and they added to this chapter a few words to say that, of the five cities in Egypt inhabited by Jews, one shall be called the City of Destruction. This may have been Onion, with its rival altar ; or it may have been Heliopolis ; as the Hebrew word Destruction is nearly the same in sound as the word Sun. At any rate, the Jews of Egypt protected themselves from the reproach, as far as they could, by calling it, in their Greek Bible, the City of Righteousness.

We have now followed the history of the Hebrew nation in its fall as far as necessary to throw light upon the ancient Hebrew books, all of which, so far as we can put dates to them, were written before this time, with the exception, perhaps, of a chapter and a half in the Book of Daniel. For the sake of chapter ix., it will be necessary to run rapidly through the history of the next hundred years, during which time the high priesthood is changed into a monarchy, and then that monarchy is put down by the Romans, and the government by an aristocracy is established in its place.

The high-priest Simon, who gained for the nation independence, was basely murdered by his son-in-law, to whom he had given the post of governor of the valley of Jericho, a post made lucrative by the palm cultivation. In the year B.C. 135, in the reign of Antiochus Sidetes of Syria, Simon was succeeded by his son John Hyrcanus, who governed the country for nine-and-twenty years with great prosperity. The struggles of the Greek kings for the throne of Syria had so far weakened that country, that John Hyrcanus was able to withhold the tribute, and for the next half century the Jews were an independent nation. This had been the case once before when Nineveh was overthrown by Babylon; and king Josiah for a year or two had no master. But excepting the few months in Josiah's reign, and excepting the moments of fitful struggles in rebellion against the foreigners, the Jews had paid tribute to Assyria, Egypt, Babylonia, Persia, or Syria, for six hundred years, ever since the reign of Ahaz.

As long as the war against Syria had continued or was feared, John Hyrcanus had leant for support on the enthusiasm of the popular party. But on the return of peace and quiet the nobles naturally came into power; and now we for the first time hear of the Pharisees and Sadducees, as two political parties, and we are thus able to justify the conjectures by which we have already connected these two names with the old parties in the state. John Hyrcanus at first favoured the Pharisees. They can only have been the country party who had supported his father Simon in the revolt against the Greco-Syrians. He afterwards took the other party, the Sadducees, into his favour. They must have been the party who had opposed his father, those who had held the castle of Jerusalem by force against him, those who had been willing to submit to Antiochus Epiphanes, and to adopt Greek manners and customs at the bidding of Antiochus, a party which, however strange it may seem, included the chief priests, the Sons of Aaron, or Sons of Zadok, as they were also called. Here, then, we have the two names explained, and the two parties identified. The old country party are now called Pharisees or *villagers;* and the city party, the party of the chief priest, the Sons of Zadok, are called Sadducees. Hitherto they have been divided in their political aims. Hereafter they will be known as sects, differing in religion.

The coins of John Hyrcanus bear the double cornucopia,

which seems to have been borrowed from the Greek coins of Egypt and Syria. His new advisers the Sadducees were the party favourable to Greek customs.

It was at the beginning of the rule of John Hyrcanus that Jesus the son of Sirach went down into Egypt, and there translated and published his grandfather's work, which has been already mentioned. How far he added to it does not **appear**. The prologue and **the** last chapter are all that seem **to be the** work of the grandson. He says that when a young man in Jerusalem he had prayed for wisdom in the courts of the Temple; that he had come to Egypt in the thirty-eighth year of Ptolemy Euergetes II; that he met with some trouble there from being falsely accused to the king, from which troubles however he was released. He was probably a teacher, **as he advises** his readers to buy learning with silver, and they will thereby gain much gold.

The First Book of Maccabees was written under John Hyrcanus. It begins with the Revolt under Judas, and relates the struggle continued under his brother Jonathan, and Jonathan's son Simon, and closes with the death of Simon the father of John Hyrcanus, thus embracing a period of twenty-eight years.

John Hyrcanus, in his wars against the Greco-Syrian king, besieged and wholly destroyed the Samaritan town of Shechem, among other towns in the northern part of the country. Upon this the Samaritan Temple on the neighbouring Mount Gerizim, once the rival to that of **Jerusalem,** was left desolate, and probably soon went to decay.

The government by a priest ended with John Hyrcanus. He was succeeded in B.C. 106 by his son, JUDAS ARISTOBULUS, **who** took the title of king. After a year, ALEXANDER JANNÆUS, the younger son of John Hyrcanus, came to the throne of Jerusalem.

It is at this time that we become acquainted with a Jewish apocryphal work, written in Greek, in Homeric verse, called the Sibylline Verses. This work would deserve little mention but for the importance which for a time it held in Rome. In B.C. 83, the Roman Capitol was burnt, and the old pagan Sibylline books were lost in the fire. On this a Jew of Erythræ, on the west coast of Lydia, published a forgery of his own under the same name. This work contains a history of the Creation, much praise of the Jews, and exhortation to Monotheism; a series of prophecies concerning Jewish and Pagan history, with a promise of God's kingdom upon earth, a time of peace and happiness, and of judgment on the wicked. This strange work had been heard of in Rome, and in B.C. 76, the consul C. Curio persuaded the senate to send an embassy to fetch it. It was then placed in the Capitol under proper care.* We now trace the influences of these Sibylline verses in the writings of Virgil, Cicero, and other Latin authors; and they seem to have been not a little helpful in spreading Monotheism among the more thoughtful Romans, and in thus preparing the way for Christianity.†

On the death of Alexander Jannæus, his **widow** ALEXANDRA governed Judea during the years B.C. 78-69. Her son Hyrcanus II made himself high-priest in B.C. 69; and then in B.C. 65, her younger son Aristobulus II set up his claim to the throne against his brother, and began his reign jointly with his own son, Alexander II.‡

Hyrcanus II and Aristobulus II by their quarrels brought into the country the Roman general Pompey, who, after making king Aristobulus his prisoner, besieged Jerusalem, and took possession of it in the year B.C. 63. Pompey then returned to Rome, carrying with him king Aristobulus as his prisoner, and leaving Hyrcanus and the young Alexander each at the head of an army and of a party in the state. Hyrcanus then for a short time gained possession of Jerusalem, and began to rebuild the walls which Pompey had thrown down; but Gabinius, the Roman general at that time commanding in Syria, brought his army down to Jerusalem, and declared the Jewish monarchy at an end. He deposed Hyrcanus, and gave to him the title of high-priest, but with no civil power, and soon afterwards conquered Alexander, and made him prisoner, while Aristobulus still remained a prisoner in Rome. Gabinius changed the form of government into AN ARISTO-CRACY. He divided what had been the kingdom into five parts, and appointed over each of these parts its own governing council. The city of Jerusalem remained in the hands of the Romans.§ In that city the council was the Sanhedrim of high-priests, elders, and scribes, and it exercised not a little authority over the nation; but in the four other cities the authority of the council was very limited.

It is to this time that the celebrated prophecy of the Seventy Weeks, in the ninth chapter of Daniel, seems to

* Fenestella in Lactantius, Div. Inst. I. 6; De Ira 23.
† Huidekoper's Judæism at Rome.
‡ Josephus Antiq. XIII. viii.—XIV. i.
§ Josephus Antiq. XIV. i.—v.; Wars, I. viii. 5.

relate. It mentions the fortifications of the Temple and of the city being repaired in sixty-nine weeks, or 483 years after the decree went forth that the Jews might return home from captivity; an anointed one being then cut off, namely, the king Aristobulus; and the people of the Ruler who **comes** making a treaty with Many, or the Roman general **setting** up an Aristocracy **in** place of the monarchy. The **whole** passage is as follows:—

Seventy weeks [or 490 years] are determined for thy people and for thy holy city to finish the transgression, and to make an end of sins, and to make atonement for iniquity, and to bring in everlasting righteousness, and to put the seal upon the vision and the prophet, and to anoint the Holy of Holies. Know, therefore, and understand, that from the going forth of the command [B.C. 538] to lead back home, and to build up Jerusalem, while there is an anointed Ruler [Zerubbabel], shall be seven weeks [or 49 years]. Then in sixty and two weeks [or 434 years] the Broad Place [of the Temple] shall be built again [B.C. 55], and the ditch, even amidst the distress of the times. And after the sixty and two weeks shall an Anointed One [king Aristobulus] be cut off, and nothing shall remain to him. And the people of the Ruler [or Roman General] that shall come will destroy the city and the Holy Place; and the end thereof will be with a flood; and until the end of the war desolations are determined. And he will confirm a treaty with Many [or the Aristocracy] for one week. And in the middle of the week [B.C. 51] he will cause the sacrifice and the meal-offering to cease and upon the battlements shall be the abominations [or idolatrous ensigns] of desolation; even until the consummation, and that which has been determined, shall be poured out upon the desolator.

Chapter xii. **is a** continuation **of** chapter ix., **and** it relates to the three times, or years, and a half time, that is, the half week which completes the seventy weeks **of** chapter ix.

In chapter xii. **2**, we meet **for** the **first** time in the Bible with the belief clearly expressed that **the** dead will hereafter **rise to** judgment:—

Many of them that sleep in the dust of the earth shall awake, some to everlasting life, and some to shame and everlasting contempt.

The prophecy of a Messiah, or *anointed* ruler, and then of a Messiah, who was to be cut off, was probably well understood at the time, at least by those for whom it was written. But as days went on, it remained only as one more added to the list of dark hints by which the prophets, in the hour of danger, had warned the people, and from which the hopeful found encouragement to look for better times. With these words the people naturally joined the former prophecy in Isaiah xlv. 1, of a Messiah, meaning king Cyrus, who was to let the captives go free, and to build up the fortunes of the

nation; and also the words of Isaiah xi., which promise a Rod
from the Stem of Jesse, with many other passages pointing to
Zerubbabel, or the house of David, as the prince by whom
Judah was to be saved, and who was to be a light to the
nations, and a salvation to the ends of the earth. Such half-
understood words led the hopeful to look for a time when they
would be fully explained.

Joined to these **was** another class **of** prophecies, which
promised, or rather threatened, a coming Day of Jehovah.
First, when the Assyrians invaded Judea, Joel had warned the
people in burning words that the Day of Jehovah was at hand,
a dreadful day of punishment, which should lead every one to
fast and repent of his evil doings. When the Babylonians
afterwards brought upon the nation a yet more dreadful misfortune, Ezekiel xiii. 5 speaks of that as the Day of Jehovah.
When Babylon was on the point of being conquered, and
Israel's prospects brightened, a prophet in Isaiah xiii. 6 again
declares that the Day of Jehovah is coming, a dreadful day,
but of punishment only on their enemies. In Nehemiah's
time the Life of Elijah was written, with **the** account of his
being taken up to heaven in a chariot of fire; and then
Malachi again foretells the great and dreadful Day of Jehovah,
but adds that Elijah will first return to earth to give the
people warning, and prepare them for it.

These scattered hints, when gathered together into one view,
became at length a grave cause of hope and fear; and their
realization was naturally looked for when John the Baptist
and Jesus of Nazareth began to call upon their hearers to
repent.

The few words in Daniel vii. 9-14, are a very late addition.
That chapter had ended with saying that at least the kingdom
over all nations will be given to "the people, the holy ones of
the Most High." But this addition of verses 9-14 interrupts
the prophecy, and describes "one like a Son of Man coming
in the clouds," to whom will be given an everlasting kingdom
over all nations. These words point to the expected coming
of the Messiah. In the other parts of this chapter the beasts
are monarchies, or lines of kings, and the horns are the kings
in succession; but in this added portion the one beast is a
king, perhaps the Roman emperor, as in Revelation xiii. 1.
He is to be slain, and the other beasts, his generals, are to
have their lives spared.

Here, then, we part with the Hebrew and Chaldee portions
of the Bible. The volume, or rather series of volumes, was

brought to a close because the Hebrew language had gone out of use as a living tongue, and the Jewish writers would have found a difficulty in adding to it, except in Syriac or Greek.

Josephus, in his Defence of the Jews against Apion, says that they have only twenty-two books, and these are justly thought to be Divine. Five of these contain the traditions about the origin of mankind until the death of Moses; thirteen continue the history until the reign of Artaxerxes; and four are hymns and precepts for the conduct of life. The five, of course, are the Pentateuch. The thirteen may be—

Joshua, Judges, Ruth, Kings, Chronicles, Ezra, Nehemiah, Esther, Isaiah, Jeremiah with Lamentations, Ezekiel, Daniel, the XII minor prophets. The four may be—

Job, Psalms, Proverbs, Ecclesiastes.

As in this arrangement he follows the Greek, not the Hebrew, we may suppose that he also follows the Greek in counting the Books of Samuel among the Books of Kings; or with the Jews he may have called Ezra and Nehemiah one book, and then Samuel and Kings may be two. But in either way, we find no place in this list for Solomon's Song.

Of the Book of Enoch, the older and larger part was written about the same time with the ninth chapter of Daniel, but probably in Syriac. It is known to us only through an Ethiopic translation, and some fragments of a Greek translation. It professes to be written by Enoch, the seventh from Adam. It may be divided into four parts. The first part in chapters i.—xxxv., relates Enoch's vision in heaven, whither he had been carried without dying. He foresees God coming down to Mount Sinai, and the Sons of God having children by the daughters of men, and the wicked race which sprang therefrom. With much that is not easily understood, he gives the names of the seven Watchers, or guardian angels, some of which we have in the Book of Daniel; and also the names of the wicked angels, among whom is Azazeel, perhaps the scape-goat of the Book of Leviticus. This portion of the book is quoted in the Epistle of Jude.

The second portion, in chapters xxxvii.—lxx., Enoch's second vision, is more modern, written probably after the Christian Era. It seems to be more modern than the Book of Revelation and Daniel vii. 9-14, because in those books

"One like a son of man " is the description of a being seen in a vision in the heavens; while in these chapters of the Book of Enoch, as in the Gospels, "the Son of Man " has become a proper name.

The third portion, chapters lxxi.—lxxiii., is astronomical. Here the angel Uriel explains to Enoch the motions of the heavenly bodies, dividing the year into 364 days, and the day into eighteen hours. From the length of the longest day, and of the shortest, we learn that this portion of the book, and probably the whole, was written to the north of Palestine, perhaps at Antioch in Syria.

The fourth and last portion of the Book of **Enoch,** chapters lxxxiv.—cv., is historical. Enoch relates his dream **to** his son Methusalah, running obscurely through the **history** of the nation, from Cain and Abel, Noah, Moses, **the Judges,** the Kings, the Captivity, the Second Temple, down to the twelve native princes after the revolt of the Maccabees. This brings us to the time of Herod, and gives a date which may belong to three out of the four portions of our Book. The whole is of very little value, except to show how mystical were the opinions now becoming common, and how ready were the writers to put a false name upon their writings.

The Book of Enoch did not gain admission into the collection of Hebrew Scriptures; and it very little deserved admission.

The Bible, however, in its Greek translation, continued to receive additions; these we now separate from the Hebrew books, under the name of the Apocrypha. Some of the Greek additions, indeed, had been written before this time; **such as the** First Book **of** Esdras; the Wisdom of Jesus the son of Sirach; and the two Books of Maccabees, which we **have** made **use of** in the latter part of this History. The more modern writings are the Book of Tobit, dated at the **time of** the Captivity of the ten tribes, but written perhaps in the reign of Herod; the Book of Judith, profess-ing to relate events in the reign of Nebuchadnezzar, but written in the time of Vespasian, whom the writer points to covertly under the name of the Babylonian king; and the Wisdom of Solomon, which seems to be a Christian work. The Second Book of Esdras, which also finds a place in the Apocrypha, is a Latin work, written after the death of the Roman Emperor Caracalla.

As the history of the Hebrew nation is chiefly valuable

for the history of its religious books, we may here bring it
to a close. It has shown us the nation in its rise and in its
fall. It has shown, as all history does, the people's crimes
and their virtues ; and though from its baldness not very
distinctly, it has shown sometimes the one and sometimes
the other on the increase. But it has shown knowledge,
and, what is chiefly to our purpose, religious knowledge,
always on the increase. If the Israelites had ever had their
religious feelings weakened by the worship of more gods
than one, it was before the beginning of trustworthy
history. When in later days their prophets reproach them
with idolatry, the blame seems to be deserved only so far as
they had wisely and humanely consented to be called one
nation with the mixed races in Canaan among whom they
had settled. The God whom they worshipped at the
beginning of our history may have been thought by the less
enlightened to have been the God of the Israelites only,
while the nations around lived each of them under its own
god. But even as early as David's reign, the Hebrew
writers had taught that there was One only God, the maker
of all things, who was to be feared and worshipped with
sacrifices. Then for more than two centuries the nation
remained cramped by priestly legislation. But after a time
the prophets taught them that God did not ask for any other
sacrifice than that they should cease to do evil, and learn to
do well. The Book of Deuteronomy, near the end of the
monarchy, had added that God was not only to be feared,
but that they ought to love God with all their heart, and
that when he afflicts or punishes, he does it as a father, for
our improvement. The Book of Job, written after the
Return from Captivity, argues that our knowledge of God's
ways, even in easier matters, such as the seasons and the
habits of animals, is so limited that we must not fancy that
we can judge of his moral justice, or hope to understand
why in each case he does so afflict us. Some years after
the Return from Captivity, the latter chapters of Leviticus
show that the nation had made another great step; they had
learned that we should not only love God, but should also
love our neighbour as ourselves.

So also in the motives for avoiding sin and doing right,
which are put forward in the Hebrew writings, our history
shows that a like change was taking place for the better.
The Book of Exodus had threatened that God would visit
sins upon the sinner's children to the third and fourth

27 *

generation.   After the Captivity, the Book of Ezekiel
taught that the son would not have to bear the sins of the
father, but "the soul **that** sinneth he shall die ; " and "if the
wicked man shall turn from all his sins and do what is right
he shall surely live, he shall not die."   The latter chapters
of Leviticus add **a** higher motive for shunning wickedness,
saying, " Be ye holy, as I Jehovah am **holy.**"   And lastly,
the twelfth chapter of Daniel, in the reign of Antiochus
Epiphanes, while adding a new motive for right actions, yet
further removed their difficulties as to God's bestowal of
rewards in this life, **by** promising them **a** state **of** being
after death, " when some will arise to everlasting life, and
some to shame and everlasting contempt."   From first to last
the Jews always based their opinion about right and wrong
upon the moral sense.   The prophets never give reasons for
their advice, but make a simple appeal **to** the conscience in
the words, " Jehovah hath said it."

Such is the history of the Jewish religion, as shown in
the Hebrew Scriptures, a religion which, when released
from the bonds of the ceremonial law, became the forerunner
of Christianity.   But while we review the past by the help of
the light which later events have thrown upon it, we must
remember that Christianity did not take its rise among
the priests who were admitted within the court of the Altar,
but among the despised Galileans, who when they come up
to the Temple were required to stand apart in the **court** of
the Gentiles.

THE
HEBREW CHRONOLOGY.

In these pages the writer ventures on no opinion about the age of the world, or the number of years that it has been inhabited by man, nor even attempts to decide the date of the Exodus of the Israelites out of Egypt under Moses. His aim is merely to show at what times the Hebrew writers place those events. He has simply taken out the spaces of time mentioned in the Bible, and placed them together in a series till they come down to the recorded eclipses. Modern science tells us with certainty how many years before our own time these eclipses happened : and thus, to the Table of years which had been made by counting forward, we are able to put our own more usual and more convenient dates by counting backwards, from the Christian Era. Thus, if an eclipse is known to have taken place 2593 years before this present year, which we call A.D. 1872, we deduct 1872 from the above number, and say that it happened B.C. 621.

The chronology of the Old Testament may conveniently be divided into two parts, the traditional chronology and the historical chronology.

The first is formed by adding together the age of each of the patriarchs at the time of the son's birth, from which we learn that Abraham left Haran in Syria in A.M. 2023; that the Exodus of the Israelites from Egypt took place in A.M. 2668; and that Solomon, in the fourth year of his reign, built the Temple of Jerusalem in A.M. 3148. Here the traditional chronology may be said to end ; and, after this time, the dates are recorded with so much greater care, and with such an evident aim at exactness, that we may safely consider that we have entered upon historical chronology. From this we learn that the building of the Temple took place in the year B.C. 973. We thus gain the opinion of the Hebrew writers that **Adam was** created in the year B.C. 4121 (=3148 + 973).

The received chronology places the creation of Adam in the year B.C. 4004, **or** 4000 years **before** the birth of Jesus; and it will not be uninteresting **to examine** the reasons for its doing so. The Epistle of Barnabas mentions an opinion held by the Jews, **that the** world was to be destroyed at the end of 6000 years from its creation, because, according to Genesis chapter i., it was created in six days, and according to 2 **Peter** iii. 8, "one day with the Lord is **as** a thousand **years**." On comparing this with our chronology, it will be **seen** that the Promises were given to Abraham in A.M. 2023, **and** that Jesus was born in A.M. 4121. Hence, a very little alteration of the dates will make the Bible seem to declare that mankind had lived 2000 years before the Promises, 2000 more before the Gospel; and this adjustment of the chronology, to make it agree with a fanciful opinion, has been made in the margin of the authorized English Bibles. This opinion also led to the natural prophecy, among those who are fond of such fanciful interpretations, that the world is to last 2000 years under the Gospel, and to come to an end in A.D. 2000, or more exactly, in A.D. 1996, because modern criticism has made it probable that Jesus was born in the year B.C. 4.

TABLE OF THE TRADITIONAL CHRONOLOGY FROM THE CREATION TO SOLOMON'S REIGN.

GENESIS.								A.M.
V. 3	Adam,	when 130 years old begat Seth				-	-	130
6	Seth,	,, 105	,,	,,	,,	Enos	-	235
9	Enos	,, 90	,,	,,	,,	Cainan	-	325
12	Cainan	,, 70	,,	,,	,,	Mahalaleel	-	395
15	Mahalaleel,	,, 65	,,	,,	,,	Jared	-	460
18	Jared,	,, 162	,,	,,	,,	Enoch	-	622
21	Enoch,	,, 65	,,	,,	,,	Methuselah	-	687
25	Methuselah,	,, 187	,,	,,	,,	Lamech	-	874
28	Lamech,	,, 182	,,	,,	,,	Noah	-	1056
32	Noah,	,, 500	,,	,,	,,	Shem	-	1556
VII. 6	,,	,, 600	,,	,,	The Flood		-	1656
XI. 10	Two years after the Flood, Shem begat Arphaxad						-	1658
12	Arphaxad when 35 years old,				,,	Salah	-	1693
14	Salah,	,, 30	,,	,,	,,	Eber	-	1723
16	Eber,	,, 34	,,	,,	,,	Peleg	-	1757
18	Peleg,	,, 30	,,	,,	,,	Reu	-	1787
20	Reu,	,, 32	,,	,,	,,	Serug	-	1819

GENESIS.					A.M.
XI. 22	Serug,	when 30 years old,	begat Nahor	.	1849
24	Nahor,	,, 29 ,, ,,	,, Terah	.	1878
26	Terah,	,, 70 ,, ,,	,, Abram	.	1948
XII. 4	Abram,	,, 75 ,, ,,	left Haran	.	2023
XXI. 5	When 100 years old, 25 years later,		begat Isaac	.	2048
XXV. 26	Isaac,	when 60 years old,	,, Jacob	.	2108
XLVII. 9	Jacob,	,, 130 ,, ,, settles in Egypt		.	2238
EXODUS.					
XII. 40	After 430 years, they leave Egypt		. . .	.	2668
1 KINGS.					
VI. 1	480 years after the Exodus is the 4th of Solomon			.	3148

ON THE BOOK OF JUDGES.

THE above-mentioned period of 480 years, which the writer of 1 Kings vi. 1 places between the Exodus and the building of the Temple by Solomon, would seem to have been learned by adding together the times mentioned in the history. In the Books of Joshua and Judges there are periods amounting to 460 years. If we continue, in the same way, to think none of the events contemporaneous, we must add to this sum :—

    1 year from the Exodus to the espying of the land.— Numb. x. 11.—xiii. 2.

40 years of David's reign.

3 years of Solomon's reign to the building of the Temple; making a total of 504 years. How the writer lessened this down to 480 it is in vain to conjecture. Sound criticism would lead us to lessen it much more by considering many events in the Book of Judges as contemporaneous.

Thus, in chapters vi.—xii. we have a continuous history, limited for the most part to the middle tribes of Ephraim and **Manasseh,** though sometimes we find Gad, Issachar, and Zebulun joined to them. This describes an invasion and conquest of their country by the Midianites and others from the east of the Jordan, and then the reigns of Gideon and Abimelech, and the judgeships of Tola and Jair (chapter x. 1, 4). These quiet reigns are followed by a second great invasion and conquest of the land. This is by the children of Ammon from the east, and by the Philistines from the south, and it is followed by the judgeships of Jephthah, Ibzan, Elon, and Abdon. The whole occupies 144 years; namely, 95 years before the second invasion, and 49 years

after it. It seems probable that these two portions embrace **the whole** period of time which the Book of Judges covers, and that the other invasions relate to other parts of the country which sometimes had judges **of** their own. Thus the wars of Benjamin against the Moabites, and the conquest of Moab, in chapter iii. 14-30, and the wars of the northern tribes against the Syrians, in chapter iii. 8-11, and against the Canaanites, in chapter iv. v. may have taken place during the first of these periods; and Samson's wars against the Philistines, in chapters xiii.—xvi., may have been included in the second period of time. This shortening of the chronology of this book will make it better agree with the genealogies; for, since Moses is the fourth **in** descent from Jacob, and David the eleventh, we cannot allow more than four, or at most five, generations of men to the time occupied by the Book of Judges.

On the other hand, the Book of Judges, in chapter xi. 26, has preserved a tradition, relating to a yet earlier time, that the Israelites had dwelt for 300 years on the east of the Jordan, between the time of the Exodus and the time of Judges ruling in Canaan. This very probable statement is expressly contradicted in Numbers xxxii. 12, xxxiv. 17, and Joshua iii.

THE CHRONOLOGY OF THE SEPTUAGINT.

WHEN the Greek Jews made the Septuagint version, in the reigns of the Ptolemies, they seem not to have been content with the very moderate antiquity for their nation and the human race given in the Hebrew books; and, accordingly, they added 1466 years to the age of the world, by making the patriarchs older at the birth of their sons. They thus add 586 in Genesis v.—vii., and 880 in Genesis xi. xii. They probably meant to add an exact Egyptian cycle of four times 365, or 1460 years. The difference of six years may be an error of the scribe. On comparing the Greek chronology with the Hebrew, sound criticism will certainly lead us to conclude that the Hebrew is what the writers originally wrote. However mistaken we may think them in supposing that the world had only been peopled with mankind for such a small number of years, yet we cannot accept the Greek chronology as the original. It is evidently a correction, an attempted improvement **on the** Hebrew.

And even as an improvement it is of very little value, since even with its help we by no means carry back the creation of man to a time early enough to satisfy the reasonable requirements of science.

A second improvement proposed by the Greek translators was to shorten the time of the Israelites' residence in Egypt —the time between Jacob's bringing his family into Egypt and Moses leading them out. This, in the above table, is quoted from Exodus xii. 40, as 430 years. But in the Greek, this period of 430 years is said to include their residence in Canaan as well as their residence in Egypt, commencing with Abraham's leaving Haran; and it thus shortens the residence in Egypt by 215 years. This certainly agrees better with the genealogies; but it cannot be accepted as what the writer originally wrote.

THE HISTORICAL PORTION OF HEBREW CHRONOLOGY.

THIS is calculated backwards from the eclipse in the 5th of Nabopulassar, B.C. 621, by the help of the years mentioned in Ezekiel, Jeremiah, and the Books of Kings. In the Books of Kings we often meet with contradictory statements. The length of the reign, as there stated, does not always agree with the length as we should calculate it to be, when the writer gives us a date for its ending, and also a date for the end of the previous reign. The latter mode of determining the length seems to be of the two the more trustworthy. The contradiction can be reconciled only upon the supposition that many of the kings reigned jointly with their fathers, and had thus been nominally reigning several years before their real reign began. This is the supposition of many of the best Biblical critics. Our Table thus makes the reign of Solomon about thirty-nine years more modern than the received chronology, which, on the other hand, supposes each king of Judah to have counted his years from his father's death. Thus with us it becomes unnecessary to place an interregnum between Jeroboam II of Israel and his son Zachariah, and a second interregnum between Pekeh of Israel and Hosea, who dethroned him.

The received chronology, which may be seen in the margin of most Bibles, is formed by simply adding up together the length of every king's reign, overlooking the difficulty caused by the double method of reckoning employed in the

Books of Kings, and overlooking the fact, certain in some cases, and probable in others, that a king's years were reckoned, not from his father's death, but from when he was associated with his father on the throne. If we had nothing to guide us but the Books of Chronicles, we should be driven to that mode of reasoning. But the Books of Kings teach us otherwise, and thus lead us to shorten the sum of the kings' reigns by thirty-nine years.

When the reigns of the Jewish kings come to an end, the Table is continued forwards by the help of Claudius Ptolemy, to the seventh year of Cambyses, which is again fixed by an eclipse; and to the second year of Darius, when the Jews had leave to rebuild the Temple.

The quotations from the historians, by which the Table is formed, are placed in the Notes at the end of it.

TABLE OF HEBREW CHRONOLOGY.

FROM DAVID TO THE REBUILDING OF THE TEMPLE.

B.C.	JUDAH.					ISRAEL.			
1016	David in **Hebron** [1]					Ish-bosheth or **Ish-** [baal			
1008				**DAVID**					
976				**SOLOMON** [2]					
936	1 of Rehoboam	.	.	.		1 of Jeroboam	.		
935	2	.	.	.	.	2	.	.	.
934	3	.	.	.	.	3	.	.	.
933	4	.	.	.	.	4	.	.	.
932	5	.	.	.	.	5	.	.	.
931	6	.	.	.	.	6	.	.	.
930	7	.	.	.	.	7	.	.	.
929	8	.	.	.	.	8	.	.	.
928	9	.	.	.	.	9	.	.	.
927	10	.	.	.	.	10	.	.	.
926	11	.	.	.	.	11	.	.	.
925	12	.	.	.	.	12	.	.	.
924	13	.	.	.	.	13	.	.	.
923	14	.	.	.	.	14	.	.	.
922	15	.	.	.	.	15	.	.	.
921	16	.	.	.	.	16	.	.	.
920	17	.	.	.	[3]	17	.	.	.
919	(18)	1 of Abijam	.	.	[4]	18	.	.	.
918	(19)	2	.	.	.	19	.	.	.
917	(20)	3 . 1 of Asa	.	.	[5]	20	.	.	.
916	(21)	2	.	.	.	21 . 1 of Nadab [6]			
915	(22)	3	.	.	.	22 . 2 . 1 of Baasha			
914	(23)	4	.	.	.	2	.	.	[7]
913	(24)	5	.	.	.	3	.	.	.
912	(25)	6	.	.	.	4	.	.	.
911	(26)	7	.	.	.	5	.	.	.
910	(27)	8	.	.	.	6	.	.	.
909	(28)	9	.	.	.	7	.	.	.
908	(29)	10	.	.	.	8	.	.	.
907	(30)	11	.	.	.	9	.	.	.

B.C.	JUDAH.					ISRAEL.	
906	(31) 12 of **Asa**	.	.	.		10 of Baasha	.
905	(32) 13 .	.	.	.	.	11	. . .
904	(33) 14 .	.	.	.	.	12	. . .
903	(34) 15 .	.	.	.	.	13	. . .
902	(35) 16 .	.	.	.	.	14	. . .
901	(36) 17 .	.	.	.	[8]	15	. . .
900	18	.	.	.	.	16	. . .
899	19	.	.	.	.	17	. . .
898	20	.	.	.	.	18	. . .
897	21	.	.	.	.	19	. . .
896	22	.	.	.	.	20	. . .
895	23	.	.	.	.	21	. . .
894	24	.	.	.	.	22	. . .
893	25	.	.	.	.	23	. . .
892	26	.	.	.	.	24 . 1 of Elah [9]	
891	27	.	.	.	.	2 . 1 . 1 of Omri	
890	28	.	.	.	.	2 . 2 & Tibni [10]	
889	29	.	.	.	.	3 . 3	
888	30	.	.	.	.	4 . 4	. .
887	31	.	.	.	.	5 . 5	. .
886	32	.	.	.	.	6 of Omri alone	
885	33	.	.	.	.	7	. . .
884	34	.	.	.	.	8	. . .
883	35	.	.	.	.	9	. . .
882	36	.	.	.	.	10	. . .
881	37	.	.	.	.	11	. . .
880	38	.	.	.	.	12 . 1 of Ahab [11]	
879	39	.	.	.	.	2	. . .
878	40	.	.	.	.	3	. . .
877	41 . 1 of Jehoshaphat	.	[12]			4	. . .
876	2	.	.	.	.	5	. . .
875	3	.	.	.	.	6	. . .
874	4	.	.	.	.	7	. . .
873	5	.	.	.	.	8	. . .
872	6	.	.	.	.	9	. . .
871	7	.	.	.	.	10	. . .
870	8	.	.	.	.	11	. . .
869	9	.	.	.	.	12	. . .
868	10	.	.	.	.	13	. . .
867	11	.	.	.	.	14	. . .

B.C.	JUDAH.					ISRAEL.		
866	12 of Jehoshaphat	.	.	.		15 of Ahab	.	
865	13 .	.	.	.	.	16	.	.	.
864	14 .	.	.	.	.	17	.	.	.
863	15 .	.	.	.	.	18	.	.	.
862	16 .	.	.	.	.	19	.	[ziah
861	17 .	.	.	.	.	20 . 1 of Aha-	[13]
860	18 .	.	.	.	.	21 . 2 . of 1 Je-	[14]
859	19 .	.	.	.	.	22 . 2	horam	.
858	20 .	.	.	.	.	3	.	.	.
857	21 .	.	.	.	.	4	.	.	.
856	22 . 1 of Jehoram	.	.	[15]	5	.	.	.
855	23 . 2	.	.	.	.	6	.	.	[16]
854	24 . 3	.	.	.	.	7	.	.	.
853	25 . 4	.	.	.	.	8	.	.	.
852	5 .	.	.	.	.	9	.	.	.
851	6 .	.	.	.	.	10	.	.	.
850	7 .	.	.	.	.	11	.	.	.
849	{ 8 . 1 of Ahaziah . . [17] { 1 of Athaliah . . [19]	(12 . . . { 1 . of Jehu [18]
848	2 .	.	.	.	.	2	.	.	.
847	3 .	.	.	.	.	3	.	.	.
846	4 .	.	.	.	.	4	.	.	.
845	5 .	.	.	.	.	5	.	.	.
844	6 .	.	.	.	.	6	.	.	.
843	7 . 1 of Jehoash	.	.	[20]	7	.	.	.
842	2 .	.	.	.	. .	8	.	.	.
841	3 .	.	.	.	.	9	.	.	.
840	4 .	.	.	.	.	10	.	.	.
839	5 .	.	.	.	.	11	.	.	.
838	6 .	.	.	.	.	12	.	.	.
837	7 .	.	.	.	.	13	.	.	.
836	8 .	.	.	.	.	14	.	.	.
835	9 .	.	.	.	.	15	.	.	.
834	10 .	.	.	.	.	16	.	.	.
833	11 .	.	.	.	.	17	.	.	.
832	12 .	.	.	.	.	18	.	.	.
831	13 .	.	.	.	.	19	.	.	.
830	14 .	.	.	.	.	20	.	.	.
829	15 .	.	.	.	.	21	.	.	.
828	16 .	.	.	.	.	22	.	.	.
827	17 .	.	.	.	.	23	.	.	.

B.C.	JUDAH.	ISRAEL.
826	18 of Jehoash	24 of Jehu
825	19	25
824	20	26
823	21	27
822	22	28
821	23	1 of Jehoahaz [21]
820	24	2
819	25	3
818	26	4
817	27	5
816	28	6
815	29	7
814	30	8
813	31	9
812	32	10
811	33	11
810	34	12
809	35	13
808	36	14
807	37	15 . 1 of Je- [22]
806	38 . 1 of Amaziah . . [23]	16 . 2 hoash
805	39 . 2	17 . 3
804	40 . 3	4 . 1 of Jeroboam
803	4	5 . 2 II jointly
802	5	6 . 3 with his
801	6 . 1 of Azariah . . [25]	7 . 4 father
800	7 . 2 when 16 years old, .	8 . 5
799	8 . 3 jointly with his	9 . 6
798	9 . 4 father .	10 . 7
797	10 . 5	11 . 8
796	11 . 6	12 . 9
795	12 . 7	13 . 10
794	13 . 8	14 . 11
793	14 . 9	15 . 12 [II
792	15 . 10	16 . 13 of Jeroboam
791	16 . 11	14 . alone [24]
790	17 . 12	15
789	18 . 13	16
788	19 . 14	17
787	20 . 15	18
786	21 . 16 of Amaziah and	19 of Jeroboam II

B.C.	JUDAH.	ISRAEL.
785	22 . 17 Azariah . . .	20 of Jeroboam II.
784	23 . 18	21 . . .
783	24 . 19	22 . . .
782	25 . 20	23 . . .
781	26 . 21	24 . . .
780	27 . 22	25 . . .
779	28 . 23	26 . . .
778	29 . 24 of Azariah or Uzziah .	27 . . .
777	25 alone . . . [26]	28 . . .
776	26	29 . . .
775	27	30 . . .
774	28	31 . . .
773	29	32 . . .
772	30	33 . . .
771	31	34 . . .
770	32	35 . . .
769	33	36 . . .
768	34	37 . . .
767	35	38 . . .
766	36	39 . . .
765	37	40 . [iah
764	38	41 . 1 of Zachar-[27]
763	39 . . . . {	1 of Shallum [28] 1 of Menahem [29]
762	40	2 . . .
761	41	3 . . .
760	42	4 . . .
759	43	5 . . .
758	44	6 . . .
757	45	7 . . .
756	46	8 . . .
755	47	9 . . .
754	48	10 . . .
753	49	(11?) . . [30]
752	50	1 of Pekahiah [31]
751	51	2 . . .
750	52	1 of Pekah . [32]
749	1 of Jotham . . . [33]	2 . . .
748	2	3 . . .
747	3	4 . . .

B.C.	JUDAH.					ISRAEL.			
746	4 of Jotham	.	.	.	.	5 of Pekah	.		.
745	5	.	.	.	.	6	.	.	.
744	6	.	.	.	.	7	.	.	.
743	7	.	.	.	.	8	.	.	.
742	8	.	.	.	.	9	.	.	.
741	9 .	1 of Ahaz	.		.	10	.	.	.
740	10 .	2 .	.	.	.	11	.	.	.
739	11 .	3 .	.	.	.	12	.	.	.
738	12 .	4 .	.	.	.	13	.	.	.
737	13 .	5 .	.	.	.	14	.	.	.
736	14 .	6 .	.	.	.	15	.	.	.
735	15 .	7 .	.	.	.	16	.	.	.
734	16 .	8 .	.	.	[34]	17	.	.	.
733	(17) .	9 .	.	.	.	18	.	.	.
732	(18) .	10 .	.	.	.	19	.	.	.
731	(19) .	11 .	.	.	.	20	.	.	.
730	(20) .	12 .	.	.	.	1 of Hoshea	.	[35]	
729	13	.	.	.	.	2	.	.	.
728	14	.	.	.	.	3	.	.	.
727	15 .	1 of Hezekiah		.	[36]	4	.	.	.
726	16 .	2 .	.	.	.	5	.	.	.
725	3	.	.	.	.	6	.	.	.
724	4	.	.	.	[37]	7	.	.	.
723	5	.	.	.	.	8	.	.	.
722	6	.	.	.	[38]	9 Shalmanezer king			
721	7	.	.	.	[39]	of Assyria.			
720	8	.	.	.	.	Sennacherib.			
719	9	.	.	.	.				
718	10	.	.	.	.				
717	11	.	.	.	.				
716	12	.	.	.	.				
715	13	.	.	.	.				
714	14	.	.	.	.				
713	15	.	.	.	.	Sennacherib's over-			
712	16	.	.	.	.	throw. Berodach			
711	17	.	.	.	.	Baladan's embassy.			
710	18	.	.	.	.				
709	19	.	.	.	.				
708	20	.	.	.	.				
707	21	.	.	.	.				

B.C.	JUDAH.	ASSYRIA.
706	22 of Hezekiah . . .	Sennacherib
705	23	
704	24	
703	25	
702	26	
701	27	
700	28	
699	29	
698	1 of Manasseh . . [40]	
697	2	
696	3	
695	4	
694	5	
693	6	
692	7	
691	8 . . .	
690	9	
689	10	
688	11	
687	12 . . .	
686	13 . . .	
685	14 . . .	
684	15 . . .	
683	16 . . .	Esarhaddon
682	17 . . .	
681	18 . . .	
680	19 . . .	
679	20 . . .	
678	21 . . .	
677	22	
676	23	
675	24	
674	25	
673	26	
672	27	
671	28 . . .	
670	29 . . .	
669	30	
668	31 . . .	Sardanapalus
667	32 . . .	

28

B.C.	JUDAH.	ASSYRIA.
666	33 of Manasseh . . .	Sardanapalus
665	34	
664	35	
663	36	
662	37	
661	38	
660	39	
659	40	
658	41	
657	42	
656	43	
655	44	
654	45	
653	46	
652	47	
651	48	
650	49	
649	50	
648	51	
647	52	
646	53	
645	54	
644	55	
643	1 of Amon . . . [41]	
642	2	
641	1 of Josiah . . . [42]	
640	2	
639	3	
638	4	
637	5	
636	6	
635	7	
634	8	
633	9	
632	10	
631	11	
630	12	
629	13	
628	14	
627	15	

B.C.	JUDAH.	BABYLON.
626	16 of Josiah	
625	17	1 of Nabopulassar
624	18	2 . . .
623	19	3 . . .
622	20	4 . . .
621	21	5 An eclipse
620	22	6 recorded [44]
619	23	7 . . .
618	24	8 . . .
617	25	9 . . .
616	26	10 . . .
615	27	11 . . .
614	28	12 . . .
613	29	13 . . .
612	30	14 . . .
611	31	15 . . .
610	{ 1 of Jehoahaz { 1 of Jehoiakim } [45]	16 . . .
609	2	17 . . .
608	3	18 . . .
607	4 . . . . [46]	19 . 1 of Nebuchad-
606	5	20 . 2 . nezzar .
605	6	21 . 3 . . .
604	7	22 . 4 . . .
603	8	23 . 5 . . .
602	9	24 . 6 . . .
601	10 . . [Captivity [47]	25 . 7 . . .
600	11 . 1 of Jehoiachin or of	26 . 8 . . .
599	2 . 1 of Zedekiah . [48]	27 . 9 . . .
598	3 . 2	28 . 10 . . .
597	4 . 3	29 . 11 . . .
596	5 . 4	30 . 12 . . [49]
595	6 . 5	31 . 13 . . .
594	7 . 6	32 . 14 . . .
593	8 . 7	33 . 15 . . .
592	9 . 8	34 . 16 . . .
591	10 . 9	35 . 17 . . .
590	11 . 10	18 . [50]
589	12 . 11. 1 of City destroyed [51]	19 . . .
588	13 . 2	20 . . .
587	14 . 3	21

28 *

B.C.	JUDAH.		BABYLON.
586	15 of Captivity	4 of City .	22 of Nebuchad-
585	16 . . .	5 destroyed	23 nezzar
584	17 . . .	6 . .	24 ,,
583	18 . . .	7 . .	25 ,,
582	19 . . .	8 . .	26 ,,
581	20 . . .	9 . .	27 ,,
580	21 . . .	10 . .	28 ,,
579	22 . . .	11 . .	29 ,,
578	23 . . .	12 . .	30 ,,
577	24 . . .	13 . .	31 ,,
576	25 . . .	14 . [52]	32 ,,
575	26 . . .	15 . .	33 ,,
574	27 . . .	16 . .	34 ,,
573	28 . . .	17 . .	35 ,,
572	29 . . .	18 . .	36 ,,
571	30 . . .	19 . .	37 ,,
570	31 . . .	20 . .	38 ,,
569	32 . . .	21 . .	39 ,,
568	33 . . .	22 . .	40 ,,
567	34 . . .	23 . .	41 ,,
566	35 . . .	24 . .	42 ,,
565	36 . . .	25 . .	43 ,,
564	37 Jehoiachin re-	26 . .	44 . 1 of Evil [53]
563	leased from	27 . .	45 . 2 Merodach
562	prison	28 . .	46 . 3 ,,
561		29 . .	47 . 4 ,,
560		30 . .	48 . 1 of Neriglis-
559		31 . .	49 . 2 sor
558		32 . .	50 . 3 ,,
557		33 . .	51 . 4 ,,
556		34 . .	52 . 5 ,,
555		35 . .	53 . 1 of Na- [54]
554		36 . .	54 . 2 bonned
553		37 . .	55 . 3 ,,
552		38 . .	56 . 4 ,,
551		39 . .	57 . 5 ,,
550		40 . .	58 . 6 ,,
549		41 . .	59 . 7 ,,
548		42 . .	60 . 8 ,,
547		43 . .	61 . 9 ,,

B.C.	JUDAH.	BABYLON.	
546	44 of City de-	62 of Nebuchad-	10 of Nabonned
545	45 stroyed	63 nezzar or of	11 ,,
544	46 .	64 Jeremiah's	12 ,,
543	47 . .	65 prophecy	13 ,,
542	48 . .	66 . . .	14 ,,
541	49 . .	67 . . .	15 ,,
540	50 . .	68 . . .	16 ,,
539	51 . .	69 . . .	17 ,,
538	52 Prince	70 . . [55]	1 of Cyaxares II
537	53 Zerub-		2 or Darius the
536	54 babel		3 Mede and of
535	55 . .		4 Cyrus in Ba-
534	56 . .		5 bylon [56]
533	57 . .		6 ,,
532	58 . .		7 ,,
531	59 . .		8 ,,
530	60 . .		9 ,,
529	61 . .		1 of Cambyses
528	62 . .		2 ,,
527	63 . .		3 ,,
526	64 . .		4 ,,
525	65 . .		5 ,,
524	66 . .		6 ,,
523	67		7 An eclipse re-
522	68 . .		8 corded [57]
521	69 . .		1 of Darius [58]
520	70 . .		2 ,,
516	The Temple finished . . .		6 of Darius [59]
483	Esther made queen of Persia .		3 of Xerxes I [60]
479	Ezra comes to Jerusalem .		3 of Xerxes I [61]
468	Eliashib chief priest . .		[62]
445	Nehemiah comes to Jerusalem .		20 of Artaxer-
433	Nehemiah returns to Susa .		32 [64] xes [63]

NOTES,

(1.) DAVID reigned forty years, namely seven years and
six months in Hebron over Judah, and then in Jerusalem
thirty-three years over both Israel and Judah; 2 Samuel
v. 5.

(2.) Solomon reigned forty years over all Israel; 1 Kings
xi. 42. Some small portion of this may have been jointly
with his father David.

(3.) Rehoboam, the son of Solomon, reigned seventeen
years over Judah; 1 Kings xiv. 21.

(4.) Abijah or Abijam, the son of Rehoboam, began to
reign in the eighteenth year of Jeroboam, and reigned
three years over Judah; 1 Kings xv. 1.

To this reign, said to be of three years, we can only
allow two; and the same dropping of a year will be
observed in many other cases. This is explained in the
Mishna, in treatise Rosh Hashanah, chapter i., where we
read that the years of a king's reign were said to end with
the New Year's day; and thus the first year of every reign
may have consisted of only a few weeks, or even a few days.
The same, of course, was the case with the last year of a
reign. Thus the last year of one king and the first of his
successor together only filled twelve months. This mode of
reckoning the regnal years was used throughout Egypt,
Babylonia, Syria, and Asia Minor, even for the Greek kings
and Roman emperors who afterwards reigned over those
countries; and it will have to be attended to when we meet
with authors who lived in those countries dating the baptism
and crucifixion of Jesus by means of the years of an
Emperor's reign.

(5.) Asa, the son of Abijam, began to reign over Judah
in the twentieth year of Jeroboam, and reigned forty-one
years; 1 Kings xv. 9.

(6.) Nadab, the son of Jeroboam, began to reign over Israel in the second year of Asa king of Judah, and reigned two years; 1 Kings xv. 25. This was in the twenty-first year of his father, and it contradicts 1 Kings xiv. 20, where we are told that Jeroboam reigned twenty-two years, unless we suppose that father and son reigned jointly.

(7.) Baasha slew Nadab, and began to reign over Israel in the third year of Asa; and he reigned in Tirzah twenty-four years; 1 Kings xv. 33.

(8.) In the thirty-sixth year of Asa, Baasha makes war against him; 2 Chron. xvi. 1. Here the years of Asa are probably counted in continuation of those of his grandfather, as Baasha died in the twenty-sixth year of Asa; 1 Kings xvi. 8.

(9.) Elah, the son of Baasha, began to reign in the twenty-sixth of Asa, and he reigned for two years; 1 Kings xvi. 8.

(10.) In the twenty-seventh of Asa, Zimri slew Elah, and reigned for seven days over Israel; 1 Kings xvi. 15. We have omitted his name from the table. Then Omri and Tibni divided the kingdom of Israel. Omri reigned twelve years, for the first six in Tirzah, and for the last six in Samaria, the new capital of Israel; 1 Kings xvi. 23. Tibni reigned five years, dying in the thirty-first of Asa, leaving Omri to reign for seven years over all Israel; 1 Kings xvi. 22.

(11.) Ahab, the son of Omri, began to reign in the thirty-eighth of Asa, and reigned over Israel in Samaria twenty-two years; 1 Kings xvi. 29.

(12.) Jehoshaphat, the son of Asa, began to reign over Judah in the fourth year of Ahab, and reigned twenty-five years; 1 Kings xxii. 41.

(13.) Ahaziah, the son of Ahab, began to reign over Israel in the seventeenth of Jehoshaphat, and reigned two years; 1 Kings xxii. 51. This contradicts 1 Kings xvi. 29, by shortening Ahab's reign, unless we suppose that the son reigned jointly with his father, which is very possible, though not allowed by 1 Kings xxii. 40, which says he reigned in his stead.

(14.) Jehoram, the son of Ahab, succeeded his brother in the eighteenth year of Jehoshaphat, and reigned twelve years over Israel; 2 Kings iii. 1. The first two years of his reign were also jointly with his father, unless, as before remarked, we shorten the father's reign.

(15.) In the fifth year of Joram king of Israel, Jehoram, the son of Jehoshaphat, began to **reign** over Judah while his father was yet alive. He reigned **eight** years; 2 Kings viii. 16, 17. As the father and son are **here** said to have reigned jointly, as did David and his son Solomon, **it is** not unreasonable to suppose that it may have **been** the same with other kings, when the historian has not expressly said so. Our chronology **is** not troubled by the words in the Hebrew " while Jehoshaphat was yet king of Judah ;" but some MSS. of the Vulgate and several printed editions have omitted them.

(16.) We read in 2 Kings i. 17, that in the second year of Jehoram king of Judah, Jehoram of Israel succeeded to his brother Ahaziah. But this **date can in no** way be reconciled with what we have learned from other passages. See notes (14) and (15).

(17.) Ahaziah king of Judah began to reign in **the** eleventh year of Joram king of Israel, 2 Kings ix. 29, or in the twelfth year, according to 2 Kings viii. 25. This latter date seems the more probable. He reigned one year. He is called Jehoahaz in 2 Chron. xxi. 17.

(18.) Jehu, who had slain Jehoram king of Israel, reigned twenty-eight years ; 2 Kings x. 36.

(19.) Ahaziah king of Judah was slain at the same time as Jehoram king of Israel, 2 Kings ix. 27, and he was succeeded by his mother Athaliah, who reigned seven years ; **2 Kings xi. 4.** In the verse before we are told that the child, the rightful king, was hidden for only six years. This may be explained by note (4), where we learn that six years may easily get counted for seven regnal years.

(20.) In the seventh year of Jehu, Jehoash began to reign **over** Judah. He reigned forty years; 2 Kings xii. 1.

(21.) In the twenty-third year of Jehoash, Jehoahaz, the son of Jehu, began to reign over Israel, and reigned seventeen years ; 2 Kings xiii. 1.

(22.) In the thirty-seventh year of Jehoash of Judah, Jehoash, the son of Jehoahaz, began to reign over Israel, and reigned sixteen years; 2 Kings xiii. 10.

(23.) In the second year of Jehoash of Israel, Amaziah, the son of Jehoash of Judah, began to reign, and he reigned twenty-nine years ; 2 Kings xiv. 1: he survived Jehoash of Israel fifteen years; 2 Kings xiv. 17. Then his son began in the so-called twenty-seventh of Jeroboam ; 2 Kings **xv. 1.**

(24.) In the fifteenth year of Amaziah, Jeroboam began to reign over Israel, and reigned forty-one years; 2 Kings xiv. 23. This can only be reconciled with other quotations by supposing that he then began to reign alone, after having reigned thirteen years jointly with his father. See note (26). Here, then, we shorten the usual chronology.

(25). Azariah, or Uzziah, son of Amaziah, reigned fifty-two years over Judah; 2 Kings xv. 2. We place his beginning in the **sixth** year of his father's reign. If we followed the usual chronology, and made him begin in the twenty-seventh of Jeroboam, we should have to place an interregnum of twelve years in Israel between Jeroboam and his son Zachariah, as is done in the **margin of the** Authorized Version of the Bible.

(26.) In the twenty-seventh **year of** Jeroboam, says the historian, Azariah began to reign; 2 Kings xv. 1. This was fifteen years after the death of Jehoash of Israel; 2 Kings xiv. 17. Hence it is clear that Jeroboam had reigned twelve **or** thirteen years jointly with his father. Our Table agrees also with Josephus, who says, in Antiq., IX. ix. 3, that Uzziah, or Azariah, began to reign in the fourteenth year **of** Jeroboam. Josephus in neither case counts the years which they had reigned with their fathers.

(27.) In the thirty-eighth year of Azariah, Zachariah began **to** reign **over** Israel. He reigned for six months; 2 Kings xv. 8. He succeeded on the death **of** Jeroboam his father; 2 Kings **xiv. 29; but the usual chronology** places an interregnum between them.

(28.) In the thirty-ninth year **of** the reign of Uzziah, Shallum reigned for one month over Israel; 2 Kings xv. 13.

(29.) Also in the thirty-ninth year of Azariah, or Uzziah, Menahem began to reign over Israel, and he reigned ten **years;** 2 Kings xv. 17.

(30.) The forty-ninth year of Azariah is unaccounted for in **Israel.** Perhaps Menahem reigned eleven years.

(31.) In the fiftieth year of Azariah, Pekahiah, the son of Menahem, began to reign over Israel, and reigned two years; 2 Kings xv. 23.

(32.) In the fifty-second year of Azariah, Pekah, having slain Pekahiah, began to reign in Israel. He reigned twenty years; 2 Kings xv. 27.

(33.) In the second year of Pekah, Jotham, the son of Uzziah, began to reign over Judah, and reigned sixteen years; 2 Kings **xv. 32.**

(34.) In the seventeenth year of Pekah, Ahaz, the son of Jotham began to reign, and reigned sixteen years; 2 Kings xvi. 1. This must be understood to mean that he then began to reign alone at the death of his father, after having reigned seven years as his colleague. This is confirmed by the quotations in the next note, and makes it unnecessary to place an interregnum between Pekah and Hoshea who slew him, as is done in the margin of the Authorized Version.

(35.) Hoshea began to reign over Israel in the twelfth year of Ahaz, and reigned nine years; 2 Kings xvii. 1. He slew his predecessor, Pekah, in the twentieth year of Jotham; 2 Kings xv. 30. The two dates mean the same year; though Jotham had been dead four years, his years were still used in dating events.

(36.) In the third year of Hoshea, Hezekiah began to reign over Judah, and reigned twenty-nine years; 2 Kings xviii. 1. But we place the beginning of his reign one year later, agreeably with the two following quotations.

(37.) The fourth year of Hezekiah was the seventh of Hoshea. In that year Shalmanezer, king of Assyria, besieged Samaria; 2 Kings xviii. 9.

(38.) The sixth year of Hezekiah was the ninth of Hoshea. In that year the monarchy of Israel came to an end; 2 Kings xvii. 6; xviii. 10.

(39.) The year B.C. 721 was the first year of Mardoc Empadus king of Babylon, by an eclipse of the moon observed in Babylon, and recorded by Claudius Ptolemy. He is called Berodach Baladan in the Hebrew; and he sends an embassy to Hezekiah, perhaps about fifteen years before the death of the latter, or about B.C. 713; 2 Kings xx. 6-12. Mardoc Empadus died B.C. 709.

(40.) Manasseh succeeded his father, or perhaps grandfather, Hezekiah, and reigned fifty-five years; 2 Kings xxi. 1. Henceforth we have no kings of Israel for the historian to make use of their years in dating the kings of Judah; hence we are left in doubt whether the first year of Manasseh is to be counted as the same year as the last of Hezekiah, or as following it. The same remark applies to the first year of Amon, and to the first year of Josiah; and thus it would be equally correct to make the accession of Solomon more modern by one, by two, or by three years.

(41.) Amon succeeded his father Manasseh, and reigned two years; 2 Kings xxi. 19.

(42.) Josiah succeeded his father Amon, and reigned thirty-one years ; 2 Kings xxii. 1.

(43.) Jeremiah begins to prophesy in the thirteenth year of Josiah ; Jerem. xxv. 3. See note (46).

(44.) The year B.C. 621 was the fifth year of Nabopulassar, king of Babylon, by an eclipse of the moon, recorded by C. Ptolemy.

(45.) Jehoahaz, called also Shallum, succeeded Josiah, and reigned three months; and then Jehoiakim, called also Eliakim, reigned eleven years ; 2 Kings xxiii. 31, 36.

(46.) The fourth year of Jehoiakim was the first of Nebuchadnezzar, and the twenty-third from the thirteenth of Josiah ; Jerem. xxv. 1. The Captivity in Babylon was to come to an end in seventy years from this time.

(47.) Jehoiachin, called also Jeconiah, and Coniah, reigned three months, and was then carried into captivity in the eighth year of Nebuchadnezzar; 2 Kings xxiv. 8-12. His series of years, we shall see, was continued under the name of "the Captivity." Some writers make the first year of "the Captivity" follow the first year of Jehoiachin; but this is contradicted by these several passages.

(**48.**) Zedekiah, called also Mattaniah, reigned eleven years, while Jehoiachin was a captive in Babylon ; 2 Kings xxiv. 18.

(49.) The fifth year of the Captivity is the year 30 of an era not named; Ezek. i. 1, 2. This is obviously of Nabopulassar.

(50.) The tenth year of Zedekiah is the eighteenth of Nebuchadnezzar ; Jerem. xxxii. 1.

(51.) The city of Jerusalem was destroyed in the twelfth year of the Captivity, Ezek. xxxiii. 21; and in the nineteenth of Nebuchadnezzar ; 2 Kings xxv. 8. This shows that the years of "the Captivity" were counted from the king's accession, not from his being carried captive. Ezekiel, in chap. iv., says that Judah shall be punished for forty years, and Israel for three hundred and ninety years ; meaning that Israel's guilt began three hundred and fifty years before that of Judah. Our chronology places Israel's Revolt three hundred and thirty-six years before the Captivity, and three hundred and forty-seven years before the City and the Temple were destroyed. We thus differ either three or fourteen years from Ezekiel's reckoning.

(52.) The twenty-fifth year of the Captivity is the fourteenth of the City destroyed ; Ezek. xl. 1.

(53.) Evil Merodach began to reign in the thirty-seventh year of the Captivity; 2 Kings xxv. 27.

(54.) The Nabonned of Cl. Ptolemy seems to be the colleague on the throne, and perhaps the father, of the Belshazzar of the Book of Daniel.

(55.) The Desolation of seventy years, mentioned in Jeremiah xxv. 11, came to an end in the first year of Cyrus; 2 Chron. xxxvi. 21; Ezra i. 1. The Jewish captives in Babylon then returned home under Prince Zerubbabel.

(56.) Xenophon, in his Cyropædia, makes Cyaxares II of Media the conqueror of Babylon; and the Book of Daniel says that it was Darius the Mede who overthrew the Babylonian monarchy. By some these two kings are thought to be the same; but by some their very existence is denied; and Cl. Ptolemy makes Cyrus of Persia the immediate successor of the last king of Babylon. But in favour of there having been such a Median conqueror, we may remark that Jerem. li. 11, and Isaiah xiii. 17, which are later additions to those books, both speak of the Medes as the conquerors of Babylon; and in Isaiah xxi. 2, those nations are spoken of as the joint conquerors. Cyrus reigned nine years.

(57.) The year B.C. 523 was the seventh of Cambyses, by an eclipse of the moon recorded by Cl. Ptolemy. Cambyses reigned eight years.

(58.) In the second year of Darius, Jerusalem had been punished seventy years; Zechariah i. 7, 12.

The years of the Babylonian kings, after the overthrow of the Assyrians and before their own overthrow, are in Cl. Ptolemy fewer by one than in our table; thus—

	As above.	In Cl. Ptolemy.
Nabopulassar	18 years.	20 years.
Nebuchadnezzar	43 „	43 „
Evil Merodach	4 „	2 „
Neriglissor	5 „	4 „
Nabonned	17 „	17 „
	87	86

(59.) The building of the second Temple was finished in the sixth year of Darius (Ezra vi. 15) by Prince Zerubbabel; Zechariah iv. 9.

(60.) Esther is made queen in Susa, the capital of Persia,

by Ahasuerus, who reigned over one hundred and twenty-seven provinces, from India to Ethiopia; Esther i. This was in the third year of his reign. He was probably Xerxes I. Her influence may have obtained for Ezra permission to return to Jerusalem.

(61.) In the seventh year of Artaxerxes, Ezra comes to Jerusalem as the Persian governor of the city; Ezra vii. 8. This was probably in the reign of Xerxes I, called Ahasuerus in the Book of Esther. This was fifty-nine years after the Decree of Cyrus which allowed the first return of the Jews. See Daniel ix. 25, where forty-nine years only are allowed to what seems to be meant for this space of time.

(62.) Eliashib is chief priest; Paschal Chronicle; and Nehem. iii. 1.

(63.) In the twentieth year, probably of Artaxerxes Longimanus, Nehemiah comes to Jerusalem; Nehemiah ii. 1.

(64.) Nehemiah returns to Susa, in the thirty-second year of Artaxerxes; Nehem. xiii. 6.

BIBLICAL INDEX.

THE END.

www.ingramcontent.com/pod-product-compliance
Lightning Source LLC
Chambersburg PA
CBHW052335110726
47901CB00005B/1231